THE COMMENTARIES OF
GAIUS

AND

RULES OF ULPIAN

TRANSLATED WITH NOTES BY

J. T. ABDY, LL.D.

JUDGE OF COUNTY COURTS,
LATE REGIUS PROFESSOR OF LAWS IN THE UNIVERSITY OF CAMBRIDGE,
AND FORMERLY FELLOW OF TRINITY HALL;

AND

BRYAN WALKER, M.A., LL.D.

LAW LECTURER OF ST JOHN'S COLLEGE, CAMBRIDGE;
LATE FELLOW AND LECTURER OF CORPUS CHRISTI COLLEGE;
AND FORMERLY LAW STUDENT OF TRINITY HALL.

Dixi saepius post scripta geometrarum nihil exstare quod vi ac subtilitate cum Romanorum jureconsultorum scriptis comparari possit, tantum nervi inest, tantum profunditatis.

LEIBNITZ.

THIRD EDITION BY BRYAN WALKER.

EDITED FOR THE SYNDICS OF THE UNIVERSITY PRESS.

THE LAWBOOK EXCHANGE, LTD.
Clark, New Jersey

ISBN 978-1-58477-548-5

Lawbook Exchange edition 2006, 2014

The quality of this reprint is equivalent to the quality of the original work.

The Lawbook Exchange, Ltd.
33 Terminal Avenue
Clark, New Jersey 07066-1321

Please see our website for a selection of our other publications and fine facsimile reprints of classic works of legal history:
www.lawbookexchange.com

Library of Congress Cataloging-in-Publication Data

Gaius.
The commentaries of Gaius and Rules of Ulpian / Gaius & Ulpian, translated with notes by J.T. Abdy and Bryan Walker.-- 3rd ed. / by Bryan Walker.
p. cm.
In Latin with parallel English translations.
Originally published: Cambridge [England] : The University Press, 1885.
Includes bibliographical references and index.
ISBN 1-58477-548-3 (alk. paper)
1. Roman law. I. Ulpianus, Domitius, ca. 160-228. II. Walker, Bryan, 1840-1887. III. Abdy, J. T. (John Thomas), 1822-1899. IV. Tituli ex corpore Ulpiani. English & Latin. V. Title.
KJA882.A3I567 2005
340.5'4--dc22 2005001886

Printed in the United States of America on acid-free paper

THE COMMENTARIES OF GAIUS

AND

RULES OF ULPIAN

TRANSLATED WITH NOTES BY

J. T. ABDY, LL.D.

JUDGE OF COUNTY COURTS,
LATE REGIUS PROFESSOR OF LAWS IN THE UNIVERSITY OF CAMBRIDGE,
AND FORMERLY FELLOW OF TRINITY HALL;

AND

BRYAN WALKER, M.A., LL.D.

LAW LECTURER OF ST JOHN'S COLLEGE, CAMBRIDGE;
LATE FELLOW AND LECTURER OF CORPUS CHRISTI COLLEGE;
AND FORMERLY LAW STUDENT OF TRINITY HALL.

Dixi saepius post scripta geometrarum nihil exstare quod vi ac subtilitate cum Romanorum jureconsultorum scriptis comparari possit, tantum nervi inest, tantum profunditatis.

LEIBNITZ.

THIRD EDITION BY BRYAN WALKER.

EDITED FOR THE SYNDICS OF THE UNIVERSITY PRESS.

Cambridge:
AT THE UNIVERSITY PRESS.
1885

Cambridge:
PRINTED BY C. J. CLAY, M.A. & SON,
AT THE UNIVERSITY PRESS.

PREFACE.

In publishing, at the request of the Syndics of the Cambridge University Press, a third edition of the Commentaries of Gaius and Rules of Ulpian, I must, first of all, express my deep regret that Dr Abdy, my co-editor in the former editions, is prevented by his increasing professional engagements from rendering me his valuable aid and counsel for this reissue of our work. I have, therefore, to undertake alone the recasting of the book into what will probably be its final form; as the Verona MS. of Gaius has all but perished in yielding up its secrets to the chemicals, employed first by Bekker and Göschen, then by Bluhme of still more potent and damaging kind, and lastly by Studemund; and the discovery of another MS. we can only hope for and hardly expect.

The principal feature, of course, in this edition, is the embodiment of the new readings of Studemund in the text; but reference has also been made to the editions and annotations which have appeared since the publication of Studemund's Apograph in 1874: principally to Goudsmit's *Kritische Aanteekeningen op Gajus*, published at Leyden, 1875, to Krüger and Studemund's edition of *Gaius*, Berlin, 1877, with Mommsen's introductory *Epistula Critica*, to Huschke's edition, Leipzig, 1878, and to Polenaar's, Leyden, 1879.

The translation has been corrected to accord with the revised text, and a few notes have been added, but strictly in accordance with the principle laid down in our first edition, and which I am happy to say has met with favour, that the notes should only be such as are necessary to elucidate the meaning of the writer, and that Gaius himself should be presented to the reader, and not Gaius hidden and overburdened with commentary. The text of Gaius is still imperfect, and it is too hazardous to attempt to reconstruct the three missing pages in the MS., after those numbered 80, 126 and 194. The pages of the MS. are marked in the margin of the text. I have supplied obvious corrections in spelling in the received text: also put in words obviously omitted, these being printed in the ordinary type and within brackets: and more conjectural emendations in italics, noting, in almost all cases, the authority for the same.

No one who watches the progress of legal literature in England can fail to observe the recent remarkable development of the study of Roman law in our country. Twenty-nine years ago the learned author of *Ancient Law*, in his admirable essay on Roman Law and Legal Education[1], pointed out the fact as even then visible. In that essay, which for its exhaustive reasoning and eloquent advocacy of the merits of the law of Rome can never be too often noticed nor too frequently perused, the writer mentions one special cause why Roman law has a peculiar value to Englishmen. "It is," he says, "not because our own jurisprudence and that of Rome were *once* alike that they ought to be studied together; it is because they *will* be alike. It is because in England we are slowly and perhaps unconsciously or unwillingly, but still steadily and certainly, accustoming ourselves to the same modes of legal thought and to the same conceptions of legal principles to which the Roman jurisconsults had attained after centuries of accumulated experience and unwearied cultivation." Nor should it be forgotten, as he points out, that the literature in which Roman legal thought and legal reasoning are enshrined is the product of men singularly remarkable for wide learning, deep research, rare gifts of logical acumen, and "all the grand qualities which we identify with one or another of the most distinguished of our own greatest lawyers and greatest thinkers."

It is then a matter for congratulation that what may be

[1] *Cambridge Essays*, published by J. W. Parker and Son in 1856.

fairly called a revival has taken place in this branch of learning; and that in our own University the study of Roman Law, which has always had a footing here, although in later times frequently but a feeble one, has fixed its hold more firmly amongst the other studies of the place. Unfortunately our knowledge of Roman Law has been for many years past circumscribed within very narrow limits. Its excellencies, literary and juridical, have been judged of from one work alone; and whilst the whole range of classical writers has been eagerly travelled over by the teacher and the student, the author and the reader, the style, the language, and the logic of some of Rome's greatest thinkers and ablest administrators have been utterly neglected, or at best noticed in vague and careless reference. If, in addition to the *Institutes* of Justinian, the reviving taste for Roman jurisprudence shall promote a closer and more careful study of the language and thought of the old jurisconsults, as exhibited in the books of the Digest, it may confidently be predicted that in every department of knowledge will the student of imperial Rome be a gainer; that our store of information as to her manners and customs, her legislation, the private life of her citizens, and, last though not least, her language itself, will be largely increased.

The University of Cambridge has for some years past included Selected Portions of the Digest in the subjects proposed for the students in Law. Of these I have had the honour to publish for the University Press Syndicate editions in most cases; but a far more valuable contribution to this branch of Legal Learning and Literature is to be found in the Introduction to *Justinian's Digest* by H. J. Roby, also published among the works which the same Syndicate have had the credit of presenting to the public.

On Gaius himself, his name, his country, the works he composed, his position amongst the lawyers of Rome, his fame in later times, the story of the loss and wonderful recovery of his Commentaries[1], and the influence of that work on the treatise of

[1] Niebuhr discovered the MS. in 1816. It then contained 126 leaves or 251 pages. One leaf, which had become detached, was found earlier,

Justinian, there is no need to dilate. All that can be told the reader on these and other points in connection with his life and writings is so fully and ably narrated in the *Dictionary of Greek and Roman Biography* by Dr Smith, that it is sufficient to refer him to it. There are, however, one or two matters deserving of more particular attention.

In the first place, as regards Gaius himself, it is important to remember that whatever reputation he acquired in later days, and however enduring has been his fame as the model for all systematic treatise-writers on law, in his own time he was only a private lecturer. Unlike many of the distinguished lawyers who preceded him, and others equally distinguished who were his contemporaries, he never had the privilege *condendi jura, in jura respondendi*. That he was a writer held in eminent distinction in Justinian's time is clear from the large number of extracts from his works to be found in the Digest[1], and there is good reason to believe that he was a successful and popular lecturer; but it is strange that with all his rare knowledge and laborious research he did not emerge from his comparative obscurity. It may be that the very learning in which he was pre-eminent unfitted him for public life. His love of investigation, his strong liking for classification and arrangement, and his studious habits, possibly gave him a distaste for actual practice, in which all these qualities are of much less importance than rapidity of judgment, prompt decision, and aptness for argumentative disputation. He was one of those men like our own John Austin; lawyers admirably fitted for the quiet thought and learned meditation of the study, but averse from the stir

and published by Maffeius in 1732 and 1742, and again by Haubold in 1816. This corresponds to what is now Book IV, §§ 134—144, beginning with the words :...TIONE FORMULAE DET...T...I, and ending PRO HEREDE AUT PRO POSSESSOR... Niebuhr's manuscript was far from complete, wanting three entire pages besides fragments of pages here and there.

[1] A catalogue of these *excerpta* will be found in the article above-mentioned in the *Dictionary of Greek and Roman Biography*. The *Index Florentinus* merely gives the titles of the books composed by Gaius. An analysis of the passages from these quoted in the Digest, of which there are as many as 535, is laboriously worked out in the *Jurisprudentia Restituta* of Abraham Wieling, pp. 7—20, and in the *Palingenesia* of C. F. Hommel, Vol. I. pp. 55—126.

and bustle of the forum; yet not the less valuable members of the profession which they silently adorn.

A comparison of the excerpts from the writings of Gaius in the Digest with those from Ulpian, Paulus, Papinian, and others, to whom was granted the privilege of uttering *responsa*, will show that there is in Gaius, as his Commentaries also evince, an unreadiness to give his own opinion upon contested questions, a strong inclination to collect and put side by side the views of opposite schools, and a constant anxiety to treat a legal doctrine from an historical rather than a judicial point of view. In Ulpian and Paulus, and men of that stamp, we meet with decisive and pithy opinions upon legal difficulties, an abundant proof of firm self-reliance and indifference to opposite views, and a lawyer-like way of looking at a doctrine as it affects the case before them, rather than accounting for its appearance as a problem of Jurisprudence or Legislature; with them it is the matter itself which is of primary importance, with Gaius it is the clearing up of everything connected with the full understanding in the abstract of the subject on which he is engaged. To this peculiar turn of his mind we are probably indebted for his keen appreciation of the help which history affords to law, and for the large amount of reference to archaic forms and ceremonies which proceeds from his pen.

From Gaius himself the transition to his Commentaries is natural. Three or four topics present themselves for notice upon that head: (1) Their nature and object; (2) the effect upon them of certain constitutional reforms that had been and at the time of their publication were being carried out at Rome; (3) the mode in which they were first presented to the public.

1st. As to the nature and object of Gaius' Commentaries:— There is an opinion pretty commonly accepted as correct, that this volume was written, like the corresponding work of Justinian, for the express purpose of giving a general sketch of the rules and principles of the private law of Rome, and that it was intended to be a preliminary text-book for students. That this gives a very incorrect notion of the aim of Gaius and the nature of his work is clear, partly from a comparison of it with that which was intended to be a student's first book on law (viz. the *Institutes* of Justinian), and partly from the analysis of its subject-matter. What Gaius really had in view was, not the publication of a systematic treatise on private law, but the enunciation, in the shape of oral lectures, of matter that would be serviceable to those who were studying with a view to practice. The work itself, as we shall show presently, was not directly prepared for publication, but was a republication in a collected form of lectures (the outline of which, perhaps, had been originally in writing and the filling-up by word of mouth,) when the cordial reception of the same by a limited class had suggested their being put into a shape which would benefit a wider circle of students. The contents of the book will bear out this view. Thus, in the first part, Gaius speaks of men as subjects of law, shows what rights they have, points out who are *personae* and who are not, who are under *potestas* and *manus*, who can act alone, and who require some legal medium to render their acts valid. In fact, the main object of the whole of this first part is to render clear to his hearers how those who are of free birth stand, not only in relation to those who are not, but in relation to the law. Hence, there is no attempt at explaining the nature of Law and Jurisprudence, no classification of the parts of Law, no aiming at philosophical arrangements and analysis, but a simple declaration of the Roman law as it affects its subjects, men, illustrated of course by historical as well as by technical references. Hence too, we understand why there is nothing in the shape of explanation of the rules relating to marriage, of the relative position of father and son, of patron and client, nothing of the learning about the *peculium*, or about the administration of the property of minors and wards. In short, this portion of the Commentaries might be styled the general Roman law of private civil rights, cleared from all rules connected with special relations. One special matter, however, is discussed with much attention and detail, viz. the position of the *Latini* in relation to private law; but of this anomaly we shall speak at more length presently.

So far for the first portion of the work:—The second is of

the same nature, viz. a declaration of the general rules of law as affecting *Res*. Here the arrangement is as follows:—In the first place Gaius gives us certain divisions of *Res*, drawn from their quality and specific nature; he then proceeds to explain the form and method of acquisition and transfer of separate individual *Res*, whether corporeal or incorporeal, prefacing his notes upon this part of his subject with a short account of the difference between *res mancipi* and *res nec mancipi:* from this he goes on to describe the legal rules relating to inheritances and to acquisitions of *Res* in the aggregate (*per universitatem*), interspersing his subject with the law relating to legacies and *fideicommissa;* last come obligations, which are discussed as incorporeal things not capable of transfer by mancipation, *in jure cessio*, or tradition, but founded on and terminated by certain special causes. In this part of his work it is very important to bear in mind[1] that the reader is not to look for a detailed account of the force and effect of obligations, and of the specific relations existing between the parties to them by their creation and extinction, for upon these matters Gaius does not dwell. His chief aim here, as it was in the subject of inheritance, is to show how they began and how they were ended. Thus, then, this second part of the Commentaries may be entitled "The objects of Law, their gain and loss."

The third part of the Commentaries is entirely confined to the subject of actions. Here too, if the book be compared with the parallel part of Justinian's Institutes, a striking difference in the nature of the two will be visible. Gaius' work is in every respect a book of practice: it considers actions as remedies for rights infringed; it discusses the history of the subject, because the actual forms of pleading in certain actions could not be explained without an examination into their early history; it dwells upon the various parts of the pleading with a care that is almost excessive; points out the necessity and importance of equitable remedies; in fact, goes into a very tech-

[1] We are indebted to Böcking's short but valuable *Adnotatio ad Tabulas systematicas* for this analysis of the Commentaries, especially for the particular fact here adverted to.

nical and very difficult subject in a way that would be uncalled for and out of place in a mere elementary treatise on law.

2nd. The influence of certain political changes then going on at Rome upon Gaius' treatise has now to be noticed. Even to an ordinary reader of the Commentaries two remarkable features in them are visible. One the elaborate attention bestowed on the relation of the *peregrini* to the existing legal institutions of Rome, the other the constant references to the effect of the establishment of the Praetorian courts with their equitable interpretations and fictions, upon the old Civil Law. A few words upon these two points will not be out of place. There is a chapter in Mr Merivale's able *History of the Romans under the Empire*, which is most deserving of consideration by the student of Gaius. It is the one in which he speaks of the events that marked the reign of the Emperor Antoninus Pius[1]. The historian there passes in review the political elements of Roman Society at that time. Among the phenomena most deserving of attention two are especially noticed, the position of the Provincials in the state and the extension of the franchise on the one hand, and the relation of the *Jus Civile* and the *Jus Gentium* on the other. On the former head the narrative treats first of the struggles of the foreigners to obtain a participation in the advantages of Quiritary proprietorship, next of the gradual extension of Latin rights, and afterwards of full Roman rights, till the latter were in the end enjoyed by all the free population of the Empire. One or two passages deserve quotation simply for the sake of their illustration of the proposition we shall maintain,—that Gaius held it a leading object to illustrate that part of the law that had the highest interest for the practitioners of the day, viz. the legal rules and the method of procedure by which the transactions and suits of the *peregrini* were affected.

Mr Merivale tells us then "that great numbers had gained their footing as Roman Citizens by serving magistracies in the Latin towns, but the Roman rights to which they had attained

[1] Ch. LXVII.

were still so far incomplete, that they had no power of deriving an untaxed inheritance from their parents. Hence, the value of citizenship thus burdened and circumscribed was held in question by the Latins. Nerva and Trajan decreed that those *new citizens*, as they were designated, who thus came in, as it was called, *through Latium*, should be put on the same advantageous footing as the old and genuine class." Again he says, "great anxiety seems to have been felt among large classes to obtain enrolment in the ranks of Rome......Hadrian was besieged as closely as his predecessor. Antoninus Pius is celebrated on medals as a multiplier of citizens." From these facts we can draw the conclusion that a large portion of the most important and lucrative business for lawyers in Rome at the period when Gaius wrote consisted of suits in which the *Peregrini* were concerned, and therefore that a knowledge of the rules of law by which they were affected was of the highest value. Hence it is easy to account for the constant and close attention bestowed by Gaius upon the *Latinitas*, and upon all legal matters relating to it, throughout the Commentaries.

It would, however, be impossible to deal with these topics apart from that very remarkable phenomenon that must catch the eye of every reader of Roman law, viz. the *Jus Gentium* and its influence upon the Praetorian Courts. Here, again, Mr Merivale must be our authority, for he has shown most clearly how useless was the civil law of Rome in respect of questions between foreigners or between citizens and foreigners. He has described the anomalous relations of the *Jus Civile* and the *Jus Gentium* in the Flavian Era, and has drawn attention to the important position occupied by the Edict of the Praetor. To his narrative we can but refer, but the inference we would draw from that narrative is that the attraction and value of Gaius' work to its first readers lay precisely in the fact that upon all these points, (points as we see of the highest value at that time to the practising lawyer,) his rare knowledge of pleading and procedure and his nice appreciation of the value of equitable remedies made him an authority of the highest rank, and that these topics were never disregarded, when an allusion to them or illustration from them was possible.

Most probably Gaius' work is written on the lines of the arrangement of the Edict. Hence we can comprehend his silence as to the subject of *dos*, *querela inofficiosi*, &c.: these topics apparently belonged in his day to the Centumviral Court, and therefore would not form the subject of Titles in the Edict.

3rd. As to the shape in which the work of Gaius was first given to the world we have already intimated our opinion. It was not a systematic treatise composed and prepared for publication, like the *Institutes* of Justinian; but a sketch of lectures to be delivered on the legal questions most discussed at the time, corrected and amplified afterwards by the lecturer's own recollections of his *viva voce* filling-up, or by reference to notes taken by some one of his auditors[1].

That the Commentaries are not intended to be a brief Compendium is plain. In a Compendium every topic is touched upon, none treated at excessive length. Gaius, on the contrary, omits many subjects altogether, as *dos*, *peculium castrense*, the rules as to *testamenta inofficiosa* and the *quarta legitima*, (although the cognate subjects of institution and disinheritance are amply discussed,) all the *real* contracts, except *mutuum*, the "innominate" contracts, quasi-contracts, and quasi-delicts, the rules as to the inheritance of child from mother or mother from child, &c. &c. Other topics he discusses at inordinate length; the subject of the *Latinitas* is explained fully twice, viz. in I. 22 et seqq., and again in III. 56 et seqq.; the description of *agnatio* in I. 156 is repeated almost word for word in III. 10, and with the very same illustrative examples; the circumstances under which the earnings of others accrue to us are catalogued in II. 86, and again in

[1] After this conclusion had been come to by the Editors they had the satisfaction of finding their views borne out by an excellent monograph, published only a few months before the publication of their first edition by Dr Dernburg of Halle, of which they have since made free use. *Die Institutionen des Gaius, ein Collegienheft aus dem Jahre 161 nach Christi Geburt.* Halle, 1869.

nearly the same phraseology in III. 163; so too there is a double discussion of the effect of the Litis Contestatio, first in III. 180, 181, secondly in IV. 106—108. Huschke, who assumes the Commentaries to have been from the beginning a systematic treatise, says that Gaius would not have investigated the same subject twice, nor have stayed the progress of the reader to recall him to what had been already described, unless he had allowed the earlier books to pass from his hands, and so could not by reference to them discover that he was passing a second time over the same ground: and hence he frames a theory that the Commentaries were published in parts. "This hypothesis," says Huschke, "explains why on many points there is a second notice fuller and more accurate than the first."

But the second reference is not always more full and accurate than the first. Many proofs of this might be given, but we will only ask the reader to compare the passages II. 35—37 and III. 85—87, and say whether the latter adds anything to the knowledge imparted to us in the former. So also in other instances, as II. 58 and III. 201.

The lecture-hypothesis explains this peculiarity far better. When a systematic treatise is composed, the author can simply refer his reader back, on the occasion of an old topic cropping up again; but in a lecture this is impossible, and to prevent a misconception, or to guard against a defect of memory on the part of his audience, the lecturer repeats his former statements even at the risk of being tedious. This too, if thoroughly acquainted with his subject, and if delivering a course of lectures, old and familiar to him by constant repetition, he is almost certain to do, as Gaius has done, in a form identical even in its verbiage with the first enunciation.

Besides these obvious arguments for the view here adopted, Dr Dernburg brings forward others of a more refined and subtle complexion. The abundance of examples, a well-known device of a lecturer to maintain attention; the commencement of a new subject with such examples, rather than with a dry state ment of a legal maxim: the introduction of sentences such as "*Nunc transeamus ad fideicommissa. Et prius de hereditatibus despiciamus*," which serve excellently to give the auditor time to make his notes in a lecture-room, but are unnecessary and wearisome in a set treatise; the repetition of an idea in a new wording for the same end of giving rest to the hearer, as in the description of the parts of a *formula* "all these parts are not found together, but some are found and some are not found," &c. &c.; the marked antithesis, such as "*heres sponsoris non tenetur*, *fidejussoris autem heres tenetur*," the identity of phraseology rivetting attention when it proceeds from a speaker, the want of change being wearisome on the part of a writer; all these circumstances are pressed into the service of his and our argument. Hence, we may fairly assert that the nature of the commentaries is such as we affirmed it to be at starting.

But whatever be the irregularities and omissions arising from the character of the work, it must still rank high, not only as the first Roman law-book, on which all other legal treatises have been based, but as possessing an intrinsic value of its own for the light it throws upon old features of Roman life and Roman customs, for its keen appreciation of the aid which History lends to Law and Legislation, and for its philological spirit. To the lawyer desirous to know the detail of Roman practice the fourth book alone would be enough to render the volume priceless; to the classical student seeking to acquaint himself with the outline of Roman law, for the better comprehension of the classical historians, orators and poets, Gaius is at once an author more agreeable to peruse, because his language although not of the golden, is still an admirable specimen of the silver age, and beyond all comparison superior to the utterly debased style of Justinian, and more valuable as an authority because his law is that of a period only a century and a half posterior to Cicero, whilst Justinian is separated from him by more than five hundred years.

We have now to touch upon a few points more intimately connected with the present translation.

In the former editions the text relied upon was in the main that of Gneist. Gneist's edition, as is well known, is a recension of all the German editions prior to 1857, the date of its publication. The chief of these editions we ought, perhaps, to enumerate; as to the others the reader will find full information in the preface to Böcking's fourth edition, published at Leipzig in 1855. The *Editio Princeps* of 1821 was brought out by Göschen, four years after Niebuhr's discovery of the manuscript. Upon Bluhme's fresh collation of the manuscript, a second edition, embodying his discoveries, corrections, and suggestions, was given to the world by Göschen in 1824. It is of this edition that Böcking remarks: "Hujus exempli quam diu nostris suus stabit honor, nunquam pretium diminuetur." Death interrupted Göschen in his task of bringing out a third edition, but his work was completed and published by Lachmann in 1842. Klenze's edition appeared in 1829, those of Böcking successively in 1837, 1841, 1850 and 1855. Heffter's elaborate commentary and carefully emended text of the fourth book bears the date 1827.

The more modern editions on which this third edition is based are mentioned in p. v of this Introduction.

Our quotations have been as much as possible confined to Text-books easy of access, to Classical authors, and to the Sources. Wherever a well-recognized authority has clearly explained the matter in hand a mere reference has been given. In quoting the Sources we have adopted the numerical mode of reference, thus *Inst.* 1. 2. 3 signifies Justinian's *Institutes*, first book, second title, third paragraph, and D. 4. 3. 2. 1 means Digest, fourth book, third title, second law, first paragraph. Those to whom the verification of passages in the Digest and Institutes is a novelty should take notice that the opening paragraph of every law in the former, and the opening paragraph of every title in the latter, bear no number, but are marked by the symbol *pr.*, an abbreviation for *principium.*

Gaius himself is quoted without name: thus II. 100 denotes the 100th paragraph of the second commentary of Gaius.

There are good reasons why the Rules of Ulpian, fragmentary as they now are, should be bound up with the Commentaries of Gaius.

In the first place these writers are the only two, (if we except Paulus,) whose works have been preserved to our day in anything like a collected form, and both treatises, so fortunately preserved, are rich in illustrations of the spirit and remarkable characteristics of the early Roman Law. No doubt, there are other names in the long list of Roman lawyers from Cicero's time to that of Alexander Severus which occupy as high a position in the annals of Roman jurisprudence as those of Gaius and Ulpian; and other text-writers who claim equal respect as authoritative interpreters of Law. Between Servius Sulpicius, "the most eloquent of jurisconsults and most learned of orators," and Papinian, the instructor of Ulpian and Paulus, lawyers of repute are numerous;—their writings and their opinions swell the pages of the Digest; their influence is felt even in the decisions of English Judges;—yet none of them have left continuous works that have survived to our day.

In the second place, between the two treatises here presented to the public there is a close affinity. Both are meant to exhibit the leading doctrines of the Roman Law as it affects persons in their private capacities, and both are compendia of law equally useful to the student and to the practitioner. Each of them throws light upon the other, and each supplies the other's deficiencies.

We have already spoken at some length of the characteristics of Gaius' work, and have said something about his reputation as a jurist and his position as a professional advocate. It behoves us to add a few words upon the claim of Ulpian to rank among the leading authorities in Roman Law. But before proceeding to this special topic, some short notice of the general influence and character of the jurisconsults of Rome will be an useful preliminary. The golden age of Jurisprudence is a well-known and almost proverbial expression for the 200 years that intervened between the accession of Augustus and the death of Alexander Severus. This period presents so many features of interest to the student of Roman Legislation that an exhaustive essay upon it might fill a volume, involving as it would the Social, Political and

Literary history of Rome. Among the various topics which must present themselves to a writer of the History of Roman Law during the period we have mentioned, the influence and character of the lawyers would necessarily be a prominent one. In the oldest days of Rome, when the interpretation of the law and the application of its mysteries to daily life were confined to the patricians, when the cultivation of Jurisprudence was seized and retained by the nobility, and when caste privileges dominated every portion of Roman society, the practical and professional element of the lawyer's life was unknown, and the knowledge of those customary observances that stood for law, and of the acts and fictions that surrounded them, was rather one of the chief instruments for attaining political power. Various causes tended to disturb this state of things; the publication of the Praetorian Edicts, the betrayal, (a well-known story,) of the forms and ceremonies by which the application of the law was masked, the extension of Roman power, the increase of a foreign element, all these things affected the position of the old dominant class. In process of time the ancient privileges of the patrician order in the state were diminished, their claim to undisturbed power interfered with, and their charmed circle invaded: but still the social position of the learned jurisconsult was maintained, and even down to the days of Cicero the attainment of legal honours and forensic reputation was regarded as one of the safest and surest roads to political distinction and rank. The accession of Augustus to Imperial honours led to an important change in the status of the Roman Bar. A rivalry so dangerous as that of a body of men formidable from their numbers, from their influence with the people, from their learning, and from their thorough acquaintance with all the forms and practices of a state-craft coeval with the constitution itself, a body moreover allied with almost every family of distinction, was not to be endured by one who meant to consolidate his authority and to reign without a rival.

No man knew better than Augustus that force and fear were wrong weapons with which to counteract this opposing element, no man knew better than himself the sacred character of Law and Jurisprudence in the eye of every citizen of Rome, his reverence for the institutions of the city, and the respect with which the professors and expounders of the laws were regarded by him: "To strike down the Jurisconsults was to strike at the city itself[1]," and therefore measures of a milder nature were requisite. A plan was devised and, as the result shows, crowned with success. This plan was to change the character of the profession by diverting its members from their ancient line of ambition. That was done by granting to a select body out of the whole number of Jurisconsults the hitherto unheard-of privilege of giving official opinions, which, though nominally published by the emperor, were in effect the authoritative decisions of certain eminent and leading lawyers. The result of this was that a new object of ambition was held up to the eyes of the Jurists and Legists of Rome,—a new incentive and one of the most stirring kind was given them to achieve distinction in the ranks of their profession, but the inducement was no longer to cultivate law as a stepping-stone to political advancement:—law was no longer the means to an end, but an end in itself:—and henceforth the aim and object of every leading advocate was to merit the approval of the emperor alone, who was to him that fountain of honour and reward which in old times the people had been. It is unnecessary to pursue the history of this movement further. The wise and politic designs of Augustus were recognized and improved upon by succeeding rulers, especially by Tiberius, Vespasian, Titus and Trajan. Under Hadrian the dignity of the Jurisconsult was still further advanced through that well-known provision[2] by which certain *Responsa* were invested with the force of law. Great as the effect of these measures was from a political point of view, from a literary point of view still greater results followed. It is impossible in these few lines to describe adequately the marvellous energy displayed in the cause of learning by the Roman Lawyers of the golden aera. Law was their proper pursuit,

[1] Giraud, *Histoire du droit Romain*, p. 270.

[2] See Gaius, I. 7.

but in every branch of literature they shone,—Philosophy, Philology, Poetry, Oratory, History, Mathematical and Physical Sciences, to all they devoted themselves and in all they were eminent.

Their varied reading was reflected in their legal writings, their profound learning gave them vantage ground in their professional labours.—"The more we study their works, the greater pleasure we derive from the perusal. The wonderful propriety of diction, the lucid structure of the sentences, the exquisite method of the argument, give to the performances of these writers a charm peculiarly their own[1]." Nor must it be forgotten that their literary fame, their zeal for learning, and their vast energy, were displayed at a time when learning and science were in their decadence. But for the Jurists of Rome the cause of Letters would have perished. Of the men of genius whose names have come down to us and whose writings or whose opinions are worked into the great body of the Roman Law we may particularize five, not so much for their own distinctive merits, as for the importance given to their writings in the celebrated Law of Citations, published about A.D. 426. Of these five, Gaius, Papinian, Modestinus, Paulus and Ulpian, the compilers of the Digest at a later period made large use. In the Theodosian law, here alluded to, the authority of Papinian was pre-eminent, whilst to the writings of Gaius himself a higher impress of authority was given than they had hitherto attained.

That Papinian was a man of undoubted reputation is clear from his position in the state, as well as from the fragments of his writings preserved in the Digest; fellow-pupil, friend and minister of Septimius Severus, he became at an early age Praetorian Prefect and drew upon himself the hatred and vengeance of Caracalla. Famous himself, he had as pupils the two most illustrious lawyers of the succeeding generation, Paulus and Ulpian. The former, a man of great and varied learning, occupied

---

1 *Introduction to the Study of Roman Law*, by John George Phillimore, p. 234.

with Ulpian the post of Assessor to the Praetorian Prefect, and attained to high honours in the state. As for Ulpian, the fact that his writings have furnished 2461 laws to the Digest shows the reputation he left and the reverence with which his name was regarded. His chief works were a Commentary on the Edict in eighty-three books; a collection of Opinions in six books and another collection of Responsa in two books. As a lawyer he ranks high for the soundness of his views, for his practical common sense, and for the logical turn of his mind. As a writer he is clear and concise, well deserving the dignity of an authoritative jurisprudent by his power of marshalling facts and applying legal principles to them. As an instance at once of his juristical skill and of his natural acumen, we may point to his celebrated calculation of the present value of a life-annuity[1], nor would it be difficult to select other examples.

Of his public life but little is known beyond his official connection with the Emperor Alexander Severus and his assassination by the Praetorian guards. He seems to have been a man of wit and a pleasant companion, whose society was sought after by the most noble and the best in the state. Of the old writers Aelius Lampridius gives us most information regarding Ulpian and his political and professional career; but we need not enter into further details, for those who are desirous to learn all that is known about him may refer to the two accounts of his life prefixed to Schulting's *Tituli ex Corpore Ulpiani*, in that author's *Jurisprudentia Vetus Antejustinianea*, one by John Bertrand, president of Thoulouse, and the other by William Groot; whilst in the *Dictionary of Greek and Roman Biography* by Smith appears a somewhat elaborate sketch of him and his writings.

Just as there is but one manuscript of Gaius' Commentaries in existence, so is there but one of Ulpian's Rules. This is now in the Vatican Library, numbered 1128 in its catalogue, having originally belonged to the abbey of St Benedict at Fleury-sur-Loire, whence it was conveyed to Rome after the

[1] D. 35. 2. 68.

destruction of that religious house by the Calvinists in 1562. It is generally believed that all the modern editions of Ulpian's Rules are derived from this Codex, Heimbach alone maintaining that the first edition of all, that of John Tilius, or Jean du Tillet, was derived from another Codex now destroyed. But whether this be so or not is after all of little practical importance, for Heimbach himself allows that the Codex Vaticanus and the Codex Tilianus, if the latter ever existed, were either transcripts of one and the same original, or one copied from the other.

Tilius described the work, when he introduced it to the learned world at Paris in 1549, as "a mere epitome of doctrines contained in a variety of works by Ulpian;" a view now quite exploded, for almost all the best modern authorities hold that the manuscript is a genuine fragment of one and only one work of Ulpian, namely the *Liber Singularis Regularum:* so that the only point still open to debate is how far it has been mutilated, and whether intentionally or by accident. It is true that Puchta holds to the epitome theory, but even he regards the codex as an epitome of the "Rules" only, and his view meets with little favour.

Mommsen's idea is, that about Constantine's time some man, "parum doctus et incredibiliter stupidus," partly abridged and partly rewrote the treatise, to make it coincide with the law of his time. Against this theory Huschke argues that the excellent lawyers of that period would never have accepted an abridgment that did not, in the main, coincide with its original: and he further points to passages, such as I. 21; XX. 2, 10; XXVII. 1, where the ancient law is *not* removed from the text. From this evidence, and also from the fact that important matters are lost which must have been treated of in the original work, and which certainly were in force in Constantine's reign, he maintains that the omissions are throughout the result of accident rather than of design, his theory being that the transcriber of the one surviving manuscript, (apparently written about the tenth century, and probably in Gaul,) put together all he could find of Ulpian's acknowledged work; but that owing partly to his inability to discover the whole, and partly to subsequent mutilation of what he managed to collect, the work has come down to us in its present dilapidated condition.

It seems pretty clear that the transcript of the tenth century, whether embracing the greater part or only a fraction of Ulpian's original treatise, has been mutilated by the loss of a large section towards its conclusion. Ulpian's work, as a whole, runs parallel with that of Gaius. It is true that topics are usually treated more briefly in the "Rules;" still they occur in the same order as in the "Commentaries." It is true also that particular attention is given in the first-named treatise to points which Gaius either omitted or dismissed with a word or two, such as *dos, donatio inter virum et uxorem* and the *Lex Papia Poppaea:* but these extended digressions either are introduced where Gaius' briefer notices occur, or when referring to matters upon which Gaius is absolutely silent, they are brought in just where we can imagine the older writer would have introduced them, if they had not been excluded by the plan of his work. And yet although Ulpian's treatise is parallel with that of Gaius so far as it goes, it stops abruptly, and omits not only all the matter touched upon by the earlier writer in his Fourth Commentary, but even the subjects contained in the sections running from the 55th to the end of the Third Commentary. From the evident appearance of a general parallelism, and from the fact of the sudden defect just mentioned, we hold that the missing portion at the conclusion of the "Rules" is not merely a few lines or even pages, but almost a half of the work.

If we must venture a theory as to the object with which Ulpian wrote, we should attach no little importance to what has been already named, the fact that he interpolates so largely, although following the arrangement of Gaius in the main. Gaius wrote a handbook for students, with the intention of putting clearly before them the leading principles of Roman Law. His object was not so much to enter into details of practice as to present his readers with a comprehensive outline of the Roman Law as a system. On the other hand, Ulpian's aim was, we venture to think, entirely different: he wished to draw up a handbook for the use of practising lawyers. Now that a book of practice is improved by a systematic arrangement is obvious: Ulpian therefore, writing in the reign of Caracalla (see XVII. 2), took, as a model, the educational treatise which his brother lawyer had published a few years previously, introducing into it important and necessary modifications. Whilst then, on the one hand, he omitted all antiquarian disquisitions as out of place in a book of practice, on the other he introduced large interpolations on such matters as *dos* and its *retentiones*. These topics Gaius, (writing for beginners,) had passed over unnoticed, because they involved more detail than principle, because also a student could very well comprehend the general scheme of the Roman Law, without any special acquaintance with them. Ulpian, on the contrary, in a work intended for practitioners, was obliged to treat at length the rules relating to matters of such practical value as those above mentioned. Divorces were everyday occurrences at Rome; so that suits with regard to *dotes* and *retentiones* must have filled the court-lists of the time, and formed a profitable branch of a lawyer's practice: a knowledge, therefore, of all the regulations on these topics was to such an one of the highest importance.

The very title prefixed to Ulpian's work bears out our view. "Principles" (*institutiones*) are for beginners, but "Rules" (*regulæ*) aid the memory of those who have passed through their course of study, and are now engaged in the active business of their profession.

We have adopted in the main Huschke's text according to his edition of 1861; but the words of the original manuscript are distinguished from that editor's suggestions by being printed in a different type, on the same principle which we have adopted in the text of Gaius. The chief editions of Ulpian prior to Huschke's were that of Tilius, already alluded to, bearing the date 1549: those of Hugo in 1788, 1811, 1814, 1822, 1834; of Böcking, 1831, 1836, 1845, 1855, and of Vahlen 1856. All these have been consulted, but Huschke's has been preferred except where the authority against him seemed overpowering; in all doubtful cases the present editors have yielded to the authority of so undoubted a master of the Roman Law.

CAMBRIDGE, *May*, 1885.

GAII INSTITUTIONUM IURIS CIVILIS COMMENTARII QUATUOR.

PRIMUS COMMENTARIUS.

P. 1 1. *Omnes populi qui legibus et moribus reguntur partim suo proprio, partim communi omnium hominum iure utuntur*[1] *: nam quod quis*que populus ipse sibi ius constituit, id ipsius proprium est vocaturque ius civile, quasi ius proprium civitatis; quod vero naturalis ratio inter omnes homines constituit, id apud omnes populos peraeque custoditur vocaturque ius gentium, quasi quo iure omnes gentes utuntur[2]. Populus itaque Roma-

1. All associations of men which are governed by laws and customs employ law that is partly peculiar to themselves, partly shared in common by all mankind[1]: for what each such association hath established as law at its own pleasure is special to itself and is called its *Jus Civile*, the particular law, so to speak, of that state: but that which natural reason hath established amongst all men is guarded in equal degree amongst all associations and is called *Jus Gentium*, the law, so to speak, which all nations employ[2]. The Roman people, therefore,

---

1 The opening words are supplied from Just. *Inst.* I. 21. The MS. commences with three lines which cannot be deciphered.

2 Gaius is attempting to draw a distinction between the Positive Law and the Positive Morality, which together rule the conduct of citizens. A custom prevalent amongst all mankind, if such there be, would, of course, prevail in any particular state, and form an element in its Positive Morality. But there would also be Customs, peculiar to the state, and not converted into Laws; and of these he

nus partim suo proprio, partim communi omnium hominum iure utitur. Quae singula qualia sint, suis locis proponemus.

2. Constant autem iura populi Romani ex legibus, plebiscitis, senatusconsultis, constitutionibus Principum, edictis eorum qui ius edicendi habent, responsis prudentium.

3. Lex est quod populus iubet atque constituit. Plebiscitum est quod plebs iubet atque constituit. Plebs autem a populo eo distat, quod populi appellatione universi cives significantur, connumeratis et patriciis; plebis autem appellatione sine patriciis ceteri cives significantur. Unde olim patricii dicebant plebiscitis se non teneri, quia sine auctoritate

make use of law which is partly their own in particular, partly common to all mankind. What these portions of their system severally are, we shall explain in their proper places.

2. The laws, then, of the Roman people consist of *leges*, *plebiscita*, *senatusconsulta*, constitutions of the emperors, edicts of those who have the right of issuing edicts, and responses of the learned in the law.

3. A *lex* is what the *populus* directs and establishes. A *plebiscitum* is what the *plebs* directs and establishes: the *plebs* differing from the *populus* herein, that by the appellation of *populus* the collective body of the citizens, including the patricians, is denoted, whilst by the appellation of *plebs* is denoted the rest of the citizens, excluding the patricians. Hence in olden times the patricians used to say that they were not bound by plebiscites, because they were passed without

makes no mention. Moreover, the Sovereign, or the *Populus* as Gaius has it, might make any Custom, general or merely national, into a Law; and such, equally with a Law originating from any other motive influencing the Sovereign, or *populus*, would be *jus civile, quod quisque populus sibi jus constituit.* Hence Gaius' discrimination is imperfect; and his mention of *Jus Naturale*, as identical with *Jus Gentium*, is still more unfortunate. Justinian in *Inst.* 1. 5. *pr.* draws the proper distinction between them, viz. that *Jus Gentium* (as understood in the later days of Roman Jurisprudence) was General Customs, as they are found existing; and *Jus Naturale*, the Customs which ought to exist, or the Unrevealed Law of God, which can be known either by Instinct or by calculation of Utility. See Austin's *Jurisprudence*, Lectures 31, 32: Maine's *Ancient Law*, ch. 3.

P. 2 eorum facta essent. sed postea | lex Hortensia lata est, qua cautum est ut plebiscita universum populum tenerent. itaque eo modo legibus exaequata sunt[1].

4. Senatusconsultum est quod senatus iubet atque constituit, idque legis vicem optinet, quamvis fuerit quaesitum[2].

their authority: but at a later period the Lex Hortensia was enacted, whereby it was provided that the plebiscites should be binding on the whole *populus*, and therefore in this way they were put on a level with *leges*[1].

4. A *senatusconsultum* is what the senate directs and establishes, and it has the force of a *lex*, although this point was at one time disputed[2].

---

1 The terms of the Lex Hortensia are thus given by Pliny (*Nat. Hist.* XVI. 15), "Q. Hortensius dictator, quum plebs secessisset in Janiculum, legem in Esculeto tulit, ut quod ea jussisset omnes Quirites teneret." Aulus Gellius (XV. 27) also says, "Plebiscita appellantur quae tribunis plebis ferentibus accepta sunt; quibus rogationibus ante patricii non tenebantur, donec Q. Hortensius dictator eam legem tulit, ut eo jure quod plebes statuisset omnes Quirites tenerentur."

Nothing could be plainer than the words of the law as given by these two writers, did we not know of pre-existing laws, which, at first sight, seem to have settled the same principle; one 163 years previously, viz. the Lex Valeria Horatia: "ut quod tributim plebes jussisset populum teneret;" Livy, III. 55: the other 53 years previously, viz. the Lex Publilia; "ut plebiscita omnes Quirites tenerent;" Livy, VIII. 12.

Ortolan's explanation is that the Lex Valeria Horatia was merely retrospective, rendering universally binding certain plebiscites already passed in the *comitia tributa*, but not yet sanctioned by the *comitia centuriata*, nor confirmed by the *auctoritas* of the senate, (for both these ratifications were in olden times necessary;) whilst the Lex Publilia abrogated entirely the necessity of a re-enactment by the *comitia centuriata* of future plebiscites, although it did not allow them to become law against or without the *auctoritas* of the senate.

The Lex Hortensia therefore went a step further and established the perfect independence and equal authority of plebiscites and *leges*, by making the *auctoritas* unnecessary for the former; just as another Lex Publilia (B.C. 340) had already made it unnecessary for the latter, or, to speak more correctly, had ordered it to be given by anticipation; "Ut legum quae comitiis centuriatis ferrentur ante initum suffragium Patres auctores fierent." Livy, VIII. 12.

The date of the Lex Hortensia was B.C. 287. Mommsen's explanation is different: for which see his *Röm. Forsch.* Vol. I. pp. 163, 200 and 215.

2 Theophilus says that the force of laws was given to Scta. by the Lex Hortensia; Theoph. lib. I. Tit. 2. 5. But see Niebuhr's remarks on this law in his *Lectures on Roman History*, Vol. I. pp. 322, 323.

5. Constitutio Principis est quod Imperator decreto vel edicto vel epistula[1] constituit. neque umquam dubitatum est quin id legis vicem optineat, cum ipse Imperator per legem imperium accipiat[2].

6. Ius autem edicendi habent magistratus populi Romani. sed amplissimum ius est in edictis duorum Praetorum, urbani et peregrini[3]: quorum in provinciis iurisdictionem Praesides earum habent; item in edictis Aedilium curulium, quorum iurisdictionem in provinciis populi Romani Quaestores habent; nam in provincias Caesaris omnino Quaestores non mittuntur, et ob id hoc edictum in his provinciis non proponitur[4].

7. Responsa prudentium sunt sententiae et opiniones eorum

5. A constitution of the emperor is what the emperor establishes by his decree, edict, or rescript[1]; nor has there ever been a doubt as to this having the force of a *lex*, since it is by a *lex* that the emperor himself receives his authority[2].

6. The magistrates of the Roman people have the right of issuing edicts: but the most extensive authority attaches to the edicts of the two praetors, *Urbanus* and *Peregrinus*[3], the counterpart of whose jurisdiction the governors of the provinces have therein: also to the edicts of the Curule Aediles, the counterpart of whose jurisdiction the Quaestors have in the provinces of the Roman people: for Quaestors are not sent at all into the provinces of Caesar, and therefore this (Aedilitian) edict is not promulged therein[4].

7. The responses of the learned in the law are the decisions

---

[1] *Decretum* = a decision given by the emperor in his capacity of judge.

Edictum = a general constitution.

Rescriptum = *epistula* = the emperor's solution of a legal difficulty propounded to him by a magistrate or private person; and if by the former, preceding such magistrate's judgment and furnishing him with principles on which to base it. See Austin, Lect. 28, p. 200 (p. 534, third edition).

[2] See note on Just. *Inst.* I. 2. 6, Abdy and Walker's edition.

[3] See Niebuhr's *Lectures on Roman History*, Vol. I. p. 403.

[4] In the Imperial times the provinces were divided into two classes, *provinciae imperatoriae* or *Caesaris*, governed by *legati* appointed by the emperor, and *provinciae senatoriae*, governed by *proconsules* nominated by the senate. In a senatorial province the fiscal authority was lodged in the hands of a *quaestor*, in an imperial province in those of a *procurator Caesaris*. This division was done away with about the middle of the 3rd century.

quibus permissum est iura condere[1]. quorum omnium si in unum sententiae concurrant, id quod ita sentiunt legis vicem optinet; si vero dissentiunt, iudici licet quam velit sententiam sequi: idque rescripto divi Hadriani significatur[2].

8. Omne autem ius quo utimur vel ad personas pertinet,
P. 3 vel | ad res, vel ad actiones. sed prius videamus de personis[3].

9. Et quidem summa divisio de iure personarum haec est, quod omnes homines aut liberi sunt aut servi.

10. Rursus liberorum hominum alii ingenui sunt, alii libertini[4].

11. Ingenui sunt, qui liberi nati sunt; libertini, qui ex iusta servitute manumissi sunt.

and opinions of those to whom license[1] has been given to lay down the law: and if the opinions of all these are in accord, that which they so hold has the force of a *lex:* but if they are not in accord, the *judex* is at liberty to follow which opinion he pleases, as is stated in a rescript of the late emperor Hadrian[2].

8. The whole body of law which we use relates either to persons or to things or to actions. But first let us consider about persons[3].

9. The primary division then of the law of persons is this, that all men are either free or slaves.

10. Of freemen again some are *ingenui*, some *libertini*[4].

11. *Ingenui* are those who have been born free: *libertini* are those who have been manumitted from servitude recognized by the law.

---

[1] The *juris prudentes* in the most ancient times took up the profession at their pleasure, and gave their advice gratuitously. Augustus commanded that none should practise without a license, and it is to this licensing that the words "quibus permissum est" refer. See D. 1. 2. 2. 47. With reference to the jurisconsults and their influence, see Maine's *Ancient Law*, ch. 11. and note on Just. *Inst.* 1. 2. 8, Abdy and Walker's edition. For the phrase *jura condere* compare C. 1. 14. 12. 1: "si enim in praesenti leges condere soli Imperatori concessum est; et leges interpretari solo dignum imperio esse oportet."

[2] See Austin, Lect. 28, on the classification of laws.

[3] Austin discusses the signification of "person" natural or legal, in Lecture 12.

The distinction between the law of persons and the law of things is treated of in Austin's Lecture 40.

[4] See Appendix (A).

12. Rursus libertinorum (*tria sunt genera*[1] *: nam aut cives Romani, aut Latini, aut dediticiorum*) numero sunt. de quibus singulis dispiciamus; ac prius de dediticiis.

13. Lege itaque Aelia Sentia cavetur[2], ut qui servi a dominis poenae nomine vincti sint, quibusve stigmata inscripta sint, deve quibus ob noxam quaestio tormentis habita sit et in ea noxa fuisse convicti sint, quique ut ferro aut cum bestiis depugnarent traditi sint, inve ludum custodiamve coniecti fuerint, et postea vel ab eodem domino vel ab alio manumissi, eiusdem condicionis liberi fiant, cuius condicionis sunt peregrini dediticii. (14.) Vocantur autem *peregrini dediticii*[3] hi qui quondam adversus populum Romanum armis susceptis pugnaverunt, deinde victi se dediderunt. (15.) Huius ergo turpitudinis servos quocumque modo et cuiuscumque aetatis manumissos, etsi pleno iure[4] dominorum fuerint, numquam aut cives Roma-

12. Of *libertini* again there are three classes[1], for they are either Roman citizens, or Latins, or in the category of the *dediticii*. Let us consider these one by one, and first as to *dediticii*.

13. It is provided then by the Lex Aelia Sentia[2], that such slaves as have been put in chains by their masters by way of punishment, or have been branded, or examined by torture on account of misdeed, and convicted of the misdeed, or have been delivered over to fight with the sword or against wild-beasts, or cast into a gladiatorial school or a prison, and have afterwards been manumitted either by the same or another master, shall become freemen of the same class whereof are *peregrini dediticii*. 14. Now those are called *peregrini dediticii*[3] who aforetime have taken up arms and fought against the Roman people, and then, when conquered, have surrendered themselves. 15. Slaves then who have been visited with such disgrace, in whatever manner and at whatever age they have been manumitted, even although they belonged to their masters in full title[4], we shall never admit to become

[1] A line has been omitted by the transcriber of the MS., but can be supplied from the *Epitome*, I. 1.

[2] Enacted A.D. 4. Ulpian, I. 11; D. 40. 9.

[3] These words are inserted in the MS. by a later hand.

[4] "Pleno jure" = "ex jure Quiritium;" *i.e.* not merely "in bonis:" for the signification of which terms see II. 40. Compare also § 17 below.

nos aut Latinos fieri dicemus, sed omni modo dediticiorum numero constitui intellegemus[1].

16. Si vero in nulla tali turpitudine sit servus, manumissum
P. 4 modo civem Romanum, modo Latinum fieri dice|mus. (17.) Nam in cuius persona tria haec concurrunt, ut maior sit annorum triginta, et ex iure Quiritium[2] domini, et iusta ac legitima manumissione liberetur, id est vindicta aut censu aut testamento[3], is civis Romanus fit: sin vero aliquid eorum deerit, Latinus erit.

18. Quod autem de aetate servi requiritur, lege Aelia Sentia introductum est. nam ea lex minores XXX annorum servos non aliter voluit manumissos cives Romanos fieri, quam si vindicta, aput consilium iusta causa manumissionis adprobata, liberati fuerint. (19.) Iusta autem causa manumissionis est veluti si quis filium filiamve, aut fratrem sororemve naturalem,

Roman citizens or Latins, but shall under all circumstances understand to be put in the category of *dediticii*[1].

16. But if a slave have fallen under no such disgrace, we shall say that when manumitted he becomes in some cases a Roman citizen, in others a Latin. 17. For in whatsoever man's person these three qualifications are united, (1) that he be above thirty years of age; (2) the property of his master by Quiritarian right[2] and (3) liberated by a regular and lawful manumission, *i.e.* by *vindicta*, *census*, or *testament*[3], such an one becomes a Roman citizen: but if any one of these qualifications be wanting, he will be a Latin.

18. The requirement as to the age of the slave was introduced by the Lex Aelia Sentia. For that *lex* prohibited slaves manumitted under thirty years of age from becoming Roman citizens unless they were liberated by *vindicta* after lawful cause for manumission had been approved before the council. 19. Now lawful cause for manumission is, for instance, where one manumits before the council a son or daughter, or a natural brother or sister, or a foster-child, or a personal atten-

1 For further information as to *dediticii* see III. 74; Ulp. I. 11.

2 I. 54, II. 40.

3 Manumission by *census* is referred to by Cicero, *De Orat.* I. 40: "cum quæritur, is qui domini voluntate census sit, continuone an ubi lustrum conditum liber sit". For testamentary manumission, see II. 267, 276. Niebuhr is of opinion that the rights which ensued upon the various kinds of manumission were not identical. *Hist. of Rome*, Vol. I. p. 594. Ulpian, I. 6, 8, 10, 12, 16.

aut alumnum, aut paedagogum, aut servum procuratoris[1] habendi gratia, aut ancillam matrimonii causa, apud consilium manumittat. (20.) Consilium autem adhibetur in urbe Roma quidem quinque senatorum et quinque equitum Romanorum puberum[2]; in provinciis autem viginti recuperatorum[3] civium Romanorum. idque fit ultimo die conventus: sed Romae certis diebus aput consilium manumittuntur. Maiores vero triginta annorum servi semper manumitti solent, adeo ut vel in transitu manumittantur, veluti cum Praetor aut Proconsule in balneum vel in

dant, or a slave with the intent of making him his *procurator*[1], or a female slave for the purpose of marrying her.

20. Now the council consists in the city of Rome of five Senators and five Knights, Romans of the age of puberty[2]: in the provinces of twenty *Recuperatores*[3], Roman citizens. And this proceeding (the manumission) takes place on the last day of their assembly, whereas at Rome men are manumitted before the council on certain fixed days. But slaves over thirty years of age can be manumitted at any time, so that they can be manumitted even *in transitu*, for instance when the Praetor or Proconsul is on his way to the bath or the

---

[1] IV. 84.

[2] I. 196.

[3] *Recuperatores* came into use at Rome at a date long subsequent to the institution of the *judex*, to whom the Praetor remitted the investigation of evidence; but their function was the same. There was never more than one *judex* in a law-suit, but *recuperatores* were always three in number, and sometimes five. It has been said, but on doubtful authority, that *recuperatores* were first employed in the trial of cases which came before the Praetor Peregrinus: and, if it were so, we may suppose that one or two were of the nationality of each litigant, and the third or fifth man on the panel a Roman: to secure at once a fair consideration of each litigant's cause, and to prevent departure from the principles of Roman Law. But *recuperatores* were afterwards employed in cases where both litigants were Roman citizens, and were themselves Roman citizens; but were not chosen from the senators in early times, as *judices* were; nor taken off the *album judicum* in later days. As *recuperatores* never acted alone, the term became applied in Imperial times, or even earlier, to any Committee; as in the present case, to the committee to consider lawful grounds of manumission. See Livy 26. 48: Cicero *in Verrem*, Lib. III. § 12: *pro Tullio*, § 8: *pro Cæcina*, § 2 and Klotz's notes thereon: Pliny, *Epp.* 3. 20.

The *conventus* was the body of Roman citizens resident in the province; who were bound to attend at the court of the Praeses held in their neighbourhood, that they might furnish the jury.

theatrum eat. (21.) Praeterea minor triginta annorum servus manumissione potest civis Romanus fieri, si ab eo domino qui solvendo non erat, testamento eum liberum et heredem re-
P. 5 (deest) lictum[1] |—[*desunt lin.* 24].
P. 6 22. ...homines Latini Juniani appellantur[2]: Latini ideo, quia adsimulati sunt Latinis coloniariis[3]; Iuniani ideo, quia per legem Iuniam[4] libertatem acceperunt, cum olim servi viderentur esse[5]. (23.) Non tamen illis permittit lex Iunia vel ipsis testamentum facere, vel ex testamento alieno capere, vel tutores[6] testamento dari. (24.) Quod autem diximus ex testamento eos capere non posse, ita intellegemus ne quid in directo

theatre. 21. Further a slave under thirty years of age can by manumission become a Roman citizen, if (it were declared) by an insolvent master in his testament that he was left free and heir[1]........

22. .... are called *Latini Juniani*[2]; *Latini* because they are put on the same footing with the Latin colonists[3]; *Juniani* because they have received their liberty under the Lex Junia[4], whereas in former times they were considered to be slaves[5]. 23. The Lex Junia does not, however, allow them either to make a testament for themselves, or to take anything by virtue of another man's testament, or to be appointed guardians[6] by testament. 24. Nevertheless our statement that they cannot take under a testament we intend thus, that we affirm that they

[1] II. 154; Ulpian, I. 14.

[2] The general sense of the lost words at the beginning of this paragraph no doubt was that those who were manumitted, when not fulfilling all the three conditions of § 17, were Junian Latins. Read III. 56. P. 5 exists in the MS. but only a word here and there can be deciphered: and the restitution of the text by Huschke is too conjectural to merit insertion here.

[3] The Latin colonists here meant are not the inhabitants of the old Latin towns (whose franchise is called *majus Latium* by Niebuhr), who obtained full civic rights by the Julian law: but the colonists and inhabitants of the towns of Cisalpine Gaul, who were raised to the rank of Latins by a law of Cn. Pompeius Strabo; the bulk of the population, however, being debarred from *conubium*, and those who held magistracies alone receiving Roman citizenship. See note on I. 95. This franchise Niebuhr calls "minus Latium." *Hist. of Rome*, Vol. II. pp. 77—81.

[4] Lex Junia Norbana, A.D. 19.

[5] In ancient times slaves manumitted irregularly only held their liberty on sufferance. Their masters could recall them into slavery, hence "olim servi videbantur esse." III. 56; Ulpian, I. 12. The Praetor, however, protected them as being *in forma libertatis*, long before any *lex* took cognizance of them.

[6] I. 144.

hereditatis legatorumve nomine eos posse capere dicamus; alioquin per fideicommissum[1] capere possunt.

25. Hi vero qui dediticiorum numero sunt nullo modo ex testamento capere possunt, non magis quam quilibet peregrinus: quin nec ipsi testamentum facere possunt secundum id quod magis placuit[2]. (26.) Pessima itaque libertas eorum est qui dediticiorum numero sunt: nec ulla lege aut senatusconsulto aut constitutione principali aditus illis ad civitatem Romanam datur. (27.) Quin et in urbe Roma vel intra centesimum urbis Romae miliarium morari prohibentur; et si contra ea fecerint, ipsi bonaque eorum publice venire iubentur ea condicione, ut ne in urbe Roma vel intra centesimum urbis Romae miliarium serviant, neve umquam manumittantur; et si manumissi fuerint, servi populi Romani esse iubentur. et haec ita lege Aelia Sentia conprehensa sunt. |

P. 7 28. Latini vero multis modis ad civitatem Romanam perveniunt. (29.) Statim enim ex lege Aelia Sentia cautum

can take nothing in the direct way of inheritance or legacy; they can, on the other hand, take by *fideicommissum*[1].

25. But those who are in the category of *dediticii* cannot take under a testament at all, any more than a foreigner can; nor can they, according to general opinion, make a testament themselves[2]. 26. The liberty, therefore, of those who are in the category of *dediticii* is of the lowest kind, nor is access to Roman citizenship allowed them by any *lex*, *senatusconsultum*, or Imperial constitution. 27. Nay more, they are forbidden to dwell within the city of Rome or within the hundredth milestone from the city of Rome, and if they transgress these rules, they themselves and their goods are ordered to be sold publicly, with the proviso that they do not serve as slaves within the city of Rome nor within the hundredth milestone from the city of Rome, and be never manumitted: and if they be manumitted, they are ordered to become slaves of the Roman people. And these things are so laid down in the Lex Aelia Sentia.

28. Latins attain to Roman citizenship in many ways. 29. For it was expressly provided by the same Lex Aelia Sentia, that slaves manumitted under the age of thirty years

[1] II. 246.

[2] III. 75; Ulp. XX. 14.

est, ut minores triginta annorum manumissi et Latini facti, si uxores duxerint vel cives Romanas, vel Latinas coloniarias, vel eiusdem condicionis cuius et ipsi essent, idque testati fuerint adhibitis non minus quam septem testibus civibus Romanis puberibus[1], et filium procreaverint, cum is filius anniculus esse coeperit, datur eis potestas per eam legem adire Praetorem vel in provinciis Praesidem provinciae, et adprobare se ex lege Aelia Sentia uxorem duxisse et ex ea filium anniculum habere; et si is apud quem causa probata est id ita esse pronuntiaverit, tunc et ipse Latinus et uxor eius, si et ipsa eiusdem (*condicionis sit, et ipsorum filius, si et ipse eiusdem*) condicionis sit, cives Romani esse iubentur[2]. (30.) Ideo autem in ipsorum

and made Latins, if they have married wives who were either Roman citizens, or Latin colonists, or of the same condition of which they themselves were, and have made attestation of this in the presence of not less than seven witnesses, Roman citizens of the age of puberty[1], and have begotten a son, when this son has attained the age of one year, the power is given them to make application in virtue of that law, to the Praetor, or in the provinces to the governor, and adduce proof that they have married a wife in accordance with the provisions of the Lex Aelia Sentia, and have by her a son a year old; and if he before whom the case is proved, shall declare that it is as they say, then both the Latin himself, and his wife, if she be of the same condition, and their son, if he also be of the same condition, are ordered to become Roman citizens[2]. 30. For

---

[1] I. 196.

[2] I. 66, 80; III. 73; Ulpian, III. 3. There is an apparent contradiction upon this subject between Gaius and Ulpian. The former, as we see, attributes the regulations respecting the proof in these cases to the Lex Aelia Sentia, whilst the latter ascribes them to the Lex Junia Norbana. Most modern writers on the history of the old Roman law agree in affixing a later date to the Junian than to the Aelian law. To reconcile this apparent discrepancy, it is supposed that the later *lex*, which was passed in the reign of Tiberius, was to a very great extent a confirmatory enactment, embracing in it most of the regulations of the prior *lex* passed in the reign of Augustus, and therefore that the authors are right in ascribing the regulations respecting the *causae probatio* to either law. There would, however, be this important difference, viz. that if Latinity, as a *legal* kind of freedom of a lower character than *civitas*, was introduced by the Lex Junia Norbana; and the Lex Aelia Sentia was an enactment of earlier date; *causae probatio* must originally have been the mode of passing from the

filio adiecimus "si et ipse eiusdem condicionis sit," quia si uxor Latini civis Romana est, qui ex ea nascitur ex novo senatusconsulto quod auctore[1] divo Hadriano factum est, civis Romanus nascitur. (31.) Hoc tamen ius adipiscendae civitatis Romanae etiamsi soli minores triginta annorum manumissi et Latini facti ex lege Aelia Sentia habuerunt, tamen postea senatusconsulto quod Pegaso et Pusione Consulibus factum est[2], etiam maioribus triginta annorum manumissis Latinis factis concessum est[3]. (32.) Ceterum etiamsi ante decesserit Latinus, quam anniculi filii causam probarit, potest
P. 8 mater eius causam probare, et sic et ipsa fiet | civis Romana ex

this reason do we add with reference to their son, "if he also be of the same condition," because if the wife of the Latin be a Roman citizen, the child born from her is a Roman citizen by birth in virtue of a recent *senatusconsultum*, which was enacted at the instance[1] of the late emperor Hadrian.

31. Although they alone, who were Latins because of manumission under thirty years of age, had this right of obtaining Roman citizenship in virtue of the Lex Aelia Sentia, yet it was afterwards granted by a *senatusconsultum*[2], enacted in the consulship of Pegasus and Pusio, to those also who were manumitted and made Latins when over thirty years of age[3]. 32. Further, even if the Latin die before he has proved his case in respect of a son one year old, the mother can tender proof, and thus she will herself also become a Roman citizen

status called "in forma libertatis" to citizenship, i.e. from a merely *equitable* freedom to *legal* freedom; and afterwards, when the Lex Junia Norbana came into force, the mode of passing from a *lower legal* freedom to the *highest legal* freedom. A French writer, M. Marchandy, has contended with considerable show of reason that the Lex Junia preceded the Lex Aelia, and was in existence in the time of Cicero: see *Themis*, Tom. 8. The subject has been discussed at length by Hollweg in his *Dissertatio de causae probatione*.

[1] The *comitia* or senate in early imperial times still legislated in appearance, but their legislation was according to the emperor's suggestion. The *comitia* being incommodious tools, the work of legislation was usually done by the senate, the smaller and more manageable body; but the senate had no free action, their *senatusconsulta* were at the *instance of the prince*. See Austin, Vol. II. p. 200 (p. 534, third edition).

[2] About A.D. 75. For Pegasus and Pusio were consuls under Vespasian, though the exact year is not known.

[3] Who were Latins, that is to say, by failure of one or other of the conditions marked (2) and (3) in § 17 above.

Latina (*desunt lin.* 3)...ipse filius civis...debet causam probare ut...*quae* supra diximus de filio anniculo dicta intellegemus *etiam de filia annicula*...(*desunt lin.* 2) (33.)...id est fiunt cives Romani, si Romae inter vigiles sex annis militaverint. Postea dicitur factum esse senatusconsultum quo data est illis civitas Romana, si triennium militiae expleverint[1]. Item edicto Claudii Latini ius Quiritium consequuntur, si navem marinam aedificaverint, quae non minus quam x milia modior*um fru*-*men*ti capiat, eaque navis vel quae in eius locum substituta *sit*, *sex* annis frumentum Romam portaverit[2]. (34.) Praeterea a*uc*-*tore Nero*ne se*natus consultum factum est*, ut si Latinus qui patrimonium HS CC milium plurisve habebit in urbe Roma domum aedificaverit, in quam non minus quam partem dimidiam patrimonii sui impenderit, ius Quiritium consequatur. Denique Traianus constituit ut si *Latinus* in urbe tr*ien*nio pistrinum exercuerit *in quo in* dies singulos non minus quam centenos modios frumenti panseret, ad ius Quiritium perveniret. |

from being a Latin...the son too will be a Roman citizen...the rules which we have stated above with regard to a son of the age of one year, we intend to apply also to a daughter of the age of one year...33....that is to say, that they become Roman citizens, if they have served six years in the guards at Rome. It is said that subsequently a *senatusconsultum* was enacted whereby Roman citizenship was conferred on them, if they completed three years of service[1]. Likewise, by an edict of Claudius Latins obtain the *ius Quiritium*, if they have built a sea-going ship which can hold not less than 10,000 bushels of corn, and that ship, or another replacing it, has carried corn to Rome for six years[2]. 34. Moreover a *senatusconsultum* was made at the instance of Nero, that if a Latin, possessing 200,000 sesterces of property or more, built a house in the city of Rome on which he expended not less than the half of his property, he should obtain the *ius Quiritium*. Lastly, Trajan issued a constitution, that if a Latin worked a mill and bakeshop in the city for three years, in which he ground each day not less than a hundred bushels of corn, he should attain to the *ius Quiritium*.

[1] Ulp. III. 5.

[2] Ulp. III. 6.

P. 9 (*desunt lin.* 14) (35.)...datur, quocunque modo ius Quiritium fuerit consecutus. *si quis alicuius et* in bonis et ex iure Quiritium sit[1], manumissus, ab eodem scilicet, et Latinus fieri potest et ius Quiritium consequi[2].

36. (*Non tamen cuicumque volenti manumittere licet*[3]. (37.) *nam is qui*) in fraudem creditorum vel in fraudem patroni manumittit[4], nihil agit, quia lex Aelia Sentia inpedit libertatem[5].

38. Item eadem lege minori xx annorum domino non aliter
P. 10 manumittere permittitur, quam si vindicta[6] aput con|silium iusta

35. If a slave belong to any man both by Bonitarian and Quiritarian right[1], he can when manumitted (by this same owner, that is to say,) either become a Latin or obtain the "Jus Quiritium" (*i.e.* become a Roman citizen[2]).

36. Moreover the law does not allow every one to manumit who chooses so to do[3]. 37. For he who manumits with the view of defrauding his creditors or his patron[4] effects nothing, since the Lex Aelia Sentia bars the gift of freedom[5].

38. Likewise by the same law a master under twenty years of age is not allowed to manumit except by *vindicta*[6], (after)

---

[1] II. 40.

[2] This passage is capable of two interpretations, either the one here given, which is in effect that a master could, under the conditions specified, confer upon his slave either the *Latinitas* or the *civitas;* (the latter would be the result of a manumission *per vindictam*;) or else it may refer to the method of manumission termed *iteratio*, and this, as Ulpian tells us, was the result of a second manumission granted to one who had already from a slave been made a Latin, the second manumittor being his original master. See Ulpian, III. 4.

[3] Two lines are left blank in the MSS. at this point. The words can be supplied from Just. *Inst.* I. 6. *pr.* See Ulpian, I. 12—25, for a complete list of the cases where manumission is not allowed.

[4] The *patronus* is the former master of a *libertinus*. The *jura patronatus* were

(α) *Obsequia:* duties attaching upon the *libertinus* by operation of law, *e.g.* to furnish ransom for the patron if taken prisoner, to assist in furnishing dower for his daughter, and to contribute to his expenses in law-suits, &c.

(β) *Jura in bonis:* rights of succession on the part of the *patronus* to the goods of the *libertinus*. III. 39 et seqq.

(γ) *Operae:* services reserved by special agreement as a consideration for the manumission.

It is scarcely necessary to say that a freedman is styled *libertinus* in respect of his class, *libertus* in reference to his former master.

[5] I. 47. Examples of the application of this clause of the Lex Aelia Sentia are to be found in D. 28. 5. 55, 57, 60 and 83.

[6] There is good reason for objecting to the words "except by *vindicta*," for though they appear in the Institutes of Justinian, they are not

causa manumissionis adprobata fuerit. (39.) Iustae autem causae manumissionis sunt: veluti si quis patrem aut matrem aut paedagogum aut conlactaneum manumittat. sed et illae causae, quas superius id est in servo minore XXX annorum exposuimus[1], ad hunc quoque casum de quo loquimur adferri possunt. item ex diverso hae causae, quas in minore XX annorum domino rettulimus, porrigi possunt et ad servum minorem XXX annorum.

40. Cum ergo certus modus manumittendi minoribus XX annorum dominis per legem Aeliam Sentiam constitutus sit, evenit, ut qui XIIII annos aetatis expleverit, licet testamentum facere possit, et in eo heredem sibi instituere legataque relinquere possit, tamen, si adhuc minor sit annorum XX, libertatem servo dare non potest. (41.) Et quamvis vel Latinum facere velit minor XX annorum dominus, tamen nihilominus

a lawful cause for manumission has been proved before the council. 39. Lawful causes of manumission are, for instance, if a man manumit his father, or mother, or personal attendant, or foster-brother. And those causes too which we enumerated above[1], *i.e.* in reference to a slave under thirty years of age, can be applied to this case also about which we are now speaking. So, conversely, those causes which we have specified with reference to a master under twenty years of age, can be extended also to the case of a slave under thirty years of age.

40. Inasmuch then as a certain limitation of manumitting has been imposed by the Lex Aelia Sentia on masters under twenty years of age, the result is that one who has completed his fourteenth year, although he can make a testament and in it institute an heir to himself and leave legacies, yet cannot, if he be still under twenty years of age, give liberty to a single slave. 41. And even though a master under twenty years of age wish to make a man merely a Latin, yet he must still

to be found in the Commentary of Theophilus nor in the fragments of Ulpian, and it need hardly be said that in matters of historical information as to the old Roman law, Justinian's treatise is valueless. Besides we see from I. 41, that a master under twenty years of age could, at any rate, after proof of cause perform the inferior manumission *inter amicos* without *vindicta*. Niebuhr and Göschen think the passage should have the following collocation of words, "non aliter vindicta manumittere permittitur quam si aput, &c."

[1] I. 19.

debet aput consilium causam probare, et ita postea inter amicos manumittere[1].

42. Praeterea lege Fufia Caninia[2] certus modus constitutus est in servis testamento manumittendis. (43.) nam ei qui plures quam duos neque plures quam decem servos habebit, usque ad partem dimidiam eius numeri manumittere permit-
P. 11 titur. ei vero qui plures | quam X neque plures quam XXX servos habebit, usque ad tertiam partem eius numeri manumittere permittitur. at ei qui plures quam XXX, neque plures quam centum habebit, usque ad partem quartam potestas manumittendi datur. novissime ei qui plures quam C habebit, nec plures quam D, non plures ei manumittere permittitur quam ad quintam partem, neque plures datur. sed praescribit lex, ne cui plures manumittere liceat quam C. *igitur*[3] si quis unum servum omnino aut duos habet, ad hanc legem non pertinet; et ideo liberam habet potestatem manumittendi.

prove cause before the council and then afterwards manumit him privately (*inter amicos*)[1].

42. Further by the Lex Fufia Caninia[2], there was established a strict limitation of the number of slaves who can be manumitted by testament: 43. for a man who has more than two, and not more than ten slaves, is allowed to manumit to the extent of half the number. A man, again, who has more than ten, and not more than thirty slaves, is allowed to manumit to the extent of one-third of the number. A man, again, who has more than thirty, and not more than a hundred, has the power of manumitting to the extent of a fourth part. Lastly, a man who has more than a hundred, and not more than five hundred, is allowed to manumit no more than a fifth part and no greater number. But the law provides that no man shall be allowed to manumit more than a hundred. If, therefore[3], any man have only one or two slaves, he does not come under the provisions of the law, and so he has unrestrained power of manumitting.

---

1 This was one of the modes of manumission arising out of custom, and recognized by the Praetor. It was a very simple affair, for all that was required was for the master to direct his slave to go free in the presence of five witnesses.

2 Passed probably in A.D. 8. Ulpian, I. 24.

3 The MS. has CQSI; Polenaer would read *contra si*, Huschke, as in the text, *igitur si*.

(44.) Ac ne ad eos quidem omnino haec lex pertinet, qui sine testamento manumittunt. itaque licet iis, qui vindicta aut censu aut inter amicos manumittunt, totam familiam suam liberare, scilicet si alia causa non inpediat libertatem. (45.) Sed quod de numero servorum testamento manumittendorum diximus, ita intellegemus ne unquam ex eo numero, ex quo dimidia aut tertia aut quarta aut quinta pars liberari potest, *pauciores manumittere* liceat, quam ex antecedenti numero licuit. et hoc ipsa *lege* provisum est. erat enim sane absurdum, ut X servorum domino quinque liberare liceret, quia usque ad dimidiam partem eius numeri manumittere ei conceditur, *ulterius*[1] autem XII servos habenti non plures liceret manumittere quam IIII.[2]

P. 12 (deest.) at eis qui plures quam X neque | [*desunt lin.* 24][3].

P. 13 (46.) Nam et si testamento scriptis in orbem servis libertas

44. Nor does this law in any way apply to those who manumit otherwise than by testament. Therefore those who manumit by *vindicta*, *census*, or *inter amicos*, may set free their whole gang, provided no other cause stand in the way of the gift of freedom. 45. But what we have said about the number of slaves which can be manumitted by testament, we shall interpret thus, that from a number out of which the half, third, fourth, or fifth part can be set free, the allowance is never to manumit fewer than could have been manumitted out of an antecedent (*i.e.* smaller) number. And this provision is found in the *lex* itself. For it would indeed be absurd that a master having ten slaves should be allowed to manumit five, because he is at liberty to manumit to the extent of half out of that number, whilst one who had a larger number[1], twelve, should not be allowed to manumit more than four[2]. But that those who have more than ten and not.........[3].

46. For also if liberty be given by testament to slaves

[1] *Ulterius* is the reading suggested by Huschke: the MS. looks like TERIU.

[2] The owner of twelve could manumit five, for he would reckon the 12 as 10, "ex antecedenti numero": and so for other cases.

[3] The lost portion of the MS. contained a further provision of the *lex*, that the slaves to be liberated should be mentioned by name, and that if the testator had nominated more than the number allowed by law, those whose names stood first on the list should be liberated in order, until the proper number had been completed. Testators having adopted the plan of writing the names in a circle to evade this regulation, the interpretation of § 46 was brought to bear against them. Ulpian, I. 25.. Gai. *Epit.* I. 2. 2.

data sit, quia nullus ordo manumissionis invenitur, nulli liberi erunt; quia lex Fufia Caninia quae in fraudem eius facta sint rescindit. sunt etiam specialia senatusconsulta, quibus rescissa sunt ea quae in fraudem eius legis excogitata sunt.

47. In summa sciendum est, (cum) lege Aelia Sentia cautum sit, ut creditorum fraudandorum causa manumissi liberi non fiant, etiam hoc ad peregrinos pertinere, senatus ita censuit ex auctoritate Hadriani; cetera vero iura eius legis ad peregrinos non pertinere.

48. Sequitur de iure personarum alia divisio. nam quaedam personae sui iuris sunt[1], quaedam alieno iuri sunt subiectae. (49.) Sed rursus earum personarum, quae alieno iuri subiectae sunt, aliae in potestate, aliae in manu, aliae in manicipio sunt[2]. (50.) Videamus nunc de iis quae alieno iuri subiectae sint: si cognoverimus quae istae personae sint, simul intellegemus quae sui iuris sint.

51. Ac prius dispiciamus de iis qui in aliena potestate sunt.

whose names are written in a circle, none of them will be free, since no order of manumission can be found: for the Lex Fufia Caninia sets aside whatever is done for its evasion. There are also special *senatusconsulta* by which devices for the evasion of that *lex* are set aside.

47. Finally, we must observe that the provision of the Lex Aelia Sentia, that those manumitted for the purpose of defrauding creditors are not to become free, applies to foreigners as well as citizens (*etiam*), the senate so decreed at the instance of Hadrian: but the other clauses of the *lex* do not apply to foreigners.

48. Next comes another division of the law of persons. For some persons are *sui juris*[1], some are subject to the *jus* (authority) of another. 49. But again of those persons who are subject to the authority of another, some are in *potestas*, some in *manus*, some in *mancipium*[2]. 50. Let us now consider about those who are subject to another's authority: if we discover who these persons are, we shall at the same time understand who are *sui juris*.

51. And first let us consider about those who are in the *potestas* of another.

---

[1] Ulpian, IV. 1.

[2] See Appendix (B).

52. In potestate itaque sunt servi dominorum. quae quidem potestas iuris gentium est[1]: nam aput omnes peraeque gentes animadvertere possumus dominis in servos vitae necisque potestatem esse. et quodcumque per servum adquiritur, id domino adquiritur[2]. (53.) Sed hoc tempore neque civibus |
P. 14 Romanis, nec ullis aliis hominibus qui sub imperio populi Romani sunt, licet supra modum et sine causa in servos suos saevire. nam ex constitutione sancti Imperatoris Antonini qui sine causa servum suum occiderit, non minus teneri iubetur[3], quam qui alienum servum occiderit. sed et maior quoque asperitas dominorum per eiusdem Principis constitutionem coercetur. nam consultus a quibusdam Praesidibus provinciarum de his servis, qui ad fana deorum vel ad

52. Slaves, then, are in the *potestas* of their masters, which *potestas* is a creation of the *jus gentium*[1], for we may perceive that amongst all nations alike masters have the power of life and death over their slaves. Also whatever is acquired by means of a slave is acquired for the master[2]. 53. But at the present day neither Roman citizens, nor any other men who are under the empire of the Roman people are allowed to practise excessive and wanton severity upon their slaves. For by a decree of the emperor Antoninus of holy memory, he who kills his own slave without cause is ordered to be no less amenable[3] than he who kills the slave of another. Further, the extravagant cruelty of masters is restrained by a constitution of the same emperor; for when consulted by certain governors of provinces with regard to those slaves who flee for

[1] But see Austin, Vol. II. p. 265 (p. 583, third edition), on the question of slavery being according to natural law or not.

[2] II. 86...Observe that the reading is *adquiritur*, not *adquiri*; so that Gaius only asserts that the *vitae necisque potestas* is a creature of the Jus Gentium: and makes no statement as to why the master had the slave's acquisitions. Savigny says that slaves were by some nations allowed to have property, *e.g.* by the Germans, and that therefore Gaius has intentionally used the indicative mood to draw our attention to the fact that the second incident springs from the Civil Law. "Savigny on Possess. translated by Perry," p. 53, note.

[3] Amenable, that is, to the penalties of the Lex Cornelia de Sicariis: for we read in D. 48. 8. 1. 2: "Et qui hominem occiderit punitur, non habita differentia cuius conditionis hominem interemit." The penalties are stated in D. 48. 8. 3. 5; "humiliores solent vel bestiis subiici, altiores vero deportantur in insulam."

statuas Principum confugiunt, praecepit, ut si intolerabilis videatur dominorum saevitia, cogantur servos suos vendere. et utrumque recte fit[1]; male enim nostro iure uti non debemus: qua ratione et prodigis interdicitur bonorum suorum administratio.

54. Ceterum cum aput cives Romanos duplex sit dominium, nam vel in bonis vel ex iure Quiritium vel ex utroque iure[2] cuiusque servus esse intellegitur, ita demum servum in potestate domini esse dicemus, si in bonis eius sit, etiamsi simul ex iure Quiritium eiusdem non sit. nam qui nudum ius Quiritium in servo habet, is potestatem habere non intellegitur.

55. Item in potestate nostra sunt liberi nostri quos iustis nuptiis procreavimus[3]. quod ius proprium civium Romanorum

refuge to the temples of the gods or the statues of the emperors, he ordered, that if the cruelty of the masters appear beyond endurance, they shall be compelled to sell their slaves. And both these rules are just[1]: for we ought not to make a bad use of our right, and on this principle too the management of their own property is forbidden to prodigals.

54. But since among Roman citizens ownership is of two kinds, for a slave is understood to belong to a man either by Bonitary title, by Quiritary title, or by both titles[2], we shall hold that a slave is in his master's *potestas* only in case he be his by Bonitary title, this being so even though he be not the same man's in Quiritary title also. For he who has the bare Quiritary title to a slave is not understood to have *potestas*.

55. Our children, likewise, whom we have begotten in lawful marriage[3], are in our *potestas:* and this right is one peculiar to

---

[1] The MS. has "Et utrumque recte fit regula," the last word being evidently a marginal annotation, which some transcriber has inserted in the text.

[2] II. 40, 41.

[3] By *justae* or *legitimae nuptiae* is meant a marriage contracted and established by the special forms prescribed by the *jus civile:* by *non justae nuptiae*, on the other hand, is not necessarily meant an illegal marriage; for this phrase generally denotes the contract which, though not completed according to all the prescribed forms of the *jus civile*, is valid according to the *jus gentium*. This was an important distinction in reference to the *causae probatio*. See App. B: "On Marriage;" Abdy and Walker's *Justinian*.

est. fere enim nulli alii sunt homines, qui talem in filios suos
P. 15 habent potestatem, qualem nos habemus. idque divi Ha|driani edicto quod proposuit de his, qui sibi liberisque suis ab eo civitatem Romanam petebant, significatur. nec me praeterit Galatarum gentem credere, in potestate parentum liberos esse.

56. (*Habent autem in potestate liberos cives Romani,*) si cives Romanas uxores duxerint, vel etiam Latinas peregrinasve cum quibus conubium habeant[1]. cum enim conubium id efficiat, ut liberi patris condicionem sequantur, evenit ut non (solum) cives Romani fiant, set et in potestate patris sint. (57.) Unde causa cognita[2] veteranis quibusdam concedi solet principalibus constitutionibus conubium cum his Latinis peregrinisve quas

Roman citizens. For there are scarcely any other men who have over their children a *potestas* such as we have. And this the late emperor Hadrian remarked in an edict which he published with regard to those who asked him for Roman citizenship for themselves and their children. I am not, however, unaware of the fact, that the race of the Galatians think that children are in the *potestas* of their ascendants.

56. Roman citizens then have their children in their *potestas*, if they have married Roman citizens or even Latin or foreign women with whom they have *conubium*[1]. For since *conubium* has the effect of making children follow the condition of their father, the result is that they are not only Roman citizens by birth, but are also under their father's *potestas*. 57. Hence by Imperial constitutions there is often granted, on cause shewn[2], to certain classes of veterans *conubium* with such Latin or foreign women as they take for their first wives

1 When two persons have *conubium* one with another they can contract *justae nuptiae*, or a marriage followed by the effects of the *jus civile*, especially *patria potestas* over the offspring and the tie of *agnatio* amongst them. For "Conubium est uxoris ducendae facultas. Conubium habent cives Romani cum civibus Romanis; cum Latinis autem et peregrinis ita si concessum sit: cum servis nullum est conubium." Ulpian, v. 3—5. The double aspect of *conubium*, viz. as it affected *status*, and as it related to degrees of relationship, had also an important bearing on the *causae probatio*; so far as the former is concerned, *conubium* existed as an undisputed right between all Roman citizens, but only by special grant (and therefore requiring proof) between citizens and Latins, or citizens and foreigners.

2 The MS. has UNDCC.

primas post missionem uxores duxerint. et qui ex eo matrimonio nascuntur, et cives Romani et in potestatem parentum fiunt[1].

58. (*Sciendum autem est non omnes nobis uxores ducere licere*[2]*:*) nam a quarundam nuptiis[3] abstinere debemus.

59. Inter eas enim personas quae parentum liberorumve locum inter se optinent nuptiae contrahi non possunt, nec inter eas conubium est, velut inter patrem et filiam, vel inter matrem et filium, vel inter avum et neptem: et si tales personae inter
P. 16 se coierint, nefarias | et incestas nuptias contraxisse dicuntur. et haec adeo ita sunt, ut quamvis per adoptionem parentum liberorumve loco sibi esse coeperint, non possunt inter se matrimonio coniungi, in tantum, ut etiam dissoluta adoptione idem iuris

after their dismissal from service; and the children of such a marriage are both Roman citizens and in the *potestas* of their ascendants[1].

58. Now we must bear in mind that we may not marry any woman we please[2], for there are some from marriage[3] with whom we must refrain.

59. Thus between persons who stand one to another in the relation of ascendants and descendants marriage cannot be contracted, nor is there *conubium* between them, for instance, between father and daughter, or mother and son, or grandfather and granddaughter; and if such persons cohabit, they are said to have contracted an unholy and incestuous marriage. And these rules hold so universally, that even if they entered into the relation of ascendants and descendants by adoption, they cannot be united in marriage; so that even if the adoption have been dissolved the same rule stands: and therefore I

---

1 Gaius does not here tell us what were the rights of a father having *patria potestas*. Originally, no doubt, the *potestas* over children was the same as over slaves, including the power of life and death, and the right to all property which the child acquired. The former power gradually fell into abeyance, and the latter in the case of sons was infringed upon by the rules which sprang up regarding *peculium castrense* and *quasi-castrense*, for which see D. 14, 6. 2, and App. A in Abdy and Walker's *Justinian*.

2 These omitted words are suggested by Just. *Inst.* I. 10. I.

3 *Nuptiae* and *matrimonium* seem to be used indiscriminately by Gaius. *Nuptiae* properly would be the ceremonies of marriage, *matrimonium* the marriage itself.

maneat: itaque eam quae mihi per adoptionem filiae sive neptis loco esse coeperit non potero uxorem ducere, quamvis eam emancipaverim[1].

60. Inter eas quoque personas quae ex transverso gradu cognatione iunguntur est quaedam similis observatio, sed non tanta[2]. (61.) Sane inter fratrem et sororem prohibitae sunt nuptiae, sive eodem patre eademque matre nati fuerint, sive alterutro eorum[3]. sed si qua per adoptionem soror mihi esse coeperit, quamdiu quidem constat adoptio, sane inter me et eam nuptiae non possunt consistere; cum vero per emancipationem adoptio dissoluta sit[4], potero eam uxorem ducere; sed et si ego emancipatus fuero, nihil inpedimento erit nuptiis.

62. Fratris filiam uxorem ducere licet: idque primum in usum venit, cum divus Claudius Agrippinam, fratris sui filiam, uxorem duxisset[5]. sororis vero filiam uxorem ducere non licet.
P. 17 et haec ita principalibus constitutionibus significantur. | item amitam et materteram uxorem ducere non licet.

cannot marry a woman who has come to be my daughter or granddaughter by adoption, even though I have emancipated her[1].

60. Between persons also who are related collaterally there is a rule of like character, but not so stringent[2]. 61. Marriage is undoubtedly forbidden between a brother and a sister, whether they be born from the same father and the same mother, or from one or other of them[3]. But if a woman become my sister by adoption, so long as the adoption stands marriage certainly cannot subsist between us; but when the adoption has been dissolved by emancipation[4], I can marry her: and moreover if I have been emancipated there will be no bar to the marriage.

62. It is lawful to marry a brother's daughter, and this first came into practice when Claudius took to wife Agrippina, the daughter of his brother[5]. But it is not lawful to marry a sister's daughter. And these things are so laid down in constitutions of the emperors. Likewise it is unlawful to marry a father's or mother's sister.

---

1 Ulpian, v. 6.

2 Ibid.

3 *i.e.* Whether they be of the whole or half blood.

4 I. 132.

5 This connection was again prohibited by Constantine, see Just. *Inst.* I. 10. § 3.

63. Item eam quae mihi quondam socrus aut nurus aut privigna aut noverca fuit. ideo autem diximus quondam, quia si adhuc constant eae nuptiae per quas talis adfinitas quaesita est, alia ratione mihi nupta esse non potest, quia neque eadem duobus nupta esse potest, neque idem duas uxores habere[1].

64. Ergo si quis nefarias atque incestas nuptias contraxerit, neque uxorem habere videtur, neque liberos. itaque hi qui ex eo coitu nascuntur, matrem quidem habere videntur, patrem vero non utique: nec ob id in potestate eius sunt, (sed) quales sunt ii quos mater vulgo concepit. nam et ii patrem habere non intelleguntur, cum is etiam incertus sit; unde solent

63. Likewise one who has aforetime been my mother-in-law or daughter-in-law or step-daughter or step-mother. The reason for our saying "aforetime" is that if the marriage still subsists whereby such affinity has been brought about, she cannot be married to me for another reason, since neither can the same woman be married to two husbands, nor can the same man have two wives[1].

64. If then any man has contracted an unholy and incestuous marriage, he is considered to have neither wife nor children. Therefore the offspring of such a cohabitation are regarded as having a mother indeed, but no father at all: and hence they are not in his *potestas*, but are as those whom a mother has conceived out of wedlock. For these too are considered to have no father at all, inasmuch as in their case also he is uncertain: and therefore they are called spurious children,

---

[1] The rules on the subject of prohibited degrees may be thus summarized:

(*a*) Ascendants and descendants can in no case marry.

(*b*) Collaterals within the fourth degree cannot marry.

(*c*) No person can marry the son or daughter of any one of his ascendants; but he may marry their grandson or granddaughter, or more remote descendant.

(*d*) The relationship created by adoption is during its continuance as complete a bar as the relationship of blood.

(*e*) The relationship created by adoption is no bar after the dissolution of the adoption, except when it has for a time put the parties in the position of ascendant and descendant.

(*f*) Affinity bars marriage with ascendants or descendants of a former consort, and with his or her collaterals of the second degree, i.e. a deceased wife's sister or deceased husband's brother. C. 5. 5. 5.

spurii filii appellari, vel a Graeca voce quasi σποράδην concepti, vel quasi sine patre filii[1].

65. (*Aliquando autem evenit, ut liberi qui statim ut*[2]) nati sunt parentum in potestate non fiant, ii postea tamen redigantur in potestatem. (66.) *Veluti si Latin*us ex lege Aelia Sentia uxore ducta filium procreaverit, aut Latinum ex Latina, aut civem Romanum ex cive Romana, non habebit eum in potestate; *sed postea causa probata*[3] *civitatem Romanam* conse*quetur cum filio*[4]*:*
P. 18 simul ergo eum in potestate | sua habere incipit.

67. Item si civis Romanus Latinam aut peregrinam uxorem duxerit per ignorantiam, cum eam civem Romanam esse crederet, et filium procreaverit, hic non est in potestate, quia ne quidem civis Romanus est, sed aut Latinus aut peregrinus, id est eius condicionis cuius et mater fuerit, quia non aliter quisquam ad patris condicionem accedit, quam si inter patrem et

either from a Greek word, being as it were conceived σποράδην (at random), or as children without a father[1].

65. Sometimes, however, it happens that descendants[2], who at the moment of their birth are not in the *potestas* of their ascendants, are subsequently brought into their *potestas*. 66. For instance, if a Latin, having married a wife in accordance with the Lex Aelia Sentia, have begotten a son, whether a Latin son by a Latin wife or a Roman citizen by a Roman wife, he will not have him in his *potestas;* but afterwards by *causae probatio*[3] he will obtain Roman citizenship for himself and his son[4]: and therefore at the same time he begins to have him in his *potestas*.

67. Likewise if a Roman citizen through ignorance have married a Latin or a foreign woman, believing her to be a Roman citizen, and have begotten a son, this son is not in his *potestas*, because he is not even a Roman citizen, but either a Latin or a foreigner, that is, of the condition of which his mother is, since a man does not follow his father's condition unless there be *conubium* between his father and mother: yet

---

1 Ulpian, IV. 2. *Sinepatrii* according to the second derivation is contracted down into *spurii*.

2 See Just. *Inst.* I. 10. 13.

3 I. 29. Ulp. VII. 4.

4 Huschke supplies these words. Böcking and Krüger suggest almost the same.

matrem eius conubium sit: sed ex senatusconsulto[1] permittitur causam erroris probare, et ita uxor quoque et filius ad civitatem Romanam perveniunt, et ex eo tempore incipit filius in potestate patris esse. idem iuris est, si eam per ignorantiam uxorem duxerit quae dediticiorum numero est, nisi quod uxor non fit civis Romana[2]. (68.) Item si civis Romana per errorem nupta sit peregrino tamquam civi Romano, permittitur ei causam erroris probare[3], et ita filius quoque eius et maritus ad civitatem Romanam perveniunt[4], et aeque simul incipit filius in potestate patris esse. idem iuris est si peregrino tamquam Latino ex lege Aelia Sentia nupta sit: nam et de hoc specialiter senatusconsulto cavetur[5]. idem iuris est aliquatenus, si ei qui dediticiorum numero est, tamquam civi Romano aut Latino e lege Aelia Sentia nupta sit: nisi quod scilicet qui dediticiorum numero est, in sua condicione permanet, et ideo filius, quamvis

by a *senatusconsultum*[1] he is allowed to prove a case of error, and so both the wife and son attain to Roman citizenship, and from that time the son begins to be in the *potestas* of his father. The rule is the same if through ignorance he marry a woman who is in the category of the *dediticii*, except that the wife does not become a Roman citizen[2]. 68. Likewise if a Roman woman by mistake be married to a foreigner thinking him to be a Roman citizen, she is allowed to prove a case of error[3], and thus both the son and the husband attain to Roman citizenship[4], and at the same time the son begins to be in his father's *potestas*. The rule is the same if she be married in accordance with the Lex Aelia Sentia to a foreigner, under the impression that he is a Latin, for as to this special provision is made by the *senatusconsultum*[5]. The rule is the same to some extent, if she be married in accordance with the Lex Aelia Sentia to one who is in the category of the *dediticii*, under the impression that he is a Roman citizen or a Latin, except, that is to say, that he who is in the category of the *dediticii* remains in his condition, and therefore the son, although he becomes a

[1] Temp. Vespasiani, according to Gans.

[2] I. 15, 26, 27.

[3] Ulp. VII. 4.

[4] See note on I. 78. At first sight it would seem that the son was already a Roman citizen, there being no *conubium* between the parents; but the Lex Minicia had ruled otherwise.

[5] I. 67.

fiat civis Romanus, in potestatem patris non redigitur. (69.)
P. 19 Item si Latina peregrino, cum eum Latinum esse cre|deret, nupserit, potest ex senatusconsulto filio nato causam erroris probare, *et ita* omnes fiunt cives Romani, et filius in potestate patris esse incipit. (70.) Idem constitutum est, si Latinus per errorem peregrinam quasi Latinam aut civem Romanam e lege Aelia Sentia uxorem duxerit. (71.) Praeterea si civis Romanus, qui se credidisset Latinum, et ob id Latinam (duxerit), permittitur ei filio nato erroris causam probare, tamquam *si* e lege Aelia Sentia uxorem duxisset. item his qui cum cives Romani essent, peregrinos se esse credidissent et peregrinas uxores duxissent, permittitur ex senatusconsulto filio nato causam erroris probare: quo facto fiet uxor civis Romana et filius *ex lege Aelia Sen*tia non solum *ad civi*tatem Romanam pervenit, sed etiam in potestatem patris redigitur. (72.) Quaecumque de filio esse diximus, eadem et de filia dicta intellegemus. (73.) Et quantum ad erroris causam probandam attinet, nihil interest cuius aetatis filius sit filiave — — — — — — — — — — — — Latinus — — — — qui — — — — — — — nisi minor anniculo

Roman citizen, is not brought under his father's *potestas*. 69. Likewise if a Latin woman be married to a foreigner, thinking him to be a Latin, she can, by virtue of the *senatusconsultum*, after a son is born, prove a case of error, and so they all become Roman citizens, and the son is thenceforward in his father's *potestas*. 70. The same is the rule laid down if a Latin by mistake marry a foreign woman in accordance with the Lex Aelia Sentia, under the impression that she is a Latin or a citizen. 71. Further, if a Roman citizen, who believed himself to be a Latin, has for that reason married a Latin woman, he is permitted, after the birth of a son, to prove a case of error, just as though he had married in accordance with the Lex Aelia Sentia. Likewise men, who, although they were Roman citizens, believed themselves to be foreigners and married foreign wives, are allowed by the *senatusconsultum*, after the birth of a son, to prove a case of error: and on this being done the foreign wife becomes a Roman citizen, and the son by virtue of the Lex Aelia Sentia not only attains to Roman citizenship, but is brought under the *potestas* of his father. 72. Whatever we have said of a son, we shall consider to be also said of a daughter. 73. And so far as regards the proving of a case

sit filius filiave, causa probari non potest[1]. nec me praeterit in aliquo rescripto divi Hadriani ita esse constitutum, tamquam quod ad erroris quoque causam probandam [*desunt lin.* 2.] Im-
P. 20 perator — — — tuendam dedit. | (74) Si peregrinus civem Romanam uxorem duxerit, an et is causam erroris *probare possit* quaeritur... (*desunt lin.* 2.]....hoc ei specialiter concessum est. sed cum peregrinus civem Romanam uxorem duxisset, et filio nato alias[2] civitatem Romanam consecutus esset, deinde cum quaereretur an causam probare posset, rescripsit Imperator Antoninus proinde posse eum causam probare atque si peregrinus mansisset. ex quo colligimus etiam peregrinum causam probare posse. (75.) Ex iis quae diximus apparet sive civis Romanus peregrinam sive peregrinus civem Romanam uxorem duxerit, eum qui nascitur peregrinum (esse, sed) si quidem per errorem tale matrimonium coniunctum fuerit, emendari vitium eius ex constitutione, (secundum) ea quae superius diximus; si vero nullus error intervenerit, (sed) scientes

of error, it matters not of what age the son or daughter be[1]..... 74. If a foreigner has married a Roman woman, it is a question whether he can prove a case of error...this is specially granted to him. But when a foreigner had married a Roman woman, and after the birth of a son had attained to Roman citizenship in some other manner[2], and thereupon the question arose whether he could prove a case of error, the Emperor Antoninus issued a rescript that he could prove a case of error all the same as if he had remained a foreigner. Whence we gather that even a foreigner can prove a case (of error). 75. From what we have said it is evident that whether a Roman citizen has married a foreign woman, or a foreigner a Roman woman, the child is a foreigner: although, if such a marriage has been made by mistake, the defect of it is remedied by the Constitution, according to what we have said before. But if no mistake

---

[1] The rest of this paragraph is corrupt, but it seems plain that Gaius goes on to say, that, although in proving a case of error the age of the child is immaterial, yet it is not so when a Junian Latin applies to the Praetor in virtue of the Lex Aelia Sentia, for his claim is not entertained unless the child is above one year of age.

[2] Sc. *militia, nave, aedificio, pistrino vel iteratione.* See §§ 33—35, above.

suam condicionem ita coierint, nullo casu emendatur vitium eius matrimonii. (76.) Loquimur autem de his scilicet (inter) quos conubium non sit. nam alioquin si civis Romanus peregrinam cum qua ei conubium est uxorem duxerit, sicut supra quoque diximus iustum matrimonium contrahit, et tunc ex iis qui nascitur civis Romanus est et in potestate patris erit. (77.) Itaque si civis Romana peregrino cum quo ei conubium est nupserit, peregrinus sane procreatur et is iustus patris filius est,
P. 21 tamquam si ex peregrina eum procreasset. | hoc tamen tempore e senatusconsulto quod auctore divo Hadriano factum est, etiam si non fuerit conubium inter civem Romanam et peregrinum, qui nascitur iustus patris filius est. (78.) Quod autem diximus inter civem Romanam peregrinumque matrimonio contracto *qui ex eo matrimonio* nascitur peregrinum esse, *id ex lege Minicia*[1] *descendit, qua cautum* est ut si iis quidem *conubium non sit, deterioris* parentis condicionem se*quatur filius.* eadem lege cautum *est ut etiam ex* cive Romano *quum pro-*

occurred, and they so cohabited knowing their status, the defect of the marriage is in no case remedied. 76. We are, however, speaking of those only who have no *conubium* one with the other; for if, on the other hand, a Roman citizen has married a foreign woman with whom he has *conubium*, then, as we have also said above, he contracts a lawful marriage, and therefore the child of such parents is a Roman citizen and will be in the *potestas* of his father. 77. And so too, if a Roman woman be married to a foreigner with whom she has *conubium*, her child is clearly a foreigner, and yet is the lawful son of his father, just as if he had begotten him from a foreign woman. At the present time, however, by a *senatusconsultum* which was enacted at the instance of the late emperor Hadrian, even if *conubium* do not exist between the Roman woman and the foreigner, the child is the lawful son of his father. 78. But when we said that on a marriage taking place between a Roman woman and a foreigner, the child is a foreigner, this is a result of the Lex Minicia[1], wherein it was provided that, if there be not *conubium* between the parents, the son shall follow the status of the inferior parent. By the same law it was also pro-

1 See Ulpian, v. 8; where, however, the law is called Lex Mensia.

creatus fuerit filius, si peregrinam cum qua conubium non sit uxorem *duxerit*, peregrinus ex eo coitu nascatur. sed hoc maxime casu necessaria lex Minicia, nam remota ea lege, qui *ex cive Romana nascitur*, *matris* condicionem seq*ueretur*, *et ob id civis Romanus fieret: ex iis enim inter quos non* est conubium qui nascitur iure gentium matris conditioni accedit. qua parte autem iubet lex ex cive Romano et peregrina peregrinum nasci supervacua videtur, nam et remota ea lege hoc utique iure gentium[1] futurum erat. (79.) Adeo autem hoc ita est ut... (*desunt lin.* 2.)...*non* solum exterae nationes et gentes sed etiam, qui Latini nominantur : sed ad alios Latinos pertinet, qui proprios populos propriasque civitates habebant et erant peregrinorum numero. (80.) Eadem ratione ex contrario ex Latino

vided that if a son has been begotten by a Roman citizen, who has married a foreign woman with whom he has no *conubium*, a foreigner is born from such connexion. But it is in the former case that the Lex Minicia is specially needed, for, if it were not for that law, the child of a Roman woman would follow his mother's status, and so be a Roman citizen; for anyone born from parents who have not *conubium* one with the other, follows his mother's status by the *jus gentium*. But where the law directs that a foreigner shall be born from a Roman citizen and a foreign woman it seems superfluous, for, even without the law, this would certainly be so by the *jus gentium*[1]....... 79. And this is so universally the rule (that we might imagine that) not only foreign nations and people (came under the provision), but also those who are called by the name of Latins. It only applies, however, to the other Latins (i.e. not to the *Latini Juniani*), who used to have their own nationalities and governments, and were reckoned as foreigners. 80. On the same

[1] See D. 1. 5. 24. The Lex Minicia only affected the children of a marriage where one party was a Roman citizen and the other a foreigner; therefore in marriages between Roman citizens and Junian Latins (since the latter are after all not foreigners, but citizens of an inferior grade, and Latins in name only and not in reality,) the ordinary rule would apply, that the mother's status regulated that of the child in cases where there was no *conubium* between the parents; but, on the other hand, Latins by birth, who had a nationality of their own, were foreigners in reality, and so the Lex Minicia applied to marriages between them and Roman citizens.

et cive Romana, sive ex lege Aelia Sentia sive aliter contractum
P. 22 fuerit matrimonium civis Romanus nascitur. fuerunt | tamen qui putaverunt ex lege Aelia Sentia contracto matrimonio Latinum nasci, quia videtur eo casu per legem Aeliam Sentiam et Iuniam conubium inter eos dari, et semper conubium efficit, ut qui nascitur patris condicioni accedat[1]: aliter vero contracto matrimonio eum qui nascitur iure gentium matris condicionem sequi, et ob id esse civem Romanum; sed hoc iure utimur ex senatusconsulto, quo auctore divo Hadriano significatur, ut omnimodo[2] ex Latino et cive Romana natus civis Romanus nascatur. (81.) His convenienter et illud senatusconsulto divo Hadriano auctore significatur[3], ut ex Latino et peregrina, item contra ex peregrino et Latina *qui* nascitur, is matris condicionem sequatur. (82.) Illud quoque his consequens est, quod ex ancilla et libero iure gentium servus nascitur, et contra ex libera

principle, in the converse case, the child of a Latin man and a Roman woman, whether the marriage has been contracted in accordance with the Lex Aelia Sentia or otherwise, is a Roman citizen by birth. Some, however, have thought that when a marriage is contracted in accordance with the Lex Aelia Sentia, the child is a Latin; because it is considered that *conubium* is granted between them in that case by the Leges Aelia Sentia and Junia, and *conubium* always has the effect that the child follows the condition of the father[1]: but that when the marriage is contracted in any other way the child by the *jus gentium* follows the condition of the mother, and therefore is a Roman citizen; but we follow the rule in the *senatusconsultum*, in which at the instance of the late emperor Hadrian it is laid down that the child of a Latin man and Roman woman is in every case[2] a Roman citizen by birth. 81. Agreeably to these principles this rule is also stated in the *senatusconsultum* passed at the instance of the late emperor Hadrian[3], that the child of a Latin man and a foreign woman, and conversely of a foreign man and a Latin woman, follows the condition of his mother. 82. With these principles too agrees the rule, that the child of a slave woman and a free man is a slave by birth by the *jus gentium*, and on the other hand that the child of a free woman and a slave is a free man by

[1] I. 30, 56, 57, Ulpian, v. 8. [2] *Omnimodo.* The MS. has QM. [3] I. 66.

et servo liber nascitur[1]. (83.) Animadvertere tamen debemus, ne quam iuris gentium regulam vel lex aliqua vel quod legis vicem optinet, aliquo casu commutaverit. (84.) Ecce enim ex senatusconsulto Claudiano poterat civis Romana quae alieno servo volente domino eius coiit, ipsa ex pactione libera permanere, sed servum procreare[2]: nam quod inter eam et dominum istius servi convenerit, ex senatusconsulto ratum esse iubetur. sed postea divus Hadrianus iniquitate rei et inelegantia[3] iuris
P. 23 motus restituit iuris gen|tium regulam, ut cum ipsa mulier libera permaneat, liberum pariat. (85.) Ex ancilla et libero poterant liberi nasci: nam ea lege[4] cavetur, ut si quis cum aliena ancilla quam credebat liberam esse coierit; si quidem masculi nascantur, liberi sint, si vero feminae, ad eum pertineant cuius mater ancilla fuerit. sed et in hac specie divus Vespasianus inele-

birth[1]. 83. We ought, however, to be on our guard lest any *lex*, or anything equivalent to a *lex*, may have changed in any instance a rule of the *jus gentium*. 84. Thus, for example, by a *senatusconsultum* of Claudius, a Roman woman who cohabited with another person's slave with the master's consent, might herself by special agreement remain free, and yet bear a slave[2]; for whatever was agreed upon between her and the master of that slave, was by the *senatusconsultum* ordered to be binding. But afterwards, the late emperor Hadrian, moved by the want of equity in the matter and the anomalous character of the rule[3], restored the regulation of the *jus gentium*, that when the woman herself remains free, the child she bears shall also be free. 85. The children of a slave woman and a free man might be born free: for it is provided by that *lex*[4] that if a man cohabited with another person's slave, whom he imagined to be free, the children, if males, should be free; if females, should belong to him whose slave the mother was. But in this instance, too, the late emperor Vespasian, moved by the ano-

---

1 Ulp. v. 9.

2 I. 91, 160. Taciti *Ann.* XII. 53.

3 See, as to this word *inelegantia*, Austin, Lect. XXX. p. 231 (p. 552, third edition).

4 Whether the Lex here referred to is the Lex Aelia Sentia or some later Lex, or whether it is the Senatusconsultum above specified, is a moot point among commentators, but not of sufficient importance to be examined at length. It is certainly improbable that so accurate a writer as Gaius should have used Lex and Senatusconsultum as convertible terms.

gantia iuris motus restituit iuris gentium regulam, ut omni modo, etiam si masculi nascantur, servi sint eius cuius et mater fuerit. (86.) Sed illa pars eiusdem legis salva est, ut ex libera et servo alieno, quem sciebat servum esse, servi nascantur[1]. itaque apud quos talis lex non est, qui nascitur iure gentium matris condicionem sequitur et ob id liber est.

87. Quibus autem casibus matris et non patris condicionem sequitur qui nascitur, iisdem casibus in potestate eum patris, etiamsi is civis Romanus sit, non esse plus quam manifestum est. et ideo superius rettulimus[2], quibusdam casibus per errorem non iusto contracto matrimonio senatum intervenire[3] et emendare vitium matrimonii, eoque modo plerumque efficere, ut in potestatem patris filius redigatur. (88.) Sed si ancilla ex cive Romano conceperit, deinde manumissa civis Romana

malous character of the rule, restored the regulation of the *jus gentium*, that in all cases, even if males were born, they should be the slaves of him to whom the mother belonged. 86. But the other part of the same law remains in force, that from a free woman and another person's slave whom she knew to be a slave, slaves are born[1]. Amongst nations, therefore, who have no such law, the child by the *jus gentium* follows the mother's condition, and therefore is free.

87. Now in all cases where the child follows the condition of the mother and not of the father, it is more than plain that he is not in the *potestas* of his father, even though he be a Roman citizen: and therefore we have stated above[2] that in certain cases, when by mistake an unlawful marriage has been contracted, the senate[3] interferes and makes good the flaw in the marriage, and thus generally causes the son to be brought under his father's *potestas*. 88. But if a female slave conceive by a Roman citizen, be then manumitted and made a Roman

---

[1] The case treated of in § 84 is that of a woman cohabiting with a slave with his master's consent; the case in § 91, that of her cohabiting with the slave against the master's warning. The present case is that of there being neither warning nor express consent.

[2] I. 67—73.

[3] Senatus here meaning the legislature by a *senatusconsultum*. The senate never interfered in cases of this sort (*erroris probatio*) directly and as a court or body. Indirectly no doubt it did, *i.e.* by the publication of an enactment on the particular subject.

P. 24 facta sit, et tunc pariat, licet civis Romanus sit qui nascitur, | sicut pater eius, non tamen in potestate patris est, quia neque ex iusto coitu conceptus est, neque ex ullo senatusconsulto talis coitus quasi iustus constituitur.

89. Quod autem placuit, si ancilla ex cive Romano conceperit, deinde manumissa pepererit, qui nascitur liberum nasci, naturali ratione fit. nam hi qui illegitime concipiuntur, statum sumunt ex eo tempore quo nascuntur: itaque si ex libera nascuntur, liberi fiunt, nec interest ex quo mater eos conceperit, cum ancilla fuerit. at hi qui legitime concipiuntur, ex conceptionis tempore statum sumunt[1]. (90.) Itaque si cui mulieri civi Romanae praegnati aqua et igni interdictum fuerit[2], eoque modo peregrina facta sit et tunc pariat, conplures distinguunt et putant, si quidem ex iustis nuptiis conceperit, civem Romanum ex ea nasci, si vero volgo conceperit, peregrinum ex ea nasci.

citizen, and then bear her child, although the child is a Roman citizen, just as much as his father is, yet he is not in his father's *potestas*, because he is neither conceived from a lawful cohabitation, nor is such a cohabitation put on the footing of a lawful one by any *senatusconsultum*.

89. The rule, however, that if a slave woman conceive by a Roman citizen, and be then manumitted and bear a child, such child is free born, is based on natural reason. For those who are conceived illegitimately take their status from the moment of birth; therefore if born from a free woman they are free, nor is it material by what man the mother conceived them when she was a slave. But those who are conceived legitimately take their status from the time of conception[1]. 90. Therefore if a Roman woman, whilst pregnant, be interdicted from fire and water[2], and so become a foreigner, and then bear her child, many authors draw a distinction, and think that if she conceived in lawful marriage, the child born from her is a Roman citizen, whilst if she conceived out of wedlock, the

---

[1] Ulpian, v. 10.

[2] It was a rule of Roman law that no one could lose his citizenship without his own consent. The interdict from fire and water brought about the result which justice required but the law could not effect. The culprit by being debarred from the necessaries of life was driven to inflict on himself banishment, and with it loss of citizenship. "Id autem ut esset faciendum, non ademptione civitatis, sed tecti et aquae et ignis interdictione faciebant." Cic. *pro Dom.* 30.

(91.) Item si qua mulier civis Romana praegnas ex senatusconsulto Claudiano ancilla facta sit ob id, quod alieno servo invito et denuntiante domino[1] eius coierit, conplures *distingu*unt et existimant, si quidem ex iustis nuptiis conceptus sit, civem Romanum ex ea nasci, si vero volgo conceptus sit, *servum* nasci eius cuius mater facta esset ancilla. (92.) Peregrina quoque si vulgo conceperit, deinde civis Romana *facta sit*, et tunc pariat, civem Romanum parit; si vero ex peregrino, |
P. 25 *cui* secundum leges moresque peregrinorum conceperit, ita videtur ex senatusconsulto quod auctore divo Hadriano factum est civem Romanum parere si et patri eius civitas Romana donetur.

93. Si peregrinus sibi liberisque civitatem Romanam petiverit non aliter filii in potestate eius fiunt, quam si Imperator eos in potestatem redegerit[2]. quod ita demum is facit, si causa cognita aestimaverit hoc filiis expedire: diligentius autem exactiusque

child born from her is a foreigner. 91. Likewise, if a Roman woman, whilst pregnant, be reduced to slavery in accordance with the *senatusconsultum* of Claudius, because she has cohabited with another man's slave against the master's will and in spite of his warning[1], many authors draw a distinction and hold that if her child was conceived in lawful marriage, he is a Roman citizen, but if he was conceived out of wedlock, he is a slave of the man to whom the mother has been made a slave. 92. Likewise if a foreign woman have conceived out of wedlock, and then be made a Roman citizen and bear her child, the child she bears is a Roman citizen: but if, on the contrary, by a foreigner to whom she bore the child according to the laws and customs of foreigners, she is considered, in accordance with a *senatusconsultum* which was made at the instance of the late emperor Hadrian, to bear a Roman citizen if Roman citizenship has also been granted to his father.

93. If a foreigner has petitioned for Roman citizenship for himself and his children, the children are not in his *potestas*, unless the emperor has subjected them to his *potestas*[2]. Which he only does if, on investigation of the circumstances, he judge this expedient for the children: for he examines a case with more than ordinary care and exactness when it relates to

[1] I. 84, 160. [2] III. 20. Pliny, *Paneg.* c. 37.

causam cognoscit de impuberibus absentibusque. et haec ita edicto divi Hadriani significantur. (94.) Item si quis cum uxore praegnante civitate Romana donatus sit, quamvis is qui nascitur, ut supra diximus, civis Romanus sit[1], tamen in potestate patris non fit: idque subscriptione divi Hadriani significatur[2]. qua de causa qui intellegit uxorem suam esse praegnatem, dum civitatem sibi et uxori ab Imperatore petit, simul ab eodem petere debet, ut eum qui natus erit in potestate sua habeat. (95.) Alia causa est eorum qui Latii iure[3] cum liberis suis ad civitatem Romanam perveniunt: nam horum in potestate

persons under the age of puberty and to absentees. And these matters are so laid down in an edict of the late emperor Hadrian. 94. Likewise if any man, and his pregnant wife with him, be presented with Roman citizenship, although their child is, as we have said above, a Roman citizen[1], yet he is not in the *potestas* of his father: and this is laid down by a (special) rescript of the late emperor Hadrian[2]. Wherefore a man who knows his wife to be pregnant, when asking for citizenship for himself and his wife from the Emperor, ought at the same time to ask him that he may have the child who shall be born in his *potestas*. 95. The case is different with those who by right of Latinity attain with their children to Roman citizenship, for their children come under their *potestas*[3].

[1] I. 92.

[2] *Subscriptio* was the emperor's reply to a case laid before him, such reply having authority upon that particular point only. It was almost equal to a Rescript or *Epistola*. See note on I. 5, and Dirksen, *Manuale Latinitatis*, sub verbo, § 2.

[3] As stated in the note on § 22, Niebuhr held that the *majus Latium* was the franchise of the old Latin towns: whilst the *minus Latium* was the franchise of the colonists north of the Po. The Julian law gave *civitas* to all the old Latin towns, and therefore according to Niebuhr's notion, the *majus Latium* long before Gaius' time had become obsolete; the only Latin franchise remaining being the *minus*. Mommsen, however, propounds another theory, that the two franchises were both existent in Gaius' time, that neither had anything to do with the old Latins, and that the difference between the two was that in the case of the *majus Latium* the full *civitas* was conferred on those who held office in the colony, and on their wives, parents, and children; whilst in the case of the *minus Latium*, the full *civitas* was conferred on the magistrate alone and not on his relations. See Mommsen, *Die Stadtrechte von Salpensa.*, and Gaius, I. 79, 131; III. 56. The restored text of Gaius shews that Mommsen had not quite discovered the difference between the two, but very nearly.

With Mommsen's view of the subject agrees the account given by Appian (*de Bello Civili*, II. 26) of the settlement of the city of Novo Como by Caesar. Appian tells us

fiunt liberi. quod ius quibusdam peregrinis civitatibus datum est vel a populo Romano vel a senatu vel a Caesare. (96.)...aut maius est Latium aut minus. maius est Latium cum et hi
P. 26 qui decuriones leguntur et hi qui honorem aliquem aut | magistratum gerunt, civitatem Romanam *cum parentibus conjugibusque ac liberis*[1] consequuntur; minus Latium est, cum hi tantum qui vel magistratum vel honorem gerunt ad civitatem Romanam perveniunt. idque conpluribus epistulis Principum significatur. (*desunt 2 lin.*)

97. (*Non solum tamen naturales liberi*[2], *secundum ea quae*) diximus, in potestate nostra sunt, verum et hi quos adoptamus.

98. Adoptio autem duobus modis fit, aut populi auctoritate[3], aut inperio magistratus, veluti Praetoris[4]. (99.) Populi aucto-

Which right has been granted to certain foreign communities either by the Roman people, or by the Senate, or by the Emperor. 96....the franchise is either the *majus Latium* or the *minus Latium:* it is the *majus Latium* when those who are elected *decuriones* and those who hold any office of honour or magistracy attain to Roman citizenship, together with their parents, and wives and children[1]: but is the *minus Latium*, when those only themselves who hold a magistracy or office of honour attain to Roman citizenship. And this is stated in many epistles of the Emperors.

97. Not only our actual children are in our *potestas*[2], according to what we have already said, but those also whom we adopt.

98. Now adoption takes place in two ways, either by authority of the *populus*[3], or under the jurisdiction of a magistrate, for instance the Praetor[4]. 99. By authority of the *populus* we

---

the inhabitants received the *jus Latii*, and that the consequence of this was that any of the citizens who held a superior magistracy for a year obtained the Roman *civitas*. So also Asconius has a passage (*in Pison.* p. 3, edit. Orell.) which may be translated: "Pompey gave to the original inhabitants the *jus Latii*, so that they might have the same privilege as the other Latin colonies, viz. that their members by holding a magistracy should attain to the Roman citizenship." The passage in Livy XLI. 8 refers to the old *jus Latii*, which was turned into full *civitas* by the Lex Julia, but it is well worth reading.

[1] These words are supplied from the *Tabula Salpensana*.

[2] The MS. has here two blank lines: but the missing words can be supplied from Just. *Inst.* I. 11. *pr.*

[3] I. 3.

[4] Ulpian, VIII. 1—3.

ritate adoptamus eos qui sui iuris sunt: quae species adoptionis dicitur adrogatio, quia et is qui adoptat rogatur, id est interrogatur an velit eum quem adoptaturus sit iustum sibi filium esse; et is qui adoptatur rogatur an id fieri patiatur; et populus rogatur an id fieri iubeat[1]. imperio magistratus adoptamus eos qui in potestate parentium sunt, sive primum gradum liberorum optineant, qualis est filius et filia, sive inferiorem, qualis est nepos, neptis, pronepos, proneptis. (100.) Et quidem illa adoptio quae per populum fit nusquam nisi Romae fit: at haec etiam in provinciis aput Praesides earum fieri solet[2]. (101.) Item per populum feminae non adoptantur; nam id magis **P. 27** placuit. aput | Praetorem vero vel in provinciis aput Proconsulem Legatumve etiam feminae solent adoptari.

102. Item inpuberem aput populum adoptari aliquando prohibitum est, aliquando permissum est. nunc ex epistula optimi Imperatoris Antonini quam scripsit Pontificibus, si iusta causa

adopt those who are *sui juris:* which species of adoption is styled *arrogatio*, for he who adopts is *rogated*, i.e. is interrogated, whether he wishes the man whom he is about to adopt to become his lawful son: and he who is adopted is *rogated* whether he submits to that being done: and the *populus* are *rogated* whether they order it to be done[1]. Under the jurisdiction of a magistrate we adopt those who are in the *potestas* of their ascendants, whether they stand in the first degree of descendants, as son or daughter, or in a lower one, as grandson, granddaughter, great-grandson, great-granddaughter. 100. That adoption which is performed by authority of the *populus* takes place nowhere but at Rome: but the other is frequently performed in the provinces also in the presence of their governors[2]. 101. Women, likewise, are not adopted by authority of the *populus:* for so it has been generally ruled. But before the Praetor, or in the provinces before the Proconsul or Legate, women as well as men may be adopted. 102. Further, there have been times when it has been forbidden to adopt by authority of the *populus* one under the age of puberty; there have been times when it has been allowed. At the present time, according to an epistle of the excellent emperor Antoninus

[1] See Appendix (C). [2] Ulpian, VIII. 4, 5.

adoptionis esse videbitur, cum quibusdam condicionibus permissum est. aput Praetorem vero, et in provinciis aput Proconsulem Legatumve, cuiuscumque aetatis adoptare possumus[1].

103. Illud vero utriusque adoptionis commune est, quia et hi qui generare non possunt, quales sunt spadones, adoptare possunt[2]. (104.) Feminae vero nullo modo adoptare possunt, quia ne quidem naturales liberos in potestate habent[3]. (105.) Item si quis per populum sive apud Praetorem vel aput Praesidem provinciae adoptaverit, potest eundem alii in adoptionem dare. (106.) Set illa quaestio, an minor natu maiorem natu adoptare possit utriusque adoptionis commune est[4].

107. Illud proprium est eius adoptionis quae per populum fit, quod is qui liberos in potestate habet, si se adrogandum dederit, non solum ipse potestati adrogatoris subicitur, set

which he wrote to the Pontifices, if the cause of adoption appear lawful, it is allowed under certain conditions. Before the Praetor, however, or in the provinces before the Proconsul or Legate, we can adopt people of any age whatever[1].

103. It is a rule common to both kinds of adoption, that those who cannot procreate, as eunuchs-born, can adopt[2]. 104. But women cannot adopt in any way, inasmuch as they have not even their actual children in their *potestas*[3]. 105. Likewise, if a man adopt by authority of the *populus*, or before the Praetor or governor of a province, he can give the same person in adoption to another. 106. But it is a moot point whether a younger man can adopt an elder, and the doubt is common to both kinds of adoption[4].

107. There is this peculiarity attaching to the kind of adoption effected by authority of the *populus*, that if one who has children in his *potestas* give himself to be arrogated, not only is he himself subjected to the *potestas* of the arrogator,

---

1 But it was generally required that the adoptor should be more than sixty years of age, D. I. 7. 15. 2, and should be at least eighteen years older than the person adopted. *Inst.* I. II. 4, D. I. 7. 40. I.

2 Ulpian, VIII. 6.

3 Ibid. 8 *a*.

4 Justinian settled that the adoptor must be older than the adopted by 18 years ("plena pubertate"). *Inst.* I. II. 4.

etiam liberi eius in eiusdem fiunt potestate tanquam nepotes[1] | (*desunt lin.* 2).

P. 28 108. (*Nunc de his personis videamus quae in manu nostra sunt, quod*) et ipsum ius proprium civium Romanorum est. (109.) Sed in potestate quidem et masculi et feminae esse solent: in manum autem feminae tantum conveniunt. (110.) Olim itaque tribus modis in manum conveniebant, usu, farreo, coemptione. (111.) Usu in manum conveniebat quae anno continuo nupta perseverabat; nam veluti annua possessione usucapiebatur[2], in familiam viri transibat filiaeque locum optinebat. itaque lege duodecim tabularum[3] cautum est ut si qua nollet eo modo in manum mariti convenire ea quotannis trinoctio abesset atque eo modo (usum) cuiusque anni interrumperet. set hoc totum ius partim legibus sublatum est, partim ipsa desuetudine

but his children also come into the *potestas* of the same man in the capacity of grandchildren[1].

108. Now let us consider about those persons who are in our *manus*. This also is a right peculiar to Roman citizens. 109. But whereas both males and females may be in our *potestas*, females alone come into *manus*. 110. Formerly they came into *manus* in three ways, by *usus*, *farreum* or *coemptio*. 111. A woman who remained married for an unbroken year came into *manus* by *usus* (usage): for she was in a manner acquired by usucapion[2] through the possession of a year, and so passed into the family of her husband, and gained the position of a daughter. Therefore it was provided by a law of the Twelve Tables[3], that if any woman was unwilling to come under her husband's *manus* in this way, she should year by year absent herself for the space of three (successive) nights, and so break the usage of each year. But all these regulations have been in part removed

---

[1] Ulpian, VIII. 8. The emperor Justinian remodelled the whole law of adoption, enacting that the actual father should lose none of his rights, and be exempted from none of his duties in respect of the child given in adoption. The only exception was in the case when the adoptor was an ascendant of the adopted. In the latter case, styled *adoptio plena*, the old law remained in force. In the other kind (*minus plena*) the adopted child had no claims on the adoptor, except that of succeeding to him in case of his intestacy, and the adoptor had no claims whatever on the adopted.

[2] For an explanation of *usucapio*, see II. 42 et seqq.

[3] Tab. VI. l. 4.

oblitteratum est. (112.) Farreo in manum conveniunt per quoddam genus sacrificii quod Jovi Farreo fit[1] in quo farreus panis adhibetur: unde etiam confarreatio dicitur. conplura praeterea huius iuris ordinandi gratia cum certis et sollemnibus verbis, praesentibus decem testibus aguntur et fiunt. quod ius etiam nostris temporibus in usu est: nam flamines maiores, id est
P. 29 Diales, Martiales, Quirinales, item | Reges Sacrorum, nisi ex farreatis nati non leguntur[2], ac ne ipsi quidem sine comfarreatione sacerdotium habere possunt. (113.) Coemptione vero in manum conveniunt per mancipationem[3], *id est* per quandam imaginariam venditionem, nam adhibitis non minus quam v. testibus, civibus Romanis puberibus, item libripende[4], asse

by enactments, in part abolished by mere disuse. 112. Women come into *manus* by *farreum* through a particular kind of sacrifice[1] offered to Juppiter Farreus, in which a cake of fine flour (*far*) is employed: whence also the proceeding is called "confarreation": and besides this there are many other ceremonies performed and done for the purpose of ratifying the ordinance, with certain solemn words used, and with ten witnesses present. This rite is in use even in our times, for we see that the superior *flamens*, i.e. the Diales, Martiales and Quirinales, as well as the *Reges Sacrorum*, unless they be born from confarreate marriage are not elected[2], and neither can they themselves hold the priesthood unless they are married by *confarreatio*. 113. Women come into *manus* by *coemptio* by means of a mancipation[3], i.e. by a kind of imaginary sale, in the presence of not less than five witnesses, Roman citizens of the age of puberty, as well as a *libripens*[4], (wherein) he

[1] Ulpian, IX. Servius thus describes a part of the ceremony used in the marriage of a Flamen and Flaminica. "Two seats were joined together and covered with the skin of a sheep that had been sacrificed; then the couple were introduced enveloped in a veil, and made to take their seats there, and the woman, to use Dido's words, was said to be *locata* to her husband." See Servius on *Aen.* IV. 104, 357.

[2] Tacit. *Ann.* IV. 16.

[3] I. 119.

[4] I. 119. Some further information on the subject of *coemptio* will be found in Boethius *ad Cic. Top.* 3. 14. Cicero's words are: Si ita Fabiae pecunia legata est a viro, si ei viro materfamilias esset: si ea in manum viri non convenerat, nihil debetur. Genus enim est uxor: eius duae formae; una matrumfamilias earum quae in manum convenerunt; altera earum, quae tantummodo uxores habentur.

emit eam[1] mulierem, cuius in manum convenit. (114.) Potest autem coemptionem facere mulier non solum cum marito suo, sed etiam cum extraneo: scilicet aut matrimonii causa facta coemptio dicitur, aut fiduciae. quae enim cum marito suo facit coemptionem, (ut) aput eum filiae loco sit, dicitur matrimonii causa fecisse coemptionem: quae vero alterius rei causa facit coemptionem cum viro suo aut cum extraneo, veluti tutelae evitandae causa, dicitur fiduciae causa fecisse coemptionem[2]. (115.) Quod est tale:

into whose *manus* the woman is coming buys her for himself with an *as*[1]. 114. Now a woman can make a coemption not only with her husband, but also with a stranger: whence a coemption is said to be made either with intent of matrimony or with fiduciary intent. For she who makes a coemption with her husband, to be to him in the place of a daughter, is said to make coemption with the intent of matrimony: but she who makes a coemption with her husband or with a stranger for any other purpose, for instance to get rid of her guardian, is said to have made coemption with fiduciary intent[2]. 115. This is

[1] The MS. has A. EMIT EUM MULIEREM, which is not difficult to interpret.

[2] *Tutela* is treated of in I. 142—200, which passage should be read in order fully to understand this paragraph. The law, as we know, allowed the woman to do no act without the sanction of her guardians, so that even her repudiation of them required authorization on their part: although, if they were unfit for their office, and yet vexatiously refused to allow a transfer, the Praetor would, as in other cases where they refused to carry out the woman's wishes, interfere and compel them (I. 190). Supposing, then, a guardian to be willing, or to be ordered by the Praetor, to transfer the woman to another guardian of her own choosing. This renunciation of a guardianship, being as contrary to the spirit of the ancient law as a renunciation of *patria potestas*, has to be carried into effect by means of fictions. The guardian, therefore, transfers the woman into the *manus* of some third person, not the intended tutor, on the pretence that this third person is about to marry her. Herein the guardian commits no breach of duty, for he ought to try to get his ward advantageously married. The third person next proceeds to sell as a slave to an innocent purchaser the woman whom he obtained from the equally innocent guardian for the purpose of marriage. The purchaser, finding out his error, rectifies it by manumitting the woman *per vindictam*, and stands to her thereby in a relation analogous to the manumittor of a slave to the freedman, and the patron of a freedman is always his guardian, if he needs one. But the woman having been manumitted out of *mancipium*, and not out of a true *potestas* (I. 123), her patron differs from the ascendant manumittor in being a *tutor fiduciarius* instead of

si qua velit quos habet tutores reponere, et alium nancisci, illis tutoribus (auctoribus) coemptionem facit; deinde a coemptio-
P. 30 natore remancipata ei cui ipsa velit, et ab eo vindicta | manumissa, incipit eum habere tutorem, a quo manumissa est: qui tutor fidúciarius dicitur, sicut inferioribus apparebit[1]. (115 a.) Olim etiam testamenti faciendi gratia fiduciaria fiebat coemptio[2]. tunc enim non aliter feminae testamenti faciendi ius habebant, exceptis quibusdam personis, quam si coemptionem fecissent remancipataeque[3] et manumissae fuissent. set hanc necessitatem coemptionis faciendae ex auctoritate divi Hadriani senatus remisit. *censetur* enim re *ipsa* femina ea ca*pite deminuta* esse. (115 b.) Si tamen mulier fiduciae causa eum *viro suo* fecerit

effected as follows: if a woman wish to get rid of the guardians she has, and obtain another, she makes a coemption with their authorization: then being by mancipation retransferred by the *coemptionator* to such person as she pleases, and by him manumitted by *vindicta*, she henceforth has for guardian him by whom she was manumitted; and he is called a fiduciary tutor, as will appear below[1]. 115 *a.* In ancient times a fiduciary coemption took place also for the purpose of making a testament[2]. For then women had no right of making a testament (certain persons excepted), unless they had made a coemption, been retransferred by mancipation[3], and manumitted. But the senate, at the instance of the late emperor Hadrian, abolished this necessity of making a coemption. For such a woman is considered as a matter of course to suffer a *capitis deminutio.* 115 *b.* But even if a woman has made a coemption with her

a *tutor legitimus* (I. 166); and therefore has smaller powers of coercion and restraint. The whole mass of fictions in this case is strikingly analogous to those employed in the processes of adoption and emancipation of freemen; to which we shall come shortly.

[1] I. 195.

[2] In ancient times the *agnati* were heirs-at-law to a woman, and also her guardians, and their succession could not be directly set aside; for no testament could be made by the woman except by consent of her guardians. The method adopted was to break the agnatic bond by removing the woman from her family by the process described in the text. She then stood alone in the world: "caput et finis familiae," and having no *agnati* to prefer a claim against her, could freely dispose of her property. III. 9—14. Cic. *pro Mur.* c. 12.

[3] *Remancipata* is the technical word for a woman mancipated out of *manus*. "Remancipatam Gallus Aelius ait quae remancipata sit ab eo cui in manum convenerit." Festus *sub verb.*

coemptionem, nihilominus filiae loco incipit esse: nam si omnino qualibet ex causa uxor in manu viri sit, placuit eam filiae iura nancisci.

116. Superest ut exponamus quae personae in mancipio sint. (117.) Omnes igitur liberorum personae, sive masculini sive feminini sexus, quae in potestate parentis sunt, mancipari ab hoc eodem modo possunt, quo etiam servi mancipari possunt. (118.) Idem iuris est in earum personis quae in manu sunt. nam feminae a coemptionatoribus eodem modo possunt (*mancipari quo liberi a parente mancipantur; adeo quidem, ut quamvis ea sola*)[1] aput coemptionatorem filiae loco sit *quae ei* nupta sit,
P. 31 tamen nihilo minus etiam | quae ei nupta non sit, nec ob id filiae loco sit ab eo mancipari possit. (118 a.) Plerumque solum et a parentibus et a coemptionatoribus mancipantur, cum velint parentes coemptionatoresque e suo iure eas personas dimittere, sicut inferius evidentius apparebit[2].

husband with fiduciary intent, she is nevertheless at once in the place of a daughter to him: for if in any case and for any reason a woman be in the *manus* of her husband, it is held that she obtains the rights of a daughter.

116. It now remains for us to explain what persons are in *mancipium*. 117. All descendants, then, whether male or female, who are in the *potestas* of an ascendant, may be mancipated by him in the same manner in which slaves also can be mancipated. 118. The same rule applies to persons who are in *manus*. For women may be mancipated by their coemptionators in the same manner in which (descendants are mancipated by an ascendant: and so universally does this hold, that although that woman alone)[1] who is married to her coemptionator stands in the place of a daughter to him, yet one also who is not married to him and so does not stand in the place of a daughter to him, can nevertheless be mancipated by him. 118 *a*. But generally persons are mancipated, whether by ascendants or coemptionators, only when the ascendants or coemptionators wish to set them free from their control, as will be seen more clearly below[2].

[1] The words printed in italics are Göschen's conjectural suggestion, and doubtless express the sense of what Gaius intended; but they are not in the MS., which seems at this point to want a line or two through omission on the part of the transcriber.

[2] I. 132.

(119.) Est autem mancipatio, ut supra quoque diximus[1], imaginaria quaedam venditio: quod et ipsum ius proprium civium Romanorum est. eaque res ita agitur. adhibitis non minus quam quinque testibus civibus Romanis puberibus, et praeterea alio eiusdem condicionis qui libram aeneam teneat, qui appellatur libripens, is qui mancipio accipit, rem tenens ita dicit: HUNC EGO HOMINEM EX IURE QUIRITIUM[2] MEUM ESSE AIO, ISQUE MIHI EMPTUS ESTO HOC AERE AENEAQUE LIBRA: deinde aere percutit libram, idque aes dat ei a quo mancipio accipit, quasi pretii loco. (120.) Eo modo et serviles et liberae personae mancipantur. animalia quoque quae mancipi sunt[3], quo in numero habentur boves, equi, muli, asini; item praedia tam urbana[4] quam rustica quae et ipsa mancipi sunt, qualia sunt Italica[5], eodem modo solent

119. Now mancipation, as we have said above[1], is a kind of imaginary sale: and this legal form too is one peculiar to Roman citizens. It is conducted thus: not less than five witnesses being present, Roman citizens of the age of puberty, and another man besides of like condition who holds a bronze balance, and is called a *libripens*, he who receives the thing by mancipation, grasping it says as follows: "I assert this man to be mine in Quiritary right[2]; and let him be bought by me by means of this coin and bronze balance:" then he strikes the balance with a coin, and gives the coin, as though by way of price, to him from whom he receives the thing by mancipation. 120. In this manner persons, both slaves and free, are mancipated. So also are those animals which are things mancipable[3], in which category are reckoned oxen, horses, mules, asses; likewise such landed properties, with or without houses on them[4], as are things mancipable, of which kind are Italic properties[5], are mancipated

---

1 I. 113.

2 II. 40, 41.

3 II. 15.

4 Ulpian, XIX. 1.

5 Italic soil was not necessarily in Italy. The name signified that portion of the Roman empire in which certain privileges and immunities were granted to the inhabitants. These were chiefly, exemption from the *vectigal* or land-tax paid by the possessors of provincial soil, the right of self-government by elected magistrates, and the presence of the Roman rules of immovable property, with their peculiarities of *mancipatio*, *cessio in jure*, *usucapio*, etc. A list of colonies possessing the Jus Italicum is given in D. 50. 15. 1. 6, 7 and 8.

mancipari. (121.) In eo solo praediorum mancipatio a ceterorum mancipatione differt, quod personae serviles et liberae, item animalia quae mancipi sunt, nisi in praesentia sint, manci-
P. 32 pari non possunt: adeo quidem, | ut eum (qui) mancipio accipit adprehendere id ipsum quod ei in mancipio datur necesse sit: unde etiam mancipatio dicitur, quia manu res capitur. praedia vero absentia solent mancipari[1]. (122.) Ideo autem aes et libra adhibetur, quia olim aereis tantum nummis utebantur; et erant asses, dipundii, semisses et quadrantes, nec ullus aureus vel argenteus nummus in usu erat, sicut ex lege XII tabularum[2] intellegere possumus; eorumque nummorum vis et potestas non in numero erat, sed in pondere nummorum. veluti asses librales erant et dipundii fuerant *bilibres;* unde etiam dupundius dictus est quasi duo pondo: quod nomen adhuc in usu retinetur. semisses quoque et quadrantes pro rata scilicet portione ad pondus examinati erant. *unde etiam* qui dabat *olim* pecuniam non

in the same manner. 121. In this respect only does the mancipation of estates differ from that of other things, that persons, slave and free, and likewise animals which are things mancipable, cannot be mancipated unless they are present; and so strictly indeed is this the case, that it is necessary for him who takes the thing by mancipation to grasp that which is given to him by mancipation: whence the term mancipation is derived, because the thing is taken with the hand: but estates can be mancipated when at a distance[1]. 122. The reason for employing the coin and balance is that in olden times men used a bronze coinage only, and there were *asses*, *dipundii*, *semisses*, and *quadrantes*, nor was any coinage of gold or silver in use, as we may see from a law of the Twelve Tables[2]: and the force and effect of this coinage was not in its number but its weight. For instance the *asses* weighed a pound each, and the *dipundii* two; whence the name *dipundius*, as being *duo pondo;* a name which is still employed. The *semisses* (half-asses) and *quadrantes* (quarter-asses) were tested by their weight, according to their fractional part of the pound. Whence also a man who gave money

---

[1] Still a sod, a brick or a tile must be brought to be handled.

[2] Probably Tab. II. l. 1.

numerabat eam sed appendebat[1]. unde servi quibus permittitur administratio pecuniae dispensatores appellati sunt et adhuc appellantur. (123.) Si tamen quaerat aliquis, quare citra coemptionem *soleant femi*nae *st*atim m*ancipa*ri[2]: ea quidem quae coemptionem fecerit de*ducta non est in* servilem condicionem, *id est* se non com*misit coemptionatori, sed contra* mancipati mancipataeve servorum loco constituuntur, adeo quidem, ut ab eo
P. 33 cuius in mancipio | sunt neque hereditates neque legata aliter capere poss*i*nt, quam (si) simul eodem testamento liberi esse iubeantur sicuti iuris est in persona servorum[3]. sed differentiae

in the olden times did not count it out, but weighed it[1]; and thus slaves who have the management of money entrusted to them were called *dispensatores* (weighers out), and are still so called. 123. But if any one should inquire why, over and above the coemption, women are usually at once mancipated[2]; it is because a woman who makes a coemption is not reduced to the condition of a slave, that is to say, she has not made herself over to the *coemptionator;* but, on the contrary, those mancipated are brought into that condition, so that they can take neither inheritances nor legacies from him in whose *mancipium* they are, unless they be also ordered in the testament to be free, as is the rule with slaves[3]. But the reason of the difference

---

1 Isidor. Orig. XVI. c. 24.

2 The reading suggested by Huschke is: "quare viro coemptione emta mancipatis distet." The MS. has only what looks like ...ARE CITRA COEMPTIO ... NEGATIM: and therefere Lachmann suggested "si tamen quaerat aliquis *quare citra coemptionem feminae etiam mancipentur.*"

3 I believe this passage to refer entirely to fiduciary coemption. In 118 *a* Gaius has told us that coemption was, in his day, usually employed to bring about an emancipation: and if a woman had a tutor, as already explained in the note on § 114, he could not, like an ascendant, pass her directly into *mancipium.* He transfers her, therefore, into the *manus* of a *coemptionator;* who thereupon transfers her again to the person who is to make her *sui iuris*, and become her tutor: and he, having her *in mancipio*, manumits her by *vindicta.* That she should be reduced to a quasi-servile position is therefore essential: and so *citra coemptionem*, "over and above" that legal act, she must pass through a *mancipatio.* Gaius then proves that she is in the required status, by showing that she is a quasi-slave in other incidents, in addition to the possibility of being manumitted by *vindicta.*

As to "being ordered to be free": see I. 138 and II. 186 and 187.

For *citra* in this sense of *ultra* or *supra* see Dirksen, *sub verb.*, and D. 3. 6. 9 and D. 20. 1. 1. 1.

ratio manifesta est, cum a parentibus et a coemptionatoribus iisdem verbis mancipio accipiuntur quibus servi; quod non similiter *fit* in coemptione[1].

124. Videamus nunc, quo modo *hi* qui alieno iuri subiecti sunt eo iure liberentur. (125.) Ac prius de his dispiciamus qui in potestate sunt. (126.) Et quidem servi quemadmodum potestate liberentur, ex his intellegere possumus quae de servis manumittendis superius exposuimus[2].

127. Hi vero qui (*in potestate pa*)rentis sunt (*mortuo eo sui iuris fiunt. sed hoc dis*)tinctionem recipit[3]. nam *mortuo pat*re sane omnimodo filii filiaeve sui iuris efficiuntur. mortuo vero avo *non omni*modo (*nepotes nepte*sve *sui*) iuris (*fiunt, sed ita, si post mortem avi*) in patris sui potestatem recasuri non sunt. *ita*que si moriente avo (*pater eorum et vivat et in potesta*)te patris

is plain, inasmuch as they are received into *mancipium* from the parents and coemptionators with the same form of words as slaves are: which is not the case in a coemption[1].

124. Now let us see by what means those who are subject to the authority of another are set free from that authority. 125. And first let us discuss the case of those who are under *potestas*. 126. How slaves are freed from *potestas* we may learn from the explanation of the manumission of slaves which we gave above[2].

127. But those who are in the *potestas* of an ascendant become *sui juris* on his death. This, however, admits of a qualification[3]. For, undoubtedly, on the death of a father sons and daughters in all cases become *sui juris*: but on the death of a grandfather grandsons or granddaughters do not become *sui juris* in all cases, but only if after the death of the grandfather they will not relapse into the *potestas* of their father. Therefore, if at the grandfather's death their father be alive and

---

1 We do not know what the words used in a *coemptio* were, but Boethius in the passage already referred to (see note on I. 113) states that the proceedings were more in the nature of a bilateral contract than a mere unilateral one, and possibly this may be the reason of the difference in the position of the wife and the mancipated person.

2 I. 13, &c. The paragraphs 124—127 are very difficult to decipher, on account of the decay of the MS., but Justinian seems to have copied them almost verbatim, and the missing words can be filled in from *Inst.* I. 12. pr.

3 Ulpian, X. 2.

fuerit, tunc post ob(*itum avi in patris*) sui potestate fiunt: si vero is, quo tempore avus moritur, aut iam mor(*tuus est, aut*) exiit de potestate (*patris, tunc hi, quia in potestatem*)[1] eius cadere non
P. 34 possunt, sui iuris fiunt. (128.) Cum | autem is cui ob aliquod maleficium ex lege Cornelia[2] aqua et igni interdicitur civitatem Romanam amittat[3], sequitur, ut qui eo modo ex numero civium Romanorum tollitur, proinde ac mortuo eo desinant liberi in potestate eius esse: nec enim ratio patitur, ut peregrinae condicionis homo civem Romanum in potestate habeat. pari ratione et si ei qui in potestate parentis sit aqua et igni interdictum fuerit, desinit in potestate parentis esse, quia aeque ratio non patitur, ut peregrinae condicionis homo in potestate sit civis Romani parentis.

129. Quod si ab hostibus captus fuerit parens[4], quamvis ser-

in the *potestas* of his father, then after the death of the grandfather they come under the *potestas* of their father: but if at the time of the grandfather's death the father either be dead or have passed from the *potestas* of his father, then the grandchildren, inasmuch as they cannot fall under his *potestas*[1], become *sui juris*. 128. Again, since he who is interdicted from fire and water for some crime under the Lex Cornelia[2] loses his Roman citizenship[3], it follows that the descendants of a man thus removed from the category of Roman citizens cease to be in his *potestas*, just as though he were dead: for it is contrary to reason that a man of foreign status should have a Roman citizen in his *potestas*. On like principle also, if one in the *potestas* of an ascendant be interdicted from fire and water, he ceases to be in the *potestas* of his ascendant: for it is equally contrary to reason that a man of foreign status should be in the *potestas* of an ascendant who is a Roman citizen.

129. If, however, an ascendant be taken by the enemy[4],

1 These words are not in the text, which runs on thus: "exiit de potestate eius cadere non possunt." They are supplied, therefore, from Just. *Inst.* I. 12. *pr.*

2 Huschke suggests that the word *veluti* has fallen out of the text, for, of course, Roman citizenship was lost for other reasons besides violation of the Lex Cornelia.

3 I. 90. Ulpian, X. 3.

4 Ulpian, X. 4. The nature of the *jus postliminii* is partly explained in the text. Its effect was that all things and persons taken by the enemy were, on recapture, replaced in their original condition. Property retaken was returned to the original owners, and not left in the hands of the recaptor; liberated captives were

vus hostium fiat, tamen pendet ius liberorum propter ius postliminii, quia hi qui ab hostibus capti sunt, si reversi fuerint, omnia pristina iura recipiunt. itaque reversus habebit liberos in potestate. si vero illic mortuus sit, erunt quidem liberi sui iuris; sed utrum ex hoc tempore quo mortuus est aput hostes parens, an ex illo quo ab hostibus captus est, dubitari potest[1]. ipse quoque filius neposve si ab hostibus captus fuerit, similiter dicemus propter ius postliminii potestatem quoque parentis in suspenso esse. (130.) Praeterea exeunt liberi virilis sexus de
P. 35 patris potestate si flamines Diales inaugurentur, et | feminini sexus si virgines Vestales capiantur[2]. (131.) Olim quoque, quo tempore populus Romanus in Latinas regiones colonias deducebat, qui iussu parentis in coloniam Latinam nomen dedissent *desinebant in potestate pa*rentis esse, quia efficerentur alterius civitatis cives[3].

although he becomes a slave of the enemy, yet by virtue of the rule of postliminy his authority over his descendants is merely suspended; for those taken by the enemy, if they return, recover all their original rights. Therefore, if he return, he will have his descendants in his *potestas;* but if he die there, his descendants will be *sui juris;* but whether from the time when the ascendant died amongst the enemy, or from the time when he was taken by the enemy, may be disputed[1]. If too the son or grandson himself be taken by the enemy, we shall say in like manner that by virtue of the rule of postliminy the *potestas* of the ascendant is merely suspended. 130. Further, male descendants escape from their ascendant's *potestas* if they be admitted flamens of Jupiter, and female descendants if elected vestal virgins[2]. 131. Formerly also, at the time when the Roman people used to send out colonies into the Latin districts, those who by command of their ascendant had given in their names for a Latin colony, ceased to be under the *potestas* of their ascendant, because they were made citizens of another state[3].

---

regarded as having never been absent. See D. 49. 15, especially ll. 4 and 12, where the technicalities of the subject are discussed and examined.

[1] Justinian decided they should be *sui juris* from the time of the capture. Inst. 1. 12. 5.

[2] Ulpian, x. 5. Taciti *Ann.* IV. 16.

[3] See notes on I. 22, I. 95. Also see Cic. *pro Caecin.* cap. 33, 34; *de*

132. *Praeterea* emancipatione desinunt liberi in potestate parentium esse[1]. set filius quidem tribus mancipationibus, ceteri vero liberi, sive masculini sexus sive feminini, una mancipatione exeunt de parentium potestate: lex enim XII tabularum[2] tantum in persona filii de tribus mancipationibus loquitur, his verbis: SI PATER FILIUM (TER) VENUMDABIT, A PATRE FILIUS LIBER ESTO. eaque res ita agitur. mancipat pater filium alicui: is eum vindicta manumittit[3]: eo facto revertitur in potestatem patris. is eum iterum mancipat vel eidem vel alii; set in usu est eidem mancipari: isque eum postea similiter *vindicta manumittit: quo facto cum* rursus in potestatem patris fuerit reversus, *tunc* tertio pater eum mancipat vel eidem vel alii; set hoc in usu est, ut eidem mancipetur: eaque mancipatione desinit *in potestate patris esse*,
P. 36 (deest) etiamsi nondum manumissus sit, set adhuc in causa mancipii[4].... |

132. Descendants also cease to be in the *potestas* of ascendants by *emancipation*[1]. And a son ceases to be in his father's *potestas* after three mancipations, other descendants, male or female, after one: for the Law of the Twelve Tables[2] only requires three mancipations in the case of a son, in the words: "If a father sell his son three times, let the son be free from the father." Which transaction is thus effected: the father mancipates the son to some one or other, who manumits him by *vindicta*[3]: this being done, he returns into his father's *potestas*: he mancipates him a second time, either to the same man or to another, but it is usual for him to be mancipated to the same: and this person afterwards manumits him by *vindicta* in the same manner, and when by this being done he returns again into his father's *potestas*, then the father a third time mancipates him either to the same man or to another: but it is usual for him to be mancipated to the same: and by this mancipation he ceases to be in his father's *potestas*, although he is not yet manumitted, but is still in the condition called *mancipium*[4]......

domo, c. 30; *pro Balbo*, c. 11—13. In fact the direct object of the practice was to enable the new colonists to take up the *civitas* of the place they were going to colonize, and so by renouncing the *civitas* or domicile of origin, escape from the *patria potestas*. It is important to notice that this was done, and it may be presumed could only be done, by permission and authority of their ascendants. By his own act and will therefore "*nemo patriam suam exuere potest.*"

1 Ulpian, X. 1.

2 Tab. IV. l. 3.

3 I. 17.

4 The rest of this passage is il-

133. (*Liberum autem arbitrium est ei qui filium et ex eo nepotem in potestate habebit, filium quidem de potestate dimittere, nepotem vero in potestate retinere; vel ex diverso filium quidem in potestate retinere, nepotem vero manumittere; vel omnes sui iuris efficere. eadem et de pronepote dicta esse intellegemus*[1].

134. *Praeterea parentes liberis in adoptionem datis in potestate eos habere desinunt; et in filio quidem, si in adoptionem datur,*
P. 37 *tres mancipationes*) | et duae intercedentes manumissiones proinde fiunt, ac fieri solent cum ita eum pater de potestate dimittit, ut sui iuris efficiatur. deinde aut patri remancipatur, et ab eo is

133. He who has in his *potestas* a son and a grandson by that son, has unrestricted power to dismiss the son from his *potestas* and retain the grandson in it; or conversely, to retain the son in his *potestas*, but manumit the grandson; or to make both *sui juris*. And we must bear in mind that the same principles apply to the case of a great-grandson[1].

134. Further, ascendants cease to have their descendants in their *potestas* when they are given in adoption: and in the case of a son, if he be given in adoption, three mancipations and two intervening manumissions take place in like manner as they take place when the father dismisses him from his *potestas* that he may become *sui juris*. Then he is either remancipated to his father, and from the father the adoptor claims him before

legible in the MS., but Gaius, no doubt, proceeded to say that the process was completed by the man who held the freeman in *mancipium* manumitting him by *vindicta;* but that a better plan still was that he should first be retransferred by another fictitious sale, the *patria potestas* being now destroyed, from the *mancipium* of the stranger into the *mancipium* of his father; the father finally manumitting him by *vindicta*. See §§ 134 and 138. The *Epitome of Gaius*, I. 6. 3, describes the process thus: "ipse naturalis pater filium suum fiduciario patri mancipat, hoc est, manu tradit; a quo fiduciario patre naturalis pater unum aut duos nummos, quasi in similitudinem pretii accipit; et iterum eum acceptis nummis fiduciario patri tradit. Hoc secundo et tertio fit, et tertio eum fiduciario patri mancipat et tradit, et sic de patris potestate exit...Tamen cum tertio mancipatus fuerit filius a patre naturali fiduciario patri, hoc agere debet naturalis pater, ut ei a fiduciario patre remancipetur, et a naturali patre manumittatur: ut, si filius ille mortuus fuerit, ei in hereditate naturalis pater, non fiduciarius, succedat." This depends on the rule that the manumittor of a slave, and therefore also the manumittor of a person in *mancipium*, became his *patronus* and *legitimus heres* (I. 165). It was obviously necessary therefore that the actual father should manumit, in order that he or his heir might succeed to the property of the emancipated person, if he died childless. See also III. 40—42.

[1] This § is restored from D. I. 7.

qui adoptat vindicat[1] aput Praetorem filium suum esse, et illo contra non vindicante a Praetore vindicanti filius addicitur, aut non remancipatur patri sed ab eo vindicat is qui adop*tat aput* quem *in tertia* mancipatione est: set sane commodius est patri remancipari. in ceteris vero liberorum personis, seu masculini seu feminini sexus, una scilicet mancipatio sufficit[2], et aut remancipantur parenti aut non remancipantur. eadem et in provinciis aput Praesidem provinciae solent fieri. (135.) Qui ex filio semel iterumve mancipato conceptus est[3], licet post tertiam mancipationem patris sui nascatur, tamen in avi potestate est, et ideo ab eo et emancipari et in adoptionem dari potest. at is qui ex eo filio conceptus est qui in tertia mancipatione est[4], non nascitur in avi potestate. set eum Labeo quidem existimat

the Praetor as being his son[1], and the father putting in no counter-claim, the son is assigned by the Praetor to the claimant, or he is not remancipated to his natural father, but the adopter claims him from the person with whom he remains after the third mancipation. But obviously the more convenient plan is for him to be remancipated to his father[2]. In the case of other classes of descendants, whether male or female, one mancipation alone is sufficient[3], and they are either remancipated to their ascendant, or not remancipated. In the provinces the same process is gone through before the governor thereof. 135. A child conceived from a son once or twice mancipated[4], although born after the third mancipation of his father, is nevertheless in the *potestas* of his grandfather, and therefore can be either emancipated or given in adoption by him. But a child conceived from a son who has gone through the third mancipation[5], is not born in the *potestas* of his grandfather. Labeo

28, an excerpt from Gaius *libro* I. *Institutionum*.

[1] *Vindicat*=claims him by *cessio in iure*. The father has the son in *mancipium*, but the claimant demands *potestas* over him. The father collusively allows judgment to go against himself, and thus the claimant obtains a more extensive power than the father possesses at the time the *cessio* is made. Hence the process resembles a Recovery in old English Law, where, although the tenant had only a limited interest, yet the demandant claimed and got by default of the tenant's warrantor a fee simple.

[2] Because, if he should die before he is transferred into the *potestas* of the adopter, his father will succeed to his inheritance, as a quasi-patron.

[3] I. 132.

[4] I. 89.

[5] "In tertiâ mancipatione." The

in eiusdem mancipio esse cuius et pater sit. utimur autem hoc iure, ut quamdiu pater eius in mancipio sit, pendeat ius eius: et si quidem pater eius ex mancipatione manumissus erit, cadat
P. 38 in eius potestatem; si vero is, dum in mancipio sit, de|cesserit, sui iuris fit. (135 a.) Eadem scilicet [*desunt lin.* 2] ut supra diximus[1], quod in filio faciunt tres manicipationes, hoc facit una mancipatio in nepote. [*desunt lin.* 3.]

136. *Mulieres, vero in manu non sunt, nisi coemtionem cum viro* fecerint,............... *hoc in Flaminica Diali*[2] *senatusconsulto confirmatur, quo ex auctoritate consulum*[3] Maximi et Turberonis cautum est, ut haec quod ad sacra tantum videatur in manu esse, quod vero ad ceteras causas proinde habeatur, atque si in manum non convenisset. *sed mulieres quae coemtionem fecerunt per mancipationem* potestate parentis liberantur:

thinks that he is in the *mancipium* of the same man as his father is: whilst we adopt the rule, that so long as his father is in *mancipium*, the child's rights are in suspense, and if indeed the father be manumitted after the mancipation, he falls into his *potestas*, whilst if the father die in *mancipium*, he becomes *sui juris*. 135 *a.* ...... as we have said above[1], what three mancipations effect in the case of a son, one mancipation effects in the case of a grandson.

136. Women, however, are not in *manus* unless they have made coemption with a husband. This rule is established in the case of the wife of a Flamen Dialis[2] by a *senatusconsultum*, wherein it was provided, at the instance of the consuls[3] Maximus and Tubero, that such an one is to be regarded as in *manus* only so far as relates to sacred matters, but in respect of other things to be as though she had not come under *manus*. But women who have made a coemption are freed from the *potestas* of their ascendant by the mancipation: nor is it material whether they be in the *manus* of their husband or of a stranger;

preposition *in* implies that he has gone through the form of mancipation, but not yet received manumission, he is *in the third mancipation*.

[1] I. 132, 134.

[2] The marriage of a Flamen and Flaminica was not by *coemptio*, but by *confarreatio*. But probably a *coemptio* was part of the ceremonial of a *confarreatio*. The co-existence of *manus* and *potestas* only dates from the time of Augustus; and was rather an alternation, than a co-existence. See App. B. in the edition of Justinian's *Institutes* by Abdy and Walker.

[3] The filling up of the missing three lines is according to Lachmann. Maximus and Tubero were consuls in B.C. 11.

nec interest, an in viri sui manu sint, an extranei; quamvis hae solae loco filiarum habeantur quae in viri manu sunt.

137. [*desunt lin.* 4] *mancipatione* desinunt in manu esse, et si ex ea mancipatione manumissae fuerint, sui iuris[1] efficiuntur·

P. 39 [*desunt lin.* 3] nihilo magis potest cogere, | quam et filia patrem. set filia quidem nullo modo patrem potest cogere, etiamsi adoptiva sit: haec autem repudio misso[2] proinde compellere potest, atque si ei numquam nupta fuisset[3].

138. Hi qui in causa mancipii sunt[4], quia servorum loco habentur, vindicta, censu, testamento manumissi sui iuris fiunt[5]. (139.) Nec tamen in hoc casu lex Aelia Sentia locum habet. itaque nihil requirimus, cuius aetatis sit is qui manumittit[6], et qui manumittitur[7]: ac ne illud quidem, an patronum creditoremve manumissor habeat[8]. ac ne numerus quidem

although those women only are accounted in the place of daughters who are in the *manus* of a husband.

137. .... cease by the mancipation to be in *manus*, and if after the mancipation they are manumitted, they become *sui juris*[1].............. can no more compel him, than a daughter can her father. But a daughter, even though adopted, can in no case compel her father; but the other (the wife), when she has had a letter of divorce sent to her[2], can compel her husband as though she had never been married to him[3].

138. Those who are in the condition called *mancipium*[4], since they are regarded as being in the position of slaves, become *sui juris* when manumitted by *vindicta*, *census* or testament[5]. 139. And in such a case the Lex Aelia Sentia does not apply. Therefore we make no enquiry as to the age of him who manumits[6], or of him who is manumitted[7], nor even whether the manumittor have a patron or creditor[8]. Nay,

---

1 I. 115, 115 *a*.

2 "Repudio misso." A messenger or letter is sent to the other party to the marriage, seven witnesses of the age of puberty being called together to hear the instructions given to the messenger, or the contents of the letter. Warnkoenig, III. p. 52.

3 "Can compel her husband to release her from *manus*, although a daughter cannot compel her father to release her from *potestas*;" the reason being that the husband by the "repudium", has failed to fulfil his share of the compact.

4 I. 132.

5 I. 17.

6 I. 17.

7 I. 38.

8 I. 37.

legis Fufiae Caniniae finitus in his personis locum habet[1]. (140.) Quin etiam invito quoque eo cuius in mancipio sunt censu libertatem consequi possunt, excepto eo quem pater ea lege mancipio dedit, ut sibi remancipetur: nam quodammodo tunc pater potestatem propriam reservare sibi videtur eo ipso, quod mancipio recipit[2]. ac ne is quidem dicitur invito eo cuius in mancipio est censu libertatem consequi, quem pater ex noxali causa mancipio dedit[3], velut quod furti eius nomine damnatus est, et eum mancipio actori dedit: nam hunc actor pro pecunia habet. (141.) In summa admonendi sumus, ad-
P. 40 versus eos quos in mancipio habemus nihil nobis | contumeliose facere licere: alioquin iniuriarum causa tenebimur[4]. ac ne diu quidem in eo iure detinentur homines, set plerumque hoc fit dicis gratia uno momento; nisi scilicet ex noxali causa manciparentur.

142. Transeamus nunc ad aliam divisionem. nam ex his

further, the number laid down by the Lex Fufia Caninia has no application to such persons[1]. 140. Moreover they can obtain their liberty by *census* even against the will of him in whose *mancipium* they are, except when a man is given in *mancipium* by his father with the understanding that he is to be remancipated to him: for then the father is regarded as reserving to himself in some measure his own *potestas*, from the very fact that he is to take him back into *mancipium*[2]. And it is held also that a man cannot by *census* obtain his liberty against the will of the person in whose *mancipium* he is, when his father has given him into *mancipium* for a noxal cause[3], for instance, because the father has been mulcted on his account for theft, and gives him up to the plaintiff into *mancipium*: for the plaintiff has him instead of money. 141. Finally, we must observe that we are not allowed to inflict any indignity on those whom we have in *mancipium*, otherwise we shall be liable on the score of injury[4]. And men are not detained in this condition long, but in general it exists, as a mere formality, for a single instance; that is to say, unless they are mancipated for a noxal cause.

142. Now let us pass on to another division: for of those

---

1 I. 42.
2 See note on I. 132.
3 IV. 75, 79.
4 III. 223, 224.

personis, quae neque in potestate neque in manu neque in mancipio sunt, quaedam vel in tutela sunt vel in curatione, quaedam neutro iure tenentur. videamus igitur quae in tutela quae in curatione sint: ita enim intellegemus de ceteris personis quae neutro iure tenentur.

143. Ac prius dispiciamus de his quae in tutela sunt.

144. Permissum est itaque parentibus liberis quos in potestate sua habent testamento tutores dare: masculini quidem sexus inpuberibus (*dumtaxat, feminini autem cuiuscumque aetatis sint, et tum quo*)que quum nuptae sint[1]. veteres enim voluerunt feminas, etiamsi perfectae aetatis sint, propter animi levitatem in tutela esse[2]. (145.) Itaque si quis filio filiaeque testamento tutorem dederit, et ambo ad pubertatem pervenerint, filius quidem desinit habere tutorem, filia vero nihilominus in tutela permanet: tantum enim ex lege Iulia et Papia Poppaea[3] iure liberorum[4] tutela liberantur feminae. loquimur

P. 41 autem | exceptis Virginibus Vestalibus quas etiam veteres in

persons who are neither in *potestas*, *manus* or *mancipium*, some are in *tutela* or *curatio*, some are under neither of these powers. Let us, therefore, consider who are in *tutela* or *curatio:* for thus we shall understand about the other persons who are under neither power.

143. And first let us consider the case of those who are under tutelage.

144. It is permitted then to ascendants to give tutors (guardians) by testament to descendants whom they have in their *potestas:* to males indeed only so long as they are under puberty, but to females of whatever age they be, and even when they are married[1]. For the ancients thought fit that women, although of full age, should for the feebleness of their intellect be under tutelage[2]. 145. If, therefore, a man has given by testament a tutor to his son and daughter, and both attain to puberty, the son indeed ceases to have the tutor, but the daughter still remains in tutelage; for by the Lex Julia et Papia Poppaea[3] it is only by the prerogative of children[4] that women are freed from tutelage. We except the Vestal Virgins,

[1] Ulpian, XI. 1, 14—16.

[2] I. 190. Cic. *pro Muraena*, 12.

[3] Temp. Augusti, A.D. 9. See note on II. 111.

[4] I. 194.

honorem sacerdotii liberas esse voluerunt: itaque etiam lege XII tabularum cautum est[1]. (146.) Nepotibus autem neptibusque ita demum possumus testamento tutores dare, si post mortem nostram in patris sui potestatem iure recasuri non sint[2]. itaque si filius meus mortis meae tempore in potestate mea sit, nepotes quos ex eo (habeo) non poterunt ex testamento meo habere tutorem, quamvis in potestate mea fuerint: scilicet quia mortuo me in patris sui potestate futuri sunt. (147.) Cum tamen in compluribus aliis causis postumi pro iam natis habeantur, et in hac causa placuit non minus postumis, quam iam natis testamento tutores dari posse: si modo in ea causa sint, ut si vivis nobis nascantur, in potestate nostra fiant. hos etiam heredes instituere possumus, cum extraneos postumos, heredes instituere permissum non sit[3]. (148.) (Uxori) quae in manu est proinde acsi filiae[4], item nurui quae in filii manu est

however, from what we are saying, whom even the ancients wished, in honour of their office, to be free: and therefore it was so provided also in a law[1] of the Twelve Tables. 146. But to grandsons and granddaughters we are only able to give tutors by testament, in the case where after our death they will not by law relapse into the *potestas* of their father[2]. Therefore if my son at the time of my death is in my *potestas*, the grandsons whom I have by him cannot have a tutor given them by my testament, although they are in my *potestas*: the reason, of course, being that after my death they will be in the *potestas* of their father. 147. But whereas in many other cases after-born children are esteemed as already born, therefore in this case too it has been held that tutors can be given by testament to after-born as well as to existing children; provided only the children are of such a character that, if born in our lifetime, they would be in our *potestas*. We may also appoint them our heirs, although we are not allowed to appoint the after-born children of strangers our heirs[3]. 148. A tutor can be given to a wife in *manus* exactly as to a daughter[4], and to a daughter-in-

1 Tab. v. l. 1.

2 I. 127.

3 A *postumus* is one born after the making of the testament, whether in the testator's lifetime or not. If born in the testator's lifetime he was called *postumus Velleianus*. (D. 28. 3. 3. 1.) A *postumus extraneus* could not be named in a testament; but a *postumus* must be named. II. 130.

4 I. 114.

proinde ac nepti tutor dari potest. (149.) Rectissime autem tutor sic dari potest: LUCIUM TITIUM LIBERIS MEIS TUTOREM DO[1]. sed et si ita scriptum sit: LIBERIS MEIS vel UXORI MEAE TITIUS TUTOR ESTO, recte datus intellegitur. (150.) In per-
P. 42 sona tamen | uxoris quae in manu est recepta est etiam tutoris optio, id est, ut liceat ei permittere quem velit ipsa tutorem sibi optare, hoc modo: TITIAE UXORI MEAE TUTORIS OPTIONEM DO. quo casu licet uxori (tutorem optare) vel in omnes res vel in unam forte aut duas[2]. (151.) Ceterum aut plena optio datur aut angusta. (152.) Plena ita dari solet, ut proxime supra diximus. angusta ita dari solet: TITIAE UXORI MEAE DUMTAXAT TUTORIS OPTIONEM SEMEL DO, aut DUMTAXAT BIS DO. (153.) Quae optiones plurimum inter se differunt. nam quae plenam optionem habet potest semel et bis et ter et saepius tutorem optare. quae vero angustam habet optionem, si dumtaxat semel data est optio, amplius quam semel optare non potest: si tantum bis, amplius quam bis optandi facultatem

law, who is in the *manus* of our son, exactly as to a grand-daughter. 149. The most regular form of appointing a tutor is: "I give Lucius Titius as tutor to my descendants[1]:" but even if the wording be: "Titius, be tutor to my descendants or to my wife," he is considered lawfully appointed. 150. In the case, however, of a wife who is in *manus*, the selection of a tutor is also allowed, *i.e.* she may be suffered to select such person as she chooses for her tutor, in this form: "I give to Titia my wife the option of a tutor." In which case the wife has power to select a tutor either for all her affairs, or, it may be, for one or two matters only[2]. 151. Moreover, the selection is allowed either without restraint or with restraint. 152. That without restraint is given in the form we have stated just above. That with restraint is usually given thus: "I give to my wife Titia the selection of a tutor once only," or "I give it twice only." 153. Which selections differ very considerably from one another. For a woman who has selection without restraint can choose her tutor once, or twice, or thrice, or more times: but she who has selection with restraint, if it be given

[1] II. 289.

[2] There is a reference to this in Livy 39. 19: "Utique Feceniae Hispalae datio, diminutio, gentis enuptio, tutoris optio item esset, quasi ei vir testamento dedisset." See also Plaut. *Truculent.* Act 4, Sc. 4. 6.

non habet. (154.) Vocantur autem hi qui nominatim testamento tutores dantur, dativi; qui ex optione sumuntur, optivi.

155. Quibus testamento quidem tutor datus non sit, iis ex lege XII agnati sunt tutores, qui vocantur legitimi[1]. (156.) Sunt autem agnati per virilis sexus personas cognatione iuncti, quasi a patre cognati[2]: veluti frater eodem patre natus, fratris
P. 43 filius neposve ex eo, item patruus et patrui | filius et nepos ex eo. at hi qui per feminini sexus personas cognatione coniunguntur non sunt agnati, sed alias naturali iure cognati. itaque inter avunculum et sororis filium non agnatio est, sed cognatio. item amitae, materterae filius non est mihi agnatus, set cognatus, et invicem scilicet sic ego illi eodem iure coniungor: quia qui nascuntur patris, non matris familiam sequuntur[3]. (157.) Sed olim quidem, quantum ad legem XII tabularum attinet, etiam feminae agnatos habebant tutores. set postea lex Claudia[4] lata est quae, quod ad feminas attinet,

her once only, cannot choose more than once; if twice only, has not the power of choosing more than twice. 154. Tutors who are given by name in a testament are called *dativi*, those who are taken by virtue of selection, *optivi.*

155. To those who have no tutor given them by testament, the agnates are tutors by a law of the Twelve Tables, and they are called statutable tutors[1]. 156. Now the agnates[2] are those united in relationship through persons of the male sex, relations, that is to say, through the father: for instance a brother born from the same father, the son of that brother, and the grandson by that son; an uncle on the father's side, that uncle's son, and his grandson by that son. But those who are joined in relationship through persons of the female sex are not agnates, but merely cognates by natural right. Therefore there is no agnation between a mother's brother and a sister's son, but only cognation. Likewise the son of my father's sister or of my mother's sister is not my agnate, but my cognate, and conversely of course I am in like manner joined to him by the same tie: because children follow the family of their father, not of their mother[3]. 157. In olden times, indeed, under the provision of the law of the Twelve Tables, women too had agnates for tutors, but afterwards the Lex Claudia[4]

[1] Ulpian, XI. 3. [2] Ibid. 4. [3] I. 80. [4] I. 171. Ulp. XI. 8.

tutelas (illas) sustulit. itaque masculus quidem inpubes fratrem puberem aut patruum habet tutorem; femina vero talem habere tutorem non potest. (158.) Sed agnationis quidem ius capitis diminutione perimitur, cognationis vero ius non commutatur: quia civilis ratio civilia quidem iura corrumpere potest, naturalia vero non potest.

159. Est autem capitis diminutio[1] prioris capitis permutatio. eaque tribus modis accidit: nam aut maxima est capitis diminutio, aut minor quam quidam mediam vocant, aut minima.

160. Maxima est capitis diminutio, cum aliquis simul et civitatem et libertatem amittit; quae accidit incensis[2], qui ex

P. 44 forma censuali | venire iubentur, quod ius pr......ex lege......

was passed, which abolished these tutelages so far as they related to women. A male, therefore, under the age of puberty will have as tutor his brother over the age of puberty or his father's brother; but a woman cannot have a tutor of that kind. 158. By *capitis diminutio* the right of agnation is destroyed, but that of cognation is not changed: because a civil law doctrine may destroy civil law rights, but it cannot destroy those of natural law.

159. *Capitis diminutio*[1] is the change of the original *caput*, and occurs in three ways; for it is either the *capitis diminutio maxima;* or the *minor*, which some call *media;* or the *minima.*

160. The *maxima capitis diminutio* is when a man loses at once both citizenship and liberty, which happens to those who do not enrol themselves on the Censor's register[2], and therefore by the regulations as to the *census* are ordered to be sold...... by the Lex......they who in breach of that *lex* have taken up

[1] Ulpian, XI. 9—13. *Status* and *caput* are not identical in Roman law: a slave is often said to have *status*, but it is also affirmed of him that he has "*nullum caput*". Austin is of opinion that "*status* and *caput* are not synonymous expressions, but that the term *caput* signifies certain conditions which are capital or principal: which cannot be acquired or lost without a mighty change in the legal position of the party." *Caput* necessarily implies the possession of rights: *status* generally implies the possession of rights, but may imply mere obnoxiousness to duties, *e.g.* the *status* of a slave. See Austin, Lecture XII. *Caput* includes (1) Liberty, (2) Citizenship, (3) Family. (1) includes (2) and (3); (2) includes (3), therefore by the *maxima capitis diminutio* all these elements are lost, by the *media* all but liberty, by the *minima* family alone.

[2] See Cicero *pro Caecina*, 34: "quum autem incensum vendit, hoc

qui contra eam legem in urbe Roma domicilium habuerint[1]; item feminae quae ex senatusconsulto Claudiano ancillae fiunt eorum dominorum, quibus invitis et denunciantibus *nihil*o min*u*s[2] cum servis eorum coierint[3].

161. Minor sive media est capitis diminutio, cum civitas amittitur, libertas retinetur. quod accidit ei cui aqua et igni interdictum fuerit[4].

162. Minima est capitis diminutio, cum et civitas et libertas retinetur, sed status hominis conmutatur. quod accidit in his qui adoptantur, item in his quae coemptionem faciunt, et in his qui mancipio dantur, quique ex mancipatione manumittantur[5]; adeo quidem, ut quotiens quisque mancipetur ut manumittatur, totiens capite diminuatur. (163.) Nec solum maioribus diminutionibus ius adgnationis corrumpitur, sed etiam minima. et ideo si ex duobus liberis alterum pater eman-

their abode in the city of Rome[1]: likewise women, who by virtue of a *senatusconsultum* of Claudius, become slaves of those masters with whose slaves, in spite of their wish and warning[2], they have cohabited[3]:

161. The *minor* or *media capitis diminutio* is when citizenship is lost, but liberty retained; which happens to a man interdicted from fire and water[4].

162. The *minima capitis diminutio* is when both citizenship and liberty are retained, but the *status* of a man is changed; which is the case with persons adopted, also with those who make a coemption, with those who are given in *mancipium*, and with those who are manumitted after mancipation[5]: so that indeed as often as a man is mancipated with a view to manumission, so often does he suffer *capitis diminutio*. 163. Not only by the greater *diminutiones* is the right of agnation de-

(populus) iudicat; quum ii qui in servitute iusta fuerunt, censu liberentur, eum qui, quum liber esset, censeri noluerit, ipsum sibi libertatem abiudicasse."

[1] This seems to refer to the regulation of the *Lex Aelia Sentia*, that *dediticii* were not to come within 100 miles of Rome, and if they did come were to be sold. Krüger and Goudsmit object to this view, that *dediticii* had not citizenship. It is true that not *full* citizenship, but both the *Latini Juniani* and the *dediticii* had a partial citizenship.

[2] The MS. has DOMINIS. Probably the original was ꞤOMINUS; Ꞥ being the abbreviation for *nihil.*

[3] I. 84, 91; Ulpian XI. 11.

[4] I. 90, 128.

[5] I. 110, 132.

cipaverit, post obitum eius neuter alteri adgnationis iure tutor esse poterit[1].

164. Cum autem ad agnatos tutela pertineat, non simul ad omnes pertinet, sed ad eos tantum qui proximo gradu sunt.
P. 45 [*desunt lin.* 17.]

165. Ex eadem lege XII tabularum libertarum et inpuberum libertorum tutela ad patronos liberosque eorum pertinet, quae et ipsa tutela legitima vocatur: non *quia nominatim* ea lege de hac tutela ca*vetur*, *sed* quia perinde accepta est per interpretationem, atque si verbis legis praecepta esset[2]. eo enim ipso,
P. 46 *quod* h*eredita*tes libertorum libertarumque, si | intestati decessissent, iusserat lex ad patronos liberosve eorum pertinere, crediderunt veteres voluisse legem etiam tutelas ad eos pertinere, quia et agnatos quos ad hereditatem vocavit, eosdem et tutores esse iusserat[3].

stroyed, but even by the least; and therefore if a father have emancipated one of two sons, neither can after his death be tutor to the other by right of agnation[1].

164. In cases, however, where the tutelage devolves on the agnates, it does not appertain to all simultaneously but only to those who are in the nearest degree..............

165. By virtue of the same law of the Twelve Tables the tutelage of freedwomen and of freedmen under puberty devolves on the patrons and their children, (and this too is styled a statutable tutelage): not because express provision is made in that law with respect to this tutelage, but because it is gathered by construction as surely as if it had been set down[2] in the words of the law. For from the very fact that the law ordered the inheritances of freedmen and freedwomen, in case of their dying intestate, to belong to the patrons or their children, the ancients concluded that the law intended their tutelages also to devolve on them, since it ordered that the agnates too, whom it called to the inheritance, should be tutors as well[3].

---

1 He is not *tutor iure agnationis*, but he is *tutor iure patronatus*, or *iure quasi-patronatus*. See App. (D).

2 The MS. has *accepta*, doubtless a mistake of the transcriber for *praecepta*.

3 The argument is:

(1) The agnates who have the inheritance, also have the tutelage.

(2) Therefore the inheritance and the tutelage, the benefit and the burden, devolve on the same persons.

(3) Now the patrons have the in-

166. Exemplo patronorum receptae sunt[1] et aliae tutelae quae fiduciariae vocantur, id est, quae ideo nobis competunt, quia liberum caput mancipatum nobis vel a parente vel a coemptionatore manumiserimus. (167.) Set Latinarum et Latinorum inpuberum *tute*la non omni modo ad manumissores libertinorum, pertinet, sed ad eos quorum ante manumissionem ex iure Quiritium[2] (*fuerunt: unde si ancilla ex iure Quiritium*)[3] tua sit, in bonis mea, a me quidem solo, non etiam a te manumissa, Latina fieri potest, et bona eius ad me pertinent, sed eius tutela tibi competit: nam ita lege Iunia cavetur. itaque si ab eo cuius et in bonis et ex iure Quiritium ancilla fuerit facta sit Latina, ad eundem et bona et tutela pertinet.

166. Other tutelages, styled fiduciary, have been admitted into use upon the precedent of patronal tutelages[1], those namely which devolve upon us because we have manumitted a free person who has been mancipated to us either by a parent or a coemptionator. 167. But the tutelage of Latin women or Latin men under puberty does not in all cases appertain to the manumittors of the freedmen, but devolves on those whose property they were by Quiritary title before manumission[2]: therefore if a female slave be yours by Quiritary[3], mine by Bonitary title, when manumitted by me alone and not by you also, she can be made a Latin, and her goods belong to me, but her tutelage devolves on you: for it is so provided by the Lex Junia. Therefore if she be made a Latin by one to whom she belonged both by Bonitary and Quiritary title, the goods and the tutelage both go to the same man.

---

heritance by the express words of the law.

(4) Therefore they also have the tutelage by implication.

[1] I. 114, 115, 195. Ulpian, XI. 5.

[2] The manumittor might be owner both "in bonis", and "ex jure Quiritium", or he might only have the title "in bonis". (See II. 40.) For by reading I. 54, we see that if the legal ownership was separated from the beneficial, the beneficial owner, *i.e.* the owner *in bonis*, having the *potestas*, had the power of manumission. The general rule in the case of tutelages which were for the profit of the tutor as well as the pupil, was that the benefit (the right of inheritance) should go with the burden (the tutelage proper), but in this paragraph Gaius is pointing out an exception. Ulpian, XI. 19.

[3] The transcriber has evidently missed out the second of two lines, which had *Quiritium* for the final word in each.

168. Agnatis et patronis et liberorum capitum manumissoribus permissum est feminarum tutelam alii in iure cedere[1]: pupillorum autem tutelam non est permissum cedere, quia non
P. 47 videtur one|rosa, cum tempore pubertatis finiatur. (169.) Is autem cui ceditur tutela cessicius tutor vocatur. (170.) Quo mortuo aut capite diminuto revertitur ad eum tutorem tutela qui cessit. ipse quoque qui cessit, si mortuus aut capite diminutus sit, a cessicio tutela discedit et revertitur ad eum, qui post eum qui cesserat secundum gradum in ea tutela habuerit. (171.) Set quantum ad agnatos pertinet, nihil hoc tempore de cessicia tutela quaeritur, cum agnatorum tutelae in feminis lege Claudia[2] sublatae sint. (172.) Sed fiduciarios quoque quidam putaverunt cedendae tutelae ius non habere, cum ipsi se oneri subiecerint. quod etsi placeat, in parente tamen qui filiam neptemve aut proneptem alteri ea lege mancipio dedit, ut sibi remanciparetur, remancipatamque manumisit, idem dici non

168. Agnates, patrons, and manumittors of free persons are allowed to transfer to others by cession in court[1] the tutelage of women; but not that of pupils, because this tutelage is not looked upon as onerous, inasmuch as it must terminate at the time of puberty. 169. He to whom a tutelage is thus ceded is called a cessician tutor: 170. and on his death or *capitis diminutio* the tutelage returns to him who ceded it. So too, if the man himself who ceded it die or suffer *capitis diminutio*, the tutelage shifts from the cessician tutor and reverts to him who had the claim to the tutelage next in succession to the cessor. 171. But so far as relates to agnates, no question now arises about cessician tutelage, inasmuch as the tutelages of agnates over women were abolished by the Lex Claudia[2]. 172. Some, however, have held that fiduciary tutors also have not power to cede a tutelage, since they have voluntarily undertaken the burden. But although this be the rule, yet the same must not be laid down in respect of an ascendant who has given a daughter, granddaughter, or great-granddaughter into the *mancipium* of another on condition that she be remancipated to him, and has manumitted her after the remancipation: since such an

[1] II. 24. Ulpian, XI. 6—8. See note on I. 134.

[2] I. 157.

debet, cum is et legitimus tutor habeatur[1]; et non minus huic quam patronis honor praestandus est.

173. Praeterea senatusconsulto mulieribus permissum est in absentis tutoris locum alium petere: quo petito prior desinit. nec interest quam longe aberit is tutor[2]. (174.) Set excipitur, nec in absentis patroni locum liceat libertae tutorem
P. 48 petere. (175.) Patroni | autem loco habemus etiam parentem qui ex eo quod ipse sibi remancipatam filiam neptemve aut proneptem manumisit legitimam tutelam nanctus est[3]. huius quidem liberi fiduciarii tutoris loco numerantur[4]: patroni autem liberi eandem tutelam adipiscuntur, quam et pater eorum habuit. (176.) Sed aliquando etiam in patroni absentis locum per*mitt*itur tutorem petere, veluti ad hereditatem adeundam[5]. (177.) Idem senatus censuit et in persona pupilli patroni filii[6]. (178.) Nam e lege Iulia de maritandis ordinibus ei quae

one is also[1] reckoned a statutable tutor, and in no less degree must respect be paid to him than to a patron.

173. Further by a *senatusconsultum* women are allowed to apply for a tutor in the place of one who is absent, and on his appointment the original tutor ceases to be in office: nor does it matter how far the original tutor has gone away[2]. 174. But there is an exception to this, that a freedwoman may not apply for a tutor in the place of an absent patron. 175. We also regard as equivalent to a patron an ascendant who has acquired by manumission statutable tutelage by the fact of personally manumitting a daughter, granddaughter, or great-granddaughter, after her remancipation to himself[3]. The children, however, of such an one are regarded as fiduciary tutors[4], whereas the children of a patron acquire the same kind of tutelage as their father also had. 176. But sometimes a woman is allowed to apply for a tutor in the place even of an absent patron, as for instance, to enter upon an inheritance[5]. 177. The senate has adopted the same rule in the case of the son of a patron being a pupil[6]. 178. For even by the *Lex Julia de maritandis ordinibus* a woman who is in the statutable tutelage of a pupil

---

1 "Also," *i.e.* in addition to the two classes of *legitimi* already named in §§ 155, 165. Conf. I. 175.

2 Ulpian, XI. 22.

3 I. 172. See also note on I. 132.

4 D. 26. 4. 4.

5 Ulpian, XI. 22.

6 Ibid. 22.

in legitima tutela pupilli sit permittitur dotis constituendae gratia a Praetore urbano tutorem petere[1]. (179.) Sane patroni filius etiamsi inpubes sit, libertae efficietur tutor, quamquam in nulla re auctor fieri potest, cum ipsi nihil permissum sit sine tutoris auctoritate agere[2]. (180.) Item si qua in tutela legitima furiosi aut muti sit, permittitur ei senatusconsulto[3] dotis constituendae gratia tutorem petere. (181.) Quibus casibus salvam manere tutelam patrono patronique filio manifestum est. (182.) Praeterea senatus censuit, ut si tutor pupilli pupillaeve suspectus a tutela remotus sit[4], sive ex iusta causa fuerit excusatus[5], in locum eius alius tutor detur, quo facto prior tutor amittet tutelam. (183.) Haec omnia similiter et Romae et in pro-|

is allowed to apply for a tutor from the Praetor Urbanus for the purpose of arranging her *dos*[1]. 179. For the son of a patron undoubtedly becomes the tutor of a freedwoman, even though he be under puberty, although he can in no instance authorize[2] her acts, since he is not allowed to do anything for himself without the authorization of his tutor. 180. Likewise, if a woman be in the statutable tutelage of a mad or dumb person, she is by the *senatusconsultum*[3] allowed to apply for a tutor for the purpose of arranging her *dos*. 181. In these cases it is plain that the tutelage remains intact for the patron and the son of the patron. 182. Further the senate has ruled that if a tutor of a pupil, male or female, be removed from his tutorship as untrustworthy[4], or be excused on some lawful ground[5], another tutor may be given in his place, and on such appointment the original tutor will lose his tutorship. 183. All these rules are observed in like manner at Rome and in the

---

[1] Ibid. 20. For an account of *dos*, see Ulp. VI. and Appendix (B) in Abdy and Walker's *Justinian*.

[2] The *auctoritas* of the tutor is the tutor's presence and assent to the deed of the pupil. The pupil himself performs the symbolical act, though his hand may need guiding to do it; and, if he can speak, he utters the words necessary to effect the transaction in hand; but his will is considered to be defective on account of his youth (or in the case of a woman, her sex); and the tutor's presence and approval add a sound will to a duly performed act, the two requisites insisted on by the law. *Auctoritas* is derived from *augeo*, and signifies the complement or supplying of a defect.

[3] Probably that referred to in I. 173, and in Ulp. XI. 21.

[4] Just. I. 26.

[5] Just. I. 25; Ulpian, XI. 23.

P. 49 vinciis observantur, scilicet et in provinciis a praeside provinciae tutor peti potest[1] — — — — — — — — — — — — — — — — (184.) Olim cum legis actiones[2] in usu erant, etiam ex illa causa tutor dabatur, si inter tutorem et mulierem pupillumve lege agendum erat: nam quia ipse tutor in re sua auctor esse non poterat, alius dabatur, quo auctore illa legis actio perageretur: qui dicebatur praetorius tutor, quia a Praetore urbano dabatur. set post sublatas legis actiones quidam putant hanc speciem dandi tutoris in usu esse desiisse; aliis *vero* placet adhuc in usu esse si legitimo iudicio agatur[3].

185. Si cui nullus omnino tutor sit, ei datur in urbe Roma ex lege Atilia[4] a Praetore urbano et maiore parte Tribunorum plebis, qui Atilianus tutor vocatur; in provinciis vero a Praesidibus provinciarum ex lege Iulia et Titia[5]. (186.) Et ideo si cui testamento tutor sub condicione aut ex die certo datus

provinces, that is to say, that in the provinces too a tutor can be asked for from the *praeses*[1].

184. Formerly when the *legis actiones*[2] were in use, a tutor used also to be given in case proceedings by *legis actio* had to be taken between a tutor and a woman or pupil: for inasmuch as the tutor could not authorize in any matter that concerned himself, another used to be appointed under whose authorization the *legis actio* was conducted: and he was called a Praetorian tutor, because he was appointed by the Praetor Urbanus. But now that *legis actiones* have been abolished, some authorities hold that this kind of tutor has become unnecessary to be appointed; but others think it is still the proper course when proceedings have to be taken by statutable action[3].

185. Supposing a person to have no tutor at all, one is given him, in the city of Rome by virtue of the Lex Atilia[4], by the Praetor Urbanus and the major part of the Tribunes of the Plebs, who is called an Atilian tutor: in the provinces, by the governors thereof, by virtue of the Lex Julia et Titia[5]. 186. And therefore if a tutor be appointed to any one by

---

[1] Ulp. XI. 20.

[2] IV. 11 seqq. Ulpian, XI. 24.

[3] Statutable as opposed to "Imperio continenti;" for which distinction see IV. 103.

[4] Ulp. XI. 18. The Lex Atilia was probably enacted about 190 B.C. M. Atilius Serranus was Praetor in A.U.C. 560, and again in A.U.C. 567, as stated in Livy 35. 10 and 39. 23.

[5] Enacted 32 or 30 B.C. Probably in the former year for the Imperial

sit, quamdiu condicio aut dies pendet, tutor dari potest; item si pure datus fuerit, quamdiu nemo heres existat[1], tamdiu ex iis legibus tutor petendus est: qui desinit tutor esse postea quam aliquis ex testamento tutor esse coeperit. (187.) Ab hostibus quoque tutore capto ex his legibus tutor peti debet, qui desinit tutor esse, si is qui captus est in civitatem reversus fuerit: nam reversus recipit tutelam iure postliminii[2]. |

P. 50 188. Ex his apparet quot sint species tutelarum. si vero quaeramus, in quot genera hae species deducantur, longa erit disputatio: nam de ea re valde veteres dubitaverunt, nosque diligentius hunc tractatum exsecuti sumus et in edicti interpretatione, et in his libris quos ex Quinto Mucio fecimus. hoc loco tantisper sufficit admonuisse, quod quidam quinque genera esse dixerunt, ut Quintus Mucius; alii tria, ut Servius Sulpicius;

testament under a condition or to act after a certain day, so long as the condition is unfulfilled or the day not arrived, another tutor may be appointed: likewise, if the tutor be appointed without condition, still for such time as no heir exists[1] another tutor must be applied for under these laws, who ceases to be tutor so soon as any one begins to act as tutor under the testament. 187. Also when a tutor is taken by the enemy, another tutor ought to be asked for under these laws, who ceases to be tutor if the captive return into the state; for having returned he recovers his tutelage by the rule of postliminy[2].

188. From the foregoing it appears how many species of tutelage there are. But if we enquire into how many classes these species may be collected, the discussion will be tedious: for the ancients held most opposite opinions on this point, and we have carefully investigated this question both in our explanation of the Edict and in those commentaries which we have based on the works of Quintus Mucius. In the present place it is sufficient to remark only, that some have held that there are five classes, as Quintus Mucius; others three, as

Provinces; and afterwards extended to the Senatorial Provinces.

[1] The institution of the heir is the main point of a Roman testament, and until he accepts the inheritance, no provision of the testament can be carried out.

[2] I. 129.

alii duo, ut Labeo[1]; alii tot genera esse crediderunt, quot etiam species essent[2].

189. Sed inpuberes quidem in tutela esse omnium civitatium iure contingit; quia id naturali rationi conveniens est, ut is qui perfectae aetatis non sit alterius tutela regatur. nec fere ulla civitas est, in qua non licet parentibus liberis suis inpuberibus testamento tutorem dare: quamvis, ut supra diximus, soli cives Romani videantur liberos suos in potestate habere[3]. (190.) Feminas vero perfectae aetatis in tutela esse[4] fere nulla preciosa ratio suasisse videtur. nam quae vulgo creditur[5], quia levitate animi plerumque decipiuntur, et aequum erat eas tutorum auctoritate regi, magis speciosa videtur quam

Servius Sulpicius; others two, as Labeo[1]; whilst others have thought that there are as many classes as species[2].

189. Now for those under puberty to be in tutelage is a rule established by the law of all communities; because it is agreeable to natural reason that he who is not of full age should be guided by the tutelage of another: and there is scarcely any community where ascendants are not allowed to give by testament a tutor to their descendants under puberty; although, as we have said above, Roman citizens alone seem to have their children in *potestas*[3]. 190. But there is scarcely any reason of weight to account for women of full age being under tutelage[4]. For the one generally received[5], that owing to their feebleness of intellect, they are so often deceived, and so it is right they should be guided by the authority of tutors, appears more

[1] This Q. M. Scaevola (son of Pub. M. Scaevola) is the man of whom Pomponius speaks as the earliest systematic writer on the Civil Law, and whom Cicero styles the most erudite, acute, and skilful lawyer of his day, "juris peritorum eloquentissimus, eloquentium juris peritissimus." See D. I. 2. 2. 41. Cic. *de Orat.* I. 39. For a memoir of Servius Sulpicius Rufus see Cicero, *Brutus*, c. 41, and for an account of Antistius Labeo, D. I. 2. 47.

[2] For an account of the various kinds of *tutelae* see Appendix (D). The five classes of Q. Mucius were probably the same as in our tabulation; S. Sulpicius may have followed the classification of Ulpian (XI. 2); "Tutores aut legitimi sunt, aut senatus-consultis constituti, aut moribus introducti:" Labeo's division may have been into testamentary and non-testamentary, or he may have combined the two first-named classes of Sulpicius, and opposed them to the third "moribus introducti."

[3] I. 55.

[4] I. 144.

[5] See Ulp. XI. 1, also Cic. *pro Muraena*, c. 12: "propter infirmitatem consilii": Cato's speech against the repeal of the Oppian Law, Livy

vera. mulieres enim quae perfectae aetatis sunt ipsae sibi negotia
P. 51 tractant, et in quibusdam | causis dicis gratia tutor interponit auctoritatem suam; saepe etiam invitus auctor fieri a Praetore cogitur[1]. (191.) Unde cum tutore nullum ex tutela iudicium mulieri datur: at ubi pupillorum pupillarumve negotia tutores tractant, eis post pubertatem tutelae iudicio[2] rationem reddunt. (192.) Sane patronorum et parentum legitimae tutelae vim aliquam habere intelleguntur eo, quod hi neque ad testamentum faciendum, neque ad res mancipi alienandas, neque ad obligationes suscipiendas auctores fieri coguntur, praeterquam si magna causa alienandarum rerum mancipi obligationisque suscipiendae interveniat. eaque omnia ipsorum causa constituta sunt, ut quia ad eos intestatarum mortuarum hereditates pertinent, neque per testamentum excludantur ab hereditate, neque alienatis pretiosioribus rebus susceptoque aere alieno minus

specious than true. For women who are of full age manage their affairs for themselves, and the tutor affords his authorization as a mere formality in certain matters; and is besides often compelled by the Praetor to authorize against his will[1]. 191. Therefore a woman is allowed no action against her tutor on account of his tutelage; but when tutors manage the business of pupils, male or female, they are accountable to them in an action of tutelage[2], after they have reached the age of puberty. 192. The statutable tutelages of patrons and ascendants may on the other hand be seen to have some binding force, from the fact that these tutors are not compelled to authorize either the making of a testament, the alienation of things mancipable, or the contracting of obligations, unless some urgent cause arise for the alienation of the things mancipable or the contracting of the obligation. And all these regulations are made for the advantage of the tutors themselves, that, since the inheritances of the women, if they die intestate, belong to them, they may neither be excluded by a testament from the inheritance, nor may the inheritance come to them depreciated in value through the more precious articles being alienated and debt

34. 2: "maiores nostri ne privatam quidem agere feminas sine auctore voluerunt: in manu esse parentum, fratrum virorum...date frenos impotenti naturae et indomito animali."

[1] II. 122. Ulpian, XI. 25.

[2] It should be noticed that Gaius uses *judicium* and *actio* as interchangeable terms.

locuples ad eos hereditas perveniat. (193.) Aput peregrinos non similiter, ut aput nos, in tutela sunt feminae; set tamen plerumque quasi in tutela sunt: ut ecce lex Bithynorum, si quid mulier (contra)hat, maritum auctorem esse iubet aut filium eius puberem.

194. Tutela autem liberantur ingenuae quidem trium (*liberorum iure, libertinae vero quattuor, si in patroni*)[1] liberorumve eius legitima tutela sint. nam et ceterae quae alterius generis tutores habent, velut Atilianos aut fiduciarios, trium liberorum |
P. 52 iure tutela liberantur[2]. (195.) Potest autem pluribus modis libertina alterius generis habere, veluti si a femina manumissa sit: tunc enim e lege Atilia petere debet tutorem, vel in provincia (e lege Iulia) et Titia: nam in tutela patronae esse non potest. Item si a masculo manumissa, (fuerit) et auctore eo coemptionem fecerit, deinde remancipata et manumissa sit, patronum quidem habere tutorem desinit, incipit autem habere

incurred. 193. Amongst foreign nations women are not in tutelage as they are with us: but yet they are generally in a position analogous to tutelage; for instance, a law of the Bithynians orders that if a woman make any contract, her husband or son over the age of puberty shall authorize it.

194. Freeborn women are freed from tutelage by prerogative of three children; freedwomen by that of four[1], if they be in the statutable tutelage of a patron or his children. For the other freedwomen who have tutors of another kind, as Atilian or fiduciary, are also freed from tutelage by the prerogative of three children. 195. Now a freedwoman may in various ways have a tutor of a different kind (from statutable), for instance if she have been manumitted by a woman; for then she must apply for a tutor in accordance with the Lex Atilia, or in the provinces in accordance with the Lex Julia et Titia: for she cannot be in the tutelage of her patroness. Besides, if she have been manumitted by a man, and with his authorization have made a coemption, and then been remancipated and manumitted, she ceases to have her patron as tutor, and begins to have as tutor him by whom she was manumitted, and

[1] The transcriber has evidently omitted one of two consecutive lines in the MS, both of which end with *liberorum*. Hollweg suggested the words printed in italics.

[2] This privilege was conferred by the Lex Papia Poppaea, A.D. 10. Ulpian, XXIX. 3.

eum tutorem a quo manumissa est, qui fiduciarius dicitur[1]. Item si patronus *sive filius eius* in adoptionem se dedit, debet liberta *e lege Atilia vel Iulia et* Titia tutorem petere. Similiter ex iisdem legibus petere debet tutorem liberta, si patronus decesserit nec ullum virilis sexus liberorum in familia reliquerit.

196. Masculi *vero quando* puberes esse coeperint, tutela liberantur[2]. P*uberem autem* Sabinus quidem et Cassius ceterique nostri praeceptores[3] eum esse putant qui habitu corporis pubertatem ostendit, id est eum qui generare potest; sed in his qui pubescere non possunt, quales sunt spadones, eam aetatem esse spectandam, cuius aetatis puberes fiunt. sed diversae scholae auctores annis putant pubertatem aestimandam,

such an one is called a fiduciary tutor[1]. Likewise, if a patron or his son have given himself in adoption, she ought to apply for a tutor for herself in accordance with the Leges Atilia and Titia. So also a freedwoman ought to apply for a tutor under these same laws, if her patron die and leave in his family no descendant of the male sex.

196. Males are freed from tutelage when they have attained the age of puberty[2]. Now Sabinus and Cassius and the rest of our authorities[3] think that a person is of the age of puberty who shows puberty by the development of his body, that is, who can procreate: but that with regard to those who cannot attain to puberty, such as eunuchs-born, the age is to be regarded at which persons (generally) attain to puberty. But the authors of the opposite school think that puberty should be reckoned by age, *i.e.* that a person is to be regarded as

[1] I. 115.

[2] Ulpian, XI. 28.

[3] Gaius was a disciple of the two great lawyers Sabinus and Cassius. The authorities of the opposite school, to whom he here refers, were Proculus and Pegasus and their followers.

These schools arose in the time of Augustus; Ateius Capito being the founder of the Sabinian sect, Antistius Labeo of the Proculian.

It is scarcely necessary to remind the reader that the Sabinians, as that school was called, were distinguished by their preference for a strict and close adherence to the letter of the law; the Proculians for their decided inclination for a broader interpretation than strict adherence to the letter permitted. Much has been written on the distinctions between the two sects, and their influences on the laws and jurisprudence of Rome: among the leading authorities are Gravina, *de Ortu et Prog. Jur. Civ.* § 45; Hoffman's *Historia Juris*, Pt. I. p. 312; Mascow, *de sectis Sab.*

P. 53 deest id est eum puberem esse existimant | (*qui XIIII annos explevit*[1]).

P. 54 197. ————[2] aetatem pervenerit in qua res suas tueri possit, sicuti[3] aput peregrinas gentes custodiri superius indicavimus. (198.) Ex iisdem causis et in provinciis a Praesidibus earum curatores dari voluit.

199. Ne tamen et pupillorum et eorum qui in curatione sunt negotia a tutoribus curatoribusque consumantur aut deminuantur, curat Praetor, ut et tutores et curatores eo nomine satisdent[4]. (200.) Set hoc non est perpetuum. nam et tutores testamento dati satisdare non coguntur, quia fides eorum et diligentia ab ipso testatore probata est; et curatores ad quos

having attained to puberty who has completed his fourteenth year[1]................ ...

197. ......— [2]shall have arrived at the age at which he can take care of his own affairs, just as we have mentioned previously the rule to be amongst foreigners[3]. 198. Under the same circumstances the law has ordained that curators shall be given in the provinces also by the governors thereof.

199. To prevent, however, the property of pupils and of those who are under curation from being wasted or diminished by their tutors and curators, the Praetor provides that both tutors and curators shall furnish sureties[4] as to this matter. 200. But this rule is not of universal application. For, firstly, tutors given by testament are not compelled to furnish sureties, because their integrity and carefulness are borne witness to by the testator himself: and, secondly, curators to whom the

et Proc.; Hugo, *Rechtsgeschichte*, translated into French by Jourdan, Tom. II. §§ 324—329; Gibbon, c. 44.

[1] Fourteenth year if a male, twelfth if a female. Just. I. 22. pr.

[2] In the missing 24 lines we may conjecture that there was an explanation of the other causes which terminated tutelage; and that then began the exposition of curatorship; see Gai. *Epitome*, I. 8. As the laws relating to curators are to be found in Just. *Inst.* I. 23 and Ulpian, XII., it is sufficient to observe that a tutor has authority over the person as well as the property of his ward, whilst the curator is only concerned with the property: and that the office of the latter begins when the ward attains the age of 14 (the tutor then ceasing to act), and continues till the ward is 25.

[3] I. 189.

[4] *Satisdare*=to find sureties (third parties); not to enter into a personal bond. The law as to sureties (*sponsores*, *fidepromissores* and *fidejussores*) will be found in III. 115—127, and IV. 88—102.

non e lege[1] curatio pertinet, set vel a Consule vel a Praetore vel a Praeside provinciae *dan*tur, plerumque non coguntur satisdare, scilicet quia satis honesti *dati sunt.* |

curation does not come by virtue of a *lex*[1], but who are appointed either by a Consul, or a Praetor, or a governor of a province, are in most cases not compelled to furnish sureties, for the reason, obviously, that men sufficiently trustworthy are appointed.

[1] Probably the reference is to the Lex Laetoria, or Plaetoria, mentioned by Cicero (de Off. III. 15). See note on Just. *Inst.* I. 23. 2, Abdy and Walker's edition.

BOOK II.

P. 55 1. (*Superiore commentario de iure personarum*) exposuimus; modo videamus de rebus: quae vel in nostro patrimonio sunt, vel extra nostrum patrimonium habentur.

2. Summa itaque rerum divisio in duos articulos diducitur: nam aliae sunt divini iuris, aliae humani[1].

3. Divini iuris sunt veluti res sacrae et religiosae. (4.) Sacrae sunt quae Diis superis consecratae sunt; religiosae, quae Diis manibus relictae sunt. (5.) Sed sacrum quidem hoc solum existimatur quod auctoritate populi Romani consecratum est, veluti lege de ea re lata aut senatusconsulto facto.

1. In the preceding commentary we have treated of the law of persons: now let us consider as to things: which are either within our patrimony or without it.

2. The chief division of things, then, is reduced to two heads: for some things are *divini juris*, others *humani juris*[1].

3. Of the class *divini juris* are things sacred or religious. 4. Things sacred are those which are consecrated to the Gods above: things religious those which are given up to the Gods below. 5. But that land only is considered sacred which has been consecrated by authority of the Roman people, for instance by the passing of a *lex* or the making of a *senatusconsultum* in respect of it.

---

[1] The distinction which Gaius draws in § 1 is equally true and valuable: but the distinction in § 2 is of little practical value; and if Gaius intends by the use of the word "itaque" to imply that the two modes of division of things are identical, he is absolutely wrong. Justinian, in *Inst.* 2. 1. *pr.*, divides things into *res communes*, *res publicae*, *res nullius*, *res universitatis*, and *res singulorum*: and of these *res singulorum* alone are *in commercio*, or *in patrimonio nostro*. Hence, a more complete and correct tabulation than that of Gaius is:—

6. Religiosum vero nostra voluntate facimus mortuum inferentes in locum nostrum, si modo eius mortui funus ad nos pertineat. (7.) Set in provinciali solo placet plerisque solum religiosum non fieri, quia in eo solo dominium populi Romani est vel Caesaris[1], nos autem possessionem tantum vel usumfructum habere videmur[2]. utique tamen etiam si non sit religiosus,

6. On the other hand, we can of our own free will make land religious by conveying a corpse into a place which is our own property, provided only that the burial of the corpse devolves on us. 7. But it has been generally held that on provincial soil land cannot be made religious, because in such land the ownership belongs to the Roman people or to Caesar[1], and we are considered to have only the possession or usufruct[2].

A. *Res in patrimonio,—Res singulorum,* or private property.

B. *Res extra patrimonium:*—(1) *Res communes:* of which the use is common to all the world; the *proprietas* in no state or individual: as the air, the high sea, an unoccupied island.

(2) *Res nullius:* where the *proprietas* and use are both retained by the State: and these the Romans subdivided into

(α) *Res sanctae:* walls, gates, ramparts, the senate-house &c.

(β) *Res religiosae:* burial places, the individual owner of the ground divesting himself of the use, and putting the burial place under state protection.

(γ) *Res sacrae:* temples; but these were to a certain extent, at any rate, not *res nullius*, but *res publicae*.

(3) *Res publicae:* where the state retains the *proprietas*, but allows the use to the citizens at large, as roads and navigable rivers, the sea-shore.

(4) *Res universitatis:* where the *proprietas* is vested in a corporation or artificial person, and the use may either be in the corporation alone, or in the public at large. In English Law, churches and churchyards are *res universitatis*, of the second type, except as to certain parts of the church itself, which are of the first.

[1] See note on I. 6.

[2] See Savigny, *On Possession*, translated by Perry, § 13.

pro religioso habetur. item quod in provinciis non ex auctoritate populi Romani consecratum est, proprie sacrum non est, tamen pro sacro habetur.

8. Sanctae quoque res, veluti muri et portae, quodammodo divini iuris sunt.

9. Quod autem divini iuris est, id nullius in bonis est: id
P. 56 vero quod humani (*desunt lin.* 11)[1] *iuris est plerumque alicuius in bonis est: potest autem et nullius in bonis esse. nam res hereditariae, antequam aliquis heres existat, nullius in bonis sunt*)[2] ......ve domino. (10.) Hae autem res quae humani iuris sunt, aut publicae sunt aut privatae. (11.) quae publicae sunt, nullius videntur in bonis esse; ipsius enim universitatis esse creduntur. privatae sunt, quae singulorum sunt.

12. Quaedam praeterea res corporales sunt, quaedam incorporales. (13.) (Corporales) hae quae tangi possunt, veluti

Still, however, such a place, although it be not religious, is considered as religious; and so too that which is consecrated in the provinces, not by authority of the Roman people, is strictly speaking not sacred, and yet is regarded as sacred.

8. Hallowed things also, for instance walls and gates, are in some degree *divini juris*.

9. Now that which is *divini juris* is the property of no one; whilst that which is *humani juris* is generally the property of some one, although it may be the property of no one. For the items of an inheritance, before some one becomes heir[2], are no one's property. 10. Those things again which are *humani juris* are either public or private. 11. Those which are public are considered to be no one's property: for they are regarded as belonging to the community; whilst private things are those which belong to individuals.

12. Further some things are corporeal, some incorporeal. 13. Corporeal things are those which can be touched, as a

---

[1] Part of the 11 missing lines can be supplied from D. 1. 8. 1, an excerpt from *Gai. libro II. Institutionum.* These accord with *Gai. Epit.* 2. 1. 1—3.

[2] The heir instituted in the testament *becomes* heir only by entering upon the office and duties, therefore in the interval between the death of the testator and the acceptance of the inheritance there is a vacancy and the *res* are *nullius*.

fundus, homo, vestis, aurum, argentum et denique aliae res innumerabiles. (14.) Incorporales quae tangi non possunt: qualia sunt ea quae in iure consistunt[1], sicut hereditas, ususfructus, obligationes quoquo modo contractae. nec ad rem pertinet, (*quod in hereditate res corporales continentur; nam*) et fructus qui ex fundo percipiuntur[2] corporales sunt, et quod
P. 57 ex aliqua obligatione nobis debetur | plerumque corporale est, veluti fundus, homo, pecunia: nam ipsum ius successionis, et ipsum ius utendi fruendi, et ipsum ius obligationis incorporale est. eodem numero sunt iura praediorum urbanorum et rusticorum, (*quae etiam servitutes vocantur*[3]. *Praediorum urbanorum*

field, a man, a garment, gold, silver and, in a word, other things innumerable. 14. Incorporeal things are such as cannot be touched: of this kind are those which consist in a right[1], as an inheritance, an usufruct, or obligations in any way contracted. Nor is it material that in an inheritance there are comprised corporeal things: for the fruits also which are gathered in[2] (by the usufructuary) from land are corporeal, and that which is due to us by virtue of any obligation is generally corporeal, as a field, a slave or money; whilst the right itself of succession, and the right itself of the usufruct, and the right itself of the obligation, are incorporeal. In the same category are rights over estates urban or rustic, which are also called servitudes[3]...... The rights over urban estates are these; the

1 We see therefore that incorporeal things are not, strictly speaking, things at all, but only the rights to things. We may also remark that "tangible" signifies in Roman law that which is perceptible by any sense, according to the Stoic notion that all senses are modifications of that of touch. Hence "acts" are corporeal things according to this classification. Austin, Lecture XIII. See Cicero, *Topica*, cap. V. The Romans were also compelled to include "forbearances" amongst *res corporales*, though these cannot in any sense whatever be "tangible."

2 Without entering into the discussion of a subject which has engaged the attention and divided the judgment of many old authorities, and which occupied a leading position in the Roman law of Possession, it is sufficient to say that it was by the *perception*, i. e. the reduction into possession, that the tenant, usufructuary, and generally every one who derived his rights to the profits from the owner, acquired the ownership of those profits. Savigny, *On Possession*, translated by Perry, Bk. II. § 24, pp. 200—204. See D. 41. 1. 48. pr., D. 7. 4. 13, D. 22. 1. 25. 1.

3 Urban and rustic estates mean respectively lands with or without buildings on them: the situation of either, whether in town or country, is immaterial: cf. D. 8. 4. 1.

iura sunt haec: ius) altius tollendi (*aedes et offici*) endi luminibus vicini aedium aut non extollendi ne luminibus vicini officiatur. item fluminum et stillicidiorum ius ut vicinus (*flumen vel stillicidium in*) aream (*recipiat vel non recipiat*)......(*Praediorum rusticorum iura sunt haec, iter actus, via*[1], *aquaeductus*)...... enim vero ius aquae ducendae......servitutes superiores......(*Est alia rerum divisio, nam omnes res aut mancipi sunt aut*) nec mancipi[2]. mancipi sunt (*veluti fundus in Italico solo*) item aedes in Italico solo[3]. [*desunt lin.* 2] item servitutes praediorum urbanorum

right of raising a house and blocking the lights of a neighbour's house, or of not raising a house higher lest a neighbour's lights should be blocked; likewise the right of running water and dropping water, that a neighbour shall receive or not receive into his premises running or dropping water......The rights over urban estates are these, *iter*, *actus*, *via*[1], *aquaeductus*, &c.... ...There is another division of things, for all things are either mancipable or non-mancipable[2]. Mancipable things are such as a field on Italic soil, or a house on Italic soil[3]: ... also servitudes over urban estates are non-mancipable: so too sti-

[1] *Iter*=right of passage for men on foot, on horseback, or in a litter.

Actus=right of passage for carriages and beasts of burden as well as for men.

Via=right of passage generally, but of a restricted breadth; see D. 8. 38; including right of dragging stones, timber, &c. across. D. 8. 3. 1 pr., D. 8. 3. 7. pr., D. 8. 3. 12.

[2] *Res mancipi*, it is clear, were such things as were objects of interest and value in the eyes of the early possessors of Roman citizen-rights, or probably of those who laid the foundations of ancient Rome. Hence we see, firstly, how few in number were these objects, secondly, that they were such only as had a value to an agricultural people, and, thirdly, that the few rights (as distinguished from material objects) which appeared among them were rights or easements that almost necessarily formed parts of some of these material objects. They were, in fact, such things as the old settlers cared to possess and as could be transferred by the hand and into the hand, *manus*, as we have said before, being the symbol of property; and since for a long time they were the only things worthy of consideration as property, they got a name in time, more for the purpose of classification and distinction than for any other. *When* is not of much consequence, but probably not till it was necessary to distinguish them from many other things that had become known to use and practice, and which by way of opposition were called *nec mancipi*. See as to this subject Maine's *Ancient Law*, chapter viii. p. 277.

[3] See note on I. 120.

nec mancipi sunt: item stipendiaria praedia et tributaria[1] nec mancipi sunt. sed quod diximus...... mancipi esse[2].

15. *Ea autem animalia quae collo dorsove domari solent*
P. 58 *nostri quidem praeceptores* | statim ut nata sunt mancipi esse putant: Nerva vero, et Proculus et ceteri diversae scholae auctores non aliter ea mancipi esse putant, quam si domita sunt; et si propter nimiam feritatem domari non possunt, tunc videri mancipi esse incipere, cum ad eam aetatem pervenerint, qua domari solent. (16.) *Sed* ferae bestiae nec mancipi sunt, velut ursi, leones, item ea animalia quae fere bestiarum numero sunt, velut elefanti et cameli; et ideo ad rem non pertinet, quod haec animalia etiam collo dorsove domari solent, nam *ne nomen* quidem eorum animalium illo tempore fuit quo constituebatur quasdam res mancipi esse, quasdam nec mancipi. (17.) Item fere omnia quae incorporalia sunt nec mancipi sunt,

pendiary and tributary lands[1] are non-mancipable. But when we say these are mancipable[2]...... 15. Those animals which are usually tamed by yoke and saddle (*lit.* by neck and back) our authorities hold to be mancipable the moment they are born: but Nerva and Proculus and other authors of the opposite school consider that they are not mancipable unless they be broken in: and if through their excessive fierceness they cannot be broken in, then they are regarded as being mancipable on arriving at the age at which animals are usually broken in. 16. But wild-beasts such as bears and lions, are non-mancipable: so are those animals which are almost wild-beasts, as elephants and camels; and therefore it is not material that such animals are often tamed by yoke and saddle, for even the name of these animals did not exist at the time when it was settled that some things should be mancipable, others non-mancipable. 17. Likewise, almost all things which

[1] See II. 21.

[2] Although a large part of p. 57 of the MS. is illegible, there are a number of key words in this corrupted portion which are perfectly legible: and we find that the substance must have been almost identical with Just. *Inst.* 2. 3; from which therefore the *lacunae* have been to some extent filled up. Ulpian, XIX. 1 is also of service for comparison.

exceptis servitutibus praediorum rusticorum, nam eas mancipi esse constat, quamvis sint ex numero rerum incorporalium.

18. Magna autem differentia est inter mancipi res et nec mancipi[1]. (19.) Nam res nec mancipi ipsa traditione pleno iure alterius fiunt, si modo corporales sunt et ob id recipiunt traditionem. (20.) Itaque si tibi vestem vel aurum vel argentum tradidero, sive ex venditionis causa sive ex donationis sive

P. 59 quavis alia ex causa, statim tua fit ea res si modo eius dominus sim iure civili. (21.) In eadem causa sunt provincialia praedia, quorum alia stipendiaria, alia tributaria vocamus. Stipendiaria sunt ea quae in his provinciis sunt, quae propriae populi Romani esse intelleguntur. Tributaria sunt ea quae in his provinciis sunt, quae propriae Caesaris esse creduntur[2]. (22.) Mancipi vero res sunt quae per mancipationem ad alium transferuntur; unde etiam mancipi res sunt dictae. quod autem valet mancipatio, (*idem valet et in iure cessio.* (23.) *Et*

are incorporeal are non-mancipable, with the exception of servitudes over rural property on Italic soil; for these are allowed to be mancipable, although they are in the category of incorporeal things.

18. Now there is a great difference between things mancipable and things non-mancipable[1]. 19. For things non-mancipable are made the property of another man by mere delivery, provided only they be corporeal, and so admit of delivery. 20. Therefore if I deliver to you a garment, or gold, or silver, whether on the ground of sale, or donation, or on any other ground, the thing at once becomes yours, if only I am owner of it at the civil law. 21. Provincial lands, some of which we call stipendiary, some tributary, are on the same footing. Stipendiary are those which are situated in the provinces regarded as specially belonging to the Roman people: tributary are those which are in the provinces considered as specially belonging to Caesar[2]. 22. But things mancipable are those which are transferred to another by mancipation: whence also they got their appellation. But whatever effect a mancipation has, the same has

[1] Cic. *pro Flacco*, c. 32. "Illud quaero, sint ista praedia censui censenda: habeant ius civile; sint, necne mancipi: subsignari apud aerarium, apud Caesarem possint?"

[2] I. 6: II. 7.

mancipatio[1]) quidem quemadmodum fiat, superiore commentario tradidimus[2]. (24.) In iure cessio autem hoc modo fit[3]. aput magistratum populi Romani, velut Praetorem, vel aput Praesidem provinciae, is cui res in iure ceditur, rem tenens ita dicit: HUNC EGO HOMINEM EX IURE QUIRITIUM MEUM ESSE AIO. deinde postquam hic vindicaverit, *Praetor interrogat* eum qui cedit, an contra vindicet. quo negante aut tacente, tunc ei qui vindicaverit eam rem addicit. idque legis actio vocatur[4]. hoc fieri potest etiam in provinciis aput Praesides earum. (25.) Plerumque tamen et fere semper mancipationibus utimur. quod enim ipsi per nos praesentibus amicis agere possumus, hoc non est necesse cum maiore difficultate aput Praetorem aut aput Praesidem provinciae agere. (26.) Quodsi neque mancipata, neque in iure cessa sit res mancipi

also a cession in court. 23. And how a mancipation[1] is effected we have explained in the preceding Commentary[2]. 24. But a cession in court is managed as follows[3]. He to whom the thing is being passed by cession, taking hold of it in the presence of a magistrate of the Roman people, for instance, a Praetor, or the Governor of a province, speaks thus: "I assert this man to be mine by Quiritary right." Then, after he has made his claim, the Praetor questions the man who is making the cession, whether he puts in a counter-claim: and on his saying no or holding his peace, the Praetor assigns the thing to him who has claimed it. And this is called a *legis actio*[4]. This can be transacted in the provinces also before the governors thereof. 25. Generally, however, and indeed almost always, we employ mancipations. For when we can do the business by ourselves in the presence of our friends, there is no need to perform it in a more troublesome manner before the Praetor or the Governor of a province. 26. But if a thing mancipable have been passed neither by mancipation nor

[1] A line has been missed out from the usual cause, that two consecutive lines of the MS. which was copied end identically: in this instance both with the word *mancipatio*.

[2] I. 119.

[3] Ulpian, XIX. 9.

[4] IV. 11 et seqq.

Deest P. 60. P. 61 | [*desunt lin* 31.][1] (27.) *In summa admo*nendi sumus *nexum Italici soli proprium* esse, provincialis soli nexum non esse: *recipit enim nexus* significationem solum non aliter, quam si mancipi est, provinciale (vero) nec mancipi est.—aliter enim veteri lingua si ius — — — — — — — — mancipa —[2].

28. *Res* incorporales traditionem non recipere manifestum est. (29.) Sed iura praediorum urbanorum in iure cedi possunt; rusticorum vero etiam mancipari possunt. (30.) Ususfructus in iure cessionem tantum recipit[3]. Nam dominus

cession in court......[1]. 27. Finally, we must take notice that *nexum* is peculiar to Italic soil: there is no *nexum* of provincial soil: for soil admits of the application of *nexum* only when it is mancipable, and provincial soil is non-mancipable[2]. For in the ancient language a different term was applied to the right......

28. That incorporeal things do not admit of delivery is obvious. 29. But rights over urban property can only be conveyed by cession in court; whilst those over rural property can be conveyed with mancipation also. 30. Usufruct[3] admits of

---

[1] Most probably Gaius went on to say that when a *res mancipi* was merely delivered, the man who received it had it in *bonis* only, and not *ex jure Quiritium*. See II. 41.

In the missing 31 lines, which comprise the whole of p. 60 and the first 7 lines of p. 61, only the following can be read. In p. 60, line 7, *plena possessio concessa:* in line 8, *ex formula quamquam:* in line 11, *fructus na:* in line 12, *item adhuc in:* in line 17, *non fuissent:* in p. 61, line 3, *est quo nomine:* in line 7, *-dem ulla libera civitas.*

[2] The early part of this § is filled up according to Göschen's conjectural reading. *Nexum* and *nexus* are both substantives, the former an old word found in the Twelve Tables as antithetical to *mancipium* (see Tab. VI. l. 1), the latter a more modern expression, used to signify obligation generally, see D. 10. 2. 33 and D. 12. 6. 26. 7.

The meaning of *nexum* is given by Varro (*de L. Lat.* VII. 105): "Nexum Mamilius scribit, omne quod per libram et aes geritur, in quo sint mancipia. Mutius, quae per aes et libram fiunt, ut obligentur, praeter quae mancipio dentur. Hoc verius esse ipsum verbum ostendit de quo quaerit. Nam idem quod obligatur per libram, neque suum fit, inde nexum dictum." See also Festus sub verb. Hence *nexum* according to Mamilius is any dealing *per aes et libram*, whether of the nature of a contract executed or executory. In § 27 *nexum* seems to be used only as a synonym for *mancipatio*, in the ordinary meaning of the latter, and does not bear the more technical sense which Mutius ascribes to it, viz. a contract *per aes et libram*, as contradistinguished from *mancipatio*, a conveyance by the same method.

[3] An account of usufruct is to be found in Just. II. 4.

proprietatis alii usumfructum in iure cedere potest, ut ille usumfructum habeat, et ipse nudam proprietatem *retineat.* Ipse usufructuarius in iure cedendo domino proprietatis usumfructum efficit, ut a se discedat et convertatur in proprietatem. alii vero in iure cedendo nihilominus ius suum retinet: creditur enim ea cessione nihil agi[1]. (31.) Sed haec scilicet in Italicis praediis ita sunt, quia et ipsa praedia mancipationem |
P. 62 et in iure cessionem recipiunt. alioquin in provincialibus praediis sive quis usumfructum sive ius eundi, agendi, aquamve ducendi, vel altius tollendi aedes, aut non tollendi, ne luminibus vicini officiatur ceteraque similia iura constituere velit, pactionibus et stipulationibus id efficere potest[2]; quia ne ipsa quidem praedia mancipationem aut in iure cessionem recipiunt. (32.) Et cum ususfructus et hominum et ceterorum animalium constitui possit, intellegere debemus horum usumfructum etiam in provinciis per in iure cessionem constitui posse[3]. (33.) Quod

cession in court only. For the owner of the property can make cession in court of the usufruct to another, so that the latter may have the usufruct, and he himself retain the bare ownership. The usufructuary again, by making cession of the usufruct to the owner of the property causes it to depart from him and be absorbed in the ownership. But if he make cession of it to another he still retains his right, for it is considered that nothing is done by such a cession[1]. 31. But these rules only apply to Italic property, because the property itself also admits of mancipation and cession in court. In provincial property on the contrary, if a man desire to establish a usufruct, or right of path, road, watercourse, raising buildings higher, or preventing buildings being raised higher lest a neighbour's lights be interfered with, and other similar rights, he can only do it by pacts and stipulations[2], because even the property itself does not admit of mancipation or cession in court. 32. Also, since it is possible for an usufruct to be established over slaves and other animals, we must understand that usufruct over them can be established by cession in court even in the provinces[3]. 33. Now when we said that usufruct

1 Just. II. 4. § 3.
2 III. 92 et seqq.
3 Slaves and animals are *res mancipi:* therefore by the principle implied in § 31, the usufruct of them can be conveyed by *cessio in jure.*

autem diximus usumfructum in iure cessionem tantum recipere, non est temere dictum, quamvis etiam per mancipationem constitui possit eo quod in mancipanda proprietate detrahi potest: non enim ipse ususfructus mancipatur, sed cum in mancipanda proprietate deducatur, eo fit, ut aput alium ususfructus, aput alium proprietas sit. (34.) Hereditas quoque in iure cessionem tantum recipit[1]. (35.) Nam si is ad quem ab intestato legitimo iure[2] pertinet hereditas in iure eam alii ante aditionem cedat, id est ante quam heres extiterit, perinde fit heres is cui in iure cesserit, ac si ipse per legem ad hereditatem vocatus esset: post obligationem vero si cesserit, nihilominus
P. 63 ipse | heres permanet et ob id a creditoribus tenebitur, debita vero pereunt, eoque modo debitores hereditarii lucrum faciunt[3];

admitted of cession in court only, we were not speaking at random, although it may be established by mancipation also, inasmuch as it may be withheld in a mancipation of the property: for in such a case the usufruct itself is not mancipated, although the result of its being withheld in mancipating the property is that the usufruct is left with one person and the property with another. 34. An inheritance also is a thing which admits of cession in court only[1]. 35. For if he to whom an inheritance on an intestacy belongs by statute law[2] make cession of it before entry, *i.e.* before he has become heir, the other to whom he has ceded it becomes heir, just as if he had himself been called by law to the inheritance: if, however, he make cession after (accepting) the obligation, he still remains heir himself, and will therefore be liable to the creditors, but the debts (due to the inheritance) perish, and so the debtors to the inheritance are benefited[3]: the corporeal items, however, of the inheritance

Further, the *cessio in jure* may take place even in the provinces; for moveable *res mancipi* are *res mancipi* all over the world, lands alone are *res mancipi* on Italic soil only.

1 Yet we see from II. 102 that a testament could be made by mancipation. There is however no contradiction: what was mancipated was a *familia* or estate, which did not become an inheritance till the death of the testator. Here we are treating of the transfer of an inheritance by the heir, not its creation by the testator.

2 *Legitimo jure*=by virtue of a rule of the Twelve Tables or some *lex*: as opposed to a rule of the Praetor's edict.

3 He is liable to the creditors because he has done an act which identifies him juridically with the deceased as to property, rights and duties. The debtors are not liable

corpora vero eius hereditatis perinde transeunt ad eum cui cessa est hereditas, ac si ei singula in iure cessa fuissent[1]. (36.) Testamento autem scriptus heres ante aditam quidem hereditatem in iure cedendo eam alii nihil agit; postea vero quam adierit si cedat, ea accidunt quae proxime diximus de eo ad quem ab intestato legitimo iure pertinet hereditas, si post obligationem in iure cedat. (37.) Idem et de necessariis heredibus diversae scholae auctores existimant, quod nihil videtur interesse utrum (aliquis) adeundo hereditatem fiat heres, an invitus existat: quod quale sit, suo loco apparebit. sed nostri praeceptores putant nihil agere necessarium heredem, cum in iure cedat hereditatem[2]. (38.) Obligationes quoquo modo contractae nihil eorum recipiunt. nam quod mihi ab aliquo debetur, id si velim tibi deberi, nullo eorum modo quibus res corporales ad alium transferuntur id efficere possum;

pass to him to whom the inheritance was ceded, just as if they had been ceded to him singly[1]. 36. But an heir appointed by testament, if he make cession before entry on the inheritance, does a void act: whilst if he cede after entry, the results are the same as those we have just named in the case of one to whom an inheritance on an intestacy devolves by statute law, if he make cession after (accepting) the obligation. 37. The authorities of the school opposed to us hold the same in regard to *heredes necessarii*, because it seems to them immaterial whether a man becomes heir by entering on an inheritance, or becomes heir against his will. What the meaning of this is will be seen in its proper place. But our authorities think that the *heres necessarius* does a void act when he makes cession of the inheritance[2]. 38. Obligations, in whatever way they be contracted, admit of none of these (forms of transfer). For if I desire that a thing which is owed to me by a certain person should be owed to you, I cannot bring this about by any of those methods whereby corporeal things are transferred to another: but it is necessary that you should

to him because he has freely given up his *rights* in the juridical identity he had established; nor are they liable to the cessionary, because they are not bound to recognize him as a successor to their creditor, the deceased. But he is not able to renounce his *duties*, and so he remains liable to the creditors.

[1] Ulpian, XIX. 12—15.

[2] II. 152; III. 87.

sed opus est, ut iubente me tu ab eo stipuleris: quae res efficit, ut a me liberetur et incipiat tibi teneri: quae dicitur novatio obligationis[1]. (39.) sine hac vero novatione non poteris tuo
P. 64 nomine agere, sed debes ex persona mea quasi cognitor | aut procurator meus experiri[2].

40. Sequitur ut admoneamus aput peregrinos quidem unum esse dominium: nam aut dominus quisque est, aut dominus non intellegitur. Quo iure etiam populus Romanus olim utebatur: aut enim ex iure Quiritium unusquisque dominus erat, aut non intellegebatur dominus. set postea divisionem accepit dominium, ut alius possit esse ex iure Quiritium dominus, alius in bonis habere. (41.) nam si tibi rem mancipi neque mancipavero neque in iure cessero, set tantum tradidero, in bonis quidem tuis ea res efficitur, ex iure Quiritium vero mea permanebit, donec tu eam possidendo usucapias: semel enim impleta usucapione proinde pleno iure incipit, id est et in bonis et ex

by my order stipulate (for the thing) from him, and the result produced by this is that he is set free from me and begins to be bound to you: and this is called a *novation* of the obligation[1]. 39. But without such novation you cannot bring a suit in your own name, but must sue in my name as my *cognitor* or *procurator*[2].

40. The next point for us to state is that amongst foreigners there is but one kind of ownership: for a man is either owner (absolutely) or is not regarded as owner (at all). And this rule the Roman people followed of old, for a man was either owner in Quiritary right, or he was not regarded as owner. But afterwards ownership became capable of division, so that one man might be owner in Quiritary, another in Bonitary right. 41. For if I neither mancipate nor pass by cession in court, but merely deliver to you, a thing mancipable, the thing becomes yours in Bonitary, but remains mine in Quiritary right, until through possessing it you acquire it by usucapion: for so soon as usucapion is completed the thing is at once yours in

[1] III. 176.

[2] A *cognitor* is an agent appointed in court and in the presence of the other party to the suit: a *procurator* is appointed by mandate, and the opposing party has not necessarily any knowledge of his appointment till the time comes for him to act. IV. 83, 84.

iure Quritium, tua res esse ac si ea mancipata vel in iure cessa (esset. (42.) Usucapio autem) mobilium quidem rerum anno completur, fundi vero et aedium biennio; et ita lege XII tabularum cautum est[1].

43. Ceterum etiam earum rerum usucapio nobis competit quae non a domino nobis traditae fuerint, sive mancipi sint eae res sive nec mancipi, si modo ea bona fide acceperimus, cum crederemus eum qui traderet dominum esse. (44.) Quod ideo receptum videtur, ne rerum dominia diutius in incerto essent: cum sufficeret domino ad inquirendam rem suam anni
P. 65 aut | biennii spatium, quod tempus ad usucapionem possessori tributum est[2].

45. Set aliquando etiamsi maxime quis bona fide alienam rem possideat, non tamen illi usucapio procedit, velut si qui rem furtivam aut vi possessam possideat; nam furtivam

full title, i.e. both Bonitary and Quiritary, just as though it had been mancipated or passed by cession. 42. Now the usucapion of moveable things is completed in a year, that of land and buildings in two years: and it is so laid down in a law of the Twelve Tables[1].

43. Moreover usucapion runs for us even in respect of those things which have been delivered to us by one not the owner, whether they be things mancipable or things non-mancipable, provided only we have received them in good faith, believing that he who delivered them was the owner. 44. This seems to have been allowed in order to prevent the ownership of things being too long in doubt: inasmuch as the space of one or two years would be enough for the owner to make inquiries after his property, and that is the time allowed to the possessor for gaining the property by usucapion[2].

45. But sometimes, although a man possess a thing most thoroughly in good faith, yet usucapion will not run in his favour, for instance if a man possess a thing stolen or taken

[1] "Usus-auctoritas fundi biennium, ceterarum rerum annus esto." Tab. VI. l. 3. Quoted by Cic. *Top.* 4. See also Cic. *pro Caecina*, 19; Ulp. XIX. 8. For the alteration of the time of usucapion see Just. *Inst.* II. 6.

[2] II. 54, 204.

lex XII tabularum[1] usucapi prohibet, vi possessam[3] lex Iulia et Plautia[2]. (46.) Item provincialia praedia usucapionem non recipiunt[4]. (47.) *Item olim*[5] mulieris quae in agnatorum tutela erat res mancipi usucapi non poterant, praeterquam si ab ipsa tutore (auctore) traditae essent[6]: id ita lege XII tabularum manifestum[7]. (48.) Item liberos homines et res sacras et religiosas usucapi non posse manifestum est.

49. Quod ergo vulgo dicitur furtivarum rerum et vi possessarum usucapionem per legem XII tabularum prohibitam esse, non eo pertinet, ut ne *ipse fur quive* per vim *possi*det, usucapere possit, nam huic alia ratione usucapio non competit,

possession of by violence: for a law of the Twelve Tables[1] forbids a stolen thing to be gotten by usucapion, and the Lex Julia et Plautia[2] does the same for a thing taken possession of by violence[3]. 46. Provincial property also does not admit of usucapion[4]. 47. Likewise, in olden times[5] the mancipable property of a woman who was in the tutelage of her agnates could not be gotten by usucapion, except it had been delivered by the woman herself with the authorization of her tutor[6]: and this is clear from a law of the Twelve Tables[7]. 48. It it also clear that free men and sacred and religious things cannot be gotten by usucapion.

49. The common saying, that usucapion of things stolen or taken possession of by violence is prohibited by a law of the Twelve Tables, does not mean that the thief himself or possessor by violence cannot get by usucapion, for usucapion does not run for him on another account, namely

---

[1] Tab. VIII. l. 17.

[2] Lex Plautia, B.C. 59; Lex Julia de vi temp. Augusti.

[3] The three requisites of a possession which will enable usucapion, are *bona fides*, *justa causa*, and *res in commercio*. The *justa causa* is deficient in the present example, for although the goods are in the possession of an innocent alienee, yet they came to him from one wrongfully possessed. See § 49 below.

[4] In the case of provincial lands the *dominium* was reserved to the Roman people, therefore obviously no private holder could avail himself of usucapion to acquire *dominium*.

[5] The MS. has "res mulieris."

[6] "Sed quaero usu an coemptione. Usu non potuit. Nihil enim potest de tutela legitima nisi omnium tutorum auctoritate deminui." Cic. *pro Flacco*, 34. "Id mirabamur te ignorare de tutela legitima in qua dicitur esse puella nihil usucapi posse." Cic. *ad Att.* I. 5.

[7] Tab. V. l. 2.

quia scilicet mala fide possidet; sed nec ullus alius, quamquam ab eo bona fide emerit, usucapiendi ius habeat. (50.) Unde in rebus mobilibus non facile p*rocedit, ut bonae fidei possessori usucapio co*mpetat, quia qui alienam rem vendidit et tradidit furtum committit; idemque accidit, etiam si ex alia causa tradatur[1]. Set tamen hoc aliquando aliter se habet. nam si
P. 66 heres rem defuncto commodatam aut locatam vel aput eum depositam, existimans eam esse here|ditariam, vendiderit aut donaverit, furtum non committit[2]. item si is ad quem ancillae ususfructus pertinet, partum etiam suum esse credens vendiderit aut donaverit, furtum non committit[3]; furtum enim sine affectu furandi non committitur. aliis quoque modis accidere potest, ut quis sine vitio furti rem alienam ad aliquem transferat et efficiat, ut a possessore usucapiatur. (51.) Fundi quoque

that he possesses in bad faith: but that no one else has the right of usucapion, even though he buy from him in good faith. 50. Whence, in respect of moveables it is difficult for usucapion to be available for a possessor in good faith, because he who has sold and delivered a thing belonging to another commits a theft: and the same rule holds also if it be delivered on any other ground[1]. Sometimes, however, it is otherwise; for if an heir thinking that a thing lent or let to the deceased or deposited with him is a part of the inheritance, has sold or given it away, he commits no theft[2]. Likewise, if he to whom the usufruct of a female slave belongs, thinking that her offspring is also his, sells it or gives it away, he commits no theft[3], for theft is not committed without the intent of thieving. It may happen in other ways also that a man may without the taint of theft deliver a thing belonging to another to a third person, and cause it to be gained through usucapion by the possessor. 51. A man may also take possession without

---

[1] Any other ground than sale, sc.

[2] D. 41. 3. 36. pr.

[3] III. 197. We see from this that the Roman lawyers excused mistakes of law as well as of fact. The reason why this particular mistake was excused is shown in D. 41. 3. 36. 1. The usufructuary supposes he has a right to the child of the *ancilla*, because the usufructuary of a flock of sheep has a right to the young of that flock.

alieni potest aliquis sine vi possessionem nancisci, quae vel ex neglegentia domini vacet, vel quia dominus sine successore decesserit vel longo tempore afuerit[1]. nam si ad alium bona fide accipientem transtulerit, poterit usucapere possessor; et quamvis ipse qui vacantem possessionem nactus est, intellegat alienum esse fundum, *tamen* nihilo m*agis bonae fidei possessori* ad usucapionem nocetur[2], (cum) improbata sit eorum sententia qui putaverint furtivum fundum fieri posse.

52. Rursus ex contrario accidit, ut qui sciat alienam rem se possidere usucapiat: velut si rem hereditariam cuius possessionem heres nondum nactus est aliquis possederit; nam ei concessum (est usu)capere, si modo ea res est quae recipit usucapionem. quae species possessionis et usucapionis pro

violence of the land of another, which is vacant either through the carelessness of the owner, or because the owner has died without a successor, or has been absent for a long time[1]. If then he transfer it to another, who receives it in good faith, this second possessor can get it by usucapion: for although the man himself who has taken the vacant possession may be aware that the land belongs to another, yet this is no hindrance to the possessor in good faith gaining it by usucapion[2], inasmuch as the opinion of those lawyers has been set aside who thought that land could be the subject of a theft.

52. Again, in the converse case, it sometimes happens that he who knows that he is in possession of a thing belonging to another may yet acquire an usucaptive title to it. For instance, if any one take possession of an item of an inheritance of which the heir has not yet obtained possession: for he is allowed to get it by usucapion, provided only it be a thing which admits of usucapion. This species of possession and usucapion

[1] This paragraph is cited almost as it stands in D. 41. 3. 37, being there stated as taken from *Gaii Lib.* II. *Institut.* Laws 36 and 38 of the same title, which are also very similar to §§ 50 and 52 of the present book, are noted as taken from Gaii Lib. II. *Rerum quotidianarum sive Aureorum.*

[2] The first taker is deficient in *bona fides*, but not so the second. But, as there is no theft of land, the first can give a good title to the second. Hence the second has both the main requisites of *civilis possessio* (possession, that is to say, which will enable usucapion), viz. *justa causa* and *bona fides.*

herede vocatur[1]. (53.) Et in tantum haec usucapio concessa
P. 67 est, | ut et res quae solo continentur anno usucapiantur. (54.) Quare autem etiam hoc casu soli rerum annua constituta sit usucapio, illa ratio est, quod olim rerum hereditariarum possessiones ut ipsae hereditates usucapi credebantur, scilicet anno. lex enim XII tabularum[2] soli quidem res biennio usucapi iussit, ceteras vero anno. ergo hereditas in ceteris rebus videbatur esse, quia soli non est, quia neque corporalis est: et quamvis postea creditum sit ipsas hereditates usucapi non posse, tamen in omnibus rebus hereditariis, etiam quae solo teneantur, annua usucapio remansit. (55.) Quare autem omnino tam improba possessio et usucapio concessa sit, illa ratio est, quod voluerunt veteres maturius hereditates adiri, ut essent qui sacra facerent: quorum illis temporibus summa observatio fuit, et ut creditores haberent a quo suum conseque-

is called *pro herede*[1]. 53. And this usucapion has been allowed to such an extent that even things appertaining to the soil are acquired by usucapion in one year. 54. The reason why in such case the usucapion of things connected with the soil is allowed to operate in one year is this; that in former times the possessions of articles appertaining to the inheritances, just as the inheritances themselves, were considered to be gained by usucapion, and that too in one year. For the law of the Twelve Tables[2] ordered that the things appertaining to the soil should be acquired by usucapion in two years, but all other things in one. An inheritance therefore was considered to be one of the "other things," because it is not connected with the soil, since it is not even corporeal: and although at a later period it was held that inheritances themselves could not be acquired by usucapion, yet the usucapion of one year remained established in respect of all the items of inheritances, even though they might be connected with the soil. 55. And the reason why so unfair a possession and usucapion have been allowed at all is this: that the ancients wished inheritances to be entered upon speedily, that there might be persons to perform the sacred rites (of the family), to which the greatest attention

[1] See D. 41. 5. [2] Tab. VI. l. 3.

rentur. (56.) Haec autem species possessionis et usucapionis etiam lucrativa vocatur: nam sciens quisque rem alienam lucrifacit. (57.) Sed hoc tempore etiam non est lucrativa. nam ex auctoritate Hadriani senatusconsultum factum est, ut tales usucapiones revocarentur; et ideo potest heres ab eo qui rem usucepit hereditatem petendo perinde eam rem consequi atque
P. 68 si usucapta non esset. | (58.) necessario[1] tamen herede extante nihil ipso iure pro herede[2] usucapi potest.

59. Adhuc etiam ex aliis causis sciens quisque rem alienam usucapit. nam qui rem alicui fiduciae causa[3] mancipio dederit vel in iure cesserit, si eandem ipse possederit, potest usucapere, anno scilicet etiam soli si sit[4]. quae species usucapionis dicitur

was paid in those times, and that the creditors might have some one from whom to obtain their own. 56. This species, then, of possession and usucapion was also called *lucrativa* (profitable): for a man with full knowledge makes profit out of that which belongs to another. 57. At the present day, however, it is not profitable; for at the instance of the late emperor Hadrain a *senatusconsultum* was passed, that such usucapions should be set aside: and therefore the heir by suing for the inheritance may recover the thing from him who has acquired it by usucapion, just as though it had not been acquired by usucapion. 58. But if the heir be of the kind called *necessarius*[1], even by the strict law there can be no usucapion *pro herede*[2].

59. There are other cases besides in which a man with full knowledge that the property is another's can get it by usucapion. For he who has transferred a thing to any one by mancipation or by cession in court under a fiduciary agreement[3], provided he get the possession of the same, can acquire it by usucapion, and that too in one year[4], even though

---

[1] II. 153.

[2] III. 201.

[3] *Fiducia* here means a pact, attached to a conveyance by *mancipatio* or *in jure cessio*, whereby the recipient of the thing or person transferred bound himself to restore it on request, or when a particular purpose has been performed. Cf. the English "bailment". See Dirksen, sub verbo, § 2. Savigny, *On Possession*, p. 216. "Pecuniam adulescentulo grandi foenore, fiducia tamen accepta, occupavisti. Hanc fiduciam commissam tibi dicis: tenes hodie ac possides." Cic. *pro Flacco*, 21.

[4] The principle is the same as in

usureceptio, quia id quod aliquando habuimus recipimus per usucapionem. (60.) Sed cum fiducia contrahitur aut cum creditore pignoris iure, aut cum amico quo tutius nostrae res aput eum essent, si quidem cum amico contracta sit fiducia, sane omni modo conpetit usus receptio; si vero cum creditore, soluta quidem pecunia omni modo competit, nondum vero soluta ita demum competit, si neque conduxerit eam rem a creditore debitor[1], neque precario rogaverit ut eam rem possidere liceret[2]; quo casu lucrativa ususcapio conpetit[3]. (61.) Item si rem obligatam sibi populus vendiderit, eamque dominus possederit, concessa est ususreceptio: sed hoc casu praedium[4] bien-

it appertain to the soil. This species of usucapion is called usureception, because we take back by usucapion what we have had once before. 60. But since this fiduciary compact is entered into either with a creditor in reference to a pledge, or with a friend for the purpose of more completely securing such property of ours as he has in his hands; if the assurance be made with a friend, usureception is in all cases allowable: but if with a creditor, then after payment of the money it is universally allowable, but before payment it is only allowed in case the debtor has neither hired the thing from the creditor[1], nor asked for its possession upon sufferance[2] and in such case "profitable usucapion" is possible[3]. 61. Likewise, if the *populus* have sold a thing pledged to them, and the original owner get possession, usureception is allowed: but in this case if the subject of the pledge be land[4], it is usu-

§ 54: the term of usucapion is one year, because the thing is a pledge, therefore one of the "caeterae res," and no account is taken of its being a pledge of *land*.

1 A hirer has no juridical possession, but is regarded as agent for the lessor: having then no possession, he can have no usucapion. D. 13. 6. 8; D. 41. 2. 3. 20. See Savigny, *On Possession*, translated by Perry, p. 206.

2 With reference to the matter here stated Savigny says, "Whoever simply permits another to enjoy property or an easement retains to himself the right of revocation at will, and the juridical relation thence arising is called *Precarium*." See Savigny, *On Possession*, p. 355, where the learning on the subject of *precarium* and the interdict connected with it is set out at length.

3 Savigny (*Treatise on Possession*, p. 51) takes this as an example of the rule "Nemo sibi causam possessionis mutare potest." The whole of the passage of Savigny pp. 49—52 is worth reading.

4 As to Praediator in the sense used in this paragraph see Cic. *pro Balbo*, c. 20, and *In Verrem*, II. 1. 54,

nio usurecipitur. et hoc est quod volgo dicitur ex praediatura possessionem usurecipi. nam qui mercatur a populo praediator appellatur.

62. Accidit aliquando[1], ut qui dominus sit alienandae rei
P. 69 potestatem non habeat, et qui dominus non sit | alienare possit. (63.) Nam dotale praedium maritus invita muliere per legem Iuliam[2] prohibetur alienare, quamvis ipsius sit vel mancipatum ei dotis causa[3] vel in iure cessum vel usucaptum. quod quidem

recepted in two years. And hence comes the common saying that possession may be usurecepted from a *praediatura*. For he who buys from the people is called a *praediator*.

62. It sometimes[1] happens that he who is owner has not the power of alienating a thing, and that he who is not owner can alienate. 63. For by the Lex Julia[2] a husband is prevented from alienating lands forming part of the *dos* against the will of his wife: although the lands are his own through having been mancipated to him for the purpose of *dos*[3], or passed by cession in court, or acquired by usucapion. Whether

---

"praedibus et praediis populo cautum est." Varro says that *praedium* properly signifies land pledged: *de L. L.* v. 40. So also does Pseudo-Asconius in his commentary on the passage from the Verrine orations quoted above.

[1] Krüger and Studemund place §§ 62—64 in their edition of Gaius between §§ 79 and 80, approving of Heimbach's suggestion, that they have been misplaced by the copyist. But Mommsen, in his letter prefixed to the Krüger and Studemund edition, objects to this change. Gaius, he says, has discussed "alienation", that is to say, the mode of acquisition wherein one person acquires what another loses; and has digressed naturally enough into the topic of "usucapion", because it is a mode of transfer of the same class, although not voluntary but law-created; and now, before passing to a new topic, acquisition *unaccompanied* by loss, he inserts his remarks on the cases where alienation can be made by a non-owner and not made by an owner. If the paragraphs are removed to the new position which Krüger and Studemund suggest, they are unconnected with the context; for alienation by a non-owner has nothing whatever to do with acquisition unaccompanied by alienation. Mommsen thinks, however, that though these paragraphs are now where Gaius originally placed them, yet that the Jurist must have added them on after thought, as they cause a certain break in the sequence of his remarks.

[2] Lex Julia de adulteriis, temp. Augusti: Paul. *S. R.* II. 21 *b.* 2. This law, which originally applied only to Italic land, was extended by Justinian to provincial land also; see Just. *Inst.* 2. 8. pr.

[3] For the law of *dos* see Ulpian, VI. and App. (B) in Abdy and Walker's edition of Justinian's *Institutes*.

ius utrum ad Italica tantum praedia, an etiam ad provincialia pertineat, dubitatur.

64. Ex diverso agnatus furiosi curator rem furiosi alienare potest ex lege XII tabularum[1]; item procurator[2], id est *cui libera administratio permissa est*[3]; item creditor pignus ex pactione, quamvis eius ea res non sit. sed hoc forsitan ideo videatur fieri, quod voluntate debitoris intellegitur pignus alienari, qui olim pactus est ut liceret creditori pignus vendere, si pecunia non solvatur[4].

65. Ergo ex his quae diximus adparet quaedam naturali iure alienari, qualia sunt ea quae traditione alienantur; quaedam civili, nam mancipationis et in iure cessionis et usucapionis ius proprium est civium Romanorum[5].

this rule is confined to Italic lands or extends also to those in the provinces is a doubtful point.

64. On the other hand, the agnate curator of a madman can by a law of the Twelve Tables[1] alienate the property of the madman: a *procurator*[2] likewise (can alienate what belongs to another), *i.e.* a person to whom absolute management is intrusted[3]: a creditor also by special agreement may alienate a pledge, although the thing is not his own. But perhaps the last-named alienation may be considered as taking place through the pledge being regarded as alienated by consent of the debtor, who originally agreed that the creditor should have power to sell the pledge, if the money were not paid[4].

65. From what we have said then it appears that some things are alienated according to natural law, such as those alienated by mere delivery: some things according to the civil law; for the right originating from mancipation, or cession in court, or usucapion, is one peculiar to Roman citizens[5].

---

1 The fragment of the law bearing on the topic (viz. Tab. v. l. 7) does not state this doctrine in so many words, but doubtless the rule given by Gaius was a direct consequence of the fact that this law gave the *potestas* over *furiosi* to their agnates. Cf. Cic. *de Invent. Rhet.* Lib. II. c. 50.

2 IV. 84.

3 These words are filled in according to the suggestion of Buchholtz.

4 On which view it is no example of one man alienating what belongs to another.

5 See Appendix (E).

66. Nec tamen ea tantum quae traditione nostra fiunt naturali nobis ratione adquiruntur, sed etiam *quae* occupando ideo *propria fec*erimus, quia antea nullius essent: qualia sunt omnia quae terra, mari, coelo capiuntur. (67.) itaque si feram bestiam aut volucrem aut piscem cep*erimus*[1], *quidquid ita* cap-
P. 70 tum *fuerit, id statim nostrum fit, et eo us*|que nostrum esse intellegitur, donec nostra custodia coerceatur[2]. cum vero custodiam nostram evaserit et in naturalem se libertatem receperit, rursus occupantis fit, quia nostrum esse desinit. naturalem autem libertatem recipere videtur, cum aut oculos nostros evaserit, aut licet in conspectu sit nostro, difficilis tamen eius rei persecutio sit.

68. In iis autem animalibus quae ex consuetudine abire et redire solent, veluti columbis et apibus, item cervis qui in silvas ire et redire solent, talem habemus regulam traditam, ut si revertendi animum habere desierint, etiam nostra esse desinant

66. But not only those things which become ours by delivery are acquired by us on natural principle, but also those which we acquire by occupation, on the ground that they previously belonged to no one: of which class are all things caught on land, in the sea, or in the air. 67. If therefore we have caught[1] a wild beast, or a bird, or a fish, anything we have so caught at once becomes ours, and is regarded as being ours so long as it is kept in our custody[2]. But when it has escaped from our custody and returned into its natural liberty, it again becomes the property of the first taker, because it ceases to be ours. And it is considered to recover its natural liberty when it has either gone out of our sight, or, although it be still in our sight, yet its pursuit is difficult.

68. With regard to those animals which are accustomed to go and return habitually, as doves, and bees, and deer, which are in the habit of going into the woods and coming back again, we have this rule handed down; that if they cease to have the intent of returning, they also cease to be ours

[1] These words are filled in according to the suggestion of Göschen.

[2] See Savigny, *On Possession*, p. 256, and also D. 41. 1. 3. 2 and 41. 1. 5. pr.

et fiant occupantium. revertendi autem animum videntur desinere habere, cum revertendi consuetudinem deseruerint.

69. Ea quoque quae ex hostibus capiuntur naturali ratione nostra fiunt.

70. Sed et id quod per adluvionem nobis adicitur eodem iure nostrum fit. per adluvionem autem id videtur adici quod ita paulatim flumen agro nostro adicit, ut aestimare non possimus quantum quoquo momento temporis adiciatur. hoc est quod volgo dicitur, per adluvionem id adici videri quod ita paulatim adicitur, ut oculos nostros fallat. (71.) Itaque si flumen partem aliquam ex tuo praedio resciderit et ad meum
P. 71 praedium pertulerit, haec pars tua ma|net.

72. At si in medio flumine insula nata sit, haec eorum omnium communis est qui ab utraque parte fluminis prope ripam praedia possident. si vero non sit in medio flumine, ad eos pertinet qui ab ea parte quae proxuma est iuxta ripam praedia habent.

73. Praeterea id quod in solo nostro ab aliquo aedificatum

---

and become the property of the first taker: and they are considered to cease to have the intent of returning when they have abandoned the habit of returning.

69. Those things also which are taken from the enemy become ours on natural principle.

70. That also which is added to us by alluvion becomes ours on the same principle. Now that is considered to be added by alluvion which the river adds so gradually to our land, that we cannot calculate how much is added at each instant: and hence the common saying, that that is regarded as added by alluvion which is added so gradually that it cheats our eyes. 71. Therefore if the river rend away a portion of your field and carry it over to mine, that portion remains yours.

72. If an island be formed in the middle of a river, it is the common property of all who have lands adjacent to the banks on either side of the river. But if it be not in the middle of the river, it belongs to those who have lands along the bank on that side which is the nearest.

73. Moreover that which is built on our ground by any

est, quamvis ille suo nomine aedificaverit, iure naturali nostrum fit, quia superficies solo cedit[1].

74. Multoque magis id accidit et in planta quam quis in solo nostro posuerit, si modo radicibus terram complexa fuerit.

75. Idem contingit et in frumento quod in solo nostro ab aliquo satum fuerit. (76.) Sed si ab eo petamus *fundum* vel aedificium, et inpensas in aedificium vel in seminaria vel in sementem factas ei solvere nolimus, poterit nos per exceptionem doli repellere[2]; utique si bonae fidei possessor fuerit.

one, even though he have built it in his own name (*i.e.* for himself), is ours by natural law, because the superstructure goes with the soil[1].

74. Much more is this the case with a plant which a man has placed in our land, provided only it have laid hold of the earth with its roots.

75. The same is the case also with corn which has been sown on our land by any one. 76. But if we claim the land or building, and will not pay the expenses incurred upon the building, or seed, or plant, he can resist us by an exception of fraud[2]: at any rate if he be a possessor in good faith.

[1] But if the builder had acted in *bona fides* and had at the time the possession of the land, he could resist the action of the owner who refused to indemnify him, by an *exceptio doli mali*. He could, however, in no case bring an *actio ad exhibendum* to get back the actual building materials. But if the house were pulled down, then he was allowed to *vindicate* them, even if the period of usucapion for the house were completed, because "he who possesses an entirety, possesses the entirety only and not each individual part by itself" (Sav. *On Poss.* p. 193): so that the good title to the land would not have cured the bad title to the materials. If he had not possession, and if the house were not demolished, there is great doubt whether he had any remedy at all. D. 41. 1. 7. 12; D. 5. 3. 38.

[2] See IV. 115 et seqq. For "fructum," the reading of the MS., Huschke suggests "fundum." This appears a better reading, for it is plain from the ending of the paragraph that Gaius is not referring to *malâ fide* possession. We know that a *bonâ fide* possessor had a right to the fruits, if they had been severed by him (see Savigny, *On Possession*, p. 201), therefore it would be useless to talk of an action for them. Such an action would be absolutely refused by the Praetor, not granted and then overthrown *in judicio* by the exception of fraud. But as the *bonâ fide* possessor was treated equitably in this matter of fruits severed, it is only consistent that he should be treated equitably in the matter of expenses too when the fruit had not yet been severed; and so although in this latter case a

77. Eadem ratione probatum est, quod in cartulis sive membranis meis aliquis scripserit, licet aureis litteris, meum esse, quia litterae cartulis sive membranis cedunt. itaque si ego eos libros easque membranas petam, nec inpensam scripturae solvam, per exceptionem doli mali summoveri potero. (78.) Sed si in tabula mea aliquis pinxerit velut imaginem,
P. 72 contra probatur: | magis enim dicitur tabulam picturae cedere. cuius diversitatis vix idonea ratio redditur. certe secundum hanc regulam si a me possidente petas imaginem tuam esse, nec solvas pretium tabulae, poteris per exceptionem doli mali summoveri. at si tu possideas, consequens est, ut utilis mihi actio[1] adversum te dari debeat: quo casu nisi solvam impensam

77. On the same principle the rule has been established that whatever any one has written on my paper or parchment, though it be in golden letters, is mine, because the letters are an accession to the paper or parchment. So too, if I claim those books and those parchments, and yet will not pay the expense of the writing, I can be resisted by an exception of fraud. 78. But if any one have painted anything on my tablet, a likeness for instance, an opposite decision is given: for the more correct doctrine is that the tablet is an accession to the picture. For which difference scarcely any satisfactory reason is given. No doubt, according to this rule, if you claim as your own the picture of which I am in possession, and yet will not pay the price of the tablet, you can be resisted by an exception of fraud. But if you be in possession, it follows that an *actio utilis*[1] ought to be allowed me against you: in which

vindicatio would lie for the *dominus* to obtain the field and the growing crops, yet it could be successfully opposed if he had refused to make good the money laid out by the defendant during his *bonâ fide* possession of the land in dispute.

[1] In assigning new actions the Praetor was careful to frame them, as far as possible, on the precedent of actions already existing under the civil or praetorian law. It might be that the precise phraseology of some enactment was not applicable to the case in question, although its principle could be turned to use; the Praetor therefore, although unable to grant an *actio directa*, could and did grant an *actio utilis*, *i.e.* an "analogous" action: —the epithet *utilis* being derived not from *uti* the verb, but *uti* the adverb.

The special circumstances of the present case are: (1) that it is a general rule that a *vindicatio* can only be brought by the *dominus*, the owner of the thing, when he is picturae, poteris me per exceptionem doli mali repellere, utique si bona fide possessor fueris. illut palam est, quod sive tu subripuisses tabulam sive alius, conpetit mihi furti actio.

79. In aliis quoque speciebus naturalis ratio requiritur: proinde si ex uvis (aut olivis aut spicis) meis vinum aut oleum aut frumentum feceris, quaeritur utrum meum sit id vinum aut oleum aut frumentum, an tuum[1]. item si ex auro aut argento meo vas aliquod feceris, aut ex tabulis meis navem aut armarium aut subsellium fabricaveris; item si ex lana mea vestimentum feceris, vel si ex vino et melle meo mulsum feceris, sive ex medicamentis meis emplastrum vel collyrium feceris: (*quaeritur, utrum tuum sit id quod ex meo effeceris*[2]), an meum. quidam materiam et substantiam spectandam esse putant, id est, ut

case if I do not tender the price of the picture, you can resist me by an exception of fraud, at any rate if you be a possessor in good faith. It is clear that if you or any one else have stolen the tablet, an action of theft lies for me.

79. In specifications also natural principles are resorted to. For instance, if you have made wine, or oil, or corn, out of my grapes, olives, or ears, the question arises whether that wine, oil, or corn is mine or yours[1]. Likewise, if you have made any vessel out of my gold or silver, or made a ship, or chest, or seat out of my planks: likewise, if you have made a garment out of my wool, or made mead out of my wine and honey, or a plaster or eye-salve out of my drugs, the question arises whether that which you have so made out of mine is yours[2] or mine. Some think the material and substance are what ought to be regarded, *i.e.* that the thing made should be considered

kept out of possession: (2) that *ipso jure* there is no separate property in an accession, so that one who claims the accession *not* through the principal thing is not a *dominus*, and hence has no action: therefore the *dominus* being in possession of the picture, the owner of the tablet has by the civil law no action for his tablet. Here then is an opportunity for the Praetor to meet the spirit, and contravene the letter of the law, by granting to the latter an *actio utilis*. See Austin, II. 303 (II. 621, third edition).

[1] The principles here stated are fully set out and in very similar language in D. 41. 1. 7. 7, which passage forms part of a long citation from another treatise of Gaius, viz. the *Liber Rerum quotidianarum sive Aureorum*.

[2] A line has been omitted in the MS. from the usual cause, that it ends with the same word (*feceris*, in this case) as the preceding line.

cuius materia sit, illius et res quae facta sit videatur esse; idque maxime placuit Sabino et Cassio[1]. alii vero eius rem esse putant qui fecerit; idque maxime diversae scholae auctoribus
P. 73 visum est: | sed eum quoque cuius materia et substantia fuerit, furti adversus eum qui subripuerit habere actionem; nec minus adversus eundem condictionem[2] ei competere, quia extinctae res, licet vindicari non possint, condici tamen furibus et quibusdam aliis possessoribus possunt.

80. Nunc admonendi sumus neque feminam neque pupillum sine tutoris auctoritate rem mancipi alienare posse; nec mancipi vero feminam quidem posse, pupillum non posse[3]. (81.) Ideoque si quando mulier mutuam pecuniam alicui sine tutoris auctoritate dederit, quia facit eam accipientis, cum scilicet ea pecunia res nec mancipi sit, contrahit obligationem[4]. (82.) At si pupillus idem fecerit, quia non *facit eam pecuniam accipientis*

to belong to him to whom the materials belong: and this opinion found favour with Cassius and Sabinus[1]. But others think that the thing belongs to him who made it, (and this view rather is upheld by the authorities of the school opposed to us,) but that he to whom the material and substance belonged has an action of theft against him who took them away: and that he has in addition a condiction[2] against the same person, because things which have been destroyed, although they cannot be recovered by vindication, yet may be the ground of a condiction as against thieves and certain other possessors.

80. We must now be informed that neither a woman nor a pupil can without the authority of the tutor alienate a thing mancipable: a thing non-mancipable a woman can alienate, and a pupil cannot[3]. 81. Therefore in all cases where a woman lends money to any one without the authorization of her tutor, she contracts an obligation, for she makes the money the property of the recipient, inasmuch as money is a thing non-mancipable[4]. 82. But if a pupil have done the same, since he does

---

1 To which school Gaius himself belonged.

2 IV. 5.

3 Ulp. XI. 27.

4 *Mutuum* is a contract perfected by delivery in cases where delivery passes the property: hence in this instance the *mutuum* is binding, money being a *res nec mancipi*, and therefore capable of transfer by mere delivery. See III. 90.

sine tutoris auctoritate, nullam contrahit obligationem. unde pupillus vindicare quidem nummos suos potest, sicubi extent, id est intendere suos ex iure Quiritium esse; mulier *autem per mutui actionem pecuniam* ab eo reo repetere potest sed non suum esse petere[1]. unde de pupillo quidem quaeritur, an nummos quos mutuos dedit, ab eo qui accepit *bona fide alienatos ulla* actione persequi possit, quoniam *nisi a possidente vindicari non potest*[2]. (83.) *At ex contrario res tam mancipi*
P. 74 *quam* nec mancipi mulieribus | et pupillis sine tutoris auctoritate solvi[3] possunt, quoniam meliorem condicionem suam facere eis etiam sine tutoris auctoritate concessum est. (84.)

not make the money the property of the recipient without the authority of his tutor he contracts no obligation. Therefore, the pupil can recover his money by vindication, as long as it is unconsumed, *i.e.* claim it to be his own in Quiritary right: but a woman can recover her money from such a debtor by action on the loan, though she cannot sue for it as being her own[1]. Whence arises this question with regard to a pupil, viz. whether he can by any action reclaim money he has lent from him who has received it, after the latter has in good faith transferred it to a third party; since a *vindicatio* can only be brought against a possessor[2]. 83. But, on the other hand, both things mancipable and things non-mancipable can be paid[3] to women and pupils without the authorization of the tutor, because they are allowed to make their condition better even without their tutor's authorization. 84. Therefore, if a

---

1 The woman's contract is valid, therefore her execution of her own part thereof, by delivery of the money, is valid. She cannot therefore assert that the actual coins are still hers, and therefore has no *vindicatio*, even if they are in the hands of the receiver or can be traced into other hands. But the contract of *mutuum* being valid, she has an *actio mutui* on the contract.

2 The pupil, we have already been told, can bring a *vindicatio* for the coins he passed to the borrower, *sicubi extent*, *i.e.* if they can be traced: but if they have been passed to another person they probably cannot be traced. Therefore the pupil has in this event no action; for his contract is void, and so he has in the case supposed neither *actio mutui*, nor *vindicatio*. The words inserted in § 82 are mainly those suggested by Huschke.

3 *Solvere* means to discharge an obligation. It is difficult to hit upon a precise equivalent in English, because the *solutio* spoken of in this paragraph may be either *dare*, *facere*, or *praestare*.

Itaque si debitor pecuniam pupillo solvat, facit quidem pecuniam pupilli, sed ipse non liberatur[1]; quia nullam obligationem pupillus sine tutoris auctoritate dissolvere potest, quia nullius rei alienatio ei sine tutoris auctoritate concessa est. set tamen si ex ea pecunia locupletior factus sit, et adhuc petat, per exceptionem doli mali summoveri potest. (85.) Mulieri vero etiam sine tutoris auctoritate recte solvi potest: nam qui solvit, liberatur obligatione. quia res nec mancipi, ut proxume diximus, a se dimittere mulier et sine tutoris auctoritate potest: quamquam hoc ita est, si accipiat pecuniam; at si non accipiat, set habere se dicat, et per acceptilationem[2] velit debitorem sine tutoris auctoritate liberare, non potest.

86. Adquiritur autem nobis non solum per nosmet ipsos, sed etiam per eos quos in potestate manu mancipiove habemus[3]; item per eos servos in quibus usumfructum habemus;

debtor pay money to a pupil, he makes the money the property of the pupil, but is not himself freed from obligation[1], because the pupil can dissolve no obligation without the authorization of the tutor, since without his tutor's authorization he is not allowed to alienate anything. But nevertheless if he have benefited by this money, and yet sue for it again, he can be resisted by an exception of fraud. 85. Payment, however, can be legally made to a woman even without the authorization of her tutor: for he who pays is freed from obligation, since, as we have said above, a woman can part with things non-mancipable even without her tutor's authorization: although this is the case only if she receive the money: but if she do not receive it, but merely say she has it, and desire to free the debtor by acceptilation[2] without the authorization of her tutor, she cannot do so.

86. Property is acquired for us not only by our own means but also by means of those whom we have under our *potestas*, *manus* or *mancipium*[3]: likewise, by means of those slaves in

[1] This does not mean that the debtor would have to pay over again in all cases, as we see from the concluding paragraph of the section. The debtor having paid a person not fit to be entrusted with money, was liable in case any loss took place, or if the pupil wastefully expended what he had received. Just. *Inst.* II. 8. 2.

[2] III. 169.

[3] Ulpian, XIX. 18.

item per homines liberos et servos alienos quos bona fide possidemus. de quibus singulis diligenter dispiciamus.

87. Igitur (quod) liberi nostri quos in potestate habemus, item quod servi mancipio accipiunt, vel ex traditione nanciscuntur, sive quid stipulentur[1], vel ex aliqualibet causa ad-
P. 75 quirunt, id nobis adquiritur: ipse enim | qui in potestate nostra est nihil suum habere potest, et ideo si heres institutus sit[2], nisi nostro iussu, hereditatem adire non potest; et si iubentibus nobis adierit hereditatem, nobis adquiritur proinde atque si nos ipsi heredes instituti essemus. et convenienter scilicet legatum per eos nobis adquiritur. (88.) dum tamen sciamus, si alterius in bonis sit servus, alterius ex iure Quiritium, ex omnibus causis ei soli per eum adquiri cuius in bonis est[3]. (89.) Non solum autem proprietas per eos quos in potestate habemus adquiritur nobis, sed etiam possessio: cuius enim rei possessionem adepti

whom we have an usufruct: likewise, by means of free men and slaves of others whom we possess in good faith. These cases let us consider carefully one by one.

87. Whatever, therefore, our children, whom we have under our *potestas*, and likewise whatever our slaves receive by mancipation, or obtain by delivery, or stipulate for[1], or acquire in any way at all, is acquired for us: for he who is under our *potestas* can have nothing of his own; and therefore if he be instituted heir[2], he cannot enter on the inheritance except by our command; and if he enter on the inheritance at our command, it is acquired for us just as though we had ourselves been instituted heirs. And in like manner of course a legacy is acquired for us by their means. 88. Let us, however, take notice that if a slave belong to one man by Bonitary and to another by Quiritary title, acquisition is in all cases made by his means for that one only whose Bonitarian property he is[3]. 89. And not only is ownership acquired for us by means of those whom we have under our *potestas*, but possession also: for of whatever thing they have obtained possession,

---

[1] III. 114.
[2] Ulpian, XIX. 19.
[3] II. 40. Ulp. XIX. 20. The owner *in bonis* has the *potestas*. I. 54.

fuerint, id nos possidere videmur. unde etiam per eos usucapio procedit[1].

90. Per eas vero personas quas in manu mancipiove habemus, proprietas quidem adquiritur nobis ex omnibus causis, sicut per eos qui in potestate nostra sunt: an autem possessio adquiratur quaeri solet, quia ipsas non possidemus[2]. (91.) De his autem servis in quibus tantum usumfructum habemus ita placuit, ut quidquid ex re nostra vel ex operis suis adquirunt, id nobis adquiratur[3]; quod vero extra eas causas, id ad dominum proprietatis pertineat. itaque si iste servus heres institutus sit legatumve quod ei datum fuerit, non mihi, sed domino proprietatis adquiritur. (92.) Idem placet de eo qui a nobis bona

P. 76 fide possidetur, | sive liber sit sive alienus servus. quod enim

that thing we are considered to possess. Hence also usucapion takes effect through their means[1].

90. Next, by means of those persons whom we have under *manus* or *mancipium* ownership, no doubt, can be acquired for us in all cases, just as it can by those who are under our *potestas*: but whether possession can be acquired is often questioned, because we do not possess the persons themselves[2]. 91. With regard to slaves in whom we have merely an usufruct, the rule is that whatever they acquire by means of our substance or their own labour is acquired for us[3]: but whatever from other sources than these, belongs to their proprietor. Therefore, if such a slave be instituted heir or any legacy be left to him, it is acquired not for me but for his proprietor. 92. The law is the same as to one who is possessed by us in good faith, whether he be free or the slave of another. For whatever holds

1 Possession, however, is not acquired for another without that other's knowledge and consent, although property may be: for the *animus domini* must exist not only in personal but also in derivative possession, such as that of a slave for his master. See Savigny, *On Poss.* § 28, p. 224.

2 Savigny points out (*Treatise on Possession*, p. 230) that if we could only acquire derivative possession through persons of whom we ourselves have possession, the father could not acquire through the son, nor the usufructuary through the slave in whom he had the usufruct (§ 91). Gaius, consistently with himself, raises a doubt as to the last-named case in § 94.

3 Ulpian, XIX. 21.

placuit de usufructuario, idem probatur etiam de bona fide possessore[1]. itaque quod extra duas istas causas adquiritur, id vel ad ipsum pertinet, si liber est, vel ad dominum, si servus sit. (93.) Sed si bonae fidei possessor eum usuceperit servum, quia eo modo dominus fit, ex omni causa per eum sibi adquirere potest: usufructuarius vero usucapere non potest, primum quia non possidet, set habet ius utendi et fruendi; deinde quia scit alienum servum esse. (94.) De illo quaeritur, an per eum servum in quo usumfructum habemus possidere aliquam rem et usucapere possumus[2], quia ipsum non possidemus. Per eum vero quem bona fide possidemus sine dubio et possidere et usucapere possumus. loquimur autem in utriusque person*a* secundum definitionem quam proxume exposuimus, id est si quid ex re nostra vel ex operis suis adquirant, id nobis adquiritur. (95.) Ex iis apparet per liberos homines, quos neque iuri nostro subiectos habemus neque bona fide possidemus, item

good as to an usufructuary also holds good as to a possessor in good faith[1]. Therefore, whatever is acquired from causes other than these two either belongs to the man himself, if he be free, or to his master, if he be a slave. 93. But if a possessor in good faith have got the slave by usucapion, since he thus becomes his master, he can acquire by his means in every case: but an usufructuary cannot get by usucapion; firstly, because he does not possess, but has the right of usufruct; and secondly, because he knows the slave to be another's. 94. Whether we can possess and get an usucaptive title to anything by means of a slave in whom we have the usufruct is a moot point[2], since we do not possess the slave himself. There is, however, no doubt that we can both possess and get by usucapion by means of a man whom we possess in good faith. But in both instances we are speaking with a reference to the qualification which we laid down just above, viz. that it is only what they acquire by our substance or their own work which is acquired for us. 95. Hence it appears that in no case can anything be acquired for us by means of free men whom we neither have

[1] Ulpian, XIX. 21.

[2] According to D. 41. 2. 1. 8 and D. 41. 2. 49. pr. it is quite clear that the usufructuary could acquire through the slave in whom he had the usufruct.

per alienos servos, in quibus neque usumfructum habemus neque iustam possessionem, nulla ex causa nobis adquiri posse, et hoc est quod volgo dicitur per extraneam personam nobis adquiri non posse. Tantum de *possessione* quaeritur, anne per pe*rsonam liberam* nobis adquiratur[1].

P. 77 96. In summa sciendum est his qui in | potestate manu mancipiove sunt nihil in iure cedi posse. cum enim istarum personarum nihil suum esse possit, conveniens est scilicet, ut nihil suum esse in iure vindicare possint.

97. (Hactenus) tantisper admonuisse sufficit quemadmodum singulae res nobis adquirantur. nam legatorum ius, quo et ipso singulas res adquirimus, opportunius alio loco referemus[2].

subject to our authority nor possess in good faith, nor by the slaves of other men of whom we have neither the usufruct nor the lawful possession. And hence comes the vulgar saying that there can be no acquisition for us through a stranger: though it is with reference to possession alone that there is a doubt, whether it can be acquired for us by a free person[1].

96. Finally, we must take note that nothing can be passed by cession in court to those who are under *potestas*, *manus* or *mancipium*. For since these persons can have nothing of their own, it clearly follows that they cannot claim anything in court as being their own.

97. This much it is sufficient to have laid down at present as to the methods whereby particular things are acquired by us. For the law of legacies, whereby also we acquire particular things, we shall state more conveniently in another place[2]. Let us therefore now consider how things are ac-

[1] This passage in the text, it will be observed, is partly filled in conjecturally. Justinian in the parallel passage says: "per liberam personam, veluti per procuratorem, placet non solum scientibus, sed etiam ignorantibus vobis adquiri possessionem, secundum divi Severi Constitutionem:" *Inst.* 2. 9. 5. The Constitution is to be found in C. 7. 32. 1. The principal, by virtue of this enactment, acquires possession through the agent at once and before he receives information of the transaction of the business, if he gave a precedent *mandatum* (commission); but only after knowledge of the taking of possession and approval of the same (*ratihabitio*) when the agent is self-appointed (*negotiorum gestor*). See Sav. *On Poss.* pp. 230—236, Paulus, *S. R.* 5. 2. 2.

[2] II. 191 et seqq.

Videamus itaque nunc quibus modis per universitatem res nobis adquirantur. (98.) Si cui heredes facti sumus, sive cuius bonorum possessionem petierimus[1], sive cuius bona emerimus[2], sive quem adoptaverimus, sive quam in manum ut uxorem receperimus, eius res ad nos transeunt.

99. Ac prius de hereditatibus dispiciamus, quarum duplex condicio est: nam vel ex testamento, vel ab intestato ad nos pertinet.

100. Et prius est, ut de his dispiciamus quae nobis ex testamento obveniunt.

101. Testamentorum autem genera initio duo fuerunt[3]. nam aut calatis comitiis testamentum faciebant[4], quae comitia bis in anno testamentis faciendis destinata erant, aut in procinctu, id est cum belli causa arma sumebant: procinctus est

quired by us in the aggregate. 98. If then we have been made heirs to any man, or if we seek the possession of any man's goods[1], or buy any bankrupt's goods[2], or adopt any man, or receive any woman into *manus* as a wife, the property of such person passes to us.

99. And first let us consider the subject of inheritances, of which there are two descriptions, for they devolve upon us either by testament or intestacy.

100. The first point is to consider about those things which come to us by testament.

101. Originally then there were two kinds of testaments[3]: for men either made a testament at the specially-summoned *comitia*[4], which *comitia* were appointed twice in the year for the purpose of testaments being made; or *in procinctu*, *i.e.* when they were arming for battle: for *procinctus* means an army pre-

[1] III. 32.

[2] III. 77.

[3] "Testamentum est mentis nostrae contestatio, in id sollemniter facta ut post mortem nostram valeat." Ulp. XX. 1.

[4] The *comitia* of which two meetings were set apart would, it is almost needless to say, be the *curiata*: as the plebeians had not in those early times risen into importance. The rule was that inheritances should descend according to law, and a Roman could only have this rule relaxed in his own case by obtaining a special enactment, (what would have been called at a later period a *privilegium*,) at the assembly of the nation, either the whole of it, the *comitia*, or in cases of emergency such portion as could readily be collected, the *procinctus*. See Festus sub verb. *procinctus*.

enim expeditus et armatus exercitus. alterum itaque in pace et in otio faciebant, alterum in proelium exituri. (102.) Accessit
P. 78 deinde tertium | genus testamenti, quod per aes et libram agitur. qui (enim) neque calatis comitiis neque in procinctu testamentum fecerat, is si subita morte urguebatur, amico familiam suam, id est patrimonium suum, mancipio dabat, eumque rogabat quid cuique post mortem suam dari vellet. quod testamentum dicitur per aes et libram, scilicet quia per mancipationem peragitur[1]. (103.) Sed illa quidem duo genera testamentorum in desuetudinem abierunt; hoc vero solum quod per aes et libram fit in usu retentum est. sane nunc aliter ordinatur atque olim solebat. namque olim familiae emptor, id est qui a testatore familiam accipiebat mancipio, heredis locum optinebat, et ob id ei mandabat testator quid cuique post mortem suam dari vellet. nunc vero alius heres testamento instituitur, a quo etiam legata relinquuntur, alius dicis gratia propter veteris iuris imitationem

pared and armed. The one kind, therefore, they made in peace and tranquillity, the other when going out to battle. 102. Afterwards there was added a third kind of testament, which is solemnized by means of the coin and scale. For a man who had made his testament neither at the *comitia calata* nor *in procinctu*, if threatened with sudden death, used to give his *familia* (*i.e.* his patrimony) by mancipation to some friend, and injoin on him what he wished to be given to each person after his death. Which testament is called "by coin and balance," clearly because it is solemnized by mancipation[1]. 103. But the two kinds of testament first-mentioned have fallen into disuse: and that alone is retained in use which is solemnized by coin and balance. It is, however, now managed in another way from that in which it used to be. For formerly the *familiae emptor*, *i.e.* he who received the estate by mancipation from the testator, held the place of heir, and therefore the testator charged him with what he wished to be given to each person after his death. But now one person is appointed heir in the testament, and on him the legacies are charged, and another, as a mere form and in imitation of the ancient law, is employed

---

[1] Ulpian, XX. 2.

familiae emptor adhibetur. (104.) Eaque res ita agitur. Qui facit testamentum, adhibitis, sicut in ceteris mancipationibus, v testibus civibus Romanis puberibus et libripende[1], postquam tabulas testamenti scripserit, mancipat alicui dicis gratia familiam suam; in qua re his verbis familiae emptor utitur: FAMILIA PECUNIAQUE TUA ENDO MANDATELAM TUAM, CUSTO-
P. 79 DELAMQUE MEAM, QUO TU IURE TESTAMENTUM | FACERE POSSIS SECUNDUM LEGEM PUBLICAM, HOC AERE, et ut quidam adiciunt AENEAQUE LIBRA, ESTO MIHI EMPTA. deinde aere percutit libram, idque aes dat testatori velut pretii loco. deinde testator tabulas testamenti tenens ita dicit: HAEC ITA UT IN HIS TABULIS CERISQUE SCRIPTA SUNT ITA DO, ITA LEGO, ITA TESTOR, ITAQUE VOS QUIRITES TESTIMONIUM MIHI PERHIBETOTE[2]. et hoc dicitur nuncupatio. nuncupare est enim palam nominare[3]; et sane quae testator specialiter in tabulis testamenti scripserit, ea videtur generali sermone nominare atque confirmare.

as *familiae emptor*. 104. The business is effected thus. The man who is making the testament, having called together, as in all other mancipations, five witnesses, Roman citizens of puberty, and a balance-holder (*libripens*)[1], after writing the tablets of his testament mancipates his estate for form's sake to some one: at which point the *familiae emptor* makes use of these words: "Be your patrimony and money purchased into your own disposition and my custody, in order that you may be able to make a testament duly according to public law, with this coin, and," as some add, "with this bronze balance." Then he strikes the balance with the coin, and gives that coin to the testator, as it were by way of price. The testator thereupon, holding the tablets of the testament, speaks thus: "These things, just as they are written in these tablets of wax, I so give, I so bequeath, and I so claim your evidence, and do you, Quirites, so afford it me[2]." And this is called the nuncupation: for to nuncupate is to declare openly[3]: and whatever the testator has written in detail on the tablets of his testament, he is regarded as declaring and confirming by this general statement.

---

[1] Ulpian, XX. 2.
[2] Ulpian, XX. 9.
[3] "Nuncupare nominare valere apparet in legibus." Varro, *de L. L.* VI. 90.

105. In testibus autem non debet is esse qui in potestate est aut familiae emptoris aut ipsius testatoris, quia propter veteris iuris imitationem totum hoc negotium quod agitur testamenti ordinandi gratia creditur inter familiae emptorem agi et testatorem: quippe olim, ut proxime diximus, is qui familiam testatoris mancipio accipiebat, heredis loco erat. itaque reprobatum est in ea re domesticum testimonium[1]. (106.) Unde et si is qui in potestate patris est familiae emptor adhibitus sit, pater eius testis esse non potest[2]; at ne is quidem qui in eadem potestate est, velut frater eius. Sed si filiusfamilias ex castrensi peculio[3] post missionem faciat testamentum, nec pater eius recte
P. 80 testis | adhibetur[4], nec is qui in potestate patris sit. (107.) De

105. Amongst the witnesses there ought not to be any one who is under the *potestas* either of the *familiae emptor* or of the testator himself, since in imitation of the old law all this business which is done for the purpose of making the testament is regarded as taking place between the *familiae emptor* and the testator: because in olden times, as we have just stated, he who received the estate of the testator by mancipation was in the place of heir. Therefore the evidence of members of the same household was refused in the matter[1]. 106. Hence also, if he who is under the *potestas* of his father be employed as *familiae emptor*, his father cannot be a witness[2]: neither can one who is under the same *potestas*, his brother for instance. And if a *filius familias* make a testament regarding his *castrense peculium*[3] after his discharge from service, his father cannot properly be employed as a witness[4], nor one who is under the *potestas* of his father. 107. We shall consider that

1 Ulpian, XX. 3.

2 Ibid. 4, 5.

3 Ulpian, XX. 10. *Peculium* originally meant property of the *paterfamilias* held on his sufferance by the son or slave, and which he could take from him at his pleasure. *Peculium castrense* dates from the time of Augustus: soldiers *in potestate parentis* were by enactment of that emperor allowed to have an independent property in their acquisitions made on service, and the rule that the property of a son was the property of the father (II. 87) was set aside in this case. If the testament were made during service, no formalities were needed (II. 109); hence the words "post missionem" are inserted in the text.

4 Marcellus, with whom Ulpian apparently agrees, held that a father could be made witness to a testament of a *filius familias* respecting his *castrense peculium*. See D. 28. 1. 20. 2.

libripende eadem quae et de testibus dicta esse intellegemus; nam et is testium numero est. (108.) Is vero qui in potestate heredis aut legatarii est, cuiusve heres ipse aut legatarius in potestate est, quique in eiusdem potestate est, adeo testis et libripens adhiberi potest, ut ipse quoque heres aut legatarius iure adhibeantur. sed tamen quod ad heredem pertinet quique in eius potestate est, cuiusve is in potestate erit, minime hoc iure uti debemus[1].

109. Set haec diligens observatio in ordinandis testamentis militibus propter nimiam inperitiam constitutionibus Principum remissa est. nam quamvis neque legitimum numerum testium adhibuerint, neque vendiderint familiam, neque nuncupaverint testamentum, recte nihilominus testantur[2]. (110.) Praeterea permissum est iis et peregrinos et Latinos instituere heredes vel iis

what has been said about the witnesses is also said about the balance-holder: for he too is in the number of the witnesses. 108. But a man who is under the *potestas* of the heir or a legatee, or under whose *potestas* the heir or a legatee himself is, or who is under the same *potestas* (with either of them), may so undoubtedly be employed as a witness or balance-holder, that even the heir or legatee himself may be lawfully so employed. Yet so far as concerns the heir, or one who is under his *potestas*, or one under whose *potestas* he is, we ought to make use of this right very sparingly[1].

109. But these strict regulations as to the making of testaments have been relaxed by constitutions of the Emperors in the case of soldiers, on account of their great want of legal knowledge. For their testaments are valid, though they have neither employed the lawful number of witnesses, nor sold (mancipated) their estate, nor nuncupated their testament[2]. 110. Moreover, they are allowed to institute foreigners or Latins as their heirs, or to leave legacies to them: although

[1] The transaction, as Gaius tells us (II. 105), was still regarded as one between the testator and the *familiae emptor*, and yet people were gradually beginning to see that this was but a fiction, and that the real parties were the testator and the heir; hence the caution at the end of II. 108, which Justinian subsequently transformed into a rule. *Inst.* II. 10. 10.

[2] The testaments of soldiers made irregularly were only valid for one year after their leaving the service. Ulpian, XXIII. 10.

legare; cum alioquin peregrini quidem ratione civili prohibeantur capere hereditatem legataque, Latini vero per legem Iuniam[1]. (111.) Caelibes quoque qui lege Iulia[2] hereditatem legataque capere vetantur, item orbi, id est qui liberos non habent, quos lex | *Papia plus quam semissem capere prohibet*[3] [desunt 21 *lin.*[4]].

112. ...auctore divo Hadriano senatusconsultum factum est quo permissum est *puberibus* feminis etiam sine coemp-
P. 82 tione[5] testamentum facere, simodo non minores essent | anno-

in other cases foreigners are prohibited by the civil law from taking inheritances, and Latins by the Lex Junia[1]. 111. Unmarried persons also, who by the Lex Julia[2] are forbidden to take an inheritance or legacies, also *orbi*, *i.e.* those who have no children, whom the Lex Papia prevents from taking more than half the inheritance[3], (can be appointed heirs by soldiers)......[4]

112. ...at the instance of the late Emperor Hadrian a *senatusconsultum* was made whereby it was permitted that women over the age of puberty should make a testament without passing through any coemption[5], provided only they were

[1] I. 23. The prohibition of Latins was not absolute. See Ulpian, XXII. 3.

[2] The *Lex Julia de maritandis ordinibus* (temp. Augusti) is meant. *Orbi* by that law could only take half of what was bequeathed to them, unless they had a child within 100 days: and *coelibes* could take nothing, unless they married within 100 days from the time when they became entitled. Ulpian, XVII. 1. The Lex Julia was enacted A.D. 4, but it did not come into operation till A.D. 10, in which year the Lex Papia Poppaea was also passed. The two laws being thus connected both in their object and their date, are generally spoken of together, and sometimes, though not quite correctly, as if they were one law, *Lex Julia et Papia*. See Appendix (G).

[3] II. 286.

[4] A leaf, i.e. two pages, of the MS. has at this point been cut out by the writer who transcribed Jerome on the top of Gaius, and in the next numbered page (p. 81) only three lines at the bottom can be deciphered, and a word or two elsewhere, as in line 1, *prohibentur hi;* in line 8, *eius more faciant;* and in line 10, XXX ann. From the *Epitome* of Gaius, 2. 2. 1—3, which corresponds to this lost portion, we see what was the substance of the missing lines: for the *Epitome* reads: "id quoque statutum est, quod non omnibus liceat facere testamentum; sicut sunt hi qui sui iuris non sunt, sed alieno iuri subiecti sunt, hoc est filii, tam ex nobis nati quam adoptivi. Item testamenta facere non possunt inpuberes, id est minores XIV annorum, aut puellae XII. Item et hi qui furiosi, id est, mente insani, non possunt facere testamenta. Sed hi qui insani sunt, per intervalla quibus sani sunt possunt facere testamenta."

[5] I. 115 *a*.

rum XII tutore auctore; scilicet ut quae tutela liberatae non essent ita testari deberent[1]. (113.) Videntur ergo melioris condicionis esse feminae quam masculi: nam masculus minor annorum XIIII testamentum facere non potest, etiamsi tutore auctore testamentum facere velit; femina vero post XII annum testamenti faciundi ius nanciscitur[2].

114. Igitur si quaeramus an valeat testamentum, imprimis advertere debemus an is qui id fecerit habuerit testamenti factionem[3]: deinde si habuerit, requiremus an secundum iuris civilis

not less than twelve years of age and made it with the authorization of their tutor; that is, that women not freed from tutelage should so make their testaments[1]. 113. Women, therefore, seem to be in a better position than men: for a male under fourteen years of age cannot make a testament, even though he desire to make it with the authorization of his tutor: but a woman obtains the right of making a testament after her twelfth year[2].

114. If then we are considering whether a testament be valid, we first ought to consider whether he who made it had *testamenti factio*[3]: then, if he had it, we shall inquire whether

---

[1] For the circumstances under which women are freed from *tutela* see I. 194.

[2] Ulpian, XX. 12, 15.

[3] *Testamenti factio* is used in three senses:

(1) The legal capacity of making a testament:

(2) The legal capacity of taking under a testament:

(3) The legal capacity of being a witness to a testament.

The phrase is here used in the first sense. All persons *sui juris*, not being *Latini* or *Dediticii* (I. 23, 25; III. 75), had this *testamenti factio*. Persons not *sui juris* might have it in the other two senses.

After the Lex Papia Poppaea was passed, the man who had *testamenti factio* in the second sense did not of necessity receive his inheritance or legacy: he had the power of doing so still, yet that power was not absolute, but conditional on his ceasing to be *coelebs* or *orbus* within one hundred days after the testament came into operation. Therefore although he had the *testamenti factio*, circumstances might still rob him of the *jus capiendi ex testamento*.

In the third sense *testamenti factio* was not an absolute but a relative right. There were persons who did not possess it at all, and those who were not so disqualified still could not be witnesses to every testament, but were without *testamenti factio* when the testator or *familiae emptor* was linked to them by *patria potestas*, as we see from II. 105—108. From this relative character of the privilege we see how apposite is Ulpian's phraseology in XX. 2: "*cum quibus* testamenti factio est."

regulam testatus sit; exceptis militibus, quibus propter nimiam inperitiam, ut diximus, quomodo velint vel quomodo possint, permittitur testamentum facere.

115. Non tamen, ut iure civili valeat testamentum, sufficit ea observatio quam supra exposuimus de familiae venditione et de testibus et de nuncupationibus. (116.) Ante omnia requirendum est an institutio heredis sollemni more facta sit: nam aliter facta institutione nihil proficit familiam testatoris ita venire, testesque ita adhibere, aut nuncupare testamentum, ut supra diximus. (117.) Sollemnis autem institutio haec est: TITIUS HERES ESTO. set et illa iam conprobata videtur:
P. 83 TITIUM HEREDEM ESSE | IUBEO. at illa non est conprobata: TITIUM HEREDEM ESSE VOLO. set et illae a plerisque improbatae sunt: HEREDUM INSTITUO, item HEREDEM FACIO[1].

118. Observandum praeterea est, ut si mulier quae in tutela est faciat testamentum, tutoris auctoritate facere debeat: alio-

he made the testament according to the rules of the civil law: except in the case of soldiers, who, as we have stated, on account of their great want of legal knowledge are allowed to make a testament as they will and as they can.

115. But to make a testament valid by the civil law, the observances which we have explained above as to the sale of the estate, and the witnesses, and the nuncupations, are not sufficient. 116. Above all things we must inquire whether the institution of the heir was made in solemn form: for if it have been made otherwise, it is of no avail for the estate of the testator to be sold, or to call in witnesses, or to nuncupate the testament, in the manner we have stated above. 117. The solemn form of institution is this: "Titius be heir." But this also seems approved: "I order Titius to be heir." This, however, is not approved: "I wish Titius to be heir." These, too, are generally disapproved: "I institute heir," and "I make heir[1]."

118. We must further observe that if a woman who is under tutelage make a testament, she ought to make it with the authorization of her tutor: otherwise she will make a testament

1 The form to be solemn must be imperative, not precative or a mere statement. Ulpian, XXI.

quin inutiliter iure civili testabitur[1]. (119.) Praetor tamen, si septem signis testium signatum sit testamentum, scriptis heredibus secundum tabulas testamenti bonorum possessionem pollicetur: si nemo sit ad quem ab intestato iure legitimo[2] pertineat hereditas, velut frater eodem patre natus aut patruus aut fratris filius, ita poterunt scripti heredes retinere hereditatem[3]. nam idem iuris est et si alia ex *causa*[4] testamentum non valeat, velut quod familia non venierit aut nuncupationis verba testator locutus non sit[5]. (120.) Sed videamus an, etiamsi frater aut patruus extent, potiores scriptis heredibus habeantur: rescripto

invalid by the civil law[1]. 119. The Praetor, however, if the testament be sealed with the seals of seven witnesses, promises to the appointed heirs possession of the property in accordance with the testament: and if there be no person to whom the inheritance belongs on intestacy by statutable right[2], as a brother born from the same father, or a father's brother, or a brother's son, the appointed heirs will in such a case retain the inheritance[3]. For the rule is the same if the testament be invalid from other causes[4] as for instance, because the estate has not been sold, or because the testator has not spoken the words of nuncupation[5]. 120. But let us consider whether a brother or father's brother, supposing such exist, will be considered to have a better title

---

[1] II. 112.

[2] *Legitimo jure* = by right based on the law of the Twelve Tables, or on some subsequent *lex*.

[3] II. 123. Ulpian, XXIII. 6. The wording here is rather loose: a *bonorum possessor* could not be heir, for the heir is marked out by law, and if the law did not recognize a person in that capacity, the praetor's grant of *bonorum possessio* was unable to give him heirship, although it gave him the benefits of heirship. Hence "hereditatem" should have been "res hereditarias," or "bona testatoris."

The Roman civil law on the subject of inheritances was so very meagre, omitting for instance all reference to cognates and disregarding the rights of emancipated children, &c., that the praetors found themselves obliged to supplement the law by these grants of *bonorum possessio*, whereby they sometimes prevented an inheritance becoming ownerless, and in other cases left the bare name of heir to the person marked out by law, but gave the practical benefits of the succession to one more justly entitled either on natural grounds, as for instance by relationship, or on account of the expressed wish of the testator, when the testator did not pass over some person on whose appointment the law insisted.

[4] The MS. has *alia ex SCto*; an obvious blunder.

[5] See on this point D. 37. 11. 1. 7—10, where several cases of this nature are examined.

enim Imperatoris Antonini significatur[1], eos qui secundum tabulas testamenti non iure factas bonorum possessionem petierint, posse adversus eos qui ab intestato vindicant hereditatem[2] defendere se per exceptionem doli mali[3]. (121.) quod sane quidem ad masculorum testamenta pertinere certum est; item ad feminarum quae ideo non utiliter testatae sunt, quod verbi gratia familiam non vendiderint aut nuncupationis
P. 84 verba locutae non sint: | an autem et ad ea testamenta feminarum quae sine tutoris auctoritate fecerint haec constitutio pertineat, videbimus. (122.) Loquimur autem de his scilicet feminis quae non in legitima parentium aut patronorum tutela sunt, sed de his quae alterius generis tutores habent, qui etiam inviti coguntur auctores fieri: alioquin parentem et patronum sine auctoritate eius facto testamento non summoveri palam est[4].

123. Item qui filium in potestate habet curare debet, ut eum

than the appointed heirs. For it is laid down in a rescript of the Emperor Antoninus[1] that those who claim possession of goods in accordance with a testament not made in due form, can defend themselves by an exception of fraud[2] against those who claim the inheritance on intestacy[3]. 121. That this (rescript) applies to testaments of men is certain: also to those of women who have made an invalid testament because, for instance, they have not sold their estate, or have not spoken the words of nuncupation: but whether the constitution also applies to those testaments of women which they have made without authorization of the tutor is a matter for us to consider. 122. But of course, we are speaking about those women who are not in the statutable tutelage of parents or patrons, but who have tutors of another kind, who are compelled to authorize even against their will: on the other hand, it is plain that a parent or a patron cannot be set aside by a testament made without his authorization[4].

123. Likewise, he who has a son under his *potestas* must take

1 Antoninus must be Marcus Aurelius: for Antoninus Pius is referred to as *divus* in II. 195.

2 The rules about *praeteritio* (see § 123 et seqq.) do not apply to any but descendants, so that the appointed heirs are preferred to a brother or father's brother. Under Justinian's legislation, however, the brother sometimes could wrest the possession from them. Just. *Inst.* II. 18. 1.

3 IV. 115, 116.

4 This paragraph is an answer to the question implied in "videbimus" at the end of § 121. The testaments of women under fiduciary tutors will

vel heredem instituat vel nominatim exheredet[1]; alioquin si eum silentio praeterierit, inutiliter testabitur; adeo quidem, ut nostri praeceptores existiment, etiamsi vivo patre filius defunctus sit, neminem heredem ex eo testamento existere posse, scilicet quia statim ab initio non constiterit institutio. sed diversae scholae auctores, siquidem filius mortis patris tempore vivat, sane impedimento eum esse scriptis heredibus et illum ab intestato heredem fieri confitentur: si vero ante mortem patris interceptus sit, posse ex testamento hereditatem adiri putant, nullo iam filio impedimento; quia scilicet existimant (non) statim ab initio inutiliter fieri testamentum filio praeterito. (124.) Ceteras vero liberorum personas si praeterierit testator, valet testamentum. praeteritae istae personae scriptis heredibus
P. 85 in | partem adcrescunt: si sui heredes sint in virilem[2]; si extranei, in dimidiam. id est si quis tres verbi gratia filios heredes

care either to appoint him heir or to disinherit him by name[1]: otherwise, if he pass him over in silence, the testament will be void: so that, according to the opinion of our authorities, even if the son die in the lifetime of his father, no heir can exist under that testament, because the institution was invalid from the very beginning. But the authors of the school opposed to us admit that if the son be alive at the time of the father's death, he undoubtedly stands in the way of the appointed heirs, and becomes heir by intestacy: but they think that if he die before the death of his father, the inheritance can be entered upon in accordance with the testament, the son being now no hindrance: holding that when a son is passed over, the testament is not invalid from the very beginning. 124. But if the testator pass over other classes of descendants, the testament stands good. These persons so passed over attach themselves upon the appointed heirs for a portion; for a proportionate share, if those appointed are *sui heredes*[2]: for a half, if strangers have been appointed. That is, if a man

be supported by the praetor's grant of *bonorum possessio secundum tabulas*, but not those of women in *tutela legitima*. See I. 192. The incompleteness of the paragraph is easily accounted for, if our hypothesis be accepted, that the work of Gaius was merely a republication of his notes for lecture. The doubt which he starts would be explained by him orally.

[1] Ulpian, XXII. 14—23, and Cic. *De Oratore*, I. 38 apud finem.

[2] II. 156. Ulp. XXII. 17.

instituerit et filiam praeterierit, filia adcrescendo pro quarta parte fit heres; et ea ratione id consequitur quod ab intestato patre mortuo habitura esset. at si extraneos ille heredes instituerit et filiam praeterierit, filia adcrescendo ex dimidia parte fit heres. Quae de filia diximus, eadem et de nepote deque omnibus liberorum personis, sive masculini sive feminini sexus, dicta intellegemus. (125.) Quid ergo est? licet eae secundum ea quae diximus scriptis dimidiam partem modo heredibus detrahant, tamen Praetor eis contra tabulas bonorum possessionem promittit, qua ratione extranei heredes a tota hereditate repelluntur: et efficiuntur sine re[1] heredes, et hoc iure utebamur quasi nihil inter feminas et masculos interesset: (126.) set nuper Imperator Antoninus[2] significavit rescripto suo non plus nancisci feminas per bonorum possessionem, quam quod iure adcrescendi consequerentur[3]. quod in emancipatarum quoque

have, for example, instituted three sons as heirs and passed over a daughter, the daughter by attachment becomes heir to one-fourth: and on this principle obtains that share which she would have received if her father had died intestate. But if the man have instituted strangers as heirs and passed over a daughter, the daughter by attachment becomes heir to one-half. All that we have said as to a daughter we shall consider to be said also of a grandson and all classes of descendants, whether of the male or female sex. 125. But what matters it? Although women, according to what we have said, take away only one-half from the appointed heirs, yet the Praetor promises them possession of all the goods in spite of the testament, by which means the stranger heirs are debarred from the entire inheritance, and become heirs without benefit[1]: and this rule we used to follow, as if there were no difference between men and women. 126. But the Emperor Antoninus[2] has lately decided by his rescript that women are to obtain no more by possession of goods than they would obtain by right of attachment[3]. A rule which must be applied to emancipated

[1] II. 148.

[2] Marcus Aurelius. See note on II. 120.

[3] "That they are to have no more by the aid of the praetor than is given to them by the *jus civile.*" Cf. Theophilus, II. 13. 3. Ulpian, XXII. 23. These points and the

persona observandum est, *nempe ut quod* adcrescendi iure habiturae essent, si in potestate fuissent, id ipsum etiam per bonorum possessionem habeant. (127.) Sed si quidem filius a patre exheredetur, nominatim exheredari *debet*, alioquin non *prodest eum* exheredari[1]. nominatim autem exheredari videtur
P. 86 sive ita exhere|detur: TITIUS FILIUS MEUS EXH*ERES ESTO sive ita: FILIUS MEUS* EXHERES ESTO non addicto proprio nomine. (128.) Ceterae vero liberorum personae vel feminini sexus vel masculini satis inter ceteros exheredantur, id est, *his ver*b*is CETERI* OMNES EXHEREDES SUNTO, *quae ver*b*a semper post* institutionem heredum adici solent. Sed hoc ita *est iure civili.*

women as well, so that they are to have by possession of goods exactly what they would have had by right of attachment, if they had been under *potestas*. 127. But if a son be disinherited by a father, he must be disinherited by name, otherwise it is useless for him to be disinherited[1]. A man is considered to be disinherited by name, if he be either disinherited in the words: "Be my son, Titius, disinherited;" or in these: "Be my son disinherited," without the addition of his proper name. 128. But other descendants, whether of the female or male sex are adequately disinherited in a general clause, i.e. in these words: "Be all others disinherited;" words which are usually added after the institution of the heirs. But these rules are so

amending rescript of Antoninus are noticed at considerable length in the Code 6. 28. 4, and we perceive that the matter still gave rise to controversy even in Justinian's time. That emperor effected a final settlement of the dispute by a rescript of the date 531 A.D.

[1] The text is corrected according to Polenaar's suggestion. Böcking proposes to continue the passage "before the appointment of the heir (*i.e.* in a part of the testament preceding the appointment of heir), or in the midst of the appointments of the heirs (if there be several), but he cannot in any case be disinherited by a general clause (*inter ceteros*)." This is a correct statement of the law; but the text does not accord with Böcking's suggestion. The meaning of the last sentence is that he must be named; no general proviso, such as "ceteri exheredes sunto," will suffice to bar him.

We may here remark that the disinheriting of sons or descendants was not allowed to a testator unless he had good cause for setting them aside. In many cases (see Just. *Inst.*, II. 18) children so disinherited could bring the *querela inofficiosi testamenti*, "complaint of the testament not being in accordance with natural affection," and have it annulled. This, however, would be application to the Centumviri, not to the Praetor, and therefore Gaius, commenting only on the Edict, omits all reference to the Querela. See App. E. to Abdy and Walker's edition of Just. *Inst.*

(129.) Nam Praetor omnes virilis sexus lib*erorum personas,* id est nepotes quoque et pronepotes *nominatim exheredari iubet, feminini vero sexus vel nominatim vel inter ceteros: qui nisi fuerint ita exhe*redati, *promittit eis contra tabulas bonorum possessionem.* (130.) Postumi quoque liberi nominatim *heredes insti*tui debent vel exheredari. (131.) Et[1] in eo par omnium conditio *est, quod et in* filio *postumo et in quolibet ex ceteris li*beris, sive *feminini sexus sive ma*sculini, praeterito, valet *quidem testamentum, sed postea adgnatione postumi si*ve postumae rumpitur[2], et ea ra*tione totum infir*matur[3]: *ideo*que si mulier ex qua *postumus aut postu*ma sperabatur abor*tum fecerit, nihil impedimento est scriptis heredibus ad hereditatem adeundam.* (132.) *Sed feminini* quidem sexus personae *vel* nom*inatim vel*

by the civil law only. 129. For the Praetor orders all descendants of the male sex, *i.e.* grandsons also and great-grandsons, to be disinherited by name, but women either by name or in a general clause: and if they be not thus disinherited, he promises them possession of the goods as against the testament. 130. After-born descendants also must either be appointed heirs or disinherited. 131. And[1] in this respect the condition of all of them is the same, that when an after-born son or any other descendant, whether male or female, is passed over, the testament is still valid, but is broken by the subsequent *agnation*[2] of the after-born descendant, male or female, and thus becomes utterly inoperative[3]. And therefore, if a woman, from whom an after-born son or daughter is expected, miscarry, there is nothing to prevent the appointed heirs from entering on the inheritance. 132. But females may

1 A considerable portion of the MS. is lost at this point, and the italicized portions in §§ 131—134. §§ 131—134 are supplied from Justinian's *Institutes* II. 13. See Ulpian, XXII. 21, 22. The meaning of the word *postumus* is discussed in the note on I. 148.

2 By *agnatio* is merely meant the fact of becoming an *agnatus*, which might be either by birth or adoption, or, as in the present case, by conception, for when there is *conubium* the child follows his father's condition, and his rights vest at the time of conception (I. 89). Therefore the testator passes over a *suus heres*, as the child's rights extend back into the testator's lifetime.

3 See Ulp. XXIII. 3; Cic. *De Oratore*, I. 57, constat adgnascendo rumpi testamentum: and *Pro Caecin.* 25, cui filius adgnatus sit, eius testamentum non esse ruptum judica.

*inter ceteros exheredari solent. dum tamen si inter ceteros exheredentur, aliquid eis legetur, ne videantur per oblivio*nem praeteritae *esse: masculini vero sexus perso*nas placuit non aliter
P. 87 recte ex*heredari, nisi nominatim* | *exheredentur, hoc scilicet modo:* *QUICUMQUE MIHI FILIUS GENITUS FUERIT EX*HERES ESTO. (133.) *Postumorum loco sunt*[1] *et hi qui in sui heredis locum succedendo quasi adgnascendo fiunt parenti*bus sui heredes. ut ecce si filium et *ex eo nepotem ne*ptem*ve in* po*testate habeam, quia filius gradu praecedit, is solus iura sui heredis habet, quamvis nepos quoque* et neptis ex *eo in eadem potestate sint; sed si filius meus me vivo moriatur, aut qualibet ratione exeat de potestate mea, incipit nepos neptisve in eius locum succedere, et* eo modo iura suorum he*redum quasi adgnatio*ne nancisci. (134.) Ne ergo eo modo rumpat mihi testa*mentum, sicut ipsum filium vel heredem* instituere vel exheredare debeo, ne non *iure faciam testamentum,*

be disinherited either by name or in a general clause; provided only that if they be disinherited in a general clause, something be left them as a legacy, that they may not seem passed over through forgetfulness. But it has been ruled that males cannot be duly disinherited except they be disinherited by name, that is, in this manner, "Whatever son shall be born to me, let him be disinherited." 133. Those also are classed as after-born children[1], who, by succeeding into the place of a *suus heres*, become *sui heredes* to their ascendants by *quasi-agnation*. For instance, if any man have under his *potestas* a son and a grandson or granddaughter by him, the son alone has the rights of *suus heres*, because he is prior in degree, although the grandson also and the granddaughter by him are under the same *potestas:* but if my son die in my lifetime or depart from my *potestas* by any means, the grandson or granddaughter at once succeeds into his place, and so obtains the rights of a *suus heres* by quasi-agnation. 134. Therefore, to prevent him or her from thus breaking my testament, it is necessary for me to appoint as heir or disinherit the grandson or granddaughter by my son, just as I ought to appoint as

[1] These paragraphs, 133 and 134 to the words: "idque lege Junia Velleia provisum est": are not only found in Just. *Inst.* 2. 13. 2, but also in D. 28. 3. 13, and stated to be taken from *Gaius, Lib. II. Institutionum.*

*ita et ne*potem neptemve ex eo necesse est mihi *vel heredem instituere vel exheredare, ne forte, me vivo filio mortuo, succedendo*
P. 88 *in locum eius nepos neptisve* | quasi adgnatione rumpat testamentum: idque lege Iunia Velleia[1] provisum est: in qua simul exheredationis modus notatur ut virilis sexus nominatim, feminini vel nominatim vel inter ceteros exheredentur, dum tamen iis qui inter ceteros exheredantur aliquid legetur.

135. Emancipatos liberos iure civili neque heredes instituere neque exheredare necesse est, quia non sunt sui heredes. sed Praetor omnes, tam feminini quam masculini sexus, si heredes non instituantur, exheredari iubet, virilis sexus nominatim, feminini vel nominatim vel inter ceteros[2]. quodsi neque heredes instituti fuerint, neque ita, ut supra diximus, exheredati, Praetor promittit eis contra tabulas bonorum possessionem. (135 a.) In potestate patris non sunt qui cum eo civitate Romana donati sunt neque in accipienda civitate Romana pater pet*iit et*

heir or disinherit the son himself to prevent me from making an informal testament: lest, perchance, if my son die in my lifetime, the grandson or granddaughter by succeeding into his place should break my testament by the quasi-agnation: and this is provided by the Lex Junia Velleia[1]: wherein also the mode of disinheritance is specified, viz. that males shall be disinherited by name, females either by name or in a general clause, provided only that some legacy be left to those disinherited in a general clause.

135. According to the civil law it is not necessary either to appoint as heirs or to disinherit emancipated children, because they are not *sui heredes*. But the Praetor orders all, both males and females, to be disinherited, if they be not instituted heirs; those of the male sex by name, those of the female sex either by name or in a general clause[2]. But if they be neither instituted heirs, nor disinherited in the manner we have stated above, the Praetor promises them possession of the goods as against the testament. 135 *a.* Descendants are not in the *potestas* of their ascendant, when they have been presented with Roman citizenship at the same time as the ascendant; if the ascendant, when receiving his citizenship, did not ask and obtain from the

---

1 Passed A.D. 10. 2 Ulpian, XXII. 23.

impetravit a Principe ut eos in potestate haberet, aut si petiit neque impetravit. nam qui in *potestatem* patris ab Imperatore rediguntur nihil differunt ab his (qui in potestate nati sunt).

136. Adoptivi filii, quamdiu manent in adoptionem, naturalium loco sunt: emancipati vero a patre adoptivo neque iure civili, neque quod ad edictum Praetoris pertinet, inter liberos numerantur. (137.) qua ratione accidit, ut ex diverso, quod ad naturalem parentem pertinet, quamdiu quidem sint in adoptiva familia, extraneorum numero habeantur. si vero emancipati
P. 89 fuerint ab adoptivo patre, tunc incipiant | in ea causa esse qua futuri essent, si ab ipso naturali patre (emancipati) fuissent[1].

138. Si quis post factum testamentum adoptaverit sibi filium, aut per populum eum qui sui iuris est, aut per Praetorem[2] eum qui in potestate parentis fuerit, omnimodo testamentum eius rumpitur quasi agnatione sui heredis. (139.) Idem iuris est si

Emperor that he should have them in his *potestas*: or if he asked and did not obtain. For those placed under the father's *potestas* by the Emperor do not differ in the least from those born *in potestate.*

136. Adopted children, so long as they remain in adoption, are in the place of actual children: but when emancipated by their adoptive father, they are not accounted as his children either by the civil law or by the provisions of the Praetor's edict. 137. From which principle it follows, on the other hand, that in respect of their actual father they are considered to be strangers so long as they are in the adoptive family. But if they have been emancipated by the adoptive father, they begin to be in the position in which they would have been, if emancipated by the actual father himself[1].

138. If any man, after making a testament, adopt a son, either one who is *sui iuris* by authority of the *populus*, or one who is under the *potestas* of an ascendant by authority of the Praetor[2], his testament is in all cases broken by this quasi-agnation of a *suus heres.* 139. The rule is the same if a man

[1] Therefore the praetor will grant them *possessio bonorum* of the goods of the actual father. The whole of the regulations as to the claims of adopted children on their actual and adoptive parents were changed by Justinian, whose new system will be found in *Inst.* I. 11. 2; II. 13. 5.

[2] I. 98, 99.

cui post factum testamentum uxor in manum conveniat, vel quae in manu fuit nubat: nam eo modo filiae loco esse incipit[1] et quasi sua. (140.) Nec prodest sive haec, sive ille qui adoptatus est, in eo testamento sit institutus institutave. nam de exheredatione eius supervacuum videtur quaerere, cum testamenti faciundi tempore suorum heredum numero non fuerit[2]. (141.) Filius quoque qui ex prima secundave mancipatione manumittitur[3], quia revertitur in potestatem patriam, rumpit ante factum testamentum. nec prodest (si) in eo testamento heres institutus vel exheredatus fuerit. (142.) Simile ius olim fuit in eius persona cuius nomine ex senatusconsulto[4] erroris causa probatur, quia forte ex peregrina vel Latina, quae per errorem quasi civis Romana uxor ducta esset, natus esset. nam sive

take a wife into *manus* after making a testament, or if a woman already in his *manus* be married to him: for owing to this she is henceforth in the place of a daughter[1] and is a *quasi sua heres*. 140. Nor does it matter if such a woman, or a man who is adopted, have been instituted heir in that testament. For as to disinheriting, it is superfluous to make inquiry, since at the time the testament was made they were not of the class of *sui heredes*[2]. 141. A son also who is manumitted after a first or second mancipation[3], breaks a testament previously made, since he returns into his father's *potestas*. Nor does it matter if he have been instituted heir or disinherited in that testament. 142. Formerly there was a similar rule as to a person with regard to whom a cause of error was proved in accordance with the *senatusconsultum*, because, for instance, he had been born from a foreign or Latin woman, who had been married by mistake, under the impression that she was a Roman citizen[4]. For whether he had been instituted heir

[1] I. 115 *b*.

[2] If they be already instituted in the testament it must be as *extranei* and not as *sui heredes*. Therefore there is a quasi-agnation all the same, there having been no recognition of them in their present character, such recognition in fact having been impossible. "As to disinheriting," Gaius says, "there is no need to make inquiry," for as they were not *sui heredes* when the testament was made there was no need to mention them at all at that time. It is the subsequent quasi-agnation which invalidates the testament, not the fact of their being named or not named in it; for if named, they must have been named in another character.

[3] I. 132—135.

[4] I. 67.

heres institutus esset a parente sive exheredatus, sive vivo patre
P. 90 causa probata sive post mortem eius, omnimodo quasi adgnatione rumpebat testamentum. (143.) Nunc vero ex novo senatusconsulto quod auctore divo Hadriano factum est, si quidem vivo patre causa probatur, aeque ut olim omnimodo rumpit testamentum: si vero post mortem patris, praeteritus quidem rumpit testamentum, si vero heres in eo scriptus est vel exheredatus, non rumpit testamentum; ne scilicet diligenter facta testamenta rescinderentur eo tempore quo renovari non possent.

144. Posteriore quoque testamento quod iure factum est superius rumpitur. nec interest an extiterit aliquis ex eo heres, an non extiterit: hoc enim solum spectatur, an existere potuerit. ideoque si quis ex posteriore testamento quod iure factum est, aut noluerit heres esse, aut vivo testatore aut post mortem eius antequam hereditatem adiret decesserit, aut per cretionem exclusus fuerit[1], aut condicione sub qua heres institutus est

by his ascendant or disinherited, and whether cause had been proved during the lifetime of his father or after his death, in all cases he broke the testament by his quasi-agnation. 143. But now, according to a new *senatusconsultum* which was made at the instance of the late Emperor Hadrian, if cause be proved in the lifetime of the father, he (the son) altogether breaks the testament just as formerly: but if it be proved after the death of the father, he breaks the testament in case he has been passed over, but does not break it in case he has been appointed heir or disinherited therein: this obviously being intended to prevent testaments carefully made from being set aside at a time when they cannot be re-executed.

144. A testament of earlier date is also broken by one duly made at a later period. And it matters not whether any one become heir under the second testament or not: for the only point regarded is whether any one could have become heir. Therefore if any one appointed under the later and duly made testament, either refuse to be heir, or die in the lifetime of the testator or after his death but before entry on the inheritance, or be excluded by cretion[1], or fail to fulfil some condition

[1] II. 168.

defectus sit, aut propter celibatum ex lege Iulia summotus fuerit ab hereditate[1]: quibus casibus paterfamilias intestatus moritur: nam et prius testamentum non valet, ruptum a posteriore, et posterius aeque nullas vires habet, cum ex eo nemo heres extiterit.

145. Alio quoque modo testamenta iure facta infirmantur, velut (cum) is qui fecerit testamentum capite diminutus sit. quod quibus modis accidat, primo commentario relatum est[2]. (146.)
P. 91 Hoc autem casu in|rita fieri testamenta dicemus, cum alioquin et quae rumpuntur inrita fiant; (*et quae statim ab initio non iure fiunt inrita sunt; sed et ea quae iure facta sunt et postea propter capitis diminutionem inrita fiunt*[3] possunt nihilominus rupta dici. sed quia sane commodius erat singulas causas singulis appellationibus distingui, ideo quaedam non iure fieri dicuntur, quaedam iure facta rumpi, vel inrita fieri[4].

under which he was instituted heir, or be debarred from the inheritance by the Lex Julia by reason of celibacy[1]: in all these cases the *paterfamilias* dies intestate, for the earlier testament is void, being broken by the later one; and the later one is equally without force, since no one becomes heir under it.

145. Testaments duly made are invalidated in another way, for instance, if the maker of the testament suffer *capitis diminutio.* In what ways this comes to pass has been explained in the first Commentary[2]. 146. But in this case we shall say that the testaments become *ineffectual;* although, on the other hand, those are also ineffectual which are broken, and those are ineffectual which are made informally from the very beginning: and those too which have been duly made, and afterwards become ineffectual through *capitis diminutio,* might just as well be called broken. But as it is plainly more convenient to distinguish particular cases by particular names, therefore some are said to be made informally, others to be broken after being formally made, or to become ineffectual[4].

---

1 II. 111. This sentence has no apodosis; for *quibus* we must read *his* to close it.

2 I. 159.

3 Two lines have been omitted by the transcriber of the MS., but can be supplied from the parallel passage in Just. *Inst.* II. 17. 5.

4 See Appendix (F).

147. Non tamen per omnia inutilia sunt ea testamenta, quae vel ab initio non iure facta sunt, vel iure facta postea inrita facta aut rupta sunt. nam si septem testium signis signata sint testamenta, potest scriptus heres secundum tabulas bonorum possessionem petere, si modo defunctus testator et civis Romanus et suae potestatis mortis tempore fuerit: nam si ideo inritum fit testamentum, quod puta civitatem vel etiam libertatem testator amisit, aut is in adoptionem se dedit (et) mortis tempore in adoptivi patris potestate fuit, non potest scriptus heres secundum tabulas bonorum possessionem petere. (148.) (Qui autem) secundum tabulas testamenti, quae aut statim ab initio non iure factae sint, aut iure factae postea ruptae vel inritae erunt, bonorum possessionem accipiunt, si modo possunt hereditatem optinere, habebunt bonorum possessionem cum re: si vero ab iis avocari hereditas potest, habebunt bonorum possessionem sine re[1]. (149.) Nam si quis heres iure civili institutus

147. Those testaments, however, are not altogether valueless which either have been made informally at the outset, or though made formally have afterwards become ineffectual or been broken. For if testaments be sealed with the seals of seven witnesses, the appointed heir can claim possession of the goods in accordance with the testament, provided only the deceased testator was a Roman citizen and *sui juris* at the time of his death; for if the testament be ineffectual because, for instance, the testator has lost citizenship, or liberty as well, or because he gave himself in adoption and at the time of his death was under the *potestas* of the adoptive father, then the appointed heir cannot claim possession of the goods in accordance with the testament. 148. Now those who receive possession of the goods in accordance with a testament, which either was made informally from the very beginning, or though made formally was afterwards broken or became ineffectual, if only they can obtain the inheritance, will have the possession of the goods with benefit (*cum re*): but if the inheritance can be wrested from them, they will have the possession of the goods without benefit (*sine re*)[1]. 149. For if any one have

[1] It may very well happen that one man is *heres* according to the civil law, and another *bonorum possessor* according to the Praetor's edict. For example, suppose a man to have a son, whom he has

sit vel ex primo vel ex posteriore testamento, vel ab intestato iure legitimo heres sit, is potest ab iis hereditatem avocare[1]. si vero
P. 92 nemo | sit alius iure civili heres, ipsi retinere hereditatem possunt, *nec* ullum ius adversus eos habent qui bona *petendi* legitimo iure deficiunt. quia aliquando, *ut supra* quoque notavimus, etiam legitimis[2] quoque *heredibus* potiores scripti heredes habentur, *velut si ideo* non *iure* factum sit testamentum quod

been instituted heir according to the civil law either in a former or a later testament, or be heir on intestacy by statutable right, he can wrest the inheritance from them[1]. But if there be no other person heir by the civil law, they may retain the inheritance, nor have those persons any title against them, who are deficient of legal right to claim the goods. Because sometimes, as we have also stated previously, the written heirs have a better title even than the heirs at law[2], as, for instance, when the testament is irregularly made merely by reason that the

---

emancipated: and also suppose a brother to be his nearest agnate, or suppose him to appoint a testamentary heir: the brother or the instituted heir is *heres*, but the Praetor will grant *bonorum possessio* to the son: hence the *hereditas* is *sine re*, the *bonorum possessio* is *cum re*. (See § 135.) Again, the Praetor allowed only a limited time for heirs, whether *scripti* or *ab intestato*, to apply to him for *bonorum possessio* (which it was an advantage to have in addition to *hereditas*, because the Interdict "Quorum Bonorum," described in IV. 144, was attached to it), and if they failed to apply within the time, the *bonorum possessio* would be granted to applicants of the class which came next in order of succession, if it were a case of intestacy; or to the heirs *ab intestato* in the case of neglect of application on the part of an instituted heir: but still in such a case, the heir having merely omitted to secure an additional advantage, and not having forfeited his claim under the civil law, could hold the inheritance against the *bonorum possessor*; and so in this case the *hereditas* was *cum re* and the *bonorum possessio* was *sine re*. See III. 36; Ulpian, XXVIII. 13.

[1] In §§ 148, 149 the two separate cases of a first testament or a second testament being void at the civil law, and *bonorum possessio* nevertheless granted under it, are taken together, and hence a slight confusion. In § 149 the solution of the legal difficulty is given: viz. that if the void testament be a second one, the heir under a valid first testament has *hereditas cum re*: if the invalid testament be the first, it is through the fact of there being a second that it is void, therefore the heir under the second has the *hereditas cum re*, or, at any rate, *bonorum possessio cum re*: if there be but one testament and that void, the *hereditas cum re* goes to the heir on an intestacy.

[2] That is, an heir *ab intestato*, pointed out by the *jus civile*. The term technically means an heir who is not a *suus*, but an *agnatus*. But probably there is here no reference to this distinction. Ulp. XXVIII. 7.

familia non venierit, aut nuncupationis verba testator locutus non sit[1]. (150.) Cum *vero ag*nati petant hereditatem, *per exceptionem doli mali* ex con*stitutione Hadriani*[2]...*remo*veri possunt, neque e lege Julia *scriptis aufertur hereditas, si bonorum* possessores *ex edicto constituti sint. nam ita demum ex ea* lege bona caduca fiunt, et ad populum deferri iubentur, si defuncto nemo *successor extiterit*[3]. (151.) Potest ut iure facta testamenta *contraria voluntate* infirmentur. apparet non posse ex *eo solo infirma*ri test*amentum quod postea* testator *id noluerit* valere[4], usque adeo ut si linum eius inciderit nihilominus iure civili valeat. quin *etiam si* deleverit quoque aut ob*leverit* tabulas testamenti, non ideo minus[5] desinunt valere *quae in testamento fuerunt scripta*, licet eorum probatio d*ifficilis* sit. quid *ergo est?* si quis ab intestate bonorum possessionem petierit, *et is qui* ex eo

estate has not been sold, or that the testator has not spoken the words of nuncupation[1]. 150. But when agnates claim the inheritance, they can be repelled by the exception of fraud in accordance with the S. C. of Hadrian[2]; and by the Lex Julia the inheritance is not taken away from the written heirs, if they are appointed *bonorum possessores* under the provisions of Edict. For according to that Lex the goods only lapse and are to be given to the *populus*, when there is no *successor* to the deceased[3]. (151.) It is possible for testaments duly made to be invalidated by the testator's change of intention. But it appears that a testament cannot be invalidated merely because the testator had a wish that it should not stand[4]; so that even if he has broken the string which tied it, it will still be good by the civil law. And even if he has inserted passages or struck out passages, what was originally in the testament will not the less[5] stand good, though the proof of what that was is difficult. What is the result then? If any one claims possession of the goods as upon an intestacy, and the heir written in

[1] II. 119.

[2] The name of the Emperor is taken from D. 28. 3. 12.

[3] See Ulpian, XVII. 1. 2; XXVIII. 7.

[4] See Just. *Inst.* II. 17. 7. The intention of the testator is not conclusively established, and the destruction of the testament being incomplete, he is rather supposed to have changed his intention that it should not stand.

[5] *Minus* in the text appears to be a mistake for *magis*.

P. 93 testamento heres est petat hereditatem (*desunt 2 lin.*) | perveniat hereditas[1], et hoc ita rescripto Imperatoris Antonini significantur.

152. Heredes autem aut necessarii dicuntur aut sui et necessarii aut extranei.

153. Necessarius heres est servus cum libertate heres institutus; ideo sic appellatus, quia, sive velit sive nolit, omnimodo post mortem testatoris protinus liber et heres est. (154.) Unde qui facultates suas suspectas habet, solet servum primo aut secundo vel etiam ulteriore gradu[2] liberum et heredem instituere, ut si creditoribus satis non fiat, potius huius heredis quam ipsius testatoris bona veneant, id est ut ignominia quae accedit ex venditione bonorum hunc potius heredem quam ipsum testatorem contingat; quamquam aput Fufidium Sabino[3]

the testament claims the inheritance,...the inheritance will pass to him[1]; and so it is stated in a rescript of the Emperor Antoninus. ....

152. Heirs are called either *necessarii*, or *sui et necessarii*, or *extranei*.

153. A necessary heir is a slave instituted with a grant of liberty: so called from the fact that whether he desire it or not, he is in all cases free and heir at once on the death of the testator. 154. Therefore a man who suspects himself to be insolvent generally appoints a slave free and heir in the first, second, or even some more remote place[2], so that if the creditors cannot be paid in full, the goods may be sold as those of this heir rather than of himself: that is to say, that the disgrace accruing from the sale of the goods may fall upon this heir rather than the testator himself: although Sabinus, according to Fufidius[3], thinks the slave should be exempted

---

1 Sc. will pass to the written heir, if the testament be sufficiently good to obtain the Praetor's grant of *bonorum possessio*.

2 II. 174.

3 The phrase "Sabino aput Fufidium" is an ambiguous one. As Fufidius probably lived about A.D. 166, and Sabinus we know was consul in A.D. 69, the translation in our text is justifiable; but there have been commentators who render it "Sabinus in a commentary on Fufidius," thus making Fufidius the earlier writer of the two. Passages where *apud* is used in each of these senses are collected in Smith's *Dict. of Roman and Greek Biography and Mythology*, in the article on Ferox, Urseius, *q.v.* Fufidius wrote a work entitled *Quaestionum*. See D. 34. 2. 5.

placeat eximendum eum esse ignominia, quia non suo vitio, sed necessitate iuris bonorum venditionem pateretur: sed alio iure utimur. (155.) Pro hoc tamen incommodo illut ei commodum praestatur, ut ea quae post mortem patroni sibi adquisierit, sive ante bonorum venditionem sive postea, ipsi reserventur[1]. et quamvis *pro portione*[2] bona venierint, iterum ex hereditaria causa bona eius non venient, nisi si quid ei
P. 94 ex hereditaria causa fuerit adquisitum, | velut si Latini *bonis quae* adquisierit, locupletior factus sit[3]; cum ceterorum hominum quorum bona venierint pro portione, si quid postea adquirant, etiam saepius eorum bona veniri solent.

156. Sui autem et necessarii heredes sunt velut filius filiave, nepos neptisve ex filio, deinceps ceteri, qui modo in potestate

from disgrace, because he suffers the sale not from fault of his own, but from requirement of the law: but we hold to the contrary rule. 155. In return, however, for this disadvantage, there is allowed to him the advantage that whatever he acquires for himself after the death of his patron, whether before the sale of the goods or after, is reserved for himself[1]. And although the goods when sold only pay a part of the debts[2], yet his goods will not be sold a second time on account of the inheritance, unless he has acquired something in connection with the inheritance; for instance[3], if he be enriched by the goods of a Latin which have accrued to him: although when the goods of other men will only pay in part, if they acquire anything afterwards, their goods are sold over and over again.

156. Heirs *sui et necessarii* are such as a son or daughter, a grandson or granddaughter by a son, and others in direct

[1] This is called the *beneficium separationis* by later writers.

[2] The MS. has *propter contractione*.

[3] The reading we have adopted is that of Huschke, and the Latin mentioned will of course be a Latin manumitted by the testator, to whose inheritance therefore the testator's heir succeeds: see III. 56. If we take the old reading "velut si Latinus acquisierit," a second *si* must be understood; "velut si, si Latinus adquisierit, locupletior factus sit." But the explanation of the sentence would be difficult, for although the goods of a deceased Latin belong to his manumittor, that manumittor had no claim on the goods of a living one, and we know of no law putting the manumittor's creditors in a better position than himself. Possibly the mere change of *Latinus* into *Latinum* would convey the same meaning as Huschke's amendment, and keep closer to the text.

morientis fuerunt. sed uti nepos neptisve suus heres sit, non sufficit eum in potestate avi mortis tempore fuisse, sed opus est, ut pater quoque eius vivo patre suo desierit suus heres esse aut morte interceptus aut qualibet ratione liberatus potestate: tum enim nepos neptisve in locum sui patris succedunt. (157.) Sed sui quidem heredes ideo appellantur, quia domestici heredes sunt, et vivo quoque parente quodammodo domini existimantur[1]. unde etiam si quis intestatus mortuus sit, prima causa est in successione liberorum. necessarii vero ideo dicuntur, quia omnimodo, *sive* velint *sive nolint*, *tam* ab intestato quam ex testamento heredes fiunt. (158.) Sed his Praetor permittit abstinere se ab hereditate, ut potius parentis bona veneant[2]. (159.) Idem iuris est et in uxoris persona quae in

descent, provided only they were under the *potestas* of the dying man. But in order that a grandson or granddaughter may be *suus heres*, it is not enough for them to have been under the *potestas* of the grandfather at the time of his death, but it is needful that their father should also have ceased to be *suus heres* in the lifetime of his father, having been either cut off by death or freed from *potestas* in some way or other: for then the grandson or granddaughter succeeds into the place of the father. 157. They are called *sui heredes* because they are heirs of the house, and even in the lifetime of their ascendant are regarded as owners (of the property) to a certain extent[1]. Wherefore, if any one die intestate, the first place in the succession belongs to his descendants. But they are called *necessarii*, because in every case, whether they wish or not, and whether on intestacy or under a testament, they become heirs. 158. But the Praetor permits them to abstain from the inheritance, in order that the goods sold may be their ascendant's (rather than their own[2]). 159. The rule is the same as to a wife who is under *manus*, because she is in

---

[1] Papinian, D. 38. 6. 7, gives another derivation: "suus heres erit cum et ipse fuerit in potestate:" *i.e.* the ascendant had him in his *potestas* and so he was *suus* "belonging to him:" just as land or a chattel was also *suum*, because he had *dominion* over it.

[2] They could not get rid of the appellation of heirs, but they could get rid of all the practical consequences of heirship by this *beneficium abstinendi;* and so the disgrace of the sale (§ 154) fell on the memory of the deceased and not on themselves.

manu est, quia filiae loco est, et in nuru quae in manu filii est, quia neptis loco est. (160.) Quin etiam similiter abstinendi P. 95 potes|tatem facit Praetor etiam ei qui in causa mancipii[1] est, cum liber et heres institutus sit; cum necessarius, non etiam suus heres sit[2], tamquam servus.

161. Ceteri qui testatoris iuri subiecti non sunt extranei heredes appellantur. itaque liberi quoque nostri qui in potestate nostra non sunt, heredes a nobis instituti sicut extranei videntur. qua de causa et qui a matre heredes instituuntur eodem numero sunt, quia feminae liberos in potestate non habent. servi quoque qui cum libertate heredes instituti sunt et postea a domino manumissi, eodem numero habentur[3].

162. Extraneis autem heredibus deliberandi potestas data est de adeunda hereditate vel non adeunda. (163.) Sed sive is cui abstinendi potestas est[4] inmiscuerit se bonis heredita-

the place of a daughter, and as to a daughter-in-law who is under the *manus* of a son, because she is in the place of a granddaughter. 160. Besides, the Praetor grants in like manner a power of abstaining to one who is in the condition called *mancipium*[1], when he is instituted free and heir: since like a slave he is a *heres necessarius*, and not *suus* also[2].

161. All others who are not subject to a testator's authority are called extraneous heirs. Thus, our deseendants not under our *potestas*, when appointed heirs by us, are regarded as extraneous. Wherefore those who are appointed by a mother are in the same class, because women have not their children under their *potestas*. Slaves also who have been instituted heirs with a grant of liberty, if afterwards manumitted by their master, are in the same class[3].

162. To extraneous heirs is allowed a power of deliberating as to entering on the inheritance or not. 163. But if one who has the power of abstaining[4] meddle with the goods

---

[1] The MS. has: Ei qui in causa id est mancipato mancipii est: the words "id est mancipato" being evidently a gloss, which has been transferred into the text.

[2] I. 138. "*Suus* also," *i.e. necessarius et suus.*

This clause explains why a mancipated person should be appointed *free and* heir. A person in *causâ mancipii* is technically a slave. I. 123.

[3] II. 188.

[4] Sc. a *heres suus et necessarius*, I. 158.

riis, sive is cui de adeunda deliberare licet[1], adierit, postea relinquendae hereditatis facultatem non habet, nisi si minor sit annorum XXV. nam huius aetatis hominibus, sicut in ceteris omnibus causis, deceptis, ita etiam si temere damnosam hereditatem susceperint, Praetor succurrit. scio quidem divum Hadrianum etiam maiori XXV. annorum veniam dedisse, cum post aditam hereditatem grande aes alienum quod aditae hereditatis tempore latebat apparuisset[2]. |

P. 96 164. Extraneis heredibus solet cretio dari, id est finis deliberandi, ut intra certum tempus vel adeant hereditatem, vel si non adeant, temporis fine summoveantur. ideo autem cretio appellata est, quia cernere est quasi decernere et constituere[3]. (165.) Cum ergo ita scriptum sit: HERES TITIUS ESTO: adicere debemus, CERNITOQUE IN CENTUM DIEBUS PROXUMIS QUIBUS

of the inheritance, or if one who is allowed to deliberate[1] as to entering on the inheritance enter, he has not afterwards the power of abandoning the inheritance, unless he be under twenty-five years of age. For, as the Praetor gives assistance in all other cases to men of this age who have been deceived, so he does also if they have thoughtlessly taken upon themselves a ruinous inheritance. I am aware, however, that the late emperor Hadrian granted this favour also to one above twenty-five years of age, when after entry on the inheritance a great debt was discovered which was unknown at the time of entry[2].

164. To extraneous heirs "cretion" is usually given, that is, a period in which to deliberate; so that within some specified time they are either to enter on the inheritance, or if they do not enter, are to be set aside at the expiration of the time. It is called cretion because the verb *cernere* means to deliberate and decide[3]. 165. When, therefore, the clause has been written, "Titius be heir," we ought to add, "and make thy cretion within the next hundred days after thou hast

---

[1] Sc. a *heres extraneus*, I. 162.

[2] Gaius does not imply that this was a standing cause of exemption from responsibility: but that it was a *privilegium*, or anomalous favour, granted by Imperial authority in a special case.

[3] Ulpian, XXII. 25—34. "Crevi valet constitui: itaque heres quum constituit se heredem esse, dicitur cernere, et quum id facit, crevisse." Varro, *de L. L.* VII. 98. See also Festus, *sub verbo*.

SCIES POTERISQUE. QUOD NI ITA CREVERIS, EXHERES ESTO. (166.) Et qui ita heres institutus est si velit heres esse, debebit intra diem cretionis cernere, id est haec verba dicere: QUOD ME PUBLIUS *MAEV*IUS TESTAMENTO SUO HEREDEM INSTITUIT, EAM HEREDITATEM ADEO CERNOQUE. quodsi ita non creverit, finito tempore cretionis excluditur: nec quicquam proficit, si pro herede gerat, id est si rebus hereditariis tamquam heres utatur[1]. (167.) At is qui sine cretione heres institutus sit, aut qui ab intestato legitimo iure ad hereditatem vocatur, potest aut cernendo aut pro herede gerendo vel etiam nuda voluntate suscipiendae hereditatis heres fieri: eique liberum est, quocumque tempore voluerit, adire hereditatem. (sed) solet Praetor postulantibus hereditariis creditoribus tempus constituere, intra quod si velit adeat hereditatem: si minus, ut liceat creditoribus bona defuncti vendere. (168.) Si quis autem cum cre-

knowledge and ability. But if thou fail so to make thy cretion be disinherited." 166. And if the heir thus instituted desire to be heir, he ought to make cretion within the time allowed for cretion, *i.e.* speak the words, "Inasmuch as Publius Maevius has instituted me heir in his testament, I enter on that inheritance and make cretion for it." But if he do not so make cretion, he is debarred at the expiration of the time limited for cretion. Nor is it of any avail for him to act as heir, *i.e.* to use the items of the inheritance as though he were heir[1]. 167. But an heir appointed without cretion, or one called to the inheritance by statute law on an intestacy, can become heir either by exercising cretion, or by acting as heir, or even by the bare wish to take up the inheritance: and it is in his power to enter on the inheritance whenever he pleases. But the Praetor usually fixes a time, on the demand of the creditors of the inheritance, within which he may enter on the inheritance if he please, but if he do not enter, then the creditors are allowed to sell the goods of the deceased. 168. Anyone who has been instituted heir with

---

[1] "Pro herede gerere est destinatione futuri dominii aliquid ex hereditariis rebus usurpari. Et ideo pro herede gerere videtur qui fundorum hereditariorum culturas rationesque disponit, et qui servis hereditariis, jumentis rebusve aliis utitur." Paulus, *S. R.* IV. 8. § 25. See also Just. *Inst.* II. 19. 7.

tione | heres institutus est, nisi creverit hereditatem, non fit heres: ita non aliter excluditur, quam si non creverit intra id tempus quo cretio finita sit. itaque licet ante diem cretionis constituerit hereditatem non adire, tamen poenitentia actus superante die cretionis cernendo heres esse potest. (169.) At is qui sine cretione heres institutus est, quique ab intestato per legem vocatur, sicut voluntate nuda heres fit, ita et contraria destinatione statim ab hereditate repellitur. (170.) Omnis autem cretio certo tempore constringitur. in quam rem tolerabile tempus visum est centum dierum: potest tamen nihilominus iure civili aut longius aut brevius tempus dari: longius tamen interdum Praetor coartat. (171.) Et quamvis omnis cretio certis diebus constringatur, tamen alia cretio vulgaris vocatur, alia certorum dierum: vulgaris illa, quam supra exposuimus[1], id est in qua dicuntur haec verba: QUIBUS SCIET POTERITQUE; certorum dierum, in qua detractis his verbis

cretion does not become heir unless he make cretion for the inheritance; so he is not debarred in any other manner than if he fail to make cretion within the time at which the cretion is limited. Therefore, although before the day limiting the cretion he may have decided not to enter on the inheritance, yet on repenting of his act he may become heir by using his cretion, if a portion of the time of cretion still remain. 169. But one who is instituted heir without cretion, or who is called in by law on an intestacy, as on the one hand he becomes heir by bare intent, so on the other, by an opposite determination he is at once excluded from the inheritance. 170. Now every cretion is tied down to some fixed time. For which object a hundred days seems a fair allowance: but nevertheless, at civil law, either a longer or a shorter time can be given, though the Praetor sometimes abridges a longer time. 171. And although every cretion is tied down to some fixed number of days, yet one kind of cretion is called common (*vulgaris*), the other cretion of fixed days (*certorum dierum*): the common is that which we have explained above[1], *i.e.* that in which are used the words, "after he has knowledge and ability:" that of fixed days is the cretion in which the rest of

[1] II. 165.

cetera scribuntur. (172.) Quarum cretionum magna differentia est. nam vulgari cretione data nulli dies conputantur, nisi quibus scierit quisque se heredem esse institutum et possit cernere. certorum vero dierum cretione data etiam nescienti se
P. 98 heredem institutum esse numerantur dies con|tinui; item ei quoque qui aliqua ex causa cernere prohibetur, et eo amplius ei qui sub condicione heres institutus est, tempus numeratur. unde melius et aptius est vulgari cretione uti. (173.) Continua haec cretio vocatur, quia continui dies numerantur. sed quia tam dura est haec cretio, altera in usu habetur: unde etiam vulgaris dicta est.

(174.) Interdum duos pluresve gradus heredum facimus, hoc modo: LUCIUS TITIUS HERES ESTO CERNITOQUE IN DIEBUS (CENTUM) PROXIMIS QUIBUS SCIES POTERISQUE. QUODNI ITA CREVERIS, EXHERES ESTO. TUM MAEVIUS HERES ESTO CERNITOQUE IN DIEBUS CENTUM et reliqua; et deinceps in quantum velimus substituere possumus. (175.) Et licet nobis

the form is written, and these words omitted. 172. Between these cretions there is a great difference: for when common cretion is appointed, no days are taken into account except those whereon the man knows that he is instituted heir, and is able to make his cretion. But when cretion of fixed days is appointed, the days are reckoned continuously, even against one who does not know that he has been instituted heir; likewise the time is counted against one who is prevented by any reason from making his cretion, and further than this, against one who is instituted heir under a condition. Therefore it is better and more convenient to employ common cretion. 173. This cretion is called "continuous," because the days are reckoned continuously. But since this cretion is so strict, the other is generally employed, and therefore is called "common."

174. Sometimes we make two or more degrees of heirs, in this manner: "Lucius Titius be heir, and make thy cretion within the next hundred days after thou hast knowledge and ability. But if thou fail so to make cretion, be disinherited. Then Maevius be heir, and make thy cretion within a hundred days," &c. And so we can substitute successively as far as we wish. 175. And it is in our power to substitute either one per-

vel unum in unius locum substituere pluresve, et contra in plurium locum vel unum vel plures substituere. (176.) Primo itaque gradu scriptus heres hereditatem cernendo fit heres et substitutus excluditur; non cernendo summovetur, etiam si pro herede gerat, et in locum eius substitutus succedit. et deinceps si plures gradus sint, in singulis simili ratione idem contingit. (177.) Set si cretio sine exheredatione sit data, id est in haec verba: SI NON CREVERIS TUM PUBLIUS MAEVIUS HERES ESTO, illut diversum invenitur, quia si prior omissa cretione pro herede gerat, substitutus in partem
P. 99 admittitur, et fiunt ambo aequis partibus | heredes[1]. quod si neque cernat neque pro herede gerat, tum sane in universo summovetur, et substitutus in totam hereditatem succedit. (178.) Sed Sabino quidem placuit, quamdiu cernere et eo modo heres fieri possit prior, etiam si pro herede gesserit, non tamen

son or several in the place of one; and on the other hand, either one or several in the place of several. 176. The heir then, who has been instituted in the first degree, becomes heir by making cretion for the inheritance, and the substitute is excluded: but by not making cretion he is excluded, even though he act as heir, and the substitute succeeds into his place. And so, if there be several degrees, the same thing happens to each successively in like manner. 177. But if cretion be given without disinheritance, *i.e.* in the words, "If thou fail to make cretion, then let Publius Maevius be heir;" this difference is found, that if the heir first named, neglecting his cretion, act as heir, the substitute is admitted to a portion, and both become heirs to equal shares[1]. But if he neither make cretion nor act as heir, he is then undoubtedly debarred altogether, and the substitute succeeds to the entire inheritance. 178. But it was held by Sabinus, that so long as the first-named heir can exercise cretion and so become heir, by his merely acting as heir the substitute is not admitted: but that, when

[1] Ulpian (XXII. 34) calls this *imperfecta cretio.* He also mentions a constitution of Marcus Aurelius by which *gestio pro herede* was made equivalent to *cretio*, and gave the whole inheritance to the heir first named. So that either Gaius has here made a slip, or the decree came out after this portion of the commentary was written. The comparison of § 178 with this paragraph would point to the latter conclusion.

admitti substitutum: cum vero cretio finita sit, tum pro herede gerente admitti substitutum: aliis vero placuit, etiam superante cretione posse eum pro herede gerendo in partem substitutum admittere et amplius ad cretionem reverti non posse.

179. Liberis nostris inpuberibus quos in potestate habemus non solum ita, ut supra diximus, substituere possumus, id est ut si heredes non extiterint, alius nobis heres sit; sed eo amplius, ut etiam si heredes nobis extiterint et adhuc inpuberes mortui fuerint, sit iis aliquis heres[1], velut hoc modo: TITIUS FILIUS MEUS MIHI HERES ESTO. SI FILIUS MEUS MIHI (*HERES NON ERIT SIVE HERES*) ERIT ET HIC PRIUS MORIATUR QUAM IN SUAM TUTELAM VENERIT, TUNC SEIUS HERES ESTO. (180.) Quo casu si quidem non extiterit heres filius, substitutus patri fit heres: (si vero) heres extiterit filius et ante pubertatem decesserit, ipsi filio fit heres substitutus. quamobrem duo quodam-
P.100 modo sunt testamenta: | aliut patris, aliut filii, tamquam si

the time for cretion has elapsed, then by his acting as heir the substitute is admitted: whilst others have held that even if the time for cretion be unexpired, yet by acting as heir he lets in the substitute to a portion, and cannot afterwards fall back upon his cretion.

179. We can substitute to our descendants under the age of puberty whom we have in our *potestas*, not only in the way we have described above, *i.e.* that if they do not become our heirs, some one else may be *our* heir: but further than this, so that even if they do become our heirs, and die whilst still under puberty, some one else shall be *their* heir[1]; for example, thus: "Titius, my son, be my heir. If my son shall not become my heir, or if he become my heir and die before he comes into his own governance, then Seius be heir." 180. In which case, if the son do not become heir, the substitute becomes heir to the father: but if the son become heir and die before puberty, the substitute becomes heir to the son himself. Wherefore there are, in a manner, two testaments: one of the father, another of the son, as though the son had

[1] Ulpian, XXIII. 7—9. In the last of these paragraphs it is laid down much more plainly than by Gaius (though he too implies the fact throughout) that the testament for the pupil must be an appendage to a testament of the ascendant, and cannot exist otherwise.

ipse filius sibi heredem instituisset; aut certe unum est testamentum duarum hereditatum.

181. Ceterum ne post obitum parentis periculo insidiarum subiectus videretur pupillus, in usu est vulgarem quidem substitutionem palam facere, id est eo loco quo pupillum heredem instituimus. vulgaris substitutio ita vocat ad hereditatem substitutum, si omnino pupillus heres non extiterit; quod accidit cum vivo parente moritur, quo casu nullum substituti maleficium suspicari possumus, cum scilicet vivo testatore omnia quae in testamento scripta sint ignorentur. illam autem substitutionem per quam, si etiam heres extiterit pupillus et intra pubertatem decesserit, substitutum vocamus, separatim in inferioribus tabulis scribimus, easque tabulas proprio lino propriaque cera consignamus; et in prioribus tabulis cavemus, ne inferiores tabulae vivo filio et adhuc inpubere aperiantur. set longe tutius est utrumque genus substitutionis separatim in inferioribus tabulis consignari, quod si ita consignatae vel separatae fuerint substitutiones, ut diximus, ex priore potest
P.101 intellegi in altera quoque idem esse substitutus. |

instituted an heir for himself: or at any rate there is one testament regarding two inheritances.

181. But lest there should be a likelihood of the pupil being exposed to foul play after the death of his ascendant, it is usual to make the vulgar substitution openly, *i.e.* in the clause where we institute the pupil heir. The vulgar substitution calls the substitute to the inheritance in case the pupil do not become heir at all: which occurs when he dies in his ascendant's lifetime, a case wherein we can suspect no evil act on the part of the substitute, since plainly whilst the testator lives, all that is written in his testament is unknown: but the other substitution whereby we call in the substitute if the pupil become heir and die under the age of puberty, we write separately in the concluding tablets, and seal up these tablets with a string and seal of their own: and we insert a proviso in the earlier tablets, that the concluding tablets are not to be opened whilst the son is alive and under puberty. But it is by far the safer method to seal up both kinds of substitution in the concluding tablets, because if the substitutions have been sealed up or separated in the manner we

182. Non solum autem heredibus institutis inpuberibus liberis ita substituere possumus, ut si ante pubertatem mortui fuerint, sit is heres quem nos voluerimus, sed etiam exheredatis. itaque eo casu si quid pupillo ex hereditatibus legatisve aut donationibus propinquorum adquisitum fuerit, id omne ad substitutum pertinet. (183.) Quaecumque diximus de substitutione inpuberum liberorum, vel heredum institutorum vel exheredatorum, eadem etiam de postumis intellegemus[1].

184. Extraneo vero heredi instituto ita substituere non possumus, ut si heres extiterit et intra aliquod tempus decesserit, alius ei heres sit: sed hoc solum nobis permissum est, ut eum per fideicommissum[2] obligemus, ut hereditatem nostram totam vel (pro) parte restituat; quod ius quale sit, suo loco trademus.

185. Sicut autem liberi homines, ita et servi, tam nostri quam alieni, heredes scribi possunt[3]. (186.) Sed noster servus

have described, it can easily be guessed from the first that the substitute is the same in the second.

182. We can not only substitute to descendants under puberty who are instituted heirs, in such manner that if they die under puberty he whom we choose shall be heir, but we can also substitute to disinherited children. In that case, therefore, if anything be acquired by the pupil from inheritances, legacies or gifts of relations, the whole of it belongs to the substitute. 183. All that we have said as to the substitution of descendants under puberty, whether instituted heirs or disinherited, we shall also understand to apply to after-born children[1].

184. But if a stranger be instituted heir, we cannot substitute to him in such manner, that if he become our heir and die within some specified time, some other person is to be his heir: but this alone is permitted us, that we may bind him by *fideicommissum*[2] to deliver over our inheritance wholly or in part: the nature of which rule we will explain in its proper place.

185. Slaves, whether our own or belonging to other people, can be appointed heirs, just as well as free men[3]. 186. But

---

[1] I. 147 *n.* [2] II. 246 et seqq.; II. 277. [3] Ulpian, XXII. 7—13.

simul et liber et heres esse iuberi debet, id est hoc modo: STICHUS SERVUS MEUS LIBER HERESQUE ESTO, vel HERES LIBERQUE ESTO. (187.) Nam si sine libertate heres institutus sit, etiam si postea manumissus fuerit a domino, heres esse non potest, quia institutio in persona eius non constitit; ideoque licet alienatus sit, non potest iussu domini novi cernere hereditatem[1].

P.102 188. Cum libertate vero heres | institutus, si quidem in eadem causa duraverit, fit ex testamento liber et inde necessarius heres[2]. si vero ab ipso testatore manumissus fuerit, suo arbitrio hereditatem adire potest. quodsi alienatus sit, iussu novi domini adire hereditatem debet, qua ratione per eum dominus fit heres: nam ipse neque heres neque liber esse potest[3]. (189.) Alienus

it is necessary to appoint our own slave simultaneously free and heir, *i.e.* in this manner: "Let Stichus, my slave, be free and heir," or "be heir and free." 187. For if he be instituted heir without a gift of liberty, although he afterwards be manumitted by his master, he cannot be heir, because the institution was invalid in his then status; and therefore, even if he be alienated, he cannot make cretion for the inheritance at the order of his new master[1].

188. When, however, he is instituted with a gift of freedom, if he remain in the same condition, he becomes by virtue of the testament free, and therefore necessary heir[2]. But if he be manumitted by the testator himself, he can enter on the inheritance at his own pleasure. If again he have been alienated, he must enter on the inheritance at the command of his new master, and so by his means the master becomes heir: for he cannot himself become either heir or free[3]. 189. When another

[1] II. 164. Justinian altered the law on this point, so that thenceforward the appointment of a slave as heir gave him liberty by implication. *Inst.* II. 14. *pr.*

[2] II. 153.

[3] The due appointment of an heir is the foundation of the whole testament (II. 116): if the appointment be invalid, the testament fails utterly; but if a legacy fail, the residue of the testament stands good. The appointment of the slave as heir, in the present case, is valid, but for juridical reasons he inherits for the benefit of another: the gift of liberty is regarded as a legacy, and therefore the impossibility of its being received is, by the above principle, a matter of minor importance, not, at any rate, causing the inheritance to fail.

quoque servus heres institutus, si in eadem causa duraverit, iussu domini hereditatem adire debet; si vero alienatus ab eo fuerit, aut vivo testatore aut post mortem eius antequam cernat, debet iussu novi domini cernere. si vero manumissus est, suo arbitrio adire hereditatem potest. (190.) Si autem servus alienus heres institutus est vulgari cretione data[1], ita intellegitur dies cretionis cedere, si ipse servus scierit se heredem institutum esse, nec ullum impedimentum sit, quominus certiorem dominum faceret, ut illius iussu cernere possit.

191. Post haec videamus de legatis[2]. quae pars iuris extra propositam quidem materiam videtur[3]; nam loquimur de his iuris figuris quibus per universitatem res nobis adquiruntur. sed cum omnimodo de testamentis deque heredibus qui testamento instituuntur locuti sumus, non sine causa sequenti loco
P.103 poterit haec iuris materia tractari.

man's slave is instituted heir, if he remain in the same condition, he must enter on the inheritance by command of his master: but if he be alienated by him, either in the testator's lifetime or after his death, and before he has made cretion, he must make cretion by order of his new master. But if he be manumitted, he can enter on the inheritance at his own pleasure. 190. Further, if another man's slave be instituted heir, and common cretion[1] appointed, the time of cretion is only considered to begin to run, when the slave knows that he is instituted heir, and there is no hindrance to his informing his master, so that he may make cretion at his command.

191. Next, let us consider legacies[2]. Which portion of law seems indeed beyond the subject we proposed to ourselves[3]: for we are speaking of those legal methods whereby things are acquired for us in the aggregate: but as we have discussed all points relating to testaments and heirs who are appointed in testaments, this matter of law may with good reason be discussed in the next place.

---

[1] II. 173.

[2] "Legatum est quod legis modo, id est imperative, testamento relinquitur. Nam ea quae precativo modo relinquuntur fideicommissa vocantur." Ulpian, XXIV. 1. "Legatum est donatio quaedam a defuncto relicta." *Inst.* II. 20. 1.

[3] II. 97. *Per universitatem.*

192. Legatorum utique genera sunt quattuor[1]: aut enim per vindicationem legamus, aut per damnationem, aut sinendi modo, aut per praeceptionem.

193. Per vindicationem hoc modo legamus: TITIO verbi gratia HOMINEM STICHUM DO LEGO. set (et) si alterutrum verbum positum sit, veluti DO aut LEGO, aeque per vindicationem legatum est. item ut magis visum est, si ita legatum fuerit: SUMITO, vel ita: SIBI HABETO, vel ita: CAPITO, aeque per vindicationem legatum est. (194.) Ideo autem per vindicationem legatum appellatur, quia post aditam hereditatem statim ex iure Quiritium res legatarii fit; et si eam rem legatarius vel ab herede vel ab alio quocumque qui eam possidet petat, vindicare[2] debet, id est intendere suam rem ex iure Quiritium esse. (195.) In eo solo dissentiunt prudentes, quod Sabinus quidem et Cassius ceterique nostri praeceptores quod ita legatum sit statim post aditam hereditatem putant fieri legatarii, etiamsi ignoret sibi

192. There are then four kinds of legacies[1]: for we either give them by vindication, by damnation, by way of permitting, or by preception.

193. We give a legacy by vindication in the following manner: "I give and bequeath the man Stichus," for example, "to Titius." But if only one of the two words be used, for instance, "I give" or "I bequeath," still it is a legacy by vindication. And further, according to the prevalent opinion, if the legacy be given thus, "let him take," or thus, "let him have for himself," or thus, "let him acquire," it is still a legacy by vindication. 194. The legacy "by vindication" is so called because, after the inheritance is entered upon, the thing at once becomes the property of the legatee by Quiritary title; and if the legatee demand the thing either from the heir or from any other person who is in possession of it, he must proceed by vindication[2], *i.e.* plead that the thing is his by Quiritary title. 195. On the following point alone do lawyers differ, for Sabinus and Cassius and the rest of our authorities hold that what is left as a legacy in this way becomes the property of the legatee at the moment when the inheritance is entered on, even if the legatee be ignorant that the legacy has

[1] Ulpian, XXIV. 2—14. [2] IV. 1—5.

legatum esse dimissum, et postea quam scierit et *spre*verit[1] legatum, tum perinde esse atque si legatum non esset: Nerva vero et Proculus ceterique illius scholae auctores non aliter putant rem legatarii fieri, quam si voluerit eam ad se pertinere.
P.104 sed hodie ex divi Pii Antonini | constitutione hoc magis iure uti videmur quod Proculo placuit. nam cum legatus fuisset Latinus per vindicationem coloniae: deliberent, inquit, decuriones an ad se velint pertinere, proinde ac si uni legatus esset. (196.) Eae autem solae res per vindicationem legantur recte quae ex iure Quiritium ipsius testatoris sunt. sed eas quidem res quae pondere, numero, mensura constant, placuit sufficere si mortis tempore sint ex iure Quiritium testatoris, veluti vinum, oleum, frumentum, pecuniam numeratam. ceteras res vero placuit utroque tempore testatoris ex iure Quiritium esse debere, id est et quo faceret testamentum et quo moreretur: alioquin inutile est legatum. (197.) Sed sane hoc

been left to him; and that only after he has become aware of it and refused it[1] is it as though it had not been bequeathed: whilst Nerva and Proculus and the other authorities of that school hold that the thing does not become the legatee's, unless he have the intent that it shall belong to him. But at the present day, judging from a constitution of the late emperor Pius Antoninus, we seem rather to follow the rule of Proculus: for when a Latin had been left as a legacy by vindication to a colony: "let the *decuriones*[2]," he said, "consider whether they wish him to belong to them, in the same manner as if he had been bequeathed to an individual." 196. Those things alone can be bequeathed effectually by vindication which belong to the testator himself by Quiritary title. But as to those things which depend on weight, number, or measure, it has been ruled that it is sufficient if they be the testator's by Quiritary title at the time of his death; for instance, wine, oil, corn, coin: whilst it has been ruled that other things ought to be the testator's by Quiritary title at both times, that is to say, both at the time he made the testament and at the time he died; otherwise the legacy is invalid. 197. This is so un-

[1] *Spreverit.* This is Niebuhr's suggestion, which Göschen and Huschke approve. The MS. has CEERIT.

[2] See Appendix (I).

ita est iure civili. postea vero auctore Nerone Caesare senatusconsultum factum est, quo cautum est, ut si eam rem quisque legaverit quae eius numquam fuerit, perinde utile sit legatum, atque si optimo iure relictum esset[1]. optumum autem ius est per damnationem legatum; quo genere etiam aliena res legari potest, sicut inferius apparebit[2]. (198.) Sed si quis rem suam legaverit, deinde post testamentum factum eam alienaverit, plerique putant non solum iure civili inutile esse legatum, sed
P.105 nec ex senatusconsulto confirmari. quod ideo dictum | est, quia etsi per damnationem aliquis rem suam legaverit eamque postea alienaverit, plerique putant, licet ipso iure debeatur legatum, tamen legatarium petentem posse per exceptionem doli mali[3] repelli quasi contra voluntatem defuncti petat. (199.) Illut constat, si duobus pluribusve per vindicationem eadem res legata sit, sive coniunctim sive disiunctim, et omnes veniant

doubtedly by the civil law. But afterwards, at the instance of Nero Caesar, a *senatusconsultum* was enacted, wherein it was provided that if a man bequeathed a thing which had never been his, the legacy should be as valid as if it had been bequeathed in the most advantageous form[1]. Now the most advantageous form is a legacy by damnation: by which kind even the property of another can be bequeathed, as will appear below[2]. 198. But if a man bequeath a thing of his own, and then after the making of his testament alienate it, it is the general opinion that the legacy is not only invalid at the civil law, but that it is not even upheld by the *senatusconsultum*. The reason of this being so laid down is that it is generally held that even if a man's bequest of his property be by damnation and he afterwards alienate it, although by the letter of the law the legacy is due, yet the legatee on demanding it will be defeated by an exception of fraud[3], because he makes demand contrary to the intent of the deceased. 199. It is an acknowledged rule that if the same thing be left to two or more persons by vindication, whether conjointly or disjointly, and if all

[1] Nero's S. C. enacted that when a legacy was invalid on account of improper words being used, and there was no other objection to be taken to it, the legacy should be upheld: "ut quod minus pactis (aptis?) verbis legatum est, perinde sit ac si optimo iure legatum esset." Ulpian, XXIV. 11 *a*.

[2] II. 202.

[3] IV. 115 et seqq.

ad legatum, partes ad singulos pertinere, et deficientis portionem collegatario adcrescere. coniunctim autem ita legatur: TITIO ET SEIO HOMINEM STICHUM DO LEGO; disiunctim ita: LUCIO TITIO HOMINEM STICHUM DO LEGO. SEIO EUNDEM HOMINEM DO LEGO. (200.) Illut quaeritur, quod sub condicione per vindicationem legatum est pendente condicione cuius esset. Nostri praeceptores heredis esse putant exemplo statuliberi[1], id est eius servi qui testamento sub aliqua condicione liber esse iussus est, quem constat interea heredis servum esse. sed diversae scholae auctores putant nullius interim eam rem esse; quod multo magis dicunt de eo quod sine condicione pure legatum est, antequam legatarius admittat legatum.

201. Per damnationem hoc modo legamus: HERES MEUS STICHUM SERVUM MEUM DARE DAMNAS ESTO. sed et si DATO
P.106 scriptum fuerit per damnationem legatum est. (202.) Eoque genere legati etiam aliena res legari potest, ita ut heres redi-

accept the legacy, equal portions go to each, and that the portion of one not taking accrues to his co-legatee. Now a legacy is left conjointly thus: "I give and bequeath the man Stichus to Titius and Seius;" disjointly, thus: "I give and bequeath to Lucius Titius the man Stichus. I give and bequeath to Seius the same man." 200. This question arises, whose is a legacy left by vindication under a condition, whilst the condition is unfulfilled? Our authorities think it belongs to the heir, after the precedent of the *statuliber*[1], *i.e.* the slave who is ordered in a testament to become free under some condition, and who, it is admitted, is the slave of the heir for the meantime. But the authorities of the opposite school think that the thing belongs to no one in the interim: and they assert this still more strongly of a thing left simply without condition, before the legatee accepts the legacy.

201. We bequeath by damnation in the following manner: "Let my heir be bound to give my slave Stichus:" and it is also a legacy by damnation if the wording be "let him give." 202. And by this kind of legacy even a thing belonging to another may be bequeathed, so that the heir has to purchase

---

[1] Ulpian, II. 1, 2.

mere et praestare aut aestimationem eius dare debeat. (203.) Ea quoque res quae in rerum natura non est, si modo futura est, per damnationem legari potest, velut fructus qui in illo fundo nati erunt, aut quod ex illa ancilla natum erit. (204.) Quod autem ita legatum est, post aditam hereditatem, etiamsi pure legatum est, non ut per vindicationem legatum continuo legatario adquiritur, sed nihilominus heredis est. et ideo legatarius in personam agere debet, id est intendere heredem sibi dare oportere[1]: et tum heres, si mancipi sit, mancipio dare[2] aut in iure cedere[3] possessionemque tradere debet; si nec mancipi sit, sufficit si tradiderit. nam si mancipi rem tantum tradiderit, nec mancipaverit, usucapione pleno iure fit legatarii: completur autem usucapio, sicut alio quoque loco diximus[4], mobilium quidem rerum anno, earum vero quae solo tenentur, biennio. (205.) Est et illa differentia huius (et) per vindicatio-

and deliver it or give its value. 203. By damnation also can be bequeathed a thing which is not in existence, if only it will come into existence, as for instance, the fruits which shall spring up in a certain field, or the offspring which shall be born from a certain female slave. 204. A thing thus bequeathed does not at once vest in the legatee after the inheritance is entered upon, like a legacy by vindication, even though it be bequeathed unconditionally, but still belongs to the heir. Therefore the legatee must bring a personal action, *i.e.* plead that the heir is bound to give him the thing[1]: and then, if it be a thing mancipable, the heir must give it by mancipation[2] or by cession in court[3], and deliver up the possession: if it be a thing non-mancipable, it is enough that he deliver it. For if he merely deliver a thing mancipable without mancipating it, it becomes the legatee's in full title by usucapion: and usucapion, as we have also said in another place[4], is completed in the case of moveable things in one year, but in the case of those connected with the soil in two. 205. There is also this difference between this legacy and one by vindication, that supposing the same thing be bequeathed to

---

[1] IV. 2.
[2] I. 119.
[3] II. 24.
[4] II. 41.

nem legati quod si eadem res duobus pluribusve per damnationem legata sit, si quidem coniunctim, plane singulis partes debentur sicut in illo vindicationis legato, si vero disiunctim,
P.107 singulis solida res debetur; ita fit | ut scilicet heres alteri rem, alteri aestimationem eius praestare debeat. et in coniunctis deficientis portio non ad collegatarium pertinet, sed in hereditate remanet.

206. Quod autem diximus deficientis portionem in per damnationem quidem legato in hereditate retineri, in per vindicationem vero collegatario accrescere, admonendi sumus ante legem Papiam hoc iure civili ita fuisse: post legem vero Papiam[1] deficientis portio caduca fit et ad eos pertinet qui in eo testamento liberos habent. (207.) Et quamvis prima causa sit in caducis vindicandis heredum liberos habentium, deinde, si heredes liberos non habeant, legatariorum liberos habentium, tamen ipsa lege Papia significatur, ut collegatarius coniunctus, si liberos habeat, potior sit heredibus, etiamsi liberos

two or more persons by damnation, if it be conjointly, clearly equal portions are due to each as in the legacy by vindication: but if disjointly, the whole thing is due to each, and so it results that the heir must give up the thing to one and its value to the other. Also, in conjoint legacies, the portion of one who fails to take does not belong to his co-legatee, but remains in the inheritance.

206. But as to our statement that the portion of one failing to take is retained in the inheritance in the case of a legacy by damnation, but accrues to the co-legatee in the case of one by vindication: we must be reminded that this was so by the civil law before the Lex Papia: but that now since the passing of the Lex Papia[1], the portion of one failing to take becomes a lapse, and belongs to those persons named in the testament who have children. 207. And although in claiming lapses, the first right belongs to the heirs who have children, and then, if the heirs have no children, the right belongs to the legatees who have children, yet it is laid down in the Lex Papia itself, that a co-legatee conjoined (with the person who fails to take), if he have children, is to have a claim prior to that of the

[1] A.D. 10. See (H) in Appendix.

habebunt. (208.) Set plerisque placuit, quantum ad hoc ius quod lege Papia coniunctis constituitur, nihil interesse utrum per vindicationem an per damnationem legatum sit.

209. Sinendi modo ita legamus: HERES MEUS DAMNAS ESTO SINERE LUCIUM TITIUM HOMINEM STICHUM SUMERE SIBIQUE HABERE. (210.) Quod genus legati plus quidem habet (quam) per vindicationem legatum, minus autem quam per damna-
P.108 tionem. nam eo modo non solum suam rem | testator utiliter legare potest, sed etiam heredis sui: cum alioquin per vindicationem nisi suam rem legare non potest; per damnationem autem cuiuslibet extranei rem legare potest. (211.) Sed si quidem mortis testatoris tempore res vel ipsius testatoris sit vel heredis, plane utile legatum est, etiamsi testamenti faciendi tempore neutrius fuerit. (212.) Quodsi post mortem testatoris ea res heredis esse coeperit, quaeritur an utile sit legatum. et plerique putant inutile esse: quit ergo est? licet aliquis eam rem legaverit quae neque eius umquam fuerit, neque postea

heirs, even though they have children. 208. But so far as concerns this right established by the Lex Papia for conjoint legatees, it is generally held that it is immaterial whether the legacy be by vindication or by damnation.

209. We bequeath "by way of permitting" thus: "Let my heir be bound to allow Lucius Titius to take the slave Stichus and have him for himself." 210. Which kind of legacy is more efficient than one by vindication, but less efficient than one by damnation. For in this way a testator can validly bequeath not only his own property, but also that of his heir: whereas, on the other hand, by vindication he cannot bequeath anything but his own property: whilst by damnation he can bequeath the property of any stranger. 211. Now if the thing at the time of the testator's death belong either to him or to the heir, the legacy is undoubtedly valid, even though it belonged to neither at the time the testament was made. 212. But if the thing commenced to be the property of the heir after the death of the testator, it is a disputed point whether the legacy is valid: and the general opinion is that it is void. What follows then? Although a man have bequeathed a thing which was neither his at any time nor ever subsequently began to be the property of his heir, yet

heredis eius umquam esse coeperit, ex senatusconsulto Neroniano proinde videtur ac si per damnationem relicta esset[1]. (213.) Sicut autem per damnationem legata res non statim post aditam hereditatem legatarii efficitur, sed manet heredis eo usque, donec is heres tradendo vel mancipando vel in iure cedendo legatarii eam fecerit; ita et in sinendi modo legato iuris est: et ideo huius quoque legati nomine in personam actio est QUIDQUID HEREDEM EX TESTAMENTO DARE FACERE OPORTET[2]. (214.) Sunt tamen qui putant ex hoc legato non videri obligatum heredem, ut mancipet aut in iure
P.109 cedat | aut tradat, sed sufficere, ut legatarium rem sumere patiatur; quia nihil ultra ei testator imperavit, quam ut sinat, id est patiatur legatarium rem sibi habere. (215.) Maior illa dissensio in hoc legato intervenit, si eandem rem duobus pluribusve disiunctim legasti: quidam putant utrisque solidum deberi, sicut per damnationem[3]: nonnulli occupantis esse me-

by the *senatusconsultum* of Nero, it is regarded as if left by damnation[1]. 213. In like manner as a thing bequeathed by damnation does not become the property of the legatee immediately the inheritance is entered on, but remains the heir's, until the heir makes it the legatee's by delivery, or mancipation, or cession in court: so also is the law regarding a legacy *sinendi modo:* and therefore in respect of this legacy also the action is personal, running thus: "whatsoever the heir ought to give or do according to the testament[2]." 214. There are, however, people who think that in this kind of legacy the heir is not to be considered bound to mancipate, make cession in court, or deliver, but that it is enough for him to allow the legatee to take the thing: because the testator laid no charge on him except that he should allow, *i.e.* suffer the legatee to have the thing for himself. 215. The following more important dispute arises with regard to this kind of legacy, if you have bequeathed the same thing to two or more disjointly: some think the whole is due to each, as in a legacy by damnation[3]: some consider that the condition of the one

[1] Ulp. XXIV. 11 *a*.
[2] IV. 2.
[3] The MS. has *per vindicationem*, an obvious blunder.

liorem condicionem aestimant, quia cum eo genere legati damnetur heres patientiam praestare, ut legatarius rem habeat, sequitur, ut si priori patientiam praestiterit, et is rem sumpserit, securus sit adversus eum qui postea legatum petierit, quia neque habet rem, ut patiatur eam ab eo sumi, neque dolo malo fecit quominus eam rem haberet.

216. Per praeceptionem hoc modo legamus: LUCIUS TITIUS HOMINEM STICHUM PRAECIPITO. (217.) Sed nostri quidem praeceptores nulli alii eo modo legari posse putant, nisi ei qui aliqua ex parte heres scriptus esset: praecipere enim esse praecipuum sumere; quod tantum in eius personam procedit qui aliqua ex parte heres institutus est, quod is extra portionem hereditatis praecipuum legatum habiturus sit[1]. (218.) Ideoque si extraneo legatum fuerit, inutile est legatum, adeo ut
P.110 Sabinus | existimaverit ne quidem ex senatusconsulto Neroniano posse convalescere: nam eo, inquit, senatusconsulto ea tantum

who first gets possession is the better, because, since in this description of legacy the heir is bound to suffer the legatee to have the thing, it follows that if he suffer the first legatee and he take the thing, he is secure against the other who subsequently demands the legacy, because he neither has the thing, so as to allow it to be taken from him; nor has he fraudulently caused himself not to have it.

216. By preception we bequeath in this manner: "Let Lucius Titius first take the man Stichus." 217. But our authorities think that a bequest cannot be made in this form to any one who is not appointed heir in part: for *praecipere* means to take in advance: which only is possible in the case of one who is appointed heir to some part, since he can have the legacy in advance and clear of his share of the inheritance[1]. 218. Therefore if the legacy have been left to a stranger, the legacy is void, so that Sabinus thought it could not even stand by virtue of Nero's *senatusconsultum:* for he says, by that *senatusconsulatum* those bequests alone are upheld which are

[1] He is ordered to take "in advance." "In advance" must mean before he takes some other benefit: now an ordinary legatee takes nothing but his legacy, and therefore *praecipito* must refer to an heir, the only legatee whom we can conceive as taking beforehand another benefit in addition to his legacy.

confirmantur quae verborum vitio iure civili non valent, non quae propter ipsam personam legatarii non deberentur. sed Iuliano ex Sexto[1] placuit etiam hoc casu ex senatusconsulto confirmari legatum: nam ex verbis etiam hoc casu accidere, ut iure civili inutile sit legatum, inde manifestum esse, quod eidem aliis verbis recte legatur, velut per vindicationem et per damnationem et sinendi modo: tunc autem vitio personae legatum non valere, cum ei legatum sit cui nullo modo legari possit, velut peregrino cum quo testamenti factio non sit[2]; quo plane casu senatusconsulto locus non est. (219.) Item nostri praeceptores quod ita legatum est nulla ratione putant posse consequi eum cui ita fuerit legatum quam iudicio familiae erciscundae[3] quod inter heredes de hereditate erciscunda, id est dividunda accipi solet: officio[4] enim iudicis id contineri, ut ei quod per praeceptionem legatum est adiudi-

invalid at the civil law through an error of wording, not those which are not due on account on the very character of the legatee. But Julianus, according to Sextus[1], thought that the legacy was in this case upheld by the *senatusconsultum:* because from the following consideration it was plain that in this case too the wording caused the invalidity of the bequest at the civil law, viz. that the legacy could be validly left in other words to the same person, as for instance, by vindication or damnation or *sinendi modo:* and (he said) that a legacy was invalid from defect of the person only when the legacy was to one to whom a legacy could by no means be given, for instance, to a foreigner with whom there is no *testamenti factio*[2]*:* in which case undoubtedly the *senatusconsultum* is inapplicable. 219. Likewise, our authorities think the legatee can obtain a legacy left in this manner by no other means than a *judicium familiae erciscundae*[3], which is usually employed between heirs for the purpose of "erciscating," *i.e.* dividing the inheritance: for it appertains to the executive power[4] of the *judex* to assign to him the legacy by

[1] Sextus has been usually understood to denote Pomponius. Mommsen, however, suggests that the reference is to Sextus Caecilius Africanus, a pupil of Julianus. Hence, he prefers the original reading of the MS., *ex*, to the interlinear correction, *et*.

[2] See note on II. 114.

[3] IV. 42.

[4] Dirksen, *sub verbo*, § 2. A. *Officium = muneris partes, exsecutio.*

cetur. (220.) Unde intellegimus nihil aliut secundum nostrorum praeceptorum opinionem per praeceptionem legari posse, nisi quod testatoris sit: nulla enim alia res quam hereditaria deducitur in hoc iudicium. itaque si non suam rem eo
P.111 modo testator legaverit, | iure quidem civili inutile erit legatum; sed ex senatusconsulto confirmabitur[1]. aliquo tamen casu etiam alienam rem per praeceptionem legari posse fatentur: veluti si quis eam rem legaverit quam creditori fiduciae causa[2] mancipio dederit; nam officio iudicis coheredes cogi posse existimant soluta pecunia solvere eam rem, ut possit praecipere is cui ita legatum sit. (221.) Sed diversae scholae auctores putant etiam extraneo per praeceptionem legari posse proinde ac si ita scribatur: TITIUS HOMINEM STICHUM CAPITO supervacuo adiecta PRAE syllaba; ideoque per vindicationem

preception. 220. We perceive from this, that according to the opinion of our authorities, nothing can be left by preception except property of the testator: for nothing but what belongs to the inheritance can be the matter of this action. If then the testator have bequeathed in this form a thing not his own, the legacy is invalid at the civil law, but will be upheld by the *senatusconsultum*[1]. In a special case, however, they admit that another man's property can be left by preception: that is to say, if any one have bequeathed a thing which he has given by mancipation to his creditors under a fiduciary agreement[2]: for they think the heirs can be compelled by the executive power of the *judex* to release the thing by payment of the money, so that he to whom it is so left may take it in advance. 221. But the authorities of the other school think that a legacy can be left by preception even to a stranger, just as if the wording were thus: "Let Titius take the slave Stichus," the syllable *prae* being added superfluously: and therefore that such a legacy appears to be one by vindication, an opinion which is

[1] Sc. of Nero, II. 197.

[2] This refers to the ancient method of transferring both property and possession, for the purpose of assuring a creditor. "Originally it was customary to transfer to the creditor the property in a subject by mancipation, with a promise, however, by the creditor, at the moment of mancipation, to deliver the property back (*pactum de emancipando, fiducia*)." Savigny, *On Possession*, translated by Perry, p. 216.

eam rem legatam videri. quae sententia dicitur divi Hadriani constitutione confirmata esse. (222.) Secundum hanc igitur opinionem, si ea res ex iure Quiritium defuncti fuerit, potest a legatario vindicari[1], sive is unus ex heredibus sit sive extraneus: quod si in bonis tantum testatoris fuerit[2], extraneo quidem ex senatusconsulto utile erit legatum, heredi vero familiae erciscundae[3] iudicis officio praestabitur. quod si nullo iure fuerit testatoris, tam heredi quam extraneo ex senatusconsulto[4] utile erit. (223.) Sive tamen heredibus, secundum nostrorum opinionem, sive etiam extraneis, secundum illorum opinionem, duobus pluribusve eadem res coniunctim aut disiunctim legata fuerit,
P.112 singuli | partes habere debent[5].

224. Sed olim quidem licebat totum patrimonium legatis

said to be confirmed by a constitution of the late emperor Hadrian. 222. According to this opinion, therefore, if the thing belonged to the deceased by Quiritary title, it can be "vindicated[1]" by the legatee, whether he be one of the heirs or a stranger: and if it only belonged to the testator by Bonitary title[2], the legacy, if left to a stranger, will be valid by the *senatusconsultum*, but if to the heir, will be paid over to him by the executive authority of the *judex* in the *actio familiae erciscundae*[3]: whilst if it belonged to the testator by no title at all, it will be valid, whether to an heir or a stranger, by reason of the *senatusconsultum*[4]. 223. If the same thing have been left to two or more conjointly or disjointly, whether it be to heirs, according to our opinion, or even to strangers, according to theirs, all must take equal shares[5].

224. In olden times it was lawful to expend the whole

---

[1] II. 194.

[2] II. 40, 41.

[3] The derivation of the word *erciscundae* is given by Festus thus: "Erctum citumque sit inter consortes, ut in libris legum Romanarum legitur. Erctum a coercendo dictum, unde et erciscundae et ercisci. Citum autem vocatum est a ciendo." The sense of this may be thus given: "Between co-heirs, as we read in the Roman law-books, property is to be *erctum citumque*. *Erctum* is a word connected with *coerceo*, to gather together, *citum* from *cio*, to portion out." Hence the notion of Festus is that *ercisci* implies "to gather together and then apportion." A joint inheritance is *erctum citumque*, an inheritance to a single heir *erctum nec citum*. See Olivetus' note on Cic. *de Orat.* I. 56.

[4] Sc. of Nero; II. 197.

[5] See Appendix (K).

atque libertatibus erogare, nec quicquam heredi relinquere praeterquam inane nomen heredis: idque lex XII tabularum permittere videbatur, qua cavetur, ut quod quisque de re sua testatus esset, id ratum haberetur, his verbis: UTI LEGASSIT SUAE REI, ITA IUS ESTO[1]. quare qui scripti heredes erant, ab hereditate se abstinebant; et idcirco plerique intestati moriebantur. (225.) Itaque lata est lex Furia[2], qua, exceptis personis quibusdam, ceteris plus mille assibus legatorum nomine mortisve causa[3] capere permissum non est. sed et haec lex non perfecit quod voluit. qui enim verbi gratia quinque milium aeris patrimonium habebat, poterat quinque hominibus singulis millenos asses legando totum patrimonium erogare. (226.) Ideo postea lata est lex Voconia[4], qua cautum est, ne cui plus legatorum nomine mortisve causa capere liceret quam heredes caperent. ex qua lege plane quidem aliquid utique heredes habere videbantur; set tamen fere vitium simile nasce-

of a patrimony in legacies and gifts of freedom, and leave nothing to the heir, except the bare title of heir: and this a law of the Twelve Tables seemed to permit, wherein it is provided, that any disposition which a man made of his property should be valid, in the words, "In accordance with the bequests of his property which a man has made, so let the right be[1]." Wherefore those who were instituted heirs often abstained from the inheritance: and on that account many persons died intestate. 225. For this reason the Lex Furia[2] was passed, whereby it was forbidden for any person, certain exceptions, however, being made, to take more than a thousand *asses* by way of legacy or donation in contemplation of death[3]. But this law did not accomplish what it intended. For a man who had, for instance, a patrimony of five thousand *asses*, could expend his whole patrimony by bequeathing a thousand *asses* to each of five men. 226. Therefore, afterwards, the Lex Voconia[4] was passed, whereby it was provided, that no one should be allowed to take more by way of legacy or donation in contemplation of death than the heirs took. Through this law the heirs seemed certain to have something at any rate:

[1] Tab. v. l. 3.

[2] B.C. 182. A different law from the *Lex Fufia Caninia* named in I. 42. Ulpian, I. 2.

[3] Just. *Inst.* II. 7. 1.

[4] B.C. 168.

batur: nam in multas legatariorum personas distributo patri-
monio poterat adeo heredi minimum relinquere, ut non expe-
P.113 diret heredi huius lucri gra|tia totius hereditatis onera sus-
tinere. (227.) Lata est itaque lex Falcidia[1], qua cautum est,
ne plus ei legare liceat quam dodrantem. itaque necesse est,
ut heres quartam partem hereditatis habeat. et hoc nunc
iure utimur. (228.) In libertatibus quoque dandis nimiam
licentiam conpescuit lex Fufia Caninia, sicut in primo com-
mentario rettulimus[2].

229. Ante heredis institutionem inutiliter legatur, scilicet quia testamenta vim ex institutione heredis accipiunt, et ob id velut caput et fundamentum intellegitur totius testamenti heredis institutio[3]. (230.) Pari ratione nec libertas ante heredis institutionem dari potest[4]. (231.) Nostri praeceptores nec tutorem eo loco dari posse existimant: set Labeo et Proculus

but yet a mischief almost similar to the other arose: for by the patrimony being distributed amongst a large number of legatees, a testator could leave so very little to his heir, that it was not worth his while for the sake of this profit to sustain the burdens of the entire inheritance. 227. Therefore, the Lex Falcidia[1] was passed, by which it was provided that the testator should not be allowed to dispose of more than three-fourths in legacies. And thus the heir must necessarily have a fourth of the inheritance. And this is the law we now observe. 228. The Lex Fufia Caninia, as we have stated in the first commentary, has also checked extravagance in the bestowal of gifts of freedom[2].

229. A legacy is invalid if set down before the institution of the heir, plainly because testaments derive their efficacy from the institution of the heir, and therefore that institution is regarded as the head and foundation of the entire testament[3]. 230. For the same reason, a gift of freedom too cannot be given before the institution of the heir[4]. 231. Our authorities think that a tutor also cannot be given in that place: but Labeo and Proculus think a tutor can be given, because no

1 B. C. 39. Ulpian, XXIV. 32.
2 I. 42.
3 Ulpian, XXIV. 15.
4 *Ibid.* I. 20.

tutorem posse dari, quod nihil ex hereditate erogatur tutoris datione.

232. Post mortem quoque heredis inutiliter legatur[1]; id est hoc modo: CUM HERES MEUS MORTUUS ERIT, DO LEGO, aut DATO. ita autem recte legatur: CUM HERES MORIETUR: quia non post mortem heredis relinquitur, sed ultimo vitae eius tempore. rursum ita non potest legari: PRIDIE QUAM HERES MEUS MORIETUR. quod non pretiosa ratione receptum vide-
P.114 tur. | (233.) Eadem et de libertatibus dicta intellegemus. (234.) Tutor vero an post mortem heredis dari possit quaerentibus eadem forsitan poterit esse quaestio, quae de (eo) agitatur qui ante heredum institutionem datur[2].

235. Poenae quoque nomine inutiliter legatur[3]. poenae autem nomine legari videtur quod coercendi heredis causa relinquitur, quo magis heres aliquit faciat aut non faciat; velut quod ita legatur: SI HERES MEUS FILIAM SUAM TITIO IN MA-

charge is laid upon the inheritance by the giving of a tutor.

232. A bequest (to take effect) after the death of the heir is also invalid[1]: that is, one in the form: "When my heir shall be dead, I give and bequeath," or "let him give." But it is valid if worded thus: "When my heir shall be dying:" because it is not left after the decease of the heir, but at the last moment of his life. Again, a legacy cannot be left thus: "The day before my heir shall die." Which rule seems adopted for no good reason. 233. The same remarks we understand to be made with regard to gifts of freedom. 234. But if it be asked whether a tutor can be given after the death of the heir, perhaps the question will be the same as that discussed regarding him who is given before the institution of the heirs[2].

235. A legacy by way of penalty is also invalid[3]. Now a legacy is considered to be by way of penalty, which is left for the purpose of constraining the heir to do or not to do something: for instance, a legacy in these terms: "If my heir shall

---

1 Ulpian, XXIV. 16.

2 II. 231.

3 Ulpian, XXIV. 17. This rule was abolished by Justinian, as were those in §§ 229, 232. See *Inst.* II. 20. 34—36.

TRIMONIUM COLLOCAVERIT, X (MILIA) SEIO DATO; vel ita; SI FILIAM TITIO IN MATRIMONIUM NON COLLOCAVERIS, X MILIA TITIO DATO. sed et si[1] heres verbi gratia intra biennium monumentum sibi non fecerit, x Titio dari iusserit, poenae nomine legatum est. et denique ex ipsa definitione multas similes species circumspicere possumus. (236.) Nec libertas quidem poenae nomine dari potest; quamvis de ea re fuerit quaesitum. (237.) De tutore vero nihil possumus quaerere, quia non potest datione tutoris heres compelli quidquam facere aut non facere; ideoque qui datur poenae nomine tutor magis[2] sub condicione quam poenae nomine datus videbitur.

238. Incertae personae legatum inutiliter relinquitur[3]. incerta autem videtur persona quam per incertam opinionem |
P.115 animo suo testator subicit, veluti si ita legatum sit: QUI PRIMUS AD FUNUS MEUM VENERIT, (EI HERES) MEUS X (MILIA) DATO.

bestow his daughter in marriage on Titius, let him give ten thousand sesterces to Seius;" or thus: "If you do not bestow your daughter in marriage on Titius, give ten thousand to Titius." And also, if[1] he shall have ordered ten thousand to be given to Titius, "if the heir do not," for example, "set up a monument to him within two years," the legacy is by way of penalty. And in fact, from the mere definition we can perceive that there are many similar examples. 236. Not even freedom can be given by way of penalty, although this point has been questioned. 237. But as to a tutor we can raise no question, because the heir cannot be compelled by the giving of a tutor to do or not to do anything: and therefore a tutor given by way of penalty[2] is considered to be given under a condition rather than by way of penalty.

238. A legacy to an uncertain person is invalid[3]. Now an uncertain person seems to be one whom the testator brings before his mind without any clear notion of his individuality, for instance, if a legacy be given in these terms: "Let my heir give ten thousand sesterces to him who first comes to my funeral." The law is the same if he have made a general

---

[1] The *si* must be repeated: "Sed et si, si heres, etc."

[2] The MS. has "quae datur poenae nomine tutor datus fuerit magis, etc."

[3] Ulpian, XXIV. 18.

idem iuris est, si generaliter omnibus legaverit: QUICUMQUE AD FUNUS MEUM VENERIT. in eadem causa est quod ita relinquitur: QUICUMQUE FILIO MEO IN MATRIMONIUM FILIAM SUAM CONLOCAVERIT, EI HERES MEUS X MILIA DATO. illut quoque in eadem causa est quod ita relinquitur: QUI POST TESTAMENTUM CONSULES DESIGNATI ERUNT, aeque incertis personis legari videtur. et denique aliae multae huiusmodi species sunt. sub certa vero demonstratione incertae personae recte legatur, velut: EX COGNATIS MEIS QUI NUNC SUNT QUI PRIMUS AD FUNUS MEUM VENERIT, EI X MILIA HERES MEUS DATO. (239.) Libertas quoque non videtur incertae personae dari posse, quia lex Fufia Caninia iubet nominatim servos liberari[1]. (240.) Tutor quoque certus dari debet.

241. Postumo quoque alieno inutiliter legatur. (est) autem alienus postumus, qui natus inter suos heredes testatori futurus non est[2]. ideoque ex emancipato quoque filio conceptus nepos extraneus postumus est: item qui in utero est eius quae

bequest to all: "Whosoever shall come to my funeral." Of the same character is a bequest thus made: "Let my heir give ten thousand to whatever man bestows his daughter in marriage on my son." And of the same character too is a bequest made thus: "Whoever shall be consuls designate after my testament (comes into operation);" for it is in like manner regarded as a legacy to uncertain persons. And there are in fine many other instances of this kind. But a legacy is validly left to an uncertain person under a definite description, for instance, "Let my heir give ten thousand to that one of my relations now alive who first comes to my funeral." 239. It is also considered not allowable for liberty to be given to an uncertain person, because the Lex Fufia Caninia orders slaves to be liberated by name[1]. 240. A person given as a tutor ought also to be definite.

241. A legacy left to an afterborn stranger is also invalid. Now an afterborn stranger is a person who, if born, would not be a *suus heres* of the testator[2]. Therefore even a grandchild conceived from an emancipated son is an afterborn stranger: likewise the child conceived by a woman who at the Civil Law

[1] Ulpian, I. 25. See also I. 45. [2] See note on I. 147.

iure civili non intellegitur uxor, extraneus postumus patri
P.116 intelle|gitur.

242. Ac ne heres quidem potest institui postumus alienus: est enim incerta persona[1]. (243.) Cetera vero quae supra diximus[2] ad legata proprie pertinent; quamquam non inmerito quibusdam placeat poenae nomine heredem institui non posse: nihil enim interest, utrum legatum dare iubeatur heres, si fecerit aliquid aut non fecerit, an coheres ei adiciatur; quia tam coheredis adiectione quam legati datione conpellitur, ut aliquid contra propositum suum faciat aut non faciat.

244. An ei qui in potestate sit eius quem heredem instituimus recte legemus, quaeritur[3]. Servius recte legari probat, sed evanescere legatum, si quo tempore dies legatorum cedere solet[4], adhuc in potestate sit; ideoque sive pure legatum sit et vivo testatore in potestate heredis esse desierit, sive sub con-

is not regarded as a wife is considered an afterborn stranger in regard to his father.

242. An afterborn stranger cannot even be appointed heir: for he is an uncertain person[1]. 243. But all the other points which we have mentioned above[2] apply to legacies solely: although some hold, not without reason, that an heir cannot be instituted by way of penalty: for it makes no difference whether the heir be directed to give a legacy in case he do or fail to do something, or whether a co-heir be joined on to him: because as well by the addition of a co-heir, as by the giving of a legacy, he is compelled to do something against his wish or not do something.

244. It is a disputed point whether we can validly give a legacy to one who is under the *potestas* of him whom we institute heir[3]. Servius maintains that the legacy is valid, but becomes void if the legatee be still under *potestas* at the usual time for the vesting of a legacy[4]; and therefore, if either the legacy be left unconditionally, and during the testator's lifetime he cease to be under the *potestas* of the heir; or under condition, and the same

---

1 II. 238.
2 II. 229, 232, 233.
3 Ulpian, XXIV. 23.
4 "Cedere diem significat incipere deberi pecuniam: venire diem, significat eum diem venisse, quo pecunia peti potest." Ulpian in D. 50. 16. 213. *pr.*

dicione et ante condicionem id acciderit, deberi legatum. Sabinus et Cassius sub condicione recte legari, pure non recte, putant: licet enim vivo testatore possit desinere in potestate heredis esse, ideo tamen inutile legatum intellegi oportere, quia quod nullas vires habiturum foret, si statim post testamentum factum decessisset testator, hoc ideo valere quia vitam
P.117 longius traxerit, absurdum esset[1]. | diversae scholae auctores nec sub condicione recte legari, quia quos in potestate habemus, eis non magis sub condicione quam pure debere possumus. (245.) Ex diverso constat ab eo qui in potestate (tua) est, herede instituto, recte tibi legari[2]: sed si tu per eum heres extiteris, evanescere legatum, quia ipse tibi legatum debere non possis; si vero filius emancipatus aut servus manumissus erit vel in alium translatus, et ipse heres extiterit aut alium fecerit, deberi legatum.

occur before fulfilment of the condition, the legacy is due. Sabinus and Cassius think that a legacy if left under condition is good, if left unconditionally is bad: for that although the legatee may happen to cease to be under the *potestas* of the heir during the testator's lifetime, yet the legacy ought to be considered invalid for this reason, that it is absurd that what would have been invalid, if the testator had died immediately after making the testament, should be valid because he has lived longer[1]. The authorities of the other school think that the legacy cannot be left validly even under a condition, because we cannot be indebted to those who are under our *potestas* any more under a condition than unconditionally. 245. On the contrary, it is allowed that a legacy can validly be given to you, payable by one under your *potestas* who is instituted heir[2]: yet if you become heir through him, the legacy is inoperative, because you cannot owe a legacy to yourself: but if the son be emancipated, or the slave manumitted or transferred to another, and become heir himself or make another heir, the legacy is due.

1 This is Cato's rule: "Quod, si testamenti facti tempore decessisset testator, inutile foret, id legatum, quandocunque decesserit, non valere." D. 34. 7. 1. *pr.*

2 Ulpian, XXIV. 24.

246. Hinc transeamus ad fideicommissa[1].

247. Et prius de hereditatibus videamus.

248. In primis igitur sciendum est opus esse, ut aliquis heres recto iure instituatur, eiusque fidei committatur, ut eam hereditatem alii restituat: alioquin inutile est testamentum in quo nemo recto iure heres instituitur. (249.) Verba autem utilia fideicommissorum haec recte maxime in usu esse videntur: PETO, ROGO, VOLO, FIDEICOMMITTO: quae proinde firma singula sunt, atque si omnia in unum congesta sint. (250.) Cum igitur scripserimus: (LUCIUS) TITIUS HERES ESTO, possumus adicere: ROGO TE, LUCI TITI, PETOQUE A TE, UT CUM PRIMUM POSSIS HEREDITATEM MEAM ADIRE, GAIO SEIO REDDAS RESTITUAS. possumus autem et de parte restituenda rogare; et liberum est
P.118 vel sub condicione vel pure relinquere | fideicommissa, vel ex die certa. (251.) Restituta autem hereditate is qui restituit

246. Now let us pass on to *fideicommissa*[1].

247. And let us begin with the subject of inheritances.

248. First, then, we must know that some heir must be instituted in due form, and that it must be intrusted to his good faith that he deliver over the inheritance to another: for if this be not done, the testament is invalid for want of an heir instituted in due form. 249. The proper phraseology for *fideicommissa* generally employed is this: "I beg, I ask, I wish, I commit to your good faith:" and these words are equally binding when employed singly, as though they were all united into one. 250. When, therefore, we have written: "Let Lucius Titius be heir;" we may add: "I ask you, Lucius Titius, and beg of you, that as soon as you can enter on my inheritance, you will render and deliver it over to Gaius Seius." We may also ask him to deliver over a part: and it is in our power to leave *fideicommissa* either under condition, or unconditionally, or from a specified day. 251. Now when the inheritance is delivered over, he who has delivered it still

[1] *Fideicommissum* was a bequest given by way of request, not by way of command; and was held to be due on the equitable ground of respecting the testator's desires; "Fideicommissum est quod non civilibus verbis, sed precative relinquitur, nec ex rigore juris civilis proficiscitur, sed ex voluntate datur relinquentis." Ulpian, XXV. 1.

nihilominus heres permanet; is vero qui recipit hereditatem, aliquando heredis loco est, aliquando legatarii. (252.) Olim autem nec heredis loco erat nec legatarii, sed potius emptoris. tunc enim in usu erat ei cui restituebatur hereditas nummo uno eam hereditatem dicis causa venire; et quae stipulationes inter (*venditorem hereditatis et emptorem interponi solent, eadem interponebantur inter*)[1] heredem et eum cui restituebatur hereditas, id est hoc modo: heres quidem stipulabatur ab eo cui restituebatur hereditas, ut quidquid hereditario nomine condemnatus fuisset, sive quid alias bona fide dedisset, eo nomine indemnis esset, et omnino si quis cum eo hereditario nomine ageret, ut recte defenderetur: ille vero qui recipiebat hereditatem invicem stipulabatur, ut si quit ex hereditate ad heredem pervenisset, id sibi restitueretur; ut etiam pateretur eum hereditarias actiones procuratorio aut cognitorio nomine exequi[2].

remains heir: but he who receives the inheritance is sometimes in the place of heir, sometimes of legatee. 252. But formerly he used to be neither in the place of heir nor of legatee, but rather of purchaser. For it was then usual for the inheritance to be sold for a single coin and as a mere formality to him to whom it was delivered over: and the same stipulations which are usually entered into between the vendor and the purchaser of an inheritance were entered into between[1] the heir and the person to whom the inheritance was delivered over, *i.e.* in the following manner: the heir on his part stipulated with him to whom the inheritance was delivered over, that he should be indemnified for any amount in which he might be mulcted in connexion with the inheritance, or for anything which he might otherwise expend *bonâ fide*, and generally, that if any one brought an action against him in connexion with the inheritance he should be duly defended: whilst the receiver of the inheritance stipulated in his turn, that whatever should come to the heir from the inheritance should be delivered over to him: and that he should also allow him to bring actions concerning the inheritance, in the capacity of *procurator* or *cognitor*[2].

---

1 A line is here omitted from the MS., for the usual reason, that it happened to end with the same word as the preceding line; in this case *inter*.

2 IV. 83, 84.

253. Sed posterioribus temporibus Trebellio Maximo et Annaeo Seneca Consulibus[1] senatusconsultum factum est, quo cautum est, ut si cui hereditas ex fideicommissi causa restituta sit, actiones quae iure civili heredi et in heredem conpeterent (ei) et in eum darentur cui ex fideicommisso restituta esset hereditas[2], post quod senatusconsultum desierunt illae cautiones in usu
P.119 haberi. | Praetor enim utiles actiones[3] ei et in eum qui recepit hereditatem, quasi heredi et in heredem dare coepit, eaeque in edicto proponuntur. (254.) Sed rursus quia heredes scripti, cum aut totam hereditatem aut paene totam plerumque restituere rogabantur, adire hereditatem ob nullum aut minimum lucrum recusabant, atque ob id extinguebantur fideicommissa, postea Pegaso et Pusione (Consulibus)[4] senatus censuit, ut ei qui rogatus esset hereditatem restituere perinde liceret quartam partem retinere, atque e lege Falcidia in legatis retinendis

253. But at a later period, when Trebellius Maximus and Annaeus Seneca were consuls[1], a *senatusconsultum* was enacted, whereby it was provided that if an inheritance were delivered over to any one on the ground of *fideicommissum*, the actions which by the civil law would lie for and against the heir, should be granted for and against him to whom the inheritance was delivered over in accordance with the *fideicommissum*[2]. And after the passing of this *senatusconsultum*, these securities (the stipulations) ceased to be used. For the Praetor began to grant *utiles actiones*[3] for and against the receiver of the inheritance, as if they were for and against the heir, and these are set forth in the edict. 254. But again, since the appointed heirs, being generally asked to deliver over the whole or nearly the whole of an inheritance, refused to enter on the inheritance for little or no gain, and thus *fideicommissa* fell to the ground, afterwards therefore in the consulship of Pegasus and Pusio[4] the senate decreed, that he who was asked to deliver over the inheritance should be allowed to retain a fourth part, just as this right of retention is permitted by the Falcidian law as a deduction from legacies. The same re-

[1] A.D. 56, as determined from an inscription found at Pompeii in A.D. 1875.

[2] The wording of the S. C. will be found in D. 36. 1. 1. 2.

[3] See note on II. 78.

[4] In the reign of Vespasian, A.D. 70—80, but the exact year uncertain.

conceditur. ex singulis quoque rebus quae per fideicommissum relinquuntur eadem retentio permissa est. per quod senatusconsultum ipse onera hereditaria sustinet; ille autem qui ex fideicommisso reliquam partem hereditatis recipit, legatarii partiarii loco est, id est eius legatarii cui pars bonorum legatur. quae species legati partitio vocatur[1], quia cum herede legatarius partitur hereditatem. unde effectum est, ut quae solent stipulationes inter heredem et partiarium legatarium interponi, eaedem interponantur inter eum qui ex fideicommissi causa recipit hereditatem et heredem, id est ut et lucrum et damnum hereditarium pro rata parte inter eos commune sit.

P.120 (255.) Ergo si quidem non plus quam dodrantem | hereditatis scriptus heres rogatus sit restituere, tum ex Trebelliano senatusconsulto restituitur hereditas, et in utrumque actiones hereditariae pro rata parte dantur[2], in heredem quidem iure civili, in eum vero qui recipit hereditatem ex senatusconsulto Trebelliano. quamquam heres etiam pro ea parte quam re-

tention was also allowed in the case of individual things left by *fideicommissum*. By this *senatusconsultum* the heir himself sustains the burdens of the inheritance, whilst he who receives the rest of the inheritance by virtue of the *fideicommissum*, is in the position of a partiary legatee, *i.e.* of a legatee to whom a portion of the goods is left. Which species of legacy is called *partitio*[1], because the legatee shares the inheritance with the heir. The result of this is that the same stipulations which are usually entered into between the heir and the partiary legatee, are also entered into between him who receives the inheritance by way of *fideicommissum* and the heir, *i.e.* that the gain and loss of the inheritance shall be shared between them in proportion to their interests.

255. If then the appointed heir be asked to deliver over not more than three-fourths of the inheritance, the inheritance is thereupon delivered over in accordance with the *senatusconsultum Trebellianum*, and actions in connexion with the inheritance are allowed against both parties according to the extent of their interests[2]: against the heir by the civil law, and against him who receives the inheritance by the *senatusconsultum Trebellianum*. Although the heir remains heir even

1 Ulpian, XXIV. 25. Cic. *de Legibus*, II. 20.

2 Ulpian, XXV. 14.

stituit heres permanet, eique et in eum solidae actiones competunt: sed non ulterius oneratur, nec ulterius illi dantur actiones, quam apud eum commodum hereditatis remanet[1]. (256.) At si quis plus quam dodrantem vel etiam totam hereditatem restituere rogatus sit, locus est Pegasiano senatusconsulto. (257.) Set is qui semel adierit hereditatem, si modo sua voluntate adierit, sive retinuerit quartam partem sive noluerit retinere, ipse universa onera hereditaria sustinet: set quarta quidem retenta quasi partis et pro parte stipulationes interponi debent tamquam inter partiarium legatarium et heredem; si vero totam hereditatem restituerit, ad exemplum emptae et venditae hereditatis stipulationes interponendae sunt. (258.) Set si recuset scriptus heres adire hereditatem, ob id quod dicat eam sibi suspectam esse quasi damnosam, cavetur Pegasiano senatusconsulto, ut desiderante

for the part he has delivered over, and actions as to the whole lie for and against him: yet he is not burdened, nor are actions granted to him (for his own benefit) beyond the interest in the inheritance which belongs to him[1]. 256. But if he be asked to deliver over more than three-fourths, or even the whole inheritance, the *senatusconsultum Pegasianum* applies. 257. But he who has once entered on the inheritance, provided only he have done it of his own free will, whether he retain or do not wish to retain the fourth part, sustains all the burdens of the inheritance himself; but when the fourth is retained, stipulations resembling those called *partis et pro parte* ought to be employed, as between a partiary legatee and an heir: whilst if he have delivered over the whole inheritance, stipulations resembling those of a bought and sold inheritance must be employed. 258. But if the appointed heir refuse to enter upon the inheritance, because he says that it is suspected by him of being ruinous, it is provided by the *senatusconsultum Pegasianum* that at the request of him to whom

[1] Gaius is here merely stating a point of pleading. The action must be laid on the fact of the deceased owing a particular sum to the plaintiff, and therefore the whole sum must be stated in the *intentio;* though, to avoid *plus petitio*, the due proportion only must be claimed in the *condemnatio*.

P.121 eo cui restituere rogatus est, iussu | Praetoris adeat et restituat, perindeque ei et in eum qui receperit actiones dentur, ac iuris esset ex senatusconsulto Trebelliano. quo casu nullis stipulationibus opus est, quia simul et huic qui restituit securitas datur, et actiones hereditariae ei et in eum transferuntur qui receperit hereditatem.

259. Nihil autem interest utrum aliquis ex asse heres institutus aut totam hereditatem aut pro parte restituere rogetur, an ex parte heres institutus aut totam eam partem aut partis partem restituere rogetur: nam et hoc casu de quarta parte eius partis ratio ex Pegasiano senatusconsulto haberi solet.

260. Potest autem quisque etiam res singulas per fideicommissum relinquere, velut fundum, hominem, vestem, argentum, pecuniam; et vel ipsum heredem rogare, ut alicui restituat, vel legatarium, quamvis a legatario legari non possit[1]. (261.) Item potest non solum propria testatoris res per fideicommissum

he is asked to deliver it over he shall enter by order of the Praetor and deliver it over, and that actions are to be allowed for and against him who has received it, as would be the rule under the *senatusconsultum Trebellianum*. In which case no stipulations are needed, because at the same time security is afforded to him who has delivered over the inheritance, and the actions attaching to it are transferred to and against him who has received it.

259. It makes no matter whether a man instituted heir to the whole inheritance be requested to deliver over the inheritance wholly or partly, or whether the heir instituted to a part be requested to deliver over the part or part of the part: for in the latter case too it is usual for a calculation to be made of the fourth of that part according to the *senatusconsultum Pegasianum*.

260. A man can also leave individual things by *fideicommissum*, as a field, a slave, a garment, plate, money: and he can ask either the heir or a legatee to deliver it over to some one, although a legacy cannot be charged upon a legatee[1]. 261. Likewise, not only can the testator's own property be left by *fideicommissum*, but that of the heir also, or of a legatee,

[1] Ulpian, XXIV. 20.

relinqui, sed etiam heredis aut legatarii aut cuiuslibet alterius[1]. itaque et legatarius non solum de ea re rogari potest, ut eam alicui restituat, quae ei legata sit, sed etiam de alia, sive ipsius legatarii sive aliena sit. sed hoc solum observandum est, ne plus quisquam rogetur aliis restituere, quam ipse ex testamento ce-
P.122 perit: nam | quod amplius est inutiliter relinquitur. (262.) Cum autem aliena res per fideicommissum relinquitur, necesse est ei qui rogatus est, aut ipsam redimere et praestare, aut aestimationem eius solvere. *sicut iuris est*, si per damnationem aliena res legata sit[2]. sunt tamen qui putant, si rem per fideicommissum relictam dominus non vendat, extingui fideicommissum; aliam autem esse causam per damnationem legati.

263. Libertas quoque servo per fideicommissum dari potest, ut vel heres rogetur manumittere, vel legatarius. (264.) N*ec interest utrum de suo propri*o servo testator roget, an de eo qui ipsius heredis aut legatarii vel etiam extranei sit[3]. (265.) Itaque

or of any one else[1]. Therefore, not only can a request for redelivery to another be addressed to the legatee with respect to the very thing left to him, but also with respect to a different thing, whether it belong to the legatee himself or to a stranger. But this only is to be observed, that no one may be asked to deliver over to others more than he himself has taken under the testament: for the bequest of the excess is inoperative. 262. But, when another man's property is left by *fideicommissum*, it is incumbent on the person requested to deliver it either to purchase the very thing and hand it over, or to pay its value. Exactly as the rule is when another man's property is legacied by damnation[2]. There are, however, those who think that if the owner will not sell a thing left by *fideicommissum*, the *fideicommissum* is extinguished: but that the case is different with a legacy by damnation.

263. A gift of liberty can also be made to a slave by *fideicommissum*, in such manner that either the heir or a legatee may be asked to manumit him. 264. Nor does it matter whether the testator make request as to his own slave, or as to one belonging to the heir himself, or to a legatee, or even to a stranger[3]. 265. And therefore, even a stranger's slave must

[1] Ibid. XXV. 5. [2] II. 202. [3] Ulpian, II. 10.

et alienus servus redimi et manumitti debet. quod si dominus eum non vendat, sane extinguitur fideicommissaria libertas, quia hoc *casu* pretii computatio nulla intervenit[1]. (266.) Qui autem ex fideicommisso manumittitur, non testatoris fit libertus etiamsi testatoris servus fuerit, set eius qui manumittit[2]. (267.) At qui directo, testamento, liber esse iubetur, velut hoc modo: STICHUS SERVUS (MEUS) LIBER ESTO, vel hoc: STICHUM SERVUM MEUM LIBERUM ESSE IUBEO, is *ipsius testa*toris fit libertus[3]. nec alius ullus directo ex testamento libertatem habere potest, quam qui utroque tempore testatoris ex iure *Quiritium*
P.123 *fuerit, et quo f*acer*et* testamentum et quo moreretur[4]. | (*desunt lin.* 2)

268. Multum autem diff*erunt ea* quae per fideicommissum relinquuntur ab his quae directo iure legantur[5]. (269.) Nam ecce per fideicommissum etiam *nutu* hereditas relinqui potest[6]: cum alioquin legatum nisi testamento facto

be bought and manumitted. But if the owner will not sell him, clearly the fideicommissary gift of liberty is extinguished, because in this case no computation of price is possible[1]. 266. Now he who is manumitted in accordance with a *fideicommissum* does not become the freedman of the testator, even though he were the testator's slave, but the freedman of the person who manumits him[2]. 267. But he who is ordered to be free by direct bequest in a testament, for instance, in the following words: "Let my slave Stichus be free," or thus, "I order my slave Stichus to be free," becomes a freedman of the testator himself[3]. No one, however, can have liberty directly by virtue of a testament, except one who belonged to the testator by Quiritary title at both times, viz. that at which he made the testament, and that at which he died[4].

268. Things left by *fideicommissum* differ much from legacies left directly[5]. 269. Thus, for instance, an inheritance can be left by *fideicommissum* even with a nod[6]: whilst, on the contrary,

[1] Ulpian, II. 11. For the alteration of this rule see Just. *Inst.* II. 24. 2.

[2] This is a point of importance, because, as stated in note on I. 37, the *libertus* owes to his *patronus* certain duties.

[3] Such a freedman is called *libertus orcinus.* Ulpian, II. 8.

[4] Ulpian, I. 23.

[5] Justinian assimilated legacies and *fideicommissa* in all respects. See *Inst.* II. 20. 3.

[6] Ulpian, XXV. 3. D. 32. 1. 21. *pr.*

inutile sit. (270.) Item intestatus moriturus potest ab eo ad quem bona eius pertinent fideicommissum alicui relinquere: cum alioquin ab eo legari non possit. (270 a.) *Item legatum codicillis* relictum[1] non aliter valet, quam si a testatore confirmati fuerint, id est nisi in testamento caverit testator, ut quidquid in codicillis scripserit id ratum sit: fideicommissum vero etiam non confirmatis codicillis relinqui potest[2]. (271.) Item a legatario legari non potest: sed fideicommissum relinqui potest[3]. quin etiam ab eo quoque cui per fideicommissum relinquimus rursus alii per fideicommissum relinquere possumus. (272.) Item servo alieno directo libertas dari non potest: sed per fideicommissum potest[4]. (273.) Item codicillis nemo heres institui potest neque exheredari, quamvis testamento confirmati sint. at is qui testamento heres institutus est potest codicillis

a legacy, unless a testament be made, is invalid. 270. Also a man about to die intestate can leave a *fideicommissum* chargeable on him upon whom his goods devolve: although, on the contrary, a legacy cannot be charged upon such an one. 270 *a*. Likewise, a legacy left in codicils[1] is not valid, unless the codicils be confirmed by the testator, *i.e.* unless the testator insert a proviso in his testament that what he has written in the codicils shall stand good; but a *fideicommissum* can be left even in unconfirmed codicils[2]. 271. Likewise, a legacy cannot be charged upon a legatee, but a *fideicommissum* can be so charged[3]. Moreover we can leave to a second person a further *fideicommissum* chargeable on a man to whom we already have left a *fideicommissum*. 272. Likewise, liberty cannot be given directly to another man's slave, but it can be given by *fideicommissum*[4]. 273. Likewise, no one can be instituted heir or disinherited by codicils, even though they be confirmed by testament. But the heir instituted by testament may be asked

---

[1] This reading corresponds with the small space illegible, and accords with Ulp. XXV. 8. Krüger, however, would read "etiam ab herede heredis relinqui potest: cum alioquin legatum ita relictum non aliter valet etc." But this filling up is far too lengthy; though the Epitome, 2. 7. 8, has something to the effect of what Krüger suggests.

[2] The law regarding codicils is to be found in Just. *Inst.* II. 25. A codicil confirmed would become part of the testament, and the legacy thus become binding. See also Ulp. XXV. 8.

[3] II. 260, 261.

[4] II. 264, 267.

rogari, ut eam hereditatem alii totam vel ex parte restituat,
P.124 quamvis testamento codicilli confirmati non sint[1]. | (274.) Item mulier quae ab eo qui centum milia aeris census est[2] per legem Voconiam heres institui non potest, tamen fideicommisso relictam sibi hereditatem capere potest. (275.) Latini quoque qui hereditates legataque directo iure lege Iunia capere prohibentur, ex fideicommisso capere possunt[3]. (276.) Item cum senatusconsulto prohibitum sit proprium servum minorem annis xxx liberum et heredem instituere, plerisque placet posse nos iubere liberum esse cum annorum xxx erit, et rogare ut tunc illi restituatur hereditas[4]. (277.) Item quamvis non (possimus)

in codicils to deliver over the inheritance, wholly or in part, to another, even though the codicils be not confirmed by testament[1]. 274. Likewise, a woman, who by the Lex Voconia could not be instituted heir by any one registered[2] as having more than 100,000 *asses*, may still take an inheritance left her by *fideicommissum*. 275. Latins also, who are prevented by the Lex Junia from taking inheritances or legacies bequeathed directly, can take by *fideicommissum*[3]. 276. Likewise, although we are forbidden by a *senatusconsultum* to appoint free and heir our own slave who is under thirty years of age, yet it is generally held that we may order him to be free when he shall arrive at the age of thirty, and ask that the inheritance be then delivered over to him[4]. 277. Likewise, although when a man

---

1 Ulpian, XXV. 11.

2 Sc. by the censors. The law is referred to by Cicero, *in Verrem*, II. I. c. 42, *Pro Balbo*, c. 8, and *De Repub.* III. c. 10. Another provision of the law is mentioned in II. 226. There seems to have been also a third, that a man who was registered for 100,000 *asses* could not leave in legacies to women more than remained to his heir, *i.e.* not more than half of his estate. Cic. *in Verrem*, II. I. c. 43.

3 I. 23, 24.

4 I. 18. It was not by a *senatusconsultum* but by a *Lex* (*Aelia Sentia*) that men were forbidden to manumit a slave under thirty: still there need be no contradiction between this passage and I. 18. Testators, to avoid the operation of the *Lex Aelia Sentia*, had probably appointed slaves under thirty, not as heirs immediately, but to be heirs when they reached the age of thirty, and this was rendered invalid by the S.C. The S.C. therefore merely applied to a particular case the well-known maxim: "Nemo partim testatus, partim intestatus decedere potest:" for there would be an intestacy from the time of the testator's death to that when the heir became thirty years old: or, if we imagine that the heir *ab intestato* might occupy during the interval, then we are confuted by the equally trite maxim: "Semel heres, semper heres."

post mortem eius qui nobis heres extiterit alium in locum eius heredem instituere[1], tamen possumus eum rogare, ut cum morietur, alii eam hereditatem totam vel ex parte restituat. et quia post mortem quoque heredis fideicommissum dari potest[2], idem efficere possumus et si ita scripserimus: CUM TITIUS HERES MEUS MORTUUS ERIT, VOLO HEREDITATEM MEAM AD PUBLIUM MAEVIUM PERTINERE. utroque autem modo, tam hoc quam illo, Titium[3] heredem suum obligatum relinquit de fideicommisso restituendo. (278.) Praeterea legata (per) formulam petimus[4]: fideicommissa vero Romae quidem aput Consulem vel aput eum Praetorem[5] qui praecipue de fideicommissis ius dicit persequimur; in provinciis vero aput Praesidem provin-
P.125 ciae. (279.) Item de fideicommissis semper | in urbe ius dicitur: de legatis vero, cum res aguntur[6]. (280.) Item fidei-

has become our heir we cannot appoint another to take his place after his death[1]; yet we can ask him to deliver over the inheritance to another, wholly or in part, when he shall be dying. And since a *fideicommissum* can be given even after the death of the heir[2], we can also produce the same effect if we word our bequest thus: "When Titius my heir shall be dead, I wish my inheritance to belong to Publius Maevius." By each of these methods, both the first and the second, the testator leaves his heir, Titius[3], bound to deliver over a *fideicommissum*. 278. Moreover, we sue for legacies by means of a *formula*[4]: but we proceed for *fideicommissa* at Rome before the Consul or the Praetor[5] who has special jurisdiction over *fideicommissa*, in the provinces before the governor. 279. Likewise, judgment regarding *fideicommissa* is given at any time in the city: but regarding legacies only on the days devoted to litigation[6]. 280. The interest and profits of *fideicommissa* are

---

[1] II. 184.

[2] But not a legacy: see II. 232.

[3] The MS. has *Titium*. Most editors alter this into *Titius*. But it is not Titius who binds his heir; but the testator who binds both Titius and Titius' heir through Titius.

[4] IV. 30 et seqq. Fideicommissary cases were tried *extra ordinem*, *i.e.* by the magistrate, without any devolution of the investigation of facts to a *judex*.

[5] "Jus omne fideicommissi non in vindicatione, sed in petitione consistit." Paulus, *S. R.* IV. 1. § 18. See also Ulpian, XXV. 12.

[6] Legal proceedings, whether *in jure* or *in judicio*, could not take place at all times: but the division of the year into working-days and holidays was different in the two cases.

The jurisdictional term, or porcommissorum usurae et fructus debentur, si modo moram solutionis fecerit qui fideicommissum debebit: legatorum vero usurae non debentur; idque rescripto divi Hadriani significatur. scio tamen Iuliano placuisse in eo legato quod sinendi modo relinquitur[1] idem iuris esse quod in fideicommissis: quam sententiam et his temporibus magis optinere video. (281.) Item legata Graece scripta non valent: fideicommissa vero valent[2]. (282.) Item si legatum per damnationem[3] relictum heres infitietur, in duplum cum eo agitur: fideicommissi vero nomine semper in simplum persecutio est. (283.) Item (quod) quisque ex fideicommisso plus debito per errorem solverit

due, in case he who has to pay a *fideicommissum* makes delay of payment: but the interest of legacies is not due: and this is stated in a rescript of the late emperor Hadrian. I know, however, that Julianus thought the rule was the same in a legacy left *sinendi modo*[1] as in *fideicommissa*, and I see that this opinion prevails at the present time too. 281. Likewise, legacies written in Greek are invalid, but *fideicommissa* are valid[2]. 282. Likewise, if the heir deny that a legacy has been left by damnation[3], the action is brought against him for double: but the suit for *fideicommissa* is always for the value only. 283. Likewise, a man can reclaim what he has paid by mistake beyond what was due under a *fideicommissum:* whilst that

tion of time during which the Praetor could sit for the transaction of purely formal business, not involving investigation of evidence or argument thereon, was regulated thus:—the year was divided into 40 *dies fasti*, 60 *dies nefasti*, 190 *dies comitiales*, and the residue *dies intercisi*. The *dies fasti* were devoted entirely to jurisdiction: the *dies intercisi* were half-holidays: the *dies comitiales* were primarily set aside for legislative assemblies, but if not required for the meeting of the *comitia* were also available for jurisdiction: whilst on the *dies nefasti* the Praetor could not sit at all.

The judicial term, or portion of the year during which evidence or argument could be gone into before a *judex*, was simply those days not set aside for games, sacrifices or solemn banquets (*ludi*, *sacrificia*, *epulae*), for holidays (*feriae*), or for the vacations, of which latter there were originally two, one in spring and the other in autumn, although their duration and the time of their occurrence were subsequently changed by several of the emperors. The days on which judicial proceedings could not be taken were *dies festi*, those on which they could were *dies profesti*, or as they are sometimes called "*cum res aguntur*," "*rerum actus*." See Puchta on the topic.

[1] II. 209.

[2] Ulpian, XXV. 9.

[3] II. 201.

repetere potest: at id quod ex causa falsa per damnationem legati plus debito solutum sit, repeti non potest[1]. idem scilicet iuris est de eo legato quod non debitum vel ex hac vel ex illa causa per errorem solutum fuerit[2].

284. Erant etiam aliae differentiae, quae nunc non sunt. (285.) Ut ecce peregrini poterant fideicommissa capere[3]: et fere haec fuit origo fideicommissorum. sed postea id prohibitum est; et nunc ex oratione divi Hadriani senatusconsultum factum est, ut ea fideicommissa fisco vindicarentur. (286.) Cae-
P.126 libes | quoque qui per legem Iuliam hereditates legataque capere prohibentur, olim fideicommissa videbantur capere posse[4]. item orbi qui per legem Papiam, ob id quod liberos non habent, dimidias partes hereditatum legatorumque perdunt, olim solida fideicommissa videbantur capere posse. sedpostea senatusconsulto Pegasiano perinde fideicommissa quoque ac legata hereditatesque capere pro semisse prohibiti sunt. eaque

which has for an erroneous reason been paid beyond what was due under a legacy by damnation cannot be recovered[1]. The same undoubtedly is the law as to a legacy which, though not due, has for some cause or other been paid by mistake[2].

284. There used to be other differences; but these do not now exist. 285. For instance, foreigners could take *fideicommissa*[3]: and this was almost the first instance of *fideicommissa*. But afterwards this was forbidden: and now a *senatusconsultum* has been enacted, at the instance of the late emperor Hadrian, that such *fideicommissa* are to be claimed for the *fiscus*. 286. Unmarried persons also, who by the Lex Julia are debarred from taking inheritances and legacies, were in olden times considered capable of taking *fideicommissa*[4]. Likewise, childless persons, who by the Lex Papia lose half their inheritances and legacies because they have no children, were in olden times considered capable of taking *fideicommissa* in full. But afterwards by the *senatusconsultum Pegasianum* they were forbidden to take one half of *fideicommissa* as well as of inheritances or legacies. And these were transferred to those persons

[1] Ulpian, XXIV. 33.

[2] In the first case the legacy is due, but there is a payment in excess: in the second case no legacy is due at all.

[3] Cf. Val. Max. Lib. IV. c. 7.

[4] II. 111 *n*.

translata sunt ad eos qui (in eo) testamento liberos habent, aut si nullus liberos habebit, ad populum, sicuti iuris est in legatis et in hereditatibus, quae eadem aut simili ex causa *caduca fiunt*[1]. (287.) Item olim incertae personae vel postumo alieno per fideicommissum relinqui poterat, quamvis neque heres institui neque legari ei possit[2]. set senatusconsulto quod auctore divo Hadriano factum est idem in fideicommissis quod in legatis hereditatibusque constitutum est. (288.) Item poenae nomine iam non dubitatur nec per fideicommissum quidem relinqui posse. (289.) Set quamvis in multis iuris partibus longe latior causa sit fideicommissorum, quam eorum quae directo relinquuntur, in quibusdam tantumdem valeant: tamen tutor non aliter testamento dari potest quam directo, veluti hoc modo: LIBERIS MEIS TITIUS TUTOR ESTO, vel ita: LIBERIS MEIS TITIUM TUTOREM DO: per fideicommissum vero dari non potest. | (*desunt lin.* 48.)

named in the testament who have children, or, if none of them have children, to the *populus*, just as the rule is regarding legacies and inheritances, which lapse from the same or a similar cause[1]. 287. Likewise, a *fideicommissum* could formerly be left to an uncertain person or after-born stranger, although such an one could not be appointed either heir or legatee[2]. But by a *senatusconsultum* which was made at the instance of the late emperor Hadrian the same rule was established with regard to *fideicommissa* as with regard to legacies and inheritances. 288. Likewise, there is now no doubt that a bequest by way of penalty cannot be made even by *fideicommissum*. 289. But although in many legal incidents the scope of *fideicommissa* is far more comprehensive than that of direct bequests, and in others the two are of equal effect, yet a tutor cannot be given in a testament in any manner except directly, for instance thus: "Titius be tutor to my children:" or thus, "I give Titius as tutor to my children:" and one cannot be given by *fideicommissum*.

1 II. 206, 207. The words *Caduca fiunt* are supplied by Polenaar. The MS. has merely EX CAUTEM.

2 II. 238—241. Ulpian, XXII. 4.

BOOK III.

P. 126* 1. *Intestatorum*[1] *hereditates lege XII tabularum primum ad suos heredes pertinent*[2]. (2.) *Sui autem heredes existimantur liberi qui in potestate morientis fuerint, veluti filius filiave, nepos neptisve ex filio, pronepos proneptisve ex nepote filio nato prognatus prognatave. nec interest utrum naturales sint liberi, an adoptivi.*

Ita demum tamen nepos neptisve et pronepos proneptisve suorum heredum numero sunt, si praecedens persona desierit in potestate parentis esse, sive morte id acciderit sive alia ratione, veluti emancipatione: nam si per id tempus quo quis moritur filius in potestate eius sit, nepos ex eo suus heres esse non potest[3]. *idem et in ceteris*

1. The inheritances[1] of intestates by a law of the Twelve Tables belong in the first place to their *sui heredes*[2]: 2. and those descendants are accounted *sui heredes* who were under the *potestas* of the dying man, as a son or daughter, grandson or granddaughter by a son, great-grandson or great-granddaughter sprung from a grandson born from a son. Nor does it matter, whether they be actual or adopted descendants.

But a grandson or granddaughter, and a great-grandson or great-granddaughter, are in the category of *sui heredes* only when the person prior to them in degree has ceased to be under the *potestas* of his ascendant, whether that has happened by death or by some other means, emancipation for instance: for if at the time when a man dies his son be under his *potestas*, the grandson by him cannot be a *suus heres*[3]. And the same we

---

[1] The first four paragraphs of this book and a portion of the fifth are filled in conjecturally by the German editors of the text, from *Lex Dei*, sive *Mosaicarum et Romanarum Legum Collatio*, XVI. 2. 1—5, as a leaf is wanting from the MS. at this point. The passage from the *Collatio* is marked as taken from Gai. *Inst.* lib. III. See also Just. *Inst.* III. 1. *pr.*—2. Gai. *Epit.* 2. 8. *pr.*

[2] II. 156. Ulpian, XXII. 14, XXVI. 1.

[3] I. 127.

deinceps liberorum personis dictum intellegemus. (3.) *Uxor quoque quae in manu est sua heres est, quia filiae loco est; item nurus quae in filii manu est, nam et haec neptis loco est*[1]. *sed ita demum erit sua heres, si filius cuius in manu erit, cum pater moritur in potestate eius non sit. idemque dicemus et de ea quae in nepotis manu matrimonii causa sit*[2], *quia proneptis loco est.* (4.) *Postumi quoque*[3], *qui si vivo parente nati essent, in potestate eius futuri forent, sui heredes sunt.* (5.) *Idem iuris est de his quorum nomine*
P.127 *ex lege Aelia Sentia vel ex senatusconsulto post* | mortem patris causa probatur: nam et hi vivo patre causa probata in potestate eius futuri essent[4]. (6.) Quod etiam de eo filio, qui ex prima secundave mancipatione post mortem patris manumittitur, intellegemus[5].

7. Igitur cum filius filiave, et ex altero filio nepotes neptesve extant, pariter ad hereditatem vocantur; nec qui gradu

understand to be laid down with regard to other classes of descendants successively. 3. A wife also who is under *manus* is a *sua heres*, because she is in the place of a daughter: likewise a daughter-in-law who is under the *manus* of a son, because she again is in the place of a granddaughter[1]. But she will only be a *sua heres* in case the son, under whose *manus* she is, be not under his father's *potestas* when his father dies. And the same we shall also lay down with regard to a woman who is under the *manus* of a grandson for matrimonial purpose[2], because she is in the place of a great-granddaughter. 4. After-born descendants[3] also, who, if they had been born in the lifetime of the ascendant, would have been under his *potestas*, are *sui heredes*. 5. The law is the same regarding those in reference to whom a case is proved after the death of their father by virtue of the Lex Aelia Sentia or the *senatusconsultum:* for these too, if the case had been proved in the lifetime of the father, would have been under his *potestas*[4]. 6. Which rule we also apply to a son who is manumitted from a first or second mancipation after the death of his father[5].

7. When therefore a son or daughter is alive, and also grandsons or granddaughters by another son, they are called

[1] II. 159.
[2] I. 114.
[3] I. 147 *n*.
[4] I. 29 et seqq.; I. 67 et seqq.
[5] I. 132, 135; II. 141—143.

proximior est ulteriorem excludit: aequum enim videbatur nepotes neptesve in patris sui locum portionemque succedere, pari ratione et si nepos neptisve sit ex filio et ex nepote pronepos proneptisve, simul omnes vocantur ad hereditatem. (8.) Et quia placebat nepotes neptesve, item pronepotes proneptesve in parentis sui locum succedere: conveniens esse visum est non in capita, sed (in) stirpes hereditates dividi, ita ut filius partem dimidiam hereditatis ferat, et ex altero filio duo pluresve nepotes alteram dimidiam; item si ex duobus filiis nepotes extent, et ex altero filio unus forte vel duo, ex altero tres aut quattuor, ad unum aut ad duos dimidia pars pertineat, et ad tres aut quattuor altera dimidia.

P.128 9. Si nullus sit suorum heredum, tunc hereditas pertinet | ex eadem lege XII tabularum ad adgnatos[1]. (10.) Vocantur autem adgnati qui legitima cognatione iuncti sunt: legitima autem cognatio est ea quae per virilis sexus personas[2] *coniungitur. ita-*

simultaneously to the inheritance: nor does the nearer in degree exclude the more remote: for it seemed fair for the grandsons or granddaughters to succeed to the place and portion of their father. On a like principle also, if there be a grandson or granddaughter by a son and a great-grandson or great-granddaughter by a grandson, they are all called simultaneously to the inheritance. 8. And since it seemed right that grandsons and granddaughters, as also great-grandsons and great-granddaughters, should succeed into the place of their ascendant: therefore it appeared consistent that the inheritance should be divided not *per capita* but *per stirpes*, so that a son should receive one-half of the inheritance, and two or more grandsons by another son the other half: also that if there were grandsons by two sons, and from one son one or two perhaps, from the other three or four, one-half should belong to the one or two and the other half to the three or four.

9. If there be no *suus heres*, then the inheritance by the same law of the Twelve Tables belongs to the agnates[1]. 10. Now those are called agnates who are united by a relationship recognized by statute law; and a relationship recognized by statute law is one traced through persons[2] of the male sex.

[1] I. 156. Tabula v. l. 4: "Si ab intestato moritur cui suus heres nec escit, adgnatus proximus familiam habeto."

[2] This page [P. 128 of the MS.] is restored from the *Collatio*. The

que eodem patre nati fratres agna*ti si*b*i sunt, qui etiam consanguinei* vocantur, nec requiritur an etiam matrem eandem habuerint. item patruus fratris filio et invicem is illi agnatus est. eodem numero sunt fratres patrueles inter se, id est qui ex duobus fratribus progenerati sunt, quos plerique etiam consobrinos vocant. qua ratione scilicet etiam ad plures gradus agnationis pervenire poterimus. (11.) Non tamen omnibus simul agnatis dat lex XII tabularum hereditatem, sed his qui tum, cum certum est aliquem intestato decessisse, proximo gradu sunt. (12.) Nec in eo iure successio est[1]: ideoque si agnatus proximus hereditatem omiserit, vel antequam adierit, decesserit, sequentibus nihil iuris ex lege competit. (13.) Ideo autem non mortis tempore quis *proxi*mus erit requirimus, sed eo tempore quo certum fuerit aliquem intestatum decessisse, quia si quis *testamento fa*cto decesserit, melius esse visum est tunc e*x* iis requiri

Brothers therefore born from the same father are agnates one to another (and are also called *consanguinei*); nor is it a matter of inquiry whether they have the same mother as well. Likewise, a father's brother is agnate to his brother's son, and conversely the latter to the former. In the same category, one relatively to the other, are *fratres patrueles, i.e.* the sons of two brothers, who are usually called *consobrini*. And on this principle evidently we may trace out further degrees of agnation. 11. But the law of the Twelve Tables does not give the inheritance to all the agnates simultaneously, but to those who are in the nearest degree at the time when it is ascertained that a man has died intestate. 12. Under this title too there is not any devolution[1]: and therefore, if the agnate of nearest degree decline the inheritance or die before he has entered, no right accrues under the law to those of the next degree. 13. And the reason why we inquire who is nearest in degree not at the time of death but at the time when it was ascertained that a man had died intestate, is that if the man died after making a testament, it seemed the better plan for the nearest agnate to be sought

three paragraphs 7, 8, 9, which are intact in one text, are also found word for word in the *Collatio;* and what can be made out of §§ 9—13 accords with the same paragraphs in the Collation. Then the two documents are both perfect, and entirely accordant, to the end of § 17.

[1] III. 22. Ulpian, XXVI. 5.

proximum, cum certum esse coeperit neminem ex eo testamento fore heredem.

P.129 14. Quod ad feminas tamen attinet, in hoc iure aliut in | ipsarum hereditatibus capiendis placuit, aliut in ceterorum bonis ab his capiendis. nam feminarum *hereditat*es perinde ad nos agnationis iure redeunt atque masculorum: nostrae vero hereditates ad feminas ultra consanguineorum gradum non pertinent[1]. itaque soror fratri sororive legitima heres est; amita vero et fratris filia legitima heres esse (*non potest. sororis autem nobis loco est*) etiam mater aut noverca quae per in manum conventionem[2] aput patrem nostrum iura filiae nancta est.

15. Si ei qui defunctus erit sit frater et alterius fratris filius, sicut ex superioribus intellegitur[3], frater prior est, quia gradu praecedit. sed alia facta est iuris interpretatio inter suos heredes[4]. (16) Quodsi defuncti nullus frater extet, (sed) sint liberi fratrum, ad omnes quidem hereditas pertinet: sed quaesitum est, si dispari forte numero sint nati, ut ex uno unus vel duo, ex altero

for when it became certain that no one would be heir under that testament.

14. With reference to women, however, one rule has been established in this matter of law as to the taking of their inheritances, another as to the taking of the goods of others by them. For the inheritances of women devolve on us by right of agnation, equally with those of males: but our inheritances do not belong to women who are beyond the degree of *consanguineae*[1]. A sister therefore is statutable heir to a brother or a sister: but a father's sister and a brother's daughter cannot be statutable heirs. A mother, however, or a stepmother, who by *conventio in manum*[2] has gained the rights of daughter in regard to our father, stands in the place of sister to us.

15. If the deceased have a brother and a son of another brother, the brother has the prior claim, as is obvious from what we have said above[3], because he is nearer in degree. But a different interpretation of the law is made in the case of *sui heredes*[4]. 16. Next, if there be no brother of the deceased, but there be children of brothers, the inheritance belongs to all of them: but it was doubted formerly, supposing the children were unequal in number, so that there were one or two, perhaps,

[1] III. 10. [2] I. 108, 115 *b*. [3] III. 11. [4] III. 7.

tres vel quattuor, utrum in stirpes dividenda sit hereditas, sicut inter suos heredes iuris est[1], an potius in capita. iamdudum tamen placuit in capita dividendam esse hereditatem. itaque quotquot erunt ab utraque parte personae, in tot portiones hereditas dividetur, ita ut singuli singulas portiones ferant.

17. Si nullus agnatus sit, eadem lex XII tabularum gentiles
P.130 ad hereditatem vocat[2]. qui sint autem gentiles, primo com|mentario rettulimus. et cum illic admonuerimus totum gentilicium ius in desuetudinem abisse, supervacuum est hoc quoque loco de eadem re curiosius tractare.

18. Hactenus lege XII tabularum finitae sunt intestatorum hereditates: quod ius quemadmodum strictum fuerit, palam est intellegere. (19.) Statim enim emancipati liberi nullum ius

from one brother, and three or four from the other, whether the inheritance should be divided *per stirpes*, as is the rule amongst *sui heredes*[1], or rather *per capita*. It has, however, for some time been decided that the inheritance must be divided *per capita*. Therefore, whatever be the number of persons in the two branches together, the inheritance is divided into that number of portions, so that each one takes a single share.

17. If there be no agnate, the same law of the Twelve Tables calls to the inheritance the *gentiles*[2]: and who the *gentiles* are we have informed you in the first Commentary. And since we told you there that the whole of the laws relating to *gentiles* had gone into disuse, it is superfluous to treat in detail of the same matter here.

18. Thus far the inheritances of intestates are limited by the law of the Twelve Tables: and how strict these regulations were is clearly to be seen. 19. For in the first place, emanci-

[1] III. 8.

[2] Tab. V. l. 5, "Si adgnatus nec escit, gentilis familiam nancitor." The explanation referred to is not now extant; it was probably contained on the page of the MS. missing between §§ 164 and 165 of the first commentary. As the subject is merely one of antiquarian interest, it will perhaps be sufficient to quote the following passage from Cicero, *Topic.* 6: "Gentiles sunt, qui inter se eodem nomine sunt. Non est satis. Qui ab ingenuis oriundi sunt. Ne id quidem satis est. Quorum majorum nemo servitutem servivit. Abest etiam nunc. Qui capite non sunt deminuti. Hoc fortasse satis est." Festus also says: "Gentilis dicitur et ex eodem genere ortus, et is qui simili nomine appellatur, ut ait Cincius: Gentiles mihi sunt qui meo nomine appellantur." An agnate would have the same *nomen* and the same *cognomen*: a *gentilis* only the same *nomen*.

in hereditatem parentis ex ea lege habent, cum desierint sui heredes esse. (20.) Idem iuris est, si ideo liberi non sint in potestate patris, quia sint cum eo civitate Romana donati, nec ab Imperatore in potestatem redacti fuerint[1]. (21.) Item agnati capite deminuti non admittuntur ex ea lege ad hereditatem, quia nomen agnationis capitis deminutione perimitur[2]. (22.) Item proximo agnato non adeunte hereditatem, nihilo magis sequens iure legitimo admittitur[3]. (23.) Item feminae agnatae quaecumque consanguineorum gradum excedunt, nihil iuris ex lege habent[4]. (24.) Similiter non admittuntur cognati qui per feminini sexus personas necessitudine iunguntur; adeo quidem, ut nec inter matrem et filium filiamve ultro citroque[5] hereditatis capiendae ius conpetat, praeter quam si per in manum conventionem consanguinitatis iura inter eos constiterint[6].

P.131 25. Sed hae iuris iniquitates edicto Praetoris emendatae | sunt.

pated descendants have, according to this law, no right to the inheritance of their ascendant, since they have ceased to be *sui heredes*. 20. The rule is the same if children be not under the *potestas* of their father, because they have been presented with Roman citizenship at the same time with him, and have not been placed under his *potestas* by the emperor[1]. 21. Likewise, agnates who have suffered *capitis diminutio* are not admitted to the inheritance under this law, because the (very) name of agnation is destroyed by *capitis diminutio*[2]. 22. Likewise, when the nearest agnate does not enter on the inheritance, the next in degree is not on that account admitted, according to statute law[3]. 23. Likewise, female agnates who are beyond the degree of *consanguineae* have no title under this law[4]. 24. So also cognates, who are joined in relationship through persons of the female sex, are not admitted: so that not even between a mother and her son or daughter is there any right of taking an inheritance devolving either the one way or the other[5], unless by means of a *conventio in manum* the rights of consanguinity have been established between them[6].

25. But by the Praetor's edict these defects from equity in

1 I. 94.
2 I. 158.
3 III. 12.
4 III. 14.
5 Viz. neither can the mother's inheritance be taken by the son (or daughter), nor the son's (or daughter's) by the mother.
6 III. 14.

(26.) Nam eos omnes qui legitimo iure deficiuntur vocat ad hereditatem proinde ac si in potestate parentum mortis tempore fuissent, sive soli sint, sive etiam sui heredes, id est qui in potestate patris fuerunt, concurrant. (27.) Adgnatos autem capite deminutos non secundo gradu post suos heredes vocat, id est non eo gradu vocat quo per legem vocarentur, si capite minuti non essent; sed tertio, proximitatis nomine: licet enim capitis deminutione ius legitimum perdiderint, certe cognationis iura retinent[1]. itaque si quis alius sit qui integrum ius agnationis habebit, is potior erit, etiam si longiore gradu fuerit. (28.) Idem iuris est[2], ut quidam putant, in eius agnati persona, qui proximo agnato omittente hereditatem, nihilo magis iure legitimo admit-

the rule have been corrected. 26. For he calls to the inheritance all those who are deficient in statutable title, just as though they had been under the *potestas* of their ascendants at the time of their death, whether they be the sole claimants, or whether *sui heredes* also, *i.e.* those who were under the *potestas* of their father, claim with them. 27. Agnates, however, who have suffered *capitis diminutio* he does not call in the next degree after the *sui heredes*, *i.e.* he does not call them in that degree in which they would have been called by statute law if they had not suffered *capitis diminutio;* but in the third degree, on the ground of nearness of blood: for although by the *capitis diminutio* they have lost their statutable right, they surely retain the rights of cognation[1]. If, therefore, there be another person who has the right of agnation unimpaired, he will have a prior claim, even though he be in a more remote degree. 28. The rule is the same[2], as some think, in the case of an agnate, who, when the nearest agnate declines the inheritance, is not on that account admitted by statute law.

---

1 "Quia civilis ratio civilia quidem jura corrumpere potest, naturalia vero non potest." I. 158.

2 That is, such a person is called in the third, not the second degree. The question here discussed is a very important one. If the agnate referred to took as one of the third class, he would take concurrently with cognates; whereas if he took in the second class, he would have the whole inheritance to the exclusion of the cognates. Further, if the agnate were thrown, in the case supposed, into the third class, he might after all get nothing from the inheritance; for instance, he might be related to the deceased in the third degree of blood, and so be excluded by cognates who were of the first or second.

titur. sed sunt qui putant hunc eodem gradu a Praetore vocari, quo etiam per legem[1] agnatis hereditas datur. (29.) Feminae certe agnatae quae consanguineorum gradum excedunt tertio gradu vocantur, id est si neque suus heres neque agnatus ullus erit. (30.) Eodem gradu vocantur etiam eae personae quae per feminini sexus personas copulatae sunt. (31.) Liberi quoque qui in adoptiva familia sunt ad naturalium parentum hereditatem hoc eodem gradu vocantur.

P.132 32. Quos autem | Praetor vocat ad hereditatem, hi heredes ipso quidem iure non fiunt. nam Praetor heredes facere non po*test*: *per legem enim tantum vel similem iuris* con*stitution*e*m* h*eredes* fiunt, veluti per senatusconsultum et constitutionem principalem: sed *cu*m *eis*dem Pr*aetor det bonorum* p*ossessionem*, loco heredum constituuntur[2].

33. A*dhu*c a*ute*m alios complures gradus f*acit Praetor in bonorum possessionibus dandis*, d*um i*d ag*it*, ne quis *sine suc*cessore *moriatur*. de quibus in his commentariis consul*to non agimus*,

But there are some who think that such a man is called by the Praetor in the same degree as that in which the inheritance is given by statute law[1] to the agnates. 29. Female agnates who are beyond the degree of *consanguineae* are undoubtedly called in the third degree, *i.e.* in the event of there being no *suus heres* or agnate. 30. In the same class moreover are called those persons who are joined in relationship through persons of the female sex. 31. Descendants also who are in an adoptive family are called in the same degree to the inheritances of their actual ascendants.

32. Now those whom the Praetor calls to the inheritance do not become heirs in strictness of law: for the Praetor cannot make heirs, as heirs exist only by virtue of a *lex* or some analogous constitution of law, for instance a *senatusconsultum* or constitution of the emperor: but since the Praetor grants to them possession of the goods, they are put into the position of heirs[2].

33. The Praetor further makes many other degrees in the giving of possession of the goods, whilst providing that no one shall die without a successor. Concerning which degrees we purposely do not treat in this work, because we have explained all

[1] Sc. Tab. V. l. 4.
[2] See Just. *Inst.* III. 9. 2: from which this corrupt passage is restored.

quia hoc ius totum propriis commentariis *exp*lica*vimus*[1]. *hoc* solum admonuisse sufficit [*desunt lin.* 38][2]. (34.)—*item ab in-*|
P.134 testato heredes suos et agnatos ad bonorum possessionem vocat. quibus casibus beneficium eius in eo solo videtur aliquam utilitatem habere, ut is qui ita bonorum possessionem petit, interdicto cuius principium est QUORUM BONORUM uti possit[3]. cuius interdicti quae sit utilitas, suo loco proponemus. alioquin remota quoque bonorum possessione ad eos hereditas pertinet iure civili.

35. Ceterum saepe quibusdam ita datur bonorum possessio, ut is cui data sit, (non) optineat hereditatem: quae bonorum possessio dicitur sine re[4]. (36.) Nam si verbi gratia iure facto testamento heres institutus creverit hereditatem[5], sed bonorum possessionem secundum tabulas testamenti petere noluerit, con-

this branch of law in a work devoted to the subject[1]. It is sufficient to make this statement only[2]...............34....likewise he calls the *sui heredes* and *agnati*, who are heirs on an intestacy, to the possession of the goods. In which cases his grant appears to bestow an advantage only in this respect, that a man who thus sues for possession of the goods can make use of the interdict commencing with the words: *Quorum Bonorum*[3]. What is the advantage of this interdict we shall explain in its proper place. As to all other incidents, even if the grant of possession of the goods were left out of question, the inheritance belongs to them by the civil law.

35. But frequently the possession of the goods is granted to people in such a manner, that he to whom it is given does not obtain the inheritance; which possession of the goods is said to be *sine re* (without benefit)[4]. 36. For, to take an example, if the heir instituted in a testament formally executed have made cretion for the inheritance[5], but have not cared to sue for possession of the goods "in accordance with the tablets," con-

---

1 Probably the treatise *Ad Edictum Urbicum* is meant.

2 At this point several lines of the MS. are illegible; but the substance of the missing portion can be gathered from Ulpian, Tit. XXVIII. and Just. *Inst.* III. 9. The only words which can be read in the MS. are: "*per* in man*us* conventionem iura consanguini*tatis* nacta" in the 4th missing line. For the subject of Bonorum Possessio, see App. (L).

3 IV. 144. Probably this paragraph began as Just. *Inst.* III. 9. 1.

4 II. 148. Ulpian, XXIII. 6; XXVIII. 13.

5 II. 164.

tentus eo, quod iure civili heres sit, nihilo minus ii, qui nullo facto testamento ad intestati bona vocantur, possunt petere bonorum possessionem: sed sine re ad eos hereditas pertinet, cum testamento scriptus heres evincere hereditatem possit[1]. (37.) Idem iuris est, si intestato aliquo mortuo suus heres noluerit petere bonorum possessionem, contentus l*egitimo iure*[2]. *nam* et agnato competit quidem bonorum possessio, sed sine re, cum evinci hereditas ab suo herede potest. et illud convenienter, si ad adgnatum iure civili pertinet hereditas et is adierit hereditatem, sed bonorum possessionem petere noluerit, et si quis ex proximis cognatus petierit, sine re habebit bonorum possessionem propter eandem rationem. (38.) Sunt et alii quidam simi-
P.135 les casus, quorum aliquos | superiore commentario tradidimus[3].

39. Nunc de libertorum bonis videamus[4]. (40.) Olim itaque

tent with the fact that he is heir by the civil law, those who are called to the goods of the intestate in the case of no testament being made can nevertheless sue for the possession of the goods: but the inheritance belongs to them *sine re*, since the appointed heir can wrest the inheritance from them[1]. 37. The law is the same, if, when a person has died intestate, his *suus heres* do not care to sue for the possession of the goods, being content with his statutable right[2]. For then the possession of the goods belongs to the agnate, but *sine re*, since the inheritance can be wrested away from him by the *suus heres*. And in like manner, if the inheritance belong to the agnate by the civil law, and he enter upon it, but do not care to sue for possession of the goods, and if one of the cognates of nearest degree sue for it, he will for the same reason have possession of the goods *sine re*. 38. There are certain other similar cases, some of which we have treated of in the preceding Commentary[3].

39. Now let us consider about the goods of freedmen[4].

---

[1] More correctly the *bonorum possessio* belongs to them, but is *sine re*, and the *hereditas* remains with the written heir, *cum re*. But Gaius is here using *hereditas* to signify "the hereditaments," rather than "the inheritance," as he does in II. 119.

[2] *Legitimo iure* is Hollweg's suggestion. The MS. has the letter *l*, not, however, very distinct, followed by about a third of a line blank.

[3] II. 119, 148, 149.

[4] Ulpian, XXVII. XXIX.

licebat liberto patronum suum impune testamento praeterire: nam ita demum lex XII tabularum[1] ad hereditatem liberti vocabat patronum, si intestatus mortuus esset libertus nullo suo herede relicto. itaque intestato quoque mortuo liberto, si is suum heredem reliquerat, nihil in bonis eius patrono iuris erat. et si quidem ex naturalibus liberis aliquem suum heredem reliquisset, nulla videbatur esse querella; si vero vel adoptivus filius filiave, vel uxor quae in manu esset sua heres esset, aperte iniquum erat nihil iuris patrono superesse. (41.) Qua de causa postea Praetoris edicto haec iuris iniquitas emendata est. sive enim faciat testamentum libertus, iubetur ita testari, ut patrono suo partem dimidiam bonorum suorum relinquat; et si aut nihil aut minus quam partem dimidiam reliquerit, datur patrono contra tabulas testamenti partis dimidiae bonorum possessio. si vero intestatus moriatur, suo herede relicto adoptivo filio, (vel) uxore quae in manu ipsius esset, vel nuru quae in manu filii eius fuerit, data est aeque patrono adversus hos suos heredes

40. Formerly then a freedman might safely pass over his patron in his testament: for a law of the Twelve Tables[1] called the patron to the inheritance of a freedman, only if the freedman had died intestate and leaving no *suus heres*. Therefore, even when a freedman died intestate, if he left a *suus heres*, his patron had no claim to his goods. And if indeed the *suus heres* he left were one of his own actual children, there seemed to be no ground for complaint; but if the *suus heres* were an adopted son or daughter, or a wife under *manus*, it was clearly inequitable that no right should survive to the patron. 41. Wherefore this defect from equity in the law was afterwards corrected by the Praetor's edict. For if a freedman make a testament, he is ordered to make it in such manner as to leave his patron the half of his goods: and if he have left him either nothing or less than the half, possession of one-half of the goods is given to the patron "as against the tablets of the testament." Further, if he die intestate, leaving as *suus heres* an adopted son, or a wife who was under his own *manus*, or a daughter-in-law who was under the *manus* of his son, possession of half the goods is still given to the patron as against these

[1] Tab. v. l. 8.

partis dimidiae bonorum possessio. prosunt autem liberto ad P.136 ex|cludendum patronum naturales liberi, non solum quos in potestate mortis tempore habet, set etiam emancipati et in adoptionem dati, si modo aliqua ex parte heredes scripti (*sint, aut praeteriti con*)tra tabulas testamenti bonorum possessionem ex edicto petierint: nam exheredati nullo modo repellunt patronum. (42.) Postea lege Papia[1] aucta sunt iura patronorum quod ad locupletiores libertos pertinet. cautum est enim ea lege, ut ex bonis eius qui sestertiorum nu*mmorum centu*m mili*um* pluris*ve* patrimonium reliquerit[2], et pauciores quam tres liberos habebit, sive is testamento facto sive intestato mortuus erit, virilis pars patrono debeatur. itaque cum unum filium unamve filiam heredem reliquerit libertus, perinde pars dimidia patrono debetur, ac si sine ullo filio filiave moreretur; cum vero duos duasve heredes reliquerit, tertia pars debetur; si tres relinquat, repellitur patronus.

43. In bonis libertinarum nullam iniuriam antiquo iure pati-

sui heredes. But all actual descendants avail the freedman to exclude his patron, not only those whom he has under his *potestas* at the time of his death, but also those emancipated or given in adoption, provided only they be appointed heirs to some portion, or, being passed over, sue for possession of the goods "as against the tablets of the testament" in accordance with the edict: for when disinherited they in no way bar the patron. 42. Afterwards by the Lex Papia[1] the rights of patrons in regard to wealthy freedmen were increased. For it was provided by that *lex* that a proportionate share shall be due to the patron out of the goods of a freedman who has left a patrimony of the value of 100,000 sesterces or more[2], and has fewer than three children, whether he die with a testament or intestate. When, therefore, the freedman leaves as heir one son or one daughter, a half is due to the patron, just as though he died without any son or daughter: but when he leaves two heirs, male or female, a third part is due: when he leaves three the patron is excluded.

43. As to the goods of freedwomen, the patrons were not

[1] A.D. 4. See note on II. 111, and App. (H).

[2] The number is filled in from Just. *Inst.* III. 7. 2.

ebantur patroni. cum enim hae in patronorum legitima tutela essent, non aliter scilicet testamentum facere poterant quam patrono auctore[1]. itaque sive auctor ad testamentum faciendum | factus e*rat*[2] *aut de se queri debebat, quod heres ab ea* relict*us*
P.137 *non erat, aut ipsum ex testamento, si heres fa*|ctus erat, *sequebatur* hereditas: si vero auctor ei fa*ctus* non erat, *et int*estata liberta moriebatur, ad *eundem, quia suos heredes femina habere non potest, hereditas per*tinebat, nec co*gita*ri ullus *casus poterat quo quis* posset patronum a bonis *libertae invitum* repellere. (44.) Sed postea lex Papia cum quattuor liberorum iure libertinas[3] tutela patronorum liberaret, et eo modo concederet eis etiam sine tutoris auctoritate con*dere testamentum, prospexit* ut pro numero liberorum *quos liberta mortis tempo* re habuerit virilis pars patrono debeatur, eique ex bonis eius quae *C milium sestertiorum pl*urisve *reliquerit patrimo-*

injuriously affected under the ancient law. For since these women were under the statutable tutelage of their patrons, they obviously could not make a testament except with the authorization of the patron[1]. Therefore, if he had lent his authorization to the making of a testament[2], either he had himself to blame that he had not been left heir by the woman; or in case he had been left heir, the inheritance belonged to him in accordance with the testament: and supposing that he had not lent her his authorization, and the freedwoman died intestate, then too the inheritance passed to him, inasmuch as a woman cannot have *sui heredes;* neither could any case be conceived in which a person could debar the patron against his will from the property of his freedwoman. 44. But afterwards, when the Lex Papia exempted freedwomen, having the prerogative of four children[3], from the tutelage of their patrons, and thereby allowed them to make a testament even without their tutor's authorization, it provided that a proportionate share should be due to the patron, according to the number of children whom the freedwoman had at the time of her death; and that a half should be due to him out of the goods of one who left an

[1] II. 118, 122.

[2] This passage is given mainly as restored by Krüger: with one amendment, suggested by Huschke and favoured by the appearance of the MS.: viz. "ad eundem quia...hereditas pertinebat," instead of Krüger's "quia suos...ad patronum pertinebat."

[3] I. 194. Ulpian, XXIX. 3.

*nium, si testamentum fecerit, dimidia pars debeatur, si vero intestata liberta decesserit, tota heredit*as ad patronum pertinet.

45. Quae diximus de patrono, eadem intellegemus et de filio patroni, item de nepote ex filio, (et de) pronepote *ex nepote fili*o nato prognato[1]. (46.) Filia vero patroni, et *neptis* ex filio, et proneptis ex nepote filio nato prognata, olim quidem *eo iure utebantur, quod* lege XII tabularum patrono datum est, Praetor *tamen vocat tantum* ma*sculini* sexus patronorum liberos:
P.138 *sed filia, ut contra tabulas* testa|menti liberti (vel) ab intestato contra filium adoptivum vel uxorem nurumve quae in manu fuerit bonorum possessionem petat, trium liberorum iure lege Papia consequitur: aliter hoc ius non habet. (47.) Set ut ex bonis libertae testatae quattuor liberos habentis virilis pars ei debeatur, ne liberorum quidem iure consequitur, ut quidam putant. set tamen intestata liberta mortua, verba legis Papiae faciunt, ut ei virilis pars debeatur. si vero testamento facto

estate worth 100,000 sesterces or more, if she made a testament; but, if the freedwoman died intestate, the whole inheritance belongs to the patron.

45. All that we have said regarding a patron we shall apply also to the son of a patron, to his grandson by a son, and to his great-grandson sprung from a grandson born from a son[1]. 46. But the daughter of a patron, and his granddaughter by a son, and his great-granddaughter sprung from a grandson born from a son, once had the same right which is given to the patron himself by the law of the Twelve Tables; yet the Praetor only calls in male descendants of the patron: but by prerogative of three children the daughter, according to the Lex Papia, obtains (the privilege) of suing for possession of goods "as against the tablets of the testament" of a freedman, or on his intestacy in opposition to his adopted son or his wife, or his daughter-in-law under *manus;* in other cases she has not this right. 47. But, as some think, not even by prerogative of children does she obtain the right that a proportionate share should be due to her out of the goods of her freedwoman who has died testate and having four children. Still, however, if the freedwoman die intestate, the words of the Lex Papia are express that she shall have a proportionate share. But if the

[1] Ulpian, XXIX. 4.

mortua sit liberta, tale ius ei datur, quale datum est contra tabulas testamenti liberti, id est quale et virilis sexus patronorum liberi contra tabulas testamenti liberti habent: quamvis parum diligenter ea pars legis scripta sit[1]. (48.) Ex his apparet extraneos heredes[2] patronorum longe remotos esse ab omni eo iure, quod vel in intestatorum bonis vel contra tabulas testamenti patrono competit.

49. Patronae olim ante legem Papiam hoc solum ius habebant in bonis libertorum, quod etiam patronis ex lege XII tabularum datum est. nec enim ut contra tabulas testamenti ingrati liberti, vel ab intestato contra filium adoptivum vel uxorem nurumve bonorum possessionem partis dimidiae peterent, Praetor similiter ut de patrono liberisque eius curabat. (50.) Sed lex Papia duobus liberis honoratae ingenuae patronae, | liber-
P.139 tinae tribus, eadem fere iura dedit quae ex edicto Praetoris

freedwoman die leaving a testament, a right is given to the patron's daughter similar to that given to her against the testament of a freedman, that is to say, similar to the right which male descendants of a patron have, "as against the tablets of the testament:" although this portion of the *lex* is not very carefully worded[1]. 48. From the foregoing it appears that extraneous heirs[2] of a patron are completely debarred from the whole of the right which appertains to the patron himself either in respect of the goods of intestates or "as against the tablets of a testament."

49. Patronesses in olden times, before the Lex Papia was passed, had only that claim upon the goods of freedmen, which was granted to patrons also by the law of the Twelve Tables. For the Praetor did not provide for them, as he did for a patron and his descendants, that they should sue for possession of half the goods "as against the tablets of a testament" of an ungrateful freedman, or as against an adopted son, or a wife, or a daughter-in-law in a case of intestacy. 50. But the Lex Papia conferred on a freeborn patroness having two children, or a freedwoman patroness having three, almost the same rights which patrons have by the

[1] For the matter contained in these two paragraphs 46, 47, see Ulpian, XXIX. 5.
[2] II. 161.

patroni habent[1]. trium vero liberorum iure honoratae ingenuae patronae ea iura dedit quae per eandem legem patrono data sunt[2]: libertinae autem patronae non idem iuris praestitit. (51.) Quod autem ad libertinarum bona pertinet, si quidem intestatae decesserint, nihil novi patronae liberis honoratae lex Papia praestat. itaque si neque ipsa patrona neque liberta capite deminuta sit, ex lege XII tabularum ad eam hereditas pertinet, et excluduntur libertae liberi; quod iuris est etiam si liberis honorata non sit patrona: numquam enim, sicut supra diximus, feminae suum heredem habere possunt[3]. si vero vel huius vel illius capitis deminutio interveniat, rursus liberi libertae excludunt patronam, quia legitimo iure capitis deminutione perempto evenit, ut liberi libertae cognationis iure potiores habeantur. (52.) Cum autem testamento facto moritur liberta, ea quidem patrona quae liberis honorata non est nihil iuris habet contra libertae testamentum: ei vero quae liberis honorata sit, hoc ius

Praetor's edict[1]; whilst to a freeborn patroness having the prerogative of three children it gave the very rights which are given by that same law to a patron[2], although it did not give the same privilege to a freedwoman patroness. 51. But with respect to the goods of freedwomen, if they die intestate, the Lex Papia gives no new privilege to a patroness having children. If, therefore, neither the patroness herself nor the freedwoman has suffered *capitis diminutio*, the inheritance belongs to the former by the law of the Twelve Tables, and the children of the freedwoman are excluded: which is the rule even if the patroness have no children: for, as we have said above, women can never have a *suus heres*[3]. But if a *capitis diminutio* of either the one or the other have taken place, the children of the freedwoman in their turn exclude the patroness, because, when the statutable right has been destroyed by a *capitis diminutio*, the result is that the children of the freedwoman are considered to have the stronger claim by right of relationship. 52. But when a freedwoman dies after making a testament, a patroness who has no children has no right against her testament: but to one who has children the same right is granted

[1] Ulpian, XXIX. 6, 7. [2] III. 42. [3] II. 161.

tribuitur per legem Papiam quod habet ex edicto patronus contra tabulas liberti.

53. Eadem lex patronae filio liberis honorato fere[1] patroni
P.140 iura dedit; sed in huius persona etiam unius | filii filiaeve ius sufficit.

54. Hactenus omnia (ea) iura quasi per indicem tetigisse satis est: alioquin diligentior interpretatio propriis commentariis exposita est[2].

55. Sequitur ut de bonis Latinorum libertinorum dispiciamus.

56. Quae pars iuris ut manifestior fiat, admonendi sumus, id quod alio loco diximus[3], eos qui nunc Latini Iuniani dicuntur olim ex iure Quiritium servos fuisse, sed auxilio Praetoris in libertatis forma servari solitos; unde etiam res eorum peculii iure ad patronos pertinere solita est: postea vero per legem

by the Lex Papia as that which a patron has by the Praetor's edict against the testament of a freedman.

53. The same *lex* grants to the son of a patroness who has children almost[1] the rights belonging to a patron: but in his case the prerogative of even one son or daughter is sufficient.

54. It is enough to have touched on all these rights to this extent, in outline as it were: a more accurate exposition is elsewhere set forth in a book specially devoted to them[2].

55. Our next task is to consider the case of the goods of freedmen who are Latins.

56. To make this part of the law more intelligible, we must be reminded, as we said in another place[3], that those who are now called Junian Latins, were formerly slaves by Quiritary title, but through the Praetor's help used to be secured in the semblance of freedom: and so their property used to belong to their patrons by the title of *peculium:* but that afterwards, in consequence of the Lex Junia, all those whom the

---

1 The MS. has CRE. Krüger suggests *fere:* Polenaar, *omnia fere:* Huschke, *prope*. These all give an identical sense; but Mommsen would read *civi Romano*, which seems quite irrelevant.

2 Whether he refers to his treatise *Ad Edictum Urbicum*, or to that *Ad Leges Juliam et Papiam*, or to that *De Manumissionibus*, is uncertain, as the subject is appropriate to any of the three.

3 I. 22.

Iuniam eos omnes quos Praetor in libertate tuebatur liberos esse coepisse et appellatos esse Latinos Iunianos: Latinos ideo, quia lex eos liberos perinde esse voluit, atque si essent cives Romani ingenui qui ex urbe Roma in Latinas colonias deducti Latini coloniarii esse coeperunt[1]: Iunianos ideo, quia per legem Iuniam liberi facti sunt, etiamsi non essent cives Romani. legis itaque Iuniae lator, cum intellegeret futurum, ut ea fictione res Latinorum defunctorum ad patronos pertinere desinerent, quia *scilicet* neque ut servi decederent, ut possent iure peculii res
P.141 eorum ad patronos pertinere, neque | liberti Latini hominis bona possent manumissionis iure ad patronos pertinere[2], necessarium existimavit, ne beneficium istis datum in iniuriam patronorum converteretur, cavere[3], ut bona eorum proinde ad manu-

Praetor protected as if free, began to be really free, and were called Junian Latins: Latins, for the reason that the *lex* wished them to be free, just as though they had been free-born Roman citizens, who had been led out from the city of Rome into Latin colonies, and become Latin colonists[1]; Junians, for the reason that they were made free by the Junian Law, though they were not Roman citizens. Wherefore, when he who carried the Lex Junia saw that the result of this fiction would be that the goods of deceased Latins would cease to belong to their patrons; because neither would they die as slaves, so that their property could belong to their patrons by the title of *peculium*, nor could the goods of a Latin freedman belong to the patrons by the title of manumission[2]; he thought it necessary, in order to prevent the benefit bestowed on these persons from proving an injury to their patrons, to insert a proviso[3], that the

---

[1] See App. (A).

[2] The *legitima hereditas* of patrons, being derived from the law of the Twelve Tables, which did not recognize any title but that *ex jure Quiritium*, could not apply to Latins who were manumitted by owners having only the title *in bonis*. Neither could it apply to slaves manumitted irregularly and so made Latins, for the Twelve Tables again recognized no manumission but one in due form of law, *i.e.* by *vindicta, census* or testament. If the *Lex Aelia Sentia* had not been passed, there might perhaps have been a *legitima hereditas* of the goods of freedmen manumitted when under thirty years of age, but as that *lex* had forbidden such freedmen to be *cives Romani*, except in special cases, here again the rules of the Twelve Tables were inadmissible. See I. 17.

[3] The MS. has the word *voluit* after *cavere:* but this is evidently superfluous.

missores pertinerent ac si lex lata non esset. itaque iure quodammodo peculii bona Latinorum ad manumissores ea lege pertinent. (57.) Unde accidit ut longe differant ea iura quae in bonis Latinorum ex lege Iunia constituta sunt, ab his quae in hereditate civium Romanorum libertorum observantur. (58.) Nam civis Romani liberti hereditas ad extraneos heredes patroni nullo modo pertinet[1]: ad filium autem patroni nepotesque ex filio et pronepotes ex nepote (filio nato) prognatos omnimodo pertinet, etiamsi (a) parente fuerint exheredati[2]: Latinorum autem bona tamquam peculia servorum etiam ad extraneos heredes pertinent, et ad liberos manumissoris exheredatos non pertinent. (59.) Item civis Romani liberti hereditas ad duos pluresve patronos aequaliter pertinet, licet dispar in eo servo dominium habuerint[3]: bona vero Latinorum pro ea parte pertinent pro qua parte quisque eorum dominus fuerit. (60.) Item in hereditate civis Romani liberti patronus alterius patroni

goods of such freedmen should belong to their manumittors in like manner as if the law had not been passed. Therefore, the goods of Latins belong to their manumittor in virtue of that law, by a title something like that of *peculium*. 57. The result of this is that the rules applied to the goods of Latins by the Lex Junia are very different from those which are observed in reference to the inheritance of freedmen who are Roman citizens. 58. For the inheritance of a freedman who is a Roman citizen in no case belongs to the extraneous heirs of his patron[1]: but belongs in all cases to the son of the patron, to his grandsons by a son, and to his great-grandsons sprung from a grandson born from a son, even though they have been disinherited by their ascendant[2]: whilst the goods of Latins belong, like the *peculia* of slaves, even to the extraneous heirs, and do not belong to the disinherited descendants of the manumittor. 59. Likewise, the inheritance of a freedman who is a Roman citizen belongs equally to two or more patrons, although they had unequal shares of property in him as a slave[3]: but the goods of Latins belong to them according to the proportion in which each was owner. 60. Likewise, in the case of an inheritance of a freedman who was a Roman citizen, one patron excludes the son of another patron:

---

[1] III. 48.

[2] II. 45.

[3] "Placuit nullam esse libertorum divisionem." D. 37. 14. 24.

filium excludit, et filius patroni alterius patroni nepotem re-
P.142 pellit[1]: bona autem Latinorum et ad ipsum patronum et ad alterius patroni heredem simul pertinent pro qua parte ad ipsum manumissorem pertinerent. (61.) Item si unius patroni tres forte liberi sunt, et alterius unus, hereditas civis Romani liberti in capita dividitur[2], id est tres fratres tres portiones ferunt et unus quartam: bona vero Latinorum pro ea parte ad successores pertinent pro qua parte ad ipsum manumissorem pertinerent. (62.) Item si alter ex iis patronis suam partem in hereditate civis Romani liberti spernat, vel ante moriatur quam cernat[3], tota hereditas ad alterum pertinet: bona autem Latini pro parte decedentis patroni caduca fiunt[4] et ad populum pertinent.

63. Postea Lupo et Largo Consulibus[5] senatus censuit, ut bona Latinorum primum ad eum pertinerent qui eos liberasset; deinde ad liberos eorum non nominatim exheredatos, uti quis-

and the son of one patron excludes the grandson of another patron[1]: but the goods of Latins belong to a patron himself and the heir of another patron conjointly, according to the proportion in which they would have belonged to the deceased manumittor himself. 61. Again, if, for instance, there be three descendants of one patron, and one of the other, the inheritance of a freedman who is a Roman citizen is divided *per capita*[2], *i.e.* the three brothers take three portions and the only son the fourth: but the goods of Latins belong to the successors in the same proportion as that in which they would have belonged to the manumittor himself. 62. Likewise, if one of these patrons refuse his share in the inheritance of a freedman who is a Roman citizen, or die before he makes cretion[3] for it, the whole inheritance belongs to the other: but the goods of a Latin, so far as regards the portion of the patron who fails, become lapses[4] and belong to the state.

63. Afterwards, in the consulship of Lupus and Largus[5], the senate decreed that the goods of Latins should devolve; firstly, on him who freed them; secondly, on the descendants of such persons (manumittors), not being expressly disinherited, accord-

[1] Ulpian, XXVII. 2, 3.

[2] Ibid. XXVII. 4.

[3] II. 164.

[4] II. 206. Göschen thinks that *decedentis* is a mistake of the transcriber, for *deficientis*.

[5] A.D. 41.

que proximus esset; tunc antiquo iure ad heredes[1] eorum qui liberassent pertinerent. (64.) Quo senatusconsulto quidam (id) actum esse putant, ut in bonis Latinorum eodem iure utamur, quo utimur in hereditate civium Romanorum libertinorum; idemque maxime Pegaso placuit. quae sententia aperte falsa est. nam civis Romani liberti hereditas numquam ad extraneos
P.143 patroni heredes | pertinet: bona autem Latinorum etiam ex hoc ipso senatusconsulto non obstantibus liberis manumissoris etiam ad extraneos heredes pertinent. item in hereditate civis Romani liberti liberis manumissoris nulla exheredatio nocet: in bonis Latinorum nocere nominatim factam exheredationem ipso senatusconsulto significatur. verius est ergo hoc solum eo senatusconsulto actum esse, ut manumissoris liberi qui nominatim exheredati non sint praeferantur extraneis heredibus. (65.) Itaque emancipatus filius patroni praeteritus, quamvis contra tabulas testamenti parentis sui bonorum possessionem non petierit, tamen extraneis heredibus in bonis Latinorum

ing to their proximity: and then, according to the ancient law, should belong to the heirs[1] of those who had freed them. 64. The result of which *senatusconsultum* some think to be that we apply the same rules to the goods of Latins which we apply to the inheritance of freedmen who are Roman citizens: and this was most strenuously maintained by Pegasus. But his opinion is plainly false. For the inheritance of a freedman who is a Roman citizen never belongs to the extraneous heirs of his patron: whilst the goods of Latins, even by this *senatusconsultum*, belong to extraneous heirs as well, if no children of the manumittor be a bar. Likewise, in regard to the inheritance of a freedman who is a Roman citizen no deherison is of prejudice to the children of the manumittor, whilst in regard to the goods of Latins it is stated in the *senatusconsultum* itself that a deherison expressly made does prejudice. It is more correct, therefore, to say that the only effect of this *senatusconsultum* is that the children of a manumittor who are not expressly disinherited are preferred to the extraneous heirs. 65. Accordingly, the emancipated son of a patron, when passed over, is considered to have a better claim to the goods of Latins than the extraneous heirs have, notwithstanding that he may

[1] Sc. *scripti heredes.*

potior habetur. (66.) Item filia ceterique sui heredes licet iure civili inter ceteros exheredati sint, et ab omni hereditate patris sui summoveantur, tamen in bonis Latinorum, nisi nominatim a parente fuerint exheredati, potiores erunt extraneis heredibus. (67.) Item ad liberos qui ab hereditate parentis se abstinuerunt, nihilominus bona Latinorum pertinent, ab hereditate quia exheredati nullo modo dici possunt, non magis quam qui testamento silentio praeteriti sunt. (68.) Ex his omnibus satis illut apparet, si is qui Latinum fecerit,—[*desunt lin.*
P.144 22.] (69.) Item illut quoque constare videtur, si solos liberos ex disparibus partibus patronus *heredes instituerit, quod pro*
P.145 *he*redi*tariis partibus, non pro virilibus*[1], *Latini bona pu*|tant ad eos pertinere, quia nullo interveniente extraneo herede senatusconsulto locus non est. (70.) (Sed) si cum liberis suis etiam extraneum heredem patronus reliquerit, Caelius Sabinus ait

not have sued for the possession of the goods of his parent "as against the tablets of the testament." 66. Likewise, a daughter and all other *sui heredes*, although disinherited, in accordance with the civil law, in a general clause, and debarred from all the inheritance of their ascendant, yet have a claim to the goods of Latins superior to that of extraneous heirs, unless they have been expressly disinherited by their ascendant. 67. Likewise, the goods of Latins belong even to descendants who have declined to take up the inheritance of their ascendant; because they can by no means be said to be disinherited from the inheritance, any more than those can who are passed over in silence in a testament. 68. From all that has been said it is quite clear that if he who has made a man a Latin...... 69. This too seems to be admitted, that if a patron has appointed his descendants alone heirs, but for unequal portions, they think that the goods of a Latin belong to them according to their shares in the inheritance, and not in equal shares[1], because, as no extraneous heir is concerned, the *senatusconsultum* does not apply. 70. But if a patron have left a stranger heir conjointly with his descendants, Caelius Sabinus says that all

[1] The filling in of the lacuna is, with two slight variations, that of Huschke. Polenaar and Krüger suggest something different in words, but the same in signification.

tota bona pro virilibus partibus ad liberos defuncti pertinere, quia cum extraneus heres intervenit, non habet lex Iunia locum, sed senatusconsultum[1]; Iavolenus autem ait tantum eam partem ex senatusconsulto liberos patroni pro virilibus partibus habituros esse, quam extranei heredes ante senatusconsultum lege Iunia habituri essent, reliquas vero partes pro hereditariis partibus ad eos pertinere. (71.) Item quaeritur, an hoc senatusconsultum ad eos patroni liberos pertineat qui ex filia nepteve procreantur, id est ut nepos meus ex filia potior sit in bonis Latini mei quam extraneus heres. item (an) ad maternos Latinos hoc senatusconsultum pertineat quaeritur, id est ut in bonis Latini materni potior sit patronae filius quam heres

the goods (of the Latin) belong to the children in equal shares, because, when an extraneous heir is introduced, the Lex Junia does not apply, but the *senatusconsultum*[1] does; Javolenus, on the other hand, says that the children of the patron will only take that portion in equal shares according to the *senatusconsultum*, which the extraneous heirs would have had by the Lex Junia before the *senatusconsultum;* but that the other parts belong to them in the ratio of their shares in the inheritance. 71. Likewise, it is a disputed point whether this *senatusconsultum* applies to descendants of a patron through a daughter or granddaughter, *i.e.* whether my grandson by my daughter has a claim to the goods of my Latin prior to that of my extraneous heir. Likewise, it is disputed whether this *senatusconsultum* applies to Latins belonging to a mother, *i.e.* whether the son of a patroness has a claim to the goods of a Latin belonging to his mother superior to that of the extra-

[1] Sc. the S. C. of Lupus and Largus. As no mention of an equal division being enjoined by the S. C. is to be found in the portion of the text of Gaius preserved to us, it must have occurred in the fragmentary paragraphs 68 and 69. The S. C. took away the goods of the Latin from the extraneous heirs, in favour of children not expressly disinherited. A clause therefore would be needed in the S. C. to say how these should be divided, whether according to the portions in which the children had been appointed heirs, (if they were appointed,) or equally. The text tells us the S. C. declared for equality of division. The *Lex Junia*, however, having laid down the opposite rule for the division amongst extraneous heirs, the difficulty of § 70 arose with regard to the forfeitures when extraneous heirs and *sui heredes* were appointed together.

extraneus matris. Cassio placuit utroque casu locum esse senatusconsulto. sed huius sententiam plerique inprobant, quia senatus de his liberis patronarum nihil sentiat, qui aliam familiam sequerentur. idque ex eo adparet, quod nominatim exheredatos summoveat: nam videtur de his sentire qui exheredari a parente solent, si heredes non instituantur; neque autem matri
P.146 filium filiamve, neque avo | materno nepotem neptemve, si eum eamve heredem non instituat, exheredare necesse est, sive de iure civili quaeramus, sive de edicto Praetoris quo praeteritis liberis contra tabulas testamenti bonorum possessio promittitur.

72. Aliquando tamen civis Romanus libertus tamquam Latinus moritur, velut si Latinus salvo iure patroni ab Imperatore ius Quiritium consecutus fuerit: *item*[1] ut divus Traianus constituit, si Latinus invito vel ignorante patrono ius Quiritium ab Imperatore consecutus sit. quibus casibus dum vivit iste

neous heir of his mother. Cassius thought that the *senatusconsultum* was applicable in either case, but his opinion is generally disapproved of, because the senate would not have these descendants of patronesses in their thoughts, inasmuch as they belong to another family. This appears also from the fact, that they debar those disinherited expressly: for they seem to have in view those who are usually disinherited by an ascendant, supposing they be not instituted heirs; whereas there is no necessity either for a mother to disinherit her son or daughter, or for a maternal grandfather to disinherit his grandson or granddaughter, if they do not appoint them heirs; whether we look at the rules of the civil law, or at the edict of the Praetor, in which possession of goods "as against the tablets of the testament" is promised to children who have been passed over.

72. Sometimes, however, a freedman who is a Roman citizen dies as a Latin; for example, if a Latin have obtained from the Emperor the Quiritary franchise with a reservation of the rights of his patron: likewise[1], as the late emperor Trajan ruled, if a Latin has obtained the Quiritary franchise from the emperor against the will or without the knowledge of his patron. In such instances, the freedman, whilst he lives, is

[1] The MS. has *nam* instead of *item*. Huschke suggests the alteration, and would also remove the words *ut divus Traianus constituit*, and insert them after *quibus casibus* in the next clause.

libertus, ceteris civibus Romanis libertis similis est et iustos liberos procreat, moritur autem Latini iure, nec ei liberi eius heredes esse possunt; et in hoc tantum habet testamenti factionem, uti patronum heredem instituat, eique, si heres esse noluerit, alium substituere possit. (73.) Et quia hac constitutione videbatur effectum ut ne unquam isti homines tamquam cives Romani morerentur, quamvis eo iure postea usi essent, quo vel ex lege Aelia Sentia[1] vel ex senatusconsulto[2] cives Romani essent: divus Hadrianus iniquitate rei motus auctor fuit senatusconsulti faciundi, ut qui ignorante vel recusante patrono ab Imperatore ius Quiritium consecuti essent, si eo iure postea usi essent, quo ex lege Aelia Sentia vel ex senatusconsulto, si Latini mansissent, civitatem Romanam consequerentur, proinde ipsi haberentur, ac si lege Aelia Sentia vel senatusconsulto ad civitatem Romanam pervenissent. |

P.147 74. Eorum autem quos lex Aelia Sentia dediticiorum[3] numero

on the same footing with other freedmen who are Roman citizens, and begets legitimate children, but he dies as a Latin, and his children cannot be heirs to him: and he has the right of making a testament only thus far, that he may institute his patron heir, and substitute another for him in case he decline to be heir. 73. Since then the effect of this constitution seemed to be that such men could never die as Roman citizens, although they had afterwards availed themselves of those means whereby, either according to the Lex Aelia Sentia[1] or the *senatusconsultum*[2], they could become Roman citizens; the late emperor Hadrian, moved by the want of equity in the matter, caused a *senatusconsultum* to be passed, that those who had obtained the Quiritary franchise from the emperor without the knowledge or against the will of their patron, if they afterwards availed themselves of the means whereby, if they had remained Latins, they would have obtained Roman citizenship according to the Lex Aelia Sentia or the *senatusconsultum*, should be regarded in the same light as if they had attained to Roman citizenship according to the Lex Aelia Sentia or the *senatusconsultum*.

74. The goods of those whom the Lex Aelia Sentia puts into the category of *dediticii*[3] belong to their patrons; some-

[1] I. 29.

[2] Sc. the S. C. of Lupus and Largus. See §§ 69, 70.

[3] I. 13.

facit bona modo quasi civium Romanorum libertorum, modo quasi Latinorum ad patronos pertinent. (75.) Nam eorum bona qui, si in aliquo vitio non essent, manumissi cives Romani futuri essent, quasi civium Romanorum patronis eadem lege tribuuntur. non tamen hi habent etiam testamenti factionem[1]; nam id plerisque placuit, nec inmerito: nam incredibile videbatur pessimae condicionis hominibus voluisse legis latorem testamenti faciundi ius concedere. (76.) Eorum vero bona qui, si non in aliquo vitio essent, manumissi futuri Latini essent, proinde tribuuntur patronis, ac si Latini decessissent. nec me praeterit non satis in ea re legis latorem voluntatem suam verbis expressisse.

77. Videamus autem et de ea successione quae nobis ex emptione bonorum competit. (78.) Bona autem veneunt aut vivorum aut mortuorum. vivorum, velut eorum qui fraudationis causa latitant, nec absentes defenduntur; item eorum

times like those of freedmen who are Roman citizens, sometimes like those of Latins. 75. For the goods of those who on their manumission would have been Roman citizens, if they had been under no taint, are by this law assigned to the patrons, like those of freedmen who are Roman citizens; but such persons have not at the same time *testamenti factio*[1]: for most lawyers are of this opinion, and rightly: since it seemed incredible that the author of the law should have intended to grant the right of making a testament to men of the lowest *status*. 76. But the goods of those who on their manumission would have been Latins, if they had been under no taint, are assigned to the patrons, exactly as though the freedmen had died Latins. I am not, however, unaware that on this point the author of the law has not clearly expressed his intention in words.

77. Now let us consider that succession which belongs to us through the purchase of an insolvent's goods. 78. The goods which are sold may belong either to living or dead persons: living persons, for instance, when men conceal themselves with a fraudulent intent, or are not defended in their

[1] *Etiam* = like other *Cives Romani liberti*. *Testamenti factio* is here used in its highest sense. See I. 25, and note on II. 114.

qui ex lege Iulia bonis cedunt[1]; item iudicatorum post tempus, quod eis partim lege XII tabularum[2], partim edicto Praetoris, ad expediendam pecuniam tribuitur. mortuorum bona veneunt velut eorum, quibus certum est neque heredes
P.148 neque bonorum possessores[3] neque ullum alium | iustum successorem existere. (79.) Si quidem vivi bona veneant, iubet

absence; likewise, when men make a voluntary assignment[1] in accordance with the Lex Julia; likewise, the goods of judgment-debtors, after the expiration of the time which is granted them, in some cases by a law of the Twelve Tables[2], in others by the Praetor's edict, for the purpose of raising the money. The goods of dead persons are also sold; for example, those of men to whom it is certain that there will be neither heirs, *bonorum possessores*[3], nor any other lawful successor. 79. If

[1] See Mackeldey, p. 456, § 2. *Cessio bonorum* was a voluntary delivery of his goods by an insolvent, which saved him from the personal penalties of the old law. These penalties were as follows: (1) On failure to meet an engagement entered into by *nexum* (*i.e.* by provisional mancipation which a man made of himself and his estate as security against non-payment) the creditor claimed the person and property of the debtor, and these were at once assigned (*addicebantur*) to him: (2) On failure to meet engagements made in any other way, a judgment had first to be obtained and then, if after thirty days' delay payment were not made, the *addictio* followed, as in the first case. An *addictus* was at once carried off and imprisoned by his creditor, but a space of 60 days was still allowed during which he might be redeemed by payment of the debt by any friend who chose to come forward; and to afford facilities for such redemption a proclamation of the amount and circumstances of the debt was made three times, on the *nundinae*, within the 60 days. If no payment were made within this time, the *addictio* became final; the debtor's *civitas* was lost, and the creditors might even kill him or sell him beyond the Tiber. If there were several creditors, the law of the Twelve Tables, quoted by A. Gellius, was applicable; "Tertiis nundinis partes secanto: si plus minusve secuerunt se (i.e. sine) fraude esto." A. Gell. XX. 1. 49.

Savigny holds that *addictio* was originally a remedy only applicable when there was a failure to repay money lent (*certa pecunia credita*); and that the patricians to increase their power over their debtors invented the transaction called *nexum*, whereby all obligations could be turned into the form of an acknowledgment of money lent, and whereby also the interest could be made a subject of *addictio* as well as the principal: for under the old law the remedy against the debtor's person was only in respect of the principal.

Niebuhr is of opinion that *addictio* of the debtor's person was done away with by the *Lex Poetilia* A.U.C. 424; see Niebuhr's *Hist. of Rome*, III. 157, translated by Smith and Schmitz, 1851.

[2] IV. 21, see XII. Tab., Tab. III. l. 3.

[3] III. 32.

ea Praetor per dies continuos XXX possideri et proscribi; si vero mortui, post dies XV postea iubet convenire creditores, et ex eo*rum* numero magistrum creari, id est eum per quem bona veneant. itaque si vivi bona veneant, in diebus X[1] fieri iubet, si mortui, in dimidio. diebus itaque vivi bona XXXX[2], mortui vero XX, emptori addici iubet. quare autem tardius viventium bonorum venditio compleri iubetur illa ratio est, quia de vivis curandum erat ne facile bonorum venditiones paterentur.

80. Neque autem bonorum possessorum[3] neque bonorum emptorum res pleno iure fiunt, sed in bonis efficiuntur; ex iure Quiritium autem ita demum adquiruntur, si usuceperunt[4].

then the goods of a living person be sold, the Praetor orders them to be taken possession of (by the creditors) and to be advertized for sale for thirty successive days: but if those of a dead person, he orders that after fifteen days the creditors shall meet, and out of their number a *magister* be appointed, *i.e.* one by whom the goods are to be sold. Also, if the goods sold be those of a living person, he orders them to be sold (for delivery) after ten[1] days, if those of a dead person (for delivery) after half as many days; and so he commands that the goods of a living person shall be assigned over to the purchaser after forty[2] days, but those of a dead person after twenty. And the reason why the sale of the goods of living persons is ordered to become binding after a longer interval is this, that care ought to be taken when living persons are concerned that they have not to submit to sales of their goods without good reason.

80. Now neither *bonorum possessores*[3] nor the purchasers of an insolvent's goods have the property by full title, but hold it by Bonitary title alone; and it is only on completion of usucapion[4] that it becomes theirs by Quiritary title: indeed some-

[1] The number of the days in this passage is given according to Mommsen's text, but the MS. appears to have V, though the figure is indistinct.

[2] The MS. has XXX, which cannot be right, on any hypotheses.

[3] *Bonorum possessores* = those whom the Praetor recognizes as successors, although they have not the *hereditas* by the Civil Law. Conf. III. 32; IV. 34. Gaius at this point digresses for an instant into the law of intestate or testamentary succession.

[4] II. 42.

interdum quidem bonorum emptoribus ne usus quidem capio contingit, velut si pere*grinus sit* bonorum emptor, *neque ex* senatusconsulto con*cessum est ius quo* quae *civibus eius populi a nostris civibus alienan*tur usucapi possint[1]. (81.) Item quae debita *sunt ei cuius fuerunt bona*, aut ipse debuit, neque bonorum possessor ne*que* bonorum emptor ipso iure debet *aut ipsis debentur: sed* de omnibus rebus uti*libus actionibus*[2] *et conveniuntur et experiuntur*, *quas* in sequenti commentario *pro*ponemus[3]. |

P.149 82. Sunt autem etiam alterius generis successiones, quae neque lege XII tabularum neque Praetoris edicto, sed eo iure (quod) consensu receptum est introductae sunt. (83.) Etenim cum paterfamilias se in adoptionem dedit, mulierve in manum convenit[4], omnes eius res incorporales et corporales quaeque ei debitae sunt, patri adoptivo coemptionatorive ad-

times not even does usucapion run for *bonorum emptores*, as, for instance, if the *bonorum emptor* be a foreigner, and by no *senatusconsultum* has been granted the right whereby things alienated by our citizens to the citizens of that community can be usucapioned[1]. 81. Likewise, debts owing to him to whom the goods belonged, or debts which he owed, are not by the letter of the law due either to the *bonorum possessor* or the purchaser in the case of insolvency, or due from them : but on all matters such persons are sued and sue by *actiones utiles*[2], of which we shall give an account in our next book[3].

82. There are besides successions of another kind, which have been introduced into practice neither by any law of the Twelve Tables, nor by the Praetor's edict, but by those rules which are received by general consent. 83. To take an instance, when a person *sui juris* has given himself in adoption, or a woman has passed under *manus*[4], all their property, incorporeal and corporeal, and all that is due to them, is acquired by the adopting father or *coemptionator*, except those

1 This paragraph is given as reconstructed from Huschke. But it must be admitted that there is very little in the fragments of the text to support his conjectures.

2 IV. 34, 35. See note on II. 78.

3 This paragraph is thus reconstructed by Lachmann and Huschke.

4 I. 108 et seqq.

quiruntur, exceptis iis quae per capitis diminutionem pereunt, quales sunt ususfructus, operarum obligatio *libertorum* quae per iusiurandum contracta est[1], et *lites quae aguntur* legitimo iudicio[2].

84. Ex diverso q*uod* is debuit *qui se in* adoptionem dedit, quae*ve* in manum convenit, *non* transit ad coemptionatorem aut ad patrem adoptivum *nisi si* hereditarium aes alienum fuerit. *tunc* enim quia ipse pater adoptivus aut coemptionator heres fit, directo tenetur iure. is *vero qui* se adoptandum dedit, quaeve in manum convenit, desinit esse heres. De eo vero quod proprio nomine eae personae debuerint, licet neque pater adoptivus teneatur neque coemptionator, *neque* ipse quidem qui se in adoptionem dedit *vel* quae in manum convenit, maneat obligatus obligatave, quia scilicet per capitis diminutionem liberetur, tamen in eum eamve utilis actio datur re-

P.150 scissa | capitis diminutione; et si adversus hanc actionem non defendantur[3], quae bona eorum futura fuissent, si se alieno

things which perish by a *capitis diminutio*, of which kind are an usufruct, an obligation to services on the part of freedmen contracted by oath[1], and matters enforceable by a statutable action[2].

84. On the other hand, a debt owing by a man who has given himself in adoption, or by a woman who has come under *manus*, does not attach to the *coemptionator* or the adopting father himself, unless the debt be inheritable; for then since such adopting father or *coemptionator* becomes heir personally he is liable by strict law; and he who has given himself to be adopted, or she who has come under *manus*, ceases to be heir by the civil law. But with regard to a debt which such persons owed on their own account, although neither the adopting father nor the *coemptionator* is liable, nor does the man who gave himself to be adopted or the woman who came under *manus* remain bound, being freed by the *capitis diminutio*, yet an *utilis actio* is granted against them, the *capitis diminutio* being treated as non-existent: and if they be not defended[3] against this action, the Praetor permits the creditors to sell all

[1] See note on I. 26.
[2] III. 181.
[3] Sc. by the *coemptionator* or adopting father.

iuri non subiecissent, universa vendere creditoribus Praetor permittit[1].

85. *Item si is*[2] *ad quem ab intestato legitimo iure pertinet hereditas eam* legitimam hereditatem, *antequam cer*nat[3] aut pro herede gerat, alii in iure cedat[4], pleno iure fit ille heres cui cessa est hereditas *proinde ac si ipse per* legem ad hereditatem vocaretur. quodsi posteaquam heres extiterit cesserit, adhuc heres manet et ob id creditoribus ipse tenebitur: sed res corporales transferet proinde ac si singulas in iure cessisset; debita vero pereunt, eoque modo debitores hereditarii lucrum faciunt. (86.) Idem iuris est, si testamento scriptus heres, posteaquam heres extiterit, in iure cesserit hereditatem, ante aditam vero hereditatem cedendo nihil agit. (87.) Suus autem et necessarius heres an aliquit agant in iure cedendo quaeritur. nostri praeceptores nihil eos agere existimant: diversae scholae

the goods which would have been theirs, if they had not rendered themselves subject to another's authority[1].

85. Likewise, if a man[2] to whom an intestate inheritance belongs by statute law, transfer this statutable inheritance by cession in court[4] to another before exercising his cretion[3] or acting as heir, he to whom the cession is made becomes heir in full title, just as if he had himself been called to the inheritance by law. But if he make the cession after he has taken up the inheritance, he still remains heir, and therefore will be held liable personally by the creditors: but he will convey the corporeal property just as if he had made cession of each article separately: the debts, however, are at an end, and thus the debtors to the inheritance are profited. 86. The rule is the same if the heir appointed in a testament make cession after taking up the inheritance; although by making cession previously to entering on the inheritance he effects nothing. 87. Whether a *suus heres* and a *necessarius heres* can effect anything by a cession in court, is disputed. Our authorities think that their act is void: the authorities of the other

[1] IV. 38, 80.

[2] Two lines are wanting in the MS., only the words *legitimam h.* being legible in the second line; but the whole passage runs parallel with II. 34—37, from which therefore the gap can be filled up.

[3] II. 164.

[4] II. 24.

auctores idem eos agere putant, quod ceteri post aditam hereditatem; nihil enim interesse, utrum aliquis cernendo aut pro herede gerendo heres fiat, an iuris necessitate hereditati adstringatur[1]. [*deest* 1 *lin.*] |

P.151 88. (*Nunc transeamus*) ad obligationes[2]. quarum summa divisio in duas species deducitur: omnis enim obligatio vel ex contractu nascitur vel ex delicto.

89. Et prius videamus de his quae ex contractu nascuntur[3]. harum autem quattuor genera sunt: aut enim re contrahitur obligatio, aut verbis, aut litteris, aut consensu.

90. Re contrahitur obligatio velut mutui datione. (quae) proprie in his fere rebus contingit quae pondere, numero,

school think that they effect the same as other heirs who have entered upon an inheritance, for that it makes no difference whether a man become heir by cretion or by acting as heir, or be compelled to (enter upon) the inheritance by necessity of law[1].

88. Now let us pass on to obligations[2]: the main division whereof is into two kinds: for every obligation arises either from contract or from delict.

89. First, then, let us consider as to those which arise from contract[3]. Of these there are four kinds, for the obligation is contracted either by the act itself, by words, by writing, or by consent.

90. An obligation is contracted *re*, for example, in the case of a loan to be returned in kind. Strictly speaking, this deals

[1] To understand this passage fully we must recollect that a *suus heres*, as well as a *necessarius*, cannot free himself from the inheritance, in name at least. See II. 157.

[2] Justinian says: "Obligatio est juris vinculum quo necessitate adstringimur alicujus solvendae rei secundum nostrae civitatis jura." *Inst.* III. 13. *pr.* The latter words of the definition indicate that no obligation was recognized by the law unless it could be enforced by action. For a full discussion of Obligation see App. (N).

[3] Gaius does not define a contract in his Commentaries. Three elements go to its constitution, an offer from the one party, an acceptance by the other, and an obligation imposed by the law compelling the parties to abide by their offer and acceptance. When the law does not impose such obligation, the agreement is only a *pactum*, and cannot found an action, although it may be used as a defence. The Roman law regarded those agreements as contracts which were solemnized in the four ways named in the text, *re*, *verbis*, *litteris*, or *consensu*. For a list of these contracts see Appendix (N).

mensura constant: qualis est pecunia numerata, vinum, oleum, frumentum, aes, argentum, aurum. quas res aut numerando aut metiendo aut pendendo in hoc damus, ut accipientium fiant et quandoque nobis non eadem, sed alia eiusdem naturae reddantur: unde etiam mutuum appellatum est, quia quod ita tibi a me datum est ex meo tuum fit. (91.) Is quoque qui non debitum accepit ab eo qui per errorem solvit re obligatur. nam proinde ei condici potest[1] SI PARET EUM DARE OPORTERE, ac si mutuum accepisset[2]. unde quidam putant pupillum aut mulierem

almost entirely with those things which are matters of weight, number and measure, such as coin, wine, oil, corn, brass, silver, gold. And these we give by counting, measuring or weighing them, with the intent that they shall become the property of the recipients, and that at some future time not the same but others of like nature shall be restored to us: whence also the transaction is called *mutuum*, because what is so given to you by me becomes yours from being mine. 91. He also who receives a payment not due to him from one who makes the payment by mistake is bound *re*. For the condiction[1] worded thus: "should it appear that he ought to give" can be brought against him, just as though he had received a loan to be returned in kind[2]. Wherefore, some hold that a pupil or a woman to whom that which is not due has been given by mistake

[1] IV. 4, 5.

[2] This is not a case of contract at all, but of what is called quasi-contract. Justinian (III. 13) divides obligations into four classes, the classes additional to those of Gaius being *quasi ex contractu, quasi ex delicto*. These quasi-contracts are, as Austin clearly explains,—"Acts done by one person to his own inconvenience for the advantage of another, but without the authority of the other, and consequently without any promise on the part of the other to indemnify him or reward him for his trouble. An obligation, therefore, arises such as would have arisen had the one party contracted to do the act and the other to indemnify or reward." A quasi-delict, on the other hand, according to Austin, though this is not what the Roman lawyers mean by the term, is "an incident by which damage is done to the obligee (though without the negligence or intention of the obligor), and for which damage the obligor is bound to make satisfaction. It is not a delict, because intention or negligence is of the essence of a delict."

The truth is that in both these cases an incident begets an obligation, and until the breach of that obligation by refusal to indemnify or make satisfaction there is neither contract nor delict, although after such refusal there is no doubt a delict. So Gaius himself says elsewhere: "Obligationes aut ex contractu nascuntur, aut ex maleficio, aut proprio quodam jure ex variis causarum figuris." D. 44. 7. 1. pr.

cui sine tutoris auctoritate[1] non debitum per errorem datum est non teneri condictione, non magis quam mutui datione. sed haec species obligationis non videtur ex contractu consistere, quia is qui solvendi animo dat magis distrahere vult negotium quam contrahere.

P.152 92. Verbis | obligatio fit ex interrogatione et responsione, velut: DARI SPONDES? SPONDEO; DABIS? DABO; PROMITTIS? PROMITTO; FIDEPROMITTIS[2]? FIDEPROMITTO; FIDEIUBES? FIDEIUBEO; FACIES? FACIAM. (93.) Sed haec quidem verborum obligatio: DARI SPONDES? SPONDEO, propria civium Romanorum est, ceterae vero iuris gentium sunt; itaque inter omnes homines, sive cives Romanos sive peregrinos valent. et quamvis ad Graecam vocem expressae fuerint, velut hoc modo: [δώσεις; δώσω· ὁμολογεῖς; ὁμολογῶ· πίστει κελεύεις; πίστει κελεύω· ποιήσεις; ποιήσω][3]; etiam haec tamen inter cives Romanos valent,

without the authorization of the tutor[1] is not liable to the condiction, any more than he or she would be in the case of a loan to be returned in kind having been given. But this species of obligation does not seem to arise from contract, since he who gives with the intent of paying wishes rather to end a contract than to begin one.

92. An obligation *verbis* originates from a question and answer, for instance: Do you engage that it shall be given? I do engage. Will you give? I will give. Do you promise? I do promise. Do you become *fidepromissor*[2]? I do become *fidepromissor*. Do you become *fidejussor*? I do become *fidejussor*. Will you do? I will do. 93. But the verbal obligation: Do you engage that it shall be given? I do engage: is peculiar to Roman citizens, whilst the others appertain to the *jus gentium*, and therefore hold good amongst all men, whether Roman citizens or foreigners. And even if they be expressed in the Greek language, as thus: δώσεις; δώσω· ὁμολογεῖς; ὁμολογῶ· πίστει κελεύεις; πίστει κελεύω· ποιήσεις; ποιήσω[3], they still hold good amongst Roman citizens,

[1] The MS. has *totae*: but this is so clearly a mistake, that there is no doubt as to replacing it by *tutoris auctoritate*.

[2] III. 115.

[3] These Greek words are not in the MS.: but are supplied from Theophilus, 3. 15. 1. The transcriber evidently did not understand Greek, and just before wrote "eregam vocem" for "Graecam vocem," and just afterwards writes "gregis sermonis" for "Graeci sermonis."

si modo Graeci sermonis intellectum habeant. et e contrario quamvis Latine enuntientur, tamen etiam inter peregrinos valent, si modo Latini sermonis intellectum habeant. at illa verborum obligatio: DARI SPONDES? SPONDEO, adeo propria civium Romanorum est, ut ne quidem in Graecum sermonem per interpretationem proprie transferri possit; quamvis dicatur a Graeca voce figurata esse[1]. (94.) Unde dicitur uno casu hoc verbo peregrinum quoque obligari posse, velut si Imperator noster principem alicuius peregrini populi de pace ita interroget: PACEM FUTURAM SPONDES? vel ipse eodem modo interrogetur; quod nimium subtiliter dictum est; quia si quid adversus pactionem fiat, non ex stipulatu agitur, sed iure belli
P.153 res vindicatur. (95.) Illut dubitari potest, si quis[2] | *interroganti*

provided only they understand Greek. And conversely, though they be pronounced in Latin, they nevertheless hold good amongst foreigners also, provided only they understand Latin. But the verbal obligation: Do you engage that it shall be given? I do engage: is so peculiar to Roman citizens that it cannot properly be translated into Greek; although it is said to be modelled upon a Greek word[1]. 94. Hence it is said that in one case a foreigner also can be bound by this word, for instance, if our Emperor interrogate the prince of some foreign people regarding peace: Do you engage that there shall be peace? or if he be himself interrogated in like manner. But this is laid down with too much refinement: because if anything be done contrary to the agreement, an action is not brought on the stipulation, but the matter is redressed according to the rules of war. 95. It may be doubted whether any one[2] is

---

[1] Sc. from *σπένδω*.

[2] Twenty-four lines are lost here; but by comparison with the Epitome we may conjecture what was the substance of the missing portion; and a word or two decipherable in the MS. here and there shows the probability of the conjecture. First the question was discussed whether the two contracting parties might speak in different languages, which probably was settled in the affirmative. Then two cases were alluded to in which a verbal contract might be unilateral in form, i.e. in which no question need precede the promise. These were (1) *dotis dictio*, or a promise of dower made by the wife, the intended wife, or the father or debtor of the intended wife, to the husband or intended husband; Ulpian, VI. 1, 2: (2) a promise made by a freedman to his patron and confirmed by oath; III. 83. We say "unilateral in form": for it is obvious that stipulations generally were bilateral in

Latine respondeat Graece, aut interroganti Graece respondeat Latine, an recte obligetur[1]. *Sunt et* aliae obligationes *quae nulla praecedente interrogatione contrahi possunt, id est, ut si mulier, sive sponso uxor futura, sive iam marito dotem dicat......* nullo... Conplicando... *Quod tam de* corporali*bus rebus quam de incorporalibus fieri potest*[2]. *Et non solum in hac obligatione ipsa mulier sed et pater eius...item* si debitor *iussu mulieris debitum suum sponso vel marito* doti dicat. *Alius vero dotis dictione* obligari *sponso vel marito* non potest.... Et ideo si quis alius *pro muliere dotem promittere velit com*muni iure obligare *se debet, id est* st*ipulanti sponso vel marito promit*tit. *Item et alio casu uno loquente et sine interrogatione alii promittente contrahitur obligatio, id est, si libertus patrono aut donum aut munus aut operas se daturum esse juravit; in qua re autem non tam verbis*

duly bound, when he replies in Greek to one who asks the question in Latin, or replies in Latin to one who asks the question in Greek[1]. There are other obligations besides which can be entered into without any precedent question, for instance, if a woman, either when about to marry states a *dos* to her betrothed husband or to an actual husband. Such statement can be made either as to corporeal things or as to incorporeal[2]. And not only can a woman enter into such an obligation, but her father also can. Likewise, if a debtor by order of the woman states as *dos* his debt to the husband, betrothed or actual. But no other person can be bound by statement of *dos* to a husband, betrothed or actual. And therefore if any other person wishes to promise a *dos* on behalf of a woman, he must bind himself in ordinary form, i.e. he promises in answer to the question of the husband, betrothed or actual. Likewise, in another instance, when one party alone speaks and promises another without question asked, an obligation is contracted, viz. if a freedman has sworn that he will give to his patron a gift, or a present or services; but in this case the obligation

form, although they were invariably unilateral in essence, the whole burden lying on one party, the whole benefit accruing to the other.

[1] See Theophilus 3. 16. 1 and D. 45. 1. 1. 6.

[2] The Epitome has: "quod tam de mobilibus rebus quam de fundis fieri potest." But the Epitome often varies considerably from the text of Gaius; and the word "corporal" is very clear in the MS.

quam jurejurando *consistit* obligatio. *praeterea* autem *nequa-*
P.154 *quam*[1] jurejurando homines | obligantur

96.— utique cum quaeritur de iure Romanorum. nam aput peregrinos quid iuris sit, singularum civitatium iura requirentes aliud intellegere poterimus *in aliis valere*[2].

97. Si id quod dari stipulamur[3] tale sit, ut dari non possit, inutilis est stipulatio: velut si quis hominem liberum quem servum esse credebat, aut mortuum quem vivum esse credebat, aut locum sacrum vel religiosum quem putabat humani iuris esse dari stipuletur[4]. (97 a.) (*item si quis rem quae in rerum natura non est aut esse non potest, velut hippocentaurum stipuletur,*)[5] aeque inutilis est stipulatio.

98. Item si quis sub ea condicione stipuletur quae existere

is founded not so much on the words as on the oath. But, except in this instance, men are not at all[1] bound by their oath.

96. .... are bound: at any rate when the question is as to Roman law. For as to the law amongst foreigners, if we inquire into the rules of individual states, we may be able to discover that one rule prevails in one, and another in another[2].

97. If that which we stipulate[3] to be given be of such a kind that it cannot be given, the stipulation is void: for instance, if a man stipulate for a free man to be given to him thinking him a slave, or a dead man thinking him alive, or a place sacred or religious thinking it *humani juris*[4]. 97 *a.* Likewise if any one stipulate for a thing which does not exist or cannot exist, for instance, a centaur[5], the stipulation is in such a case also void.

98. Likewise, if any one stipulate under a condition which

---

1 This is a suggestion by Studemund.

2 See III. 120, note.

3 Gaius uses the verb *stipulor* here for the first time, without having defined it: the *stipulator* is the interrogator in an obligation *verbis*: *stipulor* therefore signifies to ask for something in solemn form.

As to the derivation of the word *stipulatio* there are many theories: Paulus connects it with *stipulus*, an old adjective signifying firm (*S. R.* V. 7. 1): Festus and Varro with *stips*, a coin (Varro, *de Ling. Lat.* V. 182): Isidorus with *stipula*, a straw, because, he says, in olden times the contracting parties used to break a straw in two and each retain a portion, so that by reuniting the broken ends "*sponsiones suas agnoscebant.*" (*Orig. Verb.* 24, § 30.)

4 II. 2—4.

5 The line or two omitted by the copyist are supplied from Just. *Inst.* 3. 19. 1.

non potest, veluti si digito caelum tetigerit, inutilis est stipulatio. sed legatum sub inpossibili condicione relictum nostri praeceptores proinde deberi putant, ac si sine condicione relictum esset: diversae scholae auctores non minus legatum inutile existimant quam stipulationem, et sane vix idonea diversitatis ratio reddi potest. (99.) Praeterea inutilis est stipulatio, si quis ignorans rem suam esse dari sibi eam stipuletur; quippe quod alicuius est, id ei dari non potest.

100. Denique inutilis est talis stipulatio, si quis ita dari stipuletur: POST MORTEM MEAM DARI SPONDES? vel ita: (*POST MORTEM TUAM DARI SPONDES? valet autem, si quis ita dari stipuletur: CUM MORIAR DARI SPONDES? vel ita:*)[1] CUM MORIERIS
P.155 DARI | SPONDES? id est ut in novissimum vitae tempus stipulatoris aut promissoris obligatio conferatur. nam inelegans esse visum est ex heredis persona incipere obligationem. rursus ita stipulari non possumus: PRIDIE QUAM MORIAR, aut: PRIDIE

cannot come to pass, for instance, "if he touch heaven with his finger," the stipulation is void. But our authorities think that a legacy left under an impossible condition is as valid as it would be if the condition had not been attached: the authorities of the other school think the legacy no less invalid than the stipulation. And truly a satisfactory reason for the difference can scarcely be given. 99. Besides a stipulation is void, if a man in ignorance that a thing is his own stipulate for it to be given to him: for that which is a man's cannot be given to him.

100. Lastly, a stipulation of the following kind is void; if a man stipulate thus for a thing to be given: Do you engage that it shall be given after my death? or thus: Do you engage that it shall be given after your death? But it is valid if a man thus stipulate for it to be given: Do you engage that it shall be given when I am dying? or thus: Do you engage that it shall be given when you are dying? i.e. that the obligation shall be referred to the last instant of the life of the stipulator or promiser. For it seems anomalous that the obligation should begin in the person of the heir. Again, we cannot stipulate thus: Do you engage that it shall be

[1] The words in brackets were first suggested by Huschke, in accordance with what is stated in II. 232: D. 45. 1. 45. 1: D. 45. 1. 121. 2: Theophilus, 3. 20. 14.

QUAM MORIERIS, DARI SPONDES? quia non potest aliter intellegi pridie quam aliquis morietur, quam si mors secuta sit; rursus morte secuta in praeteritum redducitur stipulatio et quodammodo talis est: HEREDI MEO DARI SPONDES? quae sane inutilis est[1]. (101.) Quaecumque de morte diximus, eadem et de capitis diminutione dicta intellegimus[2].

102. Adhuc inutilis est stipulatio, si quis ad id quod interrogatus erit non responderit: velut si sestertia x a te dari stipuler, et tu nummum sestertium v milia promittas; aut si ego pure stipuler, tu sub condicione promittas.

103. Praeterea inutilis est stipulatio, si ei dari stipulemur cuius iuri subiecti non sumus: unde illut quaesitum est, si quis sibi et ei cuius iuri subiectus non est dari stipuletur in quantum valeat stipulatio. nostri praeceptores putant in universum valere, et proinde ei soli qui stipulatus sit solidum deberi, atque si

given the day before I die, or the day before you die? Because which is the day before a person dies cannot be ascertained unless death has ensued: and again, when death has ensued, the stipulation is thrown into the past, and is in a manner of this kind: Do you engage that it shall be given to my heir? which is undoubtedly invalid[1]. 101. Whatever we have said about death we also understand to be said about *capitis diminutio*[2].

102. Further, a stipulation is void if a man do not reply to the question he is asked; for instance, if I should stipulate for ten *sestertia* to be given by you, and you should promise five *sestertia*: or if I should stipulate unconditionally, and you promise under a condition.

103. Further, a stipulation is void if we stipulate for a thing to be given to a man to whose authority we are not subject: hence this question arises, if a man stipulate for a thing to be given to himself and one to whose authority he is not subject, how far is the stipulation valid? Our authorities think it is valid to the full amount, and that the whole is due to him alone who stipulated, just as though he had not added

---

[1] Justinian abolished all these distinctions, and made valid obligations for performance after the death of either party. *Inst.* III. 19. 13.

[2] I. 159 et seqq.

extranei nomen non adiecisset. sed diversae scholae auctores
P.156 | dimidium ei deberi[1] existimant, pro altera vero parte inutilem esse stipulationem. Alia causa est *si ita* stipu*latus sim: mihi aut Titio* dari spondes? *quo casu constat mihi* solidum deberi, et me solum *ex ea stipulatione agere posse* qua*mqu*am etiam Titio *solvendo* liberaris[2].

104. Item inutilis est stipulatio, si ab eo stipuler qui iuri meo subiectus est, item si is a me stipuletur. (sed) servus quidem et qui in mancipio est et *filiafamilia*s, et quae in manu est, non solum ipsi cuius iuri subiecti subiectaeve sunt obligari non possunt, sed ne alii quidem ulli.

105. Mutum neque stipulari neque promittere posse palam est. Idem etiam in surdo receptum est: quia et is qui stipulatur verba promittentis, et qui promittit verba stipulantis exaudire debet. (106.) Furiosus nullum negotium gerere potest, quia non intellegit quid agat. (107.) Pupillus omne negotium recte

the name of the stranger. But the authorities of the other school think half is due to him[1], and that the stipulation is void as to the other half. It is a different matter when I stipulate thus: Do you engage that it shall be given to me *or* to Titius: for in this case it is admitted that the whole is due to me, and that I alone am able to sue upon the stipulation, although you can discharge yourself also by payment to Titius[2]?

104. Likewise, a stipulation is void if I stipulate for payment from one who is subject to my authority, and so too if he stipulate for payment from me. But a slave, and a person in *mancipium*, and a *filiafamilias*, and a woman in *manus*, are not only unable to be under obligation to the person to whose authority they are subject, but to any one.

105. That a dumb man can neither stipulate nor promise is plain. The same is also the rule as to a deaf man: because both he who stipulates ought to hear the words of the promiser, and he who promises the words of the stipulator. 106. A madman can transact no business, because he does not understand what he is about. 107. A pupil can legally

[1] Justinian adopted the latter view. *Inst.* III. 19. 4.

[2] D. 45. 1. 56. *pr.*: D. 45. 1. 141. 3: D. 46. 3. 10.

gerit: ita tamen ut tutor, sicubi tutoris auctoritas necessaria sit, adhibeatur, velut si ipse obligetur[1]: nam alium sibi obligare etiam sine tutoris auctoritate potest[2]. (108.) Idem iuris est in feminis quae in tutela sunt[3]. (109.) Set quod diximus de pupillis, utique de eo verum est qui iam aliquem intellectum habet: nam infans et qui infanti proximus est non multum a furioso
P.157 differt, quia huius aetatis pupilli nullum intellectum habent: sed in his pupillis per utilitatem benignior iuris interpretatio facta est[4].

110. Possumus tamen[5] ad id quod stipulamur alium adhibere qui idem stipuletur, quem vulgo adstipulatorem vocamus.

transact any business, provided that his tutor be present in cases where the tutor's authorization is necessary, for instance, when the pupil binds himself[1]: for he can bind another to himself even without the authorization of the tutor[2]. 108. The law is the same with regard to women who are under tutelage[3]. 109. But what we have said regarding pupils is only true about one who has already some understanding: for an infant and one almost an infant do not differ much from a madman, because pupils of this age have no understanding: but through regard for their interests a somewhat lenient construction of the law has been made in the case of such pupils[4].

110. We can, however[5], make another person a party to that for which we stipulate, so as to stipulate for the same, and such an one we commonly call an *adstipulator*.

---

1 Ulpian, XI. 27.

2 II. 83.

3 I. 192; II. 80.

4 That is, although they have little or no understanding, their stipulations or promises backed by the tutor's authorization are binding.

For the technical interpretation of *infanti proximus*, see III. 208, note.

5 "Hoc *tamen* respicit ad § 103." Gneist. In § 103 it is stated that no man can stipulate for the benefit of another, to which statement the doctrine of adstipulators is at first sight opposed.

The subject here discussed, viz. "De adstipulatoribus," is entirely omitted from the *Institutes* of Justinian; perhaps because the well-established principle of the older law, that a right of action could not originate in the heir of the stipulator (which was one of the chief reasons for adstipulators being employed at all) was destroyed by imperial enactment. See Cod. 4. 11, where the rule, "Ab heredibus non incipere actiones nec contra heredes," is especially condemned.

(111.) Sed huic proinde actio competit, proindeque ei recte solvitur ac nobis. sed quidquid consecutus erit mandati iudicio nobis restituere cogetur[1]. (112.) Ceterum potest etiam aliis verbis uti adstipulator quam quibus nos usi sumus. itaque si verbi gratia ego ita stipulatus sim: DARI SPONDES? ille sic adstipulari potest: IDEM FIDE TUA PROMITTIS? vel IDEM FIDE IUBES? vel contra[2]. (113.) Item minus adstipulari potest, plus non potest. itaque si ego sestertia x stipulatus sum, ille sestertia v stipulari potest; contra vero plus non potest. item si ego pure stipulatus sim, ille sub condicione stipulari potest; contra vero non potest. non solum autem in quantitate, sed etiam in tempore minus et plus intellegitur[3]: plus est enim statim aliquid dare, minus est post tempus dare. (114.) In hoc autem iure quaedam singulari iure observantur. nam ad-
P.158 stipulatoris heres non habet actionem[4]. item | servus adstipu-

111. An action then will equally lie for him and payment can as properly be made to him as to us, but whatever he has obtained he will be compelled to deliver over to us by an action of mandate[1]. 112. But the adstipulator may even use other words than those which we use. Therefore if, for example, I have stipulated thus: Do you engage that it shall be given? He may adstipulate thus: Do you become *fidepromissor* for the same? or: Do you become *fidejussor* for the same? or *vice versâ*[2]. 113. Likewise, he can adstipulate for less, but not for more. Therefore if I have stipulated for ten sestertia, he can (ad)stipulate for five: but he cannot do the contrary. Likewise, if I have stipulated unconditionally, he can (ad)stipulate under a condition: but he cannot do the contrary. And the more and the less are considered with reference not only to quantity but also to time[3]: for it is more to give a thing at once, less to give it after a time. 114. As to this matter of law some peculiar rules are observed. For the heir of the adstipulator can bring no action[4]. Likewise, a slave

[1] III. 117, 155 et seqq.

[2] III. 115. We may stipulate with the principal, and the adstipulator may adstipulate with a surety (*fidepromissor* or *fidejussor*); or we may stipulate with the surety, and he adstipulate with the principal.

[3] IV. 53.

[4] IV. 113.

lando nihil agit, quamvis ex ceteris omnibus causis stipulatione domino adquirit[1]. idem de eo qui in mancipio est magis placuit; nam et is servi loco est[2]. is autem qui in potestate patris est agit aliquid sed parenti non adquirit; quamvis ex omnibus ceteris causis stipulando ei adquirat. ac ne ipsi quidem aliter actio competit, quam si sine capitis diminutione exierit de potestate parentis, veluti morte eius, aut quod ipse flamen Dialis inauguratus est[3]. eadem de filiafamilias, et quae in manu est, dicta intellegemus.

115. Pro eo quoque qui promittit solent alii obligari, quorum alios sponsores, alios fidepromissores, alios fideiussores appellamus. (116.) Sponsor ita interrogatur: IDEM DARI SPONDES? fidepromissor: IDEM FIDEPROMITTIS? fideiussor ita: IDEM FIDE TUA ESSE IUBES? videbimus de his autem quo nomine possint proprie adpellari qui ita interrogantur: IDEM DABIS? IDEM PROMITTIS? IDEM FACIES[4]? (117.) Sponsores quidem et fidepro-

who adstipulates effects nothing, although in all other cases he acquires for his master by stipulation[1]. The same is generally held with regard to one who is under *mancipium*: for he too is in the position of a slave[2]. But he who is under the *potestas* of his father does a valid act, but does not acquire for his ascendant: although in all other cases he acquires for him by stipulation. And an action does not even lie for him personally, unless he have passed from his ascendant's *potestas* without a *capitis diminutio*, for instance, by that ascendant's death, or because he himself has been instituted Flamen Dialis[3]. The same we shall consider to be said with regard to a woman under *potestas* or under *manus*.

115. For the promiser also others are frequently bound, some of whom we call *sponsores*, some *fidepromissores*, some *fidejussores*. 116. A sponsor is interrogated thus: Do you engage that the same thing shall be given? a fidepromissor: Do you become fidepromissor for the same? a fidejussor: Do you become fidejussor for the same? But by what name those should properly be called who are interrogated thus: Will you give the same? Do you promise the same? Will you do the same? is a matter for our consideration[4]. 117. We are in the

[1] II. 87.
[2] I. 123, 138.
[3] I. 130.
[4] Such an one would be a fidejussor according to Ulpian. See D. 46. 1. 8. pr.

missores et fideiussores saepe solemus accipere, dum curamus ut diligentius nobis cautum sit. adstipulatorem vero fere tunc solum adhibemus cum ita stipulamur ut aliquid post mortem nostram detur: (quod cum) stipulando nihil agimus[1], adhibetur adstipulator, ut is post mortem nostram agat: qui si quid fuerit
P.159 consecutus| de *restitue*ndo eo mandati iudicio heredi meo tenetur[2].

118. Sponsoris vero et fidepromissoris similis condicio est, fideiussoris valde dissimilis. (119.) Nam illi quidem nullis obligationibus accedere possunt nisi verborum: quamvis interdum ipse qui promiserit non fuerit obligatus, velut si (femina) aut pupillus sine tutoris auctoritate, aut quilibet post mortem suam dari promiserit. at illut quaeritur, si servus aut peregrinus spoponderit, an pro eo sponsor aut fidepromissor obligetur[3]. fideiussor vero omnibus obligationibus, id est sive re sive verbis

frequent habit of taking sponsors, fidepromissors, and fidejussors, to make certain that we are carefully secured. But we scarcely ever employ an adstipulator save when we stipulate that something is to be given us after our death: for since we effect nothing by such a stipulation[1], an adstipulator is introduced, that he may bring the action after our death: and if he obtain anything, he is liable to my heir for its delivery in an action of mandate[2].

118. The position of a sponsor and fidepromissor is very much the same, that of a fidejussor very different. 119. For the former cannot be attached to any but verbal obligations: although sometimes the promiser himself is not bound, for instance, if a woman or a pupil have promised anything without authorization of the tutor, or if any person have promised that something shall be given after his death. But if a slave or a foreigner have promised by the word *spondeo*, it is questionable whether the sponsor or fidepromissor is bound for him[3]. A fidejussor on the contrary can be attached to any obligation,

[1] III. 100.

[2] III. 155.

[3] The reason for the difference is that the Roman law regarded the promise of the woman or pupil as binding morally, but that of the slave or foreigner as entirely void. Hence the surety's engagement, concluded in due form, is in the first case an accessory to what the law does more or less recognize, and so stands good; whilst in the other case it is an accessory to a nullity, and therefore a nullity itself.

sive litteris sive consensu contractae fuerint obligationes, adici potest. at ne illut quidem interest, utrum civilis an naturalis obligatio sit cui adiciatur; adeo quidem ut pro servo quoque obligetur, sive extraneus sit qui a servo fideiussorem accipiat, sive ipse dominus in id quod sibi debeatur. (120.) Praeterea sponsoris et fidepromissoris heres non tenetur, nisi si de peregrino fidepromissore quaeramus, et alio iure civitas eius utatur[1]: fideiussoris autem etiam heres tenetur. (121.) Item sponsor et fidepromissor lege Furia[2] biennio liberantur: et quotquot erunt numero eo tempore quo pecunia peti potest, in tot partes deducitur inter eos obligatio, et singuli viriles partes *dare iu*bentur[3]. fideiussores vero perpetuo tenentur; et quotquot erunt numero,
P.160 singuli in solidum | obligantur. itaque liberum est creditori a quo *velit* solidum petere. sed nunc ex epistula divi Hadriani *compel*l*itur* creditor a singulis, qui modo solvendo sint, partes

i.e. whether it be contracted *re*, *verbis*, *litteris* or *consensu*. And it does not even matter whether it be a civil or a natural obligation to which he is attached, so that he can be bound even for a slave, whether the receiver of the fidejussor from the slave be a stranger, or the master himself for that which is due to him. 120. Besides, the heir of a sponsor and fidepromissor is not bound, unless we be considering the case of a foreign fidepromissor, and his state adopt a different rule[1]: but the heir of a fidejussor is bound as well as himself. 121. Likewise, a sponsor and a fidepromissor are freed from liability after two years, by the Lex Furia[2]: and whatever be their number at the time when the money can be sued for, the obligation is divided amongst them into so many parts, and each of them is ordered to pay one part[3]. But fidejussors are bound for ever, and whatever be their number, each is bound for the whole amount. And so it is allowable for the creditor to demand the whole from whichever of them he may choose. But now according to an epistle of the late emperor Hadrian the creditor is compelled to sue for a proportional part from each of those only

[1] From this section it would almost appear as if the notion of a *comitas gentium* existed in Roman Jurisprudence, so as to warrant the belief that there was something like *private* international law. See III. 96.

[2] Enacted probably in B.C. 95. IV. 22.

[3] The MS. has *hocabentur*.

petere. eo igitur distat haec epistula a lege Furia, quod si quis ex sponsoribus aut fidepromissoribus solvendo non sit, hoc onus (*ad ceteros non pertinet; si vero ex fideiussoribus, hoc onus*)[1] ad ceteros quoque pertinet. set cum lex Furia tantum in Italia locum habeat, evenit, ut in caeteris provinciis sponsores quoque et fidepromissores proinde ac fideiussores in perpetuo teneantur et singuli in solidum obligentur, nisi ex epistula divi Hadriani hi quoque adiuvantur in parte. (122.) Praeterea inter sponsores et fidepromissores lex Apuleia[2] quandam societatem introduxit. nam si quis horum plus sua portione solverit, de eo quod amplius dederit adversus ceteros actiones constituit. quae lex ante legem Furiam lata est, quo tempore in solidum obligabantur: unde quaeritur an post legem Furiam adhuc legis Apuleiae beneficium supersit. et utique extra Italiam superest; nam lex quidem Furia tantum in Italia valet, Apuleia vero etiam in ceteris provinciis. set an etiam *in*

who are solvent. In this respect therefore this epistle differs from the Lex Furia, viz. that if any one of a number of sponsors or fidepromissors be insolvent, the burden does not fall upon the rest; but if any one of a number of fidejussors, the burden[1] does fall on the rest. But inasmuch as the Lex Furia is of force in Italy only, it follows that in the other provinces sponsors and fidepromissors also, as well as fidejussors, are bound for ever, and each of them for the full amount, unless they too are relieved in part by the epistle of the late emperor Hadrian. 122. Further the Lex Apuleia[2] introduced a kind of partnership amongst sponsors and fidepromissors. For if any one of them have paid more than his share, it grants him actions against the others for that which he has given in excess. Now this *lex* was enacted before the Lex Furia, at the time when they were liable in full: hence the question arises whether after the passing of the Lex Furia the benefit of the Lex Apuleia still continues. And undoubtedly it continues in places out of Italy; for the Lex Furia is only applicable in Italy, but the Lex Apuleia in the other provinces also. Whether, how-

---

[1] A line has evidently been omitted from the MS.; which is replaced according to the conjecture of Huschke.

[2] B.C. 102.

Italia[1] beneficium legis Apuleiae supersit valde quaeritur. sed *ad fideiussores lex* Apuleia non pertinet. itaque si creditor ab uno totum consecutus fuerit, huius solius detrimentum erit, scilicet si is pro quo fideiussit solvendo non sit. sed *ut ex* |
P.161 supradictis apparet, is a quo creditor totum petit poterit ex epistula divi Hadriani desiderare, ut pro parte in se detur actio. (123.) Praeterea lege Cicereia[2] cautum est, ut is qui sponsores aut fidepromissores accipiat praedicat palam et declaret, et de qua re satis accipiat, et quot sponsores aut fidepromissores in eam obligationem accepturus sit: et nisi praedixerit, permittitur sponsoribus et fidepromissoribus intra diem XXX praeiudicium postulare[3], quo quaeratur, an ex ea lege praedictum sit; et si iudicatum fuerit praedictum non esse, liberantur. qua lege fideiussorum mentio nulla fit: sed in usu est, etiam si fideiussores accipiamus, praedicere.

ever, the benefit of the Lex Apuleia continues in Italy[1] too is very doubtful. But the Lex Apuleia does not apply to fidejussors. Therefore, if the creditor have obtained the whole from one of them, the loss falls on this one only, supposing, that is, that he for whom he was fidejussor be insolvent. But, as appears from what was said above, he from whom the creditor demands payment in full can, in accordance with the epistle of the late emperor Hadrian, demand that the action shall be granted against him for his share only. 123. Further by the Lex Cicereia[2] it is provided that he who accepts sponsors or fidepromissors shall make a public statement beforehand, and declare on what matter he is taking surety, and how many sponsors and fidepromissors he is about to take in respect of the obligation: and unless he thus make declaration beforehand, the sponsors and fidepromissors are allowed at any time within thirty days to demand a preliminary investigation[3], in which the matter of inquiry is whether prior declaration was made according to the law; and if it be decided that the declaration was not made, they are freed from liability. In this law no mention is made of fidejussors; but it is usual to make a prior declaration, even if we be accepting fidejussors.

1 The MS. has *sed an etiam alis.*
2 Probably in B.C. 173. There was a Praetor Cicereius in that year.
3 IV. 44.

124. sed beneficium legis Corneliae[1] omnibus commune est. qua lege idem pro eodem aput eundem eodem anno vetatur in ampliorem summam obligari creditae pecuniae quam in xx milia; et quamvis sponsor vel fidepromissor in ampl*iorem* pecuniam, velut si (in) sestertium c milia *se obligaverit, tamen dumtaxat xx tenebitur*[2]. pecuniam autem creditam dicimus non solum eam quam credendi causa damus, set omnem quam tunc (cum) contrahitur obligatio certum est debitum iri, id est (quae) sine ulla condicione deducitur in obligationem. itaque et ea pecunia quam in diem certum dari stipulamur eodem numero est, quia certum est eam debitum iri, licet post tempus petatur. appellatione autem pecuniae omnes res in ea lege significantur[3].
P.162 itaque si vinum vel frumentum, et si fundum | vel hominem stipulemur, haec lex observanda est. (125.) Ex quibusdam tamen causis permittit ea lex in infinitum satis accipere, veluti si dotis nomine, vel eius quod ex testamento tibi debeatur, aut

124. The benefit of the Lex Cornelia[1] is common to all sureties. By this *lex* the same man is forbidden on behalf of the same man, and to the same man, and within the same year to be bound for a greater sum of borrowed money than 20,000 sesterces; and although the sponsor or fidepromissor may have bound himself for more money, for instance for 100,000 sesterces, he will nevertheless be liable only for 20,000[2]. By "borrowed money" we mean not only that which we give for the purpose of a loan, but all money which at the time when the obligation is contracted it is certain will become due, *i.e.* which is made a matter of obligation without any condition. Therefore, that money also which we stipulate shall be given on a fixed day is within the category, because it is certain that it will become due, although it can be sued for only after a time. By the appellation "money" every thing is intended in this *lex*[3]. Therefore the *lex* is to be observed if we be stipulating for wine, or corn, or a piece of land, or a man. 125. In some cases, however, the law allows us to take surety for an unlimited amount, for instance, if surety be taken in reference to a *dos*, or for something due to you under a testa-

[1] B.C. 81.

[2] Huschke's reading is *tamen dumtaxat xx damnatur*. The sentence breaks off abruptly in the MS.

[3] D. 50. 16. 178. *pr.* and 222.

iussu iudicis satis accipiatur. et adhuc lege vicesima hereditatium cavetur[1], ut ad eas satisdationes quae ex ea lege proponuntur lex Cornelia non pertineat.

126. In eo quoque iure iuris par condicio est omnium, sponsorum, fidepromissorum, fideiussorum, quod ita obligari non possunt ut plus debeant quam debet is pro quo obligantur. at ex diverso ut minus debeant obligari possunt, sicut in adstipulatoris persona diximus[2]. nam ut adstipulatoris, ita et horum obligatio accessio est principalis obligationis, nec plus in accessione esse potest quam in principali re. (127.) In eo quoque par omnium causa est, quod si quis pro reo solverit, eius reciperandi causa habet cum eo mandati iudicium[3]. et hoc amplius sponsores ex lege Publilia[4] propriam habent actionem in duplum, quae appellatur depensi.

ment, or by order of a *judex*. And further, it is provided by the Lex Vicesima Hereditatium[1] that the Lex Cornelia shall not apply to certain surety-engagements specified in that law.

126. In the following legal incident the position of all, sponsors, fidepromissors and fidejussors, is alike, that they cannot be so bound as to owe more than he for whom they are bound owes. But on the other hand they may be so bound as to owe less, as we said in the case of the adstipulator[2]. For their obligation, like that of the adstipulator, is an accessory to the principal obligation, and there cannot be more in the accessory than in the principal thing. 127. In this respect also the position of all of them is the same, that if any one has paid money for his principal, he has an action of mandate[3] against him for the purpose of recovering it. And further than this, sponsors by the Lex Publilia[4] have an action peculiar to themselves for double the amount, which is called the *actio depensi*[5].

[1] The *Lex Vicesima Hereditatium* was enacted in the reign of Augustus (A.D. 6), and laid a tax of one-twentieth on all inheritances and legacies, except where the recipients were very near relations.

[2] III. 113.

[3] III. 155 et seqq.

[4] Who Publilius was is not certainly known. He is supposed to be named by Cicero in the *Orat. pro Cluent.* c. 45.

[5] The working of this action is more fully explained by Gaius in IV. 9, 22, 25.

128. Litteris obligatio fit veluti in nominibus transcripticiis[1]. fit autem nomen transcripticium duplici modo, vel a re in personam, vel a persona in personam. (129.) (*A re in personam tran*)scriptio fit, veluti si id quod ex emptionis causa aut conductionis aut societatis mihi debeas, id expensum tibi tulero. (130.) A persona in personam transcriptio fit, veluti si id quod
P.163 mihi Titius debet tibi id ex|pensum tulero, id est si Titius te (pro) se delegaverit mihi[2]. (131.) Alia causa est eorum nominum quae arcaria vocantur. in his enim rei, non litterarum

128. An obligation *litteris* arises in the instance of "transferred entries[1]." A transferred entry occurs in two ways, either from thing to person, or from person to person. 129. A transfer from thing to person takes place when I set down to your debit what you owe me on account of a sale, a letting, or a partnership. 130. A transfer from person to person takes place when I set down to your debit what Titius owes to me, *i.e.* when Titius makes you his substitute to me[2]. 131. The case is different with those entries which are called "arcarian." For in these the obligation is one *re* not *litteris:*

[1] In order to understand the nature of this obligation it is necessary to remember that among the Romans every master of a house kept regular accounts with great accuracy: and to be negligent in this matter was regarded as disreputable. The entries were first roughly made in day-books, called *Adversaria* or *Calendaria*, and were posted at stated periods in ledgers, called *Codices expensi et accepti*. *Nomen* was the general name for any entry, whether on the debtor or creditor side of the account. When any one keeping books entered a sum of money as received from Titius, he was said *ferre* or *referre acceptum Titio*, that is, to place it to the credit of Titius: when, on the other hand, he entered a sum as paid to Titius, he was said *ferre* or *referre expensum Titio*, that is, to place it to the debit of Titius. If it could be proved that an *expensum* had been set down with the debtor's consent, the absence of a corresponding *acceptum* in the debtor's ledger was immaterial, as such absence only argued fraud or negligence on his part. The solemnity therefore which in this case turned a pact into a contract was an *entry with consent*. Heineccius, basing his reasoning on a passage of Theophilus, III. 22, holds that a contract *litteris* is never an original contract, but always operates as a *novatio* of some precedent obligation. See Heineccii *Antiquit.* III. 28 § 4. Cic. *de Off.* III. 14. Cic. *pro Rosc. Com.* I.

[2] The case supposed is that Titius owes me, say, 100 *aurei*, and you owe Titius the same amount: it simplifies matters therefore if Titius, who has to receive 100 and pay 100, remove himself from the transaction altogether by remitting your debt to him and making you, with my consent, a debtor to me in his own stead.

obligatio consistit: quippe non aliter valent, quam si numerata sit pecunia; numeratio autem pecuniae rei, non (litterarum) facit obligationem. qua de causa recte dicemus arcaria nomina nullam facere obligationem, sed obligationis factae testimonium praebere. (132.) Unde proprie dicitur arcariis nominibus etiam peregrinos obligari, quia non ipso nomine, sed numeratione pecuniae obligantur: quod genus obligationis iuris gentium est[1]. (133.) Transcripticiis vero nominibus an obligentur peregrini merito quaeritur, quia quodammodo iuris civilis est talis obligatio: quod Nervae placuit. Sabino autem et Cassio visum est, si a re in personam fiat nomen transcripticium, etiam peregrinos obligari; si vero a persona in personam, non obligari. (134.) Praeterea litterarum obligatio fieri videtur chirografis et syngrafis[2], id est si quis debere se aut daturum se

inasmuch as they do not stand good unless the money has been paid over; and the paying over of money constitutes an obligation *re* not *litteris*. And therefore we shall be correct if we say that arcarian entries produce no obligation, but afford evidence of an obligation already entered into. 132. Hence it is rightly said that even foreigners are bound by arcarian entries, because they are bound not by the entry itself, but by the paying over of the money, which kind of obligation belongs to the *jus gentium*[1]. 133. But whether foreigners are bound by transferred entries is justly disputed, because an obligation of this kind is in a manner a creation of the civil law; and so Nerva thought. But it was the opinion of Sabinus and Cassius, that if the entry were from thing to person, even foreigners were bound: but if from person to person, they were not bound. 134. Further, an obligation *litteris* is considered to arise from chirographs and syngraphs[2], *i. e.* if a man state in writing that he owes or

[1] Arcarian entries are memoranda of a contract already formed, and not the very document by which one is originated. By a "transferred entry" an engagement merely equitable was converted into one furnished with an action; whilst the value of an "arcarian entry" was that it could be used for the purpose of proving a transaction which, though good in law so far as the right to sue was concerned, might otherwise have failed for want of evidence to support it.

[2] A chirograph is signed by the debtor only, a syngraph by both debtor and creditor. Chirographs and syngraphs were not mere proofs of a contract, but documents on which an action could be brought. A simple memorandum, which was good only as evidence, was termed

scribat; ita scilicet si eo nomine stipulatio non fiat[1]. quod genus obligationis proprium peregrinorum est.

135. Consensu fiunt obligationes in emptionibus et venditionibus, locationibus (et) conductionibus, societatibus, mandatis. (136.) Ideo autem istis modis consensu dicimus obligationes P.164 contrahi, quia neque verborum | neque scripturae ulla proprietas desideratur, sed sufficit eos qui negotium gerunt consensisse. unde inter absentes quoque talia negotia contrahuntur, veluti per epistulam aut per internuntium, cum alioquin verborum obligatio inter absentes fieri non possit. (137.) Item in his contractibus alter alteri obligatur de eo quod alterum alteri ex bono et aequo praestare oportet, cum alioquin in verborum obligationibus alius stipuletur, alius promittat, et in nominibus

will give something: provided only there be no stipulation made regarding the matter[1]. This kind of obligation is peculiar to foreigners.

135. Obligations arise from consent in the cases of buying and selling, letting and hiring, partnerships and mandates. 136. And the reason for our saying that in these cases obligations are contracted by consent is that no peculiar form either of words or of writing is required, but it is enough if those who are transacting the business have come to agreement. Therefore, such matters are contracted even between persons at a distance one from the other, for example, by letter or messenger, whilst on the contrary a verbal obligation cannot arise between persons who are apart. 137. Likewise, in these contracts the one is bound to the other for all that the one ought in fairness and equity to afford to the other, whilst, on the contrary, in verbal obligations one stipulates and the

in Gaius' day a *cautio*. In Justinian's time *cautiones* and chirographs were regarded as identical; but see his regulations as to the time within which an *exceptio non numeratae pecuniae* could be brought, in *Inst.* III. 21. Mühlenbruch for some inexplicable reason considers *nomina arcaria* to be identical with syngraphs and chirographs; although the word *praeterea* in § 134 shews pretty plainly that the two are contrasted; and this inference is corroborated by our observing that syngraphs and chirographs are said to be peculiar to foreigners, whilst as to *nomina arcaria* the remark occurs, *etiam peregrinos iis obligari*, the *etiam* plainly implying that these are *not* peculiar to foreigners and therefore are something different from syngraphs and chirographs.

[1] If there be, the obligation is *verbis*, and the document becomes a

alius expensum ferendo obliget, alius obligetur[1]. (138.) Sed absenti expensum ferri potest, etsi verborum obligatio cum absente contrahi non possit.

139. Emptio (*et venditio contrahitur*) cum de pretio convenerit, quamvis nondum pretium numeratum sit, ac ne arra quidem data fuerit. nam quod arrae nomine datur argumentum est emptionis et venditionis contractae[2].

140. Pretium autem certum esse debet: alioquin si ita inter nos convenerit ut quanti Titius rem aestimaverit tanti sit empta, Labeo negavit ullam vim hoc negotium habere; cuius opinionem Cassius probat: Ofilius et eam emptionem et venditionem; cuius opinionem Proculus secutus est[3].

P.165 141. Item pretium in numerata pecunia con|sistere debet.

other promises, and in litteral obligations one binds by an entry to the debit and the other is bound[1]. 138. But an entry may be made to the debit of an absent person, although a verbal obligation cannot be entered into with an absent person.

139. A buying and selling is entered into as soon as agreement is made about the price, even though the price has not yet been paid, nor even earnest given. For what is given as earnest is only evidence of a contract of buying and selling having been entered into[2].

140. Further, the price ought to be fixed: if, on the contrary, we agree that the thing shall be bought for that price at which Titius shall value it, Labeo says such a transaction has no validity, and Cassius assents to his opinion: but Ofilius thinks there is a buying and selling, and Proculus follows his opinion[3].

141. Likewise the price must consist of coined money. For

---

cautio, not absolutely conclusive, but available as evidence of the stipulation.

[1] The old contracts based on the civil law were unilateral, the new contracts by consent, springing from the *jus gentium*, were bilateral. It will be observed that Gaius says nothing here about real contracts. Possibly this is because their position was anomalous: they had been unilateral, but under the growing influence of the *jus gentium* were becoming bilateral, as is implied in the concluding words of III. 132 above.

[2] That is, is not of the essence of the contract.

[3] Justinian settled this dispute. If the referee fixed the price, the sale was valid; if he could not or would not, the agreement was void.

nam in ceteris rebus an pretium esse possit, veluti an homo[1] aut toga aut fundus alterius rei (pretium esse possit), valde quaeritur. nostri praeceptores putant etiam in alia re posse consistere pretium; unde illut est quod vulgo putant per permutationem rerum emptionem et venditionem contrahi, eamque speciem emptionis et venditionis vetustissimam esse; argumentoque utuntur Graeco poeta Homero qui aliqua parte sic ait:

> Ἔνθεν ἄρ' οἰνίζοντο καρηκομόωντες Ἀχαιοί,
> Ἄλλοι μὲν χαλκῷ, ἄλλοι δ' αἴθωνι σιδήρῳ,
> Ἄλλοι δὲ ῥινοῖς, ἄλλοι δ' αὐτῇσι βόεσσιν,
> Ἄλλοι δ' ἀνδραπόδεσσιν[2].

diversae scholae auctores dissentiunt, aliutque esse existimant permutationem rerum, aliut emptionem et venditionem: alioquin *non posse* rem expediri permutatis rebus, quae videatur res venisse et quae pretii nomine data esse; sed rursus utramque rem videri et venisse et utramque pretii nomine datam esse ab-

whether the price can consist of other things, for instance, whether a slave[1], or a garment, or a piece of land can be the price of another thing, is very doubtful. Our authorities think the price may consist of some other thing; and hence comes the vulgar notion that by the exchange of things a buying and selling is effected, and that this species of buying and selling is the most ancient: and they bring forward as an authority the Greek poet Homer, who in a certain passage says thus: "Thereupon then the long-haired Achæans obtained wine, some for brass, some for glittering steel, some for skins of cattle, some for cattle themselves, some for slaves[2]." The authorities of the other school take a different view, and think that exchange of things is one matter, buying and selling another: otherwise, they say, it could not be made clear when things were exchanged which thing was to be considered sold and which given as a price: but again for both equally to be considered to be sold, and also both given as the price, appears ridiculous.

[1] The MS. has *hoc modo:* but this is easily corrected from Just. *Inst.* III. 23. 2.

[2] *Iliad*, VII. 472—475. The quotation is supplied from Just. *Inst.* III. 23. 2. The MS. merely has "ait et reliqua."

surdum videri. set ait Caelius Sabinus, si rem tibi venalem habenti veluti fundum, acceperim, et pretii nomine hominem forte dederim, fundum quidem videri venisse, hominem autem pretii nomine datum esse ut fundus acciperetur[1].

142. Locatio autem et conductio similibus regulis constituuntur: nisi enim merces certa statuta sit, non videtur locatio et conductio contrahi. (143.) Unde si alieno arbitrio merces per-
P.166 missa sit, velut quanti Titius aestimaverit, | quaeritur an locatio et conductio contrahatur. qua de causa si fulloni polienda curandave, sarcinatori sarcienda vestimenta dederim, nulla statim mercede constituta, postea tantum daturus quanti inter nos convenerit, quaeritur an locatio et conductio contrahatur[2]; (144.) Vel si rem tibi utendam dederim et invicem aliam rem

But Caelius Sabinus says, if when you have a thing for sale, for instance a piece of land, I take it, and give a slave, say, for the price; the land is to be regarded as sold, and the slave to be given as the price in order that the land may be received[1].

142. The contract of letting and hiring is regulated by similar rules: for unless a fixed hire be determined, no letting and hiring is considered to be contracted. 143. Therefore, if the hire be left to the decision of another, such amount, for example, as Titius shall think right, it is disputed whether a letting and hiring is contracted. Wherefore, if I give garments to a fuller to be smoothed and cleaned, or to a tailor to be repaired, no hire being settled at the time, my intention being to give afterwards what shall be agreed upon between us, it is disputed whether a letting and hiring is contracted[2]. 144. Or if I give a thing to you to be used, and in return receive from

---

[1] This is not a mere dispute about words, like so many of the points debated between the Sabinians and Proculians. The old Roman Law regarded exchange as a real contract, therefore a mere agreement to exchange was not binding, and the exchange could only be enforced in case one of the parties had delivered up the thing which he was to part with: but if the Sabinians could have been victorious in their argument, and got the lawyers to admit that an exchange was a sale, exchange would have become a consensual contract, and a mere agreement to exchange have been binding.

[2] The contract is not a *locatio conductio* for want of a *merces* specified beforehand; it is not a *mandatum* because it is not gratuitous, there being an implication that a *merces* will eventually be paid: hence the remedy can only be by an *actio in factum praescriptis verbis*, as to which see App. (S).

utendam acceperim, quaeritur an locatio et conductio contrahatur[1].

145. Adeo autem emptio et venditio et locatio et conductio familiaritatem aliquam inter se habere videntur, ut in quibusdam causis quaeri soleat utrum emptio et venditio contrahatur an locatio et conductio[2]. veluti si qua res in perpetuum locata sit, quod evenit in praediis municipum quae ea lege locantur, ut quamdiu id vectigal praestetur, neque ipsi conductori neque heredi eius praedium auferatur; sed magis placuit locationem conductionemque esse[3].

146. Item si gladiatores ea lege tibi tradiderim, ut in singulos qui integri exierint pro sudore denarii xx mihi darentur,

you another thing to be used, it is disputed whether a letting and hiring is contracted[1].

145. But buying and selling and letting and hiring have so close a resemblance to one another, that in some cases it is a matter of question whether a buying and selling is contracted or a letting and hiring[2]; for instance, if a thing be let for ever, which happens with the lands of corporations which are let out on the condition that so long as so much rent be paid, the land shall not be taken away either from the hirer himself or his heir; but it is the general opinion that this is a letting and hiring[3].

146. Likewise, if I have delivered gladiators to you on condition that for each one who escapes unhurt 20 *denarii*

[1] The contract in this case is one of the innominate real contracts—*Do ut des, &c.*—therefore is only binding when one party has completed his delivery, and not on mere consent.

[2] D. 19. 2. 2. 1.

[3] This *locatio in perpetuum* or *emphyteusis* was by Zeno made a distinct kind of contract, subject to rules of its own. See *Inst.* III. 24. 3. Also read Savigny, *On Possession*, pp. 77—79; D. 6. 3.

From these authorities and others we learn that *emphyteusis* was a comparatively modern contract, a lease of lands by a private individual or corporation to a private individual; whereas the older *ager vectigalis* was always a lease proceeding from a corporation. The leases of *agri vectigales* were not always perpetual, but sometimes for a term of years. The emphyteutic leases made by a private individual were always hereditary. Hence they were closely analogous to the *fee farms* mentioned by Britton (see Nichols' translation of Britton, fol. 164), which were lands held in fee for an annual rent reserved at the time of their grant; being therefore a species of socage. In Cicero's time lands leased by corporations, whether for years or in perpetuity, were called *agri fructuarii*.

in eos vero singulos qui occisi aut debilitati fuerint denarii mille: quaeritur utrum emptio et venditio an locatio et conductio contrahatur. et magis placuit eorum qui integri exierint locationem et conductionem contractam videri, at eorum qui occisi aut debilitati sunt emptionem et venditionem esse: idque ex
P.167 accidentibus apparet, tamquam sub condicione | facta cuiusque venditione aut locatione. iam enim non dubitatur, quin sub condicione res veniri aut locari possint[1]. (147.) Item quaeritur[2], si cum aurifice mihi convenerit ut is ex auro suo certi ponderis certaeque formae anulos mihi faceret, et acciperet verbi gratia denarios CC, utrum emptio et venditio an locatio et conductio contrahatur. Cassius ait materiae quidem emptionem et venditionem contrahi, operarum autem locationem et conductionem. sed plerisque placuit emptionem et venditionem contrahi. atqui si meum aurum ei dedero, mercede pro opera constituta, convenit locationem et conductionem contrahi[3].

shall be given to me for his exertions, but for each of those who are killed or wounded 1000 *denarii:* it is disputed whether a buying and selling or a letting and hiring is contracted. And the general opinion is that there seems to be a contract of letting and hiring in regard to those who escape unhurt, but a buying and selling in regard to those who are killed or wounded: and that this is made evident by the result, the selling or letting of each being made, as it were, under condition. For there is now no doubt that things can be sold or let under a condition[1]. 147. Likewise[2], this question is raised; supposing an agreement has been made by me with a goldsmith, that he shall make rings for me from his own gold of a certain weight and certain form, and receive, for example, 200 denarii, whether is a buying and selling or a letting and hiring contracted? Cassius says that a buying and selling of the material is contracted, and a letting and hiring of the workmanship. But most authors think that it is a buying and selling which is contracted. But if I give him my own gold, a hire being agreed upon for the work, it is allowed that a letting and hiring is contracted[3].

---

[1] D. 19. 2. 20. *pr.* [2] D. 19. 2. 2. 1.
[3] D. 18. 1. 20 and D. 18. 1. 65.

148. Societatem coire solemus aut totorum bonorum, aut unius alicuius negotii, veluti mancipiorum emendorum aut vendendorum. (149.) Magna autem quaestio fuit, an ita coiri possit societas, ut quis maiorem partem lucretur, minorem damni praestet. quod Quintus Mucius etiam (*contra naturam societatis esse censuit; sed Servius Sulpicius, cuius*)[1] etiam praevaluit sententia, adeo ita coiri posse societatem existimavit, ut dixerit illo quoque modo coiri posse, ut quis nihil omnino damni praestet set lucri partem capiat, si modo opera eius tam pretiosa videatur, ut aequum sit eum cum hac pactione in societatem admitti[2]. nam et ita posse coire societatem constat,
P.168 ut unus pecuniam conferat alter non conferat, | et tamen lucrum inter eos commune sit; saepe enim opera alicuius pro

148. We are accustomed to enter into a partnership either as to all our property, or as to one particular matter, for instance, the purchase or sale of slaves.

149. But it has been a much disputed question whether a partnership can be entered into on terms that one of the partners shall have a larger share of the gain and pay a smaller share of the loss. This, Quintus Mucius says, is irreconcilable with the very nature of partnership: but Servius Sulpicius, whose[1] opinion has prevailed, so firmly held that a partnership of this kind could be entered into, that he affirmed one could also be entered into on terms that one of the parties should pay no portion whatever of the loss, and yet take a part of the gain, provided his services appeared so valuable that it was fair that he should be admitted into the partnership on this arrangement[2]. For it is undoubtedly possible to enter into a partnership on such terms, that one shall contribute money and the other none, and yet the gain be common between

[1] A line is omitted in the MS. but can be supplied from Just. *Inst.* III. 25. 2.

[2] D. 17. 2. 30. Servius in this passage assents to the doctrine of Mucius, holding that Mucius meant that there could not be a different apportionment of loss on the bad transactions, and of profit on those successful. Servius then goes on to state, as Gaius says, that if Mucius had meant that there could not be a different apportionment of gain or loss on a balance of accounts, he would have been wrong; but as he never implies that Mucius held such a view, Gaius is, as it seems, giving an unfair account of Mucius' rule in the present passage.

pecunia valet. (150.) Et illut certum est, si de partibus lucri et damni nihil inter eos convenerit, tamen aequis ex partibus commodum et incommodum inter eos commune esse. sed si in altero partes expressae fuerint velut in lucro, in altero vero omissae, in eo quoque quod omissum est similes partes erunt.

151. Manet autem societas eousque donec in eodem sensu perseverant; at cum aliquis renuntiaverit societati, societas solvitur[1]. sed plane si quis in hoc renuntiaverit societati ut obveniens aliquod lucrum solus habeat, veluti si mihi totorum bonorum socius, cum ab aliquo heres esset relictus, in hoc renuntiaverit societati ut hereditatem solus lucrifaciat, cogetur hoc lucrum communicare. si quid vero aliut lucri fecerit quod non captaverit, ad ipsum solum pertinet. mihi vero quidquid omnino post renuntiatam societatem adquiritur soli conceditur. (152.) Solvitur adhuc societas etiam morte socii; quia qui

them: for frequently the services of one are as valuable as money. 150. And this too is certain, that if there have been no agreement between them as to the shares of gain and loss, yet the gain and loss must be divided between them in equal portions. But if the portions have been specified with regard to the one case, as for instance, with regard to the gain, and not mentioned with regard to the other, the portions will be the same as to that of which mention was omitted.

151. A partnership continues so long as the partners remain in the same mind: but when any one of them has renounced the partnership, the partnership is dissolved[1]. Yet, undoubtedly, if a man renounce a partnership for the purpose of enjoying alone some anticipated gain; for instance, if my partner in all property, when left heir by some one, renounce the partnership that he may alone have the benefit of the inheritance; he will be compelled to share this gain. If, on the other hand, he chance upon some gain which he did not aim at obtaining, this belongs to him solely. But whatever is acquired from any source after the renunciation of the partnership is granted to me alone. 152. Further, a partnership is dissolved by the death of a partner, because he who makes a contract of part-

[1] Therefore if three men be in partnership and one renounce, the remaining two are no longer partners.

societatem contrahit certam personam sibi eligit. (153.) Dicitur etiam capitis diminutione solvi societatem[1], quia civili ratione capitis diminutio morti coaequatur, sed utique si adhuc consentiant in societatem, nova videtur incipere societas. (154.) Item si cuius ex sociis bona publice aut privatim veni-
P.169 erint[2], solvitur societas. sed haec quoque | societas de qua loquimur *est ea quae* consensu contrahitur nudo[3]; iuris gentium est, itaque inter omnes homines naturali ratione consistit[4].

155. Mandatum consistit sive nostra gratia mandemus sive aliena, itaque sive ut mea negotia geras, sive ut alterius mandaverim, contrahitur mandati obligatio, et invicem alter alteri tenebimur in id quod vel me tibi vel te mihi bona fide praestare oportet. (156.) Nam si tua gratia tibi mandem,

nership selects for himself a definite person. 153. It is said that a partnership is also dissolved by a *capitis diminutio*[1], because on the principles of the civil law a *capitis diminutio* is held to be equivalent to death: but certainly if the partners consent to be partners still, a new partnership is considered to arise. 154. Likewise, if the goods of any one of the partners be sold publicly or privately[2], the partnership is dissolved. But in this case too the partnership of which we speak is one which is contracted by mere consent[3]; it is based on the *jus gentium*, and therefore on natural principles stands good between any parties whatever[4].

155. A mandate is created whether we give a commission for our own benefit or for another person's; therefore, whether I give you a commission to transact my business or that of another person, the obligation of mandate arises between us, and we shall be mutually bound one to the other for that which in good faith I ought to do for you, or you for me. 156. For if I give you a commission for your own benefit, the mandate is

[1] I. 128; III. 101.

[2] III. 78.

[3] Probably some words have been omitted from the text. There seems to be a reference to the distinction between an ordinary partnership and a *societas vectigalium*; for *publicani* could not arrange a partnership by mere consent, neither could they be *peregrini*, or assign their interests to *peregrini*: the death of one *publicanus* did not dissolve the partnership of the survivors &c. See D. 17. 2. 59.

[4] We have adopted Klenze's reading, suggested in a note to his edition of 1829. The MS. has IOR where we have inserted *est ea quae*; and instead of *iuris gentium* has *iuris cogentium*.

supervacuum est mandatum; quod enim tu tua gratia facturus sis, id de tua sententia, non ex meo mandatu, facere debes: itaque si otiosam pecuniam domi te habentem hortatus fuerim ut eam fenerares, qu*amvis e*am ei mutuam dederis a quo servare non potueris, non tamen habebis mecum mandati actionem. item si hortatus sim ut rem aliquam emeres, quamvis non expedierit tibi eam emisse, non tamen tibi mandati tenebor. et adeo haec ita sunt, ut quaeratur an mandati teneatur qui mandavit tibi ut Titio pecuniam fenerares. Servius negavit, nec magis hoc casu obligationem consistere putavit quam si generaliter alicui mandetur uti pecuniam suam faeneraret. *set* sequimur Sabini opinionem contra sentientis[1], quia non aliter Titio credidisses quam si tibi mandatum esset[2].

157. Illut constat, si quis de ea re mandet quod contra

superfluous: for what you would do for your own sake, you must do of your own accord and not on my mandate: therefore, if when you have money lying idle at home, I have advised you to put it out at interest, even if you bestow it on loan to one from whom you cannot recover it, you will nevertheless have no action of mandate against me. Likewise, if I have advised you to buy something or other, even if it be not to your advantage that you made the purchase, I still shall not be answerable to you in an action of mandate. And this rule is so universally true, that it is a disputed point whether a man is liable to you for mandate who gave you a mandate to lend money on interest to Titius. Servius thought not, and held that there was no more an obligation in this case than there is when a mandate is given to any one in general terms to put out his money on interest. But we follow the opinion of Sabinus, who held the contrary[1], because you would not have lent the money to Titius, unless the mandate had been given to you[2].

157. It is certain that if any one gives a mandate for the doing of something contrary to morality, no obligation is con-

[1] *Contra sentientis* is Mommsen's suggestion. The MS. has *con sentientis*.

[2] Therefore, it is a good mandate, being for the benefit of a stranger.

P.170 bonos mores | est, non contrahi obligationem, velut si tibi mandem ut Titio furtum aut iniuriam facias.

158. Item si quis post mortem meam faciendum mandet, inutile mandatum est, quia generaliter placuit ab heredis persona obligationem incipere non posse[1].

159. Sed recte quoque consummatum mandatum, si dum adhuc integra res sit revocatum fuerit, evanescit. (160.) Item si adhuc integro mandato mors alterutrius alicuius interveniat, id est vel eius qui mandarit vel eius qui mandatum susceperit, solvitur mandatum. sed utilitatis causa receptum est, ut si mortuo eo qui mihi mandaverit, ignorans eum decessisse executus fuero mandatum, posse me agere mandati actione: alioquin iusta et probabilis ignorantia damnum mihi adferet. et huic simile est quod plerisque placuit, si debitor meus manumisso dispensatori meo per ignorantiam solverit, liberari eum: cum alioquin stricta iuris ratione non posset liberari eo quod alii solvisset quam cui solvere deberet[2].

tracted; for instance, if I give you a mandate to commit a theft or injury upon Titius.

158. Likewise, if any one gives me a mandate for the doing of something after my death, the mandate is void, because it is an universal rule that an obligation cannot begin to operate in the person of one's heir[1].

159. Even if a mandate be duly made, yet if it be recalled before the subject of it has been dealt with, it becomes void. 160. Likewise, if the death of either of the parties occur before execution of the mandate is commenced, that is, either the death of him who gave the mandate, or of him who undertook it, the mandate is made null. But for convenience the rule has been adopted, that if after the death of the mandator, I, being ignorant that he is dead, carry out the mandate, I can bring an action of mandate: otherwise, a justifiable ignorance, very likely to occur, will bring loss upon me. Similar to this is the rule generally maintained, that if my debtor make a payment by mistake to my slave-steward after I have manumitted him, he is free from his debt: although, on the other hand, by strict rule of law, he could not be free, because he had paid a person other than him whom he ought to have paid[2].

---

[1] III. 100.

[2] Payment to a slave is payment

161. Cum autem is cui recte mandaverim egressus fuerit mandatum, ego quidem eatenus cum eo habeo mandati actionem quatenus mea interest inplesse eum mandatum, si modo implere potuerit: at ille mecum agere non potest. itaque si mandaverim tibi ut verbi gratia mihi fundum sestertiis C emeres,
P.171 sestertiis CL emeris, non habebis mecum | mandati actionem, etiamsi tanti velis mihi dare fundum quanti emendum tibi mandassem. idque maxime Sabino et Cassio placuit[1]. quodsi minoris emeris, habebis mecum scilicet actionem, quia qui mandat ut C milibus emeretur, is utique mandare intellegitur ut minoris, si posset, emeretur.

162. In summa sciendum (est, quotiens faciendum) aliquid gratis dederim, quo nomine si mercedem statuissem locatio et

161. When a man to whom I have given a mandate in proper form has transgressed its terms, I have an action of mandate against him for an amount equal to the interest I have that he should have performed the mandate, provided only he could have performed it: but he has no action against me. Thus, if I have given you a mandate to buy me a piece of land, say for a hundred thousand sesterces, and you have bought it for a hundred and fifty thousand sesterces, you will have no action of mandate against me, even though you be willing to give me the land for the price at which I commissioned you to buy it. And this was decidedly the opinion of Sabinus and Cassius[1]. But if you have bought it for a smaller price, you will doubtless have an action against me; because when a man gives a mandate for a thing to be bought for a hundred thousand sesterces, it is considered obvious that he gives the mandate for its purchase at a lower price, if possible.

162. Finally, we must observe that whenever I give any thing to be done gratuitously as to which there would have been

---

to the master, for the slave has no independent *persona:* also the master, having made the slave his steward, thereby authorized strangers to pay money to him; and therefore, if the slave appropriated the money, the master had to bear the loss. After the manumission the slave has an independent *persona*, and cannot be *dispensator* any longer, that being an office tenable only by one of the *familia*. By strict law therefore the debtor's payment is void, for it is to a wrong person; but equity will not allow the debtor to suffer, if he be without notice. The same difficulty would arise if the slave were deprived of his stewardship without being emancipated.

[1] Gaius himself advocates the opposite opinion in D. 17. 1. 4; and so does Julian in D. 17. 1. 33.

conductio contraheretur, mandati esse actionem, veluti si fulloni polienda curandave vestimenta aut sarcinatori sarcienda (dederim)[1].

163. Expositis generibus obligationum quae ex contractu nascuntur, admonendi sumus adquiri nobis non solum per nosmet ipsos, sed etiam per eas personas quae in nostra potestate manu mancipiove sunt[2]. (164.) Per liberos quoque homines et alienos servos quos bona fide possidemus adquiritur nobis; sed tantum ex duabus causis, id est si quid ex operis suis vel ex re nostra adquirant[3]. (165.) Per eum quoque servum in quo usumfructum habemus similiter ex duabus istis causis nobis adquiritur[4]. (166.) Sed qui nudum ius Quiritium in servo habet, licet dominus sit, minus tamen iuris in ea re habere intellegitur quam usufructuarius et bonae fidei possessor[5]. nam placet ex nulla causa ei adquiri posse: adeo ut etsi nomi-

a contract of letting and hiring had I settled a hire, an action for mandate lies; for instance, if I gave garments to a fuller to be smoothed and cleaned, or to a tailor to be repaired[1].

163. Now that the various kinds of obligations which arise from contract have been set out in order, we must take notice that acquisition can be made for us not only by ourselves, but also by those persons whom we have under our *potestas*, *manus*, or *mancipium*[2]. 164. Acquisition is also made for us by means of free men and the slaves of other people whom we possess in good faith: but only in two cases, viz. if they acquire any thing by their own work or from our substance[3]. 165. Acquisition is also in like manner made for us in these two cases by a slave in whom we have the usufruct[4]. 166. But he who has the mere Quiritary title to a slave, although he is owner, yet is considered to have less right in this respect than an usufructuary or possessor in good faith[5]. For it is ruled that the slave can in no case acquire for him: so that even though

Justinian also inclines to the more lenient view. See *Inst.* III. 26. 9.

[1] Although there could be no payment in the case of a mandate, yet on the completion of the work the fuller or tailor, to take the example in the text, had a claim enforceable by action for his expenses and loss of time, and the liberal construction of the amount of these always made in a *bonae fidei* action would ensure the workman a due recompense.

[2] II. 86.

[3] II. 92.

[4] II. 91.

[5] II. 88. Ulp. XIX. 20.

natim ei dari stipulatus fuerit servus, mancipiove nomine eius
P.172 acceperit, | quidam existiment nihil ei adquiri.

167. Communem servum pro dominica parte dominis adquirere certum est, excepto eo, quod uni nominatim stipulando aut mancipio accipiendo illi soli adquirit, velut cum ita stipuletur: TITIO DOMINO MEO DARI SPONDES? aut cum ita mancipio accipiat: HANC REM EX IURE QUIRITIUM LUCII TITII DOMINI MEI ESSE AIO, EAQUE EI EMPTA ESTO HOC AERE AENEAQUE LIBRA. (167 a.) Illut quaeritur (an) tamquam domini nomen adiectum domini efficit, idem faciat unius ex dominis iussum intercedens. nostri praeceptores perinde ei qui iusserit soli adquiri existimant, atque si nominatim ei soli stipulatus esset servus mancipiove accepisset. diversae scholae auctores proinde utrisque adquiri putant, ac si nullius iussum intervenisset[1].

168. Tollitur autem obligatio praecipue solutione eius quod

the slave have expressly stipulated for a thing to be given to him, or have received it by mancipation in his name, some think no acquisition is made for him.

167. A slave held in common undoubtedly acquires for his owners according to their shares of ownership, with the exception that by stipulating or receiving by mancipation expressly for one he makes acquisition for that one only; for instance, when he stipulates thus: Do you engage that it shall be given to my master Titius? or when he receives by mancipation thus: I assert this thing to be the property of my master Lucius Titius by Quiritary title; and be it bought for him with this coin and bronze balance. 167 *a*. It is questionable whether the fact of a precedent command having been given by one particular master makes the thing the property of that one master, as the mention of his name would make it his. Our authorities think the acquisition is made for that one only who gave the command, just as it would be if the slave stipulated or received by mancipation for him alone. The authorities of the other school think that acquisition is made for both masters, just as if no command had preceded[1].

168. An obligation is most obviously dissolved by payment

---

[1] Justinian decided in favour of the Sabinians, "*nostri praeceptores*," both this dispute and that mentioned in the next paragraph.

debetur. unde quaeritur, si quis consentiente creditore aliut pro alio solverit, utrum ipso iure[1] liberetur, quod nostris praeceptoribus placet: an ipso iure maneat obligatus, set adversus petentem exceptione doli mali defendi debeat[2], quod diversae scholae auctoribus visum est.

169. Item per acceptilationem tollitur obligatio. acceptilatio autem est veluti imaginaria solutio; quod enim ex verborum obligatione tibi debeam, id si velis mihi remittere, poterit
P.173 sic fieri ut patiaris haec verba | me dicere: QUOD EGO TIBI PROMISI, HABESNE ACCEPTUM? et tu respondeas: HABEO. (170.) Quo genere, ut diximus, *tantum hae obligationes solvuntur quae ex verbis consistunt*[3], non etiam ceterae: consentaneum enim visum est verbis factam obligationem posse aliis verbis dissolvi. set et id quod ex alia causa debeatur[4] potest in stipulationem deduci[5] et per acceptilationem imaginaria solutione *dissolvi.*

of that which is owed. Whence arises the question, whether a man by paying one thing instead of another with consent of the creditor is free by the letter of the law[1], as our authorities think: or remains bound according to the letter of the law, and must be defended against a plaintiff by an exception of fraud[2], which is the view upheld by the authorities of the opposite school.

169. An obligation is also dissolved by *acceptilation.* Acceptilation is, as it were, a fictitious payment; for if you wish to remit to me what I owe you on a verbal obligation, this can be done by your allowing me to say these words: Do you acknowledge as received that which I promised to you? and by your replying: I do. 170. By this process, as we have said, only verbal obligations can be dissolved[3], and not the other kinds: for it seemed reasonable that an obligation made by words should be capable of being dissolved by other words. But that also which is due on other grounds[4] can be converted into a stipulation[5], and dissolved by a fictitious payment in the

---

[1] *Ipso iure*="Quod ipsa legis auctoritate, absque magistratus auxilio, et sine exceptionis ope fit." Brissonius.

[2] For *exceptio* see IV. 115 seqq.

[3] A line omitted from the MS. is replaced from Just. *Inst.* III. 29. 1.

[4] Sc. *re*, *litteris* or *consensu*.

[5] The form of words by which this was done is to be found in Justinian, III. 29. 2, and is there called

(171.) *Quamvis vero dixerimus perfici acceptilationem imaginaria solutione*[1], tamen mulier sine tutoris auctore acceptum facere non potest; cum alioquin solvi ei sine tutoris auctoritate possit[2]. (172.) Item quod debetur pro parte recte solvitur: an autem in partem acceptum fieri possit, quaesitum est[3].

173. Est etiam alia species imaginariae solutionis per aes et libram[4]; quod et ipsum genus certis in causis receptum est, veluti si quid eo nomine debeatur quod per aes et libram gestum est, sive quit ex iudicati causa debetur. (174.) Adhibemus autem non minus quam quinque testes et libripens[5]. deinde is qui liberatur ita oportet loquatur: QUOD EGO TIBI TOT MILIBUS CONDEMNATUS SUM, ME EO NOMINE RECTE SOLVO LIBEROQUE HOC AERE AENEAQUE LIBRA. HANC TIBI LIBRAM

way of acceptilation. 171. But although we have said that an acceptilation is made by an imaginary payment[1], yet a woman cannot give an acceptilation without the authorization of her tutor, although, on the contrary, an (actual) payment can be made to her without his authorization[2]. 172. Likewise, the part-payment of a debt is valid, but it is a moot point whether there can be an acceptilation in part[3].

173. There is also another mode of fictitious payment, that by coin and balance[4]: a form which is adopted in certain cases, as for instance, when any debt is due on a transaction effected by coin and balance, or when any is due by reason of a judgment. 174. We call together, therefore, not less than five witnesses and a "balance-holder[5]." Then the man who is to be freed from his obligation must speak thus: "Inasmuch as I have been adjudged to pay you so many thousand sesterces, I duly acquit and discharge myself therefrom by means of this coin and copper balance. I weigh you this weight for

---

the Aquilian stipulation. The inventor, Aquilius Gallus, was a contemporary of Cicero. The Aquilian stipulation acted as a novation. See § 176 below.

1 Another line, evidently omitted because ending like its predecessor with "imaginaria solutione," is replaced according to Huschke's suggestion.

2 II. 85.

3 But it was eventually ruled that an acceptilation in part was allowable. D. 46. 4. 13. 1—3.

4 An instance of actual payment *per aes et libram* is to be found in Livy, VI. 14.

5 I. 119.

PRIMAM POSTREMAMQUE[1] EXPENDO (SECUNDUM) LEGEM PUBLICAM. deinde asse percutit libram eumque dat ei a quo liberatur, veluti solvendi causa. (175.) Similiter legatarius heredem eodem modo liberat de legato quod per damnationem[2] relictum est, ut tamen scilicet, sicut iudicatus condemnatum se esse significat, ita heres testamento se dare damnatum esse dicat. de eo tamen tantum potest heres eo modo liberari quod pondere, numero constet; et ita, si certum sit, quidam et de eo |
P.174 quod mensura constat idem existimant.

176. Praeterea novatione tollitur obligatio, veluti si quod tu mihi debeas a Titio dari stipulatus sim. nam interventu novae personae nova nascitur obligatio et prima tollitur translata in posteriorem: adeo ut interdum, licet posterior stipulatio inutilis sit, tamen prima novationis iure tollatur[3]. veluti si quod mihi

first and last[1], according to the law of the state." Then he strikes the balance with the coin, and gives it to the person from whose claim he is being freed, as though by way of payment. 175. In like manner does a legatee release the heir from a legacy left by damnation[2], provided only that in like manner as a judgment-debtor admits himself to have been adjudged, so must the heir admit himself to be bound by the testament to give. But the heir can only be released in this manner from a debt which is a matter of weight or number: and some also think from a debt which is a matter of measure, provided it be definite.

176. An obligation is also dissolved by *novation*, for instance, if I stipulate with Titius that what you owe me shall be given me by him. For by the introduction of a new person a new obligation arises and the original one is dissolved by being transferred into the later one: so that, sometimes, although the later stipulation be void, yet the original one is dissolved by reason of the novation[3]; for example, if I stipu-

[1] See the phrase *prima postremaque* in a form of treaty given by Livy, I. 24.

[2] II. 201.

[3] The contract superseded in a novation might be of any kind, real, verbal, litteral, or consensual, but that by which it was superseded was always a stipulation: the original contract further might be natural, civil, or praetorian, and the superseding contract too might be binding either civilly or naturally. These points are clearly laid down by Ulpian, in D. 46. 2. 1. 2. The obligation entered into by a pupil is

debes a Titio post mortem eius[1], vel a muliere pupillove sine tutoris auctoritate, stipulatus fuero. quo casu rem amitto: nam et prior debitor liberatur, et posterior obligatio nulla est. non idem iuris est, si a servo stipulatus fuero: nam tunc proinde adhuc obligatus tenetur, ac si postea a nullo stipulatus fuissem. (177.) Sed si eadem persona sit a qua postea stipuler, ita demum novatio fit si quid in posteriore stipulatione novi sit, forte si condicio vel sponsor[2] aut dies adiciatur aut detrahatur. (178.) Sed quod de sponsore dixi, non constat. nam diversae scholae auctoribus placuit nihil ad novationem proficere sponsoris adiectionem aut detractionem[3]. (179.) Quod autem diximus, si condicio adiciatur, novationem fieri, sic intellegi oportet, ut ita dicamus factam novationem, si condicio extiterit: alioquin si defecerit, durat prior obligatio[4]. sed videamus, num is

late with Titius for payment by him after his death of what you owe me[1], or with a woman or a pupil without the authorization of the tutor. In such a case I lose the thing, for the original debtor is set free, and the later obligation is null. But the rule is not the same if I stipulate with a slave, for then (the original debtor) is held bound, just as though I had not subsequently stipulated with any one. 177. If the person with whom I make the second stipulation be the same as before, there is a novation only in case there be something new in the later stipulation; for instance, if a condition, or a *sponsor*[2], or a day (of payment) be inserted or omitted. 178. But what I have said about the sponsor is not universally admitted; for the authorities of the school opposed to us think the insertion or omission of a sponsor has not the effect of causing a novation[3]. 179. Also our assertion that a novation takes place if a condition be inserted must be thus understood, that we mean a novation takes place if the condition come to pass: if on the contrary it fail, the original obligation stands good[4]. But a point we have to consider is whether he

binding naturally, therefore supersedes the original contract, but will not be enforced by the civil law: that entered into by a slave is not binding either naturally or civilly, therefore causes no novation, and the old contract remains effective.

[1] III. 100.

[2] III. 115.

[3] Sponsors were obsolete in Justinian's time, but he ruled that the introduction of a fidejussor worked a novation. *Inst.* III. 29. 3.

[4] This passage is at first sight

qui eo nomine agat doli mali aut pacti conventi exceptione possit summoveri, quia videatur inter eos id actum, ut ita ea res
P.175 peteretur, si posterioris | stipulationis extiterit condicio. Servius tamen Sulpicius existimavit statim et pendente condicione novationem fieri, et si defecerit condicio ex neutra causa agi posse et eo modo rem perire. qui consequenter et illut respondit, si quis id quod sibi Lucius Titius deberet, a servo

who sues in such a case can be met by an exception of fraud or "agreement made," because proof may be adduced that the transaction between the parties was to the effect that the thing was to be sued for only in case the condition of the latter stipulation came to pass. Servius Sulpicius, however, thought that at once and whilst the condition was in suspense a novation took place, and that if the condition failed no action could be brought on either case, and so the thing was lost. And consistently with himself he also delivered this opinion, that if any one stipulated with a slave for that which Lucius

confused, but it may be thus interpreted. Supposing a new condition to be inserted, the question arises, whether is there an immediate novation or a novation conditional? If there be an immediate novation, the old agreement is swept away altogether, and the new agreement is only to be carried out on fulfilment of the condition; so that if the condition fail, the promisee will get nothing at all. This view Gaius at once discards. The novation is, according to him, presumptively conditional, and so if the condition fail, the old obligation remains intact according to the letter of the civil law. But admitting this view to be correct, all that as yet has been shewn is that an action will be granted, and not that the plaintiff will succeed, for he may be met by an exception of *dolus malus* or *pactum conventum*, because the defendant may allege that the intent of the parties was to abolish the old certain obligation and introduce a new conditional one in its place. This question Gaius leaves unsettled, it can only be decided by the circumstances of each particular case; and so we may sum up his views thus: the presumption is that it is the novation which is conditional, an action will therefore be granted on the old agreement when the condition fails; but the presumption may be rebutted by shewing that it was not the novation, but the second stipulation, that was conditional.

The latter part of the paragraph informs us that Servius Sulpicius maintained the doctrine of which Gaius disapproves, viz. that the novation was immediate; and that he regarded from a like point of view a stipulation made with a slave, considering it to work an absolute novation, and so destroy the pre-existent obligation, without, however, being itself valid. Gaius concludes the paragraph by reiterating his dislike of these principles of interpretation. See § 176. Justinian's view agrees with that of Gaius. See *Inst.* III. 29. 3.

fuerit stipulatus, novationem fieri et rem perire; quia cum servo agi non potest. sed in utroque casu alio iure utimur: nec magis his casibus novatio fit, quam si id quod tu mihi debeas a peregrino, cum quo sponsi communio[1] non est, SPONDES verbo stipulatus sim.

180. Tollitur adhuc obligatio litis contestatione[2], si modo legitimo iudicio fuerit actum. nam tunc obligatio quidem principalis dissolvitur, incipit autem teneri reus litis contestatione: set si condemnatus sit, sublata litis contestatione incipit ex causa iudicati teneri. et hoc (est) quod aput veteres scriptum est,

Titius owed him (the stipulator), a novation took place and the thing was lost; because no action can be brought against a slave. But in both these cases we adopt a different rule; for a novation no more takes place in these cases than it would if I stipulated for that which you owe to me by means of the word *spondes* with a foreigner, with whom it is impossible to deal in *sponsion*[1].

180. An obligation is also dissolved by the *litis contestatio*[2], when proceedings are taken by a statutable action. For then the original obligation is dissolved and the defendant begins to be bound by the *litis contestatio:* but if he be condemned, then, the *litis contestatio* being no longer binding (lit. being swept away), he begins to be bound on account of the judgment. And this is the meaning of what is said by ancient writers, that

1 III. 93. *Sponsus* = *sponsoris promissio.* Dirksen, *sub verb.*

2 The Roman lawyers did not consider that a contested right was a subject of litigation as soon as the plaintiff had taken the first step towards an action. The moment when it did become a subject of litigation was the *litis contestatio.* Till the preliminary proceedings before the Praetor were terminated there was room for a peaceable accommodation between the parties, and it was only at the point when the litigants were remitted to a *judex*, the instant when the proceedings *in jure* terminated and those *in judicio* began, that the matter must inevitably be left to the decision of the law. The meaning of the term *litis contestatio* is thus given by Festus: "Contestari est cum uterque reus dicit, Testes estote. Contestari litem dicuntur duo aut plures adversarii quod ordinato judicio utraque pars dicere solet, Testes estote;" where he evidently is referring to the time anterior to the introduction of the formulary process, when *legis actiones* were in use. This ceremony became in later times a mere form, but the name was still retained. Ulpian says, "proinde non originem judicii spectandam, sed ipsam judicati velut obligationem," referring to the obligation of a *reus* after award. D. 15. 1. 3. 11.

ante litem contestatam dare debitorem oportere, post litem contestatam condemnari oportere, post condemnationem iudicatum facere oportere. (181.) Unde fit, ut si legitimo iudicio debitum petiero[1], postea de eo ipso

"before the *litis contestatio* the debtor ought to give, after the *litis contestatio* he ought to suffer condemnation (submit to award), after condemnation (award) he ought to do what is adjudged." 181. Hence it follows that if I sue for a debt by statutable action[1], I cannot afterwards, by the letter of the civil

[1] The differences in procedure between *judicia legitima* and *judicia imperio continentia* are to be found in Gaius, IV. 103—109. Mühlenbruch (in his notes on Heineccius, IV. 6. 27) gives, in substance, the following account of the origin of the appellations and the reasons for the diversity of practice of the two systems: "The reason for the numerous and important differences between the two kinds of *judicia* was that in early times the statute law was confined in its application to a few persons and a narrow district, and cases involving other persons or arising outside this district were settled at the discretion and by the direct authority (*imperium*) of the magistrates: and although in later times this free action of the magistrate was restrained within well-ascertained limits, yet it continued an admitted principle, that in the *judicia* based on the *imperium* of the magistrate there was less adherence to strict rule than in those which sprung from the *leges*. See Cic. *pro Rosc.* § 5. As the state grew, the ancient distinction became a mere matter of outward form, and the one system became so interwoven with the other, that it seems a marvel the separation was kept up so long. Hence it at length died away without any direct enactment, and it is indisputable that in Justinian's time no vestiges of it remained." See also Zimmern's *Traité des actions chez les Romains*, § XXXIV.

The Praetor's edict being annual, a right of action based on one of its clauses was not necessarily recognized by the succeeding Praetor; and even if he did grant a like action, this was not because his predecessor upheld a certain rule, but because he himself had enacted the same. Hence the action was under the new edict, even though the facts on which it was based dated from the time when the old edict was in force; and the original right of action had perished with the termination of the preceding Praetor's *imperium*. Also if an action had been brought and decided under the old edict, another could still be brought under the new edict, for the offence against that had not yet been a matter of suit. Hence the need of the *exceptio*.

As we have mentioned *imperium* above, this is perhaps the place to remark that this *imperium* implies a power of carrying out sentences: a magistrate who was merely executory was said to have *imperium merum* or *potestas*: one like the Praetor, &c., who could both adjudge and carry into execution, possessed *imperium mixtum*, *i.e.* a combination of *potestas* and *jurisdictio*; for *jurisdictio*, sometimes called *notio*, is the attribute of a magistrate who can only investigate, and must apply to other functionaries to carry out his decisions: thus a *judex* had *jurisdictio* only. See Heineccius, *Antiq. Rom.* IV. 6. 5, Mühlenbruch's edition, and D. 2. 1. 3.

iure agere non possim, quia inutiliter intendo[1] DARI MIHI OPORTERE: quia litis contestatione dari oportere desiit[2]. aliter atque si imperio continenti iudicio egerim: tunc enim nihilominus obligatio durat, et ideo ipso iure postea agere possum; sed debeo per exceptionem rei iudicatae vel in iudicium deductae
P.176 summoveri[3]. quae autem legitima | iudicia et quae imperio contineantur sequenti commentario referemus[4].

182. Transeamus nunc ad obligationes quae ex delicto nascuntur[5], veluti si quis furtum fecerit, bona rapuerit, damnum dederit, iniuriam commiserit: quarum omnium rerum uno

law, bring another action for the same, because I plead[1] in vain that "it ought to be given to me," inasmuch as by the *litis contestatio* the necessity that it should be given to me ceased[2]. It is otherwise if I proceed by action coexistent with *imperium*, for then the obligation still remains, and therefore, by the letter of the law, I can afterwards bring another action: but I must be met by the exception *rei judicatae* or *in judicium deductae*[3]. Now what are statutable actions, and what are actions coexistent with *imperium*, we shall state in the next commentary[4].

182. Now let us pass on to actions which arise from delict[5], for instance, if a man have committed a theft, carried off goods by violence, inflicted damage, done injury: the obligation arising from all which matters is of one and the same

---

1 IV. 41.

2 IV. 107.

3 IV. 106. The first exception is to the effect that the matter has already been adjudicated upon, the second that it has been carried beyond the *litis contestatio*, and that thus there has been a *novatio*. See App. (T). In the last-named exception it is obviously immaterial whether the court has yet arrived at a judgment or not. See for a curious case connected with this exception, Cic. *de Orat.* I. 37.

4 See IV. 103. Besides the methods of dissolving an obligation already mentioned there were (1) *compensatio* and *deductio*, the setting off of what the creditor owes to the debtor, in order to lessen or extinguish the debt, see IV. 61—68: (2) *confusio*, when the obligation of the debtor and right of the creditor are united in the same person: (3) mutual consent, when a contract of the consensual kind has been made, but its fulfilment not yet undertaken by either party. See App. (O).

5 It must be noticed that all the actions mentioned in §§ 182—225 are civil actions on delict. *Furtum*, *rapina*, &c. were also punishable criminally, but with this fact we have at present nothing to do.

genere consistit obligatio[1], cum ex contractu obligationes in IIII genera deducantur, sicut supra exposuimus[2].

183. Furtorum autem genera Servius Sulpicius et Masurius Sabinus IIII esse dixerunt, manifestum et nec manifestum, conceptum et oblatum: Labeo duo, manifestum, nec manifestum; nam conceptum et oblatum species potius actionis esse furto cohaerentes quam genera furtorum; quod sane verius videtur, sicut inferius apparebit[3]. (184.) Manifestum furtum quidam id esse dixerunt quod dum fit deprehenditur. alii vero ulterius, quod eo loco deprehenditur ubi fit: velut si in oliveto olivarum, in vineto uvarum furtum factum est, quamdiu in eo oliveto aut vineto fur sit; aut si in domo furtum factum sit, quamdiu in ea domo fur sit. alii adhuc ulterius, eousque manifestum furtum esse dixerunt, donec perferret eo quo perferre fur destinasset.

kind[1], whereas, as we have explained above[2], obligations from contract are divided into four classes.

183. Of thefts, then, Servius Sulpicius and Masurius Sabinus say there are four kinds, manifest and nec-manifest, concept and oblate: Labeo says there are two, manifest and nec-manifest: for that concept and oblate are rather species of action attaching to theft than kinds of theft: and this view appears to be the more correct one, as will be seen below[3]. 184. Some have defined a manifest theft to be one which is detected whilst it is being committed. Others have gone further, and said it is one which is detected in the place where it is committed: for instance, if a theft of olives be committed in an oliveyard, or of grapes in a vineyard, (it is a manifest theft) so long as the thief is in the vineyard or oliveyard: or if a theft be committed in a house, so long as the thief is in the house. Others have gone still further, and said that a theft is manifest until the thief has carried the thing to the place whither he intended to carry it. Others still further,

1 They all arise *re*.

2 III. 89.

3 III. 186, 187. Gaius, with his usual dislike of definitions, does not give one of theft. Justinian's will be found in *Inst.* IV. 1. 1. Those of Sabinus given by Aulus Gellius, XI. 18, are: "Qui alienam rem adtrectavit, cum id se invito domino facere judicare deberet, furti tenetur," and "Qui alienum tacens lucri faciendi causa sustulit furti constringitur, sive scit cujus sit sive nescit." Gaius implies that this or something like it is his definition in §§ 195, 197 below.

alii adhuc ulterius, quandoque eam rem fur tenens visus fuerit; quae sententia non optinuit. set et illorum sententia qui existimaverunt, donec perferret eo quo fur destinasset, deprehensum furtum manifestum esse, ideo non videtur probari quod magnam
P.177 recipit dubitationem utrum | unius diei an etiam plurium dierum spatio id terminandum sit. quod eo pertinet, quia saepe in aliis civitatibus surreptas res in alias civitates vel in alias provincias destinat fur perferre. ex duabus itaque superioribus opinionibus alterutra adprobatur: magis tamen plerique posteriorem probant. (185.) Nec manifestum furtum quod sit ex iis quae diximus intellegitur: nam quod manifestum non est id nec manifestum est. (186.) Conceptum furtum dicitur cum aput aliquem testibus praesentibus furtiva res quaesita et inventa est[1]: nam in eum propria actio constituta est, quamvis fur non sit, quae appellatur concepti. (187.) Oblatum furtum dicitur, cum res furtiva tibi ab aliquo oblata sit, eaque aput te concepta

that it is manifest if the thief be seen with the thing in his hands at any time; but this opinion has not found favour. The opinion, too, of those who have thought a theft to be manifest if detected before the thief has carried the thing to the place he intended seems to meet with no favour, because it admits of much doubt whether theft must in respect of time be limited to one day or to several. This has reference to the fact that a thief often intends to convey things stolen in one state to other states or other provinces. Hence, one or other of the two opinions first cited is the right one; but most people prefer the second. 185. What a nec-manifest theft is, is gathered from what we have said: for that which is not manifest is "nec-manifest." 186. A theft is termed concept when the stolen thing is sought for and found in any one's possession in the presence of witnesses[1]: for there is a particular kind of action set out against him, even though he be not the thief, called the *actio concepti.* 187. A theft is called oblate, when the stolen thing has been put on your premises

---

1 The difference between nec-manifest and concept theft is that in the first the thief delivers up the stolen thing or admits his guilt without throwing on the plaintiff the trouble of a search, whilst in the other he denies his culpability but submits quietly to the search: of course, if he offer resistance, the case becomes one of *furtum prohibitum.*

sit; utique si ea mente data tibi fuerit ut aput te potius quam aput eum qui dederit conciperetur. nam tibi, aput quem concepta est, propria adversus eum qui optulit, quamvis fur non sit, constituta est actio, (quae) appellatur oblati[1]. (188.) Est etiam prohibiti furti adversus eum qui furtum quaerere volentem prohibuerit.

189. Poena manifesti furti ex lege XII tabularum capitalis erat[2]. nam liber verberatus addicebatur ei cui furtum fecerat; utrum autem servus efficeretur ex addictione, an adiudicati loco constitueretur[3], veteres quaerebant; *servum* aeque verberatum *e saxo deiciebant*[4]. postea inprobata est asperitas poenae,

by any one and is found there: that is to say, if it have been given to you with the intention that it should be found with you rather than with him who gave it: for there is a particular kind of action set out for you, in whose hands the thing is found, against him who put the thing into your hands, even though he be not the thief, called the *actio oblati*[1]. 188. There is also an *actio prohibiti furti* against one who offers resistance to a person wishing to search.

189. The penalty of a manifest theft was by a law of the Twelve Tables capital[2]. For a free man, after being scourged, was assigned over to the person on whom he had committed the theft (but whether he became a slave by the assignment, or was put into the position of an *adjudicatus*[3], was disputed amongst the ancients): a slave, after he had in like manner been scourged, they hurled from a rock[4]. In later times objec-

[1] Paulus, *S. R.* II. 31. 3.

[2] Tab. VIII. l. 14. For the meaning of "capital" see note on III. 213.

[3] *Adjudicatus*, more usually *addictus*, (but Gaius probably uses the former appellation in this passage to avoid confusion, having already written *addicebatur* in a different signification,) means an insolvent debtor delivered over to his creditor. The *adjudicati* were not reduced to slavery, (the common opinion to that effect being erroneous,) but they had to perform for their creditor servile offices. That they differed from slaves is proved by many facts: e.g. when by payment of the debt they were liberated from the creditor they were treated thenceforth as *ingenui* and not as *libertini*; the creditor to whom payment of the debt was tendered was compelled to accept it: the debtors retained their praenomen, cognomen, tribe, &c. See Heinecc. *Antiquit. Rom.* III. 29. § 2.

[4] This is Schoell's suggestion, in his edition of the XII. Tables: and is founded on what Aulus Gellius says, § 8; "jusserunt servos...verberibus adfici et e saxo praecipitari."

et tam ex servi persona quam ex liberi quadrupli actio Praetoris
P.178 edicto constituta est[1]. | (190.) Nec manifesti furti poena per legem (XII) tabularum dupli inrogatur; eamque etiam Praetor conservat[2]. (191.) Concepti et oblati poena ex lege XII tabularum tripli est: quae similiter a Praetore servatur. (192.) Prohibiti actio quadrupli est ex edicto Praetoris introducta. lex autem eo nomine nullam poenam constituit: hoc solum praecepit[3], ut qui quaerere velit nudus quaerat, linteo cinctus, lancem habens; qui si quid invenerit, iubet id lex furtum manifestum esse. (193.) Quid sit autem linteum, quaesitum est[4]. set verius est consuti genus esse, quo necessariae partes tegerentur. quare lex tota ridicula est; nam qui vestitum quaerere prohibet, is et nudum quaerere prohibiturus est: eo magis quod ita quaesita

tion was taken to the severity of the punishment, and in the Praetor's edict an action for fourfold was set forth, whether the offender were slave or free[1]. 190. The penalty of a nec-manifest theft is laid at twofold by the law of the Twelve Tables: and this the Praetor also retains[2]. 191. The penalty of concept and oblate theft is threefold by the law of the Twelve Tables: and this too is retained by the Praetor. 192. The action with fourfold penalty for prohibited theft was introduced by the Praetor's edict. For the law had enacted no penalty in this case; but had only commanded[3] that a man wishing to search should search naked, girt with a *linteum* and holding a dish; and if he found anything, the law ordered the theft to be regarded as manifest. 193. Now what a *linteum* may be is a moot point[4]: but it is most probable that it was a kind of cincture with which the private parts were covered. Hence the whole law is absurd. For any one who resists search by a man clothed, would also resist search by him naked: especially as a thing sought for in this manner is

---

1 If the master declined to pay the penalty for his slave, he could give him up as a *noxa*. IV. 75.

2 See Sir H. S. Maine's ingenious explanation of the wide differences in the ancient penalties of *furtum manifestum* and *nec manifestum*. *Ancient Law*, p. 379.

3 Tab. VIII. l. 15.

4 The *linteum* is called *licium* sometimes, e.g. in Festus: "Lance et licio dicebatur apud antiquos, quia qui furtum ibat quaerere in domo aliena, licio cinctus intrabat, lancemque ante oculos tenebat propter matrumfamilias aut virginum praesentiam."

res inventa maiori poenae subiciatur. deinde quod lancem sive ideo haberi iubeat, ut manibus occupantis nihil subiciatur, sive ideo, ut quod invenerit ibi imponat[1]: neutrum eorum procedit si id quod quaeratur eius magnitudinis aut naturae sit ut neque subici neque ibi inponi possit. certe non dubitatur cuiuscumque materiae sit ea lanx satis legi fieri. (194.) Propter hoc tamen quod lex ex ea causa manifestum furtum esse iubet, sunt qui scribunt furtum manifestum aut lege aut natura *intellegi:* lege id ipsum de quo loquimur; natura illud de quo superius exposuimus. sed verius est natura tantum manifestum furtum intellegi. neque enim lex facere potest ut qui manifestus fur non sit manifestus sit, non magis quam qui omnino fur non sit fur sit, et qui adulter aut homicida non sit adulter vel |
P.179 homicida sit: at illut sane lex facere potest, ut perinde aliquis

subjected to a heavier penalty if found. Then as to its ordering a dish to be held, whether it be that nothing might be introduced stealthily by the hands of the holder, or that he might lay on it what he found[1]: neither of these explanations is satisfactory, if the thing sought for be of such a size or character that it can neither be introduced by stealth nor placed on the dish. On this point, at any rate, there is no dispute, that the law is satisfied whatever be the material of which the dish is made. 194. Now, since the law orders that a theft shall be manifest under the above circumstances, there are writers who maintain that a theft may be regarded as manifest either by law or by nature: by law, that of which we are now speaking; by nature, that of which we treated above. But it is more correct for a theft to be considered as manifest only by nature. For a law can no more cause a man who is not a manifest thief to become manifest, than it can cause a man who is not a thief at all to become a thief, or one who is not an adulterer or homicide to become an adulterer or homicide: but this no doubt a law can do, cause a man to be liable to punishment as though he had

[1] Festus in the passage just quoted assigns a third reason. Other authors adopt that first given in the text, and say that the dish was carried on the head and supported by both hands. See Heinecc. *Antiq.* IV. 1. § 19.

poena teneatur atque si furtum vel adulterium vel homicidium admisisset, quamvis nihil eorum admiserit.

195. Furtum autem fit non solum cum quis intercipiendi causa rem alienam amovet, set generaliter cum quis rem alienam invito domino contrectat. (196.) Itaque si quis re quae aput eum deposita sit utatur, furtum committit[1]. et si quis utendam rem acceperit eamque in alium usum transtulerit, furti obligatur. veluti si quis argentum utendum acceperit, (quod) quasi amicos ad coenam invitaturus rogaverit, et id peregre secum tulerit, aut si quis equum gestandi gratia commodatum longius secum aliquo duxerit; quod veteres scripserunt de eo qui in aciem perduxisset. (197.) Placuit tamen eos qui rebus commodatis aliter uterentur quam utendas accepissent, ita furtum committere, si intellegant id se invito domino facere, eumque si intellexisset non permissurum; at si permissurum credant, extra furti crimen videri: optima sane distinctione, quia furtum sine

committed a theft, adultery or homicide, although he have committed none of them.

195. A theft takes place not only when a man removes another's property with the intent of appropriating it, but generally when any one deals with what belongs to another against the will of the owner. 196. Therefore, if any one make use of a thing which has been deposited[1] with him, he commits a theft. And if any one have received a thing to be used, and convert it to another use, he is liable for theft. For example, if a man have received silver plate to be used, asking for it on the pretext that he is about to invite friends to supper, and carry it abroad with him; or if any one take with him to a distance a horse lent him for the purpose of a ride: and the instance the ancients gave of this was a man's taking a horse to battle. 197. It has been decided, however, that those who employ borrowed things for other uses than those for which they received them, only commit a theft in case they are aware that they are doing this against the will of the owner, and that if he knew of the proceeding he would not allow it: but if they believe he would allow it, they are not considered to be chargeable with theft: the distinction being a very proper one, since theft is not committed without

[1] See note (N) in Appendix.

dolo malo non committitur. (198.) Set et si credat aliquis invito domino se rem contrectare, domino autem volente id fiat, dicitur furtum non fieri. unde illut quaesitum et probatum est cum Titius servum meum sollicitaret, ut quasdam res mihi
P.180 subriperet et ad eum perferret, | (et servus) id ad me pertulerit, ego, dum volo Titium in ipso delicto deprehendere, permiserim servo quasdam res ad eum perferre, quaesitum est utrum furti an servi corrupti iudicio teneatur Titius mihi, an neutro: responsum, neutro eum teneri[1]; furti ideo quod non invito me res contrectarit, servi corrupti ideo quod deterior servus factus non sit. (199.) Interdum autem etiam liberorum hominum furtum fit[2], velut si quis liberorum nostrorum qui in potestate nostra sunt, sive etiam uxor quae in manu nostra sit, sive etiam iudicatus[3] vel auctoratus meus[4] subreptus fuerit. (200.) Ali-

wrongful intent. 198. And even if a man believe that he is dealing with a thing against the will of its owner, whilst the proceeding is agreeable to the will of the owner, it is said there is no theft committed. Hence this question has been raised and settled; Titius having made proposals to my slave to steal certain things from me and bring them to him, and the slave having informed me of this, I, wishing to convict Titius in the act, allowed my slave to take certain things to him: the question that arose was this, is Titius liable to me either in an action of theft, or in one for corruption of a slave, or in neither: the answer was, that he was liable in neither[1], not in an action of theft, because he had not dealt with the things against my will, nor in an action for corruption of a slave, because the integrity of the slave had not been corrupted. 199. Sometimes there can be a theft even of free persons[2], for instance, if one of my descendants who are under my *potestas*, or my wife who is under my *manus*, or even my judgment-debtor[3], or one who has engaged himself to me as a gladiator[4] be abducted. 200. Some-

---

[1] See Justinian's reasons for giving an opposite decision in *Inst.* IV. I. 8.

[2] Technically styled *plagium*.

[3] IV. 21.

[4] *Auctoratus* is defined by Paulus: "qui auctoramento locatus est ad gladium:" and Dirksen explains *auctoramentum* to be an equivalent of *jusjurandum*. Gladiators were not all captives or criminals; Roman citizens sometimes sold themselves to fight in the arena.

quando etiam suae rei quisque furtum committit, veluti si debitor rem quam creditori pignori dedit subtraxerit[1], vel si bonae fidei possessori rem meam possidenti subripuerim. unde placuit eum qui servum suum, quem alius bona fide possidebat, ad se reversum celaverit furtum committere. (201.) Rursus ex diverso interdum alienas res occupare et usucapere concessum est, nec creditur furtum fieri, velut res hereditarias quarum heres non est nactus possessionem, nisi necessarius heres esset[2]; nam necessario herede extante placuit nihil pro herede usucapi posse. Item debitor rem quam fiduciae causa creditori mancipaverit aut in iure cesserit, *secun*dum ea quae in superiore commentario rettulimus, sine furto possidere et usucapere potest[3].

202. Interdum furti tenetur qui ipse furtum non fecerit:
P.181 qualis | est cuius ope consilio furtum factum est; in quo numero

times, too, a man commits a theft of his own property, for example, if a debtor take away by stealth a thing he has given in pledge to his creditor[1], or if I take by stealth my own property from a possessor in good faith. Therefore, it has been ruled that a man commits a theft who, on the return of his own slave whom another possessed in good faith, conceals him. 201. Conversely, again, we are sometimes allowed to take possession of the property of others and acquire it by usucapion, and no theft is considered to be committed: the items of an inheritance, for example, of which the heir has not previously obtained possession, provided he be not a "necessary" heir[2]: for when the heir is of the "necessary" class, it has been ruled that there can be no usucapion *pro herede.* A debtor also, according to what we have stated in the preceding Commentary, can without theft possess and gain by usucapion what he has made over to his creditor for a fiduciary purpose by mancipation or cession in court[3].

202. Sometimes a man is liable for a theft who has not himself committed it: of such kind is he by whose aid and

---

[1] III. 204.

[2] See II. 9, 52, 58. In the first and second of these passages it is not indicated that the *possessio pro herede* of a stranger is disallowed even by the civil law, when the heir is "necessary" (II. 153); but that such is the case is to be gathered from II. 57, 58, and the passage now before us.

[3] II. 59, 60.

est qui nummos tibi excussit ut eos alius surriperet, vel obstitit tibi ut alius surriperet, aut oves aut boves tuas fugavit ut alius eas exciperet; et hoc veteres scripserunt de eo qui panno rubro fugavit armentum. Sed si quid per lasciviam et non data opera ut furtum committeretur factum sit, videbimus an utilis actio dari debeat[1], cum per legem Aquiliam quae de damno lata est etiam culpa[2] puniatur.

203. Furti autem actio ei conpetit cuius interest rem salvam esse, licet dominus non sit: itaque nec domino aliter conpetit quam si eius intersit rem non perire. (204.) Unde constat creditorem de pignore subrepto furti agere posse; adeo quidem ut quamvis ipse dominus, id est ipse debitor, eam rem subripuerit, nihilominus creditori conpetat actio furti. (205.) Item

counsel a theft has been committed: and in this category must be included one who has struck money out of your hand that another may carry it off, or has put himself in your way that another may carry it off, or has scattered your oxen or sheep that another may make away with them; and the instance the ancients gave of this was a man scattering a herd by means of a red rag. But if anything be done in wantonness, and not with set purpose for a theft to be committed, we shall have to consider whether a constructive Aquilian action should be granted[1], since by the Lex Aquilia, which was passed with reference to damage, culpable negligence[2] is also punished.

203. The action of theft can be brought by any one who has an interest that the thing should be safe, even though he be not the owner: and thus again it does not lie for the owner unless he have an interest that the thing should not perish. 204. Hence it is an admitted principle that a creditor can bring an action of theft for a pledge which has been carried off: so that even if the owner himself, that is the debtor, have carried it off, still the action of theft lies for the creditor. 205. Like-

[1] The meaning of the passage is this: "in the case supposed there is no *actio furti;* the point therefore which we shall have to consider in any particular instance is whether a constructive Aquilian action will lie." *Utilis* has been explained above in the note on II. 78. The action would be *utilis* and not *directa*, because the direct action could only be brought when the damage was done *corpori corpore*, III. 219.

[2] III. 211.

si fullo polienda curandave, aut sarcinator sarcienda vestimenta mercede certa acceperit, eaque furto amiserit, ipse furti habet actionem, non dominus; quia domini nihil interest ea non periisse, cum iudicio locati a fullone aut sarcinatore suum consequi possit, si modo is fullo aut sarcinator rei praestandae plene sufficiat; nam si solvendo non est, tunc quia ab eo dominus suum consequi non potest, ipsi furti actio conpetit, quia hoc
P.182 casu ipsius interest rem salvam esse. (206.) Quae de | fullone aut sarcinatore diximus, eadem transferemus et ad eum cui rem commodavimus: nam ut illi mercedem capiendo custodiam praestant, ita hic quoque utendi commodum percipiendo similiter necesse habet custodiam praestare. (207.) Sed is aput quem res deposita est custodiam non praestat, tantumque in eo obnoxius est si quid ipse dolo fecerit[1]: qua

wise, if a fuller have taken garments to smooth or clean, or a tailor to patch, for a settled hire, and have lost them by theft, he has the action of theft and not the owner: because the owner has no interest in the thing not perishing, since he can by an action of letting recover his own from the fuller or tailor, provided the fuller or tailor have money enough fully to make good the thing: for if he be insolvent, then, since the owner cannot recover his own from him, the action lies for the owner himself, for in this case he has an interest in the thing being safe. 206. These remarks about the fuller or tailor we shall also apply to a person to whom we have lent a thing: for in like manner as the former by receiving hire become responsible for safe keeping, so does the borrower by enjoying the advantage of the use also become responsible for the same. 207. But a person with whom a thing is deposited is not responsible for its keeping, and is only answerable for what he himself does wilfully[1]: hence, if the thing which he

[1] The depositary is only liable for *dolus*, the text says. The general rule in contracts was that the person benefited was liable for *culpa levis*, i.e. for even trivial negligence, whilst the person on whom the burden was cast was only liable for *culpa lata*, gross negligence. *Dolus* imports a wilful injury; *culpa* an unintentional damage, but one caused by negligence. The depositary would be liable for *dolus* and *culpa lata*. Gaius, therefore, is not speaking with strict accuracy when he says the depositary is liable only "si quid ipse dolo fecerit;" but perhaps he had in his thoughts the well-known maxim, *culpa lata dolo aequiparatur*, in which

de causa, (si) res ei subrepta fuerit quae restituenda est, eius nomine depositi non tenetur, nec ob id eius interest rem salvam esse: furti itaque agere non potest, set ea actio domino competit.

208. In summa sciendum est quaesitum esse, an impubes rem alienam amovendo furtum faciat. plerisque placet, quia furtum ex adfectu consistit, ita demum obligari eo crimine impuberem, si proximus pubertati sit[1], et ob id intellegat se delinquere.

209. Qui res alienas rapit tenetur etiam furti: quis enim magis alienam rem invito domino contrectat quam qui rapit? itaque recte dictum est eum improbum furem esse. set propriam actionem eius delicti nomine Praetor introduxit, quae appellatur vi bonorum raptorum; et est intra annum quadrupli actio[2], post

ought to restore be stolen from him, he is not liable to an action of deposit in respect of it, and thus he has no interest that the thing should be safe; therefore he cannot bring an action of theft, but that action lies for the owner. 208. Finally, we must observe that it is a disputed point whether a child under puberty commits a theft by removing another person's property. It is generally held that as theft depends on the intent, he is only liable to the charge, if he be very near puberty[1] and therefore aware that he is doing wrong.

209. He who takes by violence the goods of another is liable for theft (as well as *rapina*): for who deals with another's property more completely against the owner's will than one who takes it by violence? And therefore it is rightly said that he is an atrocious thief. But the Praetor has introduced a special action in respect of this delict, which is called the *actio vi bonorum raptorum*, and is an action for fourfold[2] if

---

case his dictum is correct. On the subject of *culpa* see Mackeldey, *Syst. Jur. Rom.* § 342.

[1] Probably Gaius is not writing technically when he uses the expression "pubertati proximus." The sources, however, sometimes speak of a child under seven as *infanti proximus*, and one between seven and fourteen as *pubertati proximus*. See Savigny, *On Possession*, translated by Perry, p. 180, note (b).

[2] The fourfold penalty in this *actio* includes restitution of the thing, so that more correctly the penalty is threefold. In an *actio furti manifesti*, on the contrary, the penalty is really fourfold, the thing itself being recovered separately by a *vindicatio*. See IV. 8; Just. *Inst.* IV. 6. 19.

annum simpli. quae actio utilis est[1] et si quis unam rem, licet minimam, rapuerit.

210. Damni iniuriae actio constituitur per legem Aquiliam[2]. cuius primo capite cautum est, (ut) si quis hominem alienum, |
P.183 eamve quadrupedem quae pecudum numero sit, iniuria occiderit, quanti ea res in eo anno plurimi fuerit, tantum domino dare damnetur. (211.) Is iniuria autem occidere intellegitur cuius dolo aut culpa id acciderit, nec ulla alia lege damnum quod sine iniuria datur reprehenditur: itaque inpunitus est qui sine culpa et dolo malo casu quodam damnum committit. (212.) Nec solum corpus in actione huius legis aestimatur; sed sane si servo occiso plus dominus capiat damni quam pretium servi sit, id quoque aestimatur: velut si servus meus ab aliquo heres

brought within the year, and for the single value if brought after the year: and is available[1] when a man has taken by violence a single thing, however small it may be.

210. The action called *damni injuriae* (of damage done wrongfully) was introduced by the Lex Aquilia[2], in the first clause of which it is laid down that if any one have wrongfully slain another person's slave, or an animal included in the category of cattle, he shall be condemned to pay to the owner the highest value the thing has borne within that year. 211. A man is considered to slay wrongfully when the death takes place through his malice or negligence: and damage committed without wrongfulness is not punished by this or any other law: so that a man is unpunished when he commits a damage through some mischance, without negligence or malice. 212. In an action under this law the account taken is not restricted to the mere value of the thing destroyed, but undoubtedly, if by the slaying of the slave the owner receive damage over and above the value of the slave, that too is included; for instance, if a slave of mine, instituted heir by any

1 We have several times already come across the word *utilis* derived from *uti* (as), but *utilis* here is the more common adjective derived from *utor*, to use.

2 The words of this clause of the law are given in D. 9. 2. 2. pr. In D. 9. 2. 1 we are told that the *Lex Aquilia* was a plebiscite, and Theophilus assigns it to the time of the secession of the *plebs*, probably meaning that to the Janiculum, 285 B.C. The second clause was on a different subject, as Gaius tells us in § 215, the third is quoted in D. 9. 2. 27. 5.

institutus, ante quam iussu meo hereditatem cerneret[1], occisus fuerit; non enim tantum ipsius pretium aestimatur, sed et hereditatis amissae quantitas. item si ex gemellis vel ex comoedis vel ex symphoniacis unus occisus fuerit, non solum occisi fit aestimatio, sed eo amplius quoque conputatur quod ceteri qui supersunt depretiati sunt. idem iuris est etiam si ex pari mularum unam, vel etiam ex quadrigis equorum unum occiderit. (213.) Cuius autem servus occisus est, is liberum arbitrium habet vel capitali crimine reum facere eum qui occiderit[2], vel hac lege damnum persequi. (214.) Quod autem adiectum est in hac lege: QUANTI IN EO ANNO PLURIMI EA RES FUERIT, illut efficit, si clodum puta aut luscum servum occiderit, qui in eo anno integer fuerit, (*ut non quanti mortis tempore, sed quanti in eo anno plurimi fuerit,*)[3] aestimatio fiat. quo fit, ut quis plus
P.184 interdum consequatur quam ei damnum | datum est.

one, be slain before he has made cretion[1] for the inheritance at my command. For not only the price of the man himself is computed, but the amount of the lost inheritance also. So too if one of twins, or one of a band of actors or musicians be slain, not only is the value of the slaughtered slave taken into account, but besides this the amount whereby the survivors are depreciated. The rule is the same if one of a pair of mules or of a team of horses be killed. 213. A man whose slave has been slain is free to choose whether he will make the slayer defendant on a capital[2] charge or sue for damages under this law. 214. The insertion in the law of the words: "the highest value the thing had within the year," has this effect, that if a man have killed a lame or one-eyed slave, who was whole within the year, an estimate is made not of his value at the time of death, but of his best value within the year[3]. The result of which is that sometimes a

[1] II. 164.

[2] *Capitalis* does not necessarily mean "capital" in our sense of the word, but signifies "affecting either the life, liberty, or citizenship and reputation." See Dirksen *sub verbo.* The law under which the criminal suit could be brought in the present case was the *Lex Cornelia de sicariis* (72 B.C.), the penalty whereof was interdiction from fire and water, and consequently loss of citizenship; Heineccius, *Antiqq. Rom.* IV. 18. 58. According to the Code (III. 35. 3), a master whose slave had been killed could bring *both* a criminal and a civil action.

[3] An omitted line is here supplied from Just. *Inst.* IV. 3. 9.

215. Capite secundo (in) adstipulatorem[1] qui pecuniam in fraudem stipulatoris acceptam fecerit[2], quanti ea res est, tanti actio constituitur. (216.) qua et ipsa parte legis damni nomine actionem introduci manifestum est. sed id caveri non fuit necessarium, cum actio mandati[3] ad eam rem sufficeret; nisi quod ea lege adversus infitiantem in duplum agitur[4].

217. Capite tertio de omni cetero damno cavetur. itaque si quis servum vel eam quadrupedem quae pecudum numero (*est vulneraverit, sive eam quadrupedem quae pecudum numero*)[5] non est, velut canem, aut feram bestiam, velut ursum, leonem vulneraverit vel occiderit, ex hoc capite actio constituitur. in ceteris quoque animalibus, item in omnibus rebus quae anima carent, damnum iniuria datum hoc parte vindicatur. si quid enim ustum aut ruptum aut fractum (fuerit), actio hoc capite constituitur; quamquam potuerit sola rupti appellatio in omnes istas causas

master gets more than the amount of the damage he has suffered.

215. In the second clause (of the Aquilian law) an action is granted against an adstipulator[1] who has given an acceptilation[2] in defraudance of his stipulator, for the value of the thing concerned. 216. And that this provision was introduced into this part of the law on account of the damage accruing is plain; although there was no need for such a provision, since the action of mandate[3] would suffice, save only that under this (the Aquilian law) the action is for double[4] against one who denies his liability.

217. In the third clause provision is made regarding all other damage. Therefore if any one have wounded a slave or a quadruped included in the category of cattle, or either killed or wounded a quadruped not included in that category[5], as a dog or a wild beast, such as a bear or lion, the action is based on this clause. And with respect to all other animals, as well as with respect to things devoid of life, damage done wrongfully is redressed under this clause. For if anything be burnt, or broken, or shattered, the action is based on this clause: although the word "broken" (*ruptum*) would by itself have

[1] III. 110.
[2] III. 169.
[3] III. 111.
[4] IV. 9, 171.
[5] Another omitted line is here supplied from Just. *Inst.* IV. 3. 13.

sufficere: ruptum (*enim intellegitur quod quoquo modo corruptum*)[1] est. unde non solum usta aut fracta, set etiam scissa et collisa et effusa et quoquo modo vitiata aut perempta atque deteriora facta hoc verbo continentur. (218.) Hoc tamen capite non quanti in eo anno, sed quanti in diebus XXX proxumis ea res fuerit, damnatur is qui damnum dederit; ac ne PLURIMI quidem verbum adicitur: et ideo quidam putaverunt liberum esse judicium ad id tempus ex diebus XXX aestimationem redi-
P.185 gere quo plurimi | res fuit, vel ad id quo minoris fuit. sed Sabino placuit perinde habendum ac si etiam hac parte PLURIMI verbum adiectum esset: nam legis latorem contentum fuisse, (*quod prima parte eo verbo usus esset.*)[2] (219.) Et placuit ita demum ex ista lege actionem esse, si quis corpore suo damnum dederit: ideoque alio modo damno dato utiles actiones dantur[3]: velut si quis alienum hominem aut pecudem incluserit et fame necaverit, aut iumentum tam vehementer egerit, ut rumperetur;

met all these cases: for by *ruptum* is understood that which is spoiled in any way[1]. Hence not only things burnt, or shattered, but also things torn, and bruised, and spilled, and in any way spoiled or destroyed and deteriorated, are comprised in this word. 218. Under this clause, however, the committer of the damage is condemned not for the value of the thing within the year, but within the 30 days next preceding: and the word *plurimi* (the highest value) is not added; and therefore some people have thought that the *judex* is free to assess the value at that date within the thirty days when the thing had its highest value, or another day on which it had a lower one. But Sabinus held that the clause must be interpreted just as though the word *plurimi* had been inserted in this place also, for he said the author of the law thought it sufficient to have expressed the word in the first part thereof[2]. 219. Also it has been ruled that an action lies under this law only when a man has done damage by means of his own body. Therefore for damage done in any other mode *utiles actiones*[3] are granted: for instance, if a man have shut up another person's slave or beast and starved it to death, or driven a beast of burden so

[1] Some omitted words are here again replaced from Just. *Inst.* IV. 3. 13.

[2] These words are supplied from Just. *Inst.* IV. 3. 15.

[3] See note on II. 78.

item si quis alieno servo persuaserit ut in arborem ascenderet vel in puteum descenderet, et is ascendendo aut descendendo ceciderit, (et) aut mortuus fuerit aut aliqua parte corporis laesus sit. item si quis alienum servum de ponte aut ripa in flumen proiecerit et is suffocatus fuerit, quamquam hic corpore suo damnum dedisse eo quod proiecerit non difficiliter intellegi potest.

220. Iniuria[1] autem committitur non solum cum quis pugno puta aut fuste percussus vel etiam verberatus erit, sed et si cui convicium[2] factum fuerit, sive quis bona alicuius quasi debitoris sciens eum nihil debere sibi proscripserit[3], sive quis ad infamiam alicuius libellum aut carmen scripserit, sive quis matremfamilias aut praetextatum[4] adsectatus fuerit, et denique

violently as to cause its destruction: also if a man have persuaded another person's slave to go up a tree or down a well, and in going up or down he have fallen, and either been killed or injured in some part of his body. Also if a man have thrown another person's slave from a bridge or bank into a river and he have been drowned, although in this case it is plain enough that he has caused the damage with his body, inasmuch as he cast him in.

220. Injury[1] is inflicted not only when a man is struck with the fist or a stick, or lashed, but also when abusive language[2] is publicly addressed to any one, or when any person knowing that another owes him nothing advertises[3] that other's goods for sale as though he were a debtor, or when any one writes a libel or a song to bring disgrace on another, or when any one follows about a married woman or a young[4] boy, and in

[1] For the different significations of the word *injuria* see Justinian, *Inst.* IV. 4. pr., a passage which is in great measure borrowed from Paulus.

[2] An explanation of the word *convicium* is given by Ulpian in D. 47. 10. 15. 4: "Convicium autem dicitur vel a concitatione vel a conventu, hoc est, a collatione vocum, quum enim in unum complures voces conferuntur, convicium appellatur, quasi convocium." Hence *convicium* means either abusive language addressed to a man publicly, or the act of inciting a crowd to beset a man's house or to mob the man himself.

[3] Sc. obtains from the Praetor an order for possession and leave to advertise, by making false representations to that magistrate.

[4] *Praetextatus* signifies under the age of puberty, as at the age of fourteen the *toga virilis* was assumed and the *toga praetextata* discarded.

aliis pluribus modis. (221.) Pati autem iniuriam videmur non solum per nosmet ipsos, sed etiam per liberos nostros quos in
P.186 potestate habemus; | item per uxores nostras cum in manu nostra sint. itaque si Beltiae filiae meae quae Titio nupta est iniuriam feceris, non solum filiae nomine tecum agi iniuriarum potest, verum etiam meo quoque et Titii nomine. (222.) Servo autem ipsi quidem nulla iniuria intellegitur fieri, sed domino per eum fieri videtur: non tamen iisdem modis quibus etiam per liberos nostros vel uxores iniuriam pati videmur, sed ita cum quid atrocius commissum fuerit, quod aperte in contumeliam domini fieri videtur, veluti si quis alienum servum verberaverit; et in hunc casum formula proponitur[1]. at si quis servo convicium fecerit vel pugno eum percusserit, non proponitur ulla formula nec temere petenti datur[2].

223. Poena autem iniuriarum ex lege XII tabularum[3] propter

fact in many other ways. 221. We can suffer injury not only in our own persons but also in the persons of our children whom we have under our *potestas;* and so too in the persons of our wives, if they be under our *manus.* For example then, if you do an injury to my daughter, Beltia, who is married to Titius, not only can an action for injury be brought against you in the name of my daughter, but also one in my name, and one in that of Titius. 222. To a slave himself it is considered that no injury can be done, but it is regarded as done to his master through him: we are not, however looked upon as suffering injury under the same circumstances (through slaves) as through our children or wives, but only when some atrocious act is done, which is plainly seen to be intended for the insult of the master, for instance, when a man has lashed the slave of another; and a *formula* is set forth[1] to meet such a case. But if a man have used abusive language to a slave in public or struck him with his fist, no *formula* is set forth, nor is one granted to a demandant except for good reason[2].

223. By a law of the Twelve Tables[3] the penalty for in-

---

[1] Sc. in the Edict.

[2] That is to say he has neither an action framed on any known formula, nor even one "praescriptis verbis," unless there be some special circumstances of aggravation.

[3] Tab. VIII. ll. 2, 3, and 4.

membrum quidem ruptum talio erat; propter os vero fractum aut conlisum trecentorum assium poena erat, si libero os fractum erat; at si servo, CL: propter ceteras vero iniurias XXV assium poena erat constituta. et videbantur illis temporibus in magna paupertate satis idoneae istae pecuniariae poenae. (224.) Set nunc alio iure utimur[1]. permittitur enim nobis a Praetore ipsis iniuriam aestimare; et iudex vel tanti condemnat quanti nos aestimaverimus vel minoris, prout illi visum fuerit. P.187 set cum atrocem iniuriam Praetor | aestimare soleat, si simul constituerit quantae pecuniae nomine fieri debeat vadimonium[2], hac ipsa quantitate taxamus formulam[3], et iudex quamvis possit vel minoris damnare, plerumque tamen propter ipsius Praetoris auctoritatem non audet minuere condemnationem[4]. (225.) Atrox autem iniuria aestimatur vel ex facto, velut si quis

jury was like for like in the case of a limb destroyed; but for a bone broken or crushed there was a penalty of 300 *asses* if the sufferer were a free man, and 150 if he were a slave: for all other injuries the penalty was set at 25 *asses*. And these pecuniary penalties appeared sufficient in those times of great poverty. 224. But nowadays we follow a different rule[1], for the Praetor allows us to assess our injury for ourselves: and the *judex* awards damages either to the amount at which we have assessed or to a smaller amount, according to his own discretion. But in cases where the Praetor accounts an injury "atrocious," if he at the same time have settled the amount of *vadimonium*[2] which is to be given, we limit[3] the *formula* to this quantity, and although the *judex* can award a smaller amount of damages, yet generally, on account of the respect which is due to the Praetor, he dare not make his award smaller than the "condemnation[4]." 225. Now an injury is considered "atrocious" either from the character of the act, for instance, if a man be wounded, or

---

[1] The alteration is said by A. Gellius to have been occasioned by the conduct of one Veratius, "qui pro delectamento habebat os hominis liberi manus suae palma verberare, cum servus sequebatur crumenam plenam assium portitans: et quemcunque depalmaverat, numerari statim secundum duodecim tabulas viginti quinque asses jubebat." *Noct. Att.* 20. 1.

[2] IV. 184.

[3] IV. 51.

[4] IV. 39, 43.

ab aliquo vulneratus aut verberatus fustibusve caesus fuerit; vel ex loco, velut si cui in theatro aut in foro iniuria facta sit; vel ex persona, velut si magistratus iniuriam passus fuerit, vel senatoribus ab humili persona facta sit iniuria.

lashed, or beaten with sticks by another; or from the place, for instance, if the injury be done in the theatre or the forum; or from the person, for instance, if a magistrate have suffered the injury, or it have been inflicted by a man of low rank on senators.

BOOK IV.

P.189 1. (*Si quaeratur,*) quot genera actionum sint, verius videtur duo esse: in rem et in personam[1]. nam qui IIII esse dixerunt ex sponsionum generibus[2], non animadverterunt quasdam species

1. If it be asked how many classes of actions there are, the more correct answer is that there are two, those *in rem* and those *in personam*[1]: for they who have asserted that there are four, framed on the different classes of *sponsiones*[2], have not noticed the fact that some individual kinds of actions unite together and

---

[1] It is thought better to keep the terms *in rem* and *in personam*, than to employ the apparent English equivalents "real" and "personal;" for though "personal" may, and frequently does, closely correspond with the Roman term *in personam*, "real" cannot be said to be equivalent to *in rem*; for an English real action is essentially connected with land, whilst the Roman *actio in rem* applied to movables as well as immovables. This, however, is but one point of difference out of many. See Savigny, *Syst. des heut. Röm. Rechts*, translated into French by Guenoux, *Traité de dr. Rom.* v. § 207, p. 44. Austin, Vol. III. p. 215 (Vol. II. p. 1011, third edition).

[2] *Sponsiones* belong to the time of the formulary method of suit, therefore the explanation now given of them will hardly be intelligible to a reader who is not acquainted, at least in outline, with the nature of the *formulae*, which is discussed somewhat later in this book.

When a controversy was raised on any point, whether of fact or of law, one of the litigants might challenge the other in a wager (*sponsio*) "ni ita esset," *i.e.* that if it were as the challenger asserted, the challenged should pay him some amount specified: and generally, but not always, there was a *restipulatio*, or counter-wager, that if it were not as the challenger stated, the challenger should pay the same amount to the challenged.

The origin of these *sponsiones* is referred by Heffter to a period subsequent to the passing of the Lex Silia (IV. 19), which brought into use the condiction *de pecunia certa credita*, for it is evident that by the introduction of a *sponsio* an obligation of any kind whatever might be turned into an equivalent pecuniary engagement, and so be sued upon under that *lex*.

The notion of the wager was obviously derived from the old *actio* actionum inter genera se rettulisse[1]. (2.) In personam actio est qua agimus quotiens cum aliquo qui nobis vel ex contractu vel ex delicto obligatus est (*contendimus*), id est cum intendimus[2] dare, facere, praestare oportere. (3.) In rem actio est, cum aut corporalem rem intendimus nostram esse, aut ius aliquod nobis conpetere, velut utendi[3], aut utendi fruendi, eundi, agendi, aquamve ducendi, vel altius tollendi, prospiciendive. actio ex diverso adversario est negativa[4].

form themselves into classes[1]. 2. The action *in personam* is the one we resort to whenever we sue some person who has become bound to us either upon a contract or upon a delict, that is, when we assert in our "intention[2]" that he ought to give or do something, or perform some duty. 3. The action is one *in rem*, when in our "intention" we assert either that a corporeal thing is ours, or that some right belongs to us, as, for example, that of *usus*[3] or *ususfructus*, of way, of passage, of conducting water, of raising one's buildings, or of view and prospect. So, on the other hand, the opposite party's action is (also *in rem*, but) negative[4].

---

sacramenti, but, as Gaius observes, there was a difference between the two, for the sum of the *sponsio* or *restipulatio* went to the victorious litigant, whilst that of the *sacramentum* was forfeited to the state.

Heffter thinks the "four kinds of actions framed on the various classes of sponsions" were:

(1) Actions *in rem*, with a sponsion *pro praede litis et vindiciarum*, and without a restipulation (see IV. 16).

(2) Actions *in personam* for money lent or promised, with a sponsion and a restipulation *calumniae causa* (see IV. 178).

(3) Actions of any kind, where the proper matter was converted into a pecuniary sum by the introduction of a sponsion, either by consent of the parties or by order of the Praetor, and wherein there was also a restipulation.

(4) Actions *in rem* or *in personam* without a sponsion attached.

Heffter defends his introduction of the fourth class by saying that the words of Gaius only state that there were four classes of actions distinguished by their various connexion (or want of connexion) with sponsions, and not that all classes of necessity contained a sponsion.

See Heffter's *Observations on Gai. IV.* pp. 86—89.

Huschke thinks the four classes of action were: i. *actio personalis*: ii. *formula petitoria* (IV. 4 and 5): iii. *in rem actio per sponsionem* (IV. 91): iv. *in rem actio per sacramentum* (IV. 95).

[1] For example, (taking Heffter's classification in the last note,) actions *in rem* with a sponsion *pro praede litis et vindiciarum* are not a separate *genus*, but only a *species*, comprised in the *genus*, actions *in rem*.

[2] IV. 41.

[3] *Usus* is not treated of by Gaius, but a discussion of it is to be found in Just. *Inst.* II. 5.

[4] That is, the opponent in his *in*-

4. Sic itaque discretis actionibus, certum est non posse nos rem nostram ab alio ita petere, SI PARET EUM DARE OPORTERE: nec enim quod nostrum est nobis dari potest, cum scilicet id dari nobis intellegatur quod (*ita datur, ut*) nostrum fiat; nec res quae (*iam nostra est*[1]) nostra amplius fieri potest. plane odio furum, quo magis pluribus actionibus teneantur, receptum est, ut extra poenam dupli aut quadrupli rei recipiendae nomine fures ex hac actione teneantur, SI PARET EOS DARE OPORTERE[2]. quamvis sit etiam adversus eos haec actio qua rem nostram esse petimus[3]. (5.) Appellantur autem in rem quidem actiones vindicationes; in personam vero actiones, quibus dare fierive oportere intendimus[4], condictiones[5].

4. Actions, therefore, being thus classified, it is certain that we cannot claim a thing that is ours from another person by the form: "Should it appear that he ought to give it," for that cannot be given to us which is ours, inasmuch as that only can be looked upon as a gift to us which is given for the purpose of becoming ours; nor can a thing which is ours already[1] become ours more than it is. But from a detestation of thieves, in order that they may be made liable to a greater number of actions, it has been settled that besides the penalty of double or quadruple the amount (of the thing stolen), thieves may, with the object of recovering the thing, also be made liable under the action running thus: "Should it appear that they ought to give[2];" although there also lies against them the form of action whereby we sue for a thing on the ground that it is our own[3]. 5. Now actions *in rem* are called *vindications*, whilst actions *in personam*, wherein we assert that our opponent ought to give us something, or that something ought to be done by him[4], are called *condictions*[5].

tentio alleges that these rights do not belong to the claimant. Cf. Just. *Inst.* IV. 6. 2, and D. 8. 5. 2. *pr.*

[1] Some small omissions in the MS. in this paragraph can be supplied from Just. *Inst.* IV. 6. 14.

[2] Sc. a *condictio*.

[3] Sc. a *vindicatio*.

[4] Savigny says that *Dare*, in the strict terminology of the formulary system, means to transfer property *ex jure Quiritium*; whilst *Facere*, on the other hand, embraces every kind of act, whether juridical or not, and hence comprises, amongst other things, *dare, solvere, numerare, ambulare, reddere, non facere, curare ne fiat*. Cf. D. 50. 16. 175, 189, 218.

[5] It is to be noted that Gaius says that all actions *in rem* are *vindicationes*, but that a particular class of actions *in personam* are *condictiones*.

P.190 6. Agimus autem interdum ut rem tantum con|sequamur, interdum ut poenam tantum, alias ut rem et poenam. (7.) Rem tantum persequimur velut actionibus (quibus) ex contractu agimus. (8.) Poenam tantum consequimur velut actione furti[1] et iniuriarum[2], et secundum quorundam opinionem actione vi bonorum raptorum[3]; nam ipsius rei et vindicatio et condictio nobis conpetit. (9.) Rem vero et poenam persequimur velut ex his causis ex quibus adversus infitiantem in duplum agimus: quod accidit per actionem iudicati[4], depensi[5], damni iniuriae legis Aquiliae[6], aut legatorum nomine quae per damnationem certa relicta sunt[7].

10. Quaedam praeterea sunt actiones quae ad legis actionem exprimuntur, quaedam sua vi ac potestate constant[8]. quod ut manifestum fiat, opus est ut prius de legis actionibus loquamur.

11. Actiones quas in usu veteres habuerunt legis actiones

6. Sometimes the object of our action is to recover only the thing itself, sometimes only a penalty, sometimes both the thing and a penalty. 7. We sue for the thing only, as in actions arising out of a contract. 8. We obtain a penalty only, as in the actions of theft[1] and of injury[2], and, according to the views of some lawyers, in the action of goods carried off by violence[3], for to recover the thing itself there is open to us either a vindication or a condiction. 9. We sue for the thing and a penalty in those cases, for example, where we bring our action for double the amount against an opponent who denies (the fact we state): instances of which are to be found in the actions of judgment debt[4], of money laid down by a *sponsor*[5], of wrongful damage under the Lex Aquilia[6], or on account of legacies which have been left specifically by the form called "damnation[7]."

10. Moreover, there are some actions which are founded upon a *legis actio*, whilst others stand by their own strength alone[8]. In order to make this clear we must give some preliminary account of the *legis actiones*.

11. The actions which our ancestors were accustomed to

[1] III. 189, &c.
[2] III. 224.
[3] III. 209.
[4] IV. 21, 25. See for an instance of this action Cic. *pro Flacc.* 21: "frater meus decrevit ut, si judicatum negaret, in duplum iret."
[5] III. 127.
[6] III. 216.
[7] II. 201—208, 282.
[8] IV. 33.

appellabantur[1], vel ideo quod legibus proditae erant, quippe tunc edicta Praetoris quibus conplures actiones introductae sunt nondum in usu habebantur; vel ideo quia ipsarum legum verbis accommodatae erant, et ideo immutabiles proinde atque leges observabantur. unde eum qui de vitibus succisis ita egisset ut in actione vites nominaret, responsum (est) rem perdidisse, quia debuisset arbores nominare, eo quod lex XII tabularum, ex qua de vitibus succisis actio conpeteret, generaliter de arboribus succisis loqueretur[2]. (12.) Lege autem age-
P.191 batur modis | quinque: sacramento, per iudicis postulationem, per condictionem, per manus iniectionem, per pignoris captionem.

13. Sacramenti actio generalis erat: de quibus enim rebus ut aliter ageretur lege cautum non erat, de his sacramento agebatur[3], eaque actio perinde periculosa erat falsi (nomine)[4], atque

use were called *legis actiones*[1], either from the fact of their being declared by *leges*, for in those times the Praetor's edicts, whereby very many actions have been introduced, were not in use; or from the fact that they were adapted to the words of the *leges* themselves, and so were adhered to as inflexibly as those *leges* were. Hence, when in an action for vines having been cut down, the plaintiff used the word *vites* in his plaint, it was held that he must lose the case; because he ought to have used the word *arbores*, inasmuch as the law of the Twelve Tables, on which lay the action for vines cut down, spoke generally of trees (*arbores*) cut down[2]. 12. The *legis actiones*, then, were used in five forms: viz. *sacramentum*, *judicis postulatio*, *condictio*, *manus injectio*, *pignoris captio*.

13. The *actio sacramenti* was a general one; for in all cases where there was no provision made in any *lex* for proceeding in another way, the form was by *sacramentum*[3]: and this action was then just as perilous in the case of fraud[4], as at

---

[1] See the derivation given by Pomponius to the same effect, D. 1. 2. 2. 6.

[2] See D. 43. 27. 2; where, however, the old law is only referred to, not quoted.

[3] According to Varro (*de Ling. Lat.* v. § 180, p. 70, Müller's edition) the name *sacramentum* was derived from the place of deposit, a temple (*in sacro*); for it would seem that in the most ancient times the deposit was actually staked in the hands of the magistrate, and that the practice of giving sureties instead was an innovation of a later age.

[4] The word *falsi* was clear to the earlier editors: but, probably through

hoc tempore periculosa est actio certae creditae pecuniae[1] propter sponsionem qua periclitatur reus si temere neget, (et) restipulationem qua periclitatur actor si non debitum petat: nam qui victus erat summam sacramenti praestabat poenae nomine; eaque in publicum cedebat praedesque eo nomine Praetori dabantur, non ut nunc sponsionis et restipulationis poena lucro cedit adversario qui vicerit. (14.) Poena autem sacramenti aut quingenaria erat aut quinquagenaria. nam de rebus mille aeris plurisve quingentis assibus, de minoris vero quinquaginta assibus sacramento contendebatur; nam ita lege XII tabularum cautum erat[2]. (sed) si de libertate hominis controversia erat, etsi pretiosissimus homo esset, tamen ut L assibus sacramento contenderetur eadem lege cautum est, favore scilicet libertatis[3]

the present day is the action "for a definite sum of money lent[1]," on account of the sponsion whereby the defendant is imperilled, if he oppose the plaintiff's claim without good reason, and on account of the restipulation whereby the plaintiff is imperilled, if he claim a sum not due; for he who lost the suit was liable by way of penalty to the amount of the *sacramentum*, which went to the treasury, and for the securing of this sureties were given to the Praetor: the penalty not going at that time, as does the sponsional and restipulatory penalty now, into the pocket of the successful party. 14. Now the penal sum of the *sacramentum* was either one of five hundred or one of fifty (*asses*). For when the suit was for things of the value of a thousand *asses* or more, the deposit would be five hundred, but when it was for less, it would be fifty: for thus it was enacted by a law of the Twelve Tables[2]. If, however, the suit related to the liberty of a man, although a man is valuable beyond all things, yet it was enacted by the same law that the suit should be carried on with a deposit of fifty *asses*, obviously with the view of favouring liberty[3] and in

the effects of the chemicals employed, is now illegible. *Nomine* has always been conjectural.

[1] An action, that is to say, under the Lex Silia. See note on IV. 1.

[2] Tab. II. l. 1.

[3] *Adsertores* = the friends who came forward on behalf of the man held in servitude, who of course, from the disability of his status, could do nothing for himself. Cf. Plaut. *Curc.* V. 2. 68. Terent. *Adelph.* II. 1. 40; Suet. *Caes.* 80.

P.192 (deest) ne onerarentur adsertores. | (15.) [*Nunc admonendi sumus*[1], istas omnes actiones *certis quibusdam et solemnibus verbis peragi debuisse. si verbi gratia in personam agebatur contra eum qui nexu se obligaverat*[2], *actor eum apud Praetorem ita interrogabat: Quando in iure te conspicio, postulo an fias auctor*[3], *qua de re nexum mecum fecisti? et altero negante, ille dicebat: Quando* negas, sac*ramento quingenario te provoco, si propter te fidemve tuam* captus *fraudatusve siem. deinde adversarius quoque dicebat: Qua*ndo ais neque *negas me nexum fecisse tecum qua de re agitur, similiter ego te sacramento quingenario provoco, si propter me fidemve meam captus fraudatusve non*

order to prevent the defenders of liberty being burdened unduly. 15.[1] We must now be reminded that all these actions were of necessity carried on in special and formal language. If, for instance, the action were one *in personam* against an individual who had bound himself by coin and balance[2], the plaintiff used to interrogate him in the Praetor's presence in this form: "As I see you in court, I demand whether you give formal consent[3] to (the settlement of) the matter in respect of which you have entered into a mancipatory obligation with me?" Then on this person's refusal the plaintiff went on thus: "Since you say no, I challenge you in a deposit of five hundred (*asses*), if I have been deceived and defrauded through you and through trust in you." Then the opposite party also had his say, thus: "Since you assert and do not deny that I have entered into a mancipatory obligation with you in relation to the subject-matter of this action, I too challenge you with a deposit of five hundred (*asses*), in case you have not been deceived or defrauded through me or

1 We have adopted in the opening of this paragraph, down to the words "ad iudicem accipiundum venirent," the conjectural reading of Heffter. The reading may be right or not, (its sense is undoubtedly accordant with what we know of the ancient law,) but at all events it renders the passage more complete.

2 Sc. entered into a contract by mancipation; see note on II. 27.

3 That this was the form of the ancient action against an *auctor* who was present in court is clear from Cicero *pro Caecina*, c. 19, *pro Muraena*, c. 12.

Auctor, in the language of the old lawyers, was the individual who was bound by any engagement, contracted according to the forms of the civil law, to perform some specific act or to give some specific thing and all its interest and profits. See note on Just. *Inst.* IV. 6. 2: Abdy and Walker.

sies. quibus ab utraque parte peractis litigatores poscebant iudicem, et Praetor ipsis diem praestituebat, quo] ad iudicem
P.193 accipiundum | venirent; postea vero reversis dabatur. ut autem (die) XXX iudex detur per legem Pinariam factum est[1]; ante eam autem legem *nond*um dabatur iudex[2]. illut ex superioribus intellegimus, si de re minoris quam (M) aeris agebatur, quinquagenario sacramento, non quingenario eos contendere solitos fuisse. postea tamen quam iudex datus esset, comperendinum diem, ut ad iudicem venirent, denuntiabant. deinde cum ad iudicem venerant, antequam aput eum causam perorarent, solebant breviter ei et quasi per indicem rem exponere: quae dicebatur causae collectio[3], quasi causae suae in breve coactio. (16.) Si in rem agebatur, mobilia quidem et moventia, quae modo in ius adferri adducive possent, in iure vindicabantur[4]

through trust in me." At the close of these proceedings on either side the parties demanded a *judex*, and the Praetor fixed a day for them to come and receive one; who accordingly was given to them on their return. But that the *judex* should be given them on the 30th day was an enactment of the Lex Pinaria[1]; for before the passing of that *lex* it was not the practice for a *judex* to be assigned[2]. From what has been stated above, we gather that when the dispute was in respect of a matter of smaller value than one thousand *asses* the parties were wont to join issue with a deposit of fifty and not of five hundred *asses*. Next, when their *judex* had been assigned to them, they used to give notice, each to the other, to come before him on the next day but one. Then, when they had made their appearance before the *judex*, their custom was, before they argued out their cause, to set forth the matter to him briefly and, as it were, in outline: and this was termed *causae collectio*[3], being, so to speak, a brief epitome of each party's case. 16. If the action were one *in rem*, the claim used to be made in court[4] for movable and moving things that could be brought or led

1 See App. (P).

2 This translation is in accordance with Heffter's emendation of *nondum;* Hollweg reads *statim;* Studemund is also in favour of *statim;* but in his apograph the final letters of the disputed word are IIM; which I think may be *um*, but can hardly be TIM.

3 See App. (Q).

4 In later times there was another form of proceeding, viz. *ex jure*,

ad hunc modum. qui vindicabat festucam tenebat; deinde ipsam rem adprehendebat, velut hominem, et ita dicebat: HUNC EGO HOMINEM EX IURE QUIRITIUM MEUM ESSE AIO SECUNDUM SUAM CAUSAM[1] SICUT DIXI; ECCE TIBI VINDICTAM INPOSUI: et simul homini festucam inponebat. adversarius eadem similiter dicebat et faciebat. cum uterque vindicasset, Praetor dicebat: MITTITE AMBO HOMINEM. illi mittebant. qui prior

into court as follows: the claimant, having a wand in his hand, laid hold of the thing claimed, say for instance, a slave, and uttered these words: "I assert that this slave is mine by Quiritary title, in accordance with his *status*[1], as I have declared it. Look you, I lay my wand upon him:" and at the same moment he laid his wand on the slave. Then his opponent spoke and acted in precisely the same way; and each having made his claim the Praetor said: "Let go the slave, both of you." On which they let him go, and he who

which is the one specially ridiculed by Cicero in *pro Mur.* 12. The process (technically called *manus consertio*) is fully described in both its forms by Aulus Gellius, XX. 10, the sum of whose observations may be thus given: "By the phrase *manum conserere* is meant the claiming of a matter in dispute by both litigants in a set form of words and with the thing itself before them. This presence of the thing was absolutely necessary according to a Law of the Twelve Tables commencing: *Si qui in jure manum conserunt* (Tab. IV. l. 5), and the proceedings (*vindicia, manus correptio*) must take place before the Praetor." Hence we see that in olden times the Praetor must have gone with the parties to the land, when land was the subject of dispute, although movables may possibly, and probably, have been brought by them to him. Gellius proceeds: "But when from the extension of the Roman territory and the increase of their other business, the Praetors found it inconvenient to go with the parties to distant places to take part in these proceedings, a practice arose (although contrary to the directions of the Twelve Tables), that the *manus consertio* should no longer be done before the Praetor (*in jure*), but that the parties should challenge one another to its performance without his presence (*ex jure*). They then went to the land together and bringing back a clod therefrom made their claim over that clod alone in the Praetor's presence, in the name of the entire field." This method is referred to by Festus (sub verb. *vindiciae*), "Vindiciae olim dicebantur illae (glebae) quae ex fundo sumtae in jus allatae erant." In Cicero's time the proceedings seem to have been still more fictitious: the litigants went out of court, nominally *ut consererent manus*, but returned after a few minutes' absence, feigning that the *consertio* had in the meantime taken place, and then the rest of the process followed as set down by Gaius in the text.

[1] For this meaning of *causa*, see I. 138, II. 137.

vindica(*verat, ita alterum interroga*)bat: POSTULO ANNE DICAS QUA EX CAUSA VINDICAVERIS. ille respondebat: IUS FECI SICUT VINDICTAM INPOSUI. deinde qui prior vindicaverat dice-
P.194 bat: QUANDO TU INIURIA VINDICAVISTI, | D AERIS SACRAMENTO TE PROVOCO. adversarius quoque dicebat: SIMILITER EGO TE. sive[1] L asses sacramenti nominabant. deinde eadem sequebantur quae cum in personam ageretur[2]. postea Praetor secundum alterum eorum vindicias dicebat, id est interim aliquem possessorem constituebat, eumque iubebat praedes adversario dare litis et vindiciarum[3], id est rei et fructuum: alios autem praedes[4] ipse Praetor ab utroque accipiebat sacramenti[5], quod id in publi-

was the first claimant thus interrogated the other: "I ask you whether you will state the grounds of your claim." To that his opponent replied; "I did right in touching him with my wand." Then the first claimant said: "Inasmuch as you have made a claim without right to support it, I challenge you in a deposit of five hundred *asses*." "And I too challenge you," said his opponent. Or[1] the amount of the deposit they named might be fifty *asses*. Then followed the rest of the proceedings exactly as in an action *in personam*[2]. Next the Praetor used to assign the *vindiciae* to one or other of the parties, that is, give interim possession of the thing sued for to one of them, ordering him at the same time to provide his adversary with sureties *litis et vindiciarum*[3], i.e. of the thing in dispute and its profits. The Praetor also took other sureties[4] for the deposit[5] from both parties, because that deposit

1 The MS. has *scil.* = *scilicet*. This may be a correction made by the copyist: for if the price of the slave was under 1000 *asses*, the wager would be L, not D. See IV. 14.

2 IV. 15.

3 Festus says: "*Vindiciae* was the term applied to those things which were the subjects of a lawsuit; although the suit, to speak more correctly, was about the right which the *vindiciae* (the clod, tile, &c.) symbolically represented." Festus, sub verb. *vindiciae*.

4 *Praes* is a person who binds himself to the state (becomes bail, for instance, for the payment of the *sacramentum*), and is so called because when interrogated by the magistrate if he be *praes*, *i.e.* ready and willing to be surety, he replies *praes* or *praesum*, I am ready. Festus, *sub verb.*

5 We keep to the translation "deposit" because that term is a convenient one; but it is to be remembered that it was only in very early times that a deposit really took place, and that at the time of which Gaius is treating, sureties were given, and nothing actually deposited.

cum cedebat[1]. festuca autem utebantur quasi hastae loco, signo quodam iusti dominii: *quod maxime* sua esse credebant quae ex hostibus cepissent; unde in centumviralibus iudiciis hasta praeponitur[2]. (17.) Si qua res talis erat ut sine incommodo non posset in ius adferri vel adduci, velut si columna aut grex alicuius pecoris esset, pars aliqua inde sumebatur; deinde in eam partem quasi in totam rem praesentem fiebat vindicatio. itaque ex grege vel una ovis aut capra in ius adducebatur, vel etiam pilus inde sumebatur et in ius adferebatur; ex nave vero et columna aliqua pars defringebatur. similiter si de fundo vel de aedibus sive de hereditate controversia erat, pars aliqua inde sumebatur et in ius adferebatur et in eam partem perinde atque in totam rem praesentem fiebat vindicatio: velut ex fundo gleba sumebatur et ex aedibus tegula, et si de here-
P.195 ditate controversia erat, aeque| [*folium deperditum*, 48 lin.[3]].

went to the treasury[1]. The litigants made use of a wand instead of the spear, which was the symbol of legal ownership; for men considered those things above all others to be their own which they took from the enemy: and this is the reason why the spear is set up in front of the Centumviral Courts[2]. 17. When the thing in dispute was of such a nature that it could not be brought or led into court without inconvenience, for instance, if it were a column, or a flock or herd of some kind of cattle, some portion was taken therefrom, and the claim was made upon that portion, as though upon the whole thing actually present in court. Thus, one sheep or one goat out of a flock was led into court, or even a lock of wool from the same was brought thither: whilst from a ship or a column some portion was broken off. So, too, if the dispute were about a field, or a house, or an inheritance, some part was taken therefrom and brought into court, and the claim was made upon that part, as though it were upon the whole thing there present; thus for instance, a clod was taken from the field, or a tile from the house, and if the dispute were about an inheritance, in like manner[3]......For they followed the same

1 IV. 13.

2 IV. 31. See App. (P).

3 An entire leaf of the MS. is missing here. Göschen is of opinion that the matter thus lost comprised, 1st, the remaining portion of the *actio sacramenti*; 2nd, an exposition of the action *per judicis postulationem*;

— — *observabant* enim *eundem vel paene ae*qualem *modum* capiendi iudicis, *condicen*dique *diem quo* ad iudicem capiendum praesto esse de*berent.* condicere autem denuntiare est prisca lingua[1].

18. Itaque haec quidem actio proprie condictio vocabatur: nam actor adversario denuntiabat, ut ad iudicem capiendum die xxx adesset. nunc vero non proprie condictionem dicimus actionem in personam (*esse, qua*) intendimus id nobis (dari) oportere: nulla enim hoc tempore eo nomine denuntiatio fit. (19.) Haec autem legis actio constituta est per legem Siliam et Calpurniam: lege quidem Silia certae pecuniae, lege vero Calpurnia de omni certa re. (20.) Quare autem haec actio desiderata sit, cum de eo quod nobis dari oporteat potuerimus sacramento aut per iudicis postulationem agere, valde quaeritur[2].

method, or one almost identical, in "taking a *judex*" and giving notice of a day on which they ought to be present to receive their *judex*. Now *condicere* means in ancient speech the same as *denuntiare*[1]. 18. Therefore this action was with propriety called a "condiction," for the plaintiff used to give notice to his opponent to be in court on the thirtieth day for the purpose of taking a *judex*. At the present time, however, we apply the name, *condictio*, improperly to an action *in personam*, in the "intention" of which we declare that our opponent ought to give something to us, for now-a days no notice is given in such a case. 19. This *legis actio* was established by the Leges Silia and Calpurnia; being by the Lex Silia applicable to the recovery of an ascertained sum of money, and by the Lex Calpurnia to that of any ascertained thing. 20. But why this action was needed it is very difficult to say, seeing that we could sue by the *sacramentum* or the action *per judicis postulationem* for that which ought to be given to us[2].

---

and 3rd, the commencement of that which is carried on in the three following paragraphs, viz. the form of an action *per condictionem*.

1 "Condicere est denuntiare priscâ linguâ." Just. *Inst.* IV. 6. 15. So also Festus: "Condicere est dicendo denuntiare. Condictio, in diem certam ejus rei quae agitur denuntiatio."

2 See App. (R).

21. Per manus iniectionem aeque (de) his rebus agebatur de quibus ut ita ageretur lege aliqua[1] cautum est, velut iudicati lege XII tabularum[2]; quae actio talis erat. qui agebat sic dicebat: QUOD TU MIHI IUDICATUS sive DAMNATUS ES SESTERTIUM X MILIA QUANDOC NON SOLVISTI, OB EAM REM EGO TIBI SESTERTIUM X MILIUM IUDICATI MANUS INICIO; et simul aliquam partem corporis eius prendebat. nec licebat iudicato manum sibi depellere et pro se lege agere; set vindicem dabat[3] qui pro se causam agere solebat: qui vindicem non dabat domum ducebatur ab actore et vinciebatur. (22.) Postea
P.196 quaedam leges ex aliis quibusdam causis | pro iudicato manus

21. Similarly an action in the form of an arrest (*manus injectio*) lay for those cases where it was specified in any[1] *lex* that this should be the remedy; as in the case of an action upon a judgment which was given by a law of the Twelve Tables[2]. That action was of the following nature: he who brought it uttered these words: "Inasmuch as you have been adjudicated or condemned to pay me ten thousand sesterces and whereas you have not paid it, I therefore lay my hands upon you for ten thousand sesterces, a debt due on judgment:" and at the same moment he laid hold of some part of his body; nor was he against whom the judgment had been given allowed to remove the arrest and conduct his action for himself, but he named a protector (*vindex*)[3], who managed the case for him: a defendant who did not name a protector was taken off by the plaintiff to his house and put in chains there. 22. Afterwards certain *leges* allowed the action *per manus injectionem* against some specified persons under

---

1 We have here followed Göschen's reading: "lege aliqua cautum est," instead of Heffter's: "lege Aquiliâ cautum est:" 1stly, because, as the former says, it would otherwise be difficult to understand why the word *aeque* is introduced here, 2ndly, because of the next paragraph, "velut lege XII tabularum," 3rdly, because the reading accords with that in § 28 of this book. The MS. has *Aquilia*.

2 Tab. III. l. 3.

3 See IV. 46. Boethius, ad Cic. *Top.* I. 2, § 10, says: "Vindex est qui alterius causam suscipit vindicandam." There is a curious law of the Twelve Tables on this subject, "Assiduo vindex assiduus esto; proletario quoi quis volet vindex esto," Tab. I. l. 4; in which passage *assiduus* is to be interpreted *pecuniosus*. Festus thus defines *vindex:* "Vindex ab eo quod vindicat, quominus is qui prensus est ab aliquo teneatur."

iniectionem in quosdam dederunt: sicut lex Publilia in eum pro quo sponsor[1] dependisset, si in sex mensibus proximis quam pro eo depensum esset non solvisset sponsori pecuniam; item lex Furia de sponsu[2] adversus eum qui a sponsore plus quam virilem partem exegisset; et denique conplures aliae leges in multis causis talem actionem dederunt. (23.) Set aliae leges ex quibusdam causis constituerunt quasdam actiones per manus iniectionem, sed puram, id est non pro iudicato: velut lex (Furia) testamentaria adversus eum qui legatorum nomine mortisve causa plus M assibus cepisset[3], cum ea lege non esset exceptus[4], ut ei plus capere liceret; item lex Marcia[5] adversus foeneratores, ut si usuras exegissent, de his reddendis per manus iniectionem cum eis ageretur. (24.) Ex quibus legibus, et si quae aliae similes essent, cum agebatur, manum sibi depellere et pro se lege agere (licebat). nam et actor in ipsa legis actione

other particular circumstances "as though upon a judgment:" for instance, the Lex Publilia did so against him for whom a *sponsor*[1] had paid money, if he had not repaid it to the *sponsor* within the six months next after it had been paid for him: so, too, did the Lex Furia de Sponsu[2] against him who had exacted from a *sponsor* more than his proportion of a debt: and in fact many other *leges* allowed an action of the kind in various cases. 23. Other *leges* again allowed in certain cases actions *per manus injectionem*, but (made them) substantive, *i.e.* not "as though upon a judgment:" for example, the Lex Furia Testamentaria allowed such an action against a man who had taken more than a thousand *asses* by way of legacy or donation in prospect of death[3], in spite of his not being exempted[4] by the *lex* so as to have the right of taking such larger sum: and the Lex Marcia[5] allowed such an action against usurers, so that if they exacted usurious interest, proceedings for restitution of the same could be taken against them by the form *per manus injectionem*. 24. When therefore an action was brought upon these *leges* and others like them, the defendant was at liberty to remove the arrest and conduct his action for himself, for the

[1] III. 127.

[2] For an account of this law, see III. 121, 122.

[3] See Just. *Inst.* II. 7. 1.

[4] II. 225. Ulp. I. 2.

[5] See Livy VII. 21. B.C. 352.

non adiciebat hoc verbum PRO IUDICATO, sed nominata causa ex qua agebat, ita dicebat: OB EAM REM EGO TIBI MANUM INICIO; cum hi quibus pro iudicato actio data erat, nominata causa ex qua agebant, ita inferebant: OB EAM REM EGO TIBI PRO IUDICATO MANUM INICIO. nec me praeterit in forma legis Furiae testamentariae PRO IUDICATO verbum inseri, cum in ipsa
P.197 lege non sit: quod videtur | nulla ratione factum. (25.) Sed postea lege Vallia, excepto iudicato et eo pro quo depensum est, ceteris omnibus cum quibus per manus iniectionem agebatur permissum est sibi manum depellere et pro se agere. itaque iudicatus et is pro quo depensum est etiam post hanc legem vindicem dare debebant, et nisi darent, domum ducebantur. istaque quamdiu legis actiones in usu erant semper ita observabatur; unde nostris temporibus is cum quo iudicati depensive agitur[1] iudicatum solui satisdare[2] cogitur[3].

plaintiff did not in the very *legis actio* add the phrase *pro judicato* ("as though upon a judgment"), but specifying the reason why he sued, went on thus: "on that account I lay my hand on you:" whereas they to whom the action was given "as though upon a judgment," after specifying the reason why they were suing, proceeded thus; "on that account I arrest you as though upon a judgment." I have not, however, forgotten that in the form of proceeding under the Lex Furia Testamentaria the phrase, *pro judicato*, is inserted, though it does not appear in the *lex* itself; but that insertion seems made without reason. 25. Afterwards, however, permission was given by the Lex Vallia to all other persons, save him against whom a judgment had passed and him for whom money had been paid by a *sponsor*, when sued in the form *per manus injectionem*, to remove the arrest and conduct their action for themselves. A judgment-debtor, therefore, and one for whom money had been paid were compelled even after the passing of this *lex* to nominate a protector, and unless they did so they were carried off to the plaintiff's house. And these rules were always adhered to so long as *legis actiones* were in use: whence even in our times he who is defendant in an action either on a judgment or for money paid by a *sponsor*[1] is compelled to give sureties[2] for the payment of that which shall be adjudicated[3].

[1] III. 127. [2] IV. 102. [3] Those who desire further inform-

26. Per pignoris capionem lege agebatur de quibusdam rebus moribus, (de quibusdam) lege. (27.) Introducta est moribus rei militaris: nam propter stipendium licebat militi ab eo qui distribuebat, nisi daret, pignus capere: dicebatur autem ea pecunia quae stipendii nomine dabatur aes militare. item propter eam pecuniam licebat pignus capere ex qua equus emendus erat: quae pecunia dicebatur aes equestre[1]. item propter eam pecuniam ex qua hordeum equis erat conparandum; quae pecunia dicebatur aes hordiarium. (28.) Lege autem introducta est pignoris capio velut lege XII tabularum[2] adversus eum qui hostiam emisset, nec pretium redderet: item adversus eum qui

26. The *legis actio per pignoris capionem* was for some matters a remedy originating from old custom, for others one derived from a *lex*. 27. That *capio* which dealt with military proceeds was the creation of custom. For a soldier was allowed to take a pledge from the paymaster for the due discharge of his pay: and the money which was given as pay was called "military proceeds" (*aes militare*). So, too, the cavalry soldier was allowed to take a pledge for the payment of the money necessary for the purchase of his charger, and this money was called *aes equestre*[1]. So also could these soldiers take a pledge for the money necessary for the purchase of provender for their chargers, and this was called *aes hordearium*. 28. *Pignoris capio* was also (sometimes) introduced by *lex*, as, for instance, by a law of the Twelve Tables[2] against a man who purchased a victim for sacrifice and did not pay the price:

ation on the subject of *manus injectio* are referred to Heffter's *Observations on Gai. IV.* pp. 15—17. It will be seen from a perusal thereof that Gaius' enumeration of the cases wherein such action is allowed is not exhaustive.

The oft-quoted laws, 1 and 2 of Tab. I. of the Twelve, are not referred to here, because they seem to treat of a somewhat different matter, viz. arrest of a defendant who refused to appear in court at all, whereas the present subject of our author is the arrest of one who had appeared in the original action, had lost it, and had then evaded payment of the judgment laid on him. For the same reason Hor. *Sat.* I. 9. 74 and the well-known passages from Plautus (*Curcul.* and *Pers.*) are not brought forward.

[1] The money for purchasing the horses of the *equites* was provided by the state (Livy, I. 43), that for the feeding of them by widows; the pledge therefore would be taken in the former case, as for *aes militare*, from the *tribunus aerarius*, in the latter from the widow. See Aul. Gell. VII. 10.

[2] Tab. XII. l. 1.

mercedem non redderet pro eo iumento quod quis ideo locasset, ut inde pecuniam acceptam in dapem, id est in sacrificium P.198 inpenderet[1]. | item lege censoria[2] data est pignoris captio publicanis vectigalium publicorum populi Romani adversus eos qui aliqua lege vectigalia deberent. (29.) Ex omnibus autem istis causis certis verbis pignus capiebatur; et ob id plerisque placebat hanc quoque actionem legis actionem esse. quibusdam autem (non) placebat: primum quod pignoris captio extra ius peragebatur, id est non aput Praetorem, plerumque etiam absente adversario; cum alioquin ceteris actionibus non aliter uti possent quam aput Praetorem praesente adversario: praeterea quod nefasto quoque die[3], id est quo non licebat lege agere, pignus capi poterat.

30. Set istae omnes legis actiones paulatim in odium venerunt. namque ex nimia subtilitate veterum qui tunc iura condi-

as also against him who did not pay the hire of a beast of burden which some one had let out to him for the express purpose of expending the receipts therefrom on a *daps*, *i.e.* on a sacrificial feast[1]. So also a *pignoris capio* was given by a *lex censoria*[2] to the farmers of the public revenues of the Roman people against those who owed taxes under any *lex*. 29. In all these cases the pledge was taken with a set form of words; and hence it was generally held that this action too was a *legis actio*: but some authorities have dissented from that view; firstly, because the *pignoris capio* was a process transacted out of court, *i.e.* not before the Praetor, and generally too in the absence of the opposite party; whereas the plaintiff could not put other (*legis*) *actiones* in force except before the Praetor and in the presence of his opponent; and further because a pledge might be taken even on a *dies nefastus*[3], that is to say, on a day when it is not allowed to transact court-business.

30. All these *legis actiones*, however, by degrees fell into discredit, for through the excessive refinements of those who

---

1 *Daps* was the archaic word for the sacred ceremonies at the winter and spring sowing. See Festus, *sub verb.*

2 The *leges censoriae* referred chiefly to the letting out of the revenues, public lands and public works. For the concern of the censors in such matters see D. 50. 16. 203, Varro, *de R. R.* II. 1.

3 See note on II. 279.

derunt[1] eo res perducta est, ut vel qui minimum errasset litem perderet[2]. itaque per legem Aebutiam et duas Iulias[3] sublatae sunt istae legis actiones effectumque est ut per concepta verba[4], id est per formulas litigaremus. (31.) Tantum ex duabus causis permissum est lege agere: damni infecti, et si centumvirale iudicium futurum sit[5]. sane quidem cum ad centumviros itur, ante lege agitur sacramento aput Praetorem urbanum vel peregrinum[6] Praetorem. damni vero infecti nemo vult lege agere, set potius stipulatione quae in edicto[7] proposita est obligat adversarium suum: itaque et commodius ius et plenius est
P.200 (quam) per pignoris | (capionem) [*desunt* 24 *lin.*] apparet[8].
(32.) Contra in ea forma quae publicano proponitur talis fictio

at that time determined[1] the law, matters reached such a pitch that a litigant who had made the very slightest error lost his cause[2]. Therefore these *legis actiones* were got rid of by the Lex Aebutia and the two Leges Juliae[3], and the result has been that our litigious process is now carried on by directions[4] framed upon the case, *i.e.* by *formulae*. 31. In two cases only were the litigants allowed to resort to a *legis actio*, viz. in the case of anticipated damage, and in that of an action appertaining to the centumviral jurisdiction[5]. In fact, when the parties resort to the *centumviri*, there are preliminary proceedings in the form of the *actio sacramenti* before the Praetor Urbanus or Praetor Peregrinus[6]. In the case of anticipated damage, however, no one cares now to proceed by way of *legis actio*, but rather binds his opponent by the stipulation set forth in the edict (of the Praetor)[7], for this process is at once more convenient and more complete...[8]. 32. On the other hand, in the

1 *Condere* is used in this sense of determining or expounding in I. 7.

2 See an example in IV. 11.

3 See App. (P).

4 Sc. directions given to the *judex* by the Praetor.

5 See App. (P).

6 IV. 95.

7 The proceedings alluded to were as follows: he who anticipated damage from the ruinous condition of his neighbour's buildings or other nuisance, called on him to promise reparation in case injury ensued (the stipulation referred to in the text); and if this were refused, he obtained from the Praetor the *missio ex primo decreto*, whereby he was put into possession of the buildings, &c. to hold them in pledge. After a reasonable interval, the stipulation being still refused, he obtained a *missio ex secundo decreto*, and so became owner *ex jure Quiritium*, if the offender had the complete *dominium*, or obtained a juridical possession enabling usucapion, if the offender had Bonitarian ownership only. See Mackeldey, § 484, D. 39. 2.

8 Heffter has endeavoured to fill

est, ut quanta pecunia olim si pignus captum esset, id pignus is a quo captum erat luere deberet, tantam pecuniam condemnetur. (33.) Nulla autem formula ad condictionis fictionem exprimitur. sive enim pecuniam sive rem aliquam certam debitam nobis petamus, eam ipsam dari nobis oportere intendimus; nec ullam adiungimus condictionis fictionem. itaque simul intellegimus eas formulas quibus pecuniam aut rem aliquam nobis DARE OPORTERE intendimus, sua vi ac potestate valere. eiusdem naturae sunt actiones commodati[1], fiduciae[2], negotiorum gestorum et aliae innumerabiles[3].

formula which is set forth for the benefit of a revenue-collector, there is a fiction to the effect that the defendant shall be condemned in the amount at which in olden times, when a pledge was taken, he from whom that pledge had been taken would have had to ransom it. 33. But no formula is framed on the fiction of a condiction, for whether we be suing for money or some ascertained thing due to us, we state in the *intentio* that such thing itself "ought to be given to us," without adding any fictitious condiction. Hence we understand at once that those formulae in the *intentio* of which we declare that money or some thing "ought to be given to us" avail of their own special force and power. The same characteristic belongs to the actions of loan[1], of fiduciary pact[2], of gratuitous services, and to other actions innumerable[3].

up the break of 24 lines occurring at this point: his suggested reading may be translated to this effect: "At the present day there is no proper *legis actio* in the form *per pignoris capionem*, but only a fictitious process employed in certain actions; a result brought about by the *Lex Julia Judiciaria*. Of these fictions there are many, attaching to statutable and civil actions. For there are actions so based on a fictitious *legis actio*, that we insert in the *condemnatio* the amount or act which our opponent would have had to give or perform, if the *legis actio* provided for the purpose had been carried out in regular form. Hence we do not sue directly and upon the actual obligation, but indirectly upon the tie springing from the (supposed) *legis actio*. It is to be remembered, however, that we cannot now-a-days thus sue upon a fiction of *legis actio* in all cases where the old legal system allowed process by real *legis actio*, but only when the *legis actio* is of the form *per pignoris capionem*... This appears from the formulae themselves, which the Praetor has set forth in his edict, for instance," &c. &c. (as in the text).

[1] II. 59.

[2] See D. 44. 7. 5. *pr.*

[3] The topic of fictions is of importance as an introduction to the

34. Habemus adhuc alterius generis fictiones in quibusdam formulis: velut cum is qui ex edicto bonorum possessionem petit ficto se herede agit[1]. cum enim praetorio iure et non legitimo succedat in locum defuncti, non habet directas actiones[2], et neque id quod defuncti fuit potest intendere suum esse, *neque id quod ei* debebatur potest intendere (dari) sibi oportere; itaque ficto se herede intendit veluti hoc modo: IUDEX ESTO. SI AULUS AGERIUS, id est ipse actor,

34. We have besides fictions of another kind in some formulae: for instance when a person who sues for "*bonorum possessio* in accordance with the edict," brings an action upon the fiction that he is heir[1]. For since he succeeds to the position of the deceased by praetorian and not by statutable right, he has no direct actions[2], and cannot set out in his *intentio* either that what belonged to the deceased is "his own," or that that which was owed to the deceased ought to be given to himself: therefore feigning himself heir, he states his *intentio* somewhat in this fashion: "Let so and so be *judex*. If Aulus Agerius (that is the plaintiff himself) had been a heir

learning relating to the formulary system. Hence it is that Gaius has thought it necessary to give an elaborate account of the old *legis actiones*, which were, as we see, almost entirely obsolete in his day, and to explain the connexion between one of the *leges actiones* and fictions on the one hand, and the influence of fictions in pleading upon the formulary system on the other. The whole subject of fictions has been analyzed very minutely and explained most thoroughly by Savigny in his *Syst. des Röm. Rechts* (see the French translation by Guenoux, *Traité du droit Romain*, v. § ccxv. pp. 76—84). Zimmern too has given a short chapter on the same subject as introductory to the formulary system (see Zimmern translated by L. Etienne, *Traité des Actions:* 2me partie, section ii. Art. premier, § l. p. 140). The whole of Savigny's short chapter should be studied as explanatory of the sections of Gaius numbered from 34 to 60, and also as explanatory of the vast extension of pleading by the introduction of what were called *utiles actiones*, through the advantages which the use of fictions offered. One part however deserves special notice here, viz. where he points out the difference between *actiones fictitiae* and *actiones utiles*. "*Utilis actio* and *actio fictitia*," says he, "were originally exactly equivalent;" Gaius using the term *utilis*, and Ulpian the term *fictitia*. But there was this difference between them, that whereas *fictitia* expresses the form of procedure actually adopted, *utilis* expresses the very essence of the thing itself, that is to say, the extension of an institution owing to the practitioner's wants. In § 35 we have two actions *in pari materia*, one of which was *utilis* and *fictitia*, the other *utilis* but not *fictitia*.

[1] III. 32 et seqq.

[2] That is, no action is specially provided for his claim by the civil law.

LUCIO TITIO HERES ESSET[1], *TUM SI* FUNDUM DE QUO AGITUR EX IURE QUIRITIUM *EIUS ESSE OPOR*TET. si T*iti*o debeatur pecunia[2], praeposita simili*ter fictione* illa ita subicitur: TUM SI PARET NUMERIUM NEGIDIUM AULO AGERIO SESTERTIUM X MILIA DARE OPORTERE[3]. (35.) Similiter et bonorum emptor[4] ficto se herede agit. sed interdum et alio modo agere solet. |
P.201 nam ex persona eius cuius bona emerit sumpta intentione, convertit condemnationem in suam personam, id est ut quod illius esset vel illi dare oporteret, eo nomine adversarius huic condemnetur: quae species actionis appellatur Rutiliana,

of Lucius Titius[1], then if that estate about which the action is brought ought to be his by Quiritary right," &c.; or if money be due to Titius[2], a similar fiction is prefixed, and the formula runs on: "Then should it appear that Numerius Negidius ought[3] to give to Aulus Agerius 10,000 sesterces." 35. So too the purchaser of an insolvent's estate[4] sues under the fiction of being heir. Sometimes, however, he sues in another way. For commencing with an *intentio* running in the name of him whose property he has bought, he changes the *condemnatio* so as to make it run in his own name; that is (he claims) that his opponent ought to be condemned to make payment to him (the plaintiff) on account of what belonged to the other (whose estate he has bought) or on account of what he was bound to give to that other. This form of action is called *Rutilian,* because

1 The subjunctive, *esset,* in the *intentio* marks a fiction which is not to be controverted: the matter asserted by the plaintiff and denied by the defendant is in the indicative, *si paret, si oportet.*

2 The MS. at this point is very difficult to decipher: but it looks like SI TDO DEVEAT' PCUN. The P in the last word is imperfect, but there is evidently the long downstroke peculiar to P; the N also is more like I than N.

3 "The word *oportere,*" says Paulus, "does not apply to the extent of the Judex's powers, for he can give larger or smaller damages, but refers to the present value (of the subject-matter of the agreement or claim)," D. 50. 16. 37. Thus, suppose in a stipulatory contract between S. and T. the clause *Quidquid te dare facere oportet* were inserted; then in case of any dispute between the parties, the claim would be restricted to the actual sum that was due, or that the thing was worth at the time when the contract was made. See D. 45. 1. 65. 1 and 45. 1. 125.

"Hence," says Savigny (*Traité du droit Rom.* translated by Guenoux, v. p. 88), "the expression *oportere* in the *intentio* must always be understood to apply to the actual existence of a debt arising out of some strictly legal engagement or transaction, and not to a debt that may result from a judicial decision."

4 III. 77—81.

quia a Praetore Publio Rutilio, qui et bonorum venditionem[1] introduxisse dicitur, conparata est. superior autem species actionis qua ficto se herede bonorum emptor agit Serviana vocatur. (36.) (*Eiusdem generis est quae Publiciana vocatur*[2].) datur autem haec actio ei qui ex iusta causa traditam sibi rem nondum usucepit[3] eamque amissa possessione petit. nam quia non potest eam ex iure Quiritium suam esse intendere, fingitur rem usucepisse, et ita, quasi ex iure Quiritium dominus factus esset, intendit hoc modo: IUDEX ESTO. SI QUEM HOMINEM AULUS AGERIUS EMIT, IS EI TRADITUS EST, ANNO POSSEDISSET[4], TUM SI EUM HOMINEM DE QUO AGITUR EIUS EX IURE QUIRITIUM ESSE OPORTET et reliqua. (37.) Item civitas Romana peregrino fingitur[5]; si eo nomine agat aut cum eo agatur, quo nomine nostris legibus actio constituta est, si modo iustum sit

it was framed by the Praetor Publius Rutilius, who is also said to have been the inventor of the proceeding called *bonorum venditio*[1]. The form of action first named, in which the purchaser of the insolvent's estate sues under the fiction of being the heir, is called *Servian*. 36. Of the same kind is that action known as *Publician*[2]. This is granted to him who has not yet completed his usucapion[3] of something delivered to him on lawful grounds, and who having lost the possession seeks to recover the thing. For inasmuch as he cannot declare that the thing is his in Quiritary right, he is by fiction assumed to have completed his usucapion, and then, as though he had become owner by Quiritary title, he frames his *intentio* in this manner: "Let so-and-so be *judex*. Supposing Aulus Agerius to have possessed[4] for a year the slave whom he bought and who was delivered to him, then if it should appear that that slave, about whom this action is brought, ought to be his by Quiritary title," &c. 37. Again, Roman citizenship is by a fiction ascribed to a foreigner[5], if he sue or be sued in some case for which an action is granted by our laws, provided only it be just that such

[1] III. 77.

[2] The author of this law is generally supposed to be the Praetor Publicius mentioned by Cicero in *pro Cluent.* c. 45. The words of the law are quoted in D. 6. 2. 1. *pr.*

[3] II. 41.

[4] The fiction again is marked by the use of the subjunctive: the sale and delivery may be disputed, but not the possession.

[5] There is an example of this fiction in Cic. *in Verr.* II. 2. 12, "Judicia hujusmodi: qui cives Romani erant, si Siculi essent, quum Siculos eorum legibus dari oporteret. Qui Siculi, si cives Romani essent," &c.

eam actionem etiam ad peregrinum extendi, velut si furti agat peregrinus aut cum eo agatur; (*nam si cum eo agatur*) in formula ita concipitur: IUDEX ESTO. SI PARET (OPE) CONSILIOVE DIONIS HERMAEI FILII FURTUM FACTUM ESSE PATERAE AUREAE, QUAM OB REM EUM, SI CIVIS ROMANUS ESSET, PRO FURE DAMNUM DECIDERE OPORTERET[1] et reliqua. item si peregrinus furti agat, civitas ei Romana fingitur. similiter si ex lege
P.202 Aquilia peregrinus damni | iniuriae agat aut cum eo agatur, ficta civitate Romana iudicium datur. (38.) Praeterea aliquando fingimus adversarium nostrum capite diminutum non esse[2]. nam si ex contractu nobis obligatus obligatave sit et capite deminutus deminutave fuerit, velut mulier per coemptionem[3], masculus per adrogationem[4], desinit iure civili debere nobis[5], nec directo intendi potest dare eum eamve oportere; sed ne in

action should be extended to a foreigner; for instance, if a foreigner sues for a theft or an action be brought against him; for if an action be brought against him, the formula is framed thus: "Let so-and-so be *judex*. Should it appear that a theft of a golden goblet has been committed with the aid and counsel of Dio, the son of Hermaeus, for which matter, were he a Roman citizen, he would have to make satisfaction for the loss as a thief[1]," &c. Again, if a foreigner bring an action for theft, Roman citizenship is by fiction ascribed to him. Similarly, if a foreigner sue under the Lex Aquilia for damage done contrary to law, or if he be sued on such account, an action is granted on the fiction of his having Roman citizenship.

38. Besides we sometimes feign that our adversary has not suffered a *capitis diminutio*[2]. For if any one, man or woman, be bound to us on a contract, and undergo *capitis diminutio*, a woman, for instance, by coemption[3] or a man by arrogation[4], such person is no longer bound to us by the civil law[5], nor can we declare directly in our *intentio* that he or she

1 He was not the actual thief, but only an accomplice; but he was liable to an action just as though he were the actual thief. Hence *pro* is here used in precisely the same signification as in the phrase *pro judicato;* IV. 22, 24, &c. The phrase "damnum decidere" is appropriate to the *condemnatio* of an action on delict.

2 I. 159.

3 I. 113.

4 I. 99.

5 III. 84.

potestate eius sit ius nostrum corrumpere, introducta est contra eum eamve actio utilis[1], rescissa capitis deminutione, id est in qua fingitur capite deminutus deminutave non esse.

39. Partes autem formularum hae sunt: demonstratio, intentio, adiudicatio, condemnatio. (40.) Demonstratio est ea pars formulae quae praecipue ideo inseritur, ut demonstretur res de qua agitur, velut haec pars formulae: QUOD AULUS AGERIUS NUMERIO NEGIDIO HOMINEM VENDIDIT. item haec: QUOD AULUS AGERIUS APUT NUMERIUM NEGIDIUM HOMINEM DEPOSUIT. (41.) Intentio est ea pars formulae qua actor desiderium suum concludit, velut haec pars formulae: SI PARET NUMERIUM NEGIDIUM AULO AGERIO SESTERTIUM X MILIA DARE OPORTERE. item haec: QUIDQUID PARET NUMERIUM NEGIDIUM AULO AGERIO DARE FACERE (OPORTERE). item haec: SI PARET HOMINEM EX IURE QUIRITIUM AULI AGERII ESSE[2]. (42.) Adiudicatio

"ought to give:" but to prevent either of them having the power of destroying our right, an *utilis actio*[1] has been invented against them, in which their *capitis diminutio* is set aside, in which, that is to say, there is a fiction that they have not suffered any *capitis diminutio*.

39. Now the parts of a formula are these, the *demonstratio*, the *intentio*, the *adjudicatio*, and the *condemnatio*. 40. The *demonstratio* is that part of a formula which is inserted at the outset for the purpose of having the matter described about which the action is brought; this part of a formula, for example: "Inasmuch as Aulus Agerius sold a slave to Numerius Negidius:" or this: "inasmuch as Aulus Agerius deposited a slave with Numerius Negidius." 41. The *intentio* is the part of a formula in which the plaintiff declares his demand: this part of a formula, for instance: "If it appear that Numerius Negidius ought to give to Aulus Agerius 10,000 sesterces;" or this: "whatever it appears that Numerius Negidius ought to give or do for Aulus Agerius;" or this: "if it appear that the slave belongs to Aulus Agerius by Quiritary title[2]." 42. The *adjudi-*

[1] II. 78 *n.*

[2] These examples are well selected, being examples of the *intentiones* of the three most common forms of action, viz. the first an *intentio* suitable for an *actio in personam* of the character described as *certae condemnationis;* the second for an *actio in personam* of the class *incertae condemnationis;* the third for an *actio in rem.*

est ea pars formulae qua permittitur iudici rem alicui ex litigatoribus adiudicare: velut si inter coheredes familiae erciscundae agatur, aut inter socios communi dividundo, aut inter vicinos finium regundorum; nam illic ita est: QUANTUM ADIUDICARI OPORTET, IUDEX TITIO ADIUDICATO[1]. (43.) Con-
P.203 demnatio est ea pars formulae, qua iudici condemnandi | absolvendive potestas permittitur[2], velut haec pars formulae: IUDEX NUMERIUM NEGIDIUM AULO AGERIO SESTERTIUM X MILIA CONDEMNA. SI NON PARET ABSOLVE. item haec: IUDEX NUMERIUM NEGIDIUM AULO AGERIO DUMTAXAT (X MILIA) CONDEMNA. SI NON PARET ABSOLVITO. item haec: IUDEX NUMERIUM NEGIDIUM AULO AGERIO CONDEMNATO et reliqua, ut non adiciatur DUMTAXAT[3] (X MILIA). (44.) Non tamen istae

catio is that part of a formula in which the *judex* is permitted to adjudicate something to one of the litigants, as in the suit between coheirs for partition of the inheritance, or between partners for a division of the partnership effects, or between neighbouring proprietors for a setting out of their boundaries; for in such cases this part of the formula runs: "Let the *judex* adjudicate to Titius as much as ought to be adjudicated[1]." 43. The *condemnatio* is that part of a formula in which power is granted to the *judex* to condemn (*i.e.* mulct) or acquit[2]: this part of a formula, for instance: "*Judex*, condemn Numerius Negidius to pay 10,000 sesterces to Aulus Agerius; if it do not appear (that the circumstances put forth in the *intentio* are true), acquit him;" or this: "*Judex*, condemn Numerius Negidius to pay to Aulus Agerius a sum not exceeding 10,000 sesterces; if it do not appear (that the circumstances set forth in the *intentio* are true), acquit him:" or this: "*Judex*, condemn Numerius Negidius to pay to Aulus Agerius," &c. without the addition of "not exceeding[3] 10,000." 44. All these parts, however, are not

---

1 See Just. *Inst.* IV. 17. 4—7; Ulp. XIX. 16.

2 IV. 48 et seqq. Paulus says in D. 42. 1. 3: "qui damnare potest, is absolvendi quoque potestatem habet." Gaius himself says also in IV. 114: "vulgo dicitur omnia judicia absolutoria esse."

3 The writer of the MS. ought to have added to his *dumtaxat* the words *x milia*. But he has evidently been careless, omitting *x milia* after the first *dumtaxat*, where it is now replaced in the text: inserting it needlessly in the last *condemnatio* before the words *et reliqua*; and omitting it here again after *dumtaxat*, where it is wanted.

omnes partes simul inveniuntur, sed quaedam inveniuntur, quaedam non inveniuntur. certe intentio aliquando sola invenitur, sicut in praeiudicialibus formulis[1], qualis est qua quaeritur an aliquis libertus sit, vel quanta dos sit[2], et aliae complures. demonstratio autem et adiudicatio et condemnatio numquam solae inveniuntur, nihil enim omnino sine intentione vel condemnatione valet (demonstratio); item condemnatio sine demonstratione vel intentione, vel adiudicatio, nullas vires habet[3]. ob id numquam solae inveniuntur.

45. Sed eas quidem formulas in quibus de iure quaeritur in ius conceptas vocamus. quales sunt quibus intendimus nostrum esse aliquid ex iure Quiritium, aut nobis dari oportere, aut pro fure damnum (decidere oportere[4]; in) quibus iuris civilis intentio est[5]. (46.) Ceteras vero in factum

always found together in the same formula, but some appear and some do not appear. Of a certainty the *intentio* is sometimes found alone, as in praejudicial formulae[1], such, for instance, as that wherein the matter in issue is whether a person is a freedman, or what is the amount of a *dos*[2], and many others. But the *demonstratio*, the *adjudicatio* and the *condemnatio* are never found alone: for the *demonstratio* is utterly useless without an *intentio* or a *condemnatio:* and again a *condemnatio* or *adjudicatio* is of no effect without a *demonstratio* or an *intentio*[3]*:* therefore these are never found alone.

45. Now those formulae wherein the issue is upon the law, we call *in jus conceptae.* Of this kind are those in which we lay our *intentio* to the effect that something is ours by Quiritary title, or that some one ought to give us something, or ought to pay damages as though he were a thief[4]. In these the *intentio* is one of the civil law[5]. 46. All other formulae we style *in*

---

1 Praejudicial actions were essentially *in rem.* They were brought to establish some fact as preliminary to a pending action. See Zimmern's *Traité des actions chez les Romains*, § LXVI., Heineccius' *Antiqq. Rom.* IV. 6. 34, note t.

2 The subject of *dos* is discussed in Ulp. VI.

3 I have inserted *demonstratio* in the text, and have written *adjudicatio* before *nullas vires*, where the MS. has *adjudicatione.* Gaius shows by his concluding remarks that he merely had stated what parts could stand alone, not how the parts could be combined.

4 IV. 37 *n.*

5 For a full discussion of the phrases *formula in jus*, *formula in factum*, see App. (S).

An example of a *formula in jus*

conceptas vocamus, id est in quibus nulla talis intentionis conceptio est, (sed) initio formulae, nominato eo quod factum est, adiciuntur ea verba per quae iudici damnandi absolvendive potestas datur; qualis est formula qua utitur patronus contra
P.204 libertum qui eum contra edictum Praetoris in ius vocavit; | nam in ea ita est: RECUPERATORES SUNTO[1]. SI PARET ILLUM PATRONUM AB ILLO (ILLIUS) PATRONI LIBERTO CONTRA EDICTUM ILLIUS PRAETORIS IN IUS VOCATUM ESSE, RECUPERATORES ILLUM LIBERTUM ILLI PATRONO SESTERTIUM X MILIA CONDEMNATE[2]. SI NON PARET, ABSOLVITE. ceterae quoque formulae quae sub titulo DE IN IUS VOCANDO propositae sunt[3] in factum conceptae sunt: velut adversus eum qui in ius vocatus neque venerit neque vindicem dederit[4]; item contra eum qui vi ex-

factum conceptae; formulae, that is to say, in which the *intentio* is not drawn up in the manner above, but at the outset of which, after a specification of that which has been done, words are added whereby power of condemning or acquitting is conferred on the *judex*. Of this kind is the formula which the patron employs against his freedman who has summoned him into court contrary to the Praetor's edict, for it runs: "Let so-and-so be *recuperatores*[1]. Should it appear that such-and-such a patron has been summoned into court by such-and-such a freedman of the said patron contrary to the edict of such-and-such a Praetor, then let the *recuperatores* condemn the said freedman to pay to the said patron 10,000 sesterces[2]; should it not appear so, let them acquit him." The other formulae which are set forth under the title *de in jus vocando*[3] are *in factum conceptae:* as, for instance, that against him who when summoned into court has neither made his appearance nor assigned a protector[4]; also that against him who has by force

concepta is to be found in Cic. *pro Rosc. Com.* c. 4.

1 See notes on I. 20, IV. 105.

2 See Just. *Inst.* IV. 16. 3; D. 2. 4. 24 and 25. From these passages we also perceive that the copyist of the MS. has by a mistake written 10,000 for 5000 sesterces in the *condemnatio* of the formula quoted in the text.

3 These are commented on in D. 2. 4.

4 See note on IV. 21. Whether the *vindex* was in Gaius' time required in all cases where neither the summons was obeyed nor bail tendered, or was only needed in centumviral causes and actions *depensi* and *judicati*, is a disputed point. See Heffter's notes on this passage.

emerit eum qui in ius vocatur. et denique innumerabiles eiusmodi aliae formulae in albo proponuntur. (47.) Sed ex quibusdam causis Praetor et in ius et in factum conceptas formulas proponit, velut depositi et commodati[1]. illa enim formula quae ita concepta est: IUDEX ESTO. QUOD AULUS AGERIUS APUT NUMERIUM NEGIDIUM MENSAM ARGENTEAM DEPOSUIT, QUA DE RE AGITUR, QUIDQUID OB EAM REM NUMERIUM NEGIDIUM AULO AGERIO DARE FACERE OPORTET EX FIDE BONA, EIUS IUDEX NUMERIUM NEGIDIUM AULO AGERIO CONDEMNATO, NISI RESTITUAT[2]; SI NON PARET, ABSOLVITO—in ius concepta est. at illa formula quae ita concepta est: IUDEX ESTO. SI PARET AULUM AGERIUM APUT NUMERIUM NEGIDIUM MENSAM ARGENTEAM DEPOSUISSE, EAMQUE DOLO MALO NUMERII NEGIDII AULO AGERIO REDDITAM NON ESSE, QUANTI EA RES ERIT, TANTAM PECUNIAM IUDEX NUMERIUM NEGIDIUM AULO AGERIO CON-

rescued a person summoned into court. In fact there are innumerable other formulae of a like description set forth in the edict. 47. There are, however, cases in which the Praetor publishes both *formulae in jus conceptae* and *formulae in factum conceptae*, for instance, in the actions on deposit and on loan[1]; for the formula which is drawn up in this form: "Let so-and-so be *judex*. Inasmuch as Aulus Agerius has deposited a silver table with Numerius Negidius, from which transaction this suit arises, whatever Numerius Negidius ought in good faith to give or do to Aulus Agerius on account of this matter, do thou, *judex*, condemn Numerius Negidius to give or do to Aulus Agerius, unless he restore (the table)[2]; should it not so appear, acquit him," is a *formula in jus concepta*: but that which is drawn up thus: "Let so-and-so be *judex*. Should it appear that Aulus Agerius has deposited with Numerius Negidius a silver table, and that this through the fraud of Numerius Negidius has not been restored to Aulus Agerius, do thou, *judex*, condemn Numerius Negidius to pay to Aulus Agerius so much money as the thing in dispute shall

[1] IV. 60. See App. (N).

[2] In the MS. after the word *condemnato* appear the letters n. r., which Heffter thinks are incapable of any satisfactory explanation. It is Huschke's suggestion that they stand for *nisi restituat*, as inserted in our text. For this kind of formula see D. 16. 3. 1. 21 and D. 13. 6. 3. 3. See also note on IV. 141.

DEMNATO; SI NON PARET, ABSOLVITO—in factum concepta est. similes etiam commodati formulae sunt.

48. Omnium autem formularum quae condemnationem habent ad pecuniariam aestimationem condemnatio nunc con-
P.205 cepta est. itaque etsi corpus aliquod petamus, | velut fundum, hominem, vestem, aurum, argentum, iudex non ipsam rem condemnat eum cum quo actum est, sicut olim fieri solebat; (sed) aestimata re pecuniam eum condemnat. (49.) Condemnatio autem vel certae pecuniae in formula proponitur, vel incertae. (50.) Certae pecuniae velut in ea formula qua certam pecuniam petimus; nam illic ima parte formulae ita est: IUDEX NUMERIUM NEGIDIUM AULO AGERIO SESTERTIUM X MILIA CONDEMNA. SI NON PARET, ABSOLVE. (51.) Incertae vero condemnatio pecuniae duplicem significationem habet. est enim una quae est (cum) aliqua praefinitione, quae vulgo dicitur cum taxatione[1],

be worth: should it not so appear, acquit him," is a *formula in factum concepta*. There are similar formulae for loan also.

48. The *condemnatio* of all the formulae which have one is now drawn with a view to pecuniary compensation; therefore, although we be suing for some specific article, as for instance, for a field, a slave, a garment, gold, silver, the *judex* does not condemn the defendant in the thing itself, as was the custom in old times, but condemns him in money according to the valuation of the thing. 49. The *condemnatio* is drawn in the formula for a sum certain or for a sum uncertain. 50. It is for a sum certain, for instance, in the formula by which we sue for a sum certain, for at the end of the formula there occurs the direction: "Do thou, *judex*, condemn Numerius Negidius to pay to Aulus Agerius 10,000 sesterces: should it not so appear, acquit him." 51. The *condemnatio* may be for a sum uncertain in two different senses. For there is one kind with a definite maximum prefixed, which is generally styled *cum taxatione*[1]; for instance, when we are suing for some-

[1] So called because the word *dumtaxat* occurs in it, as in the instance here given and in that in IV. 43. Festus gives another explanation, connecting *taxat* and *taxatio* with *tangi*. See Festus, *sub verb*. If we regard *dumtaxat* as two words, we might accept Festus' definition, translating *dum taxat*, "so long as it touches," *i.e.* "goes as far as, does not exceed."

velut si incertum aliquid petamus; nam illic ima parte formulae ita est: IUDEX NUMERIUM NEGIDIUM AULO AGERIO DUMTAXAT SESTERTIUM X MILIA CONDEMNA. SI NON PARET, ABSOLVE. vel incerta est et infinita condemnatio, velut si rem aliquam a possidente nostram esse petamus, id est si in rem agamus, vel ad exhibendum; nam illic ita est: QUANTI EA RES ERIT, TANTAM PECUNIAM IUDEX NUMERIUM NEGIDIUM EIDEM CONDEMNA. SI NON PARET, ABSOLVITO. (52.) Qui de re vero est iudex si condemnet[1], certam pecuniam condemnare debet, etsi certa pecunia in condemnatione posita non sit. debet autem iudex at*tendere, ut* cum certae pecuniae condemnatio posita sit, neque maioris neque minoris summa *quam quae est* posita condemnet, alioquin litem suam facit[1]. item si taxatio posita sit, ne pluris condemnet quam taxatum sit,

thing uncertain, for then in the final part of the formula the wording is: "on this account, *judex*, condemn Numerius Negidius to pay to Aulus Agerius a sum not exceeding 10,000 sesterces; should it not so appear, acquit him." The other kind is that which is uncertain and unlimited; for instance, when we are claiming anything as being ours from one who is in possession thereof, that is when our action is one *in rem*, or for the purpose of having the thing produced in court, for then the *condemnatio* runs: "Do thou, *judex*, condemn Numerius Negidius to pay to Aulus Agerius as much money as the thing in dispute is worth: if it do not so appear, acquit him." 52. But if he who is *judex* in a case condemn[1], he must condemn in a specific amount, even though no specific amount have been stated in the *condemnatio*. A *judex* must on the other hand take care, when the *condemnatio* is limited to a sum specified, not to condemn for a larger or smaller amount than that which is stated, otherwise "he makes the cause his own[2]." So also where a *taxatio* has been inserted,

[1] Krüger and Studemund would read: *quid ergo est?* but the reading in the text (which is Huschke's in his earlier editions, though he afterwards adopted *quid ergo est?*) seems to accord better with the MS.

[2] "A *judex* is said 'to make the cause his own' when his decision is fraudulently and designedly given to evade the provisions of a *lex*. He will be guilty of fraud, if he be proved to have acted from favour, or enmity, or mercenary motives; and will have to pay the full value of the matter in dispute." D. 5. 1. 15. 1. The phrase is found in Cic. *de Orat.* II. 75, "Quid si, quum pro altero dicas, litem suam facias." From the passage in the text it would appear that a *judex* was liable for a wrong

alias enim similiter litem suam facit. minoris autem damnare |
P.206 ei permissum est. at si etiam (*taxatio posita non sit, quanti velit condemnare potest.* (52 a.) *Unde quia quod petit*) qui formulam acc*ipit* intendere debet, nec am(*plius iudex quam*) certa condemnatione constringi(*tur, neque ite*rum) eandem *actor formul*am accipit, (*et in condemnation*)e certam (*pecuniam quam petit ponere debet, ne consequatur min*)us quam velit[1].

53. Si quis intentione plus conplexus fuerit, *causa cadit*, id est rem perdit, nec a Praetore in integrum restituitur[2], exceptis quibusdam casibus in quibus *om*nes *actores Praetor* non patitur of*fici* (*damno ob errorem suum. nam minoribus xxv annorum*

he must not condemn for more than the sum "taxed," for otherwise he will, as before, "make the cause his own:" he may, however, condemn for less. But in the case when no *taxatio* has been inserted, he can condemn for such amount as he pleases. 52 *a*. Hence, as the receiver of a formula ought to lay his *intentio* for what he claims, and as the *judex* is limited by the *condemnatio* if stated for a sum certain, and as the plaintiff cannot have the same *formula* a second time, therefore he must state in the *condemnatio* the specific sum which he claims, lest he get less than he wishes[1].

53. Where a person has comprised in his *intentio* more (than is due to him), he fails in his cause, *i.e.* he loses the thing he is suing for, and he cannot be restored to his former position[2] by the Praetor, except in certain cases in which the Praetor does not suffer every plaintiff to be visited with loss on account of his own mistake. For as he aids persons under 25 years of

---

decision given through ignorance, as well as for one through fraud; but it is to be remembered that skilled *jurisconsulti* were appointed to assist the *judices*; see Aul. Gell. XII. 13. Read App. (Q).

1 The restoration of this corrupt passage is mainly in accordance with Huschke's suggestions. The Praetor, rather than the plaintiff, settles the *condemnatio*; but the settlement, of course, will be based upon the plaintiff's statement of facts.

2 Here *restitui in integrum* = to have the right of bringing a new action on the old facts. As soon as a litigated matter had arrived at the *litis contestatio* a *novatio* took place, and the defendant was no longer under obligation to fulfil his original engagement, but bound to carry out the award of the court: if then the court acquitted him, the plaintiff obviously could no longer sue on the old obligation, as that had been extinguished by the *novatio*. Hence *restitui in integrum* signifies that the plaintiff is freed from the damaging effects of the *novatio*, or, in other words, can bring a new action on the original case. See III. 180, 181. Paulus, *S. R.* I. 7.

semper ut in aliis causis et hic succurrit[1]. *plus autem quatuor*) modis petitur: re, tempore, loco, causa[2]. re: veluti *si quis pro x* milibus quae ei debentur, xx milia petierit, *aut* si *is cuius* ex parte res est, totam rem, aut maiore ex parte *suam* esse intenderit. *tempore: veluti si quis ante diem vel* ante *conditionem petierit. loco: veluti si quod certo loco* dari promissum *erat, id alio loco sine commemoratio*ne eius loci petatur, *velut si quis ita stipulatus erat:* X *MILIA* DARI *CAPUAE* SPONDES? de*inde* Romae p*ure intenderit eo* m*odo:* *SI* PAR*ET EX STIPULATU TE X MILIA SS.* DARE MIHI OPORTERE. plu*s* enim (*petere intellegitur, quia promissori utilitatem adimit, quam haberet, si Capuae solveret. si quis tamen eo loco agat, quo dari promissum est, potest*) |

age in other cases, so does he in this[1]. Too much is sued for in four ways, in substance, in time, in place, in quality[2]. It is sued for in substance in the case of a man seeking to recover 20,000 sesterces instead of the 10,000 owed to him, or in the case of a man who, having a share in a particular thing, lays his *intentio* for the whole or too large a part of it. It is sued for in time, in the case of a man suing before the arrival of the day named or the happening of the condition fixed. It is sued for in place, in the case of a man suing in some other place for the money which it had been promised should be paid in a particular place, without referring to the place so specified: for instance, suppose the stipulation had been in this form: "Do you engage to give me 10,000 sesterces at Capua?" and then the plaintiff were to lay his *intentio* at Rome in the general form thus: "Should it appear that you are bound by stipulation to give me 10,000 sesterces." For the plaintiff is assumed to be suing for too large an amount, because he deprives the promiser of the advantage he might have had by the payment being made at Capua. If, however, the plaintiff bring his action in the place where it was promised that the money should

[1] The latter part of this section is translated from the conjectural reading of Huschke, printed in the text above.

[2] "Causa cadimus aut loco, aut summa, aut tempore, aut qualitate. Loco, alibi: summa, plus: tempore, repetendo ante tempus: qualitate, ejusdem speciei rem meliorem postulantes." Paulus, *S. R.* I. 10. See also Just. *Inst.* IV. 6. 33, where the alterations effected by Zeno's constitution are specified, with the exception of that in respect of a *plus petitio tempore*, which was that a plaintiff should have to wait twice as long as he originally would have had to wait, and to pay all costs. C. 3. 10. 1.

P.207 petere, id est non adiecto loco. (53 *a.*) Causa plus petitur velut si quis in intentione tollat electionem debitoris quam is habet obligationis iure. velut si quis ita stipulatus sit: SESTERTIUM X MILIA AUT HOMINEM STICHUM DARE SPONDES? deinde alterutrum ex his petat; nam quamvis petat quod minus est, plus tamen petere videtur, quia potest adversarius interdum facilius id praestare quod non petitur. similiter si quis genus stipulatus sit, deinde speciem petat, velut si quis purpuram stipulatus sit generaliter, deinde Tyriam specialiter petat: quin etiam licet vilissimam petat, idem iuris est propter eam rationem quam proxime diximus. idem iuris est si quis generaliter hominem stipulatus sit, deinde nominatim aliquem petat, velut Stichum, quamvis vilissimum. itaque sicut ipsa stipulatio concepta est, ita et intentio formulae concipi debet. (54.) Illud satis apparet in incertis formulis[1] plus peti non posse, quia, cum certa quantitas non petatur, sed QUIDQUID ADVER-

be given, he can sue for it, that is, without adding the name of the place. 53 *a.* It is sued for in quality, in the case where a creditor in his *intentio* deprives his debtor of that right of election which he has by virtue of the obligation between them; as when a stipulation is worded thus: "Do you promise to give 10,000 sesterces or your slave Stichus?" and thereupon the creditor claims one or the other of these: now here, although he may actually sue for that of smaller value, yet he is regarded as suing for the larger, for it might sometimes be that his opponent could more easily give that which is not demanded. Similarly when a person having stipulated generically, sues specifically; as when the stipulation has been for purple cloth generally, and the action is specifically for Tyrian cloth: nay, even although he may be suing for that which is of least value, yet for the reason we have just stated, the rule is the same. So too is it when the stipulation has been for a slave generally, and the suit is brought for a particular slave, viz. Stichus, although he be really of the least value. Hence as the stipulation has been worded, so ought the *intentio* of the formula to be drawn. 54. Of this there is no doubt, that in what are called "uncertain formulae[1]" too large an amount cannot be sued for, because when a definite amount is not sued for,

[1] IV. 49—52.

SARIUM DARE FACERE OPORTERET intendatur, nemo potest plus intendere. idem iuris est, et si in rem incertae partis actio data sit; velut talis QUANTAM PARTEM PARET IN EO FUNDO, QUO DE AGITUR, ACTORIS ESSE: quod genus actionis in paucissimis causis dari solet. (55.) Item palam est si quis aliud pro alio intenderit, nihil eum periclitari eumque ex integro agere posse, quia nihil ante videtur egisse, velut si is qui hominem Stichum|
P.208 petere deberet Erotem petierit; aut si quis ex testamento dari sibi oportere intenderit cui ex stipulatu debebatur; aut si cognitor[1] aut procurator intenderit sibi dari oportere. (56.) Set plus quidem intendere, sicut supra diximus[2], periculosum est: minus autem intendere licet; sed de reliquo intra eiusdem praeturam agere non permittitur; nam qui ita agit per exceptionem excluditur, quae exceptio appellatur litis dividuae[3]. (57.) At si in condemnatione plus petitum sit quam oportet,

but the *intentio* is laid for "whatever our opponent ought to give or do," no one can be guilty of a *plus petitio*. The same rule also holds when an action *in rem* has been granted for an undetermined part; such as this, for instance; "such part in the land about which the action is as shall appear to belong to the plaintiff;" a kind of action which is allowed in very few instances. 55. Again, it is clear that when a man lays his *intentio* for one thing instead of another, he is not put in peril thereby, and can sue again, because he seems to have done nothing in the first suit; for instance, when a man who ought to sue for the slave Stichus sues for Eros; or when a man to whom a matter is due upon a stipulation sets forth in his *intentio* that it is due to him upon a testament; or when a *cognitor*[1] or *procurator* has worded his *intentio* that something is due to himself (instead of to his principal). 56. But although, as we have said above[2], it is dangerous to lay an *intentio* for too much, we may lay one for too little: but then we may not sue for the residue within the term of office of the same Praetor. For if we so sue, we are met successfully by the *exceptio* styled *litis dividuae*[3]. 57. Where, however, too much is comprised in the *condemnatio* the plaintiff is in no peril: but

[1] IV. 83, 84.

[2] IV. 53.

[3] IV. 122. By Zeno's constitution, referred to in note on IV. 53, the *judex* was allowed in such a case to augment the amount in giving his decision.

actoris quidem periculum nullum est, sed *reus cum*[1] iniquam formulam acceperit[2], in integrum restituitur[3] ut minuatur condemnatio. si vero minus positum fuerit quam oportet, hoc solum consequitur quod posuit[4]: nam tota quidem res in iudicium deducitur, constringitur autem condemnationis fine, quam iudex egredi non potest[5]. nec ex ea parte Praetor in integrum restituit: facilius enim reis Praetor succurrit quam actoribus. loquimur autem exceptis minoribus XXV annorum; nam huius aetatis hominibus in omnibus rebus lapsis Praetor succurrit[6]. (58.) Si in demonstratione plus aut minus positum sit, nihil in iudicium deducitur, et ideo res in integro manet: et hoc est quod dicitur falsa demonstratione rem non perimi. (59.) Sed sunt qui putant minus recte conprehendi. ut qui forte Stichum et Erotem emerit recte videtur ita demonstrare:

when the defendant[1] has received[2] an improperly-drawn formula the proceedings are quashed[3] in order that the *condemnatio* may be lessened. But if too small an amount be stated, the plaintiff only obtains what he[4] has stated: for the whole matter is laid before the *judex*, and yet is cut down by the limitation of the *condemnatio*, beyond which the *judex* must not go[5]. Nor does the Praetor in this instance allow a fresh action: for he is more ready to assist defendants than plaintiffs. But from these remarks we except those who are under 25 years of age: for the Praetor in all cases of mistake on the part of such persons grants them relief[6]. 58. If a larger or smaller sum than that due be set down in the *demonstratio*, there is nothing for the *judex* to try, and the matter remains as it was at starting: and this is what is meant by the saying, "that the matter in dispute is not brought to a conclusion by a false *demonstratio*." 59. Some lawyers, however, think that it is not bad pleading to state too small an amount in the *demonstratio*: For, to take an instance, a person who has bought Stichus and Eros

[1] *Reus cum.* These two words were inserted by Göschen.

[2] Sc. from the Praetor.

[3] See note on IV. 53. Possibly the rule in the text is laid down because an error in the *condemnatio* must be due to carelessness on the part of the magistrate who issued the formula, and not produced by a misstatement made by the plaintiff himself, as that would cause a *plus petitio* also in the *intentio*.

[4] *He* must mean the Praetor.

[5] IV. 52.

[6] II. 163.

QUOD EGO DE TE HOMINEM EROTEM EMI, et si velit, de Sticho
P.209 alia formula idem agat, quia verum est eum | qui duos emerit singulos quoque emisse: idque ita maxime Labeoni visum est[1]. sed si is qui unum emerit de duobus egerit, falsum demonstrat. idem et in aliis actionibus est, velut commodati et depositi[2]. (60.) Sed nos aput quosdam scriptum invenimus, in actione depositi et denique in ceteris omnibus quibus damnatus unusquisque ignominia notatur[3], eum qui plus quam oporteret demonstraverit litem perdere; velut si quis una re deposita duas res pluresve deposuisse demonstraverit, aut si is cui pugno mala percussa est in actione iniuriarum etiam aliam partem corporis percussam sibi demonstraverit. quod an debeamus credere verius esse, diligentius requiremus. certe cum duae sint depositi formulae, alia in ius concepta, alia in factum, sicut

is entitled to draw his *demonstratio* thus: "Inasmuch as I bought the slave Eros of you," and if he please may claim Stichus in like manner by another formula, because it is true enough that the purchaser of two slaves is also the purchaser of one of them: and this certainly was Labeo's opinion[1]. On the other hand, when the purchaser of one thing sues for two, his *demonstratio* is false. This doctrine holds in other actions also, such as those of loan and deposit[2]. 60. We have, however, found it laid down by some writers, that in the action of deposit and in all other actions where the consequence of an adverse judgment is ignominy[3], he who has stated too much in his *demonstratio* loses the suit; as when a man after making a deposit of one thing has stated two or more, or when after being struck on the cheek with a blow of the fist, he has stated in the *demonstratio* of his action for injuries that some other part of his body was also struck. We will examine this statement a little more at length to see whether we ought to consider it correct. No

---

[1] D. 16. 3. 1. 41 is perhaps the passage referred to.

[2] See App. (N).

[3] A list of the actions which carried this consequence with them is to be found in IV. 182. What was the exact effect of an ignominious verdict is not, however, very clear: but that it did seriously affect the person against whom it was recorded seems obvious from the careful enumeration of the various causes producing *ignominia* or *infamia* to be found in D. 3. 2.

supra quoque notavimus[1], et in ea quidem formula quae in ius concepta est, initio res de qua agitur demonstratorio modo designetur, deinde inferatur iuris contentio his verbis: QUIDQUID OB EAM REM ILLUM ILLI DARE FACERE OPORTET; in ea vero quae in factum concep*ta est statim* initio intentionis alio modo res de qua agitur designetur his verbis: SI PARET ILLUM APUT ILLUM DEPOSUISSE, dubitare non debemus, quin si quis in formula quae in factum composita est plures res designaverit quam deposuerit, litem perdat, quia in intentione plus posuit[2] [*desunt* 48 *lin.*].

61. *In bonae fidei iudiciis*[3] *libera potestas permitti videtur iudici ex bono et aequo aestimandi quantum actori restitui debeat.*
P.212 *in quo et illud* | continetur, ut habita ratione eius quod invicem

doubt, since there are, as we have stated above[1], two formulae for an action of deposit, one *in jus concepta*, the other *in factum concepta*, and in the former the matter in dispute is first set forth in the manner of a *demonstratio*, and then the issue of law is introduced in these words: "Whatever the one is bound on that account to give or do for the other:" whilst in the formula *in factum concepta* the thing in dispute is set forth at once in the beginning of the *intentio* in a different manner, in this form: "Should it appear that the one deposited with the other:" (all this being premised) there can be no doubt that if in a formula *in factum concepta* the plaintiff has described more things than he has deposited, he loses his suit, because he has claimed too much in the *intentio*[2].

61. In actions *bonae fidei*[3] full power is allowed to the *judex* to assess according to principles of fairness and equity the amount which ought to be paid to the plaintiff. In this commission is also contained the duty of taking account of anything which the plaintiff in his turn is bound to pay upon the

---

[1] IV. 47.

[2] Heffter, Huschke, Krüger, Studemund are all of opinion that the matter here missing was similar to that contained in Just. *Inst.* IV. 6. 36—39. The opening words of § 61 are supplied from Just. *Inst.* IV. 6. 30.

[3] The distinction between actions *stricti juris* and *bonae fidei* is treated of in Just. *Inst.* IV. 6. 28—30. As the whole subject is fully discussed and explained by Mackeldey and Zimmern, we need only refer to Mackeldey's *Systema Juris Rom.* § 197, and Zimmern's *Traité des actions chez les Romains*, § LXIII.

actorem ex eadem causa praestare oporteret, in reliquum eum cum quo actum est condemnare[1]. (62.) Sunt autem bonae fidei iudicia haec: ex empto vendito, locato conducto, negotiorum gestorum[2], mandati, depositi, fiduciae[3], pro socio, tutelae, (*commodati, pigneraticium, familiae erciscundae, communi dividundo, praescriptis*) verbis[4]. (63.) Tamen iudici nullam omnino invicem conpensationis rationem habere *in ipsis*[5] formulae verbis praecipitur; sed quia id bonae fidei iudicio conveniens videtur, ideo officio eius contineri creditur. (64.) Alia causa est illius actionis qua argentarius experitur: nam is cogitur cum conpensatione agere, et ea conpensatio verbis formulae exprimitur, *adeo quidem ut itaque* ab initio conpensatione facta minus intendit sibi dare oportere. ecce enim si sestertium x milia debeat Titio, atque ei xx debeantur, sic intendit: SI PARET TITIUM SIBI X MILIA DARE OPORTERE AMPLIUS QUAM IPSE TITIO DEBET. (65.) Item bonorum emptor[6] cum deductione

same transaction, and so condemning the defendant to pay the balance only[1]. 62. Now the *bonae fidei* actions are these: on sale, letting, voluntary agency[2], mandate, deposit, fiduciary agreement to restore[3], partnership, guardianship, loan, pledge, division of an inheritance, partition of common property, and *præscriptis verbis*[4]. 63. The *judex*, however, is not enjoined in the actual words[5] of the formula to take account of mutual set-off: but it is considered to be within the scope of his office, because it seems consonant with the notion of a *bonae fidei* action. 64. The case is different in the kind of action by which a banker sues; for he is compelled to sue *cum conpensatione*, and that set-off is expressed in the wording of the formula: so that, making the set-off therefore at the outset, the banker declares in his *intentio* that the reduced sum is due to him. Thus, suppose he owes Titius 10,000 sesterces and that 20,000 are due to him, he lays his *intentio* thus: "Should it appear that Titius is bound to give him 10,000 sesterces more than he owes to Titius." 65. Again the purchaser of an insolvent's goods[6]

1 See D. 13. 6. 18. 4.
2 See D. 44. 7. 5. *pr.*
3 II. 59, 60.
4 See App. (S). The completion of the list is taken from Just. *Inst.* IV. 6. 28. In the MS. the first portion of the list is written twice, and the rest omitted, with the exception of the concluding word *verbis*.
5 The MS. has NTRARTAE.
6 III. 77.

agere iubetur, *id est ut* in hoc solum adversarius eius condemnetur quod superest, deducto eo quod invicem ei bonorum emptor defraudatoris nomine debet. (66.) Inter conpensationem autem quae argentario interponitur et deductionem quae obicitur bonorum emptori illa differentia est, quod in conpensationem hoc solum vocatur quod eiusdem generis et naturae est. veluti pecunia cum pecunia conpensatur, triticum cum tritico, vinum
P.213 cum vino: adeo | ut quibusdam placeat non omni modo vinum cum vino, aut triticum cum tritico conpensandum, sed ita si eiusdem naturae qualitatisque sit. in deductionem autem vocatur et quod non est eiusdem generis[1]. itaque si pecuniam petat bonorum emptor, et invicem frumentum aut vinum si debeat, deducto quanti id erit, in reliquum experitur. (67.) Item vocatur in deductionem et id quod in diem debetur; conpensatur autem hoc solum quod praesenti die debetur. (68.) Praeterea conpensationis quidem ratio in intentione ponitur: quo fit, ut si facta conpensatione plus nummo uno

is directed to bring his action *cum deductione*, that is to say, for his opponent to be condemned to pay the balance only after the sum has been deducted which the purchaser of the estate reciprocally owes to him on the bankrupt's account. 66. Between the set-off made against a banker and the deduction opposed to the purchaser of an insolvent's goods there is this difference, that in the set-off nothing is taken into account except what is of the same class and character: as, for instance, money is set off against money, wheat against wheat, wine against wine; nay, some persons think that wine cannot in all cases be set off against wine, nor wheat against wheat, but only when the two parcels are of like character and quality. But in the case of a deduction things are taken into account which are not of the same class[1]. Hence if the purchaser of an insolvent's goods sue for money and himself in turn owe corn or wine, after deduction of the value thereof he claims for the balance. 67. In a deduction account is also taken of that which is due at a future time; but in a set-off only of that due at the instant. 68. Moreover the reckoning of a set-off is stated in the *intentio;* the result of which is that if the banker

[1] See Paulus, *S. R.* II. 5. 3, where the rule is thus stated: "Compensatio debiti paris speciei et causa dispari admittitur."

intendat argentarius, causa cadat et ob id rem perdat. deductio vero ad condemnationem ponitur, quo loco plus petenti periculum non intervenit[1]; utique bonorum emptore agente, qui licet de certa pecunia agat, incerti tamen condemnationem concipit.

69. Quia tamen superius mentionem habuimus[2] de actione qua in peculium filiorumfamilias servorumque agitur, opus est, ut de hac actione et de ceteris quae eorumdem nomine in parentes dominosve dari solent diligentius admoneamus.

70. Inprimis itaque si iussu patris dominive negotium gestum erit, in solidum Praetor actionem in patrem dominumve comparavit: et recte, quia qui ita negotium gerit magis patris dominive quam filii servive fidem sequitur. (71.) Eadem ratione |
P.214 comparavit duas alias actiones, exercitoriam et institoriam. tunc autem exercitoria locum habet, cum pater dominusve

on making his set-off claim too much by a single sesterce, he fails in his cause, and so loses the whole matter at issue. But a deduction is placed in the *condemnatio;* and there is no danger to a man who makes a *plus petitio* there[1]: at least when the plaintiff is the purchaser of an insolvent's goods, for although such an one sues for a specified sum, yet he frames his *condemnatio* for an uncertain one.

69. As we have already[2] mentioned the action which is brought for the *peculium* of children under *potestas* and of slaves, it is now necessary for us to explain more carefully the nature of this action and of others which are usually granted against parents or masters in the name of such persons.

70. In the first place, then, if any transaction have been entered into by the express command of the father or master, the Praetor has provided a form of action for the whole debt against such father or master; and this is very proper, because he who enters into such an engagement puts his confidence in the father or master rather than in the son or slave. 71. On the same principle the Praetor has drawn up two other actions, known respectively as "exercitorian" and "institorian." The

[1] IV. 57.

[2] Probably in the part of the MS. which immediately preceded VI. 61; for this, according to Heffter and Huschke, corresponded to *Inst.* IV. 6. 36—39, and in that part of Justinian's work the *peculium* and the actions relating to it are referred to.

filium servumve magistrum navis praeposuerit, et quid cum eo eius rei gratia cui praepositus fuit negotium gestum erit; cum enim ea quoque res ex voluntate patris dominive contrahi videatur, aequissimum esse visum est in solidum actionem dari. quin etiam, licet extraneum quisque magistrum navi praeposuerit, sive servum sive liberum, tamen ea Praetoria actio in eum redditur. ideo autem exercitoria actio appellatur, quia exercitor[1] vocatur is ad quem cottidianus navis quaestus pervenit. Institoria vero formula tum locum habet, cum quis tabernae aut cuilibet negotiationi filium servumve aut quemlibet extraneum, sive servum sive liberum, praeposuerit, et quid cum eo[2] eius rei gratia cui praepositus est contractum fuerit. ideo autem institoria vocatur, quia qui tabernae praeponitur institor appellatur. quae et ipsa formula in solidum est.

former of these is resorted to when a father or master has made his son or slave the captain of a vessel, and some engagement has been entered into with one or the other in reference to the business he was appointed to manage; for as this engagement also seems to be contracted with the consent of the father or master, it appeared most equitable that an action should be given for the full amount. And, what is more, although the owner of a vessel have placed some stranger, whether bond or free, in command, still this Praetorian action is granted against him (the owner). The reason why the action is called "exercitorian" is because the name *exercitor*[1] is given to the person to whom the daily profits of a vessel accrue. The "institorian" formula can be employed, whenever a person has placed his son, or slave, or even a stranger, whether bond or free, to manage a shop or business of any kind, and some engagement has been entered into with this manager[2] in reference to the business he has been set to manage. It derives its name "institorian" from the fact that the person who is set to manage a shop is called *institor*. This formula, too, is for the full amount.

---

1 An *exercitor* was not necessarily the owner of a vessel, but might be a charterer. See D. 14. 1. 1. 15.

2 Or with the servants or apprentices of the manager. See Paulus, *S. R.* II. 8. 3: "Quod cum discipulis eorum qui officinis vel tabernis praesunt contractum est, in magistros vel institores tabernae in solidum actio dabitur." See D. 14. 3. 3, and 14. 3. 8.

72. Praeterea tributoria quoque actio in patrem dominumve constituta est, cum filius servusve in peculiari merce sciente patre dominove negotietur. nam si quid eius rei gratia cum eo contractum fuerit, ita Praetor ius dicit, ut quidquid in his mer-
P.215 cibus[1] | *erit, quodque inde receptum erit, id inter patrem dominumve, si quid ei debebitur, et ceteros creditores pro rata portione distribuatur. et quia ipsi patri dominove distributionem permittit, si quis ex creditoribus queratur, quasi minus ei tributum sit quam oportuerit, hanc ei actionem adcommodat, quae tributoria appellatur.*

73. *Praeterea introducta est actio de peculio deque eo quod in rem patris dominive versum erit, ut quamvis sine voluntate patris dominive negotium gestum erit, tamen sive quid in rem eius versum fuerit, id totum praestare debeat, sive quid non sit in rem eius versum, id eatenus praestare debeat, quatenus peculium patitur. in rem autem patris dominive versum intellegitur quidquid ne-*

72. Besides these actions, another, called the "tributorian" action, has been granted against a father or master, when a child or slave trades with the merchandise of his *peculium* with the knowledge of his father or master. For if any contract have been entered into with such trader on account of such business, the rule ordained by the Praetor is that all the stock[1] comprised in the *peculium* and all profit which has been derived therefrom shall be divided between the father or master, if anything be due to him, and the other creditors, in proportion to their claims. And as the Praetor allows the father or master to make the distribution, therefore in case of complaint being made by any one of the creditors that his share is smaller than it ought to be, he gives this creditor the action called "tributorian."

73. In addition to the above, an action has been introduced "relating to the *peculium* and to whatever has been converted to the profit of the father or master;" so that even though the transaction in question have been entered into without the wish of the father or master, yet if, on the one hand, anything have been converted to his profit, he is bound to make satisfaction to the full amount of that profit, and if, on the other hand, there have been no profit to him, he is still bound to make satisfaction so far as the *peculium* admits. Now everything

[1] The paragraphs which follow are supplied from Just. *Inst.* IV. 7. 3 and 4, a page being lost from the MS. at this point.

cessario in rem eius impenderit filius servusve, veluti si mutuatus pecuniam creditoribus eius solverit, aut aedificia ruentia fulserit, aut familiae frumentum emerit, vel etiam fundum aut quamlibet aliam rem necessariam mercatus erit. itaque si ex decem ut puta sestertiis quae servus tuus a Titio mutua accepit creditori tuo quinque sestertia solverit, reliqua vero quinque quolibet modo consumpserit, pro quinque quidem in solidum damnari debes, pro ceteris vero quinque eatenus, quatenus in peculio sit: ex quo scilicet apparet, si tota decem sestertia in rem tuam versa fuerint, tota decem sestertia Titium consequi posse. licet enim una est actio qua de peculio deque eo quod in rem patris dominive versum sit agitur, tamen duas habet condemnationes. itaque iudex aput quem ea actione agitur ante dispicere solet, an in rem patris dominive versum sit, nec aliter ad peculii aestimationem transit, quam si aut nihil in rem patris dominive versum intellegatur, aut non totum. cum
P.216 *autem quaeritur quantum in peculio sit, ante* | deducitur quod patri dominove quique in eius potestate sit a filio servove de-

which the son or slave necessarily expends upon the father's or master's business is taken to be to the profit of the father or master; as, for example, when the son or slave has borrowed money and with it paid his father's or master's creditors, or propped up his ruinous buildings, or purchased corn for his household, or bought an estate or anything else that was wanted. Therefore if out of ten sestertia, for instance, which your slave has borrowed from Titius, he have paid five to a creditor of yours, and spent the other five in some way or other, you ought to be condemned to make good the whole of the first five, but the other five only so far as the *peculium* goes. Hence it appears that if the whole of the ten sestertia have been spent upon your business, Titius is entitled to recover them all. For although there is but one and the same form of action for obtaining the *peculium* and the amount converted to the profit of the father or master, yet it has two *condemnationes*. Therefore the *judex* before whom the action is tried ought first to ascertain whether anything has been converted to the profit of the father or master, and he can only go on to settle the amount of the *peculium* after satisfying himself that nothing, or not the whole amount in question, has been so converted. When, however, a question arises about the amount of the *peculium*, anything which is owed by the son or slave to the father or betur, et quod superest, hoc solum peculium esse intellegitur. aliquando tamen id quod ei debet filius servusve qui in potestate patris dominive est non deducitur ex peculio, velut si is cui debet in huius ipsius peculio sit[1].

74. Ceterum dubium non est, quin et is qui iussu patris dominive contraxerit, cuique vel exercitoria vel institoria formula competit, de peculio aut de in rem verso agere possit. sed nemo tam stultus erit, ut qui aliqua illarum actionum sine dubio solidum consequi possit, in difficultatem se deducat probandi habere peculium eum cum quo contraxerit, exque eo peculio posse sibi satisfieri, vel id quod prosequitur in rem patris dominive versum esse. is quoque cui tributoria actio conpetit, de peculio vel de in rem verso agere potest: sed huic sane plerumque expedit hac potius actione uti quam tributoria. nam in tributoria eius solius peculii ratio habetur quod in his mer-

master, or to a person under his *potestas*, is first deducted, and the balance alone is reckoned as *peculium*. Still, sometimes, what a son or slave owes to a person under the *potestas* of his father or master is not deducted, for instance, when he owes it to a person in his own *peculium*[1].

74. Now there is no doubt that he who has entered into a contract (with a son or slave) at the bidding of the father or master, and he who can avail himself of an exercitorian or institorian formula, may also bring the action styled *de peculio aut de in rem verso*. But no one who could recover the whole amount by one of the first-named actions would be so foolish as to involve himself in the difficult task of proving that the person with whom he contracted has a *peculium*, and that out of that *peculium* he can be paid in full, or that what he claims has been converted to the profit of the father or master. Again, he for whom a tributorian action lies, can also proceed by the action *de peculio vel de in rem verso:* but for this man it is obviously better in most cases to resort to the last-named action rather than to the tributorian action. For in the tributorian action so much only of the *peculium* is taken into consideration

[1] That is, debts owing by a *servus ordinarius* to his *servus vicarius* are not reckoned in the calculation. If the amount had been deducted as due to the *vicarius*, it would, when paid, have been again in the *peculium* of the *ordinarius*, with the *vicarius* himself, and thus the deduction would have been nugatory.

cibus est in quibus negotiatur filius servusve quodque inde receptum erit, at in actione peculii totius: et potest quisque tertia forte aut quarta vel etiam minore parte peculii negotiari, maximam vero partem in aliis rebus habere; longe magis si potest adprobari id quod contraxerit in rem patris dominive versum esse, ad hanc actionem transire debet. nam, ut supra
P.217 diximus[1], | eadem formula et de peculio et de in rem verso agitur.

75. Ex maleficio filiorumfamilias servorumve, veluti si furtum fecerint aut iniuriam commiserint, noxales actiones proditae sunt, uti liceret patri dominove aut litis aestimationem sufferre aut noxae dedere[2]: erat enim iniquum nequitiam eorum ultra ipsorum corpora parentibus dominisve damnosam esse. (76.) Constitutae sunt autem noxales actiones aut legibus aut edicto Praetoris; legibus, velut furti lege XII tabula-

as is comprised in the stock-in-trade wherewith the son or slave is trafficking, or has been taken therefrom as profit, but in the *actio peculii* the whole is considered; and it is possible for a man to traffick with a third, or fourth, or even a smaller part of his *peculium*, and to have the larger part invested in other property. Still more clearly ought the creditor to have recourse to this action, if it can be proved that the proceeds of the transaction have been altogether spent on the business of the father or master. For, as we have said above[1], the same formula deals both with the *peculium* and with outlays for the father's or master's profit.

75. For the wrongful acts of sons under *potestas* or of slaves, such as theft or injury, noxal actions have been provided, with the view of allowing the father or master either to pay the assessed damage or to give up (the offender) as a *noxa*[2]: for it would be inequitable that the offence of such persons should inflict damage on their parents or masters beyond the value of their persons. 76. Now noxal actions have been established either by *leges* or by the edict of the Praetor. By *leges*, as the action of theft under

[1] IV. 73.

[2] "Noxa est corpus quod nocuit, id est servus, noxia ipsum maleficium." Just. *Inst.* IV. 8. 1. See Festus, sub verb. *noxia*. The terminology of Justinian does not accord with that of Gaius, who in §§ 77 and 78 below uses *noxa* where according to Justinian's rule we should have had *noxia*.

rum[1], damni iniuriae velut lege Aquilia[2]: edicto Praetoris velut iniuriarum et vi bonorum raptorum. (77.) Omnes autem noxales actiones capita sequuntur[3]. nam si filius tuus servusve noxam commiserit, quamdiu in tua potestate est, tecum est actio; si in alterius potestatem pervenerit, cum illo incipit actio esse; si sui iuris coeperit esse, directa actio cum ipso est, et noxae deditio extinguitur. ex diverso quoque directa actio noxalis esse incipit: nam si pater familias noxam commiserit, et is se in adrogationem tibi dederit[4] aut servus tuus esse coeperit, (quod) quibusdam casibus accidere primo commentario tradidimus[5], incipit tecum noxalis actio esse quae ante directa fuit. (78.) Sed si filius patri aut servus domino noxam commiserit, nulla actio nascitur: nulla enim omnino inter me et eum qui in potestate mea est obligatio nasci potest. ideo-
P.218 que et si in alienam | potestatem pervenerit aut sui iuris esse

a law of the Twelve Tables[1], or that of wrongful damage under the Lex Aquilia[2]: by the edict of the Praetor, as the actions of injury and of goods taken by force. 77. Again, all noxal actions follow the persons (of the delinquents)[3]. For if your son or slave have committed a noxal act, so long as he is under your *potestas* the action lies against you: but if he pass under the *potestas* of another, the action forthwith lies against that other; if he become *sui juris*, there is a direct action against himself, and the possibility of giving him up as a *noxa* is at an end. Conversely, a direct action may become a noxal one: for if a *paterfamilias* have committed a noxal act, and then have arrogated[4] himself to you or become your slave, which we have shown in our first Commentary may happen in certain cases[5], then the action which previously was directly against the offender begins to be a noxal action against you. 78. But if a son have committed a noxal act against his father or a slave against his master, no action arises: for no obligation at all can arise between me and a person under my *potestas*. And so, though he may afterwards have passed under the *potestas* of another, or have become

[1] Tab. XII. l. 4. "Si servus furtum faxit, noxiamve nocuit, noxae dedendum esse," where the word *noxia* is used in the sense affixed to it by Justinian.

[2] III. 210.

[3] D. 9. 4. 43.

[4] I. 99.

[5] I. 160.

coeperit, neque cum ipso, neque cum eo cuius nunc in potestate est agi potest. unde quaeritur, si alienus servus filiusve noxam commiserit mihi, et is postea in mea esse coeperit potestate, utrum intercidat actio an quiescat. nostri praeceptores intercidere putant, quia in eum casum deducta sit in quo actio consistere non potuerit, ideoque licet exierit de mea potestate agere me non posse. diversae scholae auctores quamdiu in mea potestate sit quiescere actionem putant, quod ipse mecum agere non possum; cum vero exierit de mea potestate, tunc eam resuscitari[1]. (79.) Cum autem filius familias ex noxali causa mancipio datur, diversae scholae auctores putant ter eum mancipio dari debere[2], quia lege XII tabularum cautum sit, (*ne aliter filius de potestate patris*) exeat[3], quam si ter fuerit mancipatus: Sabinus et Cassius ceterique nostrae scholae auctores sufficere unam mancipationem crediderunt,

sui juris, there can be no action either against him or against the person under whose *potestas* he now is. Hence this question has been raised, whether in the event of an injury being committed against me by a slave or son of another person, who subsequently passes under my *potestas*, the right of action is altogether lost or is only in abeyance. The authorities of our school think that it is lost, because the matter has been brought into a state in which there cannot possibly be an action, and that therefore I cannot sue, although the wrongdoer have passed subsequently from under my *potestas*. The authorities of the school opposed to us think that the right of action is in abeyance so long as he is under my *potestas*, since I cannot bring an action against myself; but that it is revived when he has passed out of my *potestas*[1]. 79. Again, when a son under *potestas* is given up by mancipation for a noxal cause, the authorities of the opposed school hold that he ought to be given by mancipation thrice[2], because by a law of the Twelve Tables it has been provided that unless a son be thrice mancipated he cannot escape from the *potestas* of his father[3]: but Sabinus and Cassius and the other authorities of our school held that one mancipation is sufficient, and that the word "three" in

---

[1] Justinian decided this dispute in favour of the Sabinians. *Inst.* IV. 8. 6.

[2] I. 132, 140.

[3] Tab. IV. 1. 3.

et illam[1] TRES lege XII tabularum ad voluntarias mancipationes pertinere.

80. Haec ita de his personis quae in potestate (sunt), sive ex contractu sive ex maleficio earum nomine actio esset. quod vero ad eas personas quae in manu mancipiove sunt ita ius dicitur, ut cum ex *contr*actu earum ageretur, nisi ab eo cuius iuri subiectae sint in solidum defendantur, bona quae earum futura forent, si eius iuri subiectae non essent, veneant. sed cum rescissa diminutione[2] capitis imperio continenti iudicio |
P.219 agitur[3], *etiam cum ipsa muliere quae in manum convenit agi potest*[4], *quia tum tutoris auctoritas necessaria non est*[5]. [*desunt* 22
P.220 *lin.*] (81.) Ergo, etiamsi vel ad quam rem diximus quoque non permissum fuit ei mortuos homines dedere, tamen et si quis eum dederit qui fato suo vita excesserit, aeque liberatur[6].

the law[1] of the Twelve Tables refers to voluntary mancipations.

80. So much for those persons who are under *potestas*, when an action arises on their account either from their contract or their delict. But so far as those who are under *manus* or *mancipium* are concerned the law is thus stated: if an action be brought on their contract, unless they be defended to the full amount by him to whose authority they are subject, all the property which would have been theirs, if they had not been subject to such authority, must be sold. But when the *capitis diminutio* is treated as non-existent[2] in an action coexistent with the *imperium*[3], the action may be brought personally even against a woman under *manus*[4], because in such a case the authorization of her tutor is not required[5]... 81. Therefore although, even for the purpose we have mentioned, it was never permitted to a defendant to surrender dead slaves (instead of paying the damage they had done); yet if a man give up a slave who has died a natural death he is free from liability, as in the other case[6].

[1] The MS. has *et illam;* and, if there be no error, we must understand *vocem* = "the word, *three*, in the XII. Tables."

[2] III. 84, IV. 38. The MS. seems to have DNPTIS.

[3] IV. 103—109.

[4] I. 108.

[5] The reading here adopted is a conjecture of Huschke: founded on Ulp. XI. 27. Perhaps the words *legitimo judicio* ought to be supplied before *ageretur* in the preceding section.

[6] Zeno abolished noxal surrender of children, but that of slaves continued to Justinian's time. *Inst.* IV. 8.

82. Nunc admonendi sumus agere nos aut nostro nomine aut alieno, veluti cognitorio, procuratorio, tutorio, curatorio: cum olim, quo tempore legis actiones in usu fuissent, alieno nomine agere non liceret, praeterquam ex certis causis. (83.) Cognitor[1] autem certis verbis in litem coram adversario substituitur. nam actor ita cognitorem dat: QUOD EGO A TE verbi gratia FUNDUM PETO, IN EAM REM LUCIUM TITIUM TIBI COGNITOREM DO; adversarius ita: QUIA TU A ME FUNDUM PETIS, IN EAM REM PUBLIUM MAEVIUM COGNITOREM DO. potest ut actor ita dicat: QUOD EGO TECUM AGERE VOLO, IN EAM REM COGNITOREM DO; adversarius ita: QUIA TU MECUM AGERE VIS, IN EAM REM COGNITOREM DO. nec interest, praesens an absens cogni-

82. We must next be reminded that we can bring an action either in our own name or in the name of another; when, for instance, he sues as a *cognitor*, *procurator*, *tutor*, or *curator:* although formerly, when the *legis actiones* were in use, it was not allowable for a man to sue in the name of another, except in certain cases. 83. A *cognitor*[1] then is substituted (for a principal) in a set form of words, in order to carry on a suit, and in the opponent's presence. For the method in which the plaintiff appoints one is as follows: "Inasmuch as I am suing you for a field," to take an example, "I appoint Lucius Titius to be my *cognitor* against you for that matter:" that in which the opposite party does so is: "Since you are suing me for the field, I appoint Publius Maevius as my *cognitor* for that matter." Or it may be that the plaintiff uses these words: "As I desire to bring an action against you, I appoint a *cognitor* for the purpose;" and the defendant these: "Since you desire to bring an action against me, I appoint a *cognitor* for the purpose." The presence or absence of the *cognitor* at the time of appointment is not a material point: but if he

[1] The institution of *cognitores* was precedent in point of time to that of *procuratores*, and naturally so, because the invasion of the principle that one person could not represent another was much less barefaced in the one case than in the other. Cicero mentions the *cognitor* in the *Orat. pro Rosc. Com.* c. 18. Festus, *sub verb.*, gives the same definition as in our text: "Cognitor est qui litem ulterius suscipit coram eo cui datus est. Procurator autem absentis nomine actor fit." A *cognitor* was always appointed to conduct a suit, a *procurator* frequently for other business: Paul. *S. R.* I. 3. 2. Cognitors had become obsolete in Justinian's day.

tor detur: sed si absens datus fuerit, cognitor ita erit si cognoverit et susceperit officium cognitoris. (84.) Procurator vero nullis certis verbis in litem substituitur, sed ex solo mandato[1] et absente et ignorante adversario constituitur. quinetiam sunt qui putant eum quoque procuratorem videri cui non sit mandatum, si modo bona fide accedat ad negotium et caveat ratam rem dominum habiturum[2]. quamquam et ille cui man-
P.221 datum (est) plerumque satisdare debet, | quia saepe mandatum initio litis in obscuro est et postea aput iudicem ostenditur. (85.) Tutores autem et curatores quemadmodum constituantur, primo commentario rettulimus[3].

86. Qui autem alieno nomine agit, intentionem quidem ex persona domini sumit, condemnationem autem in suam personam convertit. nam si verbi gratia Lucius Titius pro Publio Maevio agat, ita formula concipitur: SI PARET NUMERIUM NEGIDIUM PUBLIO MAEVIO SESTERTIUM X MILIA DARE OPOR-

be absent at the time he is appointed, he will become agent only on receipt of notice and acceptance of the duty. 84. A *procurator*, on the other hand, is substituted for the purposes of the suit without any special form of words: and is appointed by simple mandate[1], and even in the absence or ignorance of the opposite party. Nay, there are some who think that even if there be no mandate given, a person may be considered a *procurator*, provided only he act in the business in good faith, and give sureties that what he does shall be ratified by his principal[2]. Although he also who has a mandate must in general give security, because a mandate is frequently kept back at the commencement of a suit, and produced afterwards before the *judex*. 85. As to the manner of appointing tutors and curators we have given information in our first Commentary[3].

86. He who sues in the name of another inserts his principal's name in the *intentio*, but in the *condemnatio* inserts his own instead. For if, for example, Lucius Titius be acting for Publius Maevius, the formula is thus drawn: "Should it appear that Numerius Negidius is bound to give 10,000 sesterces to Publius Maevius, do thou, *judex*, condemn Numerius

[1] III. 155 et seqq.

[2] Such a person was called *negotiorum gestor*, and the obligation between him and the person he represents is of the class styled *quasi ex contractu*. See App. (N).

[3] I. 144 et seqq.

TERE, IUDEX NUMERIUM NEGIDIUM LUCIO TITIO SESTERTIUM X MILIA CONDEMNA. SI NON PARET, ABSOLVE. in rem quoque si agat, intendit PUBLII MAEVII REM ESSE EX IURE QUIRITIUM, et condemnationem in suam personam convertit. (87.) Ab adversarii quoque parte si interveniat aliquis, cum quo actio constituitur, intenditur DOMINUM DARE OPORTERE; condemnatio autem in eius personam convertitur qui iudicium accepit. sed cum in rem agitur, nihil in intentione facit eius persona cum quo agitur, sive suo nomine sive alieno aliquis iudicio interveniat: tantum enim intenditur REM ACTORIS ESSE.

88. Videamus nunc quibus ex causis is cum quo agitur vel hic qui ag(it cog)atur satisdare. (89.) Igitur si verbi gratia in rem tecum agam, satis mihi dare debes. aequum enim visum est te ideo quod interea tibi rem, quae an ad te pertineat dubium est, possidere conceditur, cum satisdatione mihi cavere, ut si victus sis, nec rem[1] ipsam restituas nec litis aestimationem

Negidius to pay the 10,000 sesterces to Lucius Titius: should it not so appear, acquit him." If again the action be *in rem*, he lays his *intentio* that "such and such a thing is the property of Publius Maevius in Quiritary right," and then in the *condemnatio* changes to his own name. 87. If, again, there be on the part of the defendant some agent against whom the suit is laid, the statement in the *intentio* is to the effect that "the principal ought to give:" but in the *condemnatio* the name is changed to that of him who has undertaken the conduct of the case. But when the action is *in rem*, the name of the person against whom the action is brought has no effect on the *intentio*, whether such person be defending his own cause or acting as agent in a suit appertaining to another: for the wording of the *intentio* is simply that "the thing is the plaintiff's."

88. Let us now see under what circumstances he who is sued or he who sues is under the necessity of finding sureties. 89. If then, to take an example, I bring an action *in rem* against you, you must furnish me with sureties. For since you are allowed to have the interim-possession of the thing, in respect of which there is a doubt whether the ownership is yours or not, it has been considered equitable that you should provide me with sureties, so that if you lose the suit and will

[1] The MS. has rem n' = rem nec.

sufferas, sit mihi potestas aut tecum agendi aut cum sponso-
P.222 ribus | tuis. (90.) Multoque magis debes satisdare mihi, si alieno nomine iudicium accipias. (91.) Ceterum cum in rem actio duplex sit, (aut enim per formulam petitoriam agitur aut per sponsionem): si quidem per formulam petitoriam agitur, illa stipulatio locum habet quae appellatur iudicatum solvi[1], si vero per sponsionem, illa quae appellatur pro praede litis et vindiciarum[2]. (92.) Petitoria autem formula haec est qua actor intendit rem suam esse. (93.) Per sponsionem vero hoc modo agimus: provocamus adversarium tali sponsione: SI HOMO QUO DE AGITUR EX IURE QUIRITIUM MEUS EST, SESTERTIOS XXV NUMMOS DARE SPONDES? deinde formulam edimus

neither deliver up the subject itself nor pay the assessed value, I may have the power of proceeding either against you or your sureties. 90. And still more ought you to furnish me with sureties, if you defend an action in the name of another person. 91. Inasmuch, then, as the action *in rem* may be brought in two different forms, (for proceedings are taken either by a petitory formula or by a sponsion); if the former course be adopted, that particular stipulation is employed which has the name *judicatum solvi* (that the award of the *judex* shall be paid[1]): but if the latter, that stipulation which is called *pro praede litis et vindiciarum*[2]. 92. A petitory formula is one in which the plaintiff claims the thing to be his own. 93. The mode of procedure by sponsion is as follows: we challenge our adversary in a sponsion running thus: "if the slave who is the subject of this action be mine in Quiritary right, do you engage to give me 25 sesterces?" Then we serve him with a formula, in the *in-*

[1] "Judicatum solvi stipulatio tres clausulas in unum collatas habet: de re judicata, de re defendenda, de dolo malo:" D. 46. 7. 6. The three objects at which the *stipulatio* aimed were these, (1) to secure payment of the award of the judex, the *litis aestimatio*, in case of non-restitution of the subject of the suit, the *lis:* (2) to secure the attendance of the defendant in court: (3) to prevent any acts being done by him to the detriment of the subject of the suit. The plaintiff, if successful, could of course sue on his judgment, by *pignoris capio* for instance; but it was more convenient to sue his opponent on his stipulation; and besides, the fact of there being sureties, multiplied the chances of obtaining adequate compensation.

[2] See IV. 16 and notes thereon: also IV. 94 and Cic. *in Verr.* II. 1. c. 45 with the commentary of Pseudo-Asconius on the passage (p. 191 ed. Orell.).

qua intendimus sponsionis summam nobis dari oportere. qua formula ita demum vincimus, si probaverimus rem nostram esse[1]. (94.) Non tamen haec summa sponsionis exigitur: nec enim poenalis est, sed praeiudicialis[2], et propter hoc solum fit, ut per eam de re iudicetur. unde etiam is cum quo agitur non restipulatur: ideo autem appellata est PRO PRAEDE LITIS VINDICIARUM stipulatio, quia in locum praedium successit[3]; quia olim,

tentio of which we assert that the amount of the sponsion is due to us: and under this formula we are victorious only on our proving that the thing is ours[1]. 94. The amount of this sponsion is not, however, exacted: for it is not penal but praejudicial[2], being introduced for the sole purpose of obtaining a decision on the main issue by its means. Hence it is that the defendant does not enter into a restipulation. This stipulation, again, is called *pro praede litis et vindiciarum*, because it was substituted for the *praedes* or sureties[3],

---

1 We see then that by this device the *actio in rem* directed against no one in particular, has been converted into an *actio in personam* against our opponent. We sue him for the amount of a wager; but whether he has won or lost that wager can only be decided by the court pronouncing its opinion on our claim of ownership.

2 "*Praejudicium*," says Zimmern, "in the language of practice, was not exactly a preliminary proceeding, in the same sense as *actio praejudicialis*, but a decision which might sooner or later be appealed to as a precedent." Zimmern's *Traité des actions chez les Romains*, § XCVI.

There is some difficulty at first sight in comprehending how his victory in the sponsion benefited the plaintiff. He had certainly gained his wager, but the real object of the suit was not the winning of a trifle such as 25 sesterces, but the securing of a transfer to him by his adversary of the lands in debate. He could not proceed on his judgment, for an *actio judicati* was not intended to transfer possession, and this was what his opponent now wrongfully withheld from him. Besides, although it had been decided that the field was his, the verdict he had obtained was one for 25 sesterces, and for the double of this alone could he have brought an *actio judicati*, if such action had been allowed him at all; but we know that it was expressly refused him, for says Gaius: "nec enim poenalis est summa sed praejudicialis." How then did he proceed? On the stipulation "pro praede litis et vindiciarum," for therein his adversary had bound himself by a verbal contract to let the lands, or their value, follow the judgment as to the wager. If then the lands were not delivered, he had a personal action on this stipulation, and could, in lieu of the lands, get their value, or possibly more than their value, as the amount secured would no doubt be such as to make it worth the defendant's while to give the lands rather than forfeit his bond.

3 See note on IV. 16.

cum lege agebatur, pro lite et vindiciis, id est pro re et fructibus, a possessore petitori dabantur praedes. (95.) Ceterum si aput centumviros agitur[1], summam sponsionis non per formulam petimus, sed per legis actionem: sacramento enim reus provocatur; eaque sponsio sestertiorum CXXV nummorum fit[2],
P.223 | scilicet propter legem Creperiam. (96.) Ipse autem qui in rem agit, si suo nomine agit, satis non dat. (97.) Ac nec si per cognitorem quidem agatur, ulla satisdatio vel ab ipso vel a domino desideratur. cum enim certis et quasi sollemnibus verbis[3] in locum domini substituatur cognitor, merito domini loco habetur. (98.) Procurator vero si agat, satisdare iubetur ratam rem dominum habiturum: periculum enim est, ne iterum dominus de eadem re experiatur[4]. quod periculum (non) inter-

for in olden times, when the proceedings were by *legis actio*, such *praedes* used to be assigned by the interim-possessor to the plaintiff, for the assuring of the *lis et vindiciae*, *i.e.* the thing itself and the profits thereof. 95. But when the action is tried before the *centumviri*[1] we do not sue for the amount of the sponsion by a formula, but by a *legis actio;* for we challenge the defendant by the sacramental wager; and the sponsion arising out of it is to the amount of 125 sesterces[2], according to the Lex Creperia. 96. In the case of an *actio in rem* the plaintiff, if suing in his own name, does not furnish sureties. 97. Nay, even though a suit be brought by means of a *cognitor*, no sureties are required either from him or from his principal. For since the *cognitor* is put into the place of the principal in words of a formal and almost solemn character[3], he is fairly regarded as occupying the position of the principal. 98. But when a *procurator* brings an action, he is ordered to furnish sureties that his principal will ratify his proceedings: for there is the risk that the principal may again sue for the same thing[4]. When the proceedings are conducted by

[1] IV. 31; App. (P).

[2] We are told in IV. 14 that the *sacramentum* was 500 *asses* (or sometimes 50). As a sesterce was worth 4 *asses*, the number 125 above is correct. The sesterce was originally 2½ *asses*, but in B.C. 217, when the weight of the *as* was reduced to one ounce, the sesterce was altered to 4 *asses*, so as to be still a quarter of a *denarius:* for the *denarius* in olden times was 10 *asses*, but after B.C. 217 was 16.

[3] IV. 83.

[4] Cicero treats the subject of *satisdatio* by *cognitores* and *procuratores* at some length in his oration *Pro Quinct.* c. 7, 8.

venit, si per cognitorem actum fuit; quia de qua re quisque per cognitorem egerit, de ea non magis amplius actionem habet quam si ipse egerit. (99.) Tutores et curatores eo modo quo et procuratores satisdare debere verba edicti faciunt. sed aliquando illis satisdatio remittitur. (100.) Haec ita si in rem agatur: si vero in personam, ab actoris quidem parte quando satisdari debeat quaerentes, eadem repetemus quae diximus in actione qua in rem agitur. (101.) Ab eius vero parte cum quo agitur, si quidem alieno nomine aliquis interveniat, omnimodo satisdari debet, quia nemo alienae rei sine satisdatione defensor idoneus intellegitur[1]. sed si quidem cum cognitore agatur, dominus satisdare iubetur; si vero cum procuratore, ipse procurator. idem et de tutore et de curatore iuris est. (102.) Quod si proprio nomine aliquis iudicium aliquid accipiat
P.224 | in personam, certis ex causis satisdari solet, quas ipse Praetor significat. quarum satisdationum duplex causa est. nam aut

means of a *cognitor* this risk does not exist, because when a man sues by such an agent, he no more has a second action than he would have if he himself sued. 99. According to the letter of the edict tutors and curators ought to furnish sureties in the same manner as *procurators;* but from this necessity of finding sureties they are sometimes excused. 100. The above are the rules when the action is *in rem*, but if it be *in personam*, what we have already stated with reference to the action *in rem* will be our conclusion, if we want to know when sureties ought to be furnished on the part of the plaintiff. 101. As to the case of a defendant,—when a man defends in another's name, sureties must always be furnished, because no one is considered competent to take up another's defence unless there be sureties[1]: but the furnishing thereof is laid on the principal, when the proceedings are against a *cognitor;* whilst if they be against a *procurator*, the *procurator* himself must provide them. The latter is also the rule applying to a tutor or curator. 102. On the other hand, if a man be defendant on his own account in any action *in personam*, he has to give sureties in certain cases wherein the Praetor has so directed. For such furnishing of sureties there are two reasons, as they are provided either on account

[1] D. 3. 3. 40. 2, D. 3. 3. 46. 2, D. 3. 3. 53, D. 46. 7. 10.

propter genus actionis satisdatur, aut propter personam, quia suspecta sit. propter genus actionis, velut iudicati depensive[1], aut cum de moribus mulieris agetur[2]: propter personam, velut si cum eo agitur qui decoxerit, cuiusve bona a creditoribus possessa proscriptave sunt, sive cum eo herede agatur quem Praetor suspectum aestimaverit[3].

103. Omnia autem iudicia aut legitimo iure consistunt aut imperio continentur[4]. (104.) Legitima sunt iudicia quae in urbe Roma vel intra primum urbis Romae miliarium inter omnes cives Romanos sub uno iudice accipiuntur: eaque e lege Iulia iudiciaria[5], nisi in anno et sex mensibus iudicata fuerint expirant. et hoc est quod vulgo dicitur, e lege Iulia litem anno et sex mensibus mori[6]. (105.) Imperio vero continentur recuperatoria[7] et quae sub uno iudice accipiuntur inter-

of the nature of the action, or on account of the untrustworthy character of the person. On account of the nature of the action, in such actions as those on a judgment or for money laid down by a *sponsor*[1] or that for immorality of a wife[2]; on account of the person, when the action is against one who is insolvent, or one whose goods have been taken possession of or advertised for sale by his creditors, or when the action is brought against an heir whose conduct the Praetor considers suspicious[3].

103. All proceedings before *judices* either rest on the statute law or are coexistent with the *imperium* of the Praetor[4]. 104. Of the former kind are those which are heard before a single *judex* in the city of Rome or within the first milestone from the city of Rome, all the parties whereto are Roman citizens: and these, according to the provisions of the Lex Julia Judiciaria[5], expire unless they have been decided within a year and six months. This is what is meant by the common saying, that a suit dies in a year and six months by the Lex Julia Judiciaria[6]. 105. In the other class are comprised proceedings before *recuperatores*[7], and those which are carried

[1] IV. 25.

[2] See Ulpian, VI. 12, 13.

[3] D. 42. 5. 31, D. 42. 5. 33. 1.

[4] III. 180, 181. For the meaning of *imperium*, see note there.

[5] Temp. Augusti.

[6] D. 46. 7. 2. From the following passages it will be seen that the suffering an action to die, if done wilfully, was sometimes equivalent to fraud or *dolus*, D. 4. 3. 18. 4 and D. 42. 8. 3. 1.

[7] *Recuperatores* were possibly, at their original institution, delegates

veniente peregrini persona iudicis aut litigatoris. in eadem causa sunt quaecumque extra primum urbis Romae miliarium tam inter cives Romanos quam inter peregrinos accipiuntur. ideo autem imperio contineri iudicia dicuntur, quia tamdiu valent, quamdiu is qui ea praecepit imperium habebit. (106.) Et siquidem imperio continenti iudicio actum fuerit, sive in rem
P.225 sive in personam, sive ea formula quae in fa|ctum concepta est sive ea quae in ius habet intentionem[1], postea nihilominus ipso iure de eadem re agi potest. et ideo necessaria est exceptio rei iudicatae vel in iudicium deductae[2]. (107.) At vero (si) legitimo iudicio in personam actum sit ea formula quae iuris civilis habet intentionem, postea ipso iure de eadem re agi non potest, et ob id exceptio supervacua est. si vero vel in rem vel

on before a single *judex*, when a foreigner is concerned either as *judex* or litigant. In the same category are all proceedings taken beyond the first milestone from the city of Rome, whether the parties in them be citizens or foreigners. These proceedings are said to be "coexistent with the *imperium*," because they are effectual only during such time as the Praetor who authorized them remains in office (retains his *imperium*). 106. If then the proceedings resorted to be "coexistent with the *imperium*," whether they be *in rem* or *in personam*, and whether they have a formula the *intentio* whereof is *in factum* or one whereof the *intentio* is *in jus*[1], another action may nevertheless according to the letter of the law be brought afterwards upon the same facts. And therefore there is need of the *exceptio rei judicatae* or the *exceptio in judicium deductae*[2]. 107. But if proceedings *in personam* by statutable action be taken under a formula which has a civil law *intentio*, by the letter of the law there cannot be a second action on the same facts, and therefore the *exceptio* is superfluous. But if the action be

chosen from two nations at variance as to some right or question, to act as umpires and arrange the dispute amicably. Hence the name was subsequently applied to persons who had a function analogous to that of a *judex* in cases where foreigners were concerned. In accordance with the original notion of their being delegates chosen by different parties, they would in all cases be more than one in number; and so the name came to be applied to others who sat (two or more together) to decide cases connected with the *jus gentium*, even when both parties were Roman citizens. See note on I. 20. Also read Beaufort's *Rep. Rom.* V. 2.

[1] IV. 45, App. (S).

[2] III. 181, App. (T).

in factum actum fuerit, ipso iure nihilominus postea agi potest[1], et ob id exceptio necessaria est rei iudicatae vel in iudicium deductae. (108.) Alia causa fuit olim legis actionum. nam qua de re actum semel erat, de ea postea ipso iure agi non poterat: nec omnino ita, ut nunc, usus erat illis temporibus exceptionum. (109.) Ceterum potest ex lege quidem esse iudicium, sed legitimum non esse; et contra ex lege non esse, sed legitimum esse. nam si verbi gratia ex lege Aquilia[2] vel Ollinia[3] vel Furia[4] in provinciis agatur, imperio continebitur iudicium: idemque iuris est et si Romae aput recuperatores agamus[5], vel aput unum iudicem interveniente peregrini per-

in rem, or *in factum*, another action may nevertheless according to the letter of the law[1] be afterwards brought upon the same facts, and therefore the *exceptio rei judicatae* or that *in judicium deductae* is necessary. 108. In olden times the case was different with the *legis actiones*, for when once an action had been tried about any matter, there could not according to the letter of the law be another action on the same facts: and there was not any employment at all of *exceptiones*, as there is now. 109. Further, an action may be derived from a *lex* and yet not be "statutable," and, conversely, it may not be derived from a *lex* and yet be "statutable." For if, to take an example, an action be brought in the provinces under the Lex Aquilia[2] or Ollinia[3] or Furia[4] the action will be one "coexistent with the *imperium*:" and the rule is the same if we bring an action at Rome before *recuperatores*[5], or before one *judex* when there is a foreigner connected with the

[1] An obligation is said to be destroyed *ipso jure* in two cases; firstly when there had already been a judgment in a *legitimum judicium*, in which cases the Praetor will grant no formula for a second action; and this is the case dealt with here: secondly, when there had been no action, but a payment real or fictitious (*solutio* or *acceptilatio*), had taken place. A formula would then be granted, and the defendant would not apply for the insertion of an *exceptio*, pleading, as it were, a general issue, and establishing his defence *in judicio* by proof of the payment: this latter case is, however, foreign to the topic Gaius is here discussing. See *Thémis*, VI. p. 413.

[2] III. 210.

[3] Nothing is known about this law.

[4] The *Lex Furia de Sponsu*; for this *lex* is stated in III. 121 to be applicable to Italy only as a matter of course; and therefore if carried into effect in a province must have been a title in the edict of the *praeses* of that province, and so not "statutable," but "coexistent with the *imperium*."

[5] See note on I. 20, IV. 105.

sona[1]. et ex diverso si ex ea causa, ex qua nobis edicto Praetoris datur actio, Romae sub uno iudice inter omnes cives Romanos accipiatur iudicium, legitimum est.

110. Quo loco admonendi sumus eas quidem actiones quae ex lege senatusve consultis proficiscuntur perpetuo[2] solere Prae-
P.226 torem accommodare: | eas vero quae ex propria ipsius iurisdictione pendent plerumque intra annum dare. (111.) Aliquando tamen *has quoque perpetuo dat*[3] *scilicet cum* imitatur ius legitimum: quales sunt eae quas *bonorum possessoribus*[4] ceterisque qui heredis loco sunt *accommodat.* furti quoque manifesti actio[5], quamvis ex ipsius Praetoris iurisdictione proficiscatur, perpetuo

suit[1]. So, conversely, if in a case where an action is granted under the Praetor's edict the trial be at Rome before a single *judex*, and all the parties be Roman citizens, the action is "statutable."

110. At this point we must be reminded that the Praetor's practice is to grant at any time[2] those actions which arise from a *lex* or from *senatusconsulta*, but in general to grant those which spring from his own special jurisdiction only within one year. 111. Sometimes, however, he grants these also after any length of time[3], that is to say, when he follows the precedent of the statutable actions: for instance, in those actions which he provides for *bonorum possessores*[4] and others who occupy the position of heir. The action of manifest theft[5] also, though issuing from the jurisdiction of the Praetor himself, is granted at any time; and very properly, since the Praetor's

---

[1] Either as *judex* or litigant; see IV. 105.

[2] The Praetor granted these actions any length of time after the ground of action arose: the others he only allowed to be brought if the formula were applied for within one year. It is very likely that the rule originally was that they could only be applied for whilst the same Praetor was in office, whose year had witnessed the offence; but subsequently the space of time was a definite one, and irrespective of the possible retirement of one Praetor and succession of another. After the time of Theodosius *perpetuum* came to have a restricted meaning, and a *perpetua actio* was one which could be brought within 30, or in some cases 40 years, and no action thenceforward was actually "perpetual."

[3] The words *has quoque perpetuo dat* are supplied by Huschke, who adds to them *velut quibus*. Mommsen prefers *scilicet cum*. Neither of their suggestions accord with the traces in the MS.; but they, doubtless, express Gaius' intention.

[4] III. 32, IV. 34.

[5] III. 189.

datur; et merito, cum pro capitali poena pecuniaria constituta sit[1].

112. Non omnes actiones quae in aliquem aut ipso iure competunt aut a Praetore dantur, etiam in heredem aeque conpetunt aut dari solent. est enim certissima iuris regula, ex maleficiis poenales actiones in heredem nec conpetere nec dari solere, velut furti, vi bonorum raptorum, iniuriarum, damni iniuriae[2]: sed heredibus quidem, videlicet actoris, huiusmodi actiones competunt nec denegantur, excepta iniuriarum actione[3], et si qua alia similis inveniatur actio. (113.) Aliquando tamen ex contractu actio neque heredi neque in heredem

pecuniary penalty has been imposed instead of the capital penalty (of the Twelve Tables[1]).

112. Not every action which is either maintainable by strict law or granted by the Praetor against any one, is equally maintainable or granted against his heir. For there is a firmly-established rule of law that penal actions on delicts do not lie against the heir (of the offender), nor will usually be granted, for instance, the actions of theft, of robbery, of injury, of wrongful damage[2]: but actions of this kind lie for the heir of the same (*i.e.* of the plaintiff), and are not refused to him, except the action of injury[3] and any other action that can be shown to resemble it. 113. Sometimes, however, even an action on a contract does not lie for or against the heir of a party: for the

[1] From D. 44. 7. 35 we obtain the general rule that Praetorian actions for restitution were perpetual, those for a penalty annual. Also that annual actions did not lie against the heir of the delinquent, except to such extent as he had benefited by the wrong. The penal action for theft was an exception as to duration, but if brought against the heir, was only for the amount of his profit. However, with this limitation it was for restitution only, and so the rule still applies.

[2] III. 182—223.

[3] The reason for this is that the *actio injuriarum* was regarded by the Roman law as a purely personal remedy; "the heir had suffered no wrong," says Ulpian, in D. 47. 10. 13. pr., and Paulus, referring to a similar case, says the original action is "vindictae non pecuniae," D. 37. 6. 2. 4. But we learn from the passage of Ulpian just quoted, that if the proceedings had reached the *litis contestatio* in the life-time of the aggrieved party, they could be continued by his heir.

Other actions of like kind are those of a *patronus* against a *libertus* who has sued him without the Praetor's leave, D. 2. 4. 24; those against a man who has by violence prevented the serving of a summons, D. 2. 7. 5. 4; those against *calumniatores*, D. 3. 6. 4, &c. &c.

conpetit. nam adstipulatoris heres non habet actionem[1], et sponsoris et fide promissoris heres non tenetur[2].

114. Superest ut dispiciamus, si ante rem iudicatam is cum quo agitur post acceptum iudicium satisfaciat actori, quid officio iudicis conveniat: utrum absolvere, an ideo potius damnare, quia iudicii accipiendi tempore in ea causa fuit, ut damnari debeat[3]. nostri praeceptores absolvere eum debere
P.227 existimant: nec interesse cuius generis sit iudicium[4]. et | hoc est quod volgo dicitur Sabino et Cassio placere omnia iudicia absolutoria esse. *aliter de stricti iuris iudiciis diversae scholae auctores*[5], de bonae fidei iudiciis autem idem sentiunt quia in eiusmodi iudiciis liberum est officium iudicis. tantumdem etiam de in rem actionibus putant, quia formulae verbis id ipsum exprimatur[6].—[*desunt* 17 *lin.*].

heir of an *adstipulator* has no action[1], and the heir of a *sponsor* or *fidepromissor*[2] is not bound.

114. The next point for our consideration is this: supposing after the matter has been submitted to the *judex*, but before award, the defendant make satisfaction to the plaintiff, what is the duty of the *judex?* Ought he to acquit, or rather to condemn him, because at the time when the matter came before the *judex* he was in such a plight that he ought to be condemned[3]. Our authorities hold that the *judex* ought to acquit him: and say that the nature of the action[4] is a matter of no importance. And hence comes the common saying, that Sabinus and Cassius held "that all issues before a *judex* allow of acquittal." The authorities of the opposite school hold a different opinion with regard to *stricti juris* actions[5], but hold the same opinion with regard to actions *bonae fidei*, because in these the discretion of the *judex* is unfettered. With regard to actions *in rem* they think the same, because this very point is expressed in the words of the *formula*[6]...

---

1 III. 114.

2 III. 120.

3 His own admission, evidenced by his coming to terms, shows that he was deserving of condemnation.

4 Sc. whether it be *stricti juris* or *bonae fidei*. Justinian agreed with the Sabinians, *Inst.* IV. 12. 2.

5 These words in italics are suggestions of Krüger and Studemund.

6 These words also are suggested by Krüger and Studemund.

115. Sequitur ut de exceptionibus dispiciamus[1]. (116.)
P.228 Conparatae | sunt autem exceptiones defendendorum reorum gratia cum quibus agitur: saepe enim accidit ut quis iure civili teneatur, sed iniquum sit eum iudicio condemnari[2]: velut si stipulatus sim a te pecuniam tamquam credendi causa numeraturus, nec numeraverim; nam eam pecuniam a te peti posse certum est; dare enim te oportet, cum ex stipulatu teneris: sed quia iniquum est te eo nomine condemnari, placet per exceptionem doli mali te defendi debere. item si pactus fuero tecum, NE ID QUOD MIHI DEBEAS A TE PETAM, nihilominus

115. The next matter for our consideration is that of exceptions[1]. 116. Exceptions then are provided for the purpose of protecting defendants against whom suits are brought: for it frequently happens that a man is liable according to the civil law, and yet it would be inequitable that he should be condemned in the suit[2]: for instance, if I have stipulated for money from you on the pretence that I am about to advance you a loan, and then do not so advance it. In such a case it is clear that a suit for the money can be brought against you: for it is your duty to pay it, since you are bound by the stipulation: but as it is inequitable that you should be condemned on account thereof, it is held that you must be defended by the exception of fraud. So also, if I have made a pact with you "not to sue you for that which you owe to me," I can nevertheless claim that very thing from you by the formula "that you ought to give me it," because the obligation is not removed

[1] A defendant might reply to the plaintiff's demand in three different ways: (1) by a denial of the facts alleged, which is styled by later writers *litis contestatio mere negativa:* (2) by asserting facts which destroyed the right of action *ipso jure*, although that might originally have been well-founded, such facts for instance as payment real or fictitious (*solutio* or *acceptilatio*); of such replies the *judex* as a matter of course took notice, without any express direction in the *formula* that he should do so: (3) by asserting facts which did not destroy the right of action *ipso jure*, but on account of which the Praetor allowed a defence, *quia iniquum foret eum condemnari*; and of these the *judex* could take no notice (except in actions *ex fide bona*), unless the cognizance of them was by the *formula* expressly given to him. Such facts, included in a *formula* by means of a special clause, were *exceptiones*. See Mackeldey, *Syst. Jur. Rom.* § 200 *a.* p. 206. Exceptions then were equitable defences, creatures of the formulary system, and not in existence during the period of the *legis actiones*.

[2] See Cic. *de Invent.* II. 19, 20; *de Off.* III. 14, 15, "Cum ex eo quaereretur Quid esset dolus malus? respondebat, Cum esset aliud simulatum, aliud actum."

id ipsum a te petere possum DARI MIHI OPORTERE, quia obligatio pacto convento non tollitur: sed placet debere me petentem per exceptionem pacti conventi repelli[1]. (117.) In his quoque actionibus quae (non) in personam sunt exceptiones locum habent, velut si metu me coegeris aut dolo induxeris, ut tibi rem aliquam mancipio dem; nam si eam rem a me petas datur mihi exceptio per quam, si metus causa te fecisse vel dolo malo arguero, repelleris. item si fundum litigiosum sciens a non possidente emeris eumque a possidente petas, opponitur tibi exceptio, per quam omnimodo summoveris[2]. (118.) Exceptiones autem alias in edicto Praetor habet propositas, alias causa cognita accommodat. quae omnes vel ex legibus vel ex his quae legis vicem optinent substantiam capiunt, vel ex iurisdictione Praetoris proditae sunt.|

P.229 119. Omnes autem exceptiones in contrarium concipiuntur, quam adfirmat is cum quo agitur. nam si verbi gratia reus

by the agreement made between us; but it is held that I ought, if I sue, to be repelled by the exception of agreement made[1]. 117. Exceptions are also resorted to in actions which are not *in personam*, as for example if you have compelled me by fear, or induced me by fraud, that I am to give you something by mancipation; for if you sue me for that thing, an exception is granted me, by which you will be defeated if I prove that you acted with the intent of causing fear or with fraud. Again, if you have with knowledge purchased from a non-possessor an estate which is a subject of suit, and seek to get it from the possessor, an exception is opposed to you by which you will be completely defeated[2]. 118. Some exceptions are published by the Praetor in his edict, some he grants on cause being shown: but all of them are founded either on *leges* or enactments having the force of *leges*, or else are derived from his own jurisdiction.

119. Now all exceptions are worded in the negative of the defendant's affirmation. For if, to take an instance, the de-

1 See note on III. 89.

2 From a passage in the *Fragmenta de Jure Fisci*, § 8, it would appear that it was a somewhat serious offence to purchase a *res litigiosa*, for by an edict of Augustus a penalty of 50 sestertia was imposed, besides the bargain being declared void. See on the same subject D. 44. 6. 1 and D. 20. 3. 1. 1.

dolo malo aliquid actorem facere dicat, qui forte pecuniam petit quam non numeravit[1], sic exceptio concipitur: SI IN EA RE NIHIL DOLO MALO AULI AGERII FACTUM SIT NEQUE FIAT. item si dicat contra pactionem pecuniam peti, ita concipitur exceptio: SI INTER AULUM AGERIUM ET NUMERIUM NEGIDIUM NON CONVENIT NE EA PECUNIA PETERETUR. et denique in ceteris causis similiter concipi solet. ideo scilicet, quia omnis exceptio obicitur quidem a reo, sed ita formulae inseritur ut condicionalem faciat condemnationem, id est ne aliter iudex eum cum quo agitur condemnet, quam si nihil in ea re qua de agitur dolo actoris factum sit; item ne aliter iudex eum condemnet, quam si nullum pactum conventum de non petenda pecunia factum fuerit.

120. Dicuntur autem exceptiones aut peremptoriae aut dilatoriae. (121.) Peremptoriae sunt quae perpetuo valent, nec evitari possunt, velut quod metus causa, aut dolo malo[2],

fendant assert that the plaintiff is doing something fraudulently, suing, for example, for money which he has never paid over[1], the exception is worded thus: "if nothing has been done or is being done in this matter fraudulently on the part of Aulus Agerius." Again, if it be alleged that money is sued for contrary to agreement, the exception is thus drawn: "if it has not been agreed between Aulus Agerius and Numerius Negidius that that money shall not be sued for:" and, in a word, there is a similar mode of drawing in all other cases. The reason of this is, no doubt, because every exception is put in by the defendant, but added to the formula in such manner as to make the *condemnatio* conditional, *i. e.* that the *judex* is not to condemn the defendant unless nothing have been done fraudulently on the part of the plaintiff in the matter in question; or again that the *judex* is not to condemn him unless no agreement have been made that the money should not be sued for.

120. Exceptions are said to be either peremptory or dilatory. 121. Those are peremptory which are available at all times, and which cannot be avoided, for example the exception of intimidation, or of fraud[2], or that something has been done

[1] IV. 116.

[2] D. 4. 2. 14. 1. The penalty for intimidation, if pursued by *action*, was fourfold damages within the

aut quod contra legem senatusve consultum factum est, aut quod res iudicata est, vel in iudicium deducta est[1], item pacti conventi quo pactum est ne omnino pecunia peteretur. (122.) Dilatoriae sunt exceptiones quae ad tempus valent, veluti illius pacti conventi quod factum est verbi gratia ne intra
P.230 quinquennium peteretur: finito enim eo tempore | non habet locum exceptio. cui similis exceptio est litis dividuae et rei residuae. nam si quis partem rei petierit et intra eiusdem praeturam reliquam partem petat, hac exceptione summovetur quae appellatur litis dividuae[2]. item si is qui cum eodem plures lites habebat, de quibusdam egerit, de quibusdam distulerit, ut ad alios iudices eant, si intra eiusdem praeturam de his quas distulerit agat, per hanc exceptionem quae appellatur rei residuae summovetur. (123.) Observandum est autem ei cui dilatoria obicitur exceptio, ut differat actionem: alioquin

contrary to a *lex* or *senatus-consultum*, or that the matter has been already adjudicated upon, or laid before a *judex*[1], and so also that an agreement has been made that the money should not be sued for under any circumstances. 122. Dilatory exceptions are those which are good defences for a certain time only, as that of an agreement having been made to the effect that money should not be sued for, say, within five years; for on the expiration of that time the exception is no longer available. Similar to this is the exception *litis dividuae*, and that *rei residuae*. For if a person have brought his action for a part of the thing claimed, and then sue for the remainder within the time of office of the same Praetor, he is met by the exception styled *litis dividuae*[2]. And so too, if he who had several suits against the same defendant, have brought some and postponed others, in order that they may go before other *judices*, and then pursue those which he had postponed within the time of office of the same Praetor, he is met by the exception called *rei residuae*. 123. He then against whom a dilatory exception has been pleaded ought to be careful to put

year, simple damages afterwards.

The *action* for fraud could be brought within the year for the recovery of the loss sustained by the plaintiff; after the year there was only an *actio in factum* to receive from the defendant his gain.

[1] IV. 106, App. (T).

[2] IV. 56.

si obiecta exceptione egerit, rem perdit: nec enim post illud tempus quo integra re evitare poterat, adhuc ei potestas agendi superest, re in iudicium deducta et per exceptionem perempta[1]. (124.) Non solum autem ex tempore, sed etiam ex persona dilatoriae exceptiones intelleguntur, quales sunt cognitoriae; velut si is qui per edictum cognitorem dare non potest[2] per cognitorem agat, vel dandi quidem cognitoris ius habeat, sed eum det cui non licet cognituram suscipere. nam si obiciatur exceptio cognitoria, si ipse talis erat ut ei non liceat cognitorem dare, ipse agere potest: si vero cognitori non liceat cognituram suscipere, per alium cognitorem aut per semet ipsum liberam habet agendi potestatem, et tam hoc quam illo modo
P.231 evitare exceptionem. quod si dissi|mulaverit eam[3] et per cognitorem egerit, rem perdit. (125.) Sed peremptoria quidem

off his action: for otherwise, if he go on with his action after the exception has been pleaded, he will lose the cause: for not even after the time when he could have avoided it, if no prior proceedings had been taken, has he any longer a right of action surviving, when the matter has once been laid before a *judex* and overthrown by the exception[1]. 124. Exceptions are dilatory not only in relation to time, but also in relation to the person; of which latter kind are cognitory exceptions; as in the case of a person who, though incapacitated by the edict from nominating a *cognitor*[2], nevertheless employs one to carry on an action, or in that of a person who has the right of nominating a *cognitor*, but nominates one who is unfit for the office: for if the cognitory exception be pleaded, then, supposing the principal to be disqualified from nominating a *cognitor*, he can in person carry on the action; whilst if the *cognitor* be disqualified from undertaking the office, the principal has free choice of suing either by means of another *cognitor* or in person; and he can by either of these modes avoid the exception; but if he treat the exception with contempt[3] and sue by the first *cognitor*, he loses his case. 125. When, however, the defendant

---

1 III. 180, IV. 131.

2 IV. 83.

3 This is not the ordinary meaning of *dissimulare*, but that it here bears the sense we have assigned to it is obvious by reference to Theophilus (I. 1), who (evidently translating this sentence) writes: εἰ δὲ ὁ ἄκτωρ καταφρονήσει τῆς τοιαύτης παραγραφῆς.

exceptione si reus per errorem non fuerit usus, in integrum restituitur[1] adiciendae exceptionis gratia: dilatoria vero si non fuerit usus, an in integrum restituatur, quaeritur.

126. Interdum evenit, ut exceptio quae prima facie iusta videatur, inique noceat actori. quod cum accidat, alia adiectione opus est adiuvandi actoris gratia: quae adiectio replicatio vocatur, quia per eam replicatur atque resolvitur vis exceptionis. nam si verbi gratia pactus sum tecum, ne pecuniam quam mihi debes a te peterem, deinde postea in contrarium pacti sumus, id est ut petere mihi liceat, et si agam tecum, excipias tu, ut ita demum mihi condemneris, SI NON CONVENERIT NE EAM PECUNIAM PETEREM, nocet mihi exceptio pacti conventi; namque nihilominus hoc verum manet, etiam si postea in contrarium pacti sumus. sed quia iniquum est me excludi exceptione, replicatio mihi datur ex posteriore pacto hoc modo: SI NON POSTEA CONVENERIT[2] UT MIHI EAM PECUNIAM PETERE

has through some error not availed himself of a peremptory exception, he is restored to his former position[1] in order that the exception may be introduced: but if he have omitted to use a dilatory exception, it is doubtful whether he can be so restored.

126. It sometimes happens that an exception, which at first sight appears just, unfairly prejudices the plaintiff. When this occurs, another addition (to the formula) is needed to relieve the plaintiff, and this is called a replication, because by means of it the effect of the exception is rolled back again and untied. Thus, for example, supposing I have agreed with you not to sue you for money you owe to me, and that afterwards we make an opposite agreement, *i.e.* that I may sue you: then should I bring my action, and should you meet me with an exception that you ought to be condemned to pay me "if there have been no agreement that I should not sue for the money," this exception of agreement made is to my prejudice; for the agreement is a matter of fact, even though we have since agreed to the contrary. But as it would be unjust for me to be kept out of my rights by the exception, a replication is allowed me on the ground of the subsequent agreement, thus: "if it have not[2]

[1] *i.e.* is allowed a new trial. See note on IV. 53.

[2] We might have expected the replication to be worded: "if it *have*

LICERET. item si argentarius pretium rei quae in auctione venierit persequatur, obicitur ei exceptio, ut ita demum emptor damnetur, SI EI RES QUAM EMERIT TRADITA EST: et est iusta exceptio[1]. sed si in auctione praedictum est, ne ante emptori
P.232 traderetur quam si pretium solverit, replicatione | tali argentarius adiuvatur: AUT SI PRAEDICTUM EST NE ALITER EMPTORI RES TRADERETUR QUAM SI PRETIUM EMPTOR SOLVERIT. (127.) Interdum autem evenit, ut rursus replicatio quae prima facie iusta sit, inique reo noceat. quod cum accidat, adiectione opus est adiuvandi rei gratia, quae duplicatio vocatur. (128.) Et si rursus ea prima facie iusta videatur, sed propter aliquam causam inique actori noceat, rursus adiectione opus est qua actor adiuvetur, quae dicitur triplicatio. (129.) Quarum om-

been subsequently agreed that I may sue for the money." Again suppose a banker seeks to recover the price of a thing which has been sold at auction, and the exception is raised against him, that the purchaser is to be condemned to pay only "if the thing which he purchased has been delivered:" this is a good exception[1]; but if at the auction it has been stated at the outset that the thing is not to be delivered to the purchaser until he pay the price, the banker is relieved by a replication to the following effect: "or if it were announced at the outset that the thing was not to be delivered to the purchaser unless the purchaser paid the price." 127. But sometimes it happens that a replication in its turn, which at first sight is a fair one, presses unduly on the defendant: and when this occurs there is need of an addition (to the formula) for the purpose of assisting the defendant; which is called a duplication. 128. And if again this appear at first sight fair, but for some reason or other press unduly on the plaintiff, another addition is needed for the relief of the plaintiff; which is called a triplication. 129. The variety of

been subsequently, &c.," but the negative in the exception runs through all the succeeding sentences of the formula, and so a double negative is needed in the replication: the defendant is to be condemned when there "has not not been," i.e. when there has been, an agreement subsequent to, and in contradiction of the first agreement.

[1] The general rule is that goods need not be paid for till delivery is made, but a special agreement to the contrary is valid, as the text states.

nium adiectionum usum interdum etiam ulterius quam diximus varietas negotiorum introduxit.

130. Videamus etiam de praescriptionibus quae receptae sunt pro actore[1]. (131.) Saepe enim ex una eademque obligatione aliquid iam praestari oportet, aliquid in futura praestatione est: velut cum in singulos annos vel menses certam pecuniam stipulati fuerimus: nam finitis quibusdam annis aut mensibus, huius quidem temporis pecuniam praestari oportet, futurorum autem annorum sane quidem obligatio contracta intellegitur, praestatio vero adhuc nulla est. si ergo velimus id quidem quod praestari oportet petere et in iudicium deducere, futuram vero obligationis praestationem in integro relinquere, necesse est ut cum hac praescriptione agamus: EA RES AGATUR CUIUS REI DIES FUIT. alioquin si sine hac praescrip-

business transactions has caused the use of all these additions to be extended in some cases even beyond what we have specified.

130. Now let us consider the subject of the *praescriptiones* which are employed for the benefit of the plaintiff[1]. 131. For it often happens that in consequence of one and the same obligation there is something to be paid or done at once, and something at a future time: for instance, when we have stipulated for the payment of a certain sum of money every year or every month: for then on the termination of a certain number of years or months, there is a present obligation that the money for that period shall be paid, whilst as to the future years there is undoubtedly an obligation contracted, but as yet there is no necessity for payment. If, therefore, we wish to sue for the sum actually due and to lay the matter before a *judex*, leaving the future discharge of the obligation as it was, we must commence our action with this praescription: "Let that amount which is already due be the matter of suit." Otherwise, if we have pro-

[1] See App. (S).

"Omnis autem in quaerendo, quae viâ quadam et ratione habetur, oratio praescribere primum debet (ut quibusdam in formulis, *Ea res agatur*) ut inter quos disseritur conveniat, quid sit id de quo disseratur." Cic. *de Fin.* II. 1.

In *De Orat.* I. 37 Cicero ridicules a lawyer who had claimed the benefit of a *praescriptio* for his client, the defendant in a suit. Cicero calls it indeed an *exceptio*, but it is evident that he uses the term as synonymous with *praescriptio;* for he gives the wording "cujus pecuniae dies fuisset," a well-known praescriptive form.

P.233 tione egerimus, ea scilicet formula qua incertum petimus, | cuius intentio his verbis concepta est: QUIDQUID PARET NUMERIUM NEGIDIUM AULO AGERIO DARE FACERE OPORTERE, totam obligationem, id est etiam futuram in hoc iudicium deducimus[1], et quae ante tempus obligatio (*in iudicium deducitur, ea neque in condemnationem venit, neque postea rursus de ea agi potest*[2]). item si verbi gratia ex empto agamus, ut nobis fundus mancipio detur, debemus ita praescribere: EA RES AGATUR DE FUNDO MANCIPANDO: ut postea, si velimus vacuam possessionem nobis tradi, de tradenda (*ea vel ex stipulatu vel ex empto agere possimus. nam si obliti sic praescribere*) sumus, totius illius iuris obligatio illa incerta actione: QUIDQUID OB EAM REM NUMERIUM NEGIDIUM

ceeded without this praescription, that is, by the formula through which we sue for an uncertain sum, and the intention of which runs: "Whatever it appears that Numerius Negidius ought to give or do to Aulus Agerius;" we have included in this reference to a *judex* the whole obligation, *i.e.* even the future part of it[1]; and the obligation which is brought into court before it is exigible, cannot be included in the award, and cannot afterwards be sued for[2]. Suppose again, as another example, that we bring a suit on a purchase, for the purpose of having an estate transferred to us by mancipation; we ought to prefix this praescription: "Let the question before the court be the transfer of the land by mancipation;" so that if we subsequently desire to have the possession vacated and transferred to us, we may be able to sue for delivery either upon a stipulation or upon a purchase. For if we have forgotten so to prescribe, the binding force of the whole engagement is destroyed by the *litis contestatio* in the uncertain action: "Whatever Nu-

[1] The *litis contestatio* has worked a novation (III. 180), the original contract is transmuted into an obligation to pay the award of the court, and the court can only award the amount presently due.

It is not known why the rule was established that a formula "*quicquid dare facere oportet*" should include future as well as present undertakings: it was not so in stipulations, as we see from D. 45. 1. 76. 1. "Cum stipulamur: *quidquid te dare facere oportet*, id dumtaxat quod praesenti die debetur in stipulationem deducitur, non ut in judiciis etiam futurum: et ideo in stipulatione adicitur verbum: *oportebit*, vel ita *praesens in diemve;* hoc ideo fit, &c." This passage is reconstructed in the main according to Huschke's views.

[2] These words are suggested by Mommsen, and, no doubt, express the sense of the passage: but they do not agree with the traces in the MS.

AULO AGERIO DARE FACERE OPORTET, (*per litis contesta*)tionem consumitur, ut postea nobis agere volentibus de vacua possessione tradenda nulla supersit actio. (132.) Praescriptiones sic appellatas esse ab eo, quod ante formulas praescribuntur plus quam manifestum est.

133. Sed his quidem temporibus, sicut supra quoque notavimus[1], omnes praescriptiones ab actore proficiscuntur: olim autem quaedam et pro reo opponebantur: qualis illa erat praescriptio: EA RES AGATUR: SI IN EA RE PRAEIUDICIUM HEREDITATI NON FIAT: quae nunc in speciem exceptionis deducta est, et locum habet cum petitor hereditatis alio genere iudicii praeiudicium hereditati faciat, velut cum singulas res pet*at; esset* enim
P.234 iniquum per unius *partis*|*petitionem*[2] *maiori quaestioni de ipsa here-*
P.235 *ditate praeiudicari.* (*desunt* 24 *lin.*) *Deinde inten*|tione formulae
det*erminatum* est cui dari oportet; et sane domino dari oportet

merius Negidius ought to give or do to Aulus Agerius;" so that if we subsequently desire to bring an action for the vacation and delivery of the possession, no action will lie for us. 132. That praescriptions have their name from the fact of their being prefixed to formulae is more than evident.

133. At the present day, as we have also stated above[1], all praescriptions proceed from the plaintiff, but in olden times some of them were set up for the defendant's benefit. Such was the praescription which ran thus: "Let this be the question tried: provided only that there be thereby no prior decision as to the inheritance:" but this is now thrown into the form of an exception, and is resorted to when the claimant of an inheritance takes in some other way proceedings which affect the question of inheritance, for instance, when he brings a suit for individual portions of it; for it would be unfair to allow the more important question as to the inheritance itself to be prejudged by the petitory suit[2] for a particular part thereof....Then in the intention of the formula the person is specified to whom the payment ought to be made: and obviously it is the master to whom the subject of the slave's stipulation ought to be given.

---

[1] IV. 130. [2] IV. 92.

quod servus stipulatur. at in praescriptione de facto[1] quaeritur quod secundum naturalem significationem verum esse debet[2]. (135.) Quaecumque autem diximus de servis, eadem de ceteris quoque personis quae nostro iuri subiectae sunt dicta intellegemus. (136.) Item admonendi sumus, si cum ipso agamus qui incertum promiserit, ita nobis formulam esse propositam[3], ut praescriptio inserta sit formulae loco demonstrationis, hoc modo: IUDEX ESTO. QUOD AULUS AGERIUS DE NUMERIO NEGIDIO INCERTUM STIPULATUS EST, MODO CUIUS REI DIES FUIT, QUIDQUID OB EAM REM NUMERIUM NEGIDIUM AULO AGERIO DARE FACERE OPORTET et reliqua. (137.) Si cum sponsore aut fideiussore agatur[4], praescribi solet in persona quidem sponsoris hoc modo: EA RES AGATUR, QUOD AULUS AGERIUS DE LUCIO TITIO INCERTUM STIPULATUS EST, QUO NOMINE NUMERIUS NEGIDIUS

But it is in the praescription that the question as to the fact[1] is raised, which ought to be correctly stated[2] according to its actual purport. 135. All that we have said about slaves we shall understand to apply also to other persons who are subject to our authority. 136. We must also be reminded that if we sue the very person who has promised us a thing of uncertain value, our formula is so set forth[3] that in it a praescription is inserted in the *formula* and included in the demonstration, thus: "Let so and so be *judex*. Inasmuch as Aulus Agerius stipulated for something uncertain from Numerius Negidius; whatever in respect thereof, but only in respect of that part which is already due, Numerius Negidius ought to give or do to Aulus Agerius, &c." 137. If an action be brought against a *sponsor* or *fidejussor*[4], there is usually in the case of a *sponsor* a praescription in this form: "Let the subject of the action be the amount now due from the fact that Aulus Agerius stipulated for something uncertain from Lucius Titius, in respect whereof

1 The MS. has clearly *pacto:* but Savigny suggested *facto*, and this correction has been almost universally accepted.

2 This is Heffter's explanation of *verum:* see his note *ad locum*. In the praescription, therefore, what really took place between the stipulating parties is to be described, and the name of the slave to be given. This transaction having been examined and its real nature established, the owner of the slave is thereupon in a position to claim the money as plaintiff, for as soon as his slave's claim has been made out, he has the benefit of it.

3 Sc. in the Praetor's Edict.

4 III. 115.

SPONSOR EST, CUIUS REI DIES FUIT; in persona vero fideiussoris: EA RES AGATUR, QUOD NUMERIUS NEGIDIUS PRO LUCIO TITIO INCERTUM FIDE SUA ESSE IUSSIT, CUIUS REI DIES FUIT; deinde formula subicitur.

138. Superest ut de interdictis dispiciamus. (139.) Certis igitur ex causis Praetor aut Proconsul principaliter auctoritatem suam finiendis controversiis interponit; quod tum maxime facit cum de possessione aut quasi possessione[1] inter aliquos contenditur; et in summa aut iubet aliquid fieri, aut fieri prohibet. P.236 formulae autem verborum et conceptiones quibus in | ea re utitur interdicta decretaque vocantur. (140.) (Vocantur) autem decreta cum fieri aliquid iubet, velut cum praecipit ut aliquid exhibeatur aut restituatur: interdicta vero cum prohibet fieri, velut cum praecipit: NE SINE VITIO[2] POSSIDENTI VIS FIAT,

Numerius Negidius was *sponsor*, &c.;" and in the case of a *fidejussor:* "Let the subject of the action be the amount now due from the fact that Numerius Negidius became *fidejussor* in an unascertained sum for Lucius Titius, &c." Then follows the formula.

138. We now have to discuss the subject of interdicts. 139. In certain cases then the Praetor or Proconsul interposes his authority at the outset to bring disputes to a conclusion: and this he does more particularly in suits about possession or quasi-possession[1], summarily ordering something to be done or forbidding it to be done. The forms of words which he employs for this purpose we call interdicts or decrees. 140. They are called decrees when he orders something to be done, as when he directs that a thing shall be produced in court or be delivered up. They are called interdicts when he prohibits a thing being done, for instance, when he directs "that no violence be done to one who is in possession innocently[2]," or "that something be not done on

[1] Possession proper can only exist with reference to corporeal things: the possession of an incorporeal thing, a right, such as usufruct, is no true possession, and yet has many of the essentials of true possession, and is protected by interdicts. Quasi-possession is the term applied to the exercise of such rights, and the nature of it is fully treated of in Savigny's *Treatise on Possession* (Perry's translation), pp. 130—134.

[2] *Sine vitio = neque vi, neque clam,*

NEVE IN LOCO SACRO ALIQUID FIAT. unde omnia interdicta[1] aut restitutoria aut exhibitoria aut prohibitoria vocantur. (141.) Nec tamen cum quid iusserit fieri aut fieri prohibuerit, statim peractum est negotium, sed ad iudicem recuperatoresve itur, et ibi, editis formulis, quaeritur, AN ALIQUID ADVERSUS PRAETORIS EDICTUM[2] FACTUM SIT, vel AN FACTUM NON SIT QUOD IS FIERI IUSSERIT. et modo cum poena agitur, modo sine poena: cum poena, velut cum per sponsionem agitur; sine poena, velut cum arbiter petitur[3]. et quidem ex prohibitoriis interdictis semper per sponsionem agi solet, ex restitutoriis vero vel exhibitoriis modo per sponsionem, modo per formulam agitur quae arbitraria vocatur[4].

sacred ground." Hence all interdicts[1] are named either restitutory, exhibitory, or prohibitory. 141. The matter is not, however, at once concluded when the Praetor has commanded or forbidden the doing of something, but the parties go before a *judex* or before *recuperatores*, and there, upon the issuing of formulae, investigation is made whether anything has been done contrary to the Praetor's edict[2] or whether anything has not been done which he ordered to be done. And sometimes a penalty accompanies the action, sometimes it does not: there is a penalty attached, for instance, when the proceedings are by *sponsio;* there is no penalty, for instance, when an *arbiter*[3] is demanded. In prohibitory interdicts the course of proceeding is always by *sponsio*, in restitutory or exhibitory interdicts sometimes by *sponsio*, sometimes by the formula called *arbitraria*[4].

---

neque precario. See Savigny, *On Poss.* pp. 66, 355.

[1] Interdict is here used as a general term, including decrees also, for exhibitory and restitutory orders are plainly of the latter character. So also Justinian says in *Inst.* IV. 15. 1, *sub finem.*

[2] That is to say, against the *edictum perpetuum*, or annual edict, published by every Praetor on commencing his duties. Therefore no one was guilty of acting contrary to an interdict, unless that interdict was in accordance with the terms of the annual edict, and this is the meaning of D. 50. 17. 102. pr. The interdict was issued on an *ex parte* statement, and therefore there was a possibility that the Praetor had been misled by false representations as to the facts of the case.

[3] Cf. Cic. *pro Tull.* 53, and Justinian, *Inst.* IV. 6. 31.

[4] A *formula arbitraria* is one which has in its *condemnatio* the words

142. Principalis igitur divisio in eo est, quod aut prohibitoria sunt interdicta, aut restitutoria, aut exhibitoria. (143.) Sequens in eo est divisio[1], quod vel adipiscendae possessionis causa conparata sunt, vel retinendae, vel reciperandae.

144. Adipiscendae possessionis causa interdictum accommodatur bonorum possessori[2], cuius principium est QUORUM BONORUM : eiusque vis et potestas haec est, ut quod quisque ex his bonis quorum possessio alicui data est pro herede aut
P.237 pro possessore | possiderit, id ei cui bonorum possessio data est restituatur. pro herede autem possidere videtur tam is qui heres est, quam is qui putat se heredem esse : pro possessore is possidet qui sine causa aliquam rem hereditariam, vel etiam totam hereditatem, sciens ad se non pertinere, possidet. ideo autem

142. Of interdicts then the primary division is that they are either prohibitory, restitutory, or exhibitory. 143. There is another division[1] based on the fact that they are provided for the purpose of obtaining, retaining, or recovering possession.

144. An interdict for the purpose of obtaining possession, the first words of which are "*Quorum bonorum*," is provided for the *bonorum possessor*[2]: its force and effect being that whatever any one possesses *pro herede* or *pro possessore* out of the goods of which the possession has been given to another, is to be delivered up to that person to whom the possession of the goods has been given. Now not only the heir, but also any one who thinks himself heir, is held to possess *pro herede*: whilst a possessor *pro possessore* is any one who possesses without title any item of the inheritance or the whole inheritance, knowing that he has no claim to it. The interdict is styled

---

nisi restituat. The *condemnatio* must in all cases be for a fixed sum of money (IV. 52), but by making it depend on this condition "*nisi restituat*," the *arbiter* could compel specific performance or specific delivery. It was when such a clause was included in the *formula* transmitted to him that the functionary, generally called *judex*, received the name of *arbiter*. In assessing the alternative amount to be paid on non-compliance the reckoning was always made by him *ex bona fide* and not *ex stricto jure*.

[1] But this classification only applies to possessory interdicts. The other division is a general one, applying to interdicts for any purpose.

[2] III. 34. The words of the interdict are given in full in D. 43. 2. 1. pr.

adipiscendae possessionis vocatur, quod ei tantum utile est qui nunc primum conatur adipisci rei possessionem[1]: itaque si quis adeptus possessionem amiserit, desinit ei id interdictum utile esse. (145.) Bonorum quoque emptori[2] similiter proponitur interdictum, quod quidam possessorium vocant[3]. (146.) Item ei qui publica bona emerit, eiusdem condicionis interdictum proponitur, quod appellatur sectorium, quod sectores vocantur[4] qui publice bona mercantur. (147.) Interdictum quoque quod appellatur Salvianum adipiscendae possessionis (causa) comparatum est, eoque utitur dominus fundi de rebus coloni quas is pro mercedibus fundi pignori futuras pepigisset.

adipiscendae possessionis, because it is only available for a man who is now for the first time endeavouring to obtain possession of a thing[1]; and therefore, if after obtaining possession, he lose it again, the interdict ceases to be of service to him. 145. So too, an interdict is set forth in the edict for the benefit of the purchaser of a bankrupt's goods[2], which some call by the name *interdictum possessorium*[3]. 146. So, too, an interdict of like character is set forth for the benefit of a purchaser of public property, to which the name *interdictum sectorium* is given, because those who buy property sold for the good of the state are called *sectores*[4]. 147. The interdict also which is called *Salvianum* is provided for the purpose of obtaining possession, and the owner of land employs it with reference to the property of his tenant which the latter has pledged for the rent of his farm.

---

[1] Hence "restituatur" a few lines above does not mean to restore, but to deliver up, a sense in which the word has been frequently used before, *e.g.* in II. 248—258, passim. In fact *restituere* is a word of extremely wide signification, and also means sometimes to remove a nuisance, as in D. 43. 12. 1. 19 and D. 43. 13. 1. 11.

[2] III. 80.

[3] No trace of this interdict is to be found in the sources: probably because the later and more general interdict, "Ne vis fiat ei qui in possessionem missus erit," D. 43. 4, was found to be a sufficient protection for *bonorum emptores*, and so the other fell into disuse. Zimmern asserts that the old interdict, as well as that termed *sectorium*, was framed upon the interdict *quorum bonorum*.

[4] Festus says: "Sectores et qui secant dicuntur, et qui emta sua persequuntur." In 2 *Phil.* 26, Cicero calls Antony "Pompeii sector," and in § 29 of the same oration speaks of money "quam pro sectione debebas." For further information see Heineccius, *Antiqq. Rom.* II. 1. 22.

148. Retinendae possessionis causa solet interdictum reddi, cum ab utraque parte de proprietate alicuius rei controversia est, et ante quaeritur, uter ex litigatoribus possidere et uter petere debeat, cuius rei gratia comparata sunt UTI POSSIDETIS et UTRUBI[1]. (149.) Et quidem UTI POSSIDETIS interdictum de fundi vel aedium possessione redditur, UTRUBI vero de rerum mobilium possessione. (150.) Et si quidem de fundo vel aedi-
P.238 bus | interdicitur, eum potiorem esse Praetor iubet qui eo tempore quo interdictum redditur nec vi nec clam nec precario[2] ab adversario possideat; si vero de re mobili, eum potiorem esse iubet qui maiore parte eius anni nec vi nec clam nec precario ab adversario possidet: idque satis ipsis verbis in-

148. An interdict for the purpose of retaining possession is usually granted when two litigants both lay claim to the ownership of a particular thing, and the first question for decision is which of them ought to be possessor and which plaintiff: to this end the interdicts *uti possidetis* and *utrubi* are provided[1]. 149. The interdict *uti possidetis* is granted for the possession of land or a house, the interdict *utrubi* for the possession of moveables. 150. And if the interdict be granted for land or a house, the Praetor orders that he is to be preferred who is in possession at the time of the grant of the interdict, provided it be without violence, clandestinity, or sufferance[2] as against his opponent; but if it be granted for a moveable, he orders him to be preferred who, as against his adversary, has possessed the thing for the greater part of the year without violence, clandestinity or sufferance. This is

[1] A full account of these interdicts is to be found in Savigny's *Treatise on Possession* (Perry's translation), Book IV. §§ 40, 41. See also D. 43. 17, D. 43. 31.

[2] *Precarium* is thus defined by Savigny (*On Poss.*, p. 355 Perry's translation). "Whoever permits another to enjoy property (*i.e.* to enjoy natural possession), or to enjoy an easement, retains to himself the right of recalling permission at will, and the juridical relation arising from the transaction is called *precarium*." This name had its origin in the fact of the permission itself being usually obtained by a *prayer;* this prayer, however, is not essential, and even a tacit permission is sufficient.

Paulus says: "Precario possidere videtur non tantum qui per epistolam, vel quacunque alia ratione hoc sibi concedi postulavit, sed et is qui nullo voluntatis indicio, patiente tamen domino possidet." *S. R.* V. 6. 11. See also D. 43. 26. 1.

terdictorum significatur[1]. (151.) Sed in UTRUBI interdicto non solum sua cuique possessio prodest, sed etiam alterius quam iustum est ei accedere, velut eius cui heres extiterit, eiusque a quo emerit vel ex donatione aut dotis nomine acceperit[2]. itaque si nostrae possessioni iuncta alterius iusta possessio exsuperat adversarii possessionem, nos eo interdicto vincimus. nullam autem propriam possessionem habenti accessio temporis nec datur nec dari potest; nam ei quod nullum est nihil accedere potest. sed et si vitiosam habeat possessionem, id est aut vi aut clam aut precario ab adversario adquisitam, non datur (accessio) nam ei possessio sua nihil prodest. (152.) Annus autem retrorsus numeratur; itaque si tu verbi gratia VIII mensibus possederis prioribus, et ego VII posterioribus, ego potior ero quod trium priorum mensium possessio nihil tibi in hoc interdicto prodest, quod alterius anni possessio est. (153.) Possidere autem videmur non solum si ipsi possideamus, sed etiam si nostro

fully stated in the actual wording of the interdict[1]. 151. But in the interdict *utrubi* a person not only profits by his own possession, but also by that of any other person which lawfully accrues to him, for instance by that of one whose heir he is, or that of one from whom he has bought the thing or received it as a gift or by way of *dos*[2]. If therefore the good possession which belonged to another when joined to our possession exceed the possession of our opponent, we succeed upon this interdict. But no accession of time is allowed or can be allowed to a man who has no possession of his own: for to that which is a nullity nothing can be added. And further, if a man have a tainted possession, *i.e.* one acquired by violence, clandestinity, or sufferance as against his opponent, no accession is allowed: for his own possession does not count for him. 152. The year is reckoned backwards; therefore if you, for example, have been in possession for the first eight months, and I for the last seven, I shall be in the better position because the possession for the first three months is of no value to you as regards this interdict, because it is possession of another year. 153. We are regarded as possessors not only when we possess personally,

[1] The interdict is given in full in D. 43. 17. 1. pr. [2] I. 178, Ulp. VI.

nomine aliquis in possessione sit[1], licet is nostro iuri subiectus non sit, qualis est colonus et inquilinus. per eos quoque aput quos deposuerimus, aut quibus commodaverimus, aut quibus
P.239 gratuitam habita|tionem constituerimus, ipsi possidere videmur. et hoc est quod volgo dicitur, retineri possessionem posse per quemlibet qui nostro nomine sit in possessione. quinetiam plerique putant animo quoque *retine*ri possessionem, *id est ut, quamvis neque ipsi simus in possessione*[2] neque nostro nomine alius, tamen si non relinquendae possessionis animo sed postea reversuri inde discesserimus, retinere possessionem videamur[3].

but also when any other is in possession[1] in our name, even though he be not subject to our authority, as a tenant of land or of a house. We are also considered to possess by means of those with whom we have deposited, or to whom we have lent anything, or to whom we have given a right of habitation gratuitously. And this is the meaning of the common saying "that possession can be retained by means of any one who is in possession in our name." Moreover most lawyers think that possession can be retained by mere will, that is to say, that although we are neither in possession ourselves[2], nor any other person in our name, yet, if we departed from the subject without the intention of relinquishing possession, but intending to return again, we are considered to retain possession[3]. Now

---

[1] *Esse in possessione* does not mean the same as *possidere*, the former expression denoting the mere fact of detention, the latter that the detention is protected by means of interdicts; hence a tenant is "in possession," whereas his landlord "possesses." See Savigny *On Possession*, translated by Perry, Bk. I. § 7.

[2] A few words are here supplied from Just. *Inst.* IV. 15. 5.

[3] Savigny holds that possession is *acquired* by a conjunction of three elements, (1) the physical power of dealing with a thing and of preventing others doing so, (2) a knowledge that we have this power, (3) an intent to use it as owners of the thing and not for another's benefit. If we hold the thing with the intent of giving the ownership to another, that other acquires through us a derivative possession and we have merely detention. The first two elements make up the *factum*, the latter is the *animus*.

Possession, he says, is *retained* by the same conjunction of *animus* and *factum*, but neither need be so strongly developed as for acquisition. There need not be an active will to hold the thing, but the mere absence of any wish to cease to hold it is enough; and the *factum* is not the absolute power to deal with the thing, but the ability to reproduce that power at pleasure, coupled with a knowledge that we have such power of reproapisci vero possessionem per quos possimus secundo commentario[1] rettulimus; nec ulla dubitatio est quin animo possessionem apisci non possimus[2].

154. Reciperandae possessionis causa solet interdictum dari, si quis ex possessione *fundi vel aedium*[3] vi deiectus sit. nam ei proponitur interdictum cuius principium est: UNDE TU ILLUM VI DEIECISTI[4], per quod is qui deiecit cogitur ei restituere rei possessionem, si modo is qui deiectus est nec vi nec clam nec precario posse*derit ab alte*ro[5]: cum qui a me vi aut clam aut precario possidet inpune deici *potest*[6]. (155.) Interdum tamen

who those persons are by whom we acquire possession we have stated in our second Commentary[1]: and there is no doubt that we cannot acquire possession by mere will[2].

154. An interdict for recovering possession is generally granted when a man has been forcibly ejected from possession of land or a house[3]. For there is set forth for his benefit the interdict which commences with the words: "*Unde tu illum vi dejecisti*[4]:" by means of which the ejector is compelled to restore the possession of the thing, provided only he who was ejected did not possess as against his adversary[5] by violence, clandestinity, or sufferance: whereas anyone who possesses as against me by violence, clandestinity or sufferance, can be ejected with impunity[6]. 155. Sometimes, however, I am

duction. See Savigny's *Treatise on Possession*, translated by Perry, passim.

[1] II. 89–94.

[2] Although we can *retain* possession by merely having the power of reproduction of the original *factum*, which Gaius calls "by mere will," *animo solo;* yet to *acquire* possession, the *factum*, as stated in the note above, must be of a much more marked character, viz. an actual power of dealing.

[3] Just. *Inst.* IV. 15. 6 has: *ex possessione fundi vel aedium.*

[4] This is fully explained in Savigny's *Treatise on Possession*, Bk. IV. § 42; where the amount of violence necessary to found a claim for its benefit, and the effect of self-redress, are also entered into.

The interdict ran on "id illi restituas," *i.e.* "Restore to him that from which you have ejected him."

[5] It is a well-known principle that the possessor was not liable under the interdict, if his wrongful dealing had been directed against a person different from the applicant for the same.

[6] See Savigny's *Treatise on Possession*, p. 331. The possessor who was ejected by any of the three modes named could immediately repossess himself, and his original possession was considered by the law never to have been disturbed. See Paulus, *S. R.* V. 6. 7.

et si eum vi deiecerim, qui a me vi aut clam aut precario possideret, cogor ei restituere possessionem, velut si armis eum vi deiecerim[1]: nam propter atrocitatem delicti in tantum patior actionem ut omnimodo debeam ei restituere possessionem. armorum autem appellatione non solum scuta et gladios et galeas significari intellegemus sed et fustes et lapides.

156. Tertia divisio interdictorum in hoc est, quod aut simplicia sunt aut duplicia: (157.) simplicia velut in quibus alter actor, alter reus est: qualia sunt omnia restitutoria aut exhibi-
P.240 toria. nam actor | est qui desiderat aut exhiberi aut restitui, reus is est a quo desideratur ut exhibeat aut restituat. (158.) Prohibitoriorum autem interdictorum alia duplicia, alia simplicia sunt. (159.) Simplicia sunt veluti quibus prohibet Praetor in loco sacro aut in flumine publico ripave eius aliquid facere reum: nam actor est qui desiderat ne quid fiat, reus is qui

compelled to restore possession of the thing to a person whom I have ejected by force, even though he had got the possession as against me by violence, clandestinity, or sufferance; for instance, if I ejected him forcibly with arms[1]; for on account of the heinousness of my delict, I am liable to action to the extent that I must in any case restore to him the possession. And under the term "arms" we understand not merely shields and swords and helmets to be denoted, but also sticks and stones.

156. A third division of interdicts is based on the fact that they are simple or double. 157. Those are simple, for instance, where one party is plaintiff and the other defendant: of which kind are all restitutory or exhibitory interdicts. For the plaintiff is he who requires that the thing be produced or restored, and the defendant is he at whose hands the production or restoration is required. 158. But of prohibitory interdicts some are double, some are simple. 159. Those are simple, for instance, in which the Praetor prohibits the defendant from doing something in a sacred place, or in a public river, or on its bank: for here the plaintiff is he who desires that the thing be not done, and the defendant is he

[1] See Savigny's *Treatise on Poss.* p. 344, Cic. *pro Tullio*, c. 44, Cic. *pro Caec.* c. 32; where is described the difference between *vis quotidiana* (which was allowed against a vicious possessor) and *vis armata* (which was always prohibited).

aliquid facere conatur. (160.) Duplicia sunt, velut UTI POSSIDETIS interdictum et UTRUBI. ideo autem duplicia vocantur, quia par utriusque litigatoris in his condicio est, nec quisquam praecipue reus vel actor intellegitur, sed unusquisque tam rei quam actoris partes sustinet: quippe Praetor pari sermone cum utroque loquitur. nam summa conceptio eorum interdictorum haec est: UTI NUNC POSSIDETIS, QUOMINUS ITA POSSIDEATIS VIM FIERI VETO. item alterius: UTRUBI HIC HOMO DE QUO AGITUR MAIORE PARTE HUIUS ANNI FUIT, QUOMINUS IS EUM DUCAT VIM FIERI VETO.

161. Expositis generibus interdictorum sequitur ut de ordine et de exitu eorum dispiciamus; et incipiamus a simplicibus. (162.) Si igitur restitutorium vel exhibitorium interdictum redditur, velut ut restituatur ei possessio qui vi deiectus est, aut exhibeatur libertus[1] cui patronus operas indicere vellet, modo

who attempts to do it. 160. The double are such interdicts as *Uti possidetis* and *Utrubi:* which are called "double" from the fact that the position of each litigant in respect of them is the same, and that neither is regarded as being specially defendant or plaintiff, but each sustains the character of defendant and plaintiff at once, inasmuch as the Praetor addresses both in like language: for the general drawing of these interdicts is as follows: "I forbid violence to be employed to prevent you from possessing in the manner you now possess." So also in the case of the other interdict: "I forbid violence to be employed to prevent that man, whether of the two he be, with whom the slave who is the matter of action has been during the greater part of this year, from removing him."

161. Having now explained the different kinds of interdicts, our next task is to consider their process and result: and let us begin with the simple interdicts. 162. If then a restitutory or exhibitory interdict be granted, for instance that possession shall be restored to one who has been forcibly ejected, or that a freedman shall be produced[1] to whom his patron wishes to appoint his services, the matter is brought

[1] Sc. by means of a special interdict "de libero homine exhibendo," which, like our writ of Habeas Corpus, was a process for bringing up the body of a freeman who was under detention. "The special object of

sine periculo res ad exitum perducitur, modo cum periculo. (163.) Namque si arbitrum postulaverit is cum quo agitur, ac-
P.241 cipit formulam quae appellatur | arbitraria[1], et iudicis arbitrio si quid restitui vel exhiberi debeat, id sine periculo exhibet aut restituit et ita absolvitur: quod si nec restituat neque exhibeat, quanti ea res est condemnatur. set actor et sine poena experitur cum eo quem neque exhibere neque restituere quicquam oportet, praeterquam si calumniae iudicium[2] ei oppositum fuerit decimae partis: quamquam Proculo placuit *denegandum* calumniae iudicium ei qui arbitrum postulaverit, quasi hoc ipso confessus videatur restituere se vel exhibere debere[3]. sed alio iure utimur, et recte: plus enim *ut per modestiorem* actionem litiget arbitrum quisque petit, quam quia causae non fidit. (164.) (Ceterum) observare debet is qui vult

to a result sometimes without risk, sometimes with risk. 163. For if the defendant have demanded an *arbiter*, he receives a formula of the kind called *arbitraria*[1]; and if by the award of the *judex* he be bound to restore or produce something, he restores or produces it without risk, and so is freed from liability: but if he do not restore or produce it, he is condemned to pay its value. The plaintiff also who sues a man not under obligation to produce or restore anything, can do so without making himself liable to any penalty, unless proceedings for vexatious litigation[2] be instituted against him for the tenth part; although Proculus held that a man who had applied for an *arbiter* ought not to be allowed a suit for vexatious proceedings, since by the very fact (of demanding an *arbiter*) he seems to have made admission that he ought to restore or produce something[3]. But we very properly follow the other rule, for a man is more likely to demand an *arbiter* because he wishes to employ a less self-asserting mode of procedure, than because he has not confidence in his case. 164. He who wishes to demand an *arbiter* ought to be careful

the interdict," says Ulpian, "was to defend liberty and to prevent freemen from being held in restraint;" but it also answered the purpose specified in the text. D. 43. 29. 1. As to the freedman's *operae*, see I. 37 *n*.

1 See IV. 141 *n*.

2 IV. 174, 175.

3 The argument resembles that in IV. 114.

arbitrum petere ut statim petat antequam ex iure exeat, id est antequam a Praetore recedat: sero enim petentibus non indulgetur. (165.) Itaque si arbitrum non petierit, sed tacitus de iure exierit, cum periculo res ad exitum perducitur. nam actor provocat adversarium sponsione: NI CONTRA EDICTUM PRAETORIS NON EXHIBUERIT AUT NON RESTITUERIT: ille autem adversus sponsionem adversarii restipulatur. deinde actor quidem sponsionis formulam edit adversario; ille huic invicem restipulationis. sed actor sponsionis *formulae subicit*[1] et aliut iudicium de re restituenda vel exhibenda, ut si sponsione
P.242 vicerit, nisi ei res exhibeatur aut restituatur | (*adversarius quanti ea res sit condemnetur*[2]) [*desunt* 48 *lineae*[3]].

to do so before going out of court, that is, before he leaves the Praetor's presence; for if people make the demand at a later stage, it is not granted. 165. Hence, if the defendant do not ask for an *arbiter*, but go out of court without speaking, the matter is carried on to its issue "with risk." For the plaintiff challenges his opponent with a sponsion: "Unless he have failed to produce or restore in violation of the Praetor's edict:" and the latter again makes a restipulation in reply to his adversary's sponsion. Then the plaintiff serves his opponent with a *formula* in claim of his sponsion: and the defendant in his turn serves the other with a *formula* in claim of his restipulation. But the plaintiff tacks on to the *formula* in claim of the sponsion another precept to the *judex* in reference to the restitution or production of the thing, so that if the plaintiff succeed in his sponsion, and the thing be not produced or restored, his opponent shall be condemned for the value of the thing[2].[3]

[1] These two words are suggested by Huschke, but only the letter F after *sponsionis* is decipherable in the MS.

[2] Hollweg suggests the reading which we have put within the brackets: it is obvious that the sentence must have ended in some such manner.

It will be observed that the proceedings are identical with those described in IV. 93, the *sponsio* being in both cases prejudicial only and intended to lead up to a decision on the stipulation, *pro praede litis et vindiciarum* in the one case, *de re restituenda vel exhibenda* in the other, which stipulations were tacked on to the sponsions and really contained the gist of the case.

Hence in his *Treatise on Possession* (Book IV. § 36), Savigny says that unless the defendant on an interdict admitted the plaintiff's demand, the process on the interdict became identical with that in an ordinary action.

See Cic. *pro Caecina*, 8, *pro Tull.* 53.

[3] In the missing pages Gaius, no

P.244 166. *Et cum vicerit* | *quis* res ab eo fructus licitando, is tantisper in possessione constituitur, si modo adversario suo fructuaria stipu*latione caverit*, cuius vis et potestas haec est, ut si contra eum de possessione pronuntiatum fuerit, eam *summ*am adversario solvat[1]. haec autem licendi contentio vocatur, scilicet quia ne*utro v*olente *possessio*nem esse *adver*santis, Praetor p*ossessionem* eius rei vendit ei qui p*lus licetur*. postea alter alterum sponsione provocat: QUOD ADVERSUS EDICTUM PRAETORIS *POS*SIDENTI SIBI VIS FACTA EST[2]. et invicem ambo restipulantur adversus sponsionem vel [*desunt* 4 *lineae*[3]].—iudex aput quem de

166. And when one of the litigants has succeeded in obtaining the (disputed) property from the Praetor in the bidding for the fruits, he is put in possession temporarily, provided only he gives security to his opponent by the fructuary stipulation, the force and effect whereof is this, that if the decision shall go against him as to the possession, he must pay the amount to his opponent[1]. This contention in bidding is called the *fructus licitatio*, clearly because neither wishing the possession to belong to his adversary, the Praetor sells the possession of the thing to the one who bids highest for it. Thereafter each challenges the other in a wager: "that violence has been done to him, contrary to the Praetor's edict, whilst in possession[2]:" and each of them in turn restipulates in answer to the sponsion[3]............The *judex* before whom the suit on the

doubt, concluded his account of the process in simple interdicts, and began the account of the process in double interdicts: for which see my edition of the *Edictum Julianum*, p. 112.

[1] Krüger reads *eam summam adversario solvat*, instead of *fructus duplum praestet;* for although the double value was recovered, it was not recovered on the fructuary stipulation. That stipulation caused the forfeiture of the *simple* value, and then by a separate action the fruits themselves or another simple value could be obtained. See IV. 167. For the restitution of the other part of the passage, I have partly followed Huschke, and partly acted independently from what I can decipher in the Apograph.

For *tantisper* in the sense of *interim* see D. 9. 3. 1. 9, D. 37. 10. 3. 13, and Gaius, I. 188.

[2] The Praetor issued his order: "uti possidetis, quominus ita possideatis vim fieri veto." Each thereupon commits on the other some formal and technical violence, and each is prepared to plead that his violence was not in contravention of the Praetor's edict, being in defence of his own possession, and not in violation of the possession of his adversary.

[3] This paragraph is corrupt, and none of the conjectures made by the editors of the text seem happy enough to merit insertion.

ea re agitur illud scilicet requirit (quod) Praetor interdicto conplexus est, id est uter eorum eum fundum easve aedes per id tempus quo interdictum redditur nec vi nec clam nec precario possideret[1]. cum iudex id exploraverit, et forte secundum me iudicatum sit, adversarium mihi et sponsionis et restipulationis summas quas cum eo feci condemnat, et convenienter me sponsionis et restipulationis quae mecum factae sunt absolvit, et hoc amplius si aput adversarium meum possessio est, quia is fructus licitatione vicit, nisi restituat mihi possessionem, Cas-
P.245 celliano sive | secutorio iudicio condemnatur. (167.) Ergo is qui fructus licitatione vicit, si non probat ad se pertinere possessionem, sponsionis et restipulationis et fructus licitationis summam poenae nomine solvere et praeterea possessionem restituere iubetur, et hoc amplius fructus quos interea percepit reddit: summa enim fructus licitationis non pretium est fructuum, sed poenae nomine solvitur, quod quis alienam possessionem

subject is conducted proceeds of course to investigate the point which the Praetor dealt with in his interdict, viz. which of the parties was in possession of the land or house at the time when the interdict was granted, holding such possession without violence, clandestinity or sufferance[1]. When the *judex* has investigated this point, and his decision has been, we will suppose, in my favour, he condemns my opponent to pay the amounts of the sponsion and restipulation which I entered into with him, and consequently acquits me from the sponsion and restipulation which he entered into with me. And besides this, if the (interim-) possession be with my opponent, because he beat me in bidding for the fruits, he is condemned in a Cascellian or Secutory action, unless he restore the possession to me. 167. Therefore the successful bidder for the fruits, in case he do not prove that the possession belongs to him, is ordered to pay the amount of the sponsion and restipulation and of his bid for the fruits by way of penalty, besides restoring the possession; and further than this, he restores the fruits which he has enjoyed in the meanwhile. For the amount of the bid for the fruits is not the price of the fruits, but is paid by way of penalty for a man's attempting to retain during such

[1] IV. 150.

per hoc tempus retinere et facultatem fruendi nancisci conatus est. (168.) Ille autem qui fructus licitatione victus est, si non probaverit ad se pertinere possessionem, tantum sponsionis et restipulationis summam poenae nomine debet. (169.) Admonendi tamen sumus liberum esse ei qui fructus licitatione victus erit, omissa fructuaria stipulatione, sicut Cascelliano sive secutorio iudicio de *possess*ione reciperanda experitur, ita *similiter* et de fructus licitatione agere: in quam rem proprium iudicium conparatum est quod appellatur fructuarium, quo nomine actor iudicatum solvi satis accipit[1]. dicitur autem et hoc iudicium secutorium, quod sequitur sponsionis victoriam; sed non aeque Cascellianum vocatur. (170.) Sed quia nonnulli interdicto reddito cetera ex interdicto facere nolebant, atque
P.246 ob id non poterat res expediri, Praetor | in eam rem prospexit et comparavit interdicta quae secundaria appellamus,

(intermediate) time the possession and the power of enjoyment appertaining to another. 168. On the other hand, if he who has been beaten in the bidding for the fruits fail to prove that the possession belongs to him, he only owes by way of penalty the amount of the sponsion and restipulation. 169. We must, however, bear in mind that he who is beaten in the bidding for the fruits is at liberty, even though no fructuary stipulation have been made, to proceed similarly for the amount offered for the fruits, just as he can proceed for the recovery of the possession by the Cascellian or Secutory action: and for this purpose a special form of proceeding has been provided, called *judicium fructuarium*, by means of which the plaintiff can obtain security for the payment of the award of the *judex*[1]. This action is called "secutory" as well as the other, because it follows upon success in the sponsion, but it has not also the title Cascellian. 170. But inasmuch as some persons, after the interdict had been issued, refused to take the subsequent steps necessary to carry out the interdict, and so matters could never be brought to a conclusion, therefore the Praetor has provided for this contingency, and framed interdicts which we call "secondary," because they are granted

---

[1] IV. 91.

quod secundo loco redduntur, quorum v*is et potest*as h*aec est ut qui* cetera ex interdicto non faciat, velut qui vim non faciat aut fructus non liceatur, aut qui fructus licitatione satis non det, aut si sponsiones non faciat, sponsionisve iudicium non accipiat, sive possideat ut restituat adversario possessionem, *sive non possideat ut vim* illi possidenti non faciat. itaque et si alias potuerit interdicto UTI POSSIDETIS vincere, si cetera ex interdicto *facere noluerit, cogitur* tamen per interdictum secundarium vel *adversario restituere* possessionem, vel i*lli possidenti vim non facere*...nullum...secundarium *interdictum* Praetor (*desunt* 2 *lin.*). quamvis hanc opinionem... *Sab*inus et Cassius secuti fuerint... nobisque (*desunt* 29 *lin.*).

P.247 171. | (*Nunc admonendi sumus, ne facile homines ad litigandum procederent*[1], *iam antiquo iure placuisse temeritatem tam agentium quam eorum cum quibus ageretur, modo*) pecuniaria poena, modo iurisiurandi religione *coercendam esse:* eaque Praetor *quoque tuetur.* ideo *ex parte eius cum quo agitur* adversus *infitiantem ex*

subsequently (to the others), the force and effect whereof is this, that a man who will not take the subsequent steps to carry out the interdict, for instance, will not offer (the technical) violence, or will not bid for the fruits, or will not give security for his bidding for the fruits, or will not make his sponsion, or will not accept service in the suit for the sponsion, (is ordered), if he be in possession, to deliver over the possession to his opponent, and if he be not in possession, to abstain from offering violence to the possessor. Therefore, even if otherwise he might have succeeded in the interdict, *Uti possidetis*, still if he will not perform the acts necessary to carry out the interdict, he is compelled by the secondary interdict either to deliver the possession to his opponent, or to offer no violence to him, if in possession. 171. Now we must be reminded that to prevent men thoughtlessly proceeding to litigation[1], even in the ancient law it was found necessary to check the rashness both of plaintiffs and defendants, sometimes by pecuniary penalty, sometimes by the obligation of an oath: which regulations the Praetor also upholds. Therefore, on the side of the defendant, there is allowed in some cases an action for double the value of the matter in dispute against a man who

[1] The commencement of § 171 is supplied mainly from Just. *Inst.* IV. 16. *pr.*, and partly according to Huschke's suggestions.

P.248 *quibusdam* | causis dupli actio constituitur, velut si iudicati[1] aut depensi[2] aut damni iniuriae[3] aut legatorum per damnationem relictorum[4] nomine agitur: ex quibusdam causis sponsionem facere permittitur, velut de pecunia certa credita[5] et pecunia constituta[6]: sed certae quidem creditae pecuniae tertiae partis[7], constitutae vero pecuniae partis dimidiae. (172.) Quodsi neque sponsionis, neque dupli actionis periculum ei cum quo agitur iniungatur, ac ne statim quidem ab initio pluris quam simpli sit actio, permittit Praetor iusiurandum exigere NON CALUMNIAE CAUSA INFITIAS IRE[8]: unde quia heredes vel qui heredum loco habentur[9], *simpli* neque amplius obligati sunt[10],

denies his liability, as in the instance of the actions of judgment[1], of money laid down by a *sponsor*[2], of wrongful damage[3], or for legacies left by damnation[4]: in some cases it is allowable to enter into a sponsion, as for example in suing upon the loan of an ascertained sum[5], or for an agreed amount[6]; but in the case of an ascertained loan the sponsion is allowed for a third part[7], in the case of an agreed amount it may be for a half. 172. But if the risk neither of a sponsion nor of an action for the double amount be cast upon the defendant, or if the action at starting be not for a larger amount than the simple sum demanded, the Praetor allows the exaction of an oath, "that the traverse is not pleaded vexatiously[8]:" hence, since heirs and those who are esteemed as heirs[9] are liable for the simple value and no more[10], and since the risk of

---

1 IV. 9. 2 III. 127.

3 III. 210, 216.

4 II. 201—208, 282.

5 III. 124.

6 *Constitutum* was one of the *Pacta Praetoria*, mentioned in App. (N). It was a pact whereby a man entered into a new and special engagement to pay a debt already existing, and such debt might be owed either by the man himself or by another person. Thus a *constitutum* would render actionable a promise which previously was a mere *nudum pactum*, not giving rise to an action, and the process provided for its recovery by the Praetorian edict was that named in the text, viz. the *actio constitutae pecuniae*. See Paulus, *S. R.* II. 2.

7 Cic. *pro Rosc. Com.* 5.

8 Paulus, *S.R.* II. 1, D. 10. 2. 44. 4. From Cic. *pro Rosc. Amer.* 20 we learn that in earlier times the penalty for falsely taking the oath *de calumnia* was branding on the forehead with the letter K (for Kalumnia); and Heineccius thinks this penalty was inflicted whether the perjury took place in a civil or criminal action. See Heinecc. *Antiq.* IV. 16. 3.

9 Sc. *Bonorum possessores;* II. 119 et seqq.

10 Another reading is "jure civili non amplius obligati sunt:" the

item feminis pupillisque ex*imatur* periculum sponsionis, iubet tantum eos iurare. (173.) Statim autem ab initio pluris quam simpli actio est, velut furti manifesti quadrupli, nec manifesti dupli, concepti et oblati tripli[1]: nam ex his causis et aliis quibusdam, sive quis neget sive fateatur, pluris quam simpli est actio.

174. Actoris quoque calumnia coercetur modo calumniae iudicio, modo contrario, modo iureiurando[2], modo restipulatione. (175.) Et quidem calumniae iudicium adversus omnes actiones locum habet, et est decimae partis rei; vel adversus adsertorem[3] tertiae partis est. (176.) Liberum est autem ei cum quo agitur aut calumniae iudicium opponere, aut iusiurandum exigere NON CALUMNIAE CAUSA AGERE. (177.) Con-
P.249 trarium autem iudicium ex certis causis constituitur: | velut

the sponsion is also remitted in the case of females and minors, the Praetor orders such persons merely to take the oath. 173. Examples of actions which from their very outset are for more than the simple value of the thing in dispute are the action of manifest theft for four-fold, of non-manifest theft for double, those of concept and oblate theft for three-fold[1]; for in these and some other cases the action is for more than the simple value, whether the defendant deny or admit the claim.

174. Vexatious conduct on the part of the plaintiff too is restrained; sometimes by the action of vexatious litigation, sometimes by the cross-action, sometimes by an oath[2], sometimes by a restipulation. 175. The action of vexatious litigation is admitted in opposition to all actions whatever, and is for a tenth part of the matter in dispute; or against an *adsertor*[3] it is for the third part. 176. It is in the defendant's power to elect whether he will reply with the action of vexatious litigation, or require the oath "that the action is not brought vexatiously." 177. The cross-action is applicable to certain special cases; for instance, to that of the action

meaning of which is the same as that of "poenis nunquam obligati sunt," the reading of Huschke.

[1] III. 189—191.

[2] Similar to that referred to in IV. 172.

[3] *Adsertorem*, sc. *libertatis*. See IV. 14.

si iniuriarum agatur[1], et si cum muliere eo nomine agatur, quod dicatur ventris nomine in possessionem missa[2] dolo malo ad alium possessionem transtulisse, et si quis eo nomine agat, quod dicat se a Praetore in possessionem missum ab alio quo admissum non esse. sed adversus iniuriarum quidem actionem decimae partis datur, adversus vero duas istas quintae. (178.) Severior autem coercitio est per contrarium iudicium: nam calumniae iudicio x. partis nemo damnatur, nisi qui intellegit non recte se agere, sed vexandi adversarii gratia actionem instituit, potiusque ex iudicis errore vel iniquitate victoriam sperat quam ex causa veritatis; calumnia enim in adfectu est, sicut furti crimen[3]. contrario vero iudicio omni modo damnatur actor, si causam non tenuerit, licet aliqua opinione inductus crediderit se recte agere. (179.) Utique autem

of injury[1], and the proceedings taken against a woman when she is charged with having fraudulently transferred possession to another after having been put in possession *ventris nomine*[2]: so also to the case of a person bringing his action on the ground that, although he had received from the Praetor a grant of possession, his entry has been opposed by some one or other. When the cross-action is in reply to an action of injury it is granted for the tenth part (of the claim in that action), when it follows the two last-named it is for the fifth part. 178. The penalty involved in a cross-action is the more severe one, for in the action of vexatious litigation a man is never mulcted in the tenth unless he be aware that he is bringing his action improperly, and be taking proceedings for the mere purpose of annoying his opponent, expecting to succeed rather through the mistake or unfairness of the *judex* than through the merits of his cause: for vexatiousness like theft consists in intention[3]. In a cross-action, on the other hand, the plaintiff, if he be unsuccessful in his suit, is always mulcted, even though he were induced by some idea or other to believe that he was bringing his action properly. 179. Undoubtedly in all cases where we can proceed by cross-action,

[1] III. 224.

[2] This was when a woman on the death of her husband asserted that she was pregnant and claimed succession on behalf of the unborn child. In such a case, as we see, interim-possession of the property was given to her. See D. 3. 2. 15—19, D. 25. 5, D. 25. 6, D. 29. 2. 30. 1.

[3] III. 197, 208.

ex quibus causis contrario iudicio agere potest, etiam calumniae iudicium locum habet: sed alterutro tantum iudicio agere permittitur. qua ratione si iusiurandum de calumnia exactum fuerit, quemadmodum calumniae iudicium non datur, ita et contrarium non dari debet. (180.) Restipulationis quoque poena ex certis causis fieri solet[1]: et quemadmodum contrario iudicio omnimodo condemnatur actor[2], si causam non tenuerit, nec requiritur an scierit non recte se agere, ita etiam restipula-
P.250 tionis poena omni|modo damnatur actor. (181.) A *quo autem* restipulationis poena petitur, ei neque calumniae iudicium opponitur neque iurisiurandi religio iniungitur: nam contrarium iudicium in his causis locum non habere palam est[3].

182. Quibusdam iudiciis damnati ignominiosi fiunt[4], velut

the action of vexatious litigation can also be employed: but we are allowed to use only one of the two. According to this principle, if the oath against vexatiousness have been required, the cross-action cannot be allowed, inasmuch as the action of vexatious litigation is not (allowed). 180. The restipulatory penalty is also one applicable only to certain special cases[1]: and just as in the cross-action the plaintiff[2] is in all cases condemned to pay when he has failed in the original suit, and the question whether he did or did not know that he was suing improperly is never raised, so in the case of the restipulatory penalty is he condemned to pay in every instance. 181. When a restipulatory penalty is claimed from any one, no action of vexatious litigation can be brought against him, nor can the obligation of an oath be laid upon him; for it is plain enough that there can in such cases be no cross-action[3].

182. In some actions those against whom a judgment is given are branded with infamy[4]; for instance the actions of theft,

---

[1] IV. 13. Cic. *pro Rosc. Com.* c. 13.

[2] The plaintiff in the original action, *i.e.* the defendant in the cross-action.

[3] The meaning of this paragraph is very simple. We are told in § 174 that the *calumnia* of the plaintiff can be met in four different ways, we are now informed that the defendant must select *one* of these remedies, and that he cannot employ first one and then another. The doctrine agrees with that in § 179.

[4] The subject of *infamia* or *ignominia* is treated of in D. 3. 2. See especially 3. 2. 1, 3. 2. 4. 5, 3. 2. 6, and 3. 2. 7.

furti, vi bonorum raptorum, iniuriarum; item pro socio, fiduciae, tutelae, mandati, depositi. sed furti aut vi bonorum raptorum aut iniuriarum non solum damnati notantur ignominia, sed etiam pacti[1]: ut in edicto Praetoris scriptum est, et recte: plurimum enim interest utrum ex delicto aliquis, an ex contractu debitor sit. item illa parte edicti id ipsum nominatim *expr*i*mitur, ut qui igno*miniosus *sit plerum*que prohibeatur *pro aliis* postul*are, item cogni*torem dare, procuratorem adhibere, *vel cognitorio aut procura*torio nomine iudicio intervenire, interest enim *cum honestis* litigare[2].

183. In summa sciendum est eum qui cum alio *experiri velit, in ius vocare* oportere[3], et eum qui vocatus est, *si non sequitur, sine auctoritate* Praetoris *posse secum duc*ere. quasdam *vero personas* sine permissu Praetoris in ius vocare non licet, velut par*entes, pa*tronos patronasque, liberos et parentes pa-

robbery with violence, injury, also those in respect of partnership, fiduciary engagement, guardianship, mandate, deposit. But not only those condemned for theft, robbery, or injury are branded with ignominy, but even those who have bought the plaintiff off[1], and thus it is laid down, and very properly too, in the edict of the Praetor: for there is a considerable difference between the position of a debtor upon a delict and one upon a contract. Moreover, in this part of the edict it is expressly declared that an ignominious person is in general debarred from pleading on behalf of others, from appointing a *cognitor*, or employing a *procurator*, and from intervening in a suit in the capacity of *cognitor* or *procurator*. For it is of importance that our litigation should be with respectable persons[2].

183. In conclusion we must take note that he who wishes to sue another must summon him into court[3], and, if the man summoned will not attend, he can without further authority from the Praetor force him to come with him. But certain persons we are not allowed to summon into court without the Praetor's permission, as ascendants, patrons and patronesses, and the descendants and ascendants of a patron or patroness;

---

1 See D. 3. 2. 1. *pr.* and 6. 3.

2 The end of § 182 is filled in according to Huschke's suggestion. So also is the beginning of § 183 to some extent. See D. 3. 1. 1. 8.

3 See App. (Q).

troni patronaeve, et in eum qui adversus ea agerit poena constituitur[1]. (184.) Cum autem in ius vocatus fuerit adversarius, neque eo die finiri potuerit negotium, vadimonium ei faciendum est, id est ut promittat se certo die sisti. (185.) Fiunt autem vadimonia quibusdam ex causis pura, id est sine satisdatione,
P.251 quibusdam cum satisdatione, | quibusdam iureiurando, quibusdam recuperatoribus suppositis, id est ut qui non steterit, is protinus a recuperatoribus in summam vadimonii condemnetur: eaque singula diligenter Praetoris edicto significantur. (186.) Et si quidem iudicati depensive[2] agetur, tanti fit vadimonium quanti ea res erit; si vero ex ceteris causis, quanti actor iuraverit non calumniae causa postulare sibi vadimonium promitti, nec tamen (*pluris quam partis dimidiae, nec*) pluribus quam sestertium C milibus fit vadimonium. itaque si centum milium res erit, nec iudicati depensive agetur, non plus quam sester-

and should any one act in contravention of these regulations a penalty is appointed[1]. 184. When a defendant has been summoned to court, unless the business be concluded on the day of summons, he must enter into a *vadimonium*, that is, he must promise that he will appear on a day fixed. 185. In some cases the *vadimonia* are simple, that is, without sureties, in some they are with sureties, in some they are with an oath, in some with *recuperatores* introduced, which means that if a man fail to make appearance he will at once be condemned by the *recuperatores* for the amount of his *vadimonium*: and each of these matters is carefully explained in the Praetor's edict. 186. If then the action be upon a judgment or for money laid down by a *sponsor*[2], the amount of *vadimonium* will be the value of the matter in dispute; but if it be on other grounds, the *vadimonium* will be such amount as the plaintiff shall fix after having sworn that he does not demand a promise of *vadimonium* to himself with any vexatious object; but its amount cannot be fixed higher than half the value of the subject of the suit, or than 100,000 sesterces. If then the subject be worth 100,000 sesterces, and the action be not one on judgment or for money laid down by a *sponsor*, the

---

[1] The penalty was 5000 sesterces, IV. 46 *n*. Just. *Inst.* IV. 16. 3. See also D. 2. 4. 4.

[2] III. 115.

tium quinquaginta milium fit vadimonium. (187.) Quas autem personas sine permissu Praetoris inpune in ius vocare non possumus, easdem nec vadimonio invitas obligare nobis possumus, praeterquam si Praetor aditus permittat[1].

vadimonium cannot exceed 50,000 sesterces. 187. All persons whose appearance in court we cannot without risk compel except by the Praetor's permission[1], we are also unable to compel to furnish *vadimonium* to us against their will, save in cases where the Praetor is applied to and gives permission.

[1] IV. 183. D. 2. 6. 1—3.

THE

RULES OF ULPIAN.

TITULI EX CORPORE ULPIANI.

1. Lex aut perfecta est, aut imperfecta, aut minus quam perfecta.

Perfecta lex est, quae uetat aliquid fieri, et si factum sit, rescindit, qualis est lex Aelia Sentia......Imperfecta lex est, quae uetat aliquid fieri, et si factum sit, nec rescindit, nec poenam iniungit ei, qui contra legem fecit, qualis est lex Cincia, quae plus quam H. S....*donari* prohibet, exceptis *personis* quibusdam *uelut* cognatis, et si plus donatum sit, non rescindit[1]. 2. Minus quam perfecta lex est, quae uetat aliquid fieri, et si factum sit, non rescindit, sed poenam iniungit ei, qui contra legem fecit; qualis est lex Furia testamentaria[2], quae plus quam mille asses legati nomine mortisue causa prohibet capere praeter exceptas

1. A law is either perfect, or imperfect, or short of perfect. A perfect law is one which forbids something to be done, and rescinds it if it be done, of which kind is the Lex Aelia Sentia. An imperfect law is one which forbids something to be done, and yet, if it be done, neither rescinds it nor imposes a penalty on him who has acted contrary to the law: of which character is the Lex Cincia, prohibiting donations beyond a specified amount, except those to certain persons, relations for instance; and yet not revoking a gift in excess[1]. 2. A law short of perfect is one which forbids something to be done, and if it be done does not rescind it, but imposes a penalty on him who has acted contrary to the law: of which character is the Lex Furia Testamentaria[2], prohibiting all persons, save those specially exempted, from taking more than a thousand *asses* as a legacy or gift in

[1] The first paragraph is restored according to the conjectures of Cujas and Schilling.

[2] XXVIII. 7. Gaius, II. 225, IV. 23.

personas, et aduersus eum qui plus ceperit quadrupli poenam constituit.

3. Lex aut rogatur, id est fertur; aut abrogatur, id est prior lex tollitur; aut derogatur, id est pars prima*e legis* tollitur; aut subrogatur, id est adicitur aliquid primae legi; aut obrogatur, id est mutatur aliquid ex prima lege[1].

4. Mores sunt tacitus consensus populi, longa consuetudine inueteratus.

TIT. I. DE LIBERTIS.

5. Libertorum genera sunt tria, ciues Romani, Latini Iuniani, dediticiorum numero[2].

6. Ciues Romani sunt liberti, qui legitime *manumissi sunt, id est aut uindicta aut*[3] censu aut testamento, nullo iure inpediente[4].

7. Vindicta manumittuntur apud magistratum populi Ro-

prospect of death, and appointing a fourfold penalty against anyone who has taken a larger sum.

3. A law is either "rogated," that is to say introduced: or "abrogated," that is to say a former law is revoked: or "derogated," that is to say a part of a former law is revoked: or "subrogated," that is to say something is added to a former law: or "obrogated," that is some portion of a former law is altered[1].

4. Customs are the tacit consent of a people established by long-continued habit.

I. ON FREEDMEN.

5. There are three classes of freedmen, viz. Roman citizens, Junian Latins, and those in the category of *dediticii*[2].

6. Roman citizens are freedmen manumitted in the regular mode, that is to say by *vindicta*[3], *census* or *testament*, and in contravention of no regulation[4].

7. The manumission by *vindicta* takes place before a magis-

---

[1] See D. 50. 16. 102, and Festus on the several words, *rogare*, *abrogare*, etc.

[2] Gaius, I. 12...

[3] A line omitted from the MS. can be replaced from Gai. *Comm.* I. 17.

[4] Sc. the requirements as to age of master or of slave, I. 12, 13, Gaius, I. 17; or the consent of the *consilium*, Gaius, I. 18; or the limitations of the Lex Fufia Caninia, Gaius, I. 42.

mani, uelut consulem praetoremue uel proconsulem. 8. Censu manumittebantur olim, qui lustrali censu Romae iussu dominorum inter ciues Romanos censum profitebantur. 9. Ut testamento manumissi liberi sint, lex duodecim tabularum facit, quae confirmat *testamento datas libertates his uerbis : 'uti legassit suae rei ; ita ius esto*[1].'

10. *Latini sunt liberti, qui non legitime, uelut inter amicos, nullo iure impediente manumissi sunt, quos olim praetor tantum tuebatur in forma libertatis; nam ipso iure serui manebant*[2]. hodie autem ipso iure liberi sunt ex lege Iunia[3], qua lege Latini *I*uni*ani* nominati sunt inter amicos manumissi.

11. Dediticiorum numero sunt, qui poenae causa uincti sunt a domino, quibusue stigmata inscripta fuerunt, quiue propter noxam torti nocentesque inuenti sunt, quiue traditi sunt, ut ferro aut cum bestiis depugnarent, inue ludum uel

trate of the Roman people, as a Consul, a Praetor, or a Proconsul.

8. Manumission was effected by *census* in olden times when slaves at the quinquennial registration entered themselves on the roll amongst the Roman citizens by order of their masters. 9. The liberty of those who have been manumitted by testament results from a law of the Twelve Tables which confirms testamentary gifts of liberty in these words: "as one has disposed of his own property, so let the right be[1]."

10. Latins are freedmen who have not been manumitted in regular form, those for instance manumitted privately (*inter amicos*), and in contravention of no regulation: and these in olden times the Praetor merely used to protect in the semblance of liberty; for in strict law they remained slaves[2]. But at the present day they are free by strict law on account of the Lex Junia[3], by which *lex* those manumitted in the presence of our friends were styled Junian Latins.

11. Those are in the category of *dediticii* who have been put in chains by their masters as a punishment, or who have been branded, or who have been tortured for a misdeed and found guilty, or who have been delivered over to fight with the sword or against wild beasts, or cast into a gladiatorial school

[1] Tab. v. l. 3. Pomponius agrees with Ulpian in his interpretation of these words. See D. 50. 16. 120.

[2] The filling in of § 9 is that of Huschke, and so also that of § 10.

[3] Gaius, I. 22, III. 56.

custodiam coniecti fuerunt, deinde quoquo modo manumissi sunt[1]. idque lex Aelia Sentia facit.

12. Eadem lege cautum est, ut minor triginta annorum seruus uindicta manumissus ciuis Romanus non fiat, nisi apud consilium causa probata fuerit[2]: id est sine consilio manumissum eius aetatis seruum manere putat; testamento uero manumissum perinde haberi iubet, atque si domini uoluntate in libertate esset, ideoque Latinus fit. 13. Eadem lex eum dominum, qui minor uiginti annorum est, prohibet seruum manumittere, praeterquam si causam apud consilium probauerit[3]. 13*a*. In consilio autem adhibentur Romae quidem quinque senatores et quinque equites Romani; in prouinciis uiginti reciperatores, ciues Romani[4].

14. Ab eo domino, qui soluendo non est, seruus testamento liber esse iussus et heres institutus, etsi minor sit triginta annis, uel in ea causa sit ut dediticius fieri debeat, ciuis Romanus et heres fit; si tamen alius ex eo testamento nemo

or into a prison for the like cause, and have afterwards been manumitted by any form[1]. And these rules the Lex Aelia Sentia establishes.

12. By the same *lex* it was provided that a slave under thirty years of age when manumitted by *vindicta* should not become a Roman citizen, unless cause for manumission had been proved before the council[2]; that is, it lays down that a slave of that age manumitted without application to the council remains a slave still: but when he is manumitted by testament it directs him to be regarded as though he were holding his freedom at his master's will, and therefore he becomes a Latin. 13. The same *lex* prohibits a master under twenty years of age from manumitting a slave, unless he have proved cause before the council[3]. 13*a*. The council consists at Rome of five senators and five Roman knights, but in the provinces of twenty *reciperators*, Roman citizens[4].

14. A slave ordered to be free and instituted heir in a testament by an insolvent master, although he be under thirty years of age, or so circumstanced that he ought to become a *dediticius*, yet becomes a Roman citizen and heir: provided

[1] Gaius, I. 13.
[2] *Ib.* I. 18.
[3] *Ib.* I. 38.
[4] *Ib.* I. 20.

heres sit[1]. quod si duo pluresue liberi heredesque esse iussi sint, primo loco scriptus liber et heres fit: quod et ipsum lex Aelia Sentia facit. 15. Eadem lex in fraudem creditorum uel patroni manumittere prohibet[2].

16. Qui tantum in bonis, non etiam ex iure Quiritium[3] seruum habet, manumittendo Latinum facit. In bonis tantum alicuius seruus est uelut hoc modo, si ciuis Romanus a ciue Romano seruum emerit, isque traditus ei sit, neque tamen mancipatus ei, neque in iure cessus, neque ab ipso anno possessus sit[4]. nam quamdiu horum quid non fit, is seruus in bonis quidem emptoris, ex iure Quiritium autem uenditoris est.

17. Mulier, quae in tutela est[5], item pupillus et pupilla, nisi tutore auctore manumittere non possunt.

18. Communem seruum unus ex dominis manumittendo partem suam amittit, eaque adcrescit socio; maxime si eo modo manumiserit, quo, si proprium haberet, ciuem Romanum facturus esset. nam si inter amicos eum manumiserit, plerisque

only no one else be heir under that testament[1]. But if two or more be ordered to become free and heirs, the one first-named becomes free and heir: and this too the Lex Aelia Sentia enacts. 15. The same *lex* forbids manumissions in fraud of creditors or a patron[2].

16. He who holds a slave merely by Bonitary title and not also by Quiritary[3], makes him a Latin by manumission. A slave belongs to a man by Bonitary title only in such a case as the following: when a Roman citizen has bought a slave from another Roman citizen, and the slave has been delivered to him, but not transferred by mancipation or cession in court, nor possessed by him for a year[4]. For so long as some one of these circumstances be wanting, that slave belongs to the purchaser by Bonitary title, but to the vendor by Quiritary.

17. A woman under tutelage[5], and a pupil, male or female, cannot manumit, except with the tutor's authorisation.

18. If one of two joint owners manumit a common slave, he loses his portion and it accrues to his partner; at any rate if he manumit him in a form whereby he would have made him a Roman citizen, if he had had the sole property in him. For if he

[1] Gaius, I. 21.
[2] *Ib.* I. 37, 47.
[3] *Ib.* I. 17, 35, II. 40.
[4] *Ib.* I. 119, II. 24, 41.
[5] For *Tutela*, see Tit. XI.

placet, eum nihil egisse. 19. Seruus, in quo alterius est usus-fructus, alterius proprietas, a proprietatis domino manumissus liber non fit, sed seruus sine domino est[1].

20. Post mortem heredis aut ante institutionem heredis testamento libertas dari non potest, excepto testamento militis[2]. 21. Inter medias heredum institutiones libertas data utrisque adeuntibus non ualet; solo autem priore adeunte iure antiquo ualet. sed post legem Papiam Poppaeam, quae partem non adeuntis caducam facit, si quidem primus heres uel ius (liberorum uel ius) antiquum[3] habeat, ualere eam posse placuit; quod si non habeat, non ualere constat, quod loco non adeuntis legatarii patres heredes fiunt[4]. sunt tamen, qui

manumit him privately, it is generally held that the act is void. 19. If the usufruct of a slave belong to one man and the ownership to another, and he be manumitted by him who has the ownership, he does not become free, but is a slave without a master[1].

20. A gift of liberty cannot be bestowed in any testament, except that of a soldier, to take effect after the death of the heir, nor (can it be inserted) before the institution of the heir[2]. 21. A gift of liberty inserted between the appointments of two heirs is void, if both take up the inheritance: but if the one first-named alone take it up, the gift is valid according to the ancient law. But since the passing of the Lex Papia Poppaea, which makes to lapse the portion of one who does not take up the inheritance, it has been ruled that the gift stands good in case the heir first-named has either the right derived from children or the ancient right[3]: but when he has neither of these rights, it is decided that the gift does not stand good, because the legatees who have children become heirs in the place of the heir who fails to accept[4]: but there are persons who maintain

[1] "But only so long as the usufruct lasts; after that he becomes a Latin." Mommsen.

[2] Gaius, II. 230, 233.

[3] We see from Tit. XVIII. that ascendants and descendants of the testator to the third degree were exempted from the provisions of the Lex Papia Poppaea. These therefore are the persons referred to as having the *jus antiquum*. The words in brackets are inserted by Lachmann.

[4] These legatees are by hypothesis named in the testament subsequently to the gift of freedom, for that gift is *inter medias institutiones*. Hence, when they become heirs in the place of the first-named heir, all the heirs are posterior to the legacy of freedom; which is therefore void: for it can only subsist as a charge

et hoc casu ualere eam posse dicunt. 22. Qui testamento liber esse iussus est, mox quam uel unus ex heredibus adierit hereditatem, liber fit[1]. 23. Iusta libertas[2] testamento potest dari his seruis, qui (et) testamenti faciendi et mortis tempore ex iure Quiritium testatoris fuerunt.

24. Lex Fufia Caninia iubet, testamento ex tribus seruis non plures quam duos manumitti; et usque ad decem dimidiam partem manumittere concedit; a decem usque ad triginta tertiam partem, ut tamen adhuc quinque manumittere liceat, aeque ut ex priori numero; a triginta usque ad centum quartam partem, aeque ut decem ex superiori numero liberari possint; a centum usque ad quingentos partem quintam, simi-

that it stands good in this case too. 22. A slave who is ordered in a testament to become free, becomes free the instant that even one of the heirs takes up the inheritance[1]. 23. Full freedom[2] can be given by testament to those slaves who belonged to the testator in Quiritary right both at the time of his making the testament and at his death.

24. The Lex Fufia Caninia directs that not more than two slaves out of three shall be manumitted by testament; allows a half to be manumitted out of a number between four and ten; a third out of any number between ten and thirty, but still allowing five at least to be manumitted, just as they would have been out of the antecedent number; a fourth of any number from thirty up to a hundred, but, as before, permitting ten to be manumitted on the reckoning of the antecedent number; a fifth of any number from one hundred to five hundred, but

upon an antecedent heir, as stated in I. 20 and in Gaius, II. 229, 230.

Cujacius reads "ea lege aerarium partis haeres fiat" instead of "legatarii patres heredes fiunt," and this reading agrees with what is stated in XVII. 2, "hodie omnia caduca fisco vindicantur." Cujacius probably gives correctly the passage as altered by the abbreviator of Ulpian, whilst Huschke endeavours to go back to the original words of Ulpian himself: but in either case the words which follow in the text "sunt tamen etc." refer to the rule enunciated in XVII. 3, "caduca cum onere suo fiunt."

[1] In this case the gift of liberty is supposed to be after the institution of all the heirs, or at any rate after that of the one who accepts the inheritance. For Ulpian says elsewhere: "Testamento liber esse jussus tum fit liber, quum adita fuerit hereditas qualibet ex parte, si modo *ab eo gradu, quo liber esse jussus est*, adita fuerit, et pure quis manumissus sit." D. 40. 4. 25.

[2] Sc. *civitas Romana*, Gaius, II. 267.

liter ut ex antecedenti numero uiginti quinque possint fieri liberi. et denique praecipit, ne plures omnino quam centum ex cuiusquam testamento liberi fiant[1]. 25. Eadem lex cauet, ut libertates seruis testamento nominatim dentur[2].

TIT. II. DE STATV LIBERO (VEL STATV LIBERIS).

1. Qui sub conditione testamento liber esse iussus est, statu liber appellatur. 2. Statu liber quamdiu pendet conditio, seruus heredis (est)[3]. 3. Statu liber seu alienetur ab herede, seu usu capiatur ab aliquo[4], libertatis conditionem secum trahit. 4. Sub hac conditione liber esse iussus: SI DECEM MILIA HEREDI DEDERIT, etsi ab herede abalienatus sit, emptori dando pecuniam ad libertatem perueniet; idque lex duodecim tabularum iubet[5]. 5. Si per heredem factum sit, quominus statu liber conditioni pareat, proinde fit liber, atque

still enabling twenty-five to be liberated on the reckoning of the antecedent number; and finally it directs that not more than a hundred in all shall be set free by virtue of any man's testament[1].

25. The same *lex* provides that gifts of freedom shall be conferred on slaves by name in a testament[2].

II. ON STATULIBERI.

1. The name *statuliber* is applied to a slave ordered in a testament to become free under some condition. 2. A *statuliber*, so long as the condition is pendent, is a slave of the heir[3]. 3. The *statuliber*, whether alienated by the heir, or acquired by any one through usucapion[4], carries with him the condition of his freedom.

4. If ordered to be free under the condition: "if he give 10,000 sesterces to the heir," he will attain to freedom, even though he have been alienated by the heir, by giving the money to his purchaser; and this a law of the Twelve Tables provides[5]. 5. If anything be done by the heir to prevent the *statuliber* complying with the condition, he becomes free just as though

[1] Gaius, I. 42, 43, 45.
[2] *Ib.* II. 239.
[3] *Ib.* II. 200.
[4] *Ib.* II. 42.
[5] Supposed to be the lost law, Tab. VII. l. 12.

si conditio expleta fuisset. 6. Extraneo pecuniam dare iussus et liber esse, si paratus sit dare, et is, cui iussus est dare, aut nolit accipere, aut antequam acceperit moriatur, proinde fit liber ac si pecuniam dedisset.

7. Libertas et directo potest dari hoc modo LIBER ESTO, LIBER SIT, LIBERVM ESSE IVBEO, et per fideicommissum, ut puta ROGO, FIDEI COMMITTO HEREDIS MEI, VT STICHVM SERVVM MANVMITTAT. 8. Is, qui directo liber esse iussus est, testatoris uel orcinus fit libertus; is autem, cui per fideicommissum data est libertas, non testatoris, sed manumissoris fit libertus. 9. Cuius fidei committi potest ad rem aliquam praestandam, eiusdem etiam libertas fidei committi potest. 10. Per fideicommissum libertas dari potest tam proprio seruo testatoris, quam heredis aut legatarii, uel cuiuslibet extranei seruo. 11. Alieno seruo per fideicommissum data libertate, si dominus eum iusto pretio non uendat, extinguitur libertas, quoniam nec pretii computatio pro libertate fieri potest[1]. 12. Li-

the condition had been fulfilled. 6. If he be ordered to give money to some stranger and so become free, and be prepared to give it, but he to whom he was ordered to give it refuse to accept or die before accepting, he becomes free just as though he had given it.

7. Liberty can either be given directly, in such phrase as "Be thou free," "Let him be free," "I order him to be free:" or by *fideicommissum*, for instance in the words, "I request, I entrust to my heir's good faith that he manumit my slave Stichus." 8. One ordered in express terms to be freed becomes a freedman of the testator or *libertus orcinus:* but one whose liberty is given him by *fideicommissum* becomes the freedman of the manumittor and not of the testator. 9. Any man who can be charged by *fideicommissum* to perform anything, can also be charged by *fideicommissum* to confer freedom. 10. Liberty can be given by *fideicommissum* either to the testator's own slave, to the slave of an heir or legatee, or to the slave of any stranger. 11. If liberty be given to a stranger's slave by *fideicommissum* and the owner will not sell him for a fair price, the liberty is extinguished, because no calculation of price in lieu of liberty is possible[1]. 12. As

[1] These paragraphs, 7—11, are repeated almost verbatim in Gaius, II. 263—267, 272.

bertas sicut dari, ita et adimi tam testamento quam codicillis testamento confirmatis potest; ut tamen eodem modo adimatur, quo et data est.

TIT. III. DE LATINIS.

1. Latini ius Quiritium consequuntur his modis[1]: beneficio principali, liberis, iteratione, militia, naue, aedificio[2], pistrino[3]; praeterea ex senatusconsulto mulier quae sit ter enixa. 2. Beneficio principali Latinus ciuitatem Romanam accipit, si ab imperatore ius Quiritium impetrauerit[4]. 3. Liberis ius Quiritium consequitur Latinus, qui minor triginta annorum manumissionis tempore fuit: nam lege Iunia cautum est, ut si ciuem Romanam uel Latinam uxorem duxerit, testatione interposita quod liberorum quaerendorum causa uxorem duxerit, postea filio filiaue nato nataue et anniculo facto, possit apud praetorem uel praesidem prouinciae causam probare et fieri ciuis

liberty can be given, so also can it be taken away either by a testament or by codicils confirmed in a testament; provided only it be taken away in the same manner in which it was given.

III. ON LATINS.

1. Latins obtain Roman citizenship in the following ways[1]: by grant of the emperor, by children, by iteration, by military service, by a ship, by a building[2], by the trade of baking[3]; and besides, in virtue of a *senatus-consultum*, a woman obtains it by bearing three children. 2. A Latin obtains Roman citizenship by grant of the emperor, if he acquires the right through direct request to him[4]. 3. A Latin obtains Roman citizenship by children, if at the time of his manumission he was under the age of thirty years: for it was provided by the Lex Junia that if a Latin take to wife a Roman citizen or a Latin, making attestation that he marries her for the purpose of obtaining children, he can, after the birth of a son or daughter and their attainment of the age of one year, prove his case before the Praetor or the governor of a province and become a Roman

---

[1] Gaius, I. 28...

[2] *Ib.* I. 34.

[3] Bakers had other privileges; for instance they were allowed to decline a tutorship, see D. 27. 1. 46.

[4] Gaius, III. 72, 73.

Romanus, tam ipse quam filius filiaue eius et uxor; scilicet si et ipsa Latina sit; nam si uxor ciuis Romana sit, partus quoque ciuis Romanus est ex senatusconsulto quod auctore diuo Hadriano factum est[1]. 4. Iteratione[2] fit ciuis Romanus, qui post Latinitatem, quam acceperat maior triginta annorum, iterum iuste manumissus est ab eo, cuius ex iure Quiritium seruus fuit. sed huic concessum est ex senatusconsulto[3], etiam liberis ius Quiritium consequi. 5. Militia ius Quiritium accipit Latinus, (si) inter uigiles Romae sex annis militauerit, ex lege Visellia[4]. Praeterea ex senatusconsulto concessum est ei ut, si triennio inter uigiles militauerit, ius Quiritium consequatur. 6. Naue Latinus ciuitatem Romanam accipit, si non minorem quam decem milium modiorum nauem fabricauerit, et Romam sex annis frumentum portauerit, ex edicto diui Claudii.

citizen, both himself and his son or daughter, and his wife; that is to say if she too be a Latin; for if the wife be a Roman citizen, her offspring also is a Roman citizen by virtue of a *senatus-consultum* passed at the instance of the late emperor Hadrian[1]. 4. A Latin becomes a Roman citizen by iteration[2], if after the gift of Latinity has been conferred on him when over thirty years of age, he be a second time manumitted in due form by the person whose slave he was in Quiritary right. But by virtue of a *senatus-consultum*[3] it is allowed such an one to acquire Roman citizenship by children also.

5. A Latin receives Roman citizenship by military service in virtue of the Lex Visellia[4], if he have served six years in the Roman guards: but afterwards by a *senatus-consultum* it was allowed him to obtain Roman citizenship by serving three years in the guards. 6. A Latin receives Roman citizenship, in virtue of an edict of the late emperor Claudius, by a ship, if he have built one of the burden of not less than 10,000 *modii* and imported corn in it to Rome for six years......

---

1 Gaius, I. 29, 30.

2 *Ib.* I. 35.

3 Sc. that of Pegasus and Pusio mentioned by Gaius, I. 31.

4 Introduced by L. Visellius Varro in the time of Claudius.

TIT. IV. DE HIS QVI SVI IVRIS SVNT.

1. Sui iuris sunt familiarum suarum principes, id est pater familiae, itemque mater familiae[1].

2. Qui matre quidem (certa), patre autem incerto nati sunt, spurii adpellantur[2].

TIT. V. DE HIS QVI IN POTESTATE SVNT.

1. In potestate sunt liberi parentum ex iusto matrimonio nati.

2. Iustum matrimonium est, si inter eos qui nuptias contrahunt conubium sit, et tam masculus pubes quam femina (uiri) potens sit, et utrique consentiant si sui iuris sint, aut etiam parentes eorum si in potestate sint. 3. Conubium est uxoris iure ducendae facultas. 4. Conubium habent ciues

IV. ON THOSE WHO ARE SUI IURIS.

1. Those who are heads of their own families are *sui juris*, that is the father of a family, and the mother of a family[1]. 2. Those sprung from a known mother, but an unknown father, are called *spurious*[2].

V. ON THOSE WHO ARE UNDER POTESTAS.

1. Children born from a lawful marriage are under the *potestas* of their parents.

2. It is a lawful marriage, if there be *conubium* between those who contract the marriage, if the man be of the age of puberty as well as the woman of the age of child-bearing, and if they both consent, supposing them to be *sui juris*, or if their parents also consent, supposing them to be under *potestas*. 3. *Conubium* is the right of marrying a wife. 4. Roman citizens have *conubium*

[1] Cicero (*Top.* 3) states that a wife was *materfamilias* only when under *manus*: "Genus est uxor, ejus duae formae, una matrum-familias, earum quae in manum convenerunt, altera earum quae tantummodo uxores habentur." Aulus Gellius (18. 6) says the same. But during her husband's life-time a wife *in manu* was certainly not *princeps familiae*, for she was regarded as a daughter of her husband: she would therefore become *princeps familiae* only on the death of the husband: and her *familia* would consist of herself only, for "mulier familiae suae et caput et finis est." D. 50. 16. 195. 5.

[2] Gaius, 1. 64.

Romani cum ciuibus Romanis; cum Latinis autem et peregrinis ita si concessum sit[1]. 5. Cum seruis nullum est conubium. 6. Inter parentes et liberos infinite cuiuscumque gradus conubium non est. inter cognatos autem ex transuerso gradu olim quidem usque ad quartum gradum matrimonia contrahi non poterant: nunc autem etiam ex tertio gradu licet uxorem ducere; sed tantum fratris filiam, non etiam sororis filiam, aut amitam uel materteram, quamuis eodem gradu sint. eam denique quae nouerca uel priuigna uel nurus uel socrus nostra fuit uxorem ducere non possumus[2]. 7. Si quis eam quam non licet uxorem duxerit, incestum matrimonium contrahit: ideoque liberi in potestate eius non fiunt, sed quasi uulgo concepti spurii sunt[3].

8. Conubio interueniente liberi semper patrem sequuntur: non interueniente conubio matris conditioni accedunt, excepto eo qui ex peregrino et ciue Romana peregrinus nascitur, quoniam lex Mensia[4] ex alterutro peregrino natum deterioris

with Roman citizens; but with Latins and foreigners only when they have obtained a special grant to that effect[1]. 5. With slaves there is no *conubium*. 6. Between ascendants and descendants in any degree however distant there is no *conubium*. Formerly also marriages could not be contracted between those collaterally related within the fourth degree: but now it is allowable to take a wife even of the third degree; but only a brother's daughter, and not also a sister's daughter or the sister of a father, or of a mother, although they are in the same degree. Lastly we cannot marry one who has been our step-mother or step-daughter, daughter-in-law, or mother-in-law[2]. 7. If any man marry a woman whom he is prohibited to marry, he contracts an incestuous marriage, and therefore his children do not come under his *potestas*, but are *spurious*[3], like those born out of wedlock.

8. If there be *conubium* between the parents, the children always follow the father: if there be not *conubium*, they follow the condition of the mother: except that anyone born from a foreigner and a Roman woman is a foreigner from his birth, inasmuch as the Lex Mensia[4] orders that a child sprung

[1] Gaius, I. 57.
[2] *Ib.* I. 59—63.
[3] IV. 2. Gaius, I. 64.
[4] *Mensia* in the only MS. of Ulpian: but *Minicia* according to Studemund's apograph of Gaius.

parentis conditionem sequi iubet. 9. Ex ciue Romano et Latina Latinus nascitur, et ex libero et ancilla seruus; quoniam, cum his casibus conubia non sint, partus sequitur matrem. 10. In his qui iure contracto matrimonio nascuntur conceptionis tempus spectatur: in his autem qui non legitime concipiuntur editionis; ueluti si ancilla conceperit, deinde manumissa pariat, liberum parit; nam quoniam non legitime concepit, cum editionis tempore libera sit, partus quoque liber est[1].

TIT. VI. DE DOTIBVS.

1. Dos aut datur, aut dicitur, aut promittitur. 2. Dotem dicere[2] potest mulier quae nuptura est, et debitor mulieris, si iussu eius dicat; item parens mulieris uirilis sexus, per uirilem sexum cognatione iunctus, uelut pater, auus paternus. dare, promittere dotem omnes possunt.

from a foreigner on either side shall follow the condition of his inferior parent. 9. The offspring of a Roman citizen and a Latin woman is a Latin from his birth, and that of a free man and a slave woman is a slave; for there being no *conubium* in these cases, the offspring follows the mother. 10. The time of conception is regarded in the case of those who are born from a lawful marriage; that of birth in the case of those conceived illegitimately: for instance, if a female slave have conceived, and then after manumission bear her child, the child she bears is free: for as she did not conceive legitimately and is herself free at the time of birth, her offspring is free also[1].

VI. ON MARRIAGE-PORTIONS.

1. A marriage-portion is either given, declared or promised.
2. A woman about to marry can *declare*[2] a marriage-portion, and so can the debtor of a woman, provided he does so at her order: and so can a male ascendant of a woman related to her through a line of males, as a father or a paternal grandfather. Any person can *give* or *promise* a marriage-portion.

---

[1] Gaius, I. 89—92.

[2] *Dotis dictio* is an assignment made by the wife, her ascendant or her debtor, and not put into stipulatory form, as is more fully explained by the following extract from the

3. Dos aut profecticia dicitur, id est quam pater mulieris dedit; aut aduenticia, id est ea quae a quouis alio data est.

4. Mortua in matrimonio muliere, dos a patre profecta ad patrem reuertitur, quintis in singulos liberos in infinitum[1] relictis penes uirum. quod si pater non sit, apud maritum remanet. 5. Aduenticia autem dos semper penes maritum remanet, praeterquam si is qui dedit, ut sibi redderetur, stipulatus fuerit; quae dos specialiter recepticia dicitur.

6. Diuortio facto si quidem sui iuris sit mulier, ipsa habet rei uxoriae actionem, id est dotis repetitionem; quodsi in po-

3. A marriage-portion is said to be either "profectitious," *i. e.* one which the father of the woman has given: or "adventitious," *i. e.* one which has been given by somebody else.

4. If the woman die during the continuance of the marriage, a marriage-portion which proceeded from the father returns to the father, a fifth being retained in the husband's control for each child as far as the marriage-portion will go[1]. But if the father be no longer alive, it remains with the husband. 5. An adventitious portion, on the contrary, always remains in the husband's hands, unless the donor made a stipulation that it should be returned to him; and such a marriage-portion has the specific name of "receptitious."

6. When a divorce takes place, the woman herself has the action for the wife's property, *i. e.* the suit for recovery of the marriage-portion, if she be *sui juris;* but if she be under the

epitome of Gaius: "Sunt et aliae obligationes quae nulla praecedente interrogatione contrahi possunt, id est, ut si mulier, sive sponso uxor futura, sive jam marito, dotem dicat. Quod tam de mobilibus rebus quam de fundis fieri potest. Et non solum in hac obligatione ipsa mulier obligatur, sed et pater ejus, et debitor ipsius mulieris, si pecuniam quam illi debebat sponso creditricis ipse debitor in dotem dixerit. Hae tantum tres personae, nulla interrogatione praecedente, possunt dictione dotis legitime obligari. Aliae vero personae, si pro muliere dotem viro promiserint, communi jure obligari debent, id est, ut et interrogata respondeant et stipulata promittant." This passage from the epitome corresponds to the portion of Gaius missing after III. 94. Cujacius in his commentary of this portion of Ulpian says, "dos *dicitur* solennibus verbis sine interrogatione:" so also Lud. Charonda, "dos *dicitur* quae sine ulla stipulatione constituitur."

[1] *In infinitum* obviously cannot mean "however many children there be," for what would be done if there were six? But the phrase is introduced to show that there is no limitation like that attaching to retentions, and mentioned in § 10 below.

testate patris sit, pater adiuncta filiae persona habet actionem; nec interest aduenticia sit dos an profecticia. 7. Post diuortium defuncta muliere heredi eius actio non aliter datur, quam si moram in dote mulieri reddenda maritus fecerit.

8. Dos si pondere, numero, mensura contineatur, annua, bima, trima die redditur[1]; nisi si ut praesens reddatur, conuenerit. reliquae dotes statim redduntur.

9. Retentiones ex dote fiunt (aut propter liberos,) aut propter mores, aut propter inpensas, aut propter res donatas, aut propter res amotas.

10. Propter liberos retentio fit, si culpa mulieris aut patris, cuius in potestate est, diuortium factum sit; tunc enim singulorum liberorum nomine sextae retinentur ex dote; non plures

potestas of her father, he has the action in the joint name of his daughter and himself: and whether the marriage-portion be adventitious or profectitious makes no matter. 7. If the woman die after a divorce has taken place, an action does not lie for her heir, unless the husband have made delay in restoring the marriage-portion to his wife.

8. If the marriage-portion consist of things weighed, numbered or measured, it is restored by instalments at the end of one, two and three years respectively[1]: unless there have been an agreement for its immediate restoration. Other marriage-portions are restored at once.

9. Retentions out of a marriage-portion are made either on account of children, or on account of immorality, or on account of expenses, or on account of donations, or on account of abstractions.

10. Retention is made on account of children, if the divorce take place through the fault of the woman or of her father under whose *potestas* she is: for in such case a sixth is retained out of the marriage-portion on account of each child: but not a greater number of sixths than three. The

[1] The *dos* was usually paid over to the husband by the father in three instalments,—sometimes in more by special agreement:—therefore when returned would naturally be paid back in the same way. See D. 23. 4. 19; Cic. *Epp. ad Fam.* 6. 18. The *prima pensio* in a return of *dos* is mentioned in *Epp. ad Att.* XI. 4, the *secunda* in *Epp. ad Att.* XI. 25, the *tertia* in *Epp. ad Att.* XI. 23.

tamen quam tres. sextae in retentione sunt non in petitione[1]. 11. Dos, quae semel functa est, amplius fungi non potest, nisi aliud matrimonium sit.

12. Morum nomine, grauiorum quidem sexta[2] retinetur, leuiorum autem octaua. grauiores mores sunt adulteria tantum; leuiores omnes reliqui. 13. Mariti mores puniuntur in ea quidem dote, quae annua (bima, trima) die reddi debet[3], ita (ut) propter maiores mores praesentem dotem reddat, propter minores senum mensium die. in ea autem quae praesens reddi solet, tantum ex fructibus iubetur reddere, quantum in illa dote quae triennio redditur repraesentatio facit[4].

sixths are matters of retention, not of suit[1]. 11. A marriage-portion which has once been settled for cannot be settled for again, unless there be a subsequent marriage.

12. Retention is made for immorality;—a sixth[2] for immorality of a grosser kind, an eighth for immorality of a lighter kind. Adulteries alone constitute the grosser immorality, all others are the lighter. 13. In the case of a marriage-portion which ought to be returned by three annual instalments[3], the immorality of a husband is punished by making him restore it at once for grosser immorality, and by instalments at intervals of six months for lighter immorality: whilst in the case of that which on a voluntary divorce would be restored at once, he is ordered to restore so much out of profits, as the payment in advance would amount to in the case of a marriage-portion returnable by three yearly payments[4].

---

1 The sixths must be retained by the husband when he returns the *dos*: for he has no action for them, if he has omitted the deduction. The reason is given in § 11; that a *dos* once settled for, cannot be dealt with again, unless there be another marriage of the woman. The first marriage is completely ended, not at the divorce, but at the time of restitution of the *dos*: and the *dos* then is no longer *dos*.

2 Huschke defends the reading *sextae retinentur*, instead of *sexta retinetur* as adopted by Böcking, for he says that a woman may commit several adulteries and be fined one-sixth of her portion for each: but that there is no accumulation of penalties in the case of lesser immorality.

3 Böcking and Huschke both say that *annua die* is not to be interpreted "at the end of a year," but "by annual instalments," *i.e.* in three portions, "annua, bima, trima die." The MS. has *a die*.

4 A calculation is made of the amount he would have lost by having to pay at once the marriage-portion, if properly returnable in three instalments:—then to the mar-

14. Inpensarum species sunt tres: aut enim necessariae dicuntur, aut utiles, aut uoluptuosae. 15. Necessariae sunt impensae quibus non factis dos deterior futura est, uelut si quis ruinosas aedes refecerit. 16. Utiles sunt quibus non factis quidem deterior dos non fuerit, factis autem fructuosior effecta est, ueluti si uineta et oliueta fecerit. 17. Voluptuosae sunt quibus neque omissis deterior dos fuerit, neque factis fructuosior effecta est; quod euenit in uiridiariis et picturis similibusque rebus.

TIT. VII. DE IVRE DONATIONVM INTER VIRVM ET VXOREM.

1. Inter uirum et uxorem donatio non ualet nisi certis ex causis, id est mortis causa, diuortii causa, serui manumittendi gratia. hoc amplius principalibus constitutionibus con-

14. Of expenses there are three kinds: for they are styled either necessary, or profitable, or luxurious. 15. Expenses are "necessary" where the marriage-portion would be deteriorated by their not being incurred; as, for instance, if any one repair a dilapidated house.

16. "Profitable" expenses are such, that if they were not incurred the marriage-portion would not be deteriorated, but by their being incurred it is made more productive; as, for instance, if a man plant vineyards or oliveyards. 17. "Luxurious" expenses are such, that if they were forborne the marriage-portion would suffer no deterioration, and by their being incurred it is not made more productive; which is the case with lawns and pictures and such like.

VII. ON THE LAW OF GIFTS BETWEEN HUSBAND AND WIFE.

1. A gift between husband and wife does not stand good except in certain cases, that is, in prospect of death, in prospect of divorce, and to procure the manumission of a slave. Besides a woman is allowed by imperial constitutions to make a gift to her husband to the end that he may receive from

riage-portion, which he pays back at once according to agreement, a further sum is added equal to that loss.

cessum est mulieri in hoc donare uiro suo, ut is ab imperatore lato clauo uel equo publico similiue honore honoretur[1].

2. Si maritus diuortii causa res amouerit, rerum quoque amotarum actione tenebitur.

3. Si maritus pro muliere se obligauerit uel in rem eius inpenderit, diuortio facto eo nomine cauere sibi solet stipulatione tribunicia[2].

4. In potestate parentum sunt etiam hi liberi quorum causa probata est, per errorem contracto matrimonio inter disparis condicionis personas[3]: nam siue ciuis Romanus Latinam aut peregrinam uel eam quae dediticiorum numero est, quasi (ciuem Romanam) per ignorantiam uxorem duxerit, siue ciuis Romana per errorem peregrino uel ei qui dediticiorum numero

the emperor the distinction of senatorial or equestrian rank, or some honour of the same nature[1].

2. If the husband in prospect of a divorce abstract property of his wife, he will also be liable in the action "for things abstracted."

3. When a husband has bound himself for his wife or spent money upon her property, on the occurrence of a divorce it is usual for him to assure himself on that account by a tribunician stipulation[2].

4. Those children too are under the *potestas* of their parents whose case has been proved, after a marriage has been contracted under a misapprehension between persons of unequal condition[3]. For if a Roman citizen have in ignorance married a Latin, or foreign woman or a woman in the category of *dediticii*, taking her for a Roman citizen, or if a Roman woman have been married by mistake to a foreigner or one in the category of *dediticii*, thinking him either a Roman citizen or

[1] The constitution of Antonine is one of those referred to. See D. 24. 1. 42.

[2] "That is, the plebeian tribunes, when application is made to them by husbands called upon to restore a marriage-portion, will interfere on their behalf, unless they are secured by their wives entering into this stipulation." Huschke.

[3] Sc. *causa erroris*. Gaius, I. 65—75. The subject of *potestas* is now resumed from V. 1, the law as to marriages and marriage-portions forming a parenthesis extending from V. to VII. 3 inclusive. The rubric of Title VII. seems to be an interpolation of some transcriber; as only the first sentence relates to gifts between husband and wife.

est, (aut quasi ciui Romano) aut etiam quasi Latino ex lege Aelia Sentia[1] nupta fuerit, causa probata, ciuitas Romana datur tam liberis quam parentibus, praeter eos qui dediticiorum numero sunt; et ex eo fiunt in potestate parentum liberi.

TIT. VIII. DE ADOPTIONIBVS.

1. Non tantum naturales liberi in potestate parentum sunt, sed etiam adoptiui[2]. 2. Adoptio fit aut per populum, aut per praetorem uel praesidem prouinciae. illa adoptio quae per populum fit specialiter arrogatio dicitur. 3. Per populum qui sui iuris sunt arrogantur; per praetorem autem filiifamiliae a parentibus dantur in adoptionem. 4. Arrogatio Romae dumtaxat fit; adoptio autem etiam in prouinciis apud praesides. 5. Per praetorem uel praesidem prouinciae adoptari tam masculi quam feminae, et tam puberes quam inpuberes

even a Latin and intending to take advantage of the Lex Aelia Sentia[1]; on proof of the case Roman citizenship is given both to the children and the parents, unless the latter be in the category of *dediticii:* and thereby the children come under the *potestas* of their parents.

VIII. ON ADOPTIONS.

1. Not only are actual children under the *potestas* of their ascendants, but adopted children also[2]. 2. Adoption takes place either by authority of the *populus*, or by that of the Praetor or the governor of a province. That adoption which takes place by authority of the *populus* has the special name of arrogation. 3. By authority of the *populus* those *sui juris* are arrogated: by authority of the Praetor those under *potestas* are given in adoption by their ascendants. 4. Arrogation takes place at Rome only, but adoption in the provinces too in the presence of the governors thereof. 5. By authority of the Praetor or the governor of a province both males and females, those under puberty and those over puberty, can be adopted.

---

[1] In III. 3 Ulpian says *ex lege Junia;* and that seems to be correct: the Lex Aelia Sentia gave the right to those *in forma libertatis;* and it was the Lex Junia which made it available for Latins.

[2] Gaius, I. 97—103.

possunt. per populum uero Romanum feminae quidem non arrogantur; pupilli autem quondam non poterant arrogari[1], nunc autem possunt ex constitutione diui Antonini Pii. 6. Qui generare non potest, uelut spado, utroque modo potest adoptare; idem iuris est in persona caelibis. 7. Item is, qui filium non habet, in locum nepotis adoptare potest. 7 *a.* Feminae uero neutro modo possunt adoptare, quoniam nec naturales liberos in potestate habent[2]. 8. Si paterfamiliae arrogandum se dederit, liberi quoque eius quasi nepotes in potestate fiunt arrogatoris[3].

TIT. IX. DE HIS QVI IN MANV SVNT.

1. Farreo conuenit uxor in manum certis uerbis et testibus x praesentibus et sollemni sacrificio facto, in quo panis quoque farreus adhibetur[4].

TIT. X. QVI IN POTESTATE (MANV) MANCIPIOVE SVNT QVEMADMODVM EO IVRE LIBERENTVR.

1. Liberi parentum potestate liberantur emancipatione,

Women are not arrogated even by authority of the Roman *populus;* but pupils, who in former times could not be arrogated[1], now can by virtue of a constitution of the late emperor Antoninus Pius. 6. One who cannot procreate, as an eunuch-born, can adopt by either method. The same rule applies also to an unmarried person. 7. Likewise he who has no son, can adopt a person to stand to him as grandson. 7 *a.* But women cannot adopt by either method, because they have not even their actual children under their *potestas*[2]. 8. If a person who is *sui juris* give himself in arrogation, his children also pass under the arrogator's *potestas* in the capacity of grandchildren[3].

IX. ON THOSE WHO ARE UNDER MANUS.

1. A woman comes under *manus* by a confarreation in a set form of words uttered in the presence of ten witnesses, and by the performance of a solemn sacrifice, in which a cake of fine flour is used[4].

X. HOW THOSE WHO ARE UNDER POTESTAS, MANUS OR MANCIPIUM, ARE SET FREE FROM THE TIE.

1. Descendants are freed from the *potestas* of their ascend-

[1] Gaius, I. 102.
[2] *Ib.* I. 104.
[3] *Ib.* I. 107.
[4] *Ib.* I. 112.

id est si posteaquam mancipati fuerint manumissi sint[1]. sed filius quidem ter mancipatus ter manumissus sui iuris fit; id enim lex duodecim tabularum iubet his uerbis: 'si pater filium ter uenunduit, filius a patre liber esto[2].' ceteri autem liberi praeter filium, tam masculi quam feminae, una mancipatione manumissioneque sui iuris fiunt. 2. Morte patris filius et filia sui iuris fiunt[3]; morte autem aui nepotes ita demum sui iuris fiunt, si post mortem aui in potestate patris futuri non sunt, uelut si moriente auo pater eorum aut etiam decessit aut de potestate dimissus est: nam si mortis aui tempore pater eorum in potestate eius sit, mortuo auo in patris sui potestate fiunt. 3. Si patri uel filio aqua et igni interdictum sit patria potestas tollitur, quia peregrinus fit is cui aqua et igni interdictum est; neque autem peregrinus ciuem Romanum, neque ciuis Romanus peregrinum in potestate habere potest[4]. 4. Si pater ab hostibus captus sit, quamuis seruus hostium fiat, tamen cum reuersus fuerit omnia

ants by emancipation, *i.e.* if they are manumitted after being mancipated[1]. But a son becomes *sui juris* only after being mancipated three times and manumitted three times: for a law of the Twelve Tables directs this in the following words: "if a father sell his son three times, let the son be free from the father[2]:" whilst descendants other than a son, whether male or female, become *sui juris* by one mancipation and one manumission. 2. A son and a daughter become *sui juris* by the death of their father[3]; but grandsons become *sui juris* by the death of their grandfather only in case they will not fall under the *potestas* of their father on the grandfather's death; for example, if at the time of their grandfather's death their father either have also died or been released from *potestas*: for they come into their father's *potestas* on the death of their grandfather, if at that moment their father be in his *potestas*. 3. If the father or son be interdicted from fire and water, the parental *potestas* is destroyed, because one who is interdicted from fire and water becomes a foreigner, and neither can a foreigner have a Roman citizen under his *potestas* nor a Roman citizen a foreigner[4]. 4. If a father be taken by the enemy, although he becomes a

[1] Gaius, I. 132.
[2] Tab. IV. l. 3.
[3] Gaius, I. 127.
[4] *Ib.* I. 128.

pristina iura recipit iure postliminii. sed quamdiu aput hostes est, patria potestas eius in filio interim pendebit; et cum reuersus fuerit ab hostibus in potestate filium habebit; si uero ibi decesserit sui iuris filius erit. filius quoque si captus fuerit ab hostibus, similiter propter ius postliminii patria potestas interim pendebit[1]. 5. In potestate parentum esse desinunt et hi qui flamines Diales inaugurantur et quae uirgines Vestae capiuntur[2].

TIT. XI. DE TVTELIS.

1. Tutores constituuntur tam masculis quam feminis: sed masculis quidem inpuberibus dumtaxat propter aetatis infirmitatem; feminis autem (tam) inpuberibus quam puberibus et propter sexus infirmitatem et propter forensium rerum ignorantiam[3].

2. Tutores aut legitimi sunt, aut senatusconsultis constituti, aut moribus introducti.

3. Legitimi tutores sunt, (qui) ex lege aliqua descendunt;

slave of the enemy, yet on his return he recovers all his original rights by the rule of postliminy. But so long as he remains with the enemy, his parental *potestas* over his son is for the time suspended: and on his return he will have his son under his *potestas*, but if he die there the son will be *sui juris*. So too if the son be taken by the enemy, the parental *potestas* will in like manner be suspended for the time by the rule of postliminy[1]. 5. Those also cease to be under the *potestas* of their ascendants who are admitted flamens of Jupiter or elected vestal virgins[2].

XI. ON TUTELAGES.

1. Tutors are appointed both to males and females: but to males only whilst they remain under the age of puberty, on account of their infirmity of age: to females, however, both under and over the age of puberty, as well on account of their infirmity of sex as on account of their ignorance of forensic matters[3].

2. Tutors are either statutable, appointed by *senatus-consulta*, or introduced by custom.

3. Statutable tutors are those originating from any *lex:* but

[1] Gaius, I. 129. [2] *Ib.* I. 130, 145. [3] *Ib.* I. 144, 189—193.

per eminentiam autem legitimi dicuntur lege duodecim tabularum introducti, seu propalam, quales sunt agnati, seu per consequentiam, quales sunt patroni[1]. 4. Agnati sunt a patre cognati uirilis sexus[2], per uirilem sexum descendentes, eiusdem familiae[3], uelut patrui, filii fratris, fratres patrueles.

5. Qui liberum caput mancipatum sibi uel a parente uel a coemptionatore[4] manumisit, per similitudinem patroni tutor efficitur, qui fiduciarius tutor appellatur[5].

6. Legitimi tutores alii tutelam in iure cedere possunt[6]. 7. Is cui tutela in iure cessa est cessicius tutor appellatur[7]; qui siue mortuus fuerit, siue capite minutus, siue alii tutelam porro cesserit, redit ad legitimum tutorem tutela. sed et si legitimus decesserit aut capite minutus fuerit, cessicia quoque tutela extinguitur. 8. Quantum ad agnatos pertinet, hodie

those are more specially styled statutable who are introduced by a law of the Twelve Tables, whether in direct terms, as agnates are, or constructively, as are patrons[1]. 4. Agnates are male[2] relatives connected on the father's side, tracing through the male sex, and of the same family[3], as a father's brothers, a brother's sons, the sons of two brothers.

5. He who has manumitted a free person mancipated to him either by an ascendant or by a *coemptionator*[4], becomes tutor because of his analogy to a patron, and is called a fiduciary tutor[5].

6. Statutable tutors can transfer their tutorship to another by means of a cession in court[6]. 7. He to whom the tutorship is ceded is called a cessician tutor[7]; and if he either die, or suffer *capitis diminutio*, or cede the tutorship over to another, the tutorship returns to the statutable tutor: and so too if the statutable tutor die or suffer *capitis diminutio*, the cessician tutorship is also extinguished. 8. So far as the agnates are

[1] Gaius, I. 155, 165. In the latter paragraph we have an explanation of the "per consequentiam" of Ulpian.

[2] This is erroneous: agnates may be male and female, or both females; but they must each trace to a common male ancestor *through* an unbroken line of males.

[3] Emancipation or adoption broke the agnatic tie previously subsisting, hence the introduction of the words "eiusdem familiae."

[4] Gaius, I. 113—115, 136.

[5] *Ib.* I. 166.

[6] *Ib.* II. 24.

[7] *Ib.* I. 168—171.

cessicia tutela non procedit, quoniam permissum erat in iure cedere tutelam feminarum tantum non etiam masculorum; feminarum autem legitimas tutelas lex Claudia sustulit excepta tutela patronorum.

9. Legitima tutela capitis diminutione amittitur. 10. Capitis minutiones species sunt tres, maxima, media, minima[1]. 11. Maxima capitis diminutio est per quam et ciuitas et libertas amittitur, ueluti cum incensus aliquis uenierit, aut mulier, quod alieno seruo se iunxerit denuntiante domino, eius ancilla facta fuerit ex senatusconsulto Claudiano. 12. Media capitis diminutio dicitur per quam, sola ciuitate amissa, libertas retinetur; quod fit in eo cui aqua et igni interdicitur. 13. Minima capitis diminutio est per quam, et ciuitate et libertate salua, status dumtaxat hominis mutatur; quod fit adoptione et in manum conuentione.

14. Testamento quoque nominatim tutores dati confirmantur eadem lege duodecim tabularum his uerbis: 'uti legassit super

concerned, cessician tutorship does not exist at the present day; since it used to be allowed to make cession of the tutelages of females only and not of those of males; and the Lex Claudia abolished the statutable tutelages of women, except when held by patrons.

9. A statutable tutorship is lost by *capitis diminutio.* 10. There are three varieties of *capitis diminutio*, *maxima*, *media*, and *minima*[1]. 11. *Capitis diminutio maxima* is that by which both citizenship and liberty are lost, as in the case of a man being sold for not enrolling himself on the censor's register, or in that of a woman who cohabits with another person's slave against his master's warning, and is made his slave in accordance with the *senatus-consultum* of Claudius. 12. *Capitis diminutio media* is the name applied when citizenship alone is lost and liberty retained; which is the case with one interdicted from fire and water. 13. *Capitis diminutio minima* is that whereby the status only of a man is changed, his citizenship and liberty being unaltered; a result which follows on adoption and the passing under *manus*.

14. Tutors appointed by name in a testament are also confirmed by the same law of the Twelve Tables in these words:

[1] Gaius, I. 159—162.

pecunia tutelaue sua rei, ita ius esto[1]:' qui tutores datiui appellantur[2]. 15. Dari testamento tutores possunt liberis qui in potestate sunt[3]. 16. Testamento tutores dari possunt hi cum quibus testamenti faciendi ius est[4], praeter Latinum Iunianum; nam Latinus habet quidem testamenti factionem, sed tamen tutor dari non potest; id enim lex Iunia prohibet. 17. Si capite diminutus fuerit[5] tutor testamento datus non amittit tutelam; sed si abdicauerit se tutela, desinit esse tutor. abdicare autem est dicere, nolle se tutorem esse; in iure cedere autem tutelam testamento datus non potest; nam et legitimus in iure cedere potest, abdicare se non potest.

18. Lex Atilia iubet, mulieribus pupillisue non habentibus tutores dari a praetore et maiore parte tribunorum plebis, quos tutores Atilianos appellamus[6]. sed quia lex Atilia Romae tantum locum habet, lege Iulia et Titia prospectum est ut in

"In accordance with the testamentary disposition which a man had made regarding his money or the tutelage of his property, so let the right be[1]:" and these tutors are called dative[2]. 15. Tutors can be given in a testament to those descendants who are under *potestas*[3]. 16. Any persons with whom the testator has *testamenti factio*[4] can be appointed tutors in a testament, except a Junian Latin. For a Latin has *testamenti factio*, and yet cannot be appointed tutor; the Lex Junia forbidding it. 17. If the tutor appointed in a testament suffer *capitis diminutio*[5], he does not lose his tutorship: but if he renounce the tutorship, he ceases to be tutor; and to renounce it is to state that he declines to be tutor. Further, a testamentary tutor cannot transfer his office by cession in court; whereas a statutable tutor can get rid of it by cession in court, but not by mere renunciation.

18. The Lex Atilia orders that when women or pupils have no tutors some shall be given to them by the Praetor and the majority of the tribunes of the plebs, and these we call Atilian tutors[6]. But as the Lex Atilia is in force at Rome only, it has been provided by the Lex Julia et Titia that in the provinces

1 Tab. v. l. 3.

2 Gaius, I. 154.

3 *Ib.* I. 144.

4 The various meanings of this phrase are to be found in the note on Gaius, II. 114. Latins, according to Gaius, had no *testamenti factio* except in the sense of being competent witnesses, *i.e.* *testamenti factio relativa.* Gaius, I. 23, III. 72.

5 Sc. *minima.*

6 Gaius, I. 185.

prouinciis quoque similiter a praesidibus earum dentur tutores. 19. Lex Iunia tutorem fieri iubet Latinae uel Latini inpuberis eum cuius ea isve ante manumissionem ex iure Quiritium fuit[1]. 20. Ex lege Iulia de maritandis ordinibus tutor datur a praetore urbis ei mulieri uirginiue quam ex hac ipsa lege nubere oportet, ad dotem dandam dicendam promittendamue[2] si legitimum tutorem pupillum habeat[3]. sed postea senatus censuit ut etiam in prouinciis quoque similiter a praesidibus earum ex eadem causa tutores dentur. 21. Praeterea etiam in locum muti furiosiue tutoris alium dandum esse tutorem ad dotem constituendam senatus censuit[4]. 22. Item ex senatusconsulto tutor datur mulieri ei cuius tutor abest, praeterquam si patronus sit qui abest: nam in locum patroni absentis a liberta alter peti non potest nisi ad hereditatem adeundam et nuptias contrahendas[5]. idemque permisit in pupillo patroni filio. 23. Hoc amplius senatus censuit ut si tutor pupilli pupillaeue

also tutors shall in like manner be appointed by their governors. 19. The Lex Junia orders that the tutor of a female Latin or of a male Latin under the age of puberty shall be the person to whom they belonged in Quiritary right before their manumission[1]. 20. By the *Lex Julia de maritandis ordinibus* a tutor is given by the Praetor Urbanus to any woman or virgin bound to marry under the self-same law, in order that he may give, assign or promise her marriage-portion[2], if she have a pupil for her statutable tutor[3]. But afterwards the senate decreed that tutors should be appointed in the provinces also by the governors thereof in like manner under similar circumstances. 21. The senate has further decreed that another tutor shall be appointed in the place of a dumb or mad tutor for the purpose of settling the marriage-portion[4]. 22. Likewise by a *senatus-consultum* a tutor is appointed to a woman whose tutor is absent, unless the absentee be a patron: for one cannot be applied for by a freedwoman in the place of an absent patron, except to take up an inheritance or to arrange a marriage[5]. And it allowed the same in the case of a patron's son being a pupil. 23. Besides this the senate has decreed that if the tutor of a pupil, whether

[1] Gaius, I. 167.
[2] VI. 1.
[3] Gaius, I. 178, 183.
[4] Gaius, I. 180.
[5] *Ib.* I. 173—177, 179.

suspectus a tutela submotus fuerit, uel etiam iusta de causa excusatus, in locum eius tutor alius (detur[1]).

24. Moribus[2] tutor datur mulieri pupilloue qui cum tutore suo lege aut legitimo iudicio[3] agere uult, ut auctore eo agat, ipse enim tutor in rem suam auctor fieri non potest, qui praetorius tutor dicitur, quia a praetore urbis dari consueuit[4].

25. Pupillorum pupillarumque tutores et negotia gerunt et auctoritatem interponunt; mulierum autem tutores auctoritatem dumtaxat interponunt[5].

26. Si plures sint tutores, omnes in omni re debent auctoritatem accommodare, praeter eos qui testamento dati sunt; nam ex his uel unius auctoritas sufficit.

27. Tutoris auctoritas necessaria est mulieribus quidem in his rebus: si lege aut legitimo iudicio agant[6], si se obligent, si ciuile negotium gerant[7], si libertae suae permittant in con-

male or female, be removed from his tutorship as untrustworthy, or excused for a just reason, another tutor may be appointed in his place[1].

24. A tutor is appointed by custom[2] to a woman or pupil who wishes to sue the proper tutor under a *lex* or by statutable proceedings[3], that she may act under his authorization (for the proper tutor cannot authorize in a matter concerning himself): and such an one is called a Praetorian tutor, because it is the custom for him to be appointed by the Praetor Urbanus[4].

25. The tutors of pupils, male or female, both transact their business and give their authorization: but the tutors of women give their authorization only[5].

26. If there be several tutors, they must all give their authorization to each individual transaction, except they be testamentary tutors; for in their case the authorization of any one is enough.

27. The authorization of their tutor is needful for women in the following matters: if they take proceedings under a *lex* or by statutable action[6], if they bind themselves by contract, if they transact any business connected with the civil law[7], if they permit one of their freedwomen to cohabit with another person's

[1] Gaius, I. 182.
[2] XI. 2.
[3] Gaius, IV. 103...
[4] *Ib.* I. 184.
[5] Gaius, I. 190—192.
[6] *Ib.* IV. 103...
[7] E.g. *a cessio in jure*, or a *mancipatio*, or an *aditio hereditatis*.

tubernio alieni serui morari, si rem mancipi alienent. pupillis autem hoc amplius etiam in rerum nec mancipi alienatione tutoris auctoritate opus est.

28. Liberantur tutela masculi quidem pubertate: puberem autem Cassiani quidem eum esse dicunt qui habitu corporis pubes apparet, id est qui generare possit; Proculeiani autem eum qui quattuor decem annos expleuit, uerum Prisco uisum eum puberem esse in quem utrumque concurrit, et habitus corporis et numerus annorum[1]. 28 *a.* Feminae autem tutela (*liberantur trium liberorum iure; libertae tantum, quae in patroni tutela sunt, quattuor liberorum iure ab ea*) liberantur[2].

TIT. XII. DE CVRATORIBVS.

1. Curatores aut legitimi sunt, id est qui ex lege duodecim tabularum dantur, aut honorarii, id est qui a praetore constituuntur. 2. Lex duodecim tabularum[3] furiosum, itemque prodigum cui bonis[4] interdictum est, in curatione iubet esse

slave, if they alienate a thing mancipable. Further than this, pupils require their tutor's authorization for the alienation of things non-mancipable.

28. Males are set free from tutelage by puberty: and the Cassians say that he is of puberty who shows the fact by his bodily development, *i.e.* who can procreate; whilst the Proculians say that he is who has completed his fourteenth year; but Priscus maintains that he is of puberty in whom both requirements are fulfilled, viz. both bodily development and the number of years[1]. 28 *a.* Women on the other hand are liberated from tutelage by prerogative of three children: freedwomen, who are under the tutelage of a patron, are liberated from it only by prerogative of four children[2].

XII. ON CURATORS.

1. Curators are either statutable, *i.e.* such as are given under a law of the Twelve Tables, or honorary, *i.e.* such as are appointed by the Praetor.

2. A law of the Twelve Tables[3] orders a madman, and likewise a prodigal interdicted from the management of his property[4], to be in the curation of his agnates. 3. A curator is

[1] Gaius, I. 196.

[2] *Ib.* I. 194.

[3] Tab. V. l. 7.

[4] Huschke thinks the words "pa-

agnatorum. 3. A praetore constituitur curator, quem ipse praetor uoluerit, libertinis prodigis, itemque ingenuis qui ex testamento parentis heredes facti male dissipant bona: his enim ex lege curator dari non poterat, cum ingenuus quidem non ab intestato sed ex testamento heres factus sit patri; libertinus autem nullo modo patri heres fieri possit, qui nec patrem habuisse uidetur, cum seruilis cognatio nulla sit. 4. Praeterea dat curatorem etiam ei, qui nuper pubes factus, idonee negotia sua tueri non potest[1].

TIT. XIII. DE CAELIBE ORBO ET SOLITARIO PATRE[2].

1. Lege Iulia[3] prohibentur uxores ducere senatores quidem liberique eorum libertinas et quae ipsae quarumue pater ma-

appointed by the Praetor, being such person as the Praetor himself chooses, to prodigal freedmen, and likewise to free-born persons who are made heirs by the testament of their ascendant and criminally waste his goods: for to such persons a curator could not be given under the law, inasmuch as the freeman is heir to his father, not on intestacy, but by his testament; and the freedman cannot be heir to his father in any way, for he is not even considered to have a father, there being no relationship among slaves. 4. Moreover the Praetor gives a curator to one who has just attained puberty, but cannot properly superintend his own business[1].

XIII. ON THE UNMARRIED, THE CHILDLESS, AND THE FATHER WHO HAS LOST HIS CHILDREN[2].

1. By the Lex Julia[3] senators and their descendants are forbidden to marry freedwomen, or women who have themselves

ternis et avitis" have been lost out of the text; and probably such is the case, 1st, because something of the sort seems implied in the following paragraph and is needed to bring out its force, and 2nd, because Paulus III. 4. 7 says: "Moribus per Praetorem bonis interdicitur hoc modo: Quando tibi bona *paterna avitaque* nequitia tua disperdis, liberosque tuos ad egestatem perducis, ob eam rem tibi ea re commercioque interdico."

1 This was by virtue of the Lex Praetoria or Laetoria. See Just. *Inst.* I. 23, 2, Abdy and Walker's edition.

2 *Solitarius* may mean either the same as *orbus*, or "having only one child." As there is nothing about a *solitarius* in the Title, it is impossible to know which meaning is intended. See Dirksen, *sub verb.* The rubric seems to be a late interpolation.

3 App. (H).

terue artem ludicram fecerit; 2. ceteri autem ingenui prohibentur ducere corpore quaestum facientem, item lenam[1], et a lenone lenaue manumissam, et in adulterio deprehensam, et iudicio publico damnatam[2], et quae artem ludicram fecerit: adicit Mauricianus a senatu damnatam.

TIT. XIV. DE POENA LEGIS IVLIAE.

1. Feminis lex Iulia a morte uiri anni tribuit uacationem[3], a diuortio sex mensium: lex autem Papia a morte uiri biennii, a repudio anni et sex mensium.

TIT. XV. DE DECIMIS.

1. Vir et uxor inter se matrimonii nomine[4] decimam capere

followed the profession of the stage, or whose father or mother has done so; 2. other freeborn persons are forbidden to marry a common prostitute, or a procuress[1], or a woman manumitted by a procurer or procuress, or a woman caught in adultery, or one condemned in a public action[2], or one who has followed the profession of the stage; and Mauricianus adds one condemned by the senate...

XIV. ON THE PENALTY OF THE LEX JULIA.

1. The Lex Julia allows women a respite[3] from its requirements for one year after the death of a husband, and for six months after a divorce: but the Lex Papia allows a respite for two years after the death of a husband and for a year and six months after a divorce...

XV. ON TENTHS.

1. A husband and wife can receive one from the other a tenth on account of their marriage[4]. And if they have children

---

1 The MS. has the words in this order: "item corpore quaestum facientem. Ceteri autem ingenui prohibentur ducere lenam, etc." But Mommsen suggested a transposition, which has been adopted in the text.

2 Just. *Inst.* IV. 18; D. 23. 2. 43. The latter passage is well worth reading, as we find in it Ulpian's own interpretation of each word and expression of the portion of the Lex Julia referred to above.

3 See App. (H): where it is explained that by the *vacatio* abovenamed is meant a permission to women to take without the usual qualification legacies, inheritances or lapses devolving on them within the specified periods after their husband's death or their divorce.

4 Sc. even if *orbus* or *orba*, can receive a tenth of the deceased

possunt. quod si ex alio matrimonio liberos superstites habeant, praeter decimam quam matrimonii nomine capiunt, totidem decimas pro numero liberorum accipiunt. 2. Item communis filius filiaue post nominum diem amissus amissaue unam decimam adicit; duo autem post nominum diem amissi duas decimas adiciunt[1]. 3. Praeter decimam etiam usumfructum tertiae partis bonorum *uir et uxor* capere possunt, et quandoque liberos habuerint, eiusdem partis proprietatem; hoc amplius mulier, praeter decimam, dotem legatam sibi.

TIT. XVI. DE SOLIDI CAPACITATE INTER VIRVM ET VXOREM.

1. Aliquando uir et uxor inter se solidum capere possunt, uelut si uterque uel alteruter eorum nondum eius aetatis sint a qua lex liberos exigit, id est si uir minor annorum xxv sit, aut uxor annorum xx minor; item si utrique lege

by another marriage surviving, they can, in addition to the tenth on the title of their marriage, take further tenths in number equal to that of their children. 2. Likewise a son or daughter common to them and lost after his or her naming-day adds one tenth, and two lost after their naming-days add two tenths[1].

3. Besides the tenth, a husband or wife can also receive the usufruct of a third part of the consort's goods: and when they have had children, the ownership of the same amount: and in addition to this the wife, over and above the tenth, can take her marriage-portion, if bequeathed to her as a legacy.

XVI. ON THE POWER OF TAKING THE WHOLE AS BETWEEN HUSBAND AND WIFE.

1. Sometimes husband and wife can receive, one from the other, the entire inheritance, for instance if both or either of them be not yet of the age at which the *lex* insists on children, *i.e.* if either the husband be under 25, or the wife under 20 years of age; also if both of them have, whilst their marriage subsists,

---

partner's estate under her or his testament.

[1] Festus says the naming-day was the eighth or ninth after birth: "Lustrici dies infantium appellantur puellarum octavus, puerorum nonus, quia his lustrantur et iis nomina imponuntur."

Papia finitos annos in matrimonio excesserint, id est uir LX annos, uxor L; item si cognati inter se coierint usque ad sextum gradum. aut si uir (rei publicae causa) absit, et donec abest et intra annum postquam abesse desierit. 1 *a*. Libera inter eos testamenti factio est[1], si ius liberorum a principe inpetrauerint; aut si filium filiamue communem habeant[2], aut quattuordecim annorum filium, uel filiam duodecim amiserint; uel si duos trimos, uel tres post nominum diem amiserint, ut intra annum tamen et sex menses etiam unus cuiuscumque aetatis inpubes amissus solidi capiendi ius praestet. item si post mortem uiri intra decem menses uxor ex eo pepererit, solidum ex bonis eius capit.

2. Aliquando nihil inter se capiunt: id est, si contra legem Iuliam Papiamque Poppaeam contraxerint matrimonium, uerbi gratia si famosam quis uxorem duxerit, aut libertinam senator.

exceeded the ages limited by the Lex Papia, *i.e.* the husband 60, the wife 50; likewise, if relations within the sixth degree have married, or if the husband be absent on public business, both whilst he is still absent and within a year after he has ceased to be absent. 1 *a*. There is also complete *testamenti factio*[1] between them, if they have obtained from the emperor the privileges attaching to children, or if they have a son or daughter born from their union[2], or have lost a son of the age of fourteen or a daughter of the age of twelve: or have lost two children of the age of three years, or three after their naming-days, provided nevertheless that even one child lost at any age under puberty gives them the right of receiving the whole estate within a period of one year and six months from the death. Likewise if the wife within ten months after her husband's death bear a child by him, she takes the whole of his goods.

2. Sometimes they cannot take anything one from the other, *i.e.* when they have contracted a marriage contrary to the Lex Julia et Papia Poppaea, when for instance any freeborn man has married a woman of abandoned character, or when a senator has married a freedwoman.

---

[1] Gaius, II. 114 *n*.

[2] This is to mark the fact that the words "habet liberos, non habet liberos" in the Lex Papia Poppaea do not render it needful for two or more children to be born of the marriage, but even one will suffice. D. 50. 16. 148, 149.

3. Qui intra sexagesimum uel quae intra quinquagesimum annum neutri legi paruerit, licet ipsis legibus post hanc aetatem liberatus esset, perpetuis tamen poenis tenetur ex senatusconsulto Persiciano[1]. 4. Sed Claudiano senatusconsulto maior sexagenario si minorem quinquagenaria duxerit, perinde haberi iubetur, ac si minor sexaginta annorum duxisset uxorem. quod si maior quinquagenaria minori sexagenario nupserit, inpar matrimonium appellatur et senatusconsulto Caluitiano iubetur non proficere ad capiendas hereditates et legata et dotes. itaque mortua muliere dos caduca erit[2].

3. A man who has conformed to neither *lex* within his sixtieth year, or a woman who has not done so within her fiftieth, although after such age exempt from compliance according to the rules of the *leges* themselves, yet will be liable to their standing penalties by reason of the *senatus-consultum Persicianum*[1]. 4. But by the *senatus-consultum Claudianum* a man above sixty who marries a woman under fifty, will be accounted as if he had married whilst under sixty. But if a woman above fifty be married to a man under sixty, the marriage is styled "unequal," and by the *senatus-consultum Calvitianum* is ordered to be of no avail for taking inheritances, legacies or marriage-portions. Therefore on the death of the wife her marriage-portion will lapse[2].

---

[1] The MS. has *Pernicianum* instead of *Persicianum*.

Heineccius explains this passage at length in his *Antiquitates Romanae*, App. lib. I. cap. I. § 37. He states, in opposition to Gothofredus, that the Lex Papia *did not* forbid the marriages of men above sixty years of age with women above fifty, which idea had been deduced from a passage of Suetonius (*Claud.* 23): "Capiti Papiae Poppaeae legis a Tiberio Caesare, quasi sexagenarii generare non possent, addito obrogavit."

The Lex Papia, he says, freed men and women of the ages just named from the penalties of celibacy: and Tiberius did not forbid marriages between these persons (any more than the Lex Papia had done), but made such unions unavailing to save the parties from the penalties of the law; laying it down as a presumption *juris et de jure* that no children could be born from them: and this rule was embodied in the *senatus-consultum* of Persicus, consul three years before Tiberius' death.

The *senatus-consultum Claudianum* allowed the marriage of a man over sixty with a woman under fifty to save the former from the penalties of the law, because from such a marriage there was some chance of issue.

The *senatus-consultum Calvitianum*, on the other hand, forbade the penalties to be remitted when the wife was above fifty and the husband under sixty, because from this marriage there was no reasonable prospect of children.

[2] Mommsen says these two para-

TIT. XVII. DE CADVCIS.

1. Quod quis sibi testamento relictum, ita ut iure ciuili capere possit, aliqua ex causa non ceperit, caducum appellatur, ueluti ceciderit ab eo: uerbi gratia si caelibi uel Latino Iuniano legatum fuerit, nec intra dies centum uel caelebs legi paruerit[1], uel Latinus ius Quiritium consecutus sit[2]; aut si ex parte heres scriptus uel legatarius ante apertas tabulas decesserit uel peregrinus factus sit[3]. 2. Hodie ex constitutione imperatoris Antonini omnia caduca fisco uindicantur: sed seruato iure antiquo liberis et parentibus. 3. Caduca cum suo onere fiunt: ideoque libertates et legata et fideicommissa ab eo data, ex cuius persona hereditas caduca facta est, salua sunt: set et legata et fideicommissa cum suo onere fiunt caduca.

XVII. ON LAPSES.

1. A testamentary gift which the donee fails from any cause to take, although left to him in such manner that he could have taken it according to the civil law, is called a *lapse*, for it has in a way slipped from him; for instance, if a legacy be left to an unmarried man or to a Junian Latin, and the unmarried man do not within a hundred days conform to the *lex*[1], or the Latin do not obtain Roman citizenship[2]; or if the heir appointed to a part or if a legatee die or become a foreigner before the opening of the testament[3]. 2. At the present day, in accordance with a constitution of the emperor Antoninus, all lapses are claimed for the treasury: the ancient rule, however, being upheld for the benefit of descendants and ascendants.

3. Lapses carry with them their own burdens: and therefore gifts of freedom, legacies and *fideicommissa* charged upon him from whom the inheritance lapses, stand good, and of course legacies and *fideicommissa* also lapse subject to their burdens.

---

graphs have been retained through inadvertence by the abbreviator of Ulpian: for their provisions had been abolished by a law of Constantine; and the abbreviator in all other cases has struck out obsolete rules.

The marriage portion, which in general went to the husband or father, went instead to the *fiscus*, if the marriage had been *impar*.

1 Sc. Julia et Papia Poppaea.

2 Tit. III.

3 No doubt Ulpian proceeded to state the provisions of the Lex Julia et Papia Poppaea as to lapses (for which see Gaius, II. 206, 207), but the abbreviator has struck out this passage.

TIT. XVIII. QVI HABEANT IVS ANTIQVVM IN CADVCIS.

1. Item liberis et parentibus testatoris usque ad tertium gradum lex Papia ius antiquum dedit, ut heredibus illis institutis, quod quis ex eo testamento non capit, ad hos pertineat aut totum aut ex parte, prout pertinere possit.

TIT. XIX. DE DOMINIIS ET ADQVISITIONIBVS RERVM.

1. Omnes res aut mancipi sunt aut nec mancipi[1]. mancipi res sunt praedia[2] in Italico solo[3], (tam) rustica, qualis est fundus, quam urbana, qualis domus; item iura praediorum rusticorum, uelut uia, iter, actus, aquaeductus[4]; item serui, et quadrupedes quae dorso colloue domantur, uelut boues, muli, equi, asini. ceterae res nec mancipi sunt. elefanti et cameli quamuis collo dorsoue domentur, nec mancipi sunt, quoniam bestiarum numero sunt[5].

XVIII. WHO HAVE THE ANCIENT RIGHT IN LAPSES.

1. The Lex Papia Poppaea has further granted the ancient right to descendants and ascendants of the testator as far as the third degree. So that when these are instituted heirs anything which another person does not take under the testament belongs to them wholly or in part, according as it can belong.

XIX. ON DOMINIUM AND ACQUISITIONS OF THINGS.

1. All things are either mancipable or non-mancipable[1]. The former are praedial property[2] on Italic soil[3], both rural, as a field, and urban, as a house; also rights attaching to rural praedial property, as *via*, *iter*, *actus*, *aquaeductus*[4]; also slaves and those quadrupeds which are tamed by yoke and saddle, as oxen, mules, horses, asses. All other things are non-mancipable. Elephants and camels, although they may be tamed by yoke and saddle, are non-mancipable because they are in the category of wild beasts[5].

---

[1] Gaius, II. 15—17.

[2] *Praedium* is land or anything attached to or connected with the land. See note on Gaius, II. 61.

[3] The peculiarities of *Italicum solum* are described in a note on Gaius, I. 120.

[4] See note on Gaius, II. 15.

[5] The true reason why elephants and camels were classed with *res nec mancipi* is given by Maine in his *Ancient Law*, viz. that these animals in all probability became known to the Romans after the

2. Singularum rerum dominium nobis adquiritur mancipatione, traditione, usucapione, in iure cessione, adiudicatione, lege[1].

3. Mancipatio[2] propria species alienationis est rerum mancipi: eaque fit certis uerbis, libripende et quinque testibus praesentibus. 4. Mancipatio locum habet inter ciues Romanos, et Latinos coloniarios[3], Latinosque Iunianos, eosque peregrinos quibus commercium datum est. 5. Commercium est emendi uendundique inuicem ius[4]. 6. Res mobiles non nisi praesentes mancipari possunt[5], et non plures simul quam quot manu capi possunt; immobiles autem etiam plures simul, et quae diuersis locis sunt, mancipari possunt.

7. Traditio propria est alienatio rerum nec mancipi[6]. harum

2. We acquire ownership over individual things by mancipation, by tradition, by usucapion, by cession in court, by adjudication, and by operation of law[1].

3. Mancipation[2] is the form of transfer peculiar to things mancipable: and it is transacted with a special phraseology, and in the presence of a balance-holder (*libripens*) and five witnesses. 4. The parties to a mancipation may be Roman citizens, Latin colonists[3], Junian Latins, or those foreigners to whom the privilege of *commercium* has been given. 5. *Commercium* is the reciprocal right of purchase and sale[4]. 6. Moveable things can be mancipated only when produced before the parties[5], and then no more at one time than are able to be taken by the hand; but immoveable things can be mancipated several together, as well as lying in different localities.

7. Tradition is the method of transfer appropriate to things non-mancipable[6]. For we acquire the ownership of these

list of *res mancipi* had been settled. That list was formed in early times, and included all property likely to be important to a half-civilized community; and as writing was unknown, transfers were hedged about with formalities. When property became more extensive and more varied in character, what had originally been a protection became an inconvenience, and new articles of commerce were allowed to be alienated by simpler methods.

1 Gaius, II. 65. App. (E).

2 *Ib.* I. 119—121, II. 22.

3 App. (A).

4 But see note on XX. 13. The capacity here named is but an instance of those included in *commercium*.

5 Gaius, I. 121.

6 *Ib.* II. 19, 20, 65.

rerum dominium ipsa traditione adprehendimus, scilicet si ex iusta causa traditae sint nobis.

8. Usucapione[1] dominium adipiscimur tam mancipi rerum, quam nec mancipi. usucapio est autem dominii adeptio per continuationem possessionis anni uel biennii: rerum mobilium anni, immobilium biennii.

9. In iure cessio[2] quoque communis alienatio est et mancipi rerum et nec mancipi. quae fit per tres personas, in iure cedentis, uindicantis, addicentis: 10. in iure cedit dominus; uindicat is, cui ceditur; addicit praetor. 11. In iure cedi res etiam incorporales possunt[3], uelut usufructus et hereditas et tutela legitima libertae[4]. 12. Hereditas in iure ceditur uel antequam adeatur, uel posteaquam adita fuerit[5]: 13. antequam adeatur, in iure cedi potest legitimo ab herede: posteaquam adita est, tam a legitimo quam ab eo qui testamento heres scriptus est. 14. Si antequam adeatur, hereditas in iure cessa sit, proinde heres fit cui cessa est, ac si ipse heres legitimus

things by the delivery itself, provided always that they have been delivered to us in consequence of a transaction recognized by the law. 8. By usucapion[1] we obtain the ownership of things both mancipable and non-mancipable. Now usucapion is the acquisition of ownership through continuous possession for one or two years—one, where the things are moveable—two, where they are immoveable. 9. Cession in court[2] also is a mode of transfer common to both classes of things. It is transacted by means of three parties, the cessor in court, the claimant and the adjudicant. 10. The owner is cessor, the transferee is claimant, and the Praetor is adjudicant. 11. Even incorporeal things can be transferred by cession[3], as for instance an usufruct, and an inheritance, and the statutable tutelage of a freedwoman[4]. 12. An inheritance is transferred by cession either before or after entry[5]. 13. Before entry the transfer may be effected by a statutable heir; after entry both by a statutable heir, and by him who has been appointed heir in a testament. 14. If the inheritance have been transferred before entry, the transferee becomes heir just as if

[1] Gaius, II. 42—44.
[2] *Ib.* II. 24.
[3] *Ib.* II. 29—38.
[4] *Ib.* I. 168.
[5] *Ib.* II. 34—37, III. 85—87.

esset; quod si posteaquam adita fuerit in iure cessa sit, is qui cessit permanet heres, et ob id creditoribus defuncti manet obligatus; debita uero pereunt, id est debitores defuncti liberantur; 15. res autem corporales, quasi singulae in iure cessae essent, transeunt ad eum cui cessa est hereditas.

16. Adiudicatione[1] dominium nanciscimur per formulam familiae herciscundae, quae locum habet inter coheredes; et per formulam communi diuidundo, cui locus est inter socios; et per formulam finium regundorum, quae est inter uicinos. nam si iudex uni ex heredibus aut sociis aut uicinis rem aliquam adiudicauerit, statim illi adquiritur, siue mancipi siue nec mancipi sit.

17. Lege nobis adquiritur uelut caducum uel ereptorium ex lege Papia Poppaea[2], item legatum ex lege duodecim tabularum[3], siue mancipi res sint siue nec mancipi.

he himself had been the statutable heir; but if the transfer be made after entry, the transferor continues to be heir, and on this account remains bound to the creditors of the deceased; the debts, however, perish; in other words, the debtors of the deceased are set free; 15. but the corporeal things pass to the transferee of the inheritance just as if they had been separately transferred by cession.

16. By adjudication[1] we obtain ownership by means of the formula "for severing an estate," which is applicable to co-heirs, by means also of the formula for dividing common property, applicable to partners, and by means of the formula for setting out boundaries, applicable to neighbouring proprietors; for if a *judex* have adjudicated anything to one of several co-heirs, partners, or neighbours, acquisition thereof immediately accrues to him, whether the thing be mancipable or non-mancipable.

17. We acquire ownership by operation of law, as in the case of a lapse or an escheat by force of the Lex Papia Poppaea[2], and in that of a legacy by force of a Law of the Twelve Tables[3], whether the subject be a thing mancipable or a thing non-mancipable.

---

[1] Gaius, IV. 42.

[2] I. 21. Other instances of lapses are to be found in XVI. 4; XVII.; XXII. 3; XXIV. 12, 13; XXV. 17; XXVIII. 7.

[3] "Uti legassit super familia pecunia tutelave suae rei, ita jus esto." Tab. V. l. 3. See D. 50. 16. 130.

18. Adquiritur autem nobis etiam per eas personas, quas in potestate, manu mancipioue habemus[1]. itaque si quid eae mancipio puta acceperint, aut traditum eis sit, uel stipulatae fuerint, ad nos pertinet; 19. item si heredes institutae sint legatumue eis sit, et hereditatem iusso nostro adeuntes nobis adquirunt, et legatum ad nos pertinet. 20. Si seruus alterius in bonis, alterius ex iure Quiritium sit, ex omnibus causis adquirit ei cuius in bonis est[2]. 21. Is quem bona fide possidemus, siue liber siue alienus seruus sit, nobis adquirit ex duabus causis tantum, id est, quod ex re nostra et quod ex operis suis adquirit[3]: extra has autem causas aut sibi adquirit, si liber sit, aut domino, si alienus seruus sit. eadem sunt et in eo seruo, in quo tantum usumfructum habemus[4].

TIT. XX. DE TESTAMENTIS.

1. Testamentum est mentis nostrae iusta contestatio, in id

18. Ownership is also acquired for us by means of persons whom we have in our *potestas*, *manus* or *mancipium*[1]. If then, for instance, such persons have received something by way of mancipation, or if something have been delivered to them, or if they have stipulated for something, that thing belongs to us; 19. so too if these persons have been instituted heirs, or if a legacy have been left them, they acquire for us the inheritance upon entry therein by our direction, and the legacy belongs to us. 20. If a slave belong to one person by Bonitarian and to another by Quiritarian title, he acquires in all cases for his Bonitarian owner[2]. 21. A person whom we possess in good faith, whether he be a free man or a slave belonging to another, acquires for us in two cases only, viz. when his acquisition is the product of something belonging to us and when it is the product of his own labour[3]. Acquisitions resulting from causes other than these either belong to the man himself, if he be free, or to his owner, if he be the slave of another person (than his *bona fide* possessor). The same rules apply also to the case of a slave in whom we have only an usufruct[4].

XX. ON TESTAMENTS.

1. A testament is the legal attestation of our intentions,

[1] Gaius, II. 86—90; III. 163.
[2] *Ib.* II. 88.
[3] *Ib.* II. 92, III. 164.
[4] *Ib.* II. 91, III. 165.

sollemniter factum ut post mortem nostram ualeat. 2. Testamentorum genera fuerunt tria[1], unum quod calatis comitiis, alterum quod in procinctu[2], tertium quod per aes et libram appellatum est. sed illis duobus testamentis abolitis hodie solum in usu est quod per aes et libram fit, id est per mancipationem imaginariam. in quo testamento libripens adhibetur et familiae emptor et non minus quam quinque testes, cum quibus testamenti factio est[3]. 3. Qui in potestate testatoris est aut familiae emptoris, testis aut libripens adhiberi non potest, quoniam familiae mancipatio inter testatorem et familiae emptorem fit, et domestici testes[4] adhibendi non sunt[5]. 4. Filio *familiae* familiam emente pater eius testis esse non potest. 5. Ex duobus fratribus qui in eiusdem patris potestate sunt, alter familiae emptor, alter testis esse non potest, quoniam

made in solemn form for the express purpose of being carried out after our death. 2. There used to be three kinds of testaments[1]; one which was made at the specially-summoned *comitia*, another which was made in battle-array[2], a third which was called "by coin and balance." The two former having been abolished, the only one in use at the present day is that which is solemnized by coin and balance, that is, by means of an imaginary mancipation. And in this form of testament a balance-holder (*libripens*) is employed, also a purchaser of the estate (*familiae emptor*), and not less than five witnesses, with whom the testator can lawfully deal in testamentary matters[3]. 3. He who is in the *potestas* of the testator, or of the purchaser of the estate, cannot be employed as a witness or as a balance-holder, since the mancipation of the estate is a transaction between the testator and the purchaser of the estate, and members of their households[4] must not be employed as witnesses[5]. 4. For this reason also where a *filius familias* is the purchaser of the estate, his father cannot be a witness. 5. Of two brothers under the *potestas* of the same father, one cannot be the purchaser of the estate and the other a witness, since that which one of them takes by the mancipation he acquires for his father, for whom

[1] *Ib.* II. 101—104.

[2] "Procinctus est expeditus et armatus exercitus." Gaius, II. 101.

[3] See note on Gaius, II. 114.

[4] *Domesticus testis* is not only a son or slave, but any one amenable to coercion, as we see from D. 28. 1. 20. 1 & 3. D. 22. 5. 6.

[5] Gaius, II. 105—107.

quod unus ex his mancipio accipit adquirit patri, cui filius suus testis esse non debet. 6. Pater et qui in potestate eius est[1], item duo fratres qui in eiusdem patris potestate sunt, testes utrique, uel alter testis, alter libripens fieri possunt, alio familiam emente; quoniam nihil nocet ex una domo plures testes alieno negotio adhiberi. 7. Mutus, surdus, furiosus, pupillus, femina neque familiae emptor esse, neque testis libripensue fieri potest. 8. Latinus Iunianus et familiae emptor et testis et libripens fieri potest, quoniam cum eo testamenti factio est[2].

9. In testamento quod per aes et libram fit duae res aguntur, familiae mancipatio et nuncupatio testamenti[3]. nuncupatur testamentum in hunc modum: tabulas testamenti testator tenens ita dicit: HAEC VT IN HIS TABVLIS CERISVE SCRIPTA SVNT, ITA DO, ITA LEGO, ITA TESTOR; ITAQVE VOS, QVIRITES, TESTIMONIVM PERHIBETOTE. quae nuncupatio et testatio uocatur.

10. Filius familiae testamentum facere non potest, quoniam

his other son cannot be a witness. 6. But a father and a son under his *potestas*[1], as also two brothers under the *potestas* of the same father, may both of them be witnesses, or one may be a witness and the other the balance-holder, when some third party is the purchaser of the estate; for there is no harm in several witnesses from the same household being employed when the business affects a stranger. 7. A dumb person, a deaf person, a madman, a minor, or a woman cannot be made purchaser of the estate, or witness or balance-holder. 8. A Junian Latin can be made either purchaser of the estate, balance-holder or witness, inasmuch as testamentary dealing with him is legal[2].

9. In the form of testament by coin and balance two matters are transacted, the mancipation of the estate, and the nuncupation of the testament[3]. The testament is nuncupated after this manner: the testator holding the tablets of the testament says as follows—"These things as they are written in these tablets of wax, I so give, I so bequeath, I so claim your evidence, and do you, Quirites, so grant it me." And this is called the nuncupation and attestation.

10. A *filius-familias* cannot make a testament, inasmuch as

[1] This paragraph is quoted almost verbatim in D. 22. 5. 17.

[2] XI. 16.

[3] Gaius, II. 104.

nihil suum habet, ut testari de eo possit. sed diuus Augustus militibus[1] constituit, ut filius familiae miles de eo peculio quod in castris adquisiuit testamentum facere possit. 11. Qui de statu suo incertus est, fac eo[2], quod patre peregre mortuo ignorat se sui iuris esse, testamentum facere non potest. 12. Inpubes, licet sui iuris sit, facere testamentum non potest[3], quoni-

he has nothing of his own, so as to be able to declare any intention regarding it. But the late emperor Augustus[1] by a constitution in favour of the soldiers enacted that a *filius-familias*, being a soldier, might make a testament as to that portion of his *peculium* which he acquired whilst on service. 11. Where a man has become uncertain about his status, through ignorance, for example[2], that he is *sui juris* in consequence of his father having died abroad, he cannot make a testament. 12. A youth not of the age of puberty, though he chance to be *sui juris*, cannot make a testament[3], inasmuch as

[1] "Marcus" is the reading of Böcking, "Moribus" that of Huschke, other editors suggest "Militibus." Huschke considers that "moribus" is equivalent in sense to "per constitutiones," and he defends this notion by a reference to D. 10. 2. 2. 2, where an *utile judicium familiae erciscundae* is described as applicable to the division of a soldier's inheritance, because military testaments are valid by virtue of imperial constitutions, and not on account of any *lex*. But this argument can scarcely be accepted, since in speaking of tutors (XI. 2) Ulpian does not consider the *senatusconsultis constituti* to be a subdivision of the *moribus introducti*, but an entirely distinct class; and therefore whatever be the system of nomenclature adopted by other writers, Ulpian certainly does not adhere to that which Huschke attributes to him.

If we read "Marcus," there is the objection that earlier emperors had laid down the same regulations before Marcus' day; and therefore Böcking, although allowing that emperor's name to stand in his text, inclines in his notes to the reading "Militibus concessit," rejecting as frivolous the defence put forward for the other reading, that Ulpian wrote his Rules early in life, and was unaware at the time that the regulations of Marcus were only a republication of those of his predecessors.

[2] Böcking prefers the old reading *factus* to *fac eo* (which we have adopted from Huschke), and defends it on the ground that the uncertainty spoken of in the passage is of a peculiar kind, impossible under any circumstances to be removed at the time the testament is made. But there does not seem to be any such cardinal distinction as Böcking would make out between the present instance and others given in D. 28. 1. 14 and 15, and therefore we have followed Huschke. The principle that persons uncertain as to their status cannot make a testament is laid down in the most general terms in D. 28. 3. 6. 8, D. 29. 7. 9,—the only exception being in favour of veterans.

[3] Gaius, II. 113.

am nondum plenum iudicium animi habet. 13. Mutus, surdus, furiosus, itemque prodigus cui lege bonis interdictum est, testamentum facere non possunt: mutus, quoniam uerba nuncupationis loqui non potest; surdus, quoniam uerba familiae emptoris exaudire non potest; furiosus, quoniam mentem non habet ut testari de *su*a re possit; prodigus, quoniam commercio[1] illi interdictum est, et ob id familiam mancipare non potest. 14. Latinus Iunianus, item is qui dediticiorum numero est, testamentum facere non potest[2]: Latinus quidem, quoniam nominatim lege Iunia prohibitus est; is autem qui dediticiorum numero est quoniam nec quasi ciuis Romanus testari potest, cum sit peregrinus, nec quasi peregrinus, quoniam nullius cert*ae* ciuitatis *ciuis est*, ut *secundum*[3] leges ciuitatis suae testetur. 15. Feminae post duodecimum annum aetatis testamenta fa-

he is not yet endowed with full mental capacity. 13. A dumb person, a deaf person, a madman, and also a prodigal who is restrained by interdict from the management of his property, cannot make a testament: the dumb person because he cannot utter the nuncupatory formula, the deaf person because he cannot fully hear the words of the purchaser of the estate, the madman because he has not mental power for making testamentary disposition as to his own property, the prodigal because he has been laid under a general prohibition as to legal transactions[1], and on that account cannot mancipate his estate. 14. A Junian Latin, as also a person classed among the *dediticii*, cannot make a testament[2]: the Latin because he is specially prohibited by the Lex Junia: and he who is classed among the *dediticii* because he can neither make testamentary disposition as a Roman citizen, seeing that he is a foreigner, nor as a foreigner, seeing that he is a citizen of no ascertained state, so as to be able to make his testament in accordance with[3] the laws of his state. 15. Women after their twelfth

[1] *Commercium* was the right of being a party in those transactions, such as *mancipatio*, *cessio in jure*, etc., which were peculiar to the *jus civile*. The prodigal was interdicted from these because he was under a wider disqualification, viz. *de bonis suis*, which debarred him from all dealings equitable as well as legal.

[2] Gaius, I. 22—25.

[3] The MS. has *sciens* where we read *civis est:* and *adversus* instead of *secundum*. The last-named mistake occurs again in XXVIII. 1. A little below the MS. has *praetoriani* instead of *populi Romani*, and this mistake is also repeated, in XXIV. 28.

cere possunt, tutore auctore[1], donec in tutela sunt. 16. Seruus publicus populi Romani partis dimidiae testamenti faciendi habet ius[2].

TIT. XXI. QVEMADMODVM HERES INSTITVI DEBEAT.

1. Heres institui recte potest his uerbis: TITIVS HERES ESTO, TITIVS HERES SIT, TITIVM HEREDEM ESSE IVBEO; illa autem institutio HEREDEM INSTITVO, HEREDEM FACIO plerisque inprobata est[3].

TIT. XXII. QVI HEREDES INSTITVI POSSVNT.

1. Heredes institui possunt qui testamenti factionem cum testatore habent[4]. 2. Dediticiorum numero heres institui non potest, quia peregrinus est, cum quo testamenti factio non est[5].

year can make testaments, with the authorization of their tutors[1], as long as they are under tutelage. 16. A public slave of the Roman people has the right of making a testament as to half his *peculium*[2].

XXI. HOW AN HEIR OUGHT TO BE INSTITUTED.

1. An heir can be properly instituted by the following phraseology:—"Titius, be thou heir;" "Let Titius be heir;" "I order Titius to be heir." But an institution running thus: "I institute as heir," or "I make heir," has been generally disapproved[3].

XXII. WHO CAN BE INSTITUTED HEIRS.

1. Those can be instituted heirs who have testamentary capacity relatively to the testator[4]. 2. One who is classed among the *dediticii* cannot be instituted heir, because he is a foreigner, for whose benefit a testament cannot be made[5]. 3. A Junian

[1] Gaius, II. 113, 118.

[2] This agrees with what is said in Plin. *Epp.* VIII. 16 that a slave might, with his master's permission, make a testament for the benefit of members of the household, *intra domum;* but there are various passages in D. 28. 1, such as §§ 16, 19 and 20. 7, which assert that a slave could in no other case make a testament; and as these draw no distinction between public and private slaves, many commentators judge the present passage to be an interpolation, and false in fact.

[3] Gaius, II. 117.

[4] On the various senses of *testamenti factio*, see note on Gaius, II. 114.

[5] Gaius, I. 25, II. 110.

3. (Latinus Iunianus)[1], si quidem mortis testatoris tempore uel intra diem cretionis[2] ciuis Romanus sit, heres esse potest; quodsi Latinus manserit, lege Iunia capere hereditatem prohibetur. idem iuris est in persona caelibis propter legem Iuliam[3]. 4. Incerta persona heres institui non potest, uelut hoc modo: QVISQVIS PRIMVS AD FVNVS MEVM VENERIT, HERES ESTO; quoniam certum consilium debet esse testantis[4]. 5. Nec municipia, nec municipes heredes institui possunt, quoniam incertum corpus est, et neque cernere uniuersi, neque pro herede gerere possunt, ut heredes fiant: senatusconsulto tamen concessum est, ut a libertis suis heredes institui possint. sed fideicommissa hereditas municipibus restitui potest; denique hoc senatusconsulto prospectum est[5]. 6. Deos heredes instituere non possumus praeter eos, quos senatusconsultis constitutionibusue principum instituere concessum est, sicuti Iouem Tarpeium, Appollinem Didymaeum, Martem in Gallia, Miner-

Latin can be heir[1], provided he be a Roman citizen at the time of the testator's death, or within the period for cretion[2]; but if he have continued to be a Latin, he is prohibited from taking the inheritance by the Lex Junia. The same rule is applied to an unmarried person by reason of the Lex Julia[3]. 4. An uncertain person cannot be instituted heir, as for instance in this way: "Whoever shall first come to my funeral, let him be my heir;" for a testator's intention ought to be clear[4]. 5. Neither a municipal corporation nor its members can be instituted heirs, because the body is an uncertain one, and can neither collectively make a cretion nor act in the character of heirs, so as to become heirs: but by a *senatus-consultum* it has been conceded that they can be instituted heirs by their own freedmen. An inheritance, however, that has been left by way of *fidei-commissum* can be delivered over to the members of a municipal corporation; in fact, this is laid down by the same *senatus-consultum*[5]. 6. We cannot institute the gods as heirs, save those whose institution has been permitted by *senatus-consulta* or by imperial constitutions, as Tarpeian Jove, Didymaean Apollo, Mars in Gaul, Minerva of Ilium, Hercules

1 Gaius, I. 23, 24, II. 110.
2 XXII. 27.
3 Gaius, II. 111.
4 This rule applies to legacies also, see XXIV. 18, Gaius, II. 238.
5 Pliny, *Ep.* V. 7; D. 36. 1. 27. *pr.*; D. 38. 3. 1. 1.

uam Iliensem, Herculem Gaditanum, Dianam Efesiam, Matrem deorum Sipylensem, quae Smyrnae colitur, et Caelestem Salinensem Carthaginis.

7. Seruos heredes instituere possumus[1], nostros cum libertate, alienos sine libertate, communes cum libertate uel sine libertate. 8. Eum seruum, qui tantum in bonis noster est, nec cum libertate heredem instituere possumus, quia Latinitatem consequitur, quod non proficit ad hereditatem capiendam[2]. 9. Alienos seruos heredes instituere possumus eos tantum, quorum cum dominis testamenti factionem habemus[3]. 10. Communis seruus cum libertate recte quidem heres instituitur quasi proprius pro parte nostra; sine libertate autem quasi alienus propter socii partem[4]. 11. Proprius seruus cum libertate heres institutus, si quidem in eadem causa permanserit, ex testamento

of Gades, Diana of Ephesus, the Sipylenian mother of the gods, worshipped at Smyrna, and Salinensian Coelestis the goddess of Carthage.

7. We can institute slaves as heirs[1]; with a gift of liberty, if they belong to us; without a gift of liberty, if they are owned by other people; with or without a gift of liberty, if they are owned in common by ourselves and others. 8. A slave who is ours by Bonitary title alone we cannot institute heir even with a gift of liberty, because (by the gift of liberty) he attains the Latin status, and this is not available for the purpose of taking an inheritance[2]. 9. Slaves belonging to other people we can only institute heirs when we have testamentary capacity in reference to their masters[3]. 10. A slave who is the common property of ourselves and others is duly instituted heir with a gift of liberty, inasmuch as he is ours so far as our own share in him is concerned; and without a gift of liberty, inasmuch as he is another's property so far as our partner's share in him is concerned[4]. 11. Our own slave when instituted heir with a gift of liberty, becomes free and heir under the testament, *i.e.* "neces-

[1] Gaius, II. 185—190.

[2] XXII. 3.

[3] D. 28. 5. 31. pr.; D. 28. 5. 52.

[4] Cujacius in his commentary *ad loc.* says: "If he is instituted with a gift of liberty, he becomes the sole property of the other partner (I. 18), and therefore the whole inheritance goes to that partner: if without a gift of liberty, the inheritance is divided between the partner and the heir of the testator."

liber et heres fit, id est necessarius[1]; 12. quod si ab ipso testatore uiuente manumissus uel alienatus sit, suo arbitrio uel iussu emptoris hereditatem adire potest. sed si sine libertate sit institutus, omnino non consistit institutio[2]. 13. Alienus seruus heres institutus, si quidem in ea causa permanserit, iussu domini debet hereditatem adire; quod si uiuo testatore manumissus aut alienatus a domino fuerit, aut suo arbitrio aut iussu emptoris poterit adire hereditatem[3].

14. Sui heredes instituendi sunt uel exheredandi[4]. sui autem heredes sunt liberi quos in potestate habemus, tam naturales quam adoptiui: item uxor quae in manu est, et nurus quae in manu est filii quem in potestate habemus. 15. Postumi quoque liberi, id est, qui in utero sunt[5], si tales sunt ut nati in potestate nostra futuri sint, suorum heredum numero sunt[6]. 16. Ex suis heredibus filius quidem neque heres insti-

sary" heir, provided only he continue in the same condition[1]; 12. but if he be manumitted or alienated by the testator himself during his lifetime, he can enter upon the inheritance of his own accord or by order of his purchaser. If, however, he be instituted without a gift of liberty, the institution is altogether ineffectual[2]. 13. When a slave who is owned by some other person has been instituted heir, in the event of his continuing in the same condition, he ought to enter upon the inheritance by his master's order; but if he be manumitted or alienated by his master during the testator's lifetime he will be able to enter upon the inheritance either of his own accord or by order of his purchaser[3].

14. *Sui heredes* must be either instituted heirs or disinherited[4]. Now *sui heredes* are the descendants whom we have under our *potestas*, whether natural or adopted; also a wife who is under *manus*, and a daughter-in-law who is under the *manus* of a son who is himself under *potestas*. 15. After-born descendants too, that is, those still in the womb[5], if they be such as would have been under our *potestas* if born, are classed among *sui heredes*[6]. 16. The fact of one of the *sui heredes*

[1] Gaius, II. 188.

[2] *Ib.* II. 187. But Justinian ruled otherwise. See *Inst.* II. 14. pr.

[3] *Ib.* II. 189.

[4] *Ib.* II. 123, 138—143, 156, 159.

[5] Sc. at the time the testament is made. See note on Gaius, I. 147.

[6] Gaius, II. 130—134, III. 4.

tutus, neque nominatim exheredatus, non patitur ualere testamentum[1]. 17. Reliquae uero personae liberorum, uelut filia, nepos, neptis, si praeteritae sint, ualet testamentum, *sed* scriptis heredibus adcrescunt[2], suis quidem heredibus in partem uirilem, extraneis autem in partem dimidiam[3]. 18. Postumi quoque liberi cuiuscumque sexus omissi, quod ualuit testamentum agnatione rumpunt[4]. 19. Eos, qui in utero sunt, si nati sui heredes nobis futuri sint, possumus instituere heredes: si quidem post mortem nostram nascantur, ex iure ciuili; si uero uiuentibus nobis, ex lege Iunia.

20. Filius, qui in potestate est, si non instituatur heres, nominatim exheredari debet; reliqui sui heredes utriusque sexus aut nominatim aut inter ceteros[5]. 21. Postumus filius nominatim exheredandus est; filia postuma ceteraeque postumae feminae uel nominatim uel inter ceteros; dummodo inter ceteros

being a son, neither instituted heir nor disinherited by name, prevents the testament from being valid[1]. 17. If other classes of descendants, a daughter for instance or a grandson, or a granddaughter, be passed over, the testament is valid, but they attach themselves therein to the appointed heirs[2]; to *sui heredes*, for a proportional portion, to extraneous heirs for one-half the estate[3]. 18. Also after-born descendants of either sex, if not named, by their after-birth make void a testament which otherwise was valid[4]. 19. Those who are in the womb we can institute as heirs, supposing they would have been *sui heredes* to us in case they had been born; by virtue of the civil law, if their birth take place after our death; but if in our lifetime, by virtue of the Lex Junia.

20. If a son who is under *potestas* be not instituted heir, he ought to be disinherited by name; all other *sui heredes* of either sex may be disinherited either by name or in a general clause[5]. 21. An after-born son must be disinherited by name, an after-born daughter and other after-born female descendants either by name, or in a general clause, provided, however, that some

1 Gaius, II. 123.

2 "These omitted persons do not become heirs in opposition to the testament, but become heirs *ex testamento*, as though tacitly instituted therein." Huschke.

3 Gaius, II. 124.

4 *Ib.* II. 130—134.

5 *Ib.* II. 127, 128.

exheredatis aliquid legetur[1]. 22. Nepotes et pronepotes ceterique masculi postumi praeter filium uel nominatim uel inter ceteros cum adiectione legati sunt exheredandi; sed tutius est tamen nominatim eos exheredari; et id obseruatur magis.

23. Emancipatos liberos quamuis iure ciuili neque heredes instituere neque exheredare necesse sit, tamen praetor iubet, si non instituantur heredes, exheredari, masculos omnes nominatim, feminas (uel nominatim) uel inter ceteros; alioquin contra tabulas bonorum possessionem eis pollicetur[2].

24. Inter necessarios heredes, id est seruos cum libertate heredes scriptos, et suos et necessarios, id est liberos qui in potestate sunt, iure ciuili nihil interest: nam utrique etiam inuiti heredes sunt. sed iure praetorio suis et necessariis heredibus abstinere se a parentis hereditate permittitur; necessariis autem tantum heredibus abstinendi potestas non datur[3].

legacy be left to those who are disinherited in a general clause[1]. 22. Grandsons and great-grandsons and other after-born males, except a son, must be disinherited either by name or in a general clause, with the addition of a legacy; it is, however, safer that they be disinherited by name, and that is the more usual practice.

23. As to emancipated children of either sex, although by the civil law it is not necessary either to institute them heirs or to disinherit them, yet the Praetor orders that, unless they be instituted as heirs, they shall be disinherited, if males by name, but if females (either by name) or in general clause, otherwise he promises them possession of the goods as against the testament[2].

24. Between *heredes necessarii*, that is, slaves appointed as heirs with a gift of liberty, and *heredes sui et necessarii*, that is, descendants under *potestas*, there is no distinction according to the civil law, for both these classes are heirs even against their will; but by the Praetorian law the privilege is accorded to *heredes sui et necessarii* of renouncing their ancestor's inheritance, whilst to *heredes necessarii* alone this privilege is not accorded[3].

---

[1] Gaius, II. 130—132. It will be observed that Gaius insists on a male *postumus* being disinherited by name, and does not agree with Ulpian, that, unless he be a son, he may be disinherited *inter caeteros* with a legacy.

[2] *Ib.* II. 135.

[3] *Ib.* II. 153, 156, 158. *Heredes necessarii* had however the *bene-*

25. Extraneus heres, si quidem cum cretione sit heres institutus, cernendo fit heres; si uero sine cretione, pro herede gerendo[1]. 26. Pro herede gerit, qui rebus hereditariis tamquam dominus utitur, uelut qui auctionem rerum hereditariarum facit, aut seruis hereditariis cibaria dat. 27. Cretio est certorum dierum spatium quod datur instituto heredi ad deliberandum, utrum expediat ei adire hereditatem nec ne, uelut: TITIVS HERES ESTO CERNITOQVE IN DIEBVS CENTVM PROXIMIS, QVIBVS SCIERIS POTERISQVE. NISI ITA CREVERIS, EXHERES ESTO[2]. 28. Cernere est uerba cretionis dicere ad hunc modum: *QVOD* ME MEVIVS HEREDEM INSTITVIT, EAM HEREDITATEM ADEO CERNOQVE. 29. Sine cretione heres institutus si constituerit, nolle se heredem esse, statim excluditur ab hereditate, et amplius eam adire non potest[3]. 30. Cum cretione uero heres institutus sicut cernendo fit heres, ita non aliter excluditur, quam si intra

25. If an extraneous heir have been instituted "with cretion," he becomes heir by the act of cretion: but if he have been instituted "without cretion" he becomes heir by acting as heir[1]. 26. A man acts as heir who makes use of the effects belonging to the inheritance as though owner, as for instance when he puts up the effects to auction, or gives provisions to the slaves belonging to the inheritance. 27. "Cretion" is a space of certain days which is given to the instituted heir for the purpose of deliberating whether it be advisable for him to enter upon the inheritance or not: as for instance (in the following direction): "Titius, be thou heir and make thy cretion within the next one hundred days after thou hast knowledge and ability, but if thou dost not so make thy cretion, be disinherited[2]." 28. To make cretion is to utter the words of cretion in this way: "Since Maevius has instituted me heir, I enter upon that inheritance and make my cretion for it." 29. If he who has been instituted heir without cretion, have declared that he will not be heir, he is forthwith excluded from the inheritance, and has no further opportunity of entering upon it[3]. 30. But in like manner as he who is instituted heir with cretion becomes heir by the act of cretion, so he is not

ficium separationis, which enabled them to deduct any acquisitions they had made since the testator's death. Gaius, II. 155.

1 Gaius, II. 166—168.
2 *Ib.* II. 164—166.
3 *Ib.* II. 169.

diem cretionis non creuerit: ideoque etiamsi constituerit nolle se heredem esse, tamen, si supersint dies cretionis, paenitentia actus cernendo heres fieri potest[1].

31. Cretio aut uulgaris dicitur aut continua: uulgaris, in qua adiciuntur haec uerba: QVIBVS SCIERIS POTERISQVE; continua, in qua non adiciuntur[2]. 32. Ei qui uulgarem cretionem habet, dies illi duntaxat computantur quibus sciuit se heredem institutum esse et potuit cernere; ei uero qui continuam habet cretionem, etiam illi dies computantur quibus ignorauit se heredem institutum, aut sciuit quidem sed non potuit cernere[3].

33. Heredes aut instituti dicuntur aut substituti: (instituti), qui primo gradu scripti sunt; substituti, qui secundo gradu uel sequentibus heredes scripti sunt, uelut: TITIVS HERES ESTO CERNITOQVE IN DIEBVS PROXIMIS CENTVM QVIBVS SCIES POTERISQVE. (QVOD NI) ITA CREVERIS, EXHERES ESTO. TVNC MEVIVS

excluded on any other ground than that of not having made his cretion within the period limited; and therefore although he may have decided that he will not be heir, yet if any portion of the limited period remains, by repenting this act and by making cretion he can become heir[1].

31. Cretion is styled either common or continuous: common cretion being the one in which these words are added, "after thou hast knowledge and ability;" continuous, the one in which they are not added[2]. 32. Against him who has the common cretion those days only are reckoned during which he knew that he was instituted heir and was able to decide, whilst against him who has continuous cretion those days also are reckoned during which he was unaware of having been instituted heir, or did know it but could not decide[3].

33. Heirs are said to be either instituted or substituted. Those are instituted who have been inscribed heirs in the first degree, those are substituted who are inscribed in the second or following degrees, thus: "Titius, be thou heir, and decide within the next one hundred days after thou shalt have knowledge and ability, but unless thou shalt so decide be disinherited. In that case, Maevius, be thou my heir, and decide

---

1 Gaius, II. 168.
2 *Ib.* II. 171.
3 *Ib.* II. 172, 173.

HERES ESTO CERNITOQVE IN DIEBVS et reliqua. similiter et deinceps substitui potest[1].

34. Si sub inperfecta cretione heres institutus sit, id est non adiectis his uerbis: SI NON CREVERIS, EXHERES ESTO, sed si ita: SI NON CREVERIS, TVNC MEVIVS HERES ESTO, cernendo quidem superior inferiorem excludit; non cernendo autem sed pro herede gerendo in partem admittit substitutum[2]: sed postea diuus Marcus constituit, ut et pro herede gerendo ex asse fiat heres. quodsi neque creuerit neque pro herede gesserit, ipse excluditur, et substitutus ex asse fit heres.

TIT. XXIII. QVEMADMODVM TESTAMENTA RVMPVNTVR.

1. Testamentum iure factum infirmatur duobus modis, si ruptum aut irritum factum sit.

2. Rumpitur testamentum mutatione, id est, si postea aliud testamentum iure factum sit; item agnatione, id est, si suus

within the next one hundred days, &c." And so in similar terms can successive substitutions be made[1].

34. If an heir have been instituted under an imperfect cretion, that is, without the addition of the words: "If thou dost not decide, be disinherited," but only in this form: "If thou dost not decide, then, Maevius, be thou heir," by the act of deciding the first heir excludes the one after him, whilst by not deciding, but by acting as heir, the first heir admits the substituted heir into a half of the inheritance[2]. The Emperor Marcus, however, afterwards enacted by a Constitution, that even by acting as heir the first-named person becomes heir to the whole. But if he have neither decided nor acted as heir, he is excluded, and the substitute becomes heir to the whole inheritance.

XXIII. HOW TESTAMENTS ARE BROKEN.

1. A testament, though made in proper legal form, is invalidated in two ways, if it be broken, or if it be rendered ineffectual.

2. A testament is broken by a change, that is, if another testament have been afterwards made in proper legal form; so

[1] Gaius, II. 174.

[2] *Ib.* II. 177, 178. It is remarkable that Gaius says nothing about the constitution of Marcus.

heres agnascatur, qui neque heres institutus neque ut oportet exheredatus sit[1]. 3. Agnascitur suus heres aut agnascendo, aut adoptando[2], aut in manum conueniendo[3], aut in locum sui heredis succedendo[4], uelut nepos mortuo filio uel emancipato, aut manumissione, id est, si filius ex prima secundaue mancipatione manumissus reuersus sit in patris potestatem[5].

4. Irritum fit testamentum, si testator capite diminutus fuerit[6], aut si iure facto testamento nemo extiterit heres.

5. Si is, qui testamentum fecit, ab hostibus captus sit, testamentum eius ualet, si quidem reuersus fuerit, iure postliminii[7]; si uero ibi decesserit, ex lege Cornelia[8], quae perinde successionem eius confirmat, atque si in ciuitate decessisset.

6. Si septem signis testium signatum sit testamentum, licet iure ciuili ruptum uel irritum factum sit, praetor scriptis heredibus iuxta tabulas bonorum possessionem dat, si testator et

too it is broken by agnation, that is, when a *suus heres* is agnated who has been neither instituted heir nor disinherited in the form prescribed[1]. 3. A *suus heres* is agnated either by after-birth, or by adoption[2], or by coming under *manus*[3], or by succeeding to the position of a *suus heres*[4], as a grandson does to that of a deceased or emancipated son, or by manumission, that is, if a son who has been manumitted after a first or second mancipation has reverted to his father's *potestas*[5].

4. A testament is made ineffectual where a testator has suffered *capitis diminutio*[6], or where there is no surviving heir under a testament legally made.

5. When a person who has made a testament has been captured by the enemy, his testament is valid; if he return, by virtue of the rule of postliminy[7]; but if he die, by the Lex Cornelia[8], which confirms his succession in like manner as if he died in the state.

6. If a testament have been sealed with the seals of seven witnesses, though it may have become broken or ineffectual according to the civil law, yet the Praetor gives possession

[1] Gaius, II. 144, 131.
[2] *Ib.* II. 138.
[3] *Ib.* II. 139, III. 3.
[4] *Ib.* II. 133.
[5] *Ib.* II. 141, III. 6. As to the phrase "ex prima secundave mancipatione," see X. 1. Gaius, I. 132.
[6] Gaius, II. 145, 146.
[7] X. 4. Gaius, I. 129.
[8] For further information as to this *lex*, see D. 28. 1. 12, D. 28. 3. 15, D. 35. 2. 18. pr., D. 38. 16. 1. pr.

ciuis Romanus et suae potestatis, cum moreretur, fuit[1]; quam bonorum possessionem cum re[2], id est cum effectu, habent, si nemo alius iure heres sit.

7. Liberis inpuberibus in potestate manentibus, tam natis quam postumis, heredes substituere parentes possunt duplici modo, id est aut eo, quo extraneis, ut, si heredes non extiterint liberi, substitutus heres fiat; aut proprio iure, id est, (ut) si post mortem parentis heredes facti intra pubertatem decesserint, substitutus heres fiat[3]. 8. Etiam exheredatis filiis substituere parentibus licet[4]. 9. Non aliter inpuberi filio substituere quis heredem potest, quam si sibi (prius) heredem instituerit uel ipsum filium uel quemlibet alium[5].

10. Milites quo modo cumque fecerint testamenta ualent, id est etiam sine legitima obseruatione. nam principalibus constitutionibus permissum est illis, quo modo cumque uellent,

of the goods in accordance with the testator's directions to the appointed heirs, provided the testator was a Roman citizen and *sui juris* at the time of his death[1]; and this possession such heirs take '*cum re*[2],' that is effectually, provided there be no one else legally heir.

7. To descendants who are under the age of puberty and still subject to *potestas*, whether they be born or after-born, their ascendants can substitute heirs in two ways, viz. either in the form prescribed for making a substituted heir to extraneous heirs, so that, if the descendants do not become heirs, the substitute shall become heir; or in a special manner, so that the substitute shall become heir in case those who have been made heirs should die under the age of puberty and after their ascendant's death[3]. 8. Ascendants are allowed to make substitutions even to disinherited children[4]. 9. A person cannot substitute anybody as heir to a son under years of puberty except he have previously instituted as heir to himself either that son or some other one else[5].

10. In whatever manner soldiers may have made their testaments, they are valid, that is, even without any legal form. For by certain Imperial Constitutions they have been privileged to

[1] XXVIII. 6. Gaius, II. 119.
[2] XXVIII. 13. Gaius, II. 148, 149, III. 35—38.
[3] Gaius, II. 179—181.
[4] *Ib.* II. 182, 183.
[5] D. 28. 6. 1. 3, D. 28. 6. 2. 1—4, D. 28. 6. 10. 4.

quo modo cumque possent, testari[1]. idque testamentum (quod) miles contra iuris regulam fecit ita demum ualet, si uel in castris mortuus sit uel post missionem intra annum.

TIT. XXIV. DE LEGATIS.

1. Legatum est, quod legis modo, id est imperatiue, testamento relinquitur. nam ea, quae precatiuo modo relinquuntur fideicommissa uocantur.

2. Legamus autem quattuor modis: per uindicationem, per damnationem, sinendi modo, per praeceptionem[2]. 3. Per uindicationem his uerbis legamus: DO LEGO, CAPITO, SVMITO, SIBI HABETO[3]; 4. per damnationem his uerbis: HERES MEVS DAMNAS ESTO DARE, DATO, FACITO, HEREDEM MEVM DARE IVBEO[4]; 5. sinendi modo ita: HERES MEVS DAMNAS ESTO SINERE LVCIVM TITIVM SVMERE ILLAM REM SIBIQVE HABERE[5]. 6. per praeceptionem sic: LVCIVS TITIVS ILLAM REM PRAECIPITO[6].

declare their intentions as they will and as they can[1]. But where a soldier has made a testament contrary to the rule of law, it is only valid if he have died either on service or within a year after his discharge.

XXIV. ON LEGACIES.

1. A legacy is that which is left by testament in legal form, that is, imperatively. For those bequests which are made precatively are called *fideicommissa*.

2. Now we make legacies in four ways: by *vindicatio*, by *damnatio*, '*sinendi modo*,' by *praeceptio*[2]. 3. We give a legacy by vindication in these words: "I give and bequeath," "let him acquire," "let him take," "let him have for himself[3];" 4. by damnation in these words: "Let my heir be bound to give," "give," "do," "I order my heir to give[4];" 5. by form of sufferance thus: "Let my heir be bound to suffer Lucius Titius to take that thing and to have it for himself[5];" 6. by praeception, thus: "Let Lucius Titius first take that thing[6]."

---

1 I. 20. Gaius, II. 109—111, 114.
2 *Ib.* II. 192.
3 *Ib.* II. 193.
4 *Ib.* II. 201.
5 *Ib.* II. 209.
6 *Ib.* II. 216.

7. Per uindicationem legari possunt res quae utroque tempore ex iure Quiritium testatoris fuerunt, mortis et quando testamentum faciebat, praeterquam si pondere, numero, mensura contineantur; in his enim satis est, si uel mortis dumtaxat tempore (eius) fuerint ex iure Quiritium[1]. 8. Per damnationem omnes res legari possunt, etiam quae non sunt testatoris, dummodo tales sint quae dari possint[2]. 9. Liber homo aut res populi aut sacra aut religiosa[3] nec per damnationem legari potest, quoniam dari non potest. 10. Sinendi modo legari possunt res propriae testatoris et heredis eius[4]. 11. Per praeceptionem legari possunt res, quae etiam per uindicationem[5].

11*a*. Si ea res quae non fuit utroque tempore testatoris ex iure Quiritium per uindicationem legati sit, licet iure ciuili non ualeat legatum, tamen senatusconsulto Neroniano firmatur; quo cautum est ut quod minus pactis uerbis legatum est, per-

7. By vindication those things can be left in legacy which were the testator's property in Quiritary right at both times, *i.e.* at the time of his death and at the time when he made his testament, unless they are dependent on weight, number or measure; for as to these it is sufficient if they were the testator's property in Quiritary right at the time of his death only[1]. 8. All things can be left by damnation, even those which are not the testator's, provided, however, they are such as can be given[2]. 9. A free man, or anything belonging to the *populus*, or a thing that is sacred, or religious[3], cannot be legacied even by damnation, because it cannot be given. 10. By form of sufferance things belonging to the testator himself or his heir can be legacied[4]. 11. Anything capable of being legacied by vindication can be legacied also by praeception[5].

11*a*. Where a thing that was not the testator's property by Quiritary title at both (the above-mentioned) times has been left by vindication, though by the civil law the legacy is not valid, yet it is upheld by the *senatus-consultum Neronianum;* in which it was enacted that when a legacy is made by inapt words, it shall be the same as if it had been made in the most ad-

---

1 Gaius, II. 196.
2 *Ib.* II. 202, 203.
3 *Ib.* II. 4.
4 *Ib.* II. 210.
5 *Ib.* II. 220.

inde sit ac si optimo iure legatum esset: optimum autem ius legati per damnationem est[1].

12. Si duobus eadem res per uindicationem legata sit, siue coniunctim, uelut TITIO ET SEIO HOMINEM STICHVM DO LEGO, (siue disiunctim, uelut TITIO HOMINEM STICHVM DO LEGO, SEIO EVNDEM HOMINEM DO LEGO,)[2] concursu partes fiunt; non concurrente altero pars eius iure civili alteri adcrescebat: sed post legem Papiam Poppaeam non capientis pars caduca fit[3]. 13. Si per damnationem eadem res duobus legata sit, si quidem coniunctim, singulis partes debentur, et non capientis pars iure ciuili in hereditate remanebat, nunc autem caduca fit; quodsi disiunctim, singulis solidum debetur[4].

14. Optione autem legati per uindicationem data, legatarii electio est, uelut HOMINEM OPTATO, ELEGITO, idemque est et si tacite *legaverim optionem*[5]*:* HOMINEM *DO LEGO. at si ita:*

vantageous form, and the most advantageous form of legacy is that by damnation[1].

12. Where the same thing has been left to two persons by vindication, whether jointly, as "I give and bequeath to Titius and Seius my slave Stichus," or severally, as for instance, "I give and bequeath to Titius my slave Stichus, I give and bequeath the same slave to Seius[2];" half goes to each, if they join in accepting; but in the case of one not accepting, his part used to accrue to the other according to the civil law: but since the passing the lex Papia Poppaea, the share of him who does not take becomes a lapse[3]. 13. Where the same thing has been left by damnation to two persons, if it be jointly, then half is due to each, and the share of the one who did not take used to remain in the inheritance according to the civil law, but now becomes a lapse; but if it be severally, then the whole is due to them individually[4].

14. In the case of an optional legacy being given by way of vindication, for instance in the words: "Let him choose or select a slave," the selection is with the legatee; and the rule is also the same if the option be given tacitly[5], in this

[1] Gaius, II. 197.
[2] *Ib.* II. 199.
[3] *Ib.* II. 205—208.
[4] *Ib.* II. 205.

[5] This mutilated paragraph is filled up as Savigny suggests: *Obligationenrecht*, I. 393. In the MS. there is added in a later hand "*le-*

HERES *MEVS DAMNAS ESTO* HOMINEM DARE, heredis electio est (quem) uelit dare.

15. Ante heredis institutionem legari non potest, quoniam (uis) et potestas testamenti ab heredis institutione incipit[1]. 16. Post mortem heredis legari non potest, ne ab heredis herede legari uideatur, quod iuris ciuilis ratio non patitur. (in) mortis autem heredis tempus legari potest, uelut CVM HERES MORIETVR[2].

17. Poenae causa legari non potest. poenae autem causa legatur, quod coercendi heredis (causa) relinquitur, ut faciat quid aut non faciat, non ut (ad) legatarium pertineat[3], ut puta hoc modo: SI FILIAM TVAM IN MATRIMONIVM TITIO CONLCCAVERIS, DECEM MILIA SEIO DATO.

18. Incertae personae legari non potest, ueluti QVICVMQVE

form: "I give and bequeath a slave to him." But if it be by way of damnation, for instance, "Let my heir be bound to give a slave to Titius," the heir has a right to elect what slave he will give.

15. No legacy can be inserted before the institution of the heir, since the whole force and power of a testament start from the institution of the heir[1]. 16. Also no legacy can be left (to take effect) after the heir's death, for fear that there be an appearance of a legacy being made chargeable on the heir of the heir, which the principle of the civil law does not allow. But a legacy can be left (to take effect) at the time of the heir's death, as in this form: "When the heir shall be dying[2]."

17. A legacy cannot be left by way of penalty; and a legacy is by way of penalty when something is left for the purpose of constraining the heir to do or not to do an act, and not for the purpose of giving something to the legatee[3], as for instance in this way: "If thou bestow thy daughter in marriage on Titius, give 10,000 sesterces to Seius."

18. A legacy cannot be left to an uncertain person; for

gaverim Titio hominem *aut decem*, heres *meus dato:* hominem dare heredis electio est *nisi x* velit dare:" which is plainly wrong.

See D. 30. 1. 108. 2: D. 30. 1. 110: D. 33. 5. 2. pr. and 1.

[1] Gaius, II. 229.

[2] *Ib.* II. 232.

[3] *Ib.* II. 235. This rule, as well as those in the two preceding paragraphs, Justinian abolished; although he retained the rule that heirs could not be charged with a penalty on non-performance of an impossible, immoral or illegal act. See *Inst.* II. 20. 34—36.

FILIO MEO FILIAM SVAM IN MATRIMONIVM CONLOCAVERIT, EI HERES MEVS TOT MILIA DATO. sub certa tamen demonstratione incertae personae legari potest, uelut EX COGNATIS MEIS, QVI NVNC SVNT, QVI PRIMVS AD FVNVS MEVM VENERIT, EI HERES MEVS ILLVD DATO[1].

19. Neque ex falsa demonstratione, neque ex falsa causa legatum infirmatur[2]. falsa demonstratio est uelut TITIO FVNDVM, QVEM A TITIO EMI, DO LEGO, cum is fundus a Titio emptus non sit. falsa causa est uelut TITIO, QVONIAM NEGOTIA MEA CVRAVIT, FVNDVM DO LEGO, ut negotia eius numquam Titius curasset.

20. A legatario legari non potest[3]. 21. Legatum ab eo tantum dari potest, qui *heres institutus est*[4]: ideoque filio familiae herede instituto uel seruo, neque a patre neque a domino legari potest[5]. 22. Heredi a semet ipso legari non

instance, thus: "Whosoever shall have bestowed his daughter in marriage on my son, do thou, my heir, give him so many thousand sesterces." A legacy can however be left to an uncertain person under a definite description, for instance thus: "Do thou, my heir, give such and such a thing to him of my relations now alive who shall first come to my funeral[1]."

19. A legacy is not rendered ineffectual either by a false description or by a false consideration[2]. A false description is such as this: "The estate which I bought of Titius I give and bequeath to Titius," when in fact the estate was not bought of Titius. A false consideration is as follows: "I give and bequeath to Titius that estate, in consideration of his having managed my business," whereas Titius never had managed the testator's business.

20. A legacy cannot be charged upon a legatee[3]. 21. A legacy can only be charged upon the person who has been appointed heir in a testament[4]; and therefore if a *filius-familias* or a slave be instituted heir, a legacy cannot be charged upon his father or his master[5]. 22. A legacy cannot be left to the

[1] Gaius, II. 238.

[2] Just. *Inst.* II. 20. 30 and 31.

[3] Gaius, II. 260, 271.

[4] The words "heres institutus est" are supplied by Huschke; Cujacius suggested "ex sua persona institutus est." *Extraneus est* is inserted in the MS. in a late hand: but it is only *per damnationem* that a legacy could be charged on a stranger; though it could in all forms of legacy be charged on the heir.

[5] Sc. it cannot be charged upon them, although they get the inherit-

potest[1]. 23. Ei, qui in potestate manu mancipioue est scripti heredis sub conditione legari potest, ut requiratur quo tempore dies legati cedit in potestate heredis non sit[2]. 24. Ei cuius in potestate manu mancipioue est heres scriptus legari *potest etiam sine condicione: si tamen heres ab eo factus sit, legatum consequi* non potest[3].

25. Sicut singulae res legari possunt, ita uniuersarum quoque summa, ut puta (hoc) modo: HERES MEVS CVM TITIO HEREDITATEM MEAM PARTITO, DIVIDITO; quo casu dimidia pars bonorum legata uidetur: potest autem et alia pars, uelut tertia uel quarta, legari: quae species partitio (appellatur)[4].

26. Ususfructus legari potest iure ciuili earum rerum, qua-

heir, charged upon himself[1]. 23. A legacy can be left conditionally to a person who is under the *potestas manus* or *mancipium* of the appointed heir; so that it is required that he shall not be under the *potestas* of the heir at the time of vesting of the legacy[2]. 24. A legacy can be left even without condition to a person in whose *potestas*, *manus* or *mancipium* the appointed heir is; but if he become heir through his means he cannot take the legacy[3].

25. Just as separate things can be legacied so can an aggregate of things, as for instance in this way: "Let my heir share and divide my inheritance with Titius;" in which case half the property is regarded as legacied: but of course other shares can be legacied, as a third or a fourth, and this kind is called a partition[4].

26. By the civil law a legacy can be left of the usufruct of

ance by consenting to the son's or slave's acceptance. That this is the meaning is plain from a strikingly analogous dictum in D. 28. 6. 8. 1.

[1] An example of the application of this rule is given in D. 30. 1. 116. 1. *A* and *B* are coheirs of an estate in equal portions, and a specific field is given as a legacy to *B*, *C* and *D*: *B's* share of that field will be one-sixth, *C's* or *D's* five-twelfths. For *B*, *C*, *D* conjoin in dividing the moiety of the field which appertained to *A* as heir: but the other moiety, appertaining to *B* as heir, *C* and *D* alone divide; for *B* cannot have a legacy charged upon himself, and so as to that moiety the legacy is to *C* and *D* only.

[2] Gaius, II. 244.

[3] The italicized words in the text are supplied by Huschke. Lachmann and Böcking, without venturing on so bold an emendation, simply suggest the removal of the word *non*, which is indistinct in the MS. This had been proposed by Cujacius previously. With either alteration the doctrine agrees with Gaius, II. 245, D. 30. 1. 25, D. 30. 1. 91. pr. D. 36. 2. 17, &c.

[4] Gaius, II. 254.

rum salua substantia utendi fruendi potest esse facultas; et tam singularum rerum, quam plurium. 27. Senatusconsulto cautum est, ut etiamsi earum rerum quae in abusu continentur, ut puta uini, olei, tritici ususfructus legatus sit, legatario res tradantur, cautionibus interpositis de restituendis eis cum ususfructus ad legatarium pertinere desierit[1].

28. Ciuitatibus omnibus quae sub imperio populi Romani sunt legari potest[2]; idque a diuo Nerua introductum, postea a senatu auctore Hadriano diligentius constitutum est.

29. Legatum, quod datum est, adimi potest uel eodem testamento, uel codicillis testamento confirmatis; dum tamen eodem modo adimatur quo modo datum est[3].

30. Ad heredem legatarii legata non aliter transeunt, nisi si iam die legatorum cedente legatarius decesserit. 31. Legatorum quae pure uel in diem certum relicta sunt dies cedit

any things which admit of their usufruct being enjoyed without injury to their substance; and this usufruct may either be of separate things or of several things together. 27. By a *senatus-consultum* it was provided, that even though the usufruct legacied be that of things valuable for consumption only, as for example wine, oil, corn, the things are to be delivered to the legatee, but security must be provided for their restitution when the usufruct shall cease to belong to the legatee[1].

28. A legacy can be left to any of the civic communities which exist under the sway of the Roman people[2]; a privilege which was introduced by the late emperor Nerva, and was afterwards more definitely established by the Senate at the instance of Hadrian.

29. A legacy when given can be adeemed either by the same testament, or by codicils confirmed by the testament, provided, however, that the mode of its ademption be the same as of its bequest[3].

30. Legacies do not pass to the heir of the legatee except the death of the legatee take place after the vesting of the legacies. 31. The vesting of legacies left unconditionally, or (to be retained) until a certain day, dated from the death of the

[1] Just. *Inst.* II. 4. 2. XXII. 5.
[2] Though an inheritance cannot.
[3] Just. *Inst.* II. 21.

antiquo quidem iure ex mortis testatoris tempore; per legem autem Papiam Poppaeam ex apertis tabulis testamenti; eorum uero quae sub condicione relicta sunt cum conditio extiterit[1].

32. Lex Falcidia iubet non plus quam dodrantem totius patrimonii legari, ut omnimodo quadrans integer apud heredem remaneat[2].

33. Legatorum perperam solutorum repetitio non est[3].

TIT. XXV. DE FIDEICOMMISSIS.

1. Fideicommissum est quod non ciuilibus uerbis sed precatiue relinquitur, nec ex rigore iuris ciuilis proficiscitur sed ex uoluntate datur relinquentis. 2. Verba fideicommissorum in usu fere haec sunt: FIDEICOMMITTO, PETO, VOLO DARI et similia[4]. 3. Etiam nutu relinquere fideicommissum usu recep-

testator under the old jurisprudence; but by the Lex Papia Poppaea from the opening of the tablets of the testament; where, however, the legacies are left conditionally, the vesting dates from the time of the fulfilment of the condition[1].

32. The Lex Falcidia forbids more than three-fourths of an inheritance to be expended in legacies, so that a clear fourth may always remain with the heir[2].

33. There is no right of recovering legacies wrongly paid[3].

XXV. ON FIDEICOMMISSA.

1. A *fideicommissum* is a device expressed not in strict legal phraseology but by way of request; and does not take effect by force of the Civil Law, but is given in compliance with the wish of the person leaving it. 2. The phraseology of *fideicommissa* generally employed is such as this: "I commit to your good faith, I ask, I wish to be given," and so forth[4]. 3. It has been established by usage that a *fideicommissum* can

[1] Ulpian does not mention *legatum in diem incertum* expressly; but it is included in *legatum sub conditione*. D. 35. 1. 75: "dies incertus conditionem in testamento facit."

[2] Gaius, II. 227.

[3] *Ib.* II. 283. Huschke by comparison with this passage of Gaius suggests that the reading should be "per damnationem perperam" instead of "perperam;" for only these could be "*paid* by the heir:" the other kinds were "*taken* by the legatee."

[4] *Ib.* II. 249.

tum est[1]. 4. Fideicommissum relinquere possunt qui testamentum facere possunt, licet non fecerint: nam etiam intestato quis moriturus fideicommissum relinquere potest[2]. 5. Res per fideicommissum relinqui possunt quae per damnationem legari possunt[3]. 6. Fideicommissa dari possunt his, quibus legari potest[4]. 7. Latini Iuniani fideicommissum capere possunt, licet legatum capere non possint[5]. 8. Fideicommissum et ante heredis institutionem, et post mortem heredis, et codicillis etiam non confirmatis testamento dari potest, licet (ita) legari non possit[6]. 9. Item Graece fideicommissum scriptum ualet, licet legatum Graece scriptum non ualeat[7]. 10. Filio qui in potestate est seruoue heredibus institutis, seu his legatum sit, patris uel domini fidei committi potest, quamuis ab eo legari non possit[8]. 11. Qui testamento heres institutus est, codicillis etiam non confirmatis rogari potest, ut hereditatem totam uel ex parte alii restituat, quamuis directo heres in-

be given even by a nod[1]. 4. Those who can make a testament, although they have not made one, can leave a *fideicommissum*: for even a man about to die intestate can leave a *fideicommissum*[2]. 5. Those things can be left by *fideicommissum* which can also be left as legacies "by damnation[3]." 6. *Fideicommissa* can be given to the same persons to whom legacies can be left[4]. 7. Junian Latins can take a *fideicommissum*, though they cannot take a legacy[5]. 8. A *fideicommissum* can be given both before the institution of the heir, and (to take effect) after the death of the heir, and also by codicils unconfirmed in a testament; though legacies cannot be left in this way[6]. 9. Again a *fideicommissum* written in Greek is valid, though a legacy written in Greek is not[7]. 10. If a son under his *potestas*, or a slave be appointed heir, or if a legacy be left to them, a *fideicommissum* can be charged upon the father or owner although a legacy cannot be so charged[8]. 11. A person who has been instituted as testamentary heir can be requested by codicils, though unconfirmed, to restore the inheritance either wholly or in part to another, although an heir cannot be instituted

[1] Gaius, II. 269.
[2] *Ib.* II. 270.
[3] XXIV. 8. Gaius, II. 260—262.
[4] Gaius, II. 285—287.
[5] *Ib.* I. 24, II. 275.
[6] *Ib.* II. 277, 269.
[7] *Ib.* II. 281.
[8] XXIV. 21.

stitui ne quidem confirmatis codicillis possit[1]. 12. Fideicommissa non per formulam petuntur ut legata, sed cognitione Romae quidem consulum aut praetoris, qui fideicommissarius uocatur; in prouinciis uero praesidis prouinciae[2]. 13. Poenae causa, uel incertae personae ne quidem fideicommissa dari possunt[3].

14. Is, qui rogatus est alii restituere hereditatem, lege quidem Falcidia (locum) non habente, quoniam non plus puta quam dodrantem restituere rogatus est, ex Trebelliano senatusconsulto restituit, ut ei et in eum dentur actiones cui restituta est hereditas. lege autem Falcidia interueniente, quoniam plus dodrantem uel etiam totam hereditatem restituere rogatus est, ex Pegasiano senatusconsulto restituit, ut deducta parte quarta, ipsi qui scriptus est heres et in ipsum actiones conseruentur; is autem, qui recipit hereditatem, legatarii loco habeatur[4]. 15. Ex Pegasiano senatusconsulto restituta hereditate commoda et

directly even by confirmed codicils[1]. 12. The process for recovering *fideicommissa* is not, like that for legacies, by *formula*, but at Rome falls under the jurisdiction of the Consuls or of the Praetor called Fideicommissary Praetor; in the provinces under that of their presidents[2]. 13. Not even *fideicommissa* can be given by way of penalty, or to a foreigner, or to an uncertain person[3].

14. Where a person has been requested to hand over the inheritance to another, supposing the Lex Falcidia be not applicable, because he has not been asked to hand over more than three-fourths, he hands it over under the *senatusconsultum Trebellianum*, so that the actions are granted for and against him to whom the inheritance has been handed over. But supposing that the Lex Falcidia does apply, in consequence of his having been requested to hand over more than three-fourths or even the whole of the inheritance, then he hands it over under the *senatusconsultum Pegasianum*, so that, after the deduction of the fourth, all actions are maintained for and against him who has been appointed heir: whilst he who receives the inheritance is regarded as being in the position of legatee[4]. 15. If the inheritance have been handed over under the *senatusconsultum*

1 Gaius, II. 273.
2 *Ib.* II. 278.
3 *Ib.* II. 287, 288.
4 *Ib.* II. 253—257.

incommoda hereditatis communicantur inter heredem et eum cui reliquae partes restitutae sunt, interpositis stipulationibus ad exemplum partis et pro parte stipulationum. partis autem et pro parte stipulationes proprie dicuntur, quae de lucro et damno communicando solent interponi inter heredem et legatarium partiarium[1], id est, cum quo partitus est heres. 16. Si heres damnosam hereditatem dicat, cogitur a praetore adire et restituere totam, ita ut ei et in eum qui recipit hereditatem actiones dentur, proinde atque si ex Trebelliano senatusconsulto restituta fuisset. idque ut ita fiat, Pegasiano senatusconsulto cautum[2].

17. Si quis in fraudem tacitam fidem adcommodauerit, ut non capienti fideicommissum restituat, nec quadrantem eum deducere senatus censuit, nec caducum uindicare ex eo testamento, si liberos habeat[3].

Pegasianum, the method whereby the advantages and disadvantages of the inheritance are shared between the heir and the person to whom the residue has been handed over, is by stipulations being entered into after the model of the stipulations "of and for a part." Now those stipulations are properly called "of and for a part" which are usually entered into, for the object of sharing the gain and loss, between the heir and a partiary legatee[1], i.e. a person with whom the heir has shared the inheritance. 16. If the heir declare the inheritance to be ruinous, he is compelled by the Praetor to enter upon it and hand over the whole, so that all actions may be granted for and against the person receiving the inheritance, just as though it had been handed over under the *senatusconsultum Trebellianum;* and provisions to this effect have been enacted by the *senatusconsultum Pegasianum*[2].

17. If any one have fraudulently given a secret promise to hand over a *fideicommissum* to a person incapable of taking it, the senate has ruled that he can neither deduct a quarter, nor claim a lapse under that testament, supposing that he has children[3].

---

[1] Gaius, II. 254. For *partitio*, see XXIV. 25, above.

[2] *Ib.* II. 258. D. 36. 1. 45.

[3] This regulation was made by Antoninus, as we see from D. 49. 14. 49;—further information on the subject is to be found in D. 30. 1. 103: D. 34. 9. 11: D. 35. 2. 59. As to *caduca* see Tit. XVII. If the *fidei commissum* had been given to

18. Libertas dari potest per fideicommissum[1].

TIT. XXVI. DE LEGITIMIS HEREDIBVS.

1. Intestatorum ingenuorum hereditates pertinent primum ad suos heredes, id est liberos qui in potestate sunt, ceterosque qui in liberorum loco sunt; si sui heredes non sint, ad consanguineos, id est fratres et sorores ex eodem patre; si nec hi sint, ad reliquos agnatos proximos, id est cognatos uirilis sexus per mares descendentes eiusdem familiae[2]: id enim cautum est lege duodecim tabularum hac[3]: SI INTESTATO MORITUR, CUI SUUS HERES NEC ESCIT, AGNATUS PROXIMUS FAMILIAM HABETO[4].

2. Si defuncti sit filius, (et) ex altero filio iam mortuo nepos

18. Liberty can be given by means of a *fideicommissum*[1].

XXVI. ON STATUTABLE HEIRS.

1. The inheritances of intestate free-born persons belong first to their *sui heredes*, that is, their descendants under their *potestas* and all other persons in the position of descendants; then, if there be no *sui heredes*, to the *consanguinei*, that is, brothers and sisters begotten of the same father: then, failing these also, to the other agnates of nearest degree, that is, relations of the male sex, tracing their descent through males and of the same family[2]; for this was enacted by a law of the Twelve Tables[3] in the following words: "If any one die intestate without any *suus heres*, then let the nearest agnate have the estate[4]."

2. If the deceased leave one son and also one grandson, or

a capable person, the *fiduciarius* could have taken a full quarter, retained the amount of the legacies out of the other three-quarters, and handed the balance over to the *fidei commissarius*. So he would have profited by any lapsed legacies. *All* this profit is taken from him by the *S. C. Plancianum*, and carried to the *fiscus*.

[1] Gaius, II. 263.

[2] *Ib.* III. 1—5, 9—11.

[3] Tab. V. l. 4.

[4] Huschke is of opinion that a paragraph has been omitted between the words "habeto" and "Si defuncti"—which he supplies thus: "Si agnatus defuncti non sit, eadem lex duodecim tabularum gentiles ad hereditatem uocat his uerbis: 'si agnatus nec escit, gentiles familiam habento.' Nunc nec gentiles nec gentilicia iura in usu sunt." *i.e.* "If there be no agnate of the deceased, the same law of the Twelve Tables calls the *gentiles* to the inheritance in the following words; 'if there be also no agnate, let the *gentiles* have the estate.' At the present day neither *gentiles* nor the rules regarding *gentiles* are recognized." See Gaius, III. 17.

unus uel etiam plures, ad omnes hereditas pertinet, non ut in capita diuidatur, sed in stirpes, id est, ut filius solus mediam partem habeat et nepotes, quotquot sunt, alteram dimidiam: aequum est enim nepotes in patris sui locum succedere et eam partem habere quam pater eorum, si uiueret, habiturus esset[1].

3. Quamdiu suus heres speratur heres fieri posse, tamdiu locus agnatis non est; uelut si uxor defuncti praegnans sit, aut filius aput hostes sit[2].

4. Agnatorum hereditates diuiduntur in capita; uelut si sit fratris filius et alterius fratris duo pluresue liberi, quotquot sunt ab utraque parte personae, tot fiunt portiones, ut singuli singulas capiant[3]. 5. Si plures eodem gradu sint agnati, et quidam eorum hereditatem ad se pertinere noluerint, uel antequam adierint decesserint, eorum pars adcrescit his qui adierint: quod si nemo eorum adierit, ad insequentem gradum ex lege hereditas non transmittitur, quoniam in legitimis hereditatibus suc-

even more, born of another son deceased, the inheritance belongs to them all, not in such manner as to be divided *per capita*, but *per stirpes*, that is, that the surviving son have one half share and the grandsons, however many, have the other half: for it is fair that the grandsons should succeed to their father's place and have that share which their father would have had, were he living[1].

3. So long as there is any expectation of a *suus heres* possibly becoming heir, there is no place for the agnates, as where the wife of the deceased is pregnant, or his son is in the enemy's hands[2].

4. The inheritances of agnates are divided *per capita;* for instance, if there be a brother's son and two or more children of another brother, whatever be the number of persons in the two branches taken together, the inheritance is divided into that number of portions, so that each person may take one[3]. 5. If there be several agnates in the same degree, supposing some of them to be unwilling that the inheritance should belong to them, or to have died before their entry upon it, their share accrues to those who have entered; but if none have entered, the inheritance is not in law transmissible to the next

1 Gaius, III. 8. 2 *Ib.* III. 13. 3 *Ib.* III. 16.

cessio non est[1]. 6. Ad feminas ultra consanguineorum gradum legitima hereditas non pertinet; itaque soror fratri sororiue legitima heres fit (*amita uero uel fratris filia et deinceps legitima heres non fit*[2]). 7. Ad liberos matris intestatae hereditas sine in manum conuentione ex lege duodecim tabularum non pertinebat, quia feminae suos heredes non habent; sed postea imperatorum Antonini et Commodi oratione in senatu recitata id actum est, ut sine in manum conventione matrum legitimae hereditates ad filios pertineant, exclusis consanguineis et reliquis agnatis[3]. 8. Intestati filii hereditas ad matrem ex lege duodecim tabularum non pertinet; sed si ius liberorum habeat, ingenua trium, libertina quattuor, legitima heres fit ex senatusconsulto Tertulliano; si tamen ei filio neque suus heres sit quiue inter suos heredes ad bonorum possessionem a praetore

degree, because there is no devolution among statutable heirs[1]. 6. A statutable inheritance does not belong to women beyond the degree of *consanguineae*, therefore a sister becomes statutable heir to her brother or sister, but a father's sister or a brother's daughter &c. does not become statutable heir[2]. 7. According to the law of the Twelve Tables the inheritance of an intestate mother did not belong to her descendants, unless the marriage had been with *conventio in manum*, because women have no *sui heredes;* but at a later period the rule was made in accordance with an oration of the Emperors Antoninus and Commodus delivered in the senate, that the statutable inheritances of mothers not married with *manus* should belong to their sons, to the exclusion of the *consanguinei* and the other agnates[3]. 8. The inheritance of an intestate son does not belong to his mother by virtue of any law of the Twelve Tables; but if she have the prerogative of children, which in the case of a free-born woman is acquired by three, in that of a freedwoman by four, then she is made statutable heir by virtue of the *senatusconsultum Tertullianum;* provided only that her son have neither a *suus heres* nor any one who is called by the Praetor amongst the *sui*

---

[1] Gaius, III. 12, 22.

[2] *Ib.* III. 14, 23. Huschke suggests that the words printed in italics have been omitted by the transcriber.

[3] Gaius gives the old law in III. 24, without any mention of the enactment of Antoninus and Commodus, commonly known by the name of the S. C. Orphitianum; but Justinian devotes a title of his Institutes (III. 4) to the exposition of that *senatusconsultum*.

uocatur, neque pater ad quem lege hereditas bonorumue possessio cum re pertinet, neque frater consanguineus: quod si soror consanguinea sit, ad utrasque pertinere iubetur hereditas[1].

TIT. XXVII. DE LIBERTORVM SVCCESSIONIBVS [UEL BONIS].

1. Libertorum intestatorum hereditas primum ad suos heredes pertinet; deinde ad eos quorum liberti sunt, uelut patronum patronam liberosue patroni[2]. 2. Si sit patronus et alterius patroni filius, ad solum patronum hereditas pertinet. 3. Item patroni filius patroni nepotibus obstat[3]. 4. Ad liberos patronorum hereditas defuncti pertinet (ita) ut in capita, non in stirpes, diuidatur[4].

5. Legitimae hereditatis ius, quod ex lege duodecim tabularum[5] descendit, capitis minutione amittitur[6].

heredes to the possession of the goods, nor a father to whom in law the inheritance or the possession of the goods belongs effectively, nor a brother by the father's side; but if he have a sister by the father's side, then the inheritance is directed to belong to both (viz. the mother and this sister)[1].

XXVII. ON THE SUCCESSIONS (OR GOODS) OF FREEDMEN.

1. The inheritance of intestate freedmen belongs first to their *sui heredes;* then to those whose freedmen they are, such as their patron or patroness, or their patron's descendants[2]. 2. Should there be a patron and the son of another patron, the inheritance belongs to the patron alone. 3. The son of a patron again is preferred to the grandsons of a patron[3]. 4. The inheritance of the deceased (freedman) on going to the descendants of the patron is divisible *per capita* and not *per stirpes*[4].

5. The right of statutable inheritance originating from the law of the Twelve Tables[5] is lost by *capitis diminutio*[6].

[1] Gaius, III. 23, 24. In Gaius, however, there is no mention of the S. C. Tertullianum. That S. C. forms the subject of a title in Justinian's *Institutes* (III. 3), where full information may be found. The *jus liberorum* was conferred by the Lex Papia Poppaea, A. D. 10; see App. (H). As to the phrase "cum re" see Gaius, II. 148, 149; III. 35—37.

[2] Gaius, III. 40.

[3] *Ib.* III. 60.

[4] *Ib.* III. 61.

[5] Tab. V. l. 8.

[6] Gaius, III. 21, 27, 51.

TIT. XXVIII. DE POSSESSIONIBVS DANDIS.

1. Bonorum possessio datur aut contra tabulas testamenti, aut secundum tabulas, aut intestati[1].

2. Contra tabulas bonorum possessio[2] datur liberis emancipatis testamento praeteritis, licet legitima non ad eos pertineat hereditas[3]. 3. Bonorum possessio contra tabulas liberis tam naturalibus quam adoptiuis datur; sed naturalibus quidem emancipatis, non tamen et illis qui in adoptiua familia sunt; adoptiuis autem his tantum qui in potestate manserunt. 4. Emancipatis liberis ex edicto datur bonorum possessio, si parati sint cauere fratribus suis qui in potestate manserunt, bona quae moriente patre habuerunt se conlaturos.

5. Secundum tabulas bonorum possessio datur scriptis here-

XXVIII. ON GIVING POSSESSIONS.

1. Possession of goods is granted either in opposition to, or in accordance with the testamentary directions, or upon an intestacy[1].

2. *Bonorum possessio* in opposition to the testament[2] is given to emancipated descendants, who have been passed over in the testament, though the statutable inheritance does not belong to them[3]. 3. *Bonorum possessio* in opposition to the testamentary dispositions is given to descendants both actual and adopted: and to actual descendants even when emancipated, though not also to those who are in an adopted family; but to those adopted children alone who have remained in the *potestas* (of the adopter). 4. The *Bonorum possessio* is granted to emancipated descendants by virtue of the Edict, if they are prepared to give security to their brothers who have continued under *potestas*, that they will bring into the division the property they had at the death of their father.

5. *Bonorum possessio* in accordance with the testamentary dispositions is granted to the appointed heirs, provided there

1 The MS. has "adversus tabulas intestati." So also in XX. 14 there is *adversus* instead of *secundum*.

Gaius in his Commentaries says little on the topic of Bonorum Possessio, giving as his reason in III. 33 that he had written a special treatise on the subject, which we may conjecture to be his "Commentarii ad Edictum Urbicum."

2 D. 37. 4.

3 XXII. 23.

dibus, scilicet si eorum quibus contra tabulas[1] competit nemo sit, aut petere noluerit. 6. Etiam si iure ciuili non ualeat testamentum, forte quod familiae mancipatio uel nuncupatio defuit, si signatum testamentum sit non minus quam septem testium ciuium Romanorum signis[2], bonorum possessio datur.

7. Intestati datur bonorum possessio per septem gradus[3]: primo gradu liberis; secundo legitimis heredibus; tertio proximis cognatis; quarto familiae patroni; (quinto) patrono, patronae, item liberis uel (parentibus) patroni patronaeue; sexto uiro, uxori; septimo cognatis manumissoris, quibus per legem Furiam[4] plus mille asses capere licet: et si nemo sit ad quem bonorum possessio pertinere possit, aut sit quidem sed ius suum omiserit, populo bona deferuntur ex lege Iulia caducaria[5]. 8. Liberis bonorum possessio datur tam his qui in potestate usque in

be no one to whom possession belongs in opposition to the dispositions, or provided none of these wish to claim it[1]. 6. And further if a testament be invalid according to the Civil Law, because, perhaps, the mancipation of the estate, or the nuncupation was wanting, still *bonorum possessio* is granted if the testament have been sealed with the seals of not less than seven witnesses, Roman citizens[2].

7. *Bonorum possessio* upon an intestacy is granted through seven degrees[3]: in the first degree to descendants; in the second to statutable heirs; in the third to the nearest relations; in the fourth to the family of the patron; in the fifth to the patron or patroness, and to the descendants or ascendants of the patron or patroness; in the sixth to the husband or wife; in the seventh to the relations of the manumittor, who are allowed by the Lex Furia[4] to take more than one thousand *asses;* and if there be no one, to whom the *bonorum possessio* can belong, or if there be such an one, but he have abandoned his right, the property devolves upon the *populus* by virtue of the Lex Julia concerning lapses[5]. 8. The *bonorum possessio* "to descendants" is conferred both upon those who remained

[1] D. 37. 11.

[2] XXIII. 6. Gaius, II. 119.

[3] The first, second, third, and sixth degrees of intestate succession here named, form the subject of separate titles of the Digest, viz. 38. 6, 38. 7, 38. 8, 38. 11. The other degrees were rendered superfluous by Justinian's new regulations regarding patronage, as he himself tells us in *Inst.* III. 9. 5. See App. (L).

[4] I. 2.

[5] Gaius, II. 150.

mortis tempus fuerunt quam emancipatis[1]; item adoptiuis, non tamen etiam in adoptionem datis. 9. Proximi cognati bonorum possessionem accipiunt non solum per feminini sexus personam cognati, sed etiam agnati capite diminuti[2]: nam licet legitimum ius agnationis capitis minutione amiserint, natura tamen cognati manent.

10. Bonorum possessio datur parentibus et liberis intra annum ex quo petere potuerunt; ceteris intra centum dies. 11. Qui omnes intra id tempus si non petierint bonorum possessionem, sequens gradus amittitur, perinde atque si superiores non essent; idque per septem gradus fit.

12. Hi quibus ex successorio edicto bonorum possessio datur heredes quidem non sunt, sed heredis loco constituuntur beneficio praetoris. ideoque seu ipsi agant seu cum his agatur, ficticiis actionibus opus est in quibus heredes esse finguntur[3].

under *potestas* up to the time of the ascendant's death, and upon those who have been emancipated[1]; likewise upon those received in adoption, but not upon those given in adoption. 9. Not only do those persons receive the *bonorum possessio* "as nearest relation," who are related through a person of the female sex, but also such agnates as have undergone a *capitis diminutio*[2]: for although by the *capitis diminutio* they have lost the statutable right of agnation, they still remain relations by nature.

10. *Bonorum possessio* is granted to the ascendants and descendants within one year from the time when they became able to make their claim; to all other persons within one hundred days. 11. And when any of these classes have not made their claim within this fixed time, the next degree is admitted, just as if those preceding were non-existent, and this is the case throughout the seven degrees.

12. Those to whom *bonorum possessio* is granted by virtue of the successory edict are not indeed heirs, but are by the Praetor's grant placed in the position of heirs; and therefore whether they are themselves suing or are being sued, fictitious actions must be employed in which they are feigned to be heirs[3].

---

1 Gaius, III. 26.
2 XXVII. 5. Gaius, III. 27, 30.
3 Gaius, III. 32, IV. 34.

13. Bonorum possessio aut *cum re* datur, aut sine re[1]: cum re, (cum) is qui accipit cum effectu bona retineat; sine re, cum alius iure ciuili euincere hereditatem possit; ueluti si sit s*cript*us heres, intestati bonorum possessio sine re (est), quoniam s*cript*us heres euincere hereditatem iure legitimo potest[2].

TIT. XXIX. DE BONIS LIBERTORVM.

1. Ciuis Romani liberti hereditatem lex duodecim tabularum[3] patrono defert, si intestato sine suo herede libertus decesserit[4]: ideoque siue testamento facto decedat, licet suus heres ei non sit, seu intestato, et suus heres ei sit, quamuis non naturalis, sed uxor puta quae in manu fuit, uel adoptiuus filius, lex patrono nihil praestat. sed ex edicto praetoris, seu testamento

13. The grant of *bonorum possessio* is made either "with benefit" or "without benefit[1]." With benefit, when the recipient receives effectively, so that he can retain the property; without benefit, when some one else can by help of the Civil Law wrest the inheritance from him; for instance, if there be an heir appointed in a testament, the *bonorum possessio* on intestacy is "without benefit," because this appointed heir can by his statutable right wrest the inheritance from the *bonorum possessor*[2].

XXIX. ON THE PROPERTY OF FREEDMEN.

1. A law of the Twelve Tables[3] confers the inheritance of a Roman citizen freedman upon the patron, where the freedman has died intestate without leaving a *suus heres*[4]: and therefore if he either die after making a testament, although leaving no *suus heres*, or die intestate, and leave a *suus heres*, even one not connected by birth, but a wife, for instance, who has been under his *manus*, or an adopted son, the law abovementioned grants nothing to the patron. But by virtue of the

[1] Gaius, II. 148, 149, III. 35—37. See also above, XXIII. 6, XXVI. 8.

[2] The MS. has *suus heres* in both the places where *scriptus* is printed in the text. The *scriptus heres* could not always hold the possession against the *heres ab intestato:* he could against a *legitimus* or *cognatus proximus*, but not against a *suus praeteritus*. Hence Krüger suggests the following omission has taken place: veluti si suus heres in testa(*mento praeteritus sit, licet scriptis heredibus secundum tabulas possessio deferatur, erit tamen ea*) bonorum possessio sine re, quoniam suus heres, &c.

[3] Tab. V. l. 8.

[4] XXVII. 1. Gaius, III. 40.

(facto) libertus moriatur, ut aut nihil aut minus quam partem dimidiam bonorum patrono relinquat, contra tabulas testamenti partis dimidiae bonorum possessio illi datur, nisi libertus aliquem ex naturalibus liberis successorem sibi relinquat; siue intestato decedat, et uxorem forte in manu uel adoptiuum filium relinquat, aeque partis mediae bonorum possessio contra suos heredes patrono datur[1].

2. In bonis libertae patrono nihil iuris ex edicto datur. itaque (*seu testata decedat, id tantum iuris patronus habet, quod ei testamento ipso tutore auctore datum est;*)[2] seu intestata moriatur liberta, semper ad eum hereditas pertinet, licet liberi sint libertae, (qui) quoniam non sunt sui heredes matri, non obstant

Praetor's edict if, on the one hand, the freedman die testate, bequeathing nothing or less than half to his patron, possession of one half of the goods is granted to the patron in spite of the testamentary directions, unless the freedman leave as his successor some one of his actual descendants; and if, on the other hand, he die intestate and leave, say, a wife under *manus*, or an adopted son, possession of one half of the goods is in the same way granted to the patron to the detriment of the *sui heredes*[1].

2. No rights over the goods of a freedwoman are bestowed upon a patron by the Edict; and therefore if, on the one hand, she die testate, the patron has no rights beyond those given him in the testament, which he as guardian authorized[2]; and if, on the other hand, she die intestate, the inheritance always belongs to him, although she may have descendants, for these, not being *sui heredes* to their mother, do not stand in the

[1] Gaius, III. 41.

[2] XI. 27. Gaius, I. 192. We have filled up the lacuna according to Huschke's conjecture. Lachmann suggested: "sive auctor ad testamentum faciendum factus sit," a reading approved of by Göschen and Böcking. Something is plainly wanting to make the sense complete, and the *seu* before *intestata* cannot grammatically stand alone, but indicates that another *seu* either precedes or follows. Hence some editors have treated the sentence in the MS. as the first of the alternatives and supplied the other thus: "itaque seu intestata moriatur liberta, semper ad eum hereditas pertinet, licet liberi sint libertae, quoniam non sunt sui heredes matri: *seu testamentum jure fecerit, heres scriptus non* obst*at* patrono." The meaning of the passage is the same whichever way it is amended, for the testament of the freedwoman could only be legal if made with the consent of the patron. See Gaius, III. 43.

patrono. 3. Lex Papia Poppaea postea libertas quattuor liberorum iure tutela patronorum liberauit[1]; et cum intulerit iam posse eas sine auctoritate patronorum testari, prospexit ut pro numero liberorum libertae superstitum uirilis pars patrono debeatur[2]. 4. Liberi patroni uirilis sexus eadem iura in bonis libertorum parentum suorum habent, quae et ipse patronus[3]. 5. Feminae uero ex lege quidem duodecim tabularum[4] idem ius habent atque masculi patronorum liberi; contra tabulas autem testamenti liberti aut ab intestato contra suos heredes non naturales bonorum possessio eis non competit; sed si ius trium liberorum habuerunt, etiam haec iura ex lege Papia Poppaea nanciscuntur[5]. 6. Patronae in bonis libertorum illud ius tantum habebant quod lex duodecim tabularum introduxit; sed postea lex Papia patronae (ingenuae[6]) duobus liberis hono-

patron's way. 3. The Lex Papia Poppaea afterwards exempted freedwomen from the tutelage of patrons, by prerogative of four children[1], and having established the rule that they could thenceforth make testaments without the patron's authorization, it provided that a proportionate share of the freedwoman's property should be due to the patron, dependent on the number of her surviving children[2]. 4. The male descendants of a patron have the same rights over the goods of the freedmen of their ascendants as the patron himself has[3]. 5. Under the law of the Twelve Tables[4] female descendants have just as much right as male descendants of patrons, but *bonorum possessio* does not appertain to them either in opposition to the testamentary directions of a freedman, or on his intestacy as against those *sui heredes* who are not such by blood; yet if they have obtained the prerogative of three children, they acquire these rights also by virtue of the Lex Papia Poppaea[5].

6. Patronesses used to have only such rights over their freedmen's property as the law of the Twelve Tables established; the Lex Papia Poppaea, however, afterwards gave to a patroness of free-birth[6] enjoying the privilege of two children,

[1] Gaius, I. 194.
[2] *Ib.* III. 44.
[3] *Ib.* III. 45.
[4] Tab. V. l. 8, previously referred to in § 1.
[5] Gaius, III. 46, 47.
[6] The word *ingenuae* is not in the MS. but was inserted by Cujacius

ratae, libertinae tribus, id iuris dedit quod patronus habet ex edicto[1]. 7. Item ingenuae trium liberorum iure honoratae eadem lex id ius dedit quod ipsi patrono tribuit.

and to a freedwoman enjoying that of three, the same rights that the patron has under the Edict[1]. 7. So too the same *lex* gave to a woman of free-birth enjoying the privilege of three children all the rights which it conferred upon the patron himself.

---

and adopted by succeeding editors in accordance with the words of Gaius referred to in the next note.

[1] Gaius, III. 49, 50. But observe that Gaius says that the Lex Papia Poppaea did not give to a free-born patroness having two children or to a freedwoman patroness having three children the full rights of a patron, but *eadem fere jura*, allowing the complete rights only to a free-born patroness having three, or a freedwoman patroness having four children. This agrees with Ulpian's statement that the one class had only the rights under the Edict, the other the rights under the Lex Papia Poppaea.

APPENDIX.

(A). On *Status*, *Civitas*, *Latinitas*, &c.

ALTHOUGH Gaius gives all the more important rules as to *Status*, yet he never collects them together, so that it will be advantageous to put his scattered observations in a connected form, and to supplement them with information drawn from other sources.

Firstly, *Status* has reference to three elements, (1) Liberty, (2) Citizenship, (3) Family. This is implied rather than stated in Gaius, I. 159 et seqq.

In Gaius, I. 9, the primary element, liberty, is touched upon. All men are either free or slaves. Freemen, again, may be Romans or foreigners: if Romans they may either possess the full franchise, *Civitas*, have the lower kind denominated *Latinitas*, or be in the still inferior degree of *Dediticii*. (*Gai.* I. 12.)

Secondly, both the perfect *Civis* and the *Latinus* may possess their rights either by birth or by manumission. This fact as to *Cives* is stated explicitly in Gaius, I. 10; and that there were Latins by birth is indicated by him in III. 56. When Gaius wrote there were no *Dediticii* except emancipated slaves, but in earlier days there were *Dediticii* who had not been raised from servitude to this inferior species of freedom, but depressed into it from their absolute liberty as *Peregrini*. That this state of things had passed away may perhaps be gathered from the otherwise puzzling word *quondam* in *Gai.* I. 14.

Hence, leaving the discussion of the elements involved in *Familia* to another note, we may tabulate thus with regard to Liberty and Citizenship, denoting by A, B, C, respectively, the first, second and third grades of the members of the Roman state:

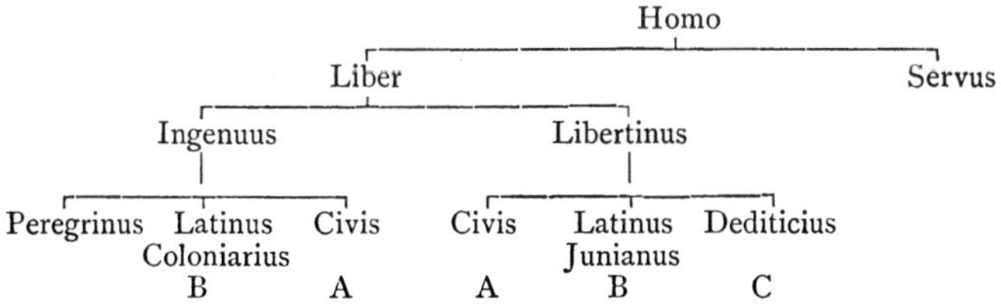

We have now to consider the various privileges of the three orders of Roman citizens. A full *Civis Romanus* had two sets of rights, those political and those private. His political rights were the *Jus Suffragii*, or capacity to vote in the Comitia, and the *Jus Honorum*, or eligibility for holding offices and magistracies. It would be foreign to our purpose to enter at length into the distinctions originally existing between Patricians and Plebeians as to these matters, for in the time of Gaius such differences had long ceased to exist. Originally the Plebeians had neither of the *jura* named above, but gradually their inferiority ceased, and they stood precisely on the same footing as the Patricians.

The private rights of a *Civis Romanus* were the *Conubium*, or capacity to contract *justae nuptiae*, whence flowed the peculiar relations of *Patria Potestas* and *Agnatio*, and the *Commercium*, which gave to its possessor the power of making contracts and conveyances (especially in reference to land) by the peculiar form styled *Mancipatio*, of writing a Testament or inheriting under one (privileges summed up in the phrase *Testamenti Factio*), of making a *Cessio in Jure*, &c. &c. From the *Conubium* too and from the *Testamenti Factio* the Plebeians had been originally debarred, but this badge of inferiority, like the other, had long died out.

The next class to *Cives* in early times was that of the *Coloni Romani* who had the *Conubium*, *Commercium* and *Testamenti Factio*, and could enjoy *Dominium ex Jure Quiritium*, but were most probably devoid of *Jus Honorum* and *Jus Suffragii*. Some, however, say that they remained *cives* in all respects, though their political rights could only be exercised at Rome. Then came the *Latini*, who had *Commercium* only. Whether this included *Testamenti Factio* or not is disputable, but probably it did involve it, for when Ulpian (XX. 14) says that the *Latini Juniani* were restrained from this by the special provisions of the *Lex Junia*, he would seem to imply that the other and older Latins had possessed it. The first Latins in alliance with Rome, and having these privileges, were the Aequi, Rutuli, Volsci and Hernici, and Latium extended along the coast from Ostia only as far as Sinuessa and the Liris. Strabo *Geog.* V. 3, 4. These Latins, generally designated *Veteres Latinii*, or *Socii Latini*, or *Socii Nominis Latini*, became full citizens after the Marsic or Social War, by the Julian Law B.C. 88; and so too did the *Coloni Romani*, if they had not the citizenship before; therefore the *Latini*, or rather *Latini Coloniarii*, of Gaius' time were a new creation (see note on Gaius, I. 95) and were barbarian in blood. The people of Nismes had the *Jus Latii;* Strabo *Geog.* IV. 1, 12, τὸ καλούμενον Λάτιον; Caesar gave it to Novo Como; Appian *de Bell. Civ.* II. 26: Pompey gave it all Transpadane Gauls, Nero to the nations of the Maritime Alps, Vespasian to all Spain; and Hadrian greatly multiplied *Latini Coloniarii*. Their privileges were the same as those of the *Veteres Latini;* and identical with those of the *Latini Juniani*, to whom accordingly we pass on.

The *Latini Juniani* had *Commercium*, and though they had not the full *Testamenti Factio*, they had a modified form of it; as they could be balance-holders and witnesses, or even be instituted heirs, for they were allowed to become purchasers of the patrimony, as Ulpian states (XX. 8), and the purchasers were in the ancient days of which he is speaking the heirs themselves. Probably, therefore, when in later days the heir was no longer allowed to be purchaser, (Gaius, II. 103) they could still be heirs. But although they could be instituted heirs (or purchasers), they could not take up the inheritance unless, prior to the time when the testament came into operation, they had attained to the full *Civitas*. Ulpian, XXII. 3.

Moreover they were debarred from the most important part of the *Testamenti Factio*, the making of a testament of their own, as we have already shown on the authority of Ulpian (XX. 14), and this is corroborated by Gaius, I. 23.

Further these Latins had no *Conubium*, although facilities were afforded for their becoming *Cives Romani*, and in such an event they would of course obtain this and all other civic rights (see Gaius, I. 28—32); and naturally they were deprived of the higher powers of voting or holding magistracies.

As to the *Dediticii*, Gaius gives so complete an account of their disqualifications in I. 25—27, that it is unnecessary to do more than call attention to the passage.

We may observe in conclusion that the son of a *Dediticius* would, on his father's death, be a *Peregrinus*, and the son of a *Latinus Junianus*, in the same event, a *Latinus Colonarius*. Over neither of them, therefore, had the patron those rights as to inheritance which he had possessed over their fathers, and which are described in Gaius, III. 56—76.

(B). On *Potestas*, *Dominium*, *Manus*, and *Mancipium*.

Potestas means primarily right or domination over oneself or something external to oneself. In many passages of the sources it is used as synonymous with *jus*, and as equivalent to full and complete ownership.

The only place in the fragments of the XII. Tables where the word occurs is the following: "Si furiosus est, adgnatorum gentiliumque in eo pecuniaque ejus potestas esto" (Tab. 5, l. 7); and what is there denoted by it is evidently a power of superintendence and direction. We may conclude then that *potestas* was not the archaic word expressing the combination of positive rights and authority possessed by the head of the household, the *paterfamilias*. Maine thinks that *manus* was the old word expressing this and all the other notions, subsequently marked with the separate and distinctive appellations of *dominium*, *potestas*, *mancipium*, and *manus*. But whatever was the comprehensive archaic term, or whether there was one at all, *potestas* in the classical jurists is the word used to express the rights and authority exercised by the *paterfamilias* over the persons of the *familia*, just as *dominium* denotes his power over the inanimate or unintelligent components of the same.

We may further observe that *potestas* has two widely different significations in the writings of the classical jurists, according as they are speaking of the authority exercised over a slave, *dominica potestas*, which they designate simply *potestas*, or that over a child, *patria potestas*. The powers involved in the first were obviously much more extensive than those involved in the second, although it is said they were identical in the earliest days of Rome. This matter, however, need not be here discussed, being fully treated of in App. A to our edition of Justinian's Institutes.

Mancipium, which originally means hand-taking (*manu capere*), is in its technical sense connected with a particular form of transfer called *mancipatio*, and stands in the sources, 1st, for the *mancipatio* itself (see Gaius, II. 59, II. 204, IV. 131); 2nd, for the rights thereby acquired; 3rd, for the subject of the *mancipatio*, the thing to be transferred; 4th, for a particular kind of transferable objects, viz. slaves, to whom it is applied, so says a law of the Digest (D. 1. 5. 4. 3), because "ab hostibus manu capiuntur;" although the more probable reason for the application of the term is to be found in the fact that slaves were viewed by the Roman lawyers as mere things, and so capable of transfer from hand to hand.

The importance of the term *mancipium*, so far as regards the historical aspect of Roman law, lies in the fact that from its connection with the word *manus* we gather a correct idea of the ancient notion of property, which was in effect the dominion over those things only that could be and were actually transferred from hand to hand.

As *potestas* came gradually to bear a restricted meaning in the law sources, and instead of being a general term for authority of any kind began to signify authority over persons only, and those too such alone as were in the *familia* of the possessor of the *potestas;* so *mancipium* became a technical term implying the power exercised over free persons whose services had been transferred by *mancipatio;* and *manus*, originally almost identical with *mancipium*, was limited to the one case of power over a wife.

A freeman held in *mancipium* was a quasi-slave relatively to his lord, although still a freeman in regard of all other members of the Roman state.

On the subject of *mancipium* read Mühlenbruch's Appendix on I. 12, in Heineccius' *Antiqq. Rom. Syntagma*, pp. 159, 160.

(C). On *Arrogation* and *Adoption.*

The process of *arrogatio* resembled the passing of a *lex*, and took place in the *Comitia Curiata.* Legislative sanction was required for so solemn an act as the absorption of the family of the *arrogatus* into that of the *arrogans* (see Gaius, I. 107) for two reasons: firstly, because the maintenance of a family and its sacred rites was viewed as a matter of religion, and as influencing the prosperity of the state; secondly, because the *populus* claimed a right of succession to all vacant inheritances as "parens omnium" (Tac. *Ann.* III. 28), and arrogation naturally prevented vacancies occurring.

This method of adoption *per populum* was practised long after the empire was established. In Cicero's time it seems to have been frequently employed, and in the *Pro Domo*, c. 29, we have a passage containing the form of words used: "Credo enim, quanquam in illâ adoptione legitime factum est nihil, tamen te esse interrogatum, Auctorne esses, ut in te P. Fonteius vitae necisque potestatem haberet, ut in filio." Augustus, Nero, and other emperors, adopted in this form, viz. by order of the *populus;* nor was it till after Galba's time that it fell into disuse, as is evident from the speech which Tacitus puts into that emperor's mouth: "Si te privatus lege curiata apud pontifices, ut moris est, adoptarem, &c." (*Hist.* I. 15.)

Adoption, or rather arrogation, by imperial rescript afterwards replaced the older method. The reader desirous of further information on this topic, the principal interest of which lies in its relation to the history of social life in ancient Rome, is referred to Heineccius' *Antiqq. Rom. Syntagma*, I. 11. pp. 143—152, Mühlenbruch's edition, and Maine's *Ancient Law*, chap. V.

(D). On *Tutors.*

Tutors may be thus tabulated according to their species:

A.	Testamentarii	(α) Dativi, Gaius, I. § 154.
		(β) Optivi, *Ib.*
B.	Legitimi	(γ) Agnati, *Ib.* § 155.
		(δ) Patroni, *Ib.* § 165.
		(ε) Quasi-patroni, *Ib.* § 175.

C. Fiduciarii { (ζ) Manumissores liberarum personarum, Gaius I. § 166. (η) Liberi quasi-patronorum, *Ib.* § 175. }

D. Cessicii (θ), *Ib.* § 168.

E. Dativi (a magistratibus dati) { (ι) Praetorii, *Ib.* §§ 176—184. (κ) Atiliani, *Ib.* §§ 185—187. }

Tutela was exercised over minors or women. Those under *tutela* were placed in that position because, either as a matter of fact or of implication of law, they were incapable of exercising the legal rights which appertained to them as persons *sui juris*. In Gaius' time the notion that women were incapable at any age of managing their affairs was exploded (Gaius, I. 190), and therefore the tutor of a woman, in many cases, had to interpose his *auctoritas* at the woman's command, and not at his own discretion. (Ulpian, XI. 27.) In the case of a minor the tutor's power to compel either acts or forbearances was unlimited; an "actio tutelae," however, to be brought by his ward on attaining puberty, hung over him, and constrained him to act for the ward's benefit (Gaius, I. 191). When the *tutela* was exercised over a woman for the benefit of tutor and ward at once, in the case, that is to say, of the two latter of the three classes of *tutelae legitimae* above, we are told that the tutor had great power to compel forbearances (*Ib.* I. 192), but we are not told whether he could insist on acts, *e.g.* whether he could compel the purchase of land, as well as stop the sale of land; but the absence of mention of this, the greater power of the two, would imply that he had not got it, as the tutor of a minor had. The *tutelae legitimae* of the *agnati* over women were abolished in Gaius' time; previously the same remarks would have applied to them.

A. *Tutores testamentarii* were allowed by the law of the Twelve Tables: "uti legassit super pecunia tutelave suae rei ita jus esto." Hence this class might be called *legitimi* equally with the succeeding, but to avoid confusion the two are marked by different appellations.

B. *Tutores legitimi* are of three kinds:—

I. The *agnati* of one to whom the *paterfamilias* had appointed no testamentary guardian. The clause of the Twelve Tables which authorized the *agnati* to act is lost, but Gaius is explicit in his statement that their authority is based on the Tables (Gaius, I. 155).

II. The *patroni* and their children (Gaius, I. 165); by implication arising from the wording of the Tables. The son very properly succeeds his father as tutor, since if there had been no manumission he would have succeeded him as *dominus*, and therefore he fairly inherits the rights reserved out of the *dominium*.

III. The manumittor of a free-born person, when that manumittor was the *paterfamilias* himself (Gaius, I. 175). If, however, the manumittor were a stranger, he would not be a *tutor legitimus*, but only a *tutor fiduciarius* (*Ib.* I. 166): and again, the children of a *tutor legitimus* of this class, which we may call the class of *quasi-patroni*, would be *tutores fiduciarii* (*Ib.* I. 175). The father is allowed to have *tutela legitima*, because, after the son has been thrice sold, and so become in the *mancipium* of the purchaser, the father buys him in turn, as a slave, (*Ib.* I. 134,) has him in *mancipium*, and manumits him by *vindicta*. He is therefore his patron or quasi-patron, and ought to have *tutela legitima*. When, however, the father is dead, the *tutela* of the brother of the *emancipatus* is only *fiduciaria;*

for, if at the father's death, both sons had been under *potestas*, after the death each would have been *sui juris;* though an elder brother, over puberty, would, as nearest agnate, have been *tutor legitimus* to a younger brother, under puberty. Therefore, in the ordinary case, his authority over his brother, the younger son, would have been less than the authority which the father had. If, then, there has been an emancipation, the elder son succeeds to his father's *tutela*, if the emancipated younger son be under puberty, for *tutela* is hereditary; but from analogy he ought in this case too to have a diminished authority, and this is effected by reducing the father's *tutela legitima* into a *tutela fiduciaria* in the brother. Whether the *tutela* is of one character or the other is no matter of indifference, if the manumitted person be a woman; for, as above observed, the coercive powers of a *tutor legitimus* were great, whilst those of a *tutor fiduciarius* were nil.

C. *Tutores fiduciarii* are of two kinds:

I. Manumittors of free persons mancipated to them by a parent or *coemptionator*. Such persons have only the tutorship of the nominal character, because when mancipation is made to a stranger for purposes of manumission, the law implies a trust that the manumittor will not use his position for his own profit (Gaius, I. 141).

II. Children of *quasi-patroni*, whose case we have discussed just above.

D. *Tutores cessicii.* This kind is fully explained in the text, and requires the less comment as it went out of use very soon after Gaius' time.

E. *Tutores dativi*:—

I. *Praetorii*, given by the praetor for various reasons (Gaius, I. 170—184); and, when given, supplanting for the time the authority of the tutor of one of the preceding classes,—deputy-tutors, in fact, for a longer or shorter period.

II. *Atiliani*, tutors appointed by the magistrate in cases where a minor or woman has no tutor at all.

(E). On *Acquisition.*

The various modes of acquisition recognized by the Roman Law are divided into two classes, (1) Natural, (2) Civil; the former existing in the jurisprudence of all nations, the latter peculiar to the Roman legal system. These and their subdivisions may be thus tabulated.

I. Natural modes of acquisition.

(*a*) Occupancy.

(1) Of animals. Gaius, II. 66, 67, 68.

(2) Of property of the enemy. *Ib.* II. 69.

(3) Of things found. Just. *Inst.* II. I. 18 and 39.

(*b*) Accession.

(1) Natural.

(α) The young of animals. Just. *Inst.* II. I. 19 and 37.

(β) Alluvion. Gaius, II. 70.

(γ) Islands rising in the sea or in a river. *Ib.* II. 72.

(δ) Channels deserted by a river. Just. *Inst.* II. I. 23.

(2) Industrial.

(α) Specification. Gaius, II. 79.

(β) Conjunction of solids. Just. *Inst.* II. I. 26.

(γ) Confusion of liquids. *Ib.* II. I. 27.

(δ) Commixtion of solids. *Ib.* II. I. 28.

(ε) Buildings. Gaius, II. 73.

(ϛ) Writing. *Ib.* II. 77.

(η) Painting. *Ib.* II. 78.

(3) Mixed.

(α) Planting. *Ib.* II. 74.

(β) Sowing. *Ib.* II. 75.

(γ) Perceptio fructuum. Just. *Inst.* II. I. 35, 36.

(*c*) Tradition (delivery). Gaius, II. 65.

(1) On sale. Just. *Inst.* II. I. 41.

(2) On gift. *Ib.*

(3) On loan (*mutuum*, which is a transfer of *property*, because the same thing has not to be restored). Gaius, III. 90.

II. Civil modes of acquisition.

(A) Universal.

(*a*) Succession on death.

(1) By legal testament (*hereditas*). Gaius, II. 98.

(2) By law, i.e. upon intestacy (*hereditas*). *Ib.* II. 98.

(3) By the Edict (*secundum tabulas*). *Ib.* II. 98, 147.

(4) By the Edict (*contra tabulas*), or *ab intestato*, II. 98, Ulp. XXVIII. 2 and 7.

(5) By *fidei commissum*, Gaius, II. 248.

(*b*) Arrogation. *Ib.* II. 98, III. 83.

(*c*) *Conventio in manum.* *Ib.* II. 98, III. 83.

(*d*) Bankruptcy. *Ib.* II. 98, III. 77.

(1) Voluntary (*cessio bonorum*). *Ib.* III. 78.

(2) Involuntary (*sectio bonorum*).

(*e*) *Addictio bonorum libertatum servandarum causa.* Just. *Inst.* III. 11. pr.

(*f*) *Cessio in jure hereditatis.* Gaius, III. 85.

(B) Singular.

(*a*) *Mancipatio.* II. 22.

(*b*) *Cessio in jure.* II. 22.

(*c*) *Usucapio.* II. 41.

(*d*) *Donatio propria,* i. e. *sine traditione.*

(1) *Inter vivos sine insinuatione:* if not more than 500 *solidi.* Just. *Inst.* VII. 2.

(2) *Inter vivos cum insinuatione:* if more than 500 *solidi.* Just. *Inst.* VII. 2.

(*e*) *Donatio impropria,* i. e. *cum traditione.*

(1) *Propter nuptias.* Just. *Inst.* II. 7. 3.

(2) *Mortis causa.* *Ib.* II. 7. 1.

(*f*) Succession on death.

(1) Legacy. Gaius, II. 97, 191.

(2) *Fideicommissum singulare.* *Ib.* II. 260.

(3) *Caducum.* *Ib.* II. 206.

(*g*) *Adjudicatio* (Ulpian, XIX. 16).

With regard to the *donationes propriae,* it is to be observed that a transfer of *property* results immediately from the gift, and thereupon is founded a right of action for transfer of the *possession* also. *Donatio mortis causa* is different, for therein the *possession* is transferred at once, together with the *property,* but the *property* is resumable at the donor's pleasure, and if he exercise his privilege, he can as proprietor recover the possession by action.

But though a transfer is necessary in a *donatio mortis causa,* if the thing given be tangible; yet the transfer may be to a stranger, in trust to pass the thing on to the donee on the testator's death: D. 39. 6. 18. 2: and in case of an incorporeal thing, as the remission of death, delivery may be impossible, and in such case a declaration in the presence of five witnesses is sufficient. D. 39. 6. 28: C. 8. 57. 4.

Ulpian (XIX. 2) mentions several of these civil titles to singular succession, and adds another, "*ex lege,*" which subdivides into *legata, caduca, donationes,* and all other methods not matters of immemorial custom, but introduced by specific enactments.

(F). On *Dominion* and *Servitudes.*

The word Servitude is used in various senses by the Roman Jurists. Sometimes they denote by it (1) every variety of property, or *Jus in rem* availing against all other people, except *Dominium,* or ownership, including even *Emphyteusis,* or a perpetual holding on condition of punctual payment of rent, or *pensio,* to the *dominus,* and of proper user of the land or property: sometimes (2) all *Jura in Rem,* except *Dominium,* and *Emphyteusis,* and *Bona Fide Possessio pro suo,* including therefore such rights as

To face p. 456.]

y

Ownership

English

1. Fee simple tenancy in capite
2. Chattel Ownership

Roman

Dominium

Personal

English

1. Fee simple tenancy of a mesne tenant
2. Fee Tail
3. Life Estate
4. Term of years

Roman

1. Emphyteusis
2. Ususfructus
3. Usus
4. Habitatio

Roman

si-Servitude

Real

English

Easement

{ 1. Affirmative or 2. Negative } Profit à prendre

{ 3. Appendant or 4. Appurtenant }

Roman

Servitude

{ 1. Positive or 2. Negative }

Usufruct, *Use* and *Habitation*, which are indefinite in user, though limited in duration; and only excluding those which are, or may be, unlimited in duration, indefinite in user, and unrestricted in point of alienation; and sometimes (3) they exclude the rights that are indefinite in user, and denote by *Servitus* those that allow a particular user only, whether for a time or in perpetuity. The second is the usual employment of the appellation: the third its more correct use.

For the full comprehension, therefore, of Servitus in its various senses, we must commence with the consideration of Ownership. Ownership is the legal power of applying a subject to all purposes not inconsistent with the absolute or relative duties of the party entitled, or with the rights, absolute or relative, of other persons. *Dominium*, then, or Ownership, admits of *modes;* for the limitations of the power of the entitled party are capable of infinite variation, according to the rights possessed by others, or the duties incumbent on himself.

In every system of Law there is some one mode of property where the liberty of user, and power of exclusion of the user of others, is indefinite in the highest degree; and where, although the right is not strictly of unlimited duration, (for no one can hold longer than his own life,) yet the party entitled can alienate the subject from all successors, who would take in default of his alienation. Such in English Law is absolute property in Chattels, or a fee simple (at any rate one held by a tenant-in-capite) in land: such too in Roman Law is *Dominium*, in the strictest sense, whether over *res mancipi* or *res nec mancipi*, or *Dominium Plenum*.

Of the inferior modes of *Dominium* there are three principal varieties: 1st where the right is of unlimited duration and indefinite user, but subject to a reversion which cannot be barred, as Emphyteusis in Roman Law, or in Old English Law a fee simple under a mesne lord, or a fee-tail prior to Taltarum's case: 2nd where the right is of limited or indefinite duration and indefinite user, as a life-estate in English Law, or an Usufruct, Use or Habitation in Roman Law: 3rd where it is of limited and definite duration and indefinite in user, as a term of years in modern English Law, or an Usufruct, Use or Habitation for a specified period in Roman Law; though an Old English lease or a Roman lease, which created no *jus in rem* at all, but only a *jus in personam* against the grantor, are, of course, not instances. In all these cases the right of owner in possession is restrained, not only by his own *general* duties, and the *general* rights of others, but by the *special* rights of those entitled to the reversion; yet the right of the owner in possession is always indefinite. For all these the name *Jus in Re Aliena* is a convenient appellation, as they are varieties of *Jus in rem*.

But the party invested with *Dominium* may be restrained, in favour of another person, from the exercise of some *definite* right of user or exclusion appertaining to his ownership; and not, as in *jus in re aliena*, of all his rights, or the bulk of his rights, of user and exclusion. These restrictions, which are also *jura in rem* when created, are technically denoted *Servitudes:* a *Servitude* being *Negative*, when merely the right of user of the owner is restricted; *Positive*, when his right of exclusion, and therefore his right of user also, is curtailed.

Either a *Servitude*, or a *Jus in re aliena*, may be conceived as (1) attached to a person, irrespective of his ownership of any specific thing; being in such case on principle inalienable; or as attached to a person, merely on the ground of his ownership of a specific thing; in which latter case the right departs from the person, if he ceases to own the thing; but devolves, in general, upon every person who successively owns the same. Thus we have the distinction of *Personal Servitudes* and *Real Servitudes: Personal Jura in Re Aliena* and *Real Jura in Re Aliena.* But *Personal Servitudes,* properly so-called, were very rare among the Romans; in fact in D. 8. 1. 8. *pr.* it is said they *could not* be created; though there were a few of a mixed character, where the right was not given to land absolutely, (in which case it would have been a *Real Servitude,*) but to the land as long as a certain man owned it, or to a man as long as he owned certain land. Thus the true Servitudes of the Romans were all either *Real Servitudes,* or *Mixt,* that is partly Real: and both in Roman and English Law they were attached only to the owner of *land,* not of *moveables.* The Roman *Jura in Re Aliena,* on the other hand, were all purely personal; for the Romans had no notion of land being given to a man, or man and his heirs, so long as they held certain other lands, which is the Old English Base Fee, a *Real Jus in Re Aliena,* or at any rate a mixed one. Thus in Roman Law *Predial Servitudes* are always *Real:* and what are called *Personal Servitudes* are invariably *Personal Jura in Re Aliena.*

(G). On *the causes rendering a Testament invalid.*

When a testament would not stand, it might be either,

Injustum, *Non jure factum,* *Imperfectum:* — owing to some original defect: as want of the proper number of witnesses: non-appointment of an heir: incapacity of the testator, heir, or witnesses:

Nullius momenti, *Nullum:* — if a *suus heres* or emancipated child be not mentioned in the testament: if the testator have not *testamenti factio:* or if the heir have it not:

Ruptum: by an agnation or quasi-agnation; by a subsequent testament: by revocation or destruction:

Inritum or *irritum;* through a *capitis diminutio* of the testator, or through no heir appearing under the testament:

Destitutum: also when no heir appears under it:

Rescissum or *Inofficiosum:* when a *querela inofficiosi* is sustained. See Just. *Inst.* II. 18.

(H). On the *Lex Julia et Papia Poppaea.*

On account of the distaste for marriage prevalent at Rome in the time of Augustus, and the consequent rapid diminution of the number of the citizens, that emperor felt bound to apply a remedy. Heineccius (XXV. 3), adduces instances of legislation to the same end in earlier days, which those who are curious on the question will find worth their perusal; and the growing evil had been a subject of anxiety to Julius, who meditated bringing forward a law to encourage marriage, but his sudden murder caused the plan to end fruitlessly. In his days the evil had grown to such a height that the extinction of the Roman name seemed imminent, for we learn from Appian that at the first census taken after the civil war, the number of citizens was only one half of that previous thereto: (Appian, *de Bell. Civ.* II. 102.) By the time of Augustus matters were still worse, and so in A. D. 4 the *Lex Julia de maritandis ordinibus* was carried. But as this enactment was not fully enforced until A.D. 9, and as the *Lex Papia Poppaea* was passed in the next year, the two are most frequently spoken of as though they were one law, and cited under the name of the *Lex Julia et Papia Poppaea.*

The most important provisions of the famous *lex* or combination of *leges* were as follows:

I. Amongst candidates for office that one should have a preference who had the greatest number of legitimate children. Tac. *Ann.* XV. 19.

II. Of the two consuls he should be senior (*qui prior sumebat fasces*) whose children were the most numerous. (Aul. Gell. *Noct. Att.* II. 15.)

III. A relief from all personal taxes and burdens should be granted to citizens who had a certain number of children:—three, if they lived at Rome; four, if they lived in Italy; five, if they lived in the Provinces.

(But we must note that this provision, though Heineccius states it to have been contained in the Lex Julia and Papia Poppaea, is a matter of dispute, and its existence is denied by Rudorff and others.)

IV. Senators should not marry freedwomen or women of a depraved character (*lenas, a lenone manumissas, quae artem ludicram exercuissent, vel filias eorum qui ejusmodi artem fecissent*): but the restriction was not extended to freedwomen in the case of other freeborn citizens, not senators.

V. Freedmen should be exempted from services (*operae*) by the *jus liberorum.*

VI. Women should be freed from tutelage by the *jus liberorum, i.e.* by bearing three children, if they were freeborn women, or four, if they were freedwomen. Gaius, I. 145, 194; Ulpian, XXIX. 3.

The *jus liberorum* conferred other privileges also, the chief being that a mother possessing it could succeed to the inheritance of her children; but this right sprang from the S. C. Tertullianum, which merely adopted the definition of *jus liberorum* in the Lex Julia et Papia Poppaea, and made it a title to the succession.

The three or four children need not be living at the time the privilege of exemption from tutelage or of succession was claimed: it was sufficient if they had been born alive. (Paulus *S. R.* IV. 9. 9.)

Closely connected with the *jus liberorum* was the rule (also contained in the Lex) that patrons, who otherwise could claim *contra tabulas* a *pars virilis* with the children of a freedman, in case the freedman died possessed of 100,000 sesterces or more, lost the right if the freedman left three children: and that patronesses obtained this same right of patrons, to share *pro virili parte* with the freedman's issue, if they themselves had three children. Gaius, III. 42, 50.

VII. Unmarried persons were to take nothing either by way of inheritance or of legacy, and married persons without children were to take only one half of the inheritance or legacy bequeathed to them. Gaius, II. 111, 144, 206—208, 286.

But it is to be observed that the Lex Papia Poppaea allowed a woman a respite from marriage, and consequently from the penalties incurred by celibacy, for two years after the death of her husband, and for eighteen months after a divorce: therein adopting the principle, although altering the detail of the Lex Julia, which had allowed a period of one year or of six months from the same terminations of a marriage respectively.

In connection with these provisions of the Lex Julia et Papia Poppaea important alterations were introduced into the law of accruals and lapses. Let us first consider the old law on the subject.

Previous to the Lex, legacies which utterly failed from the death or incapacity of the legatee, or from any original invalidity of the bequest, *lapsed* to the inheritance, and so benefited the heir. But this rule did not immediately apply to co-legacies: these only lapsed if both or all the co-legatees were unable to take.

Hence if some of the co-legatees were able to take, there might be *accrual* instead of *lapse*. Thus

(1) If the joint-legacy had been given *disjunctim* (in which case the co-legatees were styled *re conjuncti*), there was no accrual, for each legatee had from the beginning a title to the whole thing:

(2) If it had been given *conjunctim* (in which case the co-legatees were termed *re et verbis conjuncti*), accrual was generally allowed, i.e. the surviving legatee or legatees took the share of their deceased associate, the only exception being in a legacy by *damnation*, where there was a lapse (Gaius, II. 205):

(3) If the joint legacy had been given with a specification of the shares to be enjoyed by each legatee (in which case the co-legatees were said to be *verbis conjuncti*), there was no accrual, but a lapse, on account of the separation of the interests *ab initio*.

The *Lex Papia Poppaea* swept away all these regulations and left the law thus: all inheritances and legacies to unmarried and childless persons were void and were termed *caduca* (but *caelibes* by marrying within one hundred days could avoid the forfeiture; and in the case of *orbi* only one half the bequest was *caducum*, Ulpian, XVII. 1; Gaius, II. 286):

Legacies which would have lapsed or accrued by the civil law were put under the same rules, and said to be *in causâ caduci*. These rules were that *caduca* should go:

(1) to co-legatees joined *re et verbis*, or *verbis*, and having children (Gaius, II. 207); (as we said above, those joined *re* would of course get the full legacy from the universality of their original title, and therefore wanted no help from the law): failing these, they went

(2) to the heirs who had children (Gaius, II. 214): failing these again,

(3) to legatees generally, (not *conjuncti*) who had children,

(4) to the *fiscus*.

The only exception to these regulations was in the case of ascendants and descendants not more remote than the third degree, who took inheritances and accruals, whether they had children or not. Ulpian, XVIII.

All these rules were again abolished by Justinian (see Code vi. 51. 11), and the old regulations were restored almost exactly, but the exceptional law as to legacies by damnation was not re-enacted.

Caracalla had previously abrogated the *Lex Papia Poppaea*, and made *caduca* go to the *fiscus*.

VIII. The husband could not be heir or legatee of the wife, nor the wife of the husband, to an amount greater than one-tenth of the property of the defunct, together with the usufruct of another third, unless children had been born from their marriage. But there were certain exceptions to this rule, depending on the age of the parties; and there was a capacity for taking one-tenth extra by title of each child born from a precedent marriage and still alive, and one-tenth also by title of each child born from the marriage with the defunct, and lost before his or her decease; and further, the devise of the usufruct of the third was capable of being changed into a devise of the ownership, in the same case of a child being born from the marriage, and subsequently dying. Ulpian, XV. XVI.

IX. The *Lex Julia et Papia Poppaea* also contained a most complicated statement of the rights of a *patrona* and *filia patroni*, with their modifications, according to the possession or non-possession of the *jus liberorum* by these persons, or the *libertus* or *liberta;* which are fully set forth by Gaius (III. 39—76), but need no discussion here, because they refer to a stage of jurisprudence utterly alien from modern ideas, and therefore solely of antiquarian interest.

(I). On the *Decurionatus.*

The *decuriones* were the members of the senate of a *municipium*, i.e. of a town which was allowed to manage its own internal affairs. Originally the *municipes* or burgesses, convened in their general assembly, seem to have held the sovereign power: they elected the magistrates (see Cic. *pro Cluentio*, 8), and they enacted the laws (Cic. *de Leg.* III. 16): but the power of the assembly gradually declined, and the senate usurped its functions, directly administering all business, instead of adopting and passing the matters sent up to it by the *municipes*. The senate and its members are denoted by different names at different periods of Roman history, originally *ordo decurionum* (for instance, in Macrobius, *Sat.* II. 3. 11, where there is an anecdote that Caesar found it more difficult to get a *decurionatus* at Pompeii than at Rome), then *ordo* simply, finally *curia*, and the members *curiales* or *decuriones*. During this last period the magistrates of a *municipium* were nominated by the *decuriones*, and the functions of government apportioned between the two. The first infringement on the rights of the *municipes* as a body may be referred to the time of Augustus, who ordered that the right of suffrage at elections should be confined to the *decuriones:* and from that time the name of *municipes*, originally applied to all the inhabitants, is confined by writers on the subject to the members of the senate or *curia*.

As the *decuriones* were thus invested with so large an amount of power and influence, it may be asked why, in later times, it was difficult to find men willing to become members of the corporation, and why had devices to be invented to keep up the numbers of the *curia;* for instance that of allowing legitimation to be effected by enrolment of an illegitimate son as a member of the *curia* (*per oblationem curiae*). The answer is, that the absorption of all power by the emperors in later times rendered the office one of intolerable responsibility, and further, that heavy fees attended the enrolment of a new member.

Full information on the subject of the Local Magistracy under the late Emperors will be found in App. H. to our edition of Justinian's *Institutes*.

(K). On the *Classification of Legacies.*

The following table exhibits the resemblances and differences of the various forms of legacy:

	I. *Per Vindicationem.*	II. *Per Damnationem.*	III. *Sinendi modo.*	IV. *Per Praeceptionem.*
Form.	Direct bequest to the legatee.	Simple charge upon the heir.	Charge upon the heir in a peculiar form.	Direct bequest to one of several joint-heirs.
Process for recovery.	Vindicatio.	Condictio.	Condictio.	Judicium familiae erciscundae.
Subject.	Property *ex jure Quiritium* of the testator.	Anything whatever, whether belonging to the testator, the heir, or a stranger; in existence or future.	Property of the testator or the heir.	Property of the testator.
Conjoint Legacy.	Shared equally: accrual allowed.	Shared equally: no accrual allowed, but a lapse to the inheritance.	Shared equally: accrual allowed.	Shared equally: accrual allowed.
Disjoint Legacy.	Shared equally.	Paid in full to each legatee.	Paid in full to first claimant: whether to second also a disputed point.	Shared equally[1].

(L). On *Bonorum Possessio.*

In the law-sources *Bonorum Possessio* and *Possessio Bonorum* are by no means convertible terms, but the former indicates a Praetorian inheritance (if such a term may be allowed), and the latter a possession allowed to creditors, legatees and certain others.

Bonorum Possessio was either *contra tabulas testamenti*, or *secundum tabulas testamenti*, or *ab intestato.*

Of these *Bonorum Possessiones*, the second-named came earliest into existence, being granted by the Praetor in support of a testament invalid by the Civil Law through some technical informality, but yet duly evidenced by the seals of seven witnesses (Ulpian, XXVIII. 6; Gaius, II. 119). Of this *Bonorum Possessio* heirs, entitled by the Civil Law, could also avail them-

[1] The rules as to this kind of legacy are given according to Gaius and the Sabinians: the Proculians (see Gaius, II. 221, Ulpian, XXIV. 11) considered a legacy by *praeception* identical with one by vindication.

selves; and they generally did so, because of the advantage of the interdict "Quorum Bonorum," which was attached to it. Gaius, III. 34.

Next were invented the *Bonorum Possessiones ab intestato*, but of these again heirs, already entitled by the Civil Law, could avail themselves.

Last in point of time the *Bonorum Possessiones contra tabulas* came into use.

When the system was completed the order of admission under the Praetor's Edict was, firstly, those claiming *contra tabulas;* secondly, those claiming *secundum tabulas;* thirdly, those entitled *ab intestato.*

As Ulpian states all that is essential regarding the *Possessiones contra* and *secundum tabulas* in Tit. XXVIII., we may pass them over without further notice, and proceed to explain the third *Possessio*, that *ab intestato.* The difficulty in understanding the subject arises from the fact that both Ulpian and Justinian in their enumeration of the grades (seven according to the one, eight according to the other), combine in one view the successions to *ingenui*, who had never undergone a mancipation and emancipation, the successions to *ingenui* who had passed through these processes, and the successions to *liberti.* We will take the grades as they stand in the lists furnished by our authorities; but it will be seen that if the successory rights of patrons and quasi-patrons were eliminated, and the table thus made applicable to the estates of those persons only who were *ingenui* and had never been in the status called *mancipium*, the grades would be reduced to four, namely those numbered I, II, IV and VII below.

I. *Liberi* formed the first class or grade to whom the Praetor granted *Bonorum Possessio ab intestato;* and by *liberi* we understand, 1st, descendants who had never passed from their ancestor's *potestas;* 2nd, those who had been completely transferred by adoption into a stranger's *potestas*, and then ranked as *liberi* of the stranger, losing all claims both civil and praetorian on their ancestor; 3rd, those who had been emancipated, and so had lost their civil-law claims on their emancipator, (whether he were their parent by nature or by adoption), and succeeded to him only through the Praetor's aid.

II. The second class consisted of the *legitimi* or statutable heirs, i.e. all on whom the laws of the Twelve Tables or later *leges* or *senatus consulta* had conferred successory rights. Thus agnates who claimed under the rules of the Twelve Tables, mothers under the *S. C. Tertullianum*, children of intestate females under the *S. C. Orphitianum*, were admitted in this degree.

If the deceased had been emancipated, his patron or quasi-patron stood at the head of this class of successors, ranking next to those named in the first class: at any rate he did so under the laws of the Twelve Tables, but later enactments introduced from time to time so many modifications into this rule, that, to avoid confusion, we have judged it expedient to tabulate the subject separately in the next portion of the Appendix.

III. The third class, styled *Decem Personae*, is mentioned by Justinian only and not by Ulpian; doubtless because it was only of importance at an earlier stage of Roman jurisprudence, when manumissions of free persons by a stranger after mancipation were not unfrequent. The quasi-patron, or manumittor, would by the civil law have been entitled to succession on the intestacy of a quasi-freedman, in preference to the agnates of the latter; but the Praetor interfered and postponed him to the following relations of the manumitted, viz. the father, mother, grandfather, grandmother, son, daughter, grandson, grand-daughter, brother or sister. Thus the third class is hardly a class at all, but an interpolation into the second class, leaving the order of succession therein when the deceased was a manumitted *ingenuus* to be, 1st, the *decem personae;* 2nd, the *quasi-patronus* and his *sui heredes;* 3rd, the other agnates of the manumitted, not included in the *decem personae.*

When a slave was manumitted he could have no *decem personae*, for servile relationship was not acknowledged, and therefore none were agnates to him, or even cognates, except descendants born after his manumission, and these would be entitled in the first class, as *liberi.*

It may be noticed that the *decem personae* introduce another confusion into the order of succession; for they were not of necessity agnates, but in some cases cognates, and cognates properly form the next or fourth order of successors. That they were not invariably agnates is evident, for the grand parent might be maternal, and the brother or sister uterine.

IV. The fourth class consisted of the cognates of nearest degree, *cognati proximi;* and we see the reason why the word *proximi* is introduced, if we bear in mind that descendants took *per stirpes*, and were not of necessity equally near of kin to the deceased; whereas cognates took *per capita*, and as only the nearest were admitted, they must of necessity be all of one degree.

V. The fifth class (*tum quem ex familia*) was one altogether unconnected with the succession to ordinary *ingenui*, i.e. to those not manumitted, consisting of the agnates of a patron (or quasi-patron), to whom the laws of the Twelve Tables gave no rights, if they were not also *sui heredes* of the patron.

VI. The sixth class comprised the patron, patroness, and their descendants and ascendants; and although these persons seem to have been provided for already, yet we must remember that the Civil Law recognized the rights of those only who had not suffered *capitis diminutio*, and thus the present title of the successory edict was needful to bring in those patrons, &c., who had undergone such a change of status, and therefore were no longer *legitimi*. It was also needed to bring in the descendants of patronesses, who by the strict Civil Law could not claim through a female ancestor.

VII. Husband or wife were the next class, and thus a reciprocal succession was established between those who had been married without a *conventio in manum.*

VIII. The last class again had reference only to the property of *liberti* or *quasi-liberti*, conferring it, in case of failure of all other claimants, upon the cognates of the manumittor.

If a person entitled under any particular class failed to put in his claim within the prescribed period (Ulpian, XXVIII. 10), this did not absolutely destroy his rights, but merely diminished them, for he might still take concurrently with claimants of a lower order. It will be observed that the succession given by the Praetor might either be (1) in confirmation of the Civil Law, as in the case of the *possessio secundum tabulas* granted to the testamentary heir, or that *contra tabulas* to omitted children not emancipated, or that *ab intestato* to the *suus heres*, agnate or patron: (2) supplementary to the law, as in the case of the cognates, for whom the Civil Law made no provision whatever: (3) in derogation of the law, as in the case of the *possessio secundum tabulas*, when the testament was deficient in the matter of mancipation or nuncupation; or *contra tabulas*, in the case of emancipated children.

The succession of patrons (or quasi-patrons) on the intestacy of their freedmen is so entirely a matter of antiquarian interest, that for all practical ends attention need be paid to the succession to *ingenui* alone; and therefore we will conclude by giving a comparative table of those entitled on such persons' decease intestate, under the laws of the Twelve Tables and under the Praetorian Edict as it stood in Gaius' time.

Twelve Tables.	Praetorian Edict.	
I. Sui heredes.	I. (α) Sui heredes.	
	(β) Emancipated descendants. (*B. P. unde liberi.*)	
II. Agnati et agnatae.	II. Agnati et Consanguineae. (*B. P. unde legitimi.*)	
III. Gentiles.	III. (α) Agnati capite deminuti.	Gaius, III. 27.
	(β) Agnatae	...... 29.
	(γ) Agnati sequentes	...... 28.
	(δ) Liberi in adoptivâ familiâ	...... 31.
	(ε) Cognati	...... 30.
	(*B. P. unde cognati vel proximitatis causa.*)	

(M). On the *Inheritances of Freedmen and Freedwomen.*

The subject of inheritances of freedmen and freedwomen, except from an antiquarian view, is of no great interest: but for those who wish to pursue it, we subjoin the following analysis of the cases treated of by Gaius and Ulpian;

I. When a freedman died leaving his patron, or a male descendant[1] of his patron, surviving him:

(α) by the Laws of the Twelve Tables, a *suus heres* or *scriptus heres* had precedence of the patron:

(β) by the Praetorian Edict, no *suus heres* except an actual descendant, not specially disinherited, had this priority; but it was not lost by emancipation or adoption: whilst as against a *scriptus heres*, not being a descendant, or as against one who was a *suus heres* merely by operation of the civil law, the patron could claim half:

(γ) by the Lex Papia Poppaea even actual descendants, if less than three in number, and if the freedman died worth 100,000 sesterces, did not bar the patron's claim, but he took a *pars virilis* with them. In other respects the Praetorian rules were left standing. Gaius, III. 39—42, 45; Ulpian, XXIX. 1, 4.

II. When a freedwoman died leaving her patron, or a male descendant[1] of her patron, surviving her:

(α) by the Laws of the Twelve Tables, the patron excluded the descendants of the freedwoman; and she could not make a testament except with the patron's consent:

(β) the Praetor left the law as he found it:

[1] Sc. a descendant tracing through a line of males.

(γ) by the Lex Papia Poppaea the patron's right was restricted to a *pars virilis*, if the woman had the *jus liberorum:* Gaius, III. 43—45; Ulpian, XXIX. 1, 4.

III. When a freedman died, leaving a daughter of his patron, or other female descendant[1], surviving him:

(α) by the Laws of the Twelve Tables this daughter had the same claims as the son of the patron:

(β) the Praetor ignored her claims:

(γ) the Lex Papia Poppaea allowed her to rank as a son, if she had three children. Gaius, III. 46; Ulpian, XXIX. 5.

IV. When a freedwoman died, leaving a daughter of her patron, or other female descendant[1], surviving her:

(α) by the Laws of the Twelve Tables this daughter had the same claims as a son of the patron:

(β) the Praetor ignored her claims:

(γ) the Lex Papia Poppaea allowed her to rank as a son, if she had three children, and the freedwoman less than four; but if the freedwoman had four children, and made a testament in their favour, the *filia patroni* had no claim; if the freedwoman died intestate, the *filia patroni* claimed a *pars virilis:* if the freedwoman made a testament, and disinherited her children for cause, a moiety went to the *filia patroni.* Gaius, III. 47.

V. When a freedman died leaving his patroness, or a male descendant[1] of his patroness, surviving him:

(α) by the Laws of the Twelve Tables the rights of a patroness were the same as those of a patron, but her descendants had no rights.

(β) the Praetor admitted the descendants to the rights of the patroness herself, under the title of "Bonorum possessio unde liberi patroni patronaeque et parentes eorum." See App. (L).

(γ) by the Lex Papia Poppaea, if the patroness had three children and was freeborn, she had the full rights granted to the patron by the same Lex; and if she had two children, being herself freeborn, or had three children, being herself a freedwoman, she was entitled to the rights conferred on patrons by the Edict. Gaius, III. 49, 50; Ulpian, XXIX. 6, 7.

VI. When a freedwoman died leaving her patroness, or a male descendant[1] of her patroness, surviving her:

(α) by the Laws of the Twelve Tables, the rights of a patroness were the same as those of a patron; but her descendants had no rights:

(β) the Praetor admitted her descendants to the same rights:

(γ) the Lex Papia Poppaea adopted the Civil and Praetorian rules, unless the freedwoman died testate[2], in which case the patroness with children had the rights of a patron under the Edict. Gaius, III. 51, 52.

---

[1] Sc. a descendant tracing through a line of males.

[2] But she could not die testate, unless she was *liberis honorata:* and even then, she could not make a will in favour of a stranger, unless her children were dead, or deserved disinheritance.

VII. When a freedman died leaving a daughter of his patroness or other female descendant[1], surviving him:

(α) by the Laws of the Twelve Tables, such daughter had no rights:

(β) but under the Praetorian Edict, she was admitted:

(γ) by the Lex Papia Poppaea she was again excluded, unless she had a child. Gaius, III. 53.

VIII. When a freedwoman died leaving a daughter of her patroness or other female descendant[1] surviving her:

(α) by the Laws of the Twelve Tables, such daughter had no right:

(β) but under the Praetorian edict, she was admitted:

(γ) by the Lex Papia Poppaea she was again excluded, unless she had a child. Gaius, III. 53.

It will be observed that the rights of the patron over a Roman citizen freedman are transmitted, if transmitted at all, to his descendants and not to the heirs appointed in his testament. Gaius, III. 48, 58.

The inheritance of a Latin on the contrary belonged in all cases to the patron and his appointed heir. Gaius, III. 58.

(N). On the *Classification of Obligations.*

Obligations according to the Roman law are divided into (A) Natural and (B) Civil.

A. Natural obligations again are divided into (a) those which the civil law absolutely reprobates (see Warnkoenig's *Commentaries*, Vol. II. p. 158, Mackeldey's *Systema Jur. Rom.*, §§ 332, 442), and (b) those on which an action cannot be founded, but which can be used as an exception or ground of defence: *nuda pacta.*

B. Civil obligations are also subdivided into (α) civil obligations in the strictest sense, i.e. obligations furnished with an action by the civil law, (β) praetorian obligations, which are enforced by an action granted through the later legislation of the Praetor's edict.

(α) Of these civil obligations in the strictest sense there are two subdivisions, viz. (I) those which are altogether unconnected with the *jus gentium* and based on the civil law only, *legibus constitutae:* (II) those recognized by the *jus gentium*, and received into and furnished with an action by the civil law, *jure civili comprobatae.*

Under (I) we may classify (1) obligations springing from contracts *stricti juris*, which were actionable, because entered into with special forms which the civil law prescribed: (2) obligations by delict: (3) what were called *obligationes ex variis causarum figuris*, (D. 44. 7. 1. *pr.*) arising chiefly from quasi-contracts or quasi-delicts, but not entirely confined to these.

Under (II) we may range (1) contracts of the kinds styled real and consensual: (2) two descriptions of pact (see A. b. above), of which the law took cognizance in later times, viz. *Pacta adjecta* and *Pacta legitima*, an explanation of which will be found below.

A real contract is one wherein execution by either party is a ground for compelling execution by the other: a consensual contract, one which binds

[1] Sc. a descendant tracing through a line of males.

both parties immediately upon their settlement of the terms. A formal contract (*verbis* or *litteris*) is one which binds the parties only when to their presumed consent is superadded a formality prescribed by the Law.

(β) The Praetorian obligations on contract were chiefly those called (1) *constitutum pecuniae*, i.e. a promise to pay a debt of our own already existing according to natural law, but not enforceable by action, or to pay a debt, legal or moral, of another person; for the exaction of which, after the promise had passed, the Praetor in his edict furnished an action: (2) *praecarium*, a grant of the use of a thing during the pleasure of the grantor, who again could only recover possession by means of a remedy (the *interdictum de precario*) provided by the edict: (3) *receptum*, or the obligation of a tavern-keeper or ship-master to make good any damage, not purely accidental, which befell goods deposited with him in the course of his trade: also (4) *transactio*, an agreement made by two persons in settlement of matters in dispute between them, on which either could sue the other, if he that became plaintiff had fulfilled his part (D. 2. 15): and (5) *compromissum*, an agreement by two persons to refer disputed matters to arbitration, in which case either could compel the other to abide by the award of the arbitrator.

The Praetor also provided two delict actions for cases where fraud or intimidation induced innocent persons to acts or forbearances injurious to their interests, but not such as to constitute one of the Civil Law delicts on the part of the offender.

Dismissing these Praetorian obligations, we will briefly indicate the species included under the genera numbered I. and II. above:—

Contracts *stricti juris* (I. 1, above) were formal, i.e. either *verbal* or *literal;* the *verbal* being the *stipulationes*, *sponsiones*, *fidepromissiones*, *fidejussiones* and *adstipulationes*, so fully described by Gaius (III. 92—127); the *literal* being the *nomina*, *chirographae* and *syngraphae*, as to which he also says enough (III. 128—134) to render further particulars unnecessary here.

To these ought to be added, *nexum*, a contract solemnized *per aes et libram;* of which little mention is made by Gaius, its employment being in his day almost a thing of the past.

The obligations from delict (I. 2, above) were fourfold, as Gaius tells us (III. 182—225), arising either from *furtum*, *rapina*, *damnum injuriâ datum*, or *injuriae*. To these must be added *amotio rerum*, theft by husband on wife, or wife on husband.

As to the *variae causarum figurae* (I. 3, above), Gaius says but little, and that little indirectly and inferentially (*e.g.* in III. 91). We stated above that these *figurae* included two important branches, quasi-contracts and quasi-delicts: of the former subdivision we may bring forward especially the instances of (1) *Negotiorum gestio*, business transacted for a man without his knowledge or consent, whereby a jural relation arises, which is described in detail by Mackeldey in his *Systema Juris Romani*, §§ 460—462; (2) *solutio indebiti*, touched upon by Gaius slightly, but as to which Mackeldey also gives full information in §§ 468—470; (3) *communio incidens*, a community of interest cast upon two or more persons, without agreement of their own, for which we shall again refer the reader to Mackeldey, §§ 464—467; (4) *tutela* (*Inst.* 3. 27. 2); and (5) *curatela* or *curatio*.

In all these cases there is no contract, express or implied, but there is one *inferred* by Law: and so the *quasi-contract* in Roman Law may be defined as an *inferred* contract.

The *quasi-delicts* were injurious acts of slaves and descendants, and sometimes of inmates of a house for which the master, ascendant or householder was held responsible. These were different from quasi-contracts, as the latter were *inferred*, and the *quasi-delicts imputed.*

In the *variae figurae* were also reckoned, though without any generic name, the *imputed* obligations of masters or ascendants arising from contracts of their slaves or descendants, enforced by the actions *quod jussu* (IV. 70), *exercitoria* and *institoria* (IV. 71), *tributoria* (IV. 72), *de peculio et in rem verso* (IV. 73): and the two first-named actions could also be brought against the appointer of a free agent. In the *variae figurae* also were included a class of inferred delicts, as *damnum infectum* and *exhibitio negata*.

The action *de pauperie*, and that against a *judex qui litem suam fecit*, though included with the *variae figurae*, are true delict actions, for the judge errs through fraud or culpable carelessness; and the owner of the animal, which commits *pauperies*, is punished only if he has been negligent in his custody of an animal known to be dangerous: and if he has been negligent, he has committed a delict personally.

We now need only specify the chief contracts and *pacts* giving rise to an action, which fall under Class II. above, and our enumeration of obligations is completed.

Real contracts, then, are *mutuum*, a loan where the borrower has not to return the identical thing lent, but an equivalent: *commodatum*, a loan where the borrower has to return the identical thing he has received: *depositum*, a loan for the benefit of the lender, or in other words a deposit of a thing for the sake of custody; with which is classed *sequestratio*, the placing of a thing in the hands of some third person till its ownership is decided by a suit: *pignus*, a deposit as a pledge: *hypotheca*, a pledge without an actual deposit, but with one implied. Besides these there are certain contracts, which for want of a more specific name are styled *innominati*, and by the Roman lawyers are ranked in four subdivisions, viz., *Do ut des*, *Do ut facias*, *Facio ut des*, *Facio ut facias;* and the first of which, though called innominate, has a name, *permutatio*.

Consensual contracts are *Emptio Venditio*, *Locatio Conductio*, *Societas* and *Mandatum*, treated of by Gaius (III. 135—162), *Emphyteusis*, or a lease perpetual, on condition of the regular payment of a rent, and *Superficies*, a lease of a similar character, but referring only to the building on a particular plot of land, and not affecting the land, and therefore terminated by the destruction of the building. *Mandatum*, however, is not properly classed as a consensual contract, for either party may withdraw from the engagement *re integra*, i.e. unless either (1) the *mandatarius* has begun to execute the mandate, or (2) has incurred expense in preparing to execute it. In the former case the mandate is really binding *re*, i.e. by the part performance: and only in the latter is the contract purely consensual; and English lawyers would say that it had become binding by the fact of "negative consideration" arising. In all the other so-called consensual contracts there is clearly reciprocal consideration of a positive kind on either side. So that all these are binding, though the Roman lawyers did not recognize the fact, through the operation of consideration: or in the case of *Mandatum*, either through the operation of consideration, or because the contract by the act of one of the parties has become *real*.

The contracts described as real or consensual are *bonae fidei*, with the exception of *mutuum*, that is to say, the *judex* who has to decide cases arising out of them may entertain equitable pleas or answers without their being pleaded before the Praetor *in jure*, and inserted by him as *exceptiones* in the *formula*. So also are the quasi-contracts, with the exception of *indebitum*.

Pacta adjecta and *Pacta legitima* (see II. 2 above) still remain to be mentioned. The former are agreements attached to *bonae fidei* contracts, and regarded by the law of later times as forming part of the contract, so that on their breach an action may be brought. The principal varieties are, an agreement that the vendor shall have a right of preemption, in case the purchaser desires to resell, (*pactum protimeseos*): or a right of demanding a re-sale, even against the will of the purchaser, (*pactum de retrovendendo*); or a right to rescind a contract, if a better offer be received within a specified time, (*pactum addictionis in diem*): the reservation of the rights of ownership till the price is paid, (*pactum reservati dominii*): an agreement that no guarantee of the vendor against eviction of the purchaser shall be presumed, (*pactum de evictione non praestanda*): *pactum commissorium*, or *lex commissoria*, whereby the parties to a contract agree that either may rescind the agreement, if the other make delay, instead of pursuing him in damages: akin to which is an agreement that either party may within a certain time set the bargain aside, (*pactum displicentiae*): finally, an agreement that the receiver shall not part with the thing received except by consent of the party who has delivered it, (*pactum de non alimando*) (see Mackeldey, § 419). *Pacta legitima* are of various kinds, but the chief are the *pactum donationis* and that *de dote constituenda*. These again are too minute in their nature to be discussed in an elementary treatise, and we refer the reader desirous of information to Mackeldey, §§ 420—428.

(O). On the *Dissolution of Obligations*.

The subject of dissolution of obligations being touched upon but briefly by Gaius, and altogether omitted by Ulpian, it is deemed advisable to state here the Roman rules on the matter, with such brevity as is consistent with a thorough comprehension of the subject.

The modes of dissolution we shall discuss are the following: solution and oblation, acceptilation, compensation, confusion, novation, and loss or destruction of the subject (*interitus rei*).

I. First, then, as to *solution:*

This is defined in the Digest to be the actual performance of the matter of the obligation[1], and took place whenever the debtor or some one on his account performed and discharged the obligation contracted, without change or modification. The fundamental rule of the Roman law applicable to the *ipso jure* dissolution of obligations was that every obligation must be dissolved in the same way in which it was contracted[2]. Therefore, unless the subject-matter of the obligation was really and effectually performed, given or transferred, no *solution* resulted. "Actual solution," says Pothier[3], "means the actual accomplishment of that to which a man is bound; where therefore his obligation is to do something, its solution is effected only by doing that thing; where it is to give something or to transfer the property in something, only by actually giving in the one case, or by transferring the property in the other." Examples showing how strictly the rule against alteration into an equivalent was enforced are abundant in the Digest.

So far for the subject-matter of the obligation. As regarded the parties the requisites were:

(1) That the payer or transferor possessed full power to give or transfer. Supposing that established, it mattered little whether the solution had been

[1] D. 50. 16. 176.
[2] D. 50. 17. 35 and 100.
[3] *Traité des Obligations*, Part III. ch. I. § 494.

made by the debtor directly or by another party on his account; for when it could be shown that the thing given or transferred really belonged to the payer, and also that the gift or transfer was made and received expressly to relieve the debtor from the claim, any opposition on his part on the ground of ignorance or unwillingness was fruitless[1].

(2) That the gift or transfer was made to the creditor himself or his properly-constituted agent; whose constitution might be either by precedent appointment, or subsequent ratification, or even by mere knowledge when the withholding of ratification was fraudulent[2].

As regarded the place for payment, the rule was that if this had been specially provided for, the parties were bound by their agreement; but if no place had been specified, then payment was to be made at the place where the subject-matter of the obligation had been received; or if that was impossible, at the place where the debtor resided.

When a time was fixed for the payment, the agreement on this head was to be observed; but we see from D. 45. 1. 135. 2, that equitable excuses for delay were not always rejected. When no time had been fixed, the payment was due at once, but no action could be brought till formal demand had been made.

When the contracting party made the duration of a right which must have some end depend upon his own will, the right ceased at his death. Thus in a lease or a tenancy at will, with the proviso that the lessor or landlord was to enter upon the land when he wished, it was held that upon his death the lease or tenancy was at once terminated[3].

In general the party obliged was at liberty to perform his obligation before the time appointed, unless it could be shown that the stipulation as to time was made for the convenience of the other party[4].

Under the head of *solution* should be noticed one method of dissolving an obligation, which from the mode of proceeding has been termed by later commentators *oblation*, and consisted of an offer of performance or payment made by the debtor at the proper place and time. This oblation or tender, as we see from Marcellus' words in the Digest[5], was not originally equivalent in law to a payment, and so did not *ipso jure* destroy the creditor's right of action against the debtor, but the latter was allowed to prove the facts under his plea of *dolus* (want of equity). In later times, however, the debtor's position was much improved; and tender, when properly made, was as valid a dissolution of an obligation as any of the forms expressly recognized: for, according to an imperial decision in the time of Diocletian and Maximian, it was held that tender accompanied with a deposit of the money, solemnly sealed, in the hands of a competent magistrate or in some public place, was the same as payment, and barred the creditor's claim to the debt[6].

II. *Acceptilation* is described by Gaius (III. 169—172), and was originally a method of dissolution applicable only to verbal contracts. But the Aquilian stipulation, of which a full account is given by Justinian (III. 29. 2), enabled all contracts to be *novated*, or changed into verbal agreements, and thus acceptilation became possible, whatever the nature of the original contract might be.

---

[1] D. 46. 3. 23 and 53.

[2] D. 46. 3. 49, 58, 64: D. 44. 4. 6.

[3] D. 19. 2. 4.

[4] See cases in illustration collected in Lindley's *Study of Jurisprudence*, § 93, p. 86.

[5] D. 46. 3. 72. pr.

[6] This was the law in Papinian's time, as is clear from D. 22. 1. 7.

III. *Compensation* was a setting-off of one claim against another, and so causing the dissolution of both or the diminution of one by the amount of the other.

The characteristics of this mode of dissolution were:

1st. That in Gaius' days it was raised in the pleadings, either by the plaintiff himself making a set-off and suing for the balance, or by its introduction into the formula by the defendant in the way of plea; so that compensation was in this latter case unlike solution, resembling more the English set-off, which must be pleaded specially.

2nd. That it was allowed in actions *bonae fidei* only, owing its introduction into Roman procedure to equitable reasons; for, as Pomponius says, its necessity is obvious, when we consider how much more equitable and simple it is to allow a method of settling cross-claims by one action, and so by mutual payments avoid a multiplicity of suits[1].

3rd. That the debts to which compensation applied were debts of a certain fixed quantity, or, as we should term them, liquidated.

4th. That the time for payment of the debt proposed to be set-off must have arrived.

5th. That the debts which could be set-off were debts of the same kind or nature; money, for instance, against money, corn against corn, &c., for *compensatio debiti ex pari specie licet ex causa dispari admittitur*[2].

IV. *Confusion*, as its name imports, arose from the combination of creditor and debtor in one and the same person, either through the creditor becoming heir of the debtor, or the debtor heir of the creditor, or when some third person became heir to both of them. In these cases the entire obligation with all its accessories was extinguished[3].

But where a confusion intervened between the principal debtor and his surety, or between the creditor and a surety of the debtor, the result was an extinction of the accessory obligation only, the original one (between the immediate parties) remaining unaltered[4].

A point of great importance is discussed in D. 46. 1. 71, viz. whether a confusion intervening between a creditor and one of two joint-debtors sets free the other joint-debtor or a surety bound for both of them. The Treasury in a certain case had succeeded to the estate of the creditor, who had died intestate and without heirs, and to the estate of one of his debtors on a forfeiture; proceedings were taken by the Treasury, not against the joint-debtor, but against a *mandator*, on whose guarantee the money had been advanced; and the Treasury won the cause; for although by the *confusion* the mandator's liability on behalf of the one debtor was gone, his liability on behalf of the other still remained; and that other one could have been sued with effect, inasmuch as the creditor had originally a right of suing either debtor *in solidum*, had, in fact, two separate rights of action, of which *either*, though *not both*, could be used, and the Treasury as representing the creditor still retained one of them, and so could enforce it either against the co-debtor or his surety.

---

[1] D. 16. 2. 3.

[2] Paulus, *S. R.* II. 5. 3.

[3] In D. 46. 3. 107, Pomponius explains the two kinds of dissolution of verbal obligations; viz. dissolution in fact, *i.e.* by *solution*, and dissolution in law, of which *acceptilation* and *confusion* are instances.

[4] D. 46. 3. 43; 46. 3. 93.

V. We now come to *novation*. The importance of this part of the Roman Law of Obligations to the English student has been comparatively recently demonstrated. In the European Assurance Arbitration Cases re Blundell, Lord Westbury, in speaking of the rules governing the question of novation, said, "It is strange that our Legislature adopted in fact the rule of the Civil Law, from which we have borrowed the term Novation[1]." He then cites the well-known passage of the *Institutes* of Justinian[2]; and, after commenting upon it, remarks on the necessity in the mind of Justinian that there should be a definite rule on the subject which should exclude presumption, and attributes to him an enactment that no novation should be arrived at, save upon written evidence of the intention of the parties[3].

A somewhat more extended survey of the Roman Law of *novation* will not, it is hoped, be out of place, as we cannot quite assent to the statement of Lord Westbury just quoted.

The definition of novation, as given in the Digest, is very precise: "A transfer of a pre-existing debt into another obligation (be it a strictly legal or an equitable one) accompanied by its complete fusion therein[4]." Therefore to establish novation two distinct obligations must have existed; and so, when after an advance of money without any stipulatory contract, it was agreed that a stipulation should be added, as these two transactions were not distinct, it was held that there was only one contract created by them, and consequently no resulting novation[5]. And the same view was recognized in a case where the stipulation was entered into at one time and the money advanced at another, for payment was simply the carrying out of the verbal contract, and not a transformation of it into a real one[6].

From the definition of novation we proceed to consider, 1st, the obligations that might be novated; 2nd, the obligations that were capable of effecting a novation; 3rd, the parties who could make it; 4th, the form; and 5th, the effect of novation.

And here it should be noticed that the novation now under discussion is the one known by the term *voluntary*, in contradistinction to another form effected by *litis contestatio*[7].

1st. What obligations could be novated? The answer to this is simple enough, viz. every obligation[8]; natural, civil, or praetorian; verbal, real, literal, consensual[9]. All were susceptible of novation, and so, whether the contract had been entered into by stipulation or in any other way, it could be novated into a verbal obligation, provided only there was clear proof of intention that such should be the case; for, in the absence of such proof, the result would be two separate obligations, one appendant to the other[10].

Whether the obligation to be novated was dependent upon the arrival of a fixed time, or upon the happening of an uncertain event or the arrival of an uncertain time, was a matter of great importance. If it was dependent on a time certain to arrive, the obligation, being vested, was equivalent to an absolute one, and could be at once novated, even before the advent of the day fixed:—but not so when it was dependent on an uncertain time or an uncertain event: the novation was then only conditional on the event coming to pass, and therefore if the event failed, the first agree-

1 See "Times" newspaper, Nov. 7, 1871.
2 *Inst.* III. 29. 3.
3 C. 8. 42. 8.
4 D. 46. 2. 1.
5 D. 46. 2. 6. 1.
6 *Ibid.*
7 Gaius III. 180.
8 Gaius III. 176 n.
9 D. 46. 2. 1. 1.
10 D. 46. 2. 2.

ment had fallen through before it could be transformed into another[1]. But the fulfilment of the condition affecting the first obligation might be contemporaneous with the creation of the substituted obligation, as we see from an example given by Ulpian[2]; this, however, leaves the principle intact that a prior conditional obligation cannot be novated till it becomes vested.

2nd. As to the obligation by which the first one was novated, the rule was equally simple—it must be a verbal one, and must be entered into with the intention of producing novation. If in itself certain, it acted on the previous obligation at once, if that was either certain or dependent upon a fixed time; but if the previous obligation was uncertain either as to time or condition, the novation, as we have already said, was postponed[3]. On the other hand, if the new stipulation was conditional, the establishment of the novation was always deferred until the condition was fulfilled; unless the condition was one certain to be fulfilled, in other words no true condition; "for he who stipulates for a condition certain to come to pass, really enters into an absolute stipulation[4]." Thus the general rule was that the existence of a condition deferred the contemplated novation, and whether the condition appeared in the first obligation or in the second, the result was the same[5].

3rd. As to the parties by whom novation might be made.

All persons to whom valid payment could be made might make novation of an obligation, and no others. On this ground, therefore, it was held that neither a minor unauthorized by his guardian, nor a spendthrift interdicted from the management of his affairs could do such an act[6].

As all persons to whom debts could be paid might, as a rule, make novation, an important question was raised as to the power of one of several co-creditors *in solido* to do this. Paulus held that it was beyond his power[7], but Venuleius, who has examined the law on the subject with great care, held that he might, though he admits that it was a doubtful matter (*quaeritur*)[8]. He bases his conclusion on the fact that either co-creditor could take payment, sue or acceptilate. Modern views are all on the side of Venuleius, and we may refer those who wish to investigate the question more fully to the arguments of Pothier and Maynz[9].

4th. As to the form of a novation. According to Ulpian there must be a stipulation made *animo novandi*[10]. After Justinian's legislation the stipulating form was not absolutely needful, but the *animus* remained as important as ever. The reason why stipulation had been insisted upon is simple enough. Stipulation, as the text of Gaius shows, was a mode of contracting of a very precise and formal character. Each party stated his views in the most direct and positive language; the question was clear, distinct and express, and the answer exactly tallied with it. Hence from these circumstances and from the publicity of the proceeding there could be no doubt about what was meant, and no difficulty in showing by proof what had been offered and accepted. Thus the old law insisted on stipulation because that most clearly brought out the intention. But with an increasing population, a larger development of commerce, a steady flow of

[1] D. 46. 2. 8. 1; 46. 2. 14. 1. Gaius in III. 179 gives a similar rule for the converse case of novation of an absolute agreement into an agreement conditional.
[2] D. 46. 2. 8. 2.
[3] D. 46. 2. 5.
[4] D. 46. 2. 9. 1.
[5] D. 46. 2. 14.
[6] D. 46. 2. 3; 46. 2. 20. 1.
[7] D. 46. 2 10.
[8] D. 46. 2. 31. 1.
[9] Pothier, *On Obligations*, Vol. 1. Part III. ch. 2, § 3. Maynz, *Elémens du droit Romain*, Tom. 2, § 173, note 5.
[10] D. 46. 2. 1 and 2.

foreigners to Rome, and an inclination for innovation in all branches of the law, especially in that relating to contracts, the exact and technical nature of stipulatory agreements became distasteful. Other forms of contract were preferred, and stipulations were conducted with less precision and less regard to their peculiar phraseology than had formerly been imperative. In consequence of this the intention of the parties was frequently obscure, and a variety of presumptions were invented by which the lawyers sought to fix the intention of loosely-worded agreements, and decide whether they were of a supplementary or a novating character. "The old lawyers," says Justinian[1], "held that novation took place only when the parties entered into the second obligation with the intent of novating; and as upon this point doubts arose, resulting in the introduction of presumptions varying in different cases, we have laid down that novation takes place only when the contracting parties have *expressly declared* that their intention in making the second contract is to effect a novation of the first." The enactment to which Justinian refers is a Constitution of the year 530 A.D., in the consulship of Lampadius and Orestes, which concludes with these words: "our general declaration is that novation must be effected by expressed intention only, and not presumed from agreement or covenant; and where there is no express statement of such intention, the matter in dispute is without novation, or to use the Greek form ἄνευ καινότητος[2]."

It will be seen therefore from this Constitution that the fixed rule was that so long as the parties could prove to the court not only that they intended to novate, but that they used words which would make their intention beyond all doubt, that was sufficient. In what form the declaration was made, whether in writing or not, was of no importance. And therefore, although writing was, perhaps, generally resorted to, because of its being more permanent and better calculated to establish proof of the intention of the parties, still it would be going too far to admit with Lord Westbury that "no novation could be arrived at, save upon written evidence of intention."

The 5th head, viz. the effect of the novation, has now to be considered. The primary effect was, as we have already seen, that the former debt or obligation was as completely extinguished as if it had been paid or performed, and hence it followed that the hypothecations which were accessory to the old debt were extinguished with it[3], although, of course, the creditor might transfer these accessory hypothecations to the second obligation by the stipulations upon which the novation was formed[4]. But if the things pledged did not belong to the first debtor, or if the novation was in the nature of a change of debtor, whether with or without an alteration of the obligation itself, the consent of the person to whom the hypothecation belonged was necessary[5].

And this mention of a change of debtor leads us to remark that besides the method of novation by the transfer of one obligation into another, there was another method called *delegation*, by which without alteration of the obligation a third party was accepted by the creditor in place of his original debtor. To this form of dissolution three parties were necessary, viz. 1st the old debtor, the party delegating, 2nd the new debtor, the party delegated, who entered into an obligation either to the creditor or to some one appointed by him, and 3rd the creditor, who by the substitution of the new debtor discharged the old one. All that was needed

1 *Inst.* 3. 29. 3.
2 C. 8. 42. 8.
3 D. 46. 2. 18.
4 D. 20. 4. 3 *pr.*; 20. 4. 12. 5.
5 D. 46. 2. 30.

to establish delegation was proof of consent on the part of the creditor to accept the change, and a stipulatory agreement on the part of the new debtor to accept the obligation imposed on him[1]. It should be noticed that the introduction of a condition had the same effect upon a delegation as upon an ordinary novation; viz. that it suspended the operation of the delegation until the condition was fulfilled; for inasmuch as the obligation of the substitute depended upon the accomplishment of the condition, so also did the discharge of the delegant from his precedent obligation[2].

VI. On dissolution by the destruction, loss or changed form of the subject-matter of the obligation (*interitu rei*), we need not dilate. It is enough to give Mackeldey's short but terse and clear enunciation of the rules on this topic[3]. For more extensive information the reader may have recourse to the *Pandectae Justinianae* by Pothier, or the same author's Treatise upon Obligations.

The rules of Mackeldey are:—when the subject-matter of the obligation was a particular specific thing, and its loss, destruction or change was accidental, the debtor was discharged from the performance of his obligation;—when the obligation was alternative and both subjects were lost, destroyed or changed accidentally, the debtor was, as before, set free: but if one only of the subjects perished, the debtor was bound to give the other. When, however, the loss, destruction or change of a specific subject or of one of several alternative subjects was caused by the fault of one of the parties, the result varied according as the creditor or debtor was blameable. If the creditor was in fault, the destruction of the subject, if single, or of any one of the subjects, if alternative, set the debtor free absolutely: but if the debtor was in fault, the creditor could demand the price of what was destroyed, lost or changed: or if the obligation was alternative, he could elect between this price and any of the subjects still surviving.

We have been obliged in this note to confine our attention to those dissolutions which operate *ipso jure*, but it is to be borne in mind that dissolutions were in numerous cases brought about by the use of pleas or exceptions. These we do not discuss; firstly because of their highly technical character, and secondly because the ancient and modern systems of pleading have so little in common, that it is scarcely of practical value and is certainly beyond the scope of our elementary treatise to dwell on such points. We will simply mention some of these pleas, which are referred to most frequently in the Law sources;—viz. Pacti Conventi, Pacti ne petatur, Transacti, Juris jurandi, Praescriptionis, Rei judicatae, Rei in judicium deductae, Conditionis expletae, Diei venientis, &c., as to which full information can be obtained in Warnkoenig's *Commentarii Juris Romani Privati*[4].

---

[1] D. 46. 2. 22.

[2] For further information, see Pothier *On Obligations*, translated by Evans, Vol. I. Part III. ch. 2.

[3] *Systema Juris Romani*, § 494.

[4] Tom. II. Lib. III. Cap. III. §§ 1, 2.

(P). On the *Decemviri, Centumviri, Lex Pinaria, Lex Aebutia, Leges Juliae.*

A. The *Decemviri stlitibus judicandis.*

From the time of the XII Tables *decemviri* seem always to have existed in the Roman state, a fact which is indicated by Livy (III. 55) in the words he quotes from a law of the consulship of Valerius and Horatius: "ut qui tribunis plebis aedilibus judicibus *decemviris* nocuisset, ejus caput Jovi sacrum esset, familia ad aedem Cereris Liberi Liberaeque venum iret." Livy further tells us that the Decemviri, so called by preeminence, by whom the XII Tables were drawn up, themselves exercised judicial functions, "singuli decimo quoque die," (III. 33). When the consular government was re-established a court of *decemviri* was still kept in existence, and, according to Heffter, had the cognizance of almost all suits up to the date of the institution of the Praetor's office (B.C. 367). Until that event Heffter also holds that there was no giving of a *judex*, except in cases where the law specially provided for suits being conducted *per judicis postulationem:* grounding his opinion on Tab. I. l. 7: "Ni pagant, in comitio aut in foro ante meridiem causam conjicito, quom perorant ambo praesentes post meridiem praesenti stlitem addicito:" so that the *decemviri* had what in later times was styled *cognitio extraordinaria* in all sacramentary cases.

B. The *Lex Pinaria.*

This *lex*, enacted about B.C. 350, effected a great change in the functions of the *decemviri.* A large number of actions had already been withdrawn from their cognizance, and transferred to that of the Praetor; and the *Lex Pinaria* seems to have given him the power of appointing a *judex* in all cases, and not merely in those tried *per judicis postulationem* during the period of the *legis actiones.* This quickly led to the Praetor's absorbing much of the residue of the business of the Decemviral Court, and so a new function was found for the *Decemviri stlitibus judicandis*, viz. that they should preside over the *hasta*, or Centumviral Court. So we understand Pomponius in D. 1. 2. 2. 29: "deinde quum esset necessarius magistratus qui hastae praeesset, decemviri litibus judicandis sunt constituti. Eodem tempore et quatuorviri...et triumviri monetales...et triumviri capitales." And the date of this new function is fixed as the same as that of the creation of the *triumviri capitales*, which is known from the Epitome of Livy XI. to be B.C. 286.

Clearly Pomponius does not say that the Decemviri were first created in B.C. 286; for we know they had existed long before; but that they were then appointed presidents of the *hasta*, which stood in need of presidents: and *hasta* is a well-known name for the Centumviri, as we see from Valerius Max. 7. 8. 1 and 4: Quintil. *Inst. Orat.* 5. 2 and especially from a well-known passage in Martial (*Epigramm.* 7. 63. 7)

Hunc miratur adhuc centum gravis hasta virorum.

Suetonius speaks of the Decemviri being wont "centumviralem hastam cogere": and this office of theirs is also hinted at in Pliny *Epp.* 5. 21: "Sedebant judices, decemviri venerant, observabantur advocati; silentium longum; tandem a Praetore nuntius: dimittuntur centumviri."

C. *The Lex Aebutia.* Gaius says that by this law and the two Julian laws the *legis actiones* were abolished, save in two cases, viz. actions referring to *damnum infectum* and actions tried before the *centumviri.* Those who wish to know exactly how much was effected by the *Lex Aebutia* and the *Leges Juliae* respectively, should consult Heffter's *Observations on Gaius* IV. pp. 18—41, a portion of his work too long for transcription here. The results he arrives at are these: the *Lex Aebutia* was enacted about 150 to 160 B.C., and may be divided into two principal clauses; 1st that the *centumviri* should judge in all sacramentary cases of a private nature, save only that the cognizance of questions touching liberty or citizenship should be left to the *decemviri stlitibus judicandis*[1], 2nd that all other causes which had previously been sued out *per judicis arbitrive postulationem*, or *per condictionem*, should thenceforth be matters of *formula*, the Praetor having the jurisdiction thereof and appointing a *judex*, who must give a decision within eighteen months from his appointment.

D. *The Centumviri.* This college consisted of 105 members, three from each of the thirty-five tribes[2], and Cicero gives a list, the concluding words of which imply that it is not an exhaustive one, of their functions: "jactare se in causis centumviralibus, in quibus usucapionum, tutelarum, gentilitatum, agnationum, alluvionum, circumluvionum, nexorum, mancipiorum, parietum, luminum, stillicidiorum, testamentorum, caeterarumque rerum innumerabilium jura versentur." (*De Orat.* I. 38.)

E. *The Leges Juliae.* In the reign of Augustus important changes in the constitution of the centumviral courts took place. The number of the *centumviri* was increased to 180, and they were divided into two or four tribunals, (some think more,) which in some cases sat separately, although in others of more importance the whole body acted together as judges. Whether much alteration was made by the Julian laws in their cognizance is a disputed point: some jurists have held that they could no longer deal with *actiones in rem*, which thenceforth were all *per formulam*, others have denied this statement; but there is very little evidence either way.

F. *The Form of Process in a Centumviral Cause.* The plaintiff first made application to the Praetor Urbanus or Peregrinus[3], (having previously given notice to his adversary of his intention to do so,) for leave to proceed before the *centumviri*. If leave were granted, formalities similar to those described by Gaius in IV. 16 were gone through, *sponsiones*, however, forfeitable to the opposing party, taking the place of the old *sacramenta*, forfeitable to the state. The *decemviri* then convened the *centumviri*, or those divisions of them who had to decide on the question, according to the nature of the case. The rest of the process presented no peculiar features.

(Q). On the *Proceedings in a Roman Civil Action.*

In the present note it is proposed to describe the various steps of a Roman action at law from its commencement to its termination.

We shall, however, first briefly notice the nature and extent of the jurisdiction of those higher officials, by whom all points of pleading and technical preliminaries were decided.

It is, of course, unnecessary to speak here of the early history of Roman actions, or to examine the historical account of the changes by which juris-

---

[1] See Cic. *pro Caecina*, 35: *pro Domo*, 29.

[2] See Festus, sub verb.

[3] Heffter maintains that application could in some cases be made to the Praetor Peregrinus. See *Obs.* p. 39.

diction in civil suits was supposed to have passed from the kings, (if it ever was in their hands,) to the consuls.

It is sufficient to take up the narrative at the time when the Praetors were the supreme Judges, invested with that twofold legal authority which is described by the technical terms *jurisdictio* and *imperium*. (See III. 181, n.) Two functions were comprised in the *jurisdictio*, one that of issuing decrees, the other that of assigning a *judex*, (*judicis datio*).

When, therefore, the litigants had made up their minds to settle their disputes by law, they were accustomed to appear before the Praetor in a place specially assigned for trials. In old times this place was always the *comitium*[1]: at a later period the *Comitium* or *Forum* was reserved for *Judicia Publica*, whilst private suits were tried under cover in the *Basilica*. If the Praetor heard the cause in his superior seat of justice, he was said to preside *pro tribunali*, if in his ordinary seat, he was said to try *de plano*[2].

The applications for relief at his hands were, of course, much more unimportant and informal at the sittings *de plano* than at those *pro tribunali*, where all those cases were investigated which required a special argument. Hence it became customary for the Praetor, whenever some very important business was brought before him *pro tribunali*, to obtain the assistance of a *consilium*, the members of which sat behind ready to instruct him when difficult points of law arose in the course of the hearing[3]. "Often," says Pliny[4], "have I pleaded, often have I acted as *judex*, often have I sat in the *consilium*."

The Praetor's court was closed on certain days, for, as is well known, there were *dies fasti*, *dies nefasti* and *dies intercisi*[5]. "On the former days," says Varro (*de Ling. Lat.* VI. 28—30, 53), "the Praetor could deliver his opinions without offence, on the *dies nefasti*, or close days, the Praetor was forbidden to utter his solemn injunctions *Do, Dico, Addico*:" consequently on those days no suits could be heard. The business before the court was distributed methodically over the *dies fasti*; thus on one day *postulationes* only would be taken, on another *cognitiones*, on a third decrees, on a fourth manumissions, and so on, an arrangement perfectly familiar to the practising English lawyer, who takes care to provide himself with the cause lists and public notices of the courts he has to attend[6].

From this short notice of the superior courts and their characteristics, we proceed to describe the actual method in which suits were conducted. Before resorting to law it was usual to endeavour to bring about an amicable settlement of the matters of difference by means of the intervention of friends. If their efforts were unavailing, the dispute was referred to Court, and the first step in the suit was the process termed *In jus vocatio*. In old times this *In jus vocatio* was of a very primitive character. The plaintiff on meeting the defendant bade him follow him into court; should the defendant refuse or delay to obey the mandate, the plaintiff called on the bystanders to bear witness to what he was doing, touching them on the ear[7] as he did so, after which he could drag his opponent off to court in any

---

[1] See Plautus, *Poenulus*, III. 6. 12, "cras mane quaeso in comitio estote obviam."

[2] Hence Martial's allusion,

> Sedeas in alto tu licet tribunali
> Et e curuli jura gentibus reddas.
> *Epig.* XI. 98.

[3] Cf. Cic. *de Oratore*, I. 37. The governors of provinces were similarly assisted by a body of Jurisconsults called assessors, cf. D. I. 22.

[4] *Epist.* I. 20.

[5] See note on Gaius, II. 279.

[6] The Praetors, be it noticed, used to go on circuits, for the despatch of business, to certain specified places; hence *Forum Claudii*, *Cornelii*, *Domitii*, &c.

[7] See Horace, *Sat.* I. 9. 74, and Plautus, *Curculio*, V. 2. 23.

way he pleased. In course of time this rough and ready form of summons was got rid of, and at length the method of direct application to the Praetor was adopted, by whom a fine was imposed in case his order for appearance was disobeyed. The defendant, if he obeyed the summons and made his appearance, was able to obtain an interim discharge, either by procuring some one to become surety for his further appearance, or by entering into what was called a *transactio*[1], that is, a settlement of all matters in dispute. Should neither of these courses have been adopted, on the defendant announcing his intention to fight the case, the next step in the business was the *editio actionis*. This moved from the plaintiff, and was in effect the actual commencement of the case itself. By it the defendant was formally challenged, and upon it he might, or rather was obliged, either to accept service, or to ask for a short delay in order to consider as to the propriety of accepting. The plaintiff, however, might if he pleased declare his aim and object to the defendant at the time when the *vocatio in jus* was issued[2], or after its issue he might informally and out of court state his demand to his opponent, or tell him the form of action he intended to adopt[3]. Whichever mode he did adopt, the result was that the presiding magistrate and the defendant learned from the plaintiff that he intended to "postulate[4]," i. e. make a formal demand of a *formula*.

No particular phraseology or formal language was imposed upon the plaintiff in the publication of the *editio*.

As the selection of the particular form of action was entirely in the plaintiff's power, he was permitted to vary the form at any time before the final settlement of the pleadings (that is, between the *actionis editio* and the *deductio in judicium*), for "*edita actio speciem futurae litis demonstrat*" says the Code[5].

Of course such changes on the plaintiff's part were met on the defendant's side by applications for delay, and the costs consequent upon these delays were thrown upon the plaintiff. Sometimes the form of action prayed for was inadmissible in itself, sometimes the mode in which it was presented to the court was objectionable: in either of these events the Praetor refused to allow it, and whether this refusal were immediately upon the *actionis editio* or at a later period, the Praetor was not bound to declare such refusal by a *decretum*, but could if he chose simply pay no attention to the application. Hence, during the régime of the *legis actiones*, the importance of strict and precise compliance with the rules of pleading, for the consequence of ill-drawn or badly-worded pleading on the part of the plaintiff was failure, or, to use the technical phraseology, *causa cadebat*. During the formulary period there was not so much risk of this mishap, for the Praetor himself used then to mark the verbal mistakes and errors in the plaintiff's *intentio*, and neither was the issue of fact fixed, nor the case sent for trial to the *judex*, till the *formula* was properly drawn. Thus time and opportunity were given by the court for the correction of all technical omissions and mistakes before trial. Still the plaintiff, even under the formulary procedure[6], incurred the danger we are speaking of; for the trial

[1] See D. 2. 15.

[2] See Plautus, *Pers.* 4. 9. 8—10.

[3] Technically called *denunciatio*, D. 5. 2. 7, and D. 5. 3. 20. 11.

[4] The term *postulatio* embraced all applications for *formulae* to the Praetor. It frequently happened that the delivery of the formulae depended upon long arguments, in which the skill and knowledge in pleading of the advocates were fully called into play. These arguments always took place in the superior court, *in Jure*, and *pro tribunali*.

[5] C. 2. 1. 3.

[6] Thus Cicero, "Ita jus civile habemus constitutum, ut causa cadat is qui non quemadmodum oportet egerit." *De Inventione*, II. 19. See also Quint. *Inst. Or.* III. 6. 69.

being at his risk and peril, if it turned out eventually that the *formula* adopted did not fit in with his cause of action, he failed in his suit, although the shape of the action had been settled by the Praetor.

It is clear then that up to this stage the chief, if not the only active part in the proceedings was played by the plaintiff, and that whilst it was open to the defendant to take advantage of all his opponent's mistakes, he himself was called upon to do nothing, so far as his defence was concerned, before the *vadimonium* was settled.

These preliminaries, therefore, being completed, the plaintiff's next step was *vadari reum*, that is, in a particular and set form of words to pray that the defendant might find sureties to give bail for his appearance in court on a fixed day, generally the day after that following the application. That this form taxed largely the skill and care of the jurisconsults of the day is evidenced by Cicero's words[1]: "Cæsar asserts that there is not one man out of the whole mass before him who can frame a *vadimonium*." The form itself is lost[2], we may, however, surmise something of its nature from a passage in the oration *Pro Quinctio*. It seems clear that in the ordinary *vadimonium* were fixed the day and place[3] when and where the parties were to appear before the Praetor in order to have the *formula* drawn up[4], whilst in cases where the trial was to take place out of Rome the name of the magistrate in the provinces who was to give the *formula* was inserted, and on the contrary, where a defendant who was living in the provinces claimed a right of trial before a Roman tribunal, there was a statement of the name of the magistrate in Rome by whom the *formula* was to be drawn up.

Various other technicalities attached to the *vadimonia*. Two or three only need be specified. In the first place, as we have seen, bail might be exacted when a man entered into a *vadimonium*; but it might also be entered into without any bail or surety, and then it was termed *purum*; again the defendant might be called upon to swear to the faithful discharge of his promise, or *recuperatores* might be named with authority to condemn the defendant in costs to the full amount of his *vadimonium* in case of non-appearance[5]. If the defendant answered to his bail he was said *vadimonium sistere*; if he forfeited his recognizances, *vadimonium deserere*; if the day of appearance were put off, *vadimonium differre* was the technical phrase[6]. The consequences that ensued after the entry into a *vadimonium* were as follows: where the two parties appeared in person upon the day fixed, the object of the *vadimonium* being thus secured, the *vadimonium* itself was at an end, and the proceedings went on in the regular way which will presently be described: if, however, one or the other of them failed to appear when the Praetor directed their case to be called on (*citavit*), the result, in case the plaintiff made default, was that he lost his case (*causa cadebat*), but the judgment was not final and in bar of all further proceedings. In case the defendant made default, his *vadimonium* was said to be *desertum*, and the plaintiff was authorized to sue him or his bail (which he pleased) *ex stipulatu*, for the amount stated in the vadimonial formula.

Another means of securing attendance in court was a *sponsio*, entered into by the parties themselves without the intervention of sureties; and

[1] *Ad Quint. Frat.* II. 15.

[2] Unless the lines in the *Curculio*, I. 3. 5, have preserved it.

[3] In the event of the venue not being necessarily fixed by the circumstances of the case.

[4] Cic. *pro Quinct.* 8, and Gaius, IV. 184.

[5] Gaius, IV. 185. The Praetor's edict made special provision for all these cases.

[6] So Juvenal, *Sat.* III. 213, "differt vadimonia Praetor."

then on default of appearance a *missio in possessionem* was granted. This was given by the Praetor's edict, and enabled the plaintiff to be put in possession of the defendant's goods[1].

Such was the process by which care was taken on the one hand to prevent frivolous and vexatious actions, and on the other to bring the parties to joinder of issue, or to that stage where a *formula* could be granted. For this purpose the forms were these.—The Praetor having taken his seat in court, ordered the list of all the actions that had been entered and demanded two days back to be gone through, and the parties to them to be called into court. His object in doing this was to dispose of the *vadimonia* and to fix the different *judicia*. The case, therefore, being called on, supposing both parties were ready, in reply to the citation, "Where art thou who hast put me to my bail? where art thou who hast cited me?" the defendant said, "See here I am ready to meet thee; do thou on thy side be ready to meet me." The plaintiff to this replied, "Here I am:" then the defendant said, "What sayest thou?" The plaintiff rejoined, "I say that the goods which thou possessest are mine and that thou shouldest make transfer of them to me." This colloquy being ended, the next step was for the plaintiff to make his *postulatio* to the Praetor for a *formula* and a *judex*. These the Praetor could refuse, in some cases at once, in others upon cause shown. Supposing he assented to the *postulatio*, he granted a *formula*, but first heard both parties upon the application. At this stage the defendant was allowed either to argue that there was no cause of action, or to urge the insertion of some particular plea; the plaintiff on the other hand was entitled to ask for a *judicium purum*, that is, a simple issue without any special plea, or to press for a replication to such plea as was granted, and to this the defendant might rebut (*triplicare*), and the plaintiff sur-rebut (*quadruplicare*), and so on. These preliminary arguments took place *pro tribunali*, the technical term for them being *constitutio judicii*[2]. On their conclusion the *formula* was settled, and the *postulatio judicis* having been made, the final act followed by which an end was put to the pleadings, the issue of fact being drawn and sent in the *formula* to the *judex* or to *recuperatores*. If the issue had proved to be one of law, the matter would have never gone to a *judex* at all, but have been settled *in jure* by the Praetor. The *formula* itself and its component parts are so fully and clearly described in the text of Gaius that it is needless to do more than refer to that for explanation of them[3].

We have now arrived at the period of the proceedings when the parties were in a position to have the real question between them settled; that is to say, when they were before a *judex*, whose business it was to try the point remitted to him in the *formula*[4]. A few words, then, upon the nature and

[1] This *missio in possessionem* was granted against any one who was to blame for preventing a suit from going on regularly. Its consequences were so severe in their effect upon the defendant's property and character that Cicero denounced in strong language the hardship of granting a *sponsio* in case of Quinctius. See *Pro Quinct.* 8, 9, and 27.

[2] See Cic. *Oratoriae Partitiones*, 28, "Ante judicium de constituendo ipso judicio solet esse contentio;" and Cic. *de Inv.* II 19.

[3] IV. 39.

[4] The matter was now *in judicio*, as opposed to the previous enquiries, which were *in jure*.

It is beyond the scope of this note to dwell at full length on the important subject of Roman Pleading. There are, therefore, many matters which cannot now be explained; such as the consequences resulting from the *litis contestatio*; the novation effected by the *litis contestatio* (III. 176, 180, and D. 46. 2. 29); the plaintiff's power of interrogating *in jure* (not very unlike our own common law interrogatories); confessions and acknowledgments; the oath tendered by the parties each to the other before the Praetor; the *prima* extent of the jurisdiction of the *judex* will not be out of place. The *judex* was a private person, not a trained lawyer[1]; his position with reference to the parties was a combination of arbitrator and juryman; arbitrator, because he was entrusted with what in effect was the settlement of the matter in dispute between the parties; juryman, because his action was confined simply to announcing his decision. If he had been able to complete the inquiry by giving a decisive judgment and enforcing it himself, his powers would have been very similar to those of an English county court judge. They were, however, more limited. Yet, though he was bound by the terms of the *formula* to try the question of fact, he was not so completely confined to it, as to be unable to examine and decide upon such matters of law as were incidentally connected therewith. To protect him against the chance of mistakes in law he was allowed to claim and receive the advice of the Praetor or Praeses[2]: and in later times, if not in the days of Cicero, he was also able to obtain advice from a *consilium* who sat on benches near him[3]. And, further, his decisions upon legal points were subject to the control and review of the Praetor, who might annul the sentence, and either refuse to execute it or, if necessary, send it for a further hearing.

In the trial itself his authority was strictly confined to the facts specially laid before him; in other words, he had no power to travel out of the record and decide upon collateral matters of fact, at least in actions *stricti juris*, for he was able to add pleas in equitable actions (*actiones bonae fidei*). The *intentio* and the *condemnatio* were his guiding lights; from them he learned the real nature of the inquiry, and by them he was strictly limited. From the one he knew what the plaintiff was to establish; by means of the other he was at little or no difficulty in making his decision[4].

The cause then was called on, and the parties were summoned into court, *in judicium*. On their appearance, the oath of *calumnia* was administered to them[5], and when it had been taken, the advocates (*patroni*) were expected to open the cases of their clients. This they did with a very short outline of the facts. After this brief narrative, called *causae collectio*[6], the evidence was adduced, and at the close of the evidence each advocate made a second speech, urging all that could be said in his client's favour and commenting on the evidence that had been brought forward. The time occupied by these speeches was not left to the discretion of the advocates, but limited to so many *clepsydrae*[7]. When the cause had thus been fairly gone through, the last stage in the *judicium* was the sentence. Here the *judex* was, as we have mentioned above, strictly limited by the *formula*,

and *secunda actio* and the *causae ampliatio;* the law terms and times of trial at Rome and in the Provinces; and other matters of a similar nature, which would fill the pages of a more exhaustive commentary on the Roman Procedure than this assumes to be.

[1] A list of Judices selected from the body of *cives* was drawn up by each Praetor on the commencement of his year of office, and entered in his *Album*. From this list the litigants made their own selection (cf. *pro Cluentio*, 43). Strictly speaking, the plaintiff nominated the Judex, but the defendant's acceptance was necessary. Cic. *de Orat.* II. 70.

[2] This assistance was confined entirely to questions of law: for as to matters of fact, the Judex was to rely upon his own judgment and to decide "prout relligio suggerit." D. 5. 1. 79. 1. The important and varied work of the *judices* is evidenced by the fact that a book of the *Digest*, containing upwards of 80 laws, is devoted to the Judicia, D. 5. 1.

[3] Aul. Gell. *Noct. Att.* XIV. c. 2.

[4] "Ultra id quod in judicium deductum est excedere potestas judicis non potest." D. 10. 3. 18.

[5] IV. 172, 176. The *judex* himself, on taking his seat, had to swear to do his duty faithfully and legally. This he did in a set form of words, and with his hand on the altar (the *puteal Libonis*).

[6] IV. 15. In the *Digest* it is called *causae conjectio*. D. 50. 17. 1.

[7] Pliny, *Ep.* II. 11, IV. 9, VI. 2.

and if he travelled out of it, and either assumed to decide upon what was not before him or touched upon collateral matter, he was said *litem suam facere*[1], and was liable to a penalty for his mistake. With the announcement of his sentence his power and authority in the suit ended. The execution of the sentence rested with the Praetor, but a delay of 30 days was allowed between the sentence and its execution. When that time had expired the sentence became what was called a *res judicata*, and upon it the successful party could bring his action (*actio judicati*) for twice the amount of money awarded by the *judex*, and could also obtain a *missio in possessionem*, until his opponent's property was sold to pay the judgment-debt. All this part of the cause was in the hands of the Praetor, whose *imperium* enabled him to direct proceedings against the party refusing to comply with the decision of a *judex*.

(R). On the *Legis Actio per Judicis Postulationem*.

The strict nature of the *actio sacramenti*, and the serious risk attaching to it of losing the amount deposited by way of *sacramentum*, must have led to devices for withdrawing the settlement of litigious matters from that action and getting them tried in a less strict form, in fact, to the introduction of a process in which equitable constructions might be permitted. It is here, then, that we may find the germ of those equitable actions which, under the name of *actiones bonae fidei*, formed so important and valuable an adjunct to the Roman system of procedure.

That the custom of demanding a *judex* was a very ancient one even in Cicero's time we learn from a passage in the *de Officiis* (III. 10), where he speaks of it as "that excellent custom handed down from the practice of our forefathers."

Various well-established facts show not only the early efforts made to mitigate the severity of the old common-law forms by equitable expedients, but the direction that those efforts took, viz. the withdrawal of suits from the common-law judges and from the trammels of common-law forms.

Hence, we may reasonably conclude in the first place, that all actions which might by any possibility be treated equitably, were allowed to be heard by a *judex* or an *arbiter*, and next with equal reason infer, that all actions of strict law which could be settled in a clearer and safer manner by some process not so narrow or so unsuited to the question at issue as that of the *actio sacramenti*, such as suits about boundaries, about injuries caused by rainfalls and waterflows, all matters requiring technical knowledge and skilled witnesses, or, as in the case of the *actio familiae erciscundae*, careful and detailed treatment, and all actions requiring an adjustment and rateable allotment of claim, or a division of damages and interest instead of an assignment of the thing itself, were referred to a *judex*, withdrawn from the sacramental process, and handed over to that called *judicis postulatio*. See Cic. *de Legg.* III. 21, D. 43. 8. 5, D. 39. 3. 24, D. 10. 2. 1.

[1] IV. 52.

(S). On the terms *Formula in jus concepta*, *Formula in factum concepta*, *Actio directa*, *Actio in factum*.

At first sight it would seem as though there were a close analogy between the English lawyers' distinction of an issue of law and an issue of fact, and Gaius' classification of *formulae in jus conceptae* and *formulae in factum conceptae;* but on nearer inspection, the analogy proves altogether fallacious.

For when the facts were admitted by both parties to a suit, and they prayed only for an application of the known law to those facts, no *formula* was issued at all : the question of law was settled by the Praetor himself, *in jure*, and so the suit terminated. The Praetor only remitted a case to a Judex either (1) that he might ascertain certain disputed facts, and then apply to them a known law; or (2) that he might simply ascertain the facts and then report his finding, in which latter case the *formula* was termed *praejudicialis*, and the decision was a mere preliminary to further litigation; or (3) that he might ascertain the facts, and apply to his finding certain rules of equity which the Praetor judged fair and fitting, although neither the Civil Law nor the Edict contained a regulation exactly applicable to the question in debate.

For litigation falling under the first head *formulae*, common forms as they might be styled, were provided beforehand, and embodied in the Edict. But it was essential that the Judex should have an intimation whether the law to be applied by him should be civil or praetorian, and this for two reasons, viz. because the plaintiff had in many cases a choice of remedies, one civil and one praetorian, and because the powers of the *judex* and the pleas he could admit depended on the character of the law he was applying.

Such intimation was conveyed to him by the manner in which the *formula* was worded. Supposing the plaintiff's claim to be based on some enactment of the civil law, and the action provided to be *stricti iuris*, there was no *demonstratio;* but in the *intentio* a technical word or two as *designatio* would be inserted to denote the character of the action: as "si paret rem esse *ex jure Quiritium* Auli Agerii:" "si paret *ex stipulatu* Numerium Negidium Aulo Agerio debere:" "si paret Numerium Negidium Aulo Agerio *pro fure* damnum decidere oportere." Supposing it, however, to be based on some enactment of the civil law, but the action provided to be *bonae fidei* (for it is a mistake to suppose that only actions on the Edict were *bonae fidei:* see Gai. IV. 62); there was a *demonstratio* and an *intentio*, the former containing the facts admitted by both parties. And supposing it to be founded on the Edict, the action then being of necessity *bonae fidei*, there would be no *demonstratio* in separate form; but an *intentio* only, containing the admitted facts as its *designatio*. And so also would the *formula* be framed when the Praetor extended by constructive interpretation, *ex aequitate*, the spirit of a Lex or clause of his own Edict to a case not falling within its actual words.

Hence, when the jurists speak of *conceptio in jus* and *conceptio in factum*, they are not referring to the nature of the issue to be tried, whether of law or of fact, but to the nature of the enactment, civil or praetorian, on which the litigation turned.

The action, indeed, was *directa* or *vulgaris*, whether its issue were one of fact or one of law, provided only the legal point as to the applicability of which there was a dispute, or the legal principle to be applied after the disputed facts had been investigated, was set down in express terms either in a *lex* or *senatusconsultum* or in the Edict. And of these *actiones directae* there was a subdivision according to the source of the determining legal principle. When that principle was contained in a *lex* or *senatusconsultum*, the *formula* of the *actio directa* was *in jus concepta;* when it was contained in a clause of the Edict, the *formula* of the *actio directa* was *in factum concepta*. Gaius, IV. 45 *sub fin.*

A *lex* might have been furnished with an action by the Praetor in addition to the remedy attaching under the *jus civile*, or the Praetor might by his Edict have supplemented the deficiencies of such a *lex*, and granted an express action in cases arising on these supplementary provisions: and so we can understand the statement of Gaius (IV. 47) about the double *formulae*, *in factum* as well as *in jus*, given in certain cases.

Thus we conclude that all actions wherein proceedings were taken on the known law were *directae:* that they would never get beyond the step called *in jure*, if there were no controverted facts, but only a dispute as to whether the law was or was not applicable to admitted facts: that, on the contrary, a *formula* would be issued, and proceedings *in judicio* would follow, if facts were in dispute and evidence had to be taken; and then the *formula* would be *in jus concepta* or *in factum concepta* according as the law which was to settle the dispute was civil or praetorian.

But besides the *actiones directae* and the *actiones praejudiciales* there was the third class already mentioned, viz. actions to be tried by certain equitable rules which the Praetor set forth, *pro re nata* and according to his own opinion of what was proper, in cases which fell under no existing enactment, but yet involved a manifest wrong. These were the *actiones non vulgares*, more often called *actiones in factum*, and the *formulae* issued on their behalf were of necessity *in factum conceptae*, for their decision was in no way dependent on the Civil Law. So that a *formula in factum concepta* was attached to all *actiones in factum*, and to some *actiones directae*.

Of *actiones non vulgares* or *in factum* there were three kinds, their point of union being that in all the Praetor had either to make, or at any rate to modify a *formula*, and that to none of them did a common *formula* apply exactly as it stood in the Edict:

These three kinds were

(1) *Actiones utiles*, or actions resembling some *actio directa* (their name being derived from *uti*, the adverb, not from *uti* the verb). The Praetor in such an action allowed a *formula* to be, as it were, borrowed, and applied to a case which it was not originally intended to meet, but which closely resembled that for which it had been framed.

Actiones fictitiae were a particular branch of *actiones utiles*.

(2) *Actiones cum praescriptione;* granted where the circumstances out of which they sprang constituted a civil or praetorian obligation, but the common *formula* provided was too large in its scope, so that a plaintiff who made use of it would be liable to be met by the exception called *plus petitionis*. The common *formula*, therefore, was cut down to its proper limits by the addition of a *praescriptio* prefixed with the Praetor's approval. Gaius, IV. 130.

(3) *Actiones in factum praescriptis verbis:* purely equitable actions for the remedy of some wrong for which the law (civil or praetorian) had altogether failed to make provision, and for which therefore the Praetor drew up a new and special *formula*, with an account of the circumstances of the case included, and containing in its *condemnatio* a remedy of the Praetor's own invention, which was to be applied in the event of plaintiff being able to establish his case.

See Heineccius, IV. 6. 26, Mackeldey, § 194, Zimmern's *Traité des Actions chez les Romains*, § LI.

(T). On the Exceptions *Rei Judicatae* and *In Judicium Deductae.*

In IV. 106—108 Gaius draws the attention of his class to a rule of practice in pleading, by which it was laid down that in certain actions the defences of "judgment recovered" and "matter already in issue" could be set up, as of course, and under the general issue, whilst in certain other actions they could only be made use of when specially pleaded. A few words about these two pleas and the rule of practice relating to them will not perhaps be out of place. The plea, technically called *exceptio rei in judicium deductae*, meant that the exact question in controversy between the parties had already been argued before the Praetor, and had been settled by him in the shape of a *formula*. That is to say, the plaintiff on some former occasion had raised the same points, and had called upon the defendant to reply to them *in jure*, and every step in pleading up to the *litis contestatio* had been taken. The other plea, *rei judicatae*, meant that matters had gone even further than the *litis contestatio*. That is to say, that the Praetor had drawn the *formula*, and sent it down to the *judex* with the precise question of fact for trial, and that the decision of the *judex* had been given.

Now there were three sets of actions in which the effect of these defences required consideration.

There was, first, a class of actions based on the *imperium* of the Praetor and unconnected with the strict rules and technicalities of the old civil law, and for which a time of limitation was prescribed coexistent with the duration of each particular Praetor in office.

Next, there was a class of actions arising from obligations and dependent upon the old civil law, both by their very nature and from the fact that the declaration or *intentio* was of a civil law form, i.e. not standing alone, but preceded by a *demonstratio*; or without *demonstratio*, and with only technical legal terms as *designatio*.

Lastly, there was a class of actions, either real and arising from *dominium*, or personal upon the case (*in factum*) and independent not only of the old strict civil law, but of all standing rules, civil or praetorian, and allowed merely *ex aequitate Praetoris*.

In the first of these sets the rule was that the defence of "judgment recovered," and "matter still in issue," had to be specially pleaded. There were two reasons for this: firstly, because being praetorian remedies they were not affected by rules of pleading applicable to the old civil law actions; and therefore, as there was nothing in strict law to prevent a second action being brought, it was necessary to allow a protection to the defendants in the shape of a plea: and secondly, because during any succeeding Praetor's year of office the nature and subject of the actions tried by his predecessor might easily be forgotten, and therefore a reminder in the shape of a special plea like the one before us was absolutely necessary: and probably, as the Praetorian Law in early times varied from year to year, records of judgments of this kind would not be kept.

In the second set of actions the rule was that where the same plaintiff brought a second action upon the same facts against the same defendant, the defence of "judgment recovered" or "matter still in issue" was available as part of the defendant's proof under the general issue, and without any special plea. The reason for this was that, inasmuch as these were strictly legal actions with a civil law *intentio*, the plaintiff was *ipso jure*, by force of the civil law itself, barred from attempting any further claim: and moreover the law being stable, records were valuable as precedents, and could probably be quoted *in jure.*

In the third class there are two sets of actions, one founded on *dominium* or *jus in re*, the other to a certain extent founded on obligation, but not of the same kind as in the old civil law personal actions; and the rule applicable to such actions was that in order to avail himself of his special defence, it was necessary for the defendant to raise the point by his pleas.

It is clear that in the actions of the latter kind, i.e. personal actions *in factum*, both the reasons which have been given above for requiring special pleas in actions based on the *imperium* apply with extra force. For if proceedings founded on standing rules of a particular Praetor's edict were not *ipso jure* a bar to further proceedings before a new Praetor, still less could those proceedings be such a bar which had been allowed by the former Praetor merely because of his own personal theories of equity, enunciated at the time application for redress was made to him, and never cast into the form of general rules; and again, the details of such matters were even more liable to be forgotten than were those of the other kind.

Then as to those actions springing out of *dominium*, i.e. real actions, the reason why a special plea of "judgment recovered" or "matter still in issue" was necessary is obvious. In all these actions the plaintiff is maintaining a right against the whole world, and has no particular aforeknown person by whom this general right can be imperilled. As then he has to meet any and every opponent, so it is clear a victory over this or that person may not entirely and as a matter of course silence even him, for he may renew the attack on new grounds: and still less is a *jus in rem* successfully maintained against one plaintiff, secure against another plaintiff. In the case of an obligation-claim between A and B, where the judge decides that B has not to perform the particular obligation, the processes are few and simple and the ground of attack is single, but in a claim, founded on a *jus in re*, there may be a variety of proofs in support of a claim, shaped in more ways than one, and the grounds of attack may be varied in proportion to the intricacy of the right at stake. Here then there is nothing in strict law (*ipso jure*) to prevent a plaintiff who has failed once from trying to succeed a second time, and therefore, as in the first set of actions, so here, to prevent vexatious litigation, the defendant is allowed to resort to his plea of "judgment recovered" or "matter still in issue;" which, as the text says, is a matter of necessity.

INDEX.

B.

C.

J.

M.

N.

O.

P.

U.

V.

W.

CAMBRIDGE: PRINTED BY C. J. CLAY, M.A. & SON, AT THE UNIVERSITY PRESS.